Mac OS X Bible:
Jaguar Edition

Mac OS X Bible: Jaguar Edition

Lon Poole, Dennis R. Cohen, and Steve Burnett

Wiley Publishing, Inc.

Mac OS X Bible: Jaguar Edition

Published by
Wiley Publishing, Inc.
909 Third Avenue
New York, NY 10022
www.wiley.com

Copyright © 2003 by Wiley Publishing, Inc., Indianapolis, Indiana

Library of Congress Catalog Control Number: 2003101811

ISBN: 0-7645-3731-8

Manufactured in the United States of America

10 9 8 7 6 5 4 3 2 1

1O/RZ/QR/QT/IN

Published by Wiley Publishing, Inc., Indianapolis, Indiana
Published simultaneously in Canada

About the Authors

Lon Poole is the award-winning author or coauthor of over two dozen computer books, including seven books about other versions of the Mac OS, four additional Mac books, and numerous others. His popular "Quick Tips" column ran in *Macworld* magazine for over 15 years, and he has written 65 magazine feature articles on Mac topics. He has a B.A. in Computer Science from the University of California, Berkeley. Lon lives in northern California with his wife and two sons. He enjoys hiking, bicycling, carpentry, and traveling.

Dennis R. Cohen has written or contributed to many books, including *Macworld Microsoft Office 2001 Bible*, *Macworld AppleWorks 6 Bible*, *AppleWorks 6 for Dummies*, and *Mac Secrets*, 6th Edition as well as being the technical editor for over fifty titles in just the last few years. A software developer for over 20 years and a Mac developer since 1984, he brings a history not only with the Mac, but also with other platforms. Dennis lives in Sunnyvale, California, with his Boston Terrier, Spenser.

Steve Burnett is a system administrator, technical writer, and author working and living in the Research Triangle Park area of North Carolina with his wife. His first Mac was a SE in 1986. When he's not typing he plays Chapman Stick and theremin.

Credits

Acquisitions Editor
Michael Roney

Coordinating Editor
Beth Taylor

Technical Editor
Debbie Gates

Copy Editor
Maarten Reilingh

Editorial Manager
Rev Mengle

Vice President and Executive Group Publisher
Richard Swadley

Vice President and Executive Publisher
Bob Ipsen

Vice President and Publisher
Barry Pruett

Project Coordinator
Ryan Steffen

Graphics and Production Specialists
Jennifer Click, Sean Decker,
Heather Pope, Erin Zeltner

Quality Control Technicians
John Tyler Connoley, David Faust,
John Greenough, Andy Hollandbeck,
Angel Perez, Dwight Ramsey

Proofreading and Indexing
TECHBOOKS Production Services

My special thanks go to my wife, Karin, and my sons, Adam and Ethan. Without your love and support, my effort on this book would have been pointless. —L.P.

Thanks for the support of friends, family, and especially Spenser (who got me out from in front of the computer for regular exercise). —drc

My thanks for this book are to my wife, who kept assuring me I'd finish on time. —sfb

Foreword

I admit it: Mac OS X scares me just a bit. Don't get me wrong — I know the Macintosh desperately needs the under-the-hood improvements that Mac OS X provides. And I'm gradually coming to terms with the new operating system's flashy Aqua user interface.

What scares me about Mac OS X is that it's so, well, *different.* When I start exploring Mac OS X, I feel like Henry Ford might feel if he was to look under the hoods of today's cars. Sure, some things are familiar, but I also see a lot of things I don't recognize.

For a veteran of the Macintosh world, Mac OS X is almost like starting all over again. You have to learn new ways of adjusting system settings. You have to develop new troubleshooting techniques. And you have a vast new array of customizing and optimizing options.

But exploring a new frontier can be exciting if you have the right guides, and that's where this book comes in. Plenty of Mac OS X books are out there, but this one is the best.

I can say that because I know its authors, and I know that they're the most qualified people on the planet to demystify Apple's new operating system. I've known Lon Poole since the earliest days of the Macintosh — I vividly remember devouring his articles in the very first issue of *Macworld* magazine and feeling like I really understood how the Mac was put together.

That same feeling would hit me many times in the years that followed. Every time I saw something written by Lon, I knew what I'd be getting, and it's exactly what you get in this book: crystal-clear explanations and rock-solid advice, delivered with smart-bomb accuracy.

And Dennis Cohen? Our paths first crossed back in 1986, when I was writing a book about dBASE Mac, a database program from Ashton-Tate. (Both the program and the company are now gone, and boy, does that make me feel old.) Dennis was a member of the dBASE Mac development team and was the technical editor of my book. He would go on to tech-edit many of my books, and his breadth of knowledge and attention to detail never failed to amaze me.

And that's why I'm certain that the book you're holding right now is the best Mac OS X book available.

Mac OS X, with its potent combination of power and design elegance, has the potential to be the most exciting operating system in the personal computer world. Lon and Dennis have created the ultimate guide to exploring this new frontier. Happy travels.

Jim Heid
"Mac Focus" columnist, *Los Angeles Times*
Contributing Editor, *Macworld*® magazine

Acknowledgments

Lon wishes to thank Seth Novogrodsky for writing a first draft of Chapter 2 and Julie Bernstein for writing a first draft of Chapter 6. They had to do their work based on preliminary versions of Mac OS X, and I revised their work according to the finished version of Mac OS X. Therefore, any errors or omissions in their chapters are my responsibility.

Dennis would like to thank the contributors to the Mac OS X for Users mailing lists for their postings, Jennifer Brabson for loaning me an OS X-compatible printer, and Mike Rossetti for letting me use his USB camera in the preparation of this material.

Steve wants to thank his agent David Fugate for finding this opportunity, Lon and Dennis for being articulate coauthors, and Mike Roney and Beth Taylor at Wiley for being great to work with. As well, I'd also like to thank the contributors to the Triangle Macintosh User Group mailing list and the macosx community on LiveJournal for their postings. Steve Champeon deserves singling out for both his continual counsel and loan of a Wacom tablet in time of need. Other people I want to acknowledge for their advice and support to me on this project are Laura G. Ammons, Fred Brackett, Rush Combs, Paul Cory, Jay Cuthrell, Jacob Frelinger, Adrian Likins, Hal Meeks, Phi Sanders, Stephen Schaefer, Jason Sullivan, Francis Sheperd, and Scott Zekanis.

Contents at a Glance

Contents

Part II: At Work with Mac OS X   269

Chapter 9: Printing Documents 271

Chapter 10: Accessing Files Via Local Network and Internet 291

Part III: Beyond the Basics of Mac OS X   491

Chapter 16: Managing User Accounts and Privileges 493

Part IV: Making the Most of Mac OS X   649

Part V: Appendixes 783

Introduction

According to popular legend, a Mac is so easy to use that you don't need to read books about it. Alas, if only that were true. In fact, discovering all the power that Mac OS X gives your computer would take months of exploring and experimenting. Yes, exploring and experimenting can be fun. But do you really have months to devote to your computer's operating system? Save your time for having fun with games and multimedia, exploring the Internet, or maybe getting some work done. Benefit from the experience of others (in this case, the authors). Read this book so that you can put the full power of Mac OS X to work for you without a lot of poking around the Mac desktop.

Maybe you think you don't need this book because you have Apple's manuals and onscreen help. It's true these are good sources of information. But the *Mac OS X Bible:* Jaguar Edition contains a great deal of information you won't find in the manuals or help screens. This book also provides a different perspective on subjects you may not quite understand after reading the manuals. And because this book describes Mac OS X completely, you can use it instead of Apple's manuals if you don't happen to have them. (They tend to be rather thin these days, anyway.)

Who Should Read This Book

This book is meant for people who already know Mac OS fundamentals, such as choosing commands from menus, moving icons on the desktop, and selecting and editing text. If you have spent more than a few days with any Mac OS computer, you know how to do these things and are ready for what's inside this book.

Read this book to learn all about Mac OS X—how to use it if you have it, and why you should get it if you don't. If you haven't used Macintosh computers before, this book takes you from the basic concepts and techniques through all the advanced features of Mac OS X. If you have used earlier versions of the Mac OS, read this book to learn all about the new techniques and features of Mac OS X. Whether you're interested in learning the basics or ferreting out every last detail, this book helps you get the most from your sessions with Apple's latest OS.

What's Inside

Mac OS X Bible: Jaguar Edition covers all of Mac OS X's features — new, updated, and existing from previous versions — in five parts:

✦ Part I starts with an overview of Mac OS X features. Use it to get started right away or to see the big picture. Then Part I describes in depth what you encounter when you start using Mac OS X. Windows, icons, and menus appear when you start up a Mac, but look closely and you may find some new and useful aspects of these elements. When you go beyond looking around the desktop, you can organize your disks, folders, and files with the Finder. You get right to work by opening programs and documents (including documents from Windows and DOS computers), moving document contents around, and saving documents. You learn about the tools included with Mac OS X for exploring the Web, e-mail, and other parts of the Internet. You also learn how to search your computer and the Internet using the Sherlock tool and the Find command. This part of the book also shows you how to get help on screen.

✦ Part II tells you how to use some important Mac OS capabilities. You learn how to print documents and how to harness other standard services. You discover how to obtain files from the Internet and how to access files on your local network (if your computer is connected to a local network). You learn to take charge of fonts and deal with typography. In this part, you find out why Mac OS X deserves its reputation as the multimedia leader among personal computer operating systems. You also learn how to adjust a multitude of system preference settings.

✦ Part III takes you beyond Mac OS X basics — way beyond. You learn how to set up accounts for other people who use your computer. You get to know how Mac OS X can speak text and recognize your spoken commands. You learn how to set up a simple network of computers, share your files with others on the network, and provide other services on your network. This part of the book also introduces AppleScript and teaches you how to use it to automate repetitive tasks.

✦ Part IV presents many ways to make the most of Mac OS X. You learn that the accessory programs included with Mac OS X come in handy on occasion. If these programs are not enough, Part IV also includes a chapter devoted to describing low-cost software utilities you can use to enhance Mac OS X. Another chapter presents dozens of Mac OS tips and secrets. Another chapter guides you through maintenance procedures. Part IV also explains the basics of using Unix commands to control your Mac.

✦ Part V contains reference information. Here, you find the instructions for installing Mac OS X and application programs. A summary of Mac OS X keyboard shortcuts is also in this section. In addition, this part includes a glossary filled with special terms you're bound to encounter while using Mac OS X, including quite a few that Webster hasn't gotten around to yet.

If you read this book from front to back, you will find that some information appears in more than one place. In particular, everything that Chapter 1 covers in summary appears in more detail elsewhere in the book. Also, some of the tips and secrets in Chapter 24 first appear amidst relevant subject matter throughout earlier chapters. This duplication is intentional and is meant for your benefit.

Conventions Used in This Book

We make use of certain conventions in this book in an effort to help guide you through the material.

Mac OS Version References

Apple regularly updates Mac OS X, and each update carries a new version number. This version number is separate from the Roman numeral in the Mac OS X name. For simplicity, we use the name Mac OS X to refer collectively to all versions. If we need to describe features of a different Mac OS X version, we include the version number. For example, Mac OS X 10.0.4 refers to the fourth minor update prior to the release of Mac OS X 10.1. The first version of Mac OS X is numbered 10.0. Minor updates are numbered sequentially by adding another decimal point and digit in this manner: 10.0.1, 10.0.2, and so on. When Apple releases a major update with significant new features, the second decimal digit is reset to zero and dropped, and the first decimal digit increases by one. Thus Mac OS X 10.2 is the second major update, and its first minor update is Mac OS X 10.2.1.

In addition, we refer frequently to Mac OS 9 in this book. We do this because Mac OS X uses Mac OS 9 to create the Classic compatibility environment in which you can use existing applications that have not been revised to work with Mac OS X directly. Apple has updated Mac OS 9 several times since its initial release. Each update has a different version number such as 9.0.4, 9.1, and 9.2.2. For simplicity, we follow the precedent set by Apple and refer to all versions collectively as Mac OS 9. If we need to refer to a specific version, we include the full version number. For example, we refer to application programs that work in the Classic environment as Mac OS 9 applications. In fact, a Mac OS 9 application may also run in versions of Mac OS 8 and even in earlier Mac OS versions. When we refer to the Mac OS 9 used by the Classic environment, we usually specify Mac OS 9.1 or later. (The Classic environment can't use Mac OS 9.0.4 and earlier.)

Sidebars

Certain discussions in this book are expanded with sidebars. These are shaded boxes that contain background information, expert tips and advice, and other helpful information.

Icon paragraphs

We augment the description of Mac OS X features with special information that is set apart from the regular text and marked with a distinctive icon. The icon indicates the type of special information — note, caution, or tip, — as explained in the following examples.

A Note icon calls attention to an interesting or unexpected aspect of the topic at hand.

A Caution icon alerts you to potential problems with an issue under discussion. Solutions and ways to avoid the situation are also included.

A Tip icon introduces a useful tip, trick, or secret.

Getting to Know Mac OS X

What Is Mac OS X?

Mac OS X marks a new beginning for Macintosh computers. It's the start of the next generation of the Macintosh operating system. Mac OS X has a fresh new look and new behaviors, and yet it still strongly resembles its predecessors, so most long-time Macintosh users will quickly become comfortable with it. Despite this family resemblance, Mac OS X is very different on the inside. It has two new state-of-the-art graphics modules. One module handles two-dimensional graphics, and the other renders three-dimensional graphics. At the core of Mac OS X is the renowned, rock-solid Unix operating system. From Unix, Mac OS X inherits strength, speed, and resiliency.

Considering all that's new in Mac OS X, it's not surprising that existing application programs must be revised to take advantage of the new look and feel, advanced graphics, and improved dependability and performance. Nevertheless, you can still use almost all of your applications that work with Mac OS 9.1 – 9.2.2. You use these existing applications in the Mac OS X special Classic compatibility environment. This Classic environment makes the transition from Mac OS 9 to Mac OS X much easier. You can continue using the applications you've been using with Mac OS 9.1 – 9.2.2 and upgrade them over time to get the increased benefits of Mac OS X applications. If you're using Mac OS 9.0.4 or earlier, you need to upgrade to Mac OS 9.1 – 9.2.2, and you may need to upgrade some applications for compatibility with Mac OS 9.1 – 9.2.2 before you can use those applications with the Mac OS X Classic environment.

This chapter gives you an aerial view of all the changes that Mac OS X brings to appearance, behavior, graphics, core services, and application compatibility. The chapter concludes by discussing the system requirements of Mac OS X.

You won't get a lot of detail in this chapter, and you may encounter some concepts and terminology that you don't fully understand. Just imagine that you're on a helicopter sightseeing tour looking over the Mac OS X terrain below. When you finish the tour in this chapter, the rest of the book describes the details and explains the concepts that interest you.

New Looks and Methods

The moment you see Mac OS X, you know that it's different from any other computer operating system, including earlier Mac OS versions. Nothing else looks like it. Yet, use it a bit and it feels familiar because Apple has taken great pains to make it work a lot like Mac OS 9. Use Mac OS X a while longer, and you realize that your first impression wasn't so far off after all. Although the basic skills you learn with Mac OS 9 or even earlier versions still apply when you start using Mac OS X, the little tricks that make you really proficient are another matter. A lot of details have changed in Mac OS X.

Aqua looks liquid

Apple designed a new user interface for Mac OS X and named it Aqua. What does this mean? Does it mean that Aqua is simply a new skin for the same old Mac OS? Yes, Aqua is a new look. You see semitransparent menus, controls that look like polished gemstones, shadows for objects such as windows and menus, larger icons with greater detail, and increased use of animation such as buttons that pulsate and controls that change appearance when you move the mouse pointer over them.

This list of Aqua features is all visual, but the change is more than skin deep. Aqua also gives Mac OS X a distinct feel that is different from the Mac OS 9 Platinum user interface. So Aqua is a new appearance *and* a new set of behaviors. For example, you still find controls for closing, minimizing, and maximizing windows in Aqua. But these controls look different than their counterparts in Mac OS 9. Some of these controls are in different places on Aqua windows. And as you'll see, one of these controls shrinks an Aqua window in an entirely different way than the equivalent Mac OS 9 button shrinks a window. You'll notice many more changes to the way windows look and feel in OS X. Figure 1-1 displays the Platinum user interface characteristic of OS 9.

Figure 1-1: Applications running within the Classic environment use the Platinum interface familiar from OS 9.

Besides revamped windows, Aqua has redesigned menus, buttons, and icons. These elements look completely different than the same elements in Mac OS 9; and in some cases, they behave differently as well. Figure 1-2 displays the Aqua user interface of OS X.

Figure 1-2: The appearance and controls of windows in the Mac OS X Aqua interface differ from windows in the OS 9 Platinum interface.

For details on Aqua windows, menus, and controls, see Chapter 2.

Dock appears

Mac OS X is not just a new look and feel; it also has many new features. The most noticeable new feature is the strip of icons normally located at the bottom of the screen. This strip is called the Dock. The icons on the Dock represent frequently used applications, documents, folders, and Internet locations. Other icons represent applications that are currently open. Additional icons represent minimized windows. You can customize the Dock by adding and removing icons. The Dock essentially replaces the Mac OS 9 Application Switcher, Control Strip, pop-up windows, collapsible windows, and some functions of the Apple menu.

You can make Dock icons huge or tiny, or let the Dock adjust the size automatically so that all icons fit. If the icons are small, you can have the Dock magnify them one at a time as you run the mouse pointer over them. Because many icons look alike at small sizes, the Dock displays the name of an icon when you point at it. Figure 1-3 shows the Dock with some magnified icons.

Every icon in the Dock has a pop-up menu of useful commands. For example, the pop-up menu for a Mac OS X application on the Dock lists its current windows, and the pop-up menu for a folder lists its contents. You can go to a listed item by choosing it from the pop-up menu.

Figure 1-3: The Dock displays the name of the icon you're pointing at and can magnify the icon as well.

If you find the Dock intrusive, you can configure it to hide itself except when you move the mouse pointer to the bottom of the screen. You can also move the Dock to the left side or the right side of the screen.

Cross-Reference   You can learn more about the Dock in Chapter 2.

Apple menu changes jobs

Because you can use the Dock to open frequently used applications, documents, and folders, the Apple menu no longer needs to provide that capability. Accordingly, the Apple menu has a simplified role in Mac OS X. As in Mac OS 9, you use the Apple menu to display basic information about the Mac and to open a recently used application or document. In addition, the Apple menu has commands for setting systemwide preferences and for restarting the computer, shutting it down, or putting it to sleep. You can also use the Apple menu to force an application to quit. Figure 1-4 shows the Apple menu in Mac OS X.

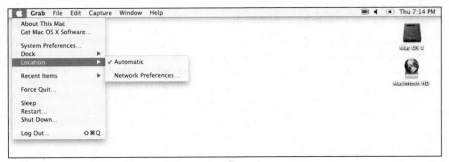

Figure 1-4: The Apple menu has a simplified role in Mac OS X.

 Cross-Reference You'll find more information about the Apple menu in Chapters 2 and 5.

Application menu moves

Like the Apple menu, the Application menu has a new job in Mac OS X. You no longer need the Application menu to switch between open applications because you have the Dock for that. The Application menu in Mac OS X contains commands dedicated to the application you're currently using, such as About, Preferences, Hide, and Quit. (Note that the About, Preferences, and Quit commands are in other menus in Mac OS 9.) In keeping with its new role, the Application menu has moved from the right end of the menu bar to the left of the File menu, and it is identified by the name of the application you're currently using. These changes take some getting used to, but they're actually more logical than the previous arrangement. Figure 1-5 shows the Application menu for the Finder.

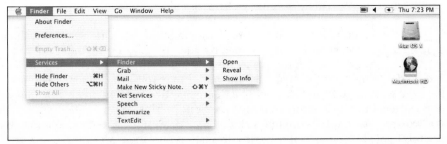

Figure 1-5: The Application menu lists commands that apply to the active application as a whole.

 Cross-Reference For additional information on the Application menu, see Chapter 5.

Finder changes its views

When the active application is the Finder, you can use its menu commands and windows to view, organize, and open applications, documents, folders, and other items stored on your Mac's hard drive, an inserted CD, and so forth. As always, you can view the contents of folders and disks as icons or as a list in a Finder window. In addition, Mac OS X introduces a third view: as columns that show you several levels of folder nesting at a glance. Figure 1-6 shows an example of the column view.

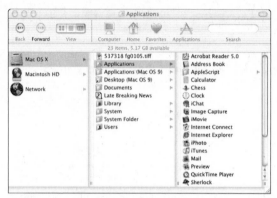

Figure 1-6: The Finder's column view shows several levels of folder hierarchy at a glance.

Regardless of the type of view, each Finder window can have a toolbar at the top. The toolbar has buttons that you can click to change the view, go back to the previous location displayed in the same window, or go to a special folder. You can customize the toolbar in each window, and you can hide it. You can also set the background color or a background picture for each window.

⬭ Finder windows don't tend to proliferate in Mac OS X with quite the wild abandon of its predecessors. When you open a folder, the Mac OS X Finder doesn't create a new window in which to display the folder's contents. Instead, the Finder uses the window from which you opened the folder to display the folder's contents. This new behavior is quite efficient but takes some getting used to if you're a Mac veteran. Change this behavior by clicking the nondescript control in the upper-right corner of a Finder window. When you do this, the window's toolbar becomes hidden, and opening a folder in this window causes the Finder to spawn a new window to display the folder's contents, just like the Mac OS 9 Finder.

Cross-Reference   You can learn more about Finder window views and toolbars in Chapters 3 and 4.

Finder changes its menus

Besides changes to Finder windows, Finder menus are changed in Mac OS X. A new Go menu can take you directly to any one of several commonly used folders. This menu also gives you quick access to the items you have designated as Favorites and to the folders you have most recently used. In addition, you can use it to connect to a network file server or an Internet location whose address you know. Figure 1-7 shows an example of the Go menu.

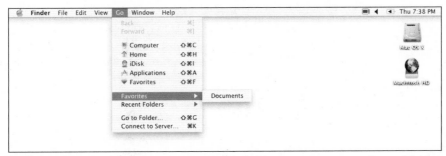

Figure 1-7: The Finder's Go menu gives you quick access to commonly used folders, your Favorites, recently used folders, and network file servers.

A less obvious change to the Finder menus concerns the Undo command, which has always been present at the top of the Edit menu. For the first time in Mac OS history, this command can actually undo common Finder operations, including moving, copying, and renaming items.

Cross-Reference   For details on Finder menus, see Chapters 3 and 4.

Folders get reorganized

When you browse through Finder windows, you notice a significantly different disk and folder organization in Mac OS X. For starters, Mac OS X has a new primary level known as Computer, and it contains an icon for each hard drive and inserted CD. If you open the startup disk, you see it contains only a handful of folders. All applications are supposed to go in the Applications folder. All of your folders and documents are supposed to go in your home folder, which bears your user name and is inside the Users folder. If other people use the same Mac, they have their own home folders in the Users folder. Figure 1-8 shows where home folders fit in the hierarchy.

Cross-Reference   You can learn more about folder organization in Chapter 3.

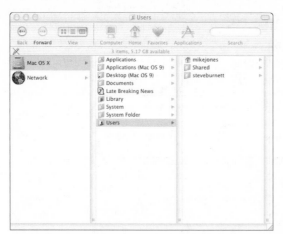

Figure 1-8: The canonical hierarchy in Mac OS X has a new primary level, Computer; a simplified root level for the startup disk and home folders for each user.

Desktop deserted

Look below the menu bar and behind the Finder windows and notice that the Desktop is practically empty in Mac OS X. All you see is a disk icon (or a couple of disk icons if you have more than one disk drive or a CD inserted) and an icon for accessing the Mac OS 9 Desktop. The Trash icon, which has traditionally anchored the lower-right corner of every Mac OS Desktop, is gone. In case you hadn't noticed, it is now at the end of the Dock, where program windows cannot cover it. The Dock also has icons for a Web browser, an e-mail program, and the Sherlock searching tool, all of which normally show up on the Desktop in Mac OS 9.

You can move icons to the Desktop if you want to, but it's actually an inconvenient location because the Desktop is usually covered by windows. You can also go extreme and configure the Finder not to show disk icons on the Desktop. There's no need to have them there, because they're always visible at the Computer level in any Finder window.

Also missing from the Mac OS X Desktop are pop-up windows. They can be handy, but the Dock (with its pop-up menus) does duplicate much of their functionality.

Cross-Reference   You'll find more about the Desktop in Chapters 3 and 4.

Icons look different

The icons you see in Finder windows and on the Desktop are much higher quality in Mac OS X. Apple has given all the icons it created a photo-realistic appearance and is encouraging other application developers to do the same. As in previous Mac OS versions, you can adjust the icon size in each window, but many more sizes are available, and the largest size is positively huge. When scaled up, OS X icons still look crisp and sharp. Figure 1-9 shows Mac OS X icons in several sizes.

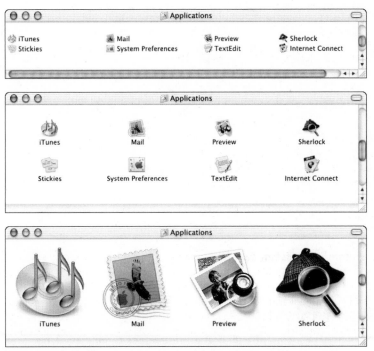

Figure 1-9: Icons in Mac OS X have a photo-realistic quality and scale smoothly to many sizes.

 For more information on icons, see Chapter 2.

Control panels supplanted

Although the Finder has undergone significant changes in Mac OS X, control panels have been entirely supplanted by a new mechanism for setting a broad range of system preferences. You no longer set options by opening individual control panels from a Control Panels folder. In Mac OS X, you select an icon in the System Preferences window and then set options related to the icon. For instance, select the Display icon to set options related to the display screen. Incidentally, long-time Macintosh users may recognize this design as reminiscent of the Control Panel from before System 7. Figure 1-10 shows the System Preferences window.

Figure 1-10: Set system-wide preferences in the Mac OS X System Preferences window.

 System Preferences are covered in Chapter 15.

Control Strip vanishes

Another means of setting frequently changed preferences in Mac OS 9, the Control Strip, is not available in Mac OS X. However, you can add some equivalent capabilities to the menu bar. Dock icons can also provide some of the same capabilities as Control Strip modules. For example, the iTunes icon in the Dock has a pop-up menu that includes commands for playing and pausing songs. Figure 1-11 shows the menu bar with an icon for changing the display resolution or number of colors.

Figure 1-11: The menu bar provides some of the capabilities of the defunct Control Strip.

For details on using Dock pop-up menus, see Chapter 4. For details on showing and hiding a Displays icon, Sound icon, or clock in the menu bar, see Chapter 15. For details on showing or hiding Modem, PPPoE, and AirPort status icons in the menu bar, see Chapter 18.

Different Internet applications bundled

The Dock always includes several applications for accessing Internet services, and there are additional Internet applications not on the Dock. As you'd expect, Internet Explorer is there for Web browsing, and Sherlock is there for searching. Mac OS X also includes a new e-mail program (aptly named Mail) and a coordinating Address Book application for managing e-mail addresses along with phone numbers and other contact information. You can use the Internet Connect application to manage Internet connections via modem, DSL, or cable modem with PPPoE, and AirPort. Figure 1-12 shows the Mail and Address Book applications.

Mac OS X also fully integrates Apple's .Mac accounts, which provide e-mail, disk storage, Web page hosting, and file sharing over the Internet. All you do to access these services is provide your iDisk account name and password. You don't have to install software in Mac OS X as you do in Mac OS 9.

 Internet applications are covered in Chapter 6.

Figure 1-12: The Mac OS X Mail application can handle your e-mail, and its Address Book application manages your contact information.

Sheets attach to windows

When you save or print a document in a Mac OS X application, a new kind of dialog descends at the top of the document window and partly covers the window like a translucent sheet. This dialog, called a *sheet*, does not block you from other windows belonging to the same application or the application's menus. A sheet remains attached to its document window even if you move the window around or switch to another window. Because of this attachment, you can't lose track of which document a sheet belongs to. Sheets are not universal in Mac OS X applications. Applications must be designed to use sheets and may use them for purposes other than saving and printing. Figure 1-13 shows an example of a sheet.

Figure 1-13: A sheet is attached to one window and does not block you from doing other work in other windows of the same application.

Cross-Reference You can find additional information on saving and printing with sheets in Chapters 5 and 9.

Open dialogs go columnar

Although not a sheet in Mac OS X, the standard Open dialog has changed a lot. In Mac OS 9, Open dialogs show a view of your files and folders that's a variation on the list view in the Finder. The Mac OS X Open dialogs show a view like the column view available in Mac OS X Finder windows. This view makes it easy to see where you are in your folder hierarchy, but you can't sort items by modification date as you can in Mac OS 9 (that is, in Mac OS 9 dialogs that use Navigation Services). Figure 1-14 shows an example of the Open dialog in Mac OS X.

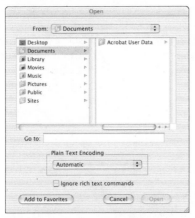

Figure 1-14: The Open dialog in Mac OS X applications displays files and folders in a column view.

For more on opening documents, see Chapter 5.

Printing gets simpler

In addition to the standard Print and Page Setup dialogs becoming sheets in Mac OS X, printing is simpler overall, especially if you use more than one printer. Instead of juggling individual Desktop printer icons as in Mac OS 9, you manage all printers and print jobs from the Print Center application. It automatically finds printers that are connected to your Mac's USB ports or are available on your local network, and you tell it which ones you want to use. Then you can choose any of these printers at the time you print from a Mac OS X application. The Print Center application opens whenever you print a document, so you can monitor the print job's progress, postpone printing, or cancel printing. The ability to preview printing on-screen is a standard feature of Mac OS X printing, as is the ability to save a PDF file in lieu of printing. Figure 1-15 shows an example of Print Center's list of available printers and the queue for one of them.

Figure 1-15: The Print Center application manages printers and their print queues for Mac OS X.

Cross-Reference   To learn more about printing, see Chapter 9.

Users account required

Although Mac OS X makes printing simpler, it makes another aspect of using a Mac a bit more complicated in the interest of improved security. Mac OS X requires you to set up at least one user account, which means only that you must specify a name and password for at least one user of the computer. You select an account name (or type an account name) and type a password during startup to log in as an authorized user, or you can configure Mac OS X to log in a user automatically. User accounts and logging in are optional in Mac OS 9. The login window is less sophisticated in Mac OS X than in Mac OS 9; you can't use your voice instead of a password. You can, however, log out with a voice command. Figure 1-16 shows the Mac OS X login window.

Cross-Reference   Logging in and logging out are covered in Chapter 2. User accounts are covered in Chapter 16.

Figure 1-16: Mac OS X requires logging in with a valid user name and password to start up, although this window can be bypassed by using the automatic login feature.

Improved Graphics

Many of the Mac OS X capabilities and much of its Aqua appearance wouldn't be possible without its new graphics engine called Quartz. It's based on Adobe's Portable Document Format (PDF) that's now a standard on the Internet. Quartz, together with OpenGL for rendering 3D graphics and QuickTime for displaying movies and other time-based media, delivers graphics performance and quality never before seen on a Mac.

Quartz does Aqua

Quartz instantly renders a complex screen image composed of menus, icons, windows, controls, and window content with special visual effects and keeps up with changes as you click controls, move and close windows, and use menus. A menu doesn't just disappear; it fades away. A sheet slides smoothly in and out of a window's title. An entire window, not just its outline, glides along as you drag it across the screen. A QuickTime movie playing in a window continues playing without interruption as you drag the window or minimize it to an icon in the Dock. A minimized window flows smoothly to and from the Dock like a genie flowing into and out of a bottle. And everywhere you look, translucency and blended drop shadows add depth to windows, menus, buttons, and other controls.

Quartz does PDF

Besides composing the screen image on the fly, Quartz enables you to create electronic documents in the PDF format simply by printing from any Mac OS X application. You specify that instead of sending the document to a printer, you want it saved as a PDF file. The PDF format preserves a document's fonts, formatting, colors, and graphics regardless of the application used to create the document. PDF enables you to preview print jobs by using the Preview application included with Mac OS X. Other people can view PDF files on all kinds of other computers by using the ubiquitous (and free) Adobe Acrobat Reader application. Figure 1-17 shows how easy it is to create a PDF file or preview a print job.

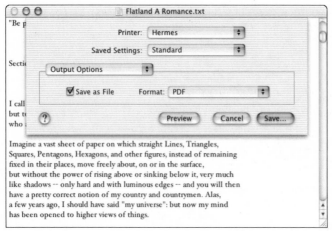

Figure 1-17: Create a PDF file or preview a print job right from the Print dialog of any Mac OS X application.

Cross-Reference   You can find more on print previews and PDF files in Chapter 9.

OpenGL does 3D

Mac OS X calls on a second graphics engine to render 3D objects and scenes with accurate lighting, shading, texture, motion blur, transparency, fog, and more special effects and for games, animation, and industrial design applications. For 3D graphics in Mac OS X, Apple licensed OpenGL from Silicon Graphics. In rendering 3D objects and scenes, OpenGL gets a speed boost from the Velocity Engine in the PowerPC G4 processor of a Mac that has one (or more) G4s. OpenGL also harnesses the 3D acceleration hardware built into all new Power Mac G4, iMac, iBook, and PowerBook computers. OpenGL delivers its fully rendered 3D objects and scenes to Quartz for compositing in the overall screen image. Software developers favor OpenGL because it works across platforms — Windows, Linux, Mac OS 9, and now Mac OS X — making it relatively easy to move a game or other application from one platform to another.

QuickTime does movies, MP3s, and more

Of course, Mac OS X has QuickTime for watching and listening to movies, MP3 music, streaming live TV and radio on the Internet, and more. QuickTime powers Apple's iMovie video-editing application and enables all Mac OS X applications to include just about every kind of image, sound, and video on the Internet. A version of QuickTime 6 is integrated into Mac OS X, where it can coordinate quickly with Quartz for optimum performance.

 Cross-Reference   For more information on QuickTime and iMovie, see Chapter 13. For more information on MP3 and Internet radio, see Chapter 14.

Modern Core

As nice as pretty graphics are, there's more to an operating system. Quartz, OpenGL, QuickTime, Aqua, and application programs all rest on a foundation dubbed Darwin. Darwin is a full-fledged Unix operating system in its own right. Darwin provides extremely stable, high-performance services, such as preemptive multitasking, symmetric multiprocessing, protected memory, advanced virtual memory, dynamic memory allocation, advanced device support, multiple file systems, advanced networking, and multiuser security. Most of these are long and eagerly awaited improvements to the Mac OS.

Preemptive multitasking

Mac OS X, like all Mac OS versions since System 7, allows more than one application to be open and operating at the same time. This is a capability called *multitasking*. It's like eating lunch while talking on the phone and driving a car. These tasks all appear to get done at the same time, but in reality you're quickly switching your attention to each task as necessary. Notice that some tasks, such as eating your lunch, take longer to complete when you're doing other tasks simultaneously.

Mac OS X eliminates a problem with multitasking as it exists in Mac OS 9 and earlier. The problem is that, in these earlier operating systems, applications must cooperatively share the system's processing time. Cooperative multitasking is fine in theory, but in practice, the system may feel unresponsive to you. With Mac OS 9, the application you're currently using may respond slowly to mouse and keyboard because other applications operating in the background aren't relinquishing control of the system often enough. The preemptive multitasking in Mac OS X deals with this problem. Darwin preempts each open application as needed to ensure that the application you're actively using doesn't get bogged down by other applications operating in the background. Those background applications won't get bogged down either, although they won't work as fast as the application you're actively using.

Symmetric multiprocessing

While making a Mac feel more responsive with preemptive multitasking, Darwin also speeds up a Mac that has two G4 processors by efficiently routing multiple tasks through both processors. It's like eating lunch in the car while someone else drives, and the two of you take turns talking on the phone so that while you're chewing, the driver is talking.

Darwin automatically routes separate tasks through two or more G4 processors, balancing the load to keep all processors busy. The tasks can be applications or parts of applications known as *threads,* which software engineers have separated out explicitly for multiprocessing. The tasks that Darwin routes through multiple processors also include separate threads of Mac OS X itself. Darwin routes all these application and operating system tasks through all available processors for best efficiency. By comparison, Mac OS 9 uses one processor for most of its tasks and for all applications that haven't been divided into separate threads. The only tasks that Mac OS 9 routes to a second processor are threads that software engineers have previously separated out for multiprocessing.

Protected memory

An advanced operating system like Mac OS X shouldn't allow serious problems in one application to bring down the whole system. Darwin's protected memory mechanism takes care of this by allocating each Mac OS X application its own memory space and preventing any application from going outside its allocated space. If an application goes haywire, Darwin forces it to quit. All other applications — as well as Quartz, OpenGL, QuickTime, Aqua, and Darwin itself — keep on going as if nothing happened. You can reopen the application that failed if you want to, but you don't have to restart the computer.

Advanced virtual memory

In addition to its protected memory mechanism, Darwin handles virtual memory and memory allocation much more effectively than Mac OS 9 and earlier. Although all Mac OS versions back to System 7 have been able to use hard drive space as if it were RAM, the technique that's the hallmark of virtual memory, Darwin does it more efficiently. In fact, the benefits of the Mac OS X virtual memory are so strong and its performance is so good that you can't turn it off.

What's more, Darwin also automatically adjusts the amount of memory allocated to each application. When an application needs more memory, Darwin allocates exactly the needed amount. This means that you don't have to bother with manually setting application memory sizes as in Mac OS 9.

Advanced device support

The contents of memory are transient, with large amounts of data moving in and out of memory to and from devices, such as hard drive, CD or DVD, printer, and digital video camcorder. Darwin's input/output (I/O) subsystem handles all the data transfer quickly. It even allows multiple applications to access multiple devices concurrently. As you would expect, the I/O subsystem is plug and play. Darwin recognizes when you plug in or unplug USB and FireWire devices into a USB or FireWire port, add PCI expansion cards, install or remove storage devices, and so on.

Multiple file systems

Storage devices, such as hard drives and CDs, use file systems to organize their contents, and Darwin enables Mac OS X to read and write many types of file systems. Naturally, it works with the established Mac OS Extended format (also known as HFS Plus) and the ISO 9660 format used by some CD-ROMs. Mac OS X can also read disks that use the older Mac OS Standard (HFS Standard) format, but you shouldn't plan to use Mac OS Standard format with new disks. In addition, Mac OS X extends support to Universal File System (UFS) format, which is similar to the standard format of most Unix volumes. Software developers can further extend Mac OS X to still more file systems, such as the Windows NT file system (NTFS).

Advanced networking

Through Darwin, Mac OS X also provides access to network file servers as though they were local drives. It can connect via the Apple File Protocol (AFP) to AppleShare file servers and Macs that use the personal file sharing built into Mac OS X and earlier (as far back as System 7). Mac OS X can connect via the Network File System (NFS) protocol to Unix file servers. And it can connect to Internet file servers that use the WebDAV protocol. Software developers can also extend Mac OS X with plug-in software that supports other file-server protocols. Mac OS 10.2 also introduced the instant networking called Rendezvous. Rendezvous is networking code that allows a Jaguar system to automatically discover and connect to devices over any IP network, using a concept called *zero configuration*. A general user needs to know only that Rendezvous works to make connecting to other computers easier.

 Cross-Reference   You can find additional information on HFS Plus and other file systems in Chapter 4.

Kernel

The core component of Darwin is called the *kernel*. One part of the kernel manages the processor (or processors) and memory. This part of the kernel is based on the Mach 3.0 technology from Carnegie-Mellon University. The other part of the Darwin kernel provides basic multiuser security and access to file systems, networking, and other services used by Quartz, OpenGL, QuickTime, Rendezvous, Aqua, and applications. This second part of the Darwin kernel is based on the BSD 4.4 technology from the University of California at Berkeley. BSD also provides a Unix command-line interface, which you can use to control Mac OS X by typing commands instead of using windows, icons, and menus. Both BSD and Mach are very highly regarded operating system components.

Cross-Reference   You can learn more about Unix commands in Chapter 26.

Classic Applications

At first, you may not see much of the Aqua interface outside of the Desktop application and the Web browser and Sherlock and a handful of other applications. That's because most, if not all, of your older applications have to be updated to use Aqua. Until a developer revises an application and you install the upgrade, you see the application in the Platinum look of Mac OS 9. A Classic application's windows, menus, buttons, and other controls all have the Platinum look, and they work like Mac OS 9 windows, menus, buttons, and so forth.

Classic environment

Classic applications have the look and behavior of Mac OS 9 because they actually operate under Mac OS 9.1 – 9.2.2 in a special environment inside Mac OS X. In fact, the Classic environment must start up before you can use a Classic application. This startup process is very similar to starting up a Mac with Mac OS 9: You can see the Welcome to Mac OS 9 message and the march of startup items (extensions and control panels), but these things appear in a Mac OS X window. (You can shrink the Classic startup window to show only a progress bar.) The startup window goes away altogether after the Classic environment has started up, and Classic windows mingle with Mac OS X windows on the screen. You get a gray Mac OS 9-style menu bar when you use a Classic application and an Aqua menu bar when you use a Mac OS X application. The Dock is still available at the bottom or the side of the screen. Figure 1-18 shows an example of a Classic application in Mac OS X.

Classic limitations

If you have more than one Classic program open at the same time, they share the Classic environment by using cooperative multitasking exactly as they do in OS 9. The Classic application you're using may get bogged down by other Classic applications that are working in the background.

Classic applications don't have protected memory, at least not from each other. This lack of protected memory means that if one Classic application fails, it may make other Classic programs that are open fail as well (or make them unreliable). When a Classic program fails, you need to restart the entire Classic environment and all the Classic programs you were using.

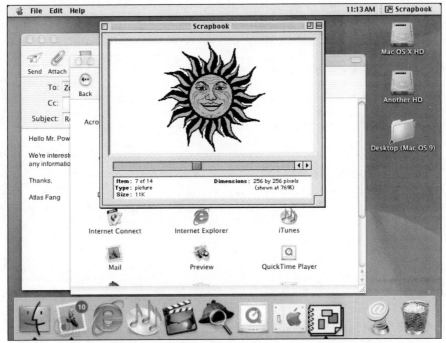

Figure 1-18: Old applications operating under Mac OS 9 in a special Classic environment mingle with Mac OS X applications.

Although individual Classic applications don't benefit from protected memory and preemptive multitasking, the Classic environment as a whole does. Problems in the Classic environment have no ill effect on Mac OS X applications or on Mac OS X itself. To them, the Classic environment is just an OS X application. If a Classic application quits unexpectedly, you restart only the Classic environment, not the whole computer. Conversely, a problem in a Mac OS X application does not affect the Classic environment or any Classic applications.

Mac OS X Applications

Old applications can be revised, and new applications can be developed to take advantage of the Aqua interface and other Mac OS X features. Apple provides software developers several frameworks for revising and creating Mac OS X applications: Carbon, Cocoa, Java, and Unix.

Carbon applications

Mac applications originally developed for Mac OS 9 and earlier can become full-fledged Mac OS X applications by revising them for the Carbon framework. The revision process is analogous to renovating a house to bring it up to modern building codes and give it the latest conveniences. Carbon can be used for developing new Mac OS X applications as well.

Applications that use the Carbon framework have an Aqua interface and take full advantage of all the advanced features of Mac OS X. Besides being first-class citizens of Mac OS X, Carbon applications can be used with Mac OS 8.1 – 9.2.2. This dual citizenship is important for many software developers because they want their applications to operate on old Macs as well as new ones.

Cocoa applications

Applications built on the Cocoa framework are also first-class citizens of Mac OS X. They have an Aqua interface and take full advantage of the advanced features of Mac OS X. Software developers who use the Cocoa framework don't care about backwards compatibility because Cocoa applications can't be used with Mac OS 9.2.2 and earlier. Developers choose Cocoa for its modern object-oriented programming techniques and rapid application development tools, which make application development significantly faster and easier than for Carbon.

Java applications and applets

The Java framework makes developing and using Java applications and applets possible with Mac OS X. Java applications and applets are noted for their portability across computing platforms, but Apple's Java framework enables developers to incorporate the Aqua interface, automatic multiprocessor support, and other Mac OS X features. Java programmers can also create Cocoa applications by using the Java programming language.

Unix applications

A number of applications run directly on a Unix kernel, and many of these applications can be made to run on the Mac OS X Unix kernel without too much effort. Average Mac OS X users aren't likely to find Unix applications very interesting, but enterprises with custom Unix applications may want to have them modified for the Mac OS X Unix kernel. Then their employees can run the custom Unix applications on a Mac together with general business applications. Individuals already knowledgeable in Unix or Linux topics are likely to be able to run many of their preferred applications.

System Requirements for Mac OS X

You can install Mac OS X on most Apple computers that were factory-equipped with a G3 or G4 processor. One exception is the original PowerBook G3 model, which can't use Mac OS X. (This model has a rainbow-colored Apple logo on its case. Other

PowerBook G3 models have a large white Apple logo.) Apple doesn't certify that Mac OS X works on older computers that have been upgraded with G3 or G4 processors, although makers of some of these processor upgrades hope to make it work.

In addition to a factory-installed G3 or G4 processor, your computer needs at least 128MB of RAM installed, and for better performance you need 256MB or more. As for disk space, plan on having 1.5GB available for the Mac OS X installation process. After installation, Mac OS X occupies about 1GB. To use applications made for Mac OS 9.1 – 9.2.1 in the Classic environment, you also need another 350MB for Mac OS 9.1 – 9.2.2. This 350MB can be on the same disk volume as Mac OS X or on another disk volume.

Your Mac must also have one of the following: a built-in display, a built-in video port, or a video card supplied by Apple.

Cross-Reference   For more information about installing Mac OS X, see Appendix A.

Summary

After reading this chapter, you know that Mac OS X looks and feels different from earlier Mac OS versions. Basic skills you have learned with earlier versions still apply, but many details have changed in Mac OS X, notably the following:

✦ The Aqua interface features redesigned windows, menus, icons, buttons, and other controls.

✦ Icons in the Dock provide quick access to applications, documents, folders, Internet locations, and minimized windows.

✦ The Apple menu provides control over the whole system, and the Application menu provides control over the active application.

✦ In the Finder, you can view windows as columns, and each window can display a toolbar.

✦ The Finder also has a Go menu and a more useful Undo command.

✦ The startup disk has a new folder organization, and the Desktop has fewer icons.

✦ Icons are higher quality, and you can scale them across a wider range of sizes.

✦ The System Preferences window replaces individual control panels.

✦ The Control Strip is not available, but the menu bar and Dock can provide some of its functions.

✦ Bundled Internet software now includes the Mail and Address Book applications for e-mail and contact information. Mac OS X also integrates an .Mac account with iDisk, which provides e-mail, disk storage, Web page hosting, and file sharing over the Internet.

✦ A sheet for detailed information about printing, saving, or some other operation in one window doesn't block other operations in the same application.

✦ Dialogs for opening files show a view of files and folders like the column view available in Finder windows.

✦ The Print Center application replaces Desktop printer icons. Print preview and saving as a PDF file are standard features of printing.

✦ At least one user account is required. Login is also required during startup, but login can be automated.

These externally visible changes are nothing compared to the internal changes in Mac OS X. The performance and quality of the Mac OS X Quartz graphics software, which is based on PDF technology, make the Aqua appearance possible. Quartz coordinates with OpenGL software for 3D graphics and with QuickTime for video and audio. The Unix-based core of Mac OS X, Darwin, provides preemptive multitasking, symmetric multiprocessing, protected memory, advanced virtual memory, dynamic memory allocation, advanced device support, multiple file systems, fast networking, and multiuser security.

You can use most Mac OS 9 applications with Mac OS X, but they operate in the Classic environment. The Classic environment has the Platinum look and feel of Mac OS 9 and doesn't provide many of the improvements listed in the preceding paragraph. Existing applications that software developers revise to use the Carbon framework can have all the advantages of Mac OS X and can still be used with Mac OS 8.1 – 9.2.2. Building new applications for Mac OS X is easier and faster with Cocoa. Cross-platform Java applications and applets work with Mac OS X, and many Unix applications can be made to run on Mac OS X as well.

Mac OS X can be installed on a Mac that was factory-equipped with a G3 or G4 processor and has at least 128MB of RAM, 1.5GB of hard drive space, and a display or video port supplied by Apple. Using the Classic environment requires additional hard drive space.

✦   ✦   ✦

Exploring the Environment

Mac OS X provides a consistent, comfortable envi-
ronment in which you work (and play) on your
Macintosh computer. Apple calls this environment Aqua
and promotes it heavily. But like the environments of
previous Mac OS versions, Aqua is made up of menus,
windows, icons, and an assortment of controls. It's important
that you know how all these Aqua objects look and operate
because you use them constantly. This chapter familiarizes
you with the Mac OS X Aqua menu bar, pop-up menus,
contextual menus, regular windows, dialogs, alerts, sheets,
window controls, other controls, and the Dock.

Not only does Mac OS X provide the Aqua environment for
you, it also enables you to work concurrently in the Classic
environment of Mac OS 9. In the Classic environment, the
menu bar, windows, and controls look different and operate
somewhat differently than their Mac OS X counterparts. In
case you haven't used Mac OS 9 or earlier, and for comparison's sake if you have, this chapter describes both Classic
and Mac OS X environments.

Before describing menus, windows, icons, and controls, this
chapter explains how you start a session in the Mac OS X
environment and how the Classic environment may then start
automatically. Finally, this chapter concludes by explaining
how you log out, restart, or shut down to end a Mac OS X
session.

Starting Up and Logging In

As you're probably aware, your computer must go through a startup process when you turn it on. Startup begins with a small, permanent program loading the full operating system software — Mac OS X — into the computer's memory from a disk. When enough of Mac OS X has loaded that it can take control of the computer, it goes through a login procedure in an effort to keep unauthorized people from using the computer. The login procedure is mandatory but can be automated. In fact, Mac OS X is initially configured for automatic login and remains that way unless someone sets it for manual login, as described in Chapter 15.

After Mac OS X starts up, you can use the Finder and other application programs made for Mac OS X. We cover the Finder in Chapters 3 and 4 and discuss using other applications in Chapter 5.

Starting up your computer with Mac OS X

You start up a Macintosh by pressing any of the following:

✦ Power button on the computer

✦ Power key on the keyboard, if the keyboard has one

✦ Power button on some Apple flat-panel displays (on some display models, the power button only turns the display on or off)

Prior to 10.2, the familiar Happy Mac icon displayed in the center of the screen while Mac OS X was loading. As of 10.2 the Happy Mac is gone, replaced by a solid Apple logo. A spinning set of bars below the Apple logo indicates that the computer is busy.

Soon a Mac OS X greeting appears together with a gauge that measures startup progress, and a sequence of brief messages reports steps in the startup process. The spinning disk changes to an arrow-shaped pointer. This pointer tracks mouse movement, but clicking the mouse button has no effect at this time. Figure 2-1 illustrates this part of the startup process.

Figure 2-1: A progress gauge and a series of messages report on the startup process.

What happens next depends on whether your computer has been configured for automatic or manual login. If your computer is configured for manual login, Mac OS X displays a login window, and you must provide an account name and password before the startup process can continue. We cover the login procedure under the next heading.

If your computer is configured for automatic login, you do not see the login screen. Instead the startup process continues, and eventually you see the Mac OS X menu bar at the top of the screen. You can find a description of the menu bar later in this chapter in the section "Investigating Menus."

Note   Your computer can be set to start up with Mac OS 9 instead of Mac OS X. In this case, a Mac OS 9 greeting appears during startup and the Mac OS X environment is not available after startup. We explain how to select the system to be used for startup in Chapter 15.

Logging in to Mac OS X

Before Mac OS X finishes starting up, it may require you to log in manually. If so, the startup process halts and you see a login window. The login window may show a list of users with accounts on your computer, or the screen may have spaces labeled Name and Password. Figure 2-2 shows examples of both types of login window.

Figure 2-2: When logging in to Mac OS X, you may get to select a user account from a list (top) or you may have to type a valid account name (bottom).

Logging in with a list of user accounts

If the login window shows a list of users who have accounts on your computer, log in by following these steps:

1. **Use the mouse to click your account name.** The initial login window goes away and is replaced by a second login window, which has a space for entering a password. Figure 2-3 shows an example of the second login window.

   If your user account name is not listed, you may be able to log in by typing your user account name. To do this, click Other in the list of account names and continue at Step 1 in the next procedure. If the account list doesn't include Other, you can't log in by entering an account name. Get help from the person who configured the computer for multiple users.

Instead of logging in, you can shut down or restart your computer by clicking the appropriate button in the window.

2. **Type your password.** You won't be able to read what you type because, for privacy, the password is displayed as a sequence of dots. Capitalization matters in the password; upper- and lowercase letters are not interchangeable. If you don't know the password for the selected user account, click the Go Back button to return to the initial login window and select a different user. If you don't know the password for any account, check with the person who configured your computer for multiple users.

3. **Press Return on the keyboard or use the mouse to click Log In.** The login window goes away, and soon the Mac OS X menu bar appears, possibly together with windows, icons, and the Dock. You can read more about the menu bar and the other objects in later sections of this chapter.

Figure 2-3: After clicking one of the account names listed in the initial login window, you must enter the password for the account.

Logging in without a list of user accounts

If the login window shows spaces in which to enter a user account name and password, as shown previously in Figure 2-2, follow these steps to log in:

1. **Type your user account name, press the Tab key, and then type your password.** You can read the name you type, but for privacy, the password is displayed as a sequence of dots. Capitalization matters in the name and the password. If you don't know your account name and password, check with the person who configured your computer for multiple users.

2. **Press Return on the keyboard or use the mouse to click Log In.** The login window goes away, and soon the Mac OS X menu bar appears, possibly together with windows, icons, and the Dock. You can read more about the menu bar and the other objects in later sections of this chapter.

3. **Instead of logging in, you can shut down or restart your computer by clicking the appropriate button in the window.**

Dealing with login problems

If the login window shakes back and forth like someone shaking his head no, either the password you entered was not correct for the user account name you specified or Mac OS X did not recognize the user account name you entered. The Password space clears so that you can retype the password and press Return or click Log In. If you typed a user account name and you need to retype it, press the tab key to highlight the Name space. If you selected a user account from a list, you can select a different account by clicking the Go Back button.

Mac OS X is flexible enough to accommodate alternate login procedures, such as voice authentication. If any such alternatives become available and you install one on your computer, the login procedure will be different than the basic procedures described here. Mac OS X doesn't by itself support voice commands for logging in, but you can log out with a voice command.

Why Is Security Important?

Mac OS X is the first general release of the Macintosh system software that incorporates truly deep-seated security. It comes at a time when security has become an important issue for many Mac users. Just a few years ago, Macs mostly stood alone in homes or were connected in fairly small, tightly controlled local networks. Today, your Mac is probably connected to countless computers around the world via the Internet. And with some types of high-speed Internet connections, your Mac may be on the Internet 24 hours a day.

Previous releases of the Mac OS, although elegant and easy to use, can be controlled only to a limited extent via the Internet. In contrast, a Mac OS X system that has been set to allow remote login via the Internet is wide open to an unscrupulous user (a *hacker* or *cracker*) who knows the right user account name and password. For example, you might set Mac OS X to allow remote login so that you could use it from another location. If a cracker were to learn your account name and guess the corresponding password, that cracker could use your computer remotely to attack other machines on the Internet. These attacks could overload entire networks, cause machines to crash, or destroy or steal data. Mac OS X is more open to misuse because it's based on Unix, which has had over 30 years of evolution and use to find solutions to security as a multiuser operating system. The first line of defense against unauthorized access is a tough password that you keep secret. (For advice on picking a good password, see Appendix A.)

What login accomplishes

The login procedure accomplishes two things. First, it proves that you are authorized to use the computer. Second, it establishes which user you are, and this user identity determines what you can see and do on the computer. Even if you're the only person who uses your computer, some of what's stored on it is protected so that you normally can't change it or remove it. This protects the integrity of the computer.

Your user identity is especially important if your computer has been set up for multiple users, such as members of a family or several workers in an office, because each user has personal preference settings and private storage areas. For example, each user may prefer a different background picture on the screen, and you may not want other users to have access to everything you have stored on the computer or all the application programs you use. You can find information on setting up Mac OS X for multiple users in Chapter 16.

Starting the Classic Environment

If you want to use applications made for Mac OS 9, you must start up the Classic environment after starting up Mac OS X. You can have Mac OS X start the Classic environment automatically after login, so we describe the Classic startup process and the Classic environment in this chapter. Chapter 5 has more information on using application programs in the Classic environment.

Starting Classic after login

On your computer, Mac OS X may be configured to start the Classic environment automatically after login. If so, you see a gauge that measures the progress of the Classic environment starting. This progress gauge appears in a window whose title begins *Classic Environment is starting* and ends with the name of the source of Mac OS 9 being used. This window may appear behind other windows because starting the Classic environment does not monopolize the computer. While Classic starts, you can use the computer for other tasks. As soon as the Classic environment has started, the progress window disappears. Figure 2-4 shows the progress window alone near the top of the Mac OS X screen.

Figure 2-4: Mac OS X monitors the Classic environment start process.

Who Needs Classic?

Applications and other software made for Mac OS 9 and earlier don't work in Mac OS X because it's an entirely new operating system for the Mac. Knowing that you would need to use older software after installing Mac OS X, Apple engineers figured out how to make Mac OS 9 work inside Mac OS X. The result is the Classic environment. As noted in Chapter 1, applications in the Classic environment don't get all the benefits of advanced Mac OS X features, such as protected memory and preemptive multitasking. Furthermore, Mac OS X applications have the Platinum look of the Mac OS 9 environment, not the Aqua look of the Mac OS X environment. Additionally, some software made for Mac OS 9 doesn't work in the Classic environment, especially software that needs direct access to the computer's hardware components. Classic's drawbacks are relatively minor. The important point is that Classic makes Mac OS X compatible with most Mac OS 9 application programs.

If you want to use the Classic environment, your computer must have Mac OS 9 (technically, Mac OS 9.1 or a later version of Mac OS 9) installed as well as Mac OS X. We cover Mac OS installation in Appendix A.

Note   The very first time the Classic environment starts on your computer, Mac OS X may display an alert saying it needs to add or update some Classic-specific resources in the Mac OS 9 System Folder. This means that some of the system files in your Mac OS 9 System Folder are not compatible with the Classic environment. Click OK to allow Mac OS X to add or update the files.

Expanding the window

▶ While the Classic environment starts, you can expand the progress window by clicking the triangle on the left side of the window. The expanded window reveals that Mac OS 9 is in fact behind the Classic curtain. In the expanded window, you see the Mac OS 9 welcome message and a sequence of icons marching across the bottom of the window. These icons represent system extensions being loaded as Mac OS 9 gets under way. Click the triangle again to collapse the window. Figure 2-5 shows the expanded window.

Stopping Classic

`Stop`   You can stop Classic before it gets started by clicking the Stop button on the right of the Classic Environment starting window. Avoid forcing Classic to stop because doing so may lead to problems in the Classic environment. If you do click Stop, Mac OS X displays a warning as shown in Figure 2-6 that asks if you're sure you want to stop Classic in the midst of starting. Click the Continue Startup button unless you absolutely must force Classic to stop by clicking the Stop Classic button.

You can safely stop Classic after it has started by using the System Preferences application as described in Chapter 15. You can also stop Classic by logging out of Mac OS X, shutting down, or restarting the computer as described at the end of this chapter.

Figure 2-5: Expand the window that monitors the Classic environment getting started and see what's really starting up.

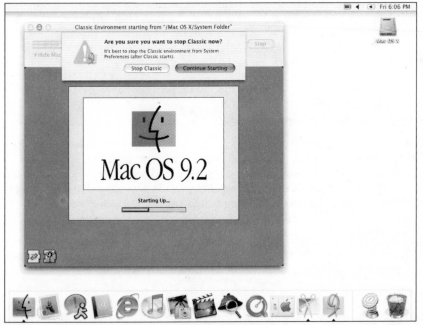

Figure 2-6: It's possible to stop Classic while it's starting up but doing so isn't recommended.

Starting Classic at other times

Don't be concerned if the Classic environment does not start automatically after Mac OS X starts up. If the Classic environment isn't already started, it will start automatically when it's needed. For example, the Classic environment starts automatically when you open a Mac OS 9 application, as described in Chapter 5. You can also start Classic manually at any time by using the System Preferences application, as described in Chapter 15.

Investigating Menus

The Mac OS has always used menus to present lists of commands or attributes. You can put a command or attribute into effect by choosing it from its menu using the mouse. Choosing a command or attribute generally takes action on an object or changes the state of an object. This object may be something you selected in advance, such as some words that you want to make a certain size that you choose. The object of a menu command may instead be an implicit part of the command, such as the list of preference settings that are displayed when you choose the Preferences command from a menu.

Menus take up a lot of space on the screen, so they're normally hidden except for their titles. When you want to see one, you click its title with the mouse.

You see menus in many different places, but you almost always see menu titles in the menu bar at the top of the screen. Menus can also appear outside the menu bar. For example, a pop-up menu appears outside the menu bar when you click its title, which should be labeled with a distinctive arrow. In addition, the Mac OS can display menus in some places based solely on the context of the mouse pointer. This section describes menus in the menu bar, pop-up menus, and contextual menus.

Why One Menu Bar?

The Mac OS has a permanent menu bar at the top of the screen for several reasons. One reason is that a menu bar at the top of the screen is an easy target to hit with the mouse. You can quickly slide the mouse pointer to the top of the screen, where it automatically stops at the menu bar. If the menu bar were at the top of a window in the middle of the screen (like on a Microsoft Windows OS), you would have to take more time to position the pointer carefully over the menu bar.

A second reason is that having a permanent menu bar at the top of the screen gives you a reliable place for every application's commands. If each window on the screen had its own menu bar, you'd have to think about which one you wanted to use.

Using the menu bar

The menus in the menu bar at the top of the screen contain commands that are relevant to the application you are using at the time. The menus may also contain attributes that apply to objects that you work with in the application. Menu titles appear in the menu bar, and you can use the mouse to display one menu at a time beneath its title. Figure 2-7 shows the menu bar as it appears initially in Mac OS X, with one of its menus displayed.

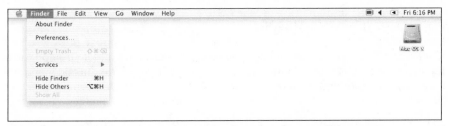

Figure 2-7: The menu bar is a permanent fixture at the top of the screen.

Using the Mac OS X menu bar

To use the menu bar, you position the mouse pointer over a menu title and click or press the mouse button. The menu opens beneath the menu title so that you can see the items in it and choose one, if you like.

To choose a menu item, position the pointer over it, highlighting it. Then click the mouse button. The menu item you choose flashes briefly and then the menu fades away.

If a menu item is dim, it is not available under the current circumstances. For example, you can't empty the computer's Trash container if it is currently empty. Another example: A menu item for setting the format of text is probably available only when some text is selected.

In Mac OS X, unlike previous Mac OS versions, a menu stays open indefinitely until you click again. With a menu displayed, you can leave your finger off the mouse button and move the pointer up and down the menu, highlighting each menu item as the pointer passes over it. You can close a menu without choosing an item from it by clicking the mouse button when the pointer is on the menu's title or anywhere outside the menu.

While looking at any menu in the menu bar, you go to and see a different menu by moving the pointer over the menu's title. Click any menu item you see to choose it or click outside any menu to stop looking at menus in the menu bar.

Tip   If you're used to the way Macintosh menus originally worked, you can still use them that way. If you click a menu title and keep holding down the mouse button while moving the pointer, the menu goes away as soon as you release the mouse button. To choose a menu item, just click and hold, move to the menu item, and release. With this method, you click only once, but you have to keep pressing the mouse button.

Using the Classic menu bar

The menu bar and menus are a little different in the Classic environment. Classic menus have the Platinum look of Mac OS 9, and they don't stay open indefinitely. A Classic menu does stay open when you click it, and it remains open as long as you keep moving the mouse. You don't have to hold down the mouse button to keep a menu open. However, a Classic menu disappears automatically if you don't move the mouse for 15 seconds. Figure 2-8 shows an example of the Classic menu bar, with one of its menus displayed.

Figure 2-8: The Classic menu bar has the Platinum look of Mac OS 9.

Standard Mac OS X menus

In most Mac OS X applications, the menu bar includes several of the following standard menus:

✦ **Apple menu** is at the left end of the menu and has a miniature solid Apple logo for its title, as compared to the six-color striped Apple menu log in OS 9. Use this menu to get basic information about your Macintosh, change system preference settings, change Dock preference settings, or change the network location. You can also use this menu to open a recently used application or document or force applications to quit. In addition, the Apple menu has commands for putting the computer into sleep mode, restarting it, shutting it down, or logging out.

✦ **Application menu** is next to the Apple menu and has the name of the application that you are currently using for its title. This menu includes commands that apply to the application as a whole. Use the Application menu to get information about the current application, change preference settings, get services from other applications (as described in Chapter 11), hide the current application or all others, or quit the application when you are done using it.

✦ **File menu** is next to the Application menu and contains commands that affect a whole document, such as New, Open, Close, Save, and Print. Usually, applications that don't have documents don't have a File menu. You can find more information on most of these commands in Chapter 5; we cover the Print command in Chapter 9.

✦ **Edit menu** is to the right of the File menu and contains commands that you can use to change a document's contents, such as Undo, Cut, Copy, Paste, and Select All. Read more about these commands in Chapter 5.

✦ **Window menu** enables you to zoom (maximize), minimize the active window, or bring all the listed windows in front of windows belonging to other applications. In addition, the Window menu lists other windows that belong to the same application and may have additional commands for window manipulation. We describe zooming and minimizing windows later in this chapter.

✦ **Help menu** gives you access to on-screen help. This menu is located immediately to the right of the last application-specific menu in the menu bar. In some cases the application may have its own help menu and the OS X Help menu may not be present. If this is true and you want to open the OS X Help, you can either switch to an application such as the Finder, or use the keyboard shortcut of the ⌘-? key. Chapter 8 has more information on the Help menu.

✦ **Clock menu** is normally at the right end of the menu bar and has a digital clock or an analog clock as its title. Click this menu to see the current date as well as the time, to switch between digital and analog clocks, and to open Date & Time pane of the System Preferences application, which we cover in Chapter 15.

✦ **Sound menu** normally appears next to the clock in the menu bar and enables you to adjust the computer's sound level. This menu has a speaker icon as its title, and it indicates the current sound level. A setting in the Sound pane of the System Preferences application determines whether the Sound menu appears in the menu bar, as described in Chapter 15.

✦ **AirPort menu** normally appears next to the Sound menu if your computer has an AirPort wireless networking card installed. This menu's title icon shows four arcs that indicate the strength of the wireless network signal. You can use the AirPort menu to join a wireless network, create a wireless network, or turn the AirPort card off and on. You can also use this menu to open the Internet Connect application, which we cover in Chapter 6. Chapter 18 has much more information on AirPort.

Each application may omit some of these menus and may add its own menus between the Edit menu and the Help menu. The menus on the right side of the menu bar may be in a different order. In addition, the menu bar may have more icons with menus on the right side of the menu bar. For example, the menu bar may have a modem icon with a menu and a PPPoE icon, each with a menu for monitoring and controlling connections via modem and PPPoE, as described in Chapters 6 and 18.

Tip Don't count on your kinesthetic memory helping you to move efficiently to a particular standard menu. Menu positions are less predictable in Mac OS X than in previous Mac OS versions. All menus to the right of the Application menu may appear in slightly different positions on the menu bar depending on the application you are currently using, because the width of the Application menu's title varies according to the length of the application's name.

Standard Classic menus

The Classic environment's menu bar has its own set of standard menus. In most Classic applications, the menu bar includes these five menus:

✦ **Apple menu** is at the left end of the menu and has a miniature multicolored Apple logo for its title. This menu usually includes an About item, which describes the application you are currently using, followed by an alphabetical list of programs, documents, and other items that can be opened. Some of the items may not work properly in the Mac OS X Classic environment; they may work only if you start up the computer with Mac OS 9. One example of an OS 9 application that will not run in the Classic environment is the Network Browser.

✦ **File menu** is next to the Apple menu and contains commands that affect a whole document, such as New, Open, Close, Save, and Print. The last item is usually Quit, which you use when you are done working with an application.

✦ **Edit menu** is to the right of the File menu and contains commands that you can use to change a document's contents, such as Undo, Cut, Copy, Paste, and Clear. The Edit menu is also the standard location for a Preferences command in Classic applications, although some applications put their Preferences command in a different menu.

✦ **Help menu** gives you access to on-screen help. This menu is immediately to the right of the last application-specific menu in the menu bar.

✦ **Application menu,** which is located at the right end of the menu bar, displays an alphabetical list of the applications that are currently running on the computer. Choosing an application makes it the active application so that you can use it. You can also use this menu to hide the active application or show or hide the other applications that are running (including Mac OS X applications).

Note   Although the names of the standard Classic menus are the same as standard Mac OS X menus, only the Edit and Help menu have similar functions. The Apple, File, and Application menus have distinct differences between Classic and Mac OS X menu bars.

Each Classic application may add its own menus between the Edit menu and the Help menu. In addition, the menu bar in the Classic environment normally includes a digital clock near the right end of the menu bar. Clicking the menu bar clock switches between the time and date display.

Using pop-up menus

A *pop-up menu* appears outside the menu bar when you click the pop-up menu's title. The title may be a text label or an icon, and the title is marked with an arrowhead to indicate that clicking it will display a pop-up menu. The arrowhead may point down or to the right. It may also be double-headed and point up and down.

Only one pop-up menu can be displayed at a time. If a pop-up menu is open, it goes away automatically if you click the title of another pop-up menu. Figure 2-9 shows examples of pop-up menus in the Mac OS X Aqua and Classic environments.

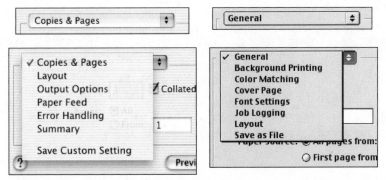

Figure 2-9: An arrowhead marks a pop-up menu in a Mac OS X application (left) and in a Classic application (right).

Using contextual menus

Rooting through menus to find a particular command isn't much fun. Wouldn't it be better if all you saw were relevant commands? That's the point of contextual menus — they offer commands that make sense in a given context. You can display a contextual menu by holding down the Control key while clicking an icon, a window, or some selected text for which you want to choose a command or attribute. The contextual menu lists commands that are relevant to the item that you Control-click. Figure 2-10 shows an example of a contextual menu for an icon.

Figure 2-10: Pressing the Control key while clicking an item may display a contextual menu.

You can Control-click one item or a selection of several items. Control-clicking a selection of several items displays a contextual menu of commands that pertain to the whole group. We explain how to make a selection of several items later in this chapter.

Tip   If your Mac has a two-button mouse or trackball, you may be able to display contextual menus by pressing the right button without holding Control. If your multi-button mouse or trackball does not already work this way, you may be able to program it to simulate a Control-click whenever you press the right button. For instructions on programming a multibutton mouse or trackball, see the documentation that came with it. These alternative pointing devices are made by a number of companies, including Kensington Technology (www.kensington.com/) and Logitech (www.logitech.com/), but not by Apple; check with the vendor to see whether the device supports multiple buttons in Mac OS X.

Menu symbols

A menu item may be accompanied by a variety of symbols. A triangle pointing to the right at the end of an item indicates that the menu has a submenu. An ellipsis (...) at the end of the item name indicates that choosing the item brings up a dialog in which you must supply additional information before the command can be completed. Generally, the same symbols appear in both Mac OS X and Classic applications. The following list summarizes these symbols and their meanings:

✓ Blue   Designates an item that is currently selected or an attribute that applies to everything that is currently selected

– Italic   Designates an attribute that applies only to some things that are currently selected

● Great   Designates a document that has unsaved changes; some applications use it instead of ✓ to designate an attribute that applies to everything that is currently selected

◆ Docu   Designates, in some applications, a window that is minimized in the Dock; designates, in the Classic environment's Application menu, an application that requires your attention

▶   Designates a menu item with a submenu

Other symbols are used to specify keyboard shortcuts for menu items. Pressing a specified combination of keys has the same effect as choosing the menu item. For example, pressing ⌘-X is equivalent to choosing the Cut command from the Edit menu. The following symbols represent keys:

⌘	Represents the Command key
△	Represents the Shift key
o	Represents the Option key
c	Represents the Control key
⊠	Represents the Delete key

When you use a keyboard shortcut for a command in a menu, the title of the menu may flash briefly to signal that the command has been issued.

Looking into Windows

You view and interact with the content of files and folders in windows. Most windows are rectangular, but some are other shapes. This section describes how different types of Mac OS windows look and work.

Recognizing different window types

You see several types of Mac OS windows, and each is designed to display a specific kind of information. Some windows display the files and other items stored on disks. Other window types display the actual contents of files, which may be text, pictures, movies, or other kinds of information. Windows called *dialogs* display options that you can set. A *sheet* is a dialog that applies to and is attached to another window, ensuring you won't lose track of which window the dialog applies to. *Alerts* are dialogs in which the Mac OS or an application program notifies you of a hazardous situation, a limitation in your proposed course of action, or an error condition. *Palettes*, also called panels and utility windows, contain controls or tools or display auxiliary information for the application that you're currently using.

Each type of window has a standard look, but it looks different in the Mac OS X Aqua environment than in the Classic environment. Two types of windows exist only in one environment. Sheets exist only in the Aqua environment, so only applications made for Mac OS X can have sheets. Classic applications can't have sheets, but some of them have a type of dialog that can't be moved (a dubious distinction). Figure 2-11 shows examples of the different types of Aqua windows, and Figure 2-12 shows examples of the different types of Classic windows.

Regular Aqua window

⊙ ○ ○ 📄 $30,000 Bequest.txt

This file is a public domain electronic text

THE $30,000 BEQUEST
and Other Stories

by
Mark Twain
(Samuel L. Clemens)

The $30,000 Bequest
A Dog's Tale
Was It Heaven? Or Hell?

Aqua sheet

○ ○ ○ 📄 $30,000 Bequest.txt

Do you want to save changes to this document before closing?

If you don't save, your changes will be lost.

(Don't Save) (Cancel) (Save)

Ordinary Aqua dialog

Connect to Server

Choose a server from the list, or enter a server address

At: 📟 192.168.1.104 ⬦ ▼

Address: afp://192.168.1.104

(Add to Favorites) (Cancel) (Connect)

Aqua alert

Do you really want to delete the index for "Another HD"?

Deleting the index will disable content searches for this item.

(Cancel) (OK)

Aqua palette

○ ○ ○ Font

Family	Typeface	Sizes
Courier New	Light	12
Didot	Light Italic	9
Futura	Regular	10
Gadget	Italic	11
Geneva	Bold	12
Georgia	Bold Italic	13
Gill Sans		14

(Extras... ▾)

Figure 2-11: The Mac OS X Aqua environment has several different types of windows.

Regular Classic window

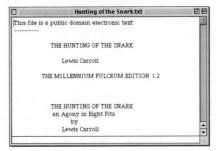

Immovable Classic dialog

Movable Classic dialog

Classic alert

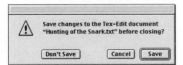

Classic palette

Figure 2-12: The Classic environment has several types of windows.

Using the Mac OS X Aqua window controls

The design of a window has as much to do with function as with form. Many parts of a window's frame are actually control surfaces that you can use to move the window, size it, close it, or change the view of its contents. Figure 2-13 shows examples of Aqua window controls.

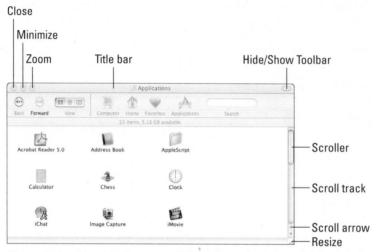

Figure 2-13: Mac OS X's Aqua windows have many controls.

The controls in Aqua windows have these effects:

✦ **Title bar.** Drag to move the window. Double-clicking the title bar minimizes the window the same as the Minimize button described below.

✦ **Close button.** Click to make the window go away. The Close button is normally red, and when you move the pointer near this button, an X appears in its center. In some applications, notably the Finder, press the Option key and click to close all the application's windows.

✦ **Minimize button.** Click to place a miniature replica of the window in the Dock. The Minimize button is normally yellow, and when you move the pointer near it, a minus sign (–) appears in it.

✦ **Zoom button.** Click to make the window as large as it needs to be to show all its contents, up to the size of the screen. Click again to make the window resume its previous size and location. (A zoomed window may leave a margin at the bottom of the screen for the Dock.) The Zoom button is normally green, and when you move the pointer near it, a plus sign (+) appears inside it. If a window cannot be resized, its Zoom button is dim, and a plus sign does not appear in its center.

✦ **Toolbar button.** Click to hide the toolbar at the top of the window. If the tool-bar is already hidden, click this button to show the toolbar. The toolbar button is present only on a window that can have a toolbar.

✦ **Scroll arrows, scroller, and scroll track.** Click a scroll arrow to move the window's contents a little; press an arrow to move smoothly; click the scroll track to move in chunks; drag the scroller to bring another part of the window's contents quickly in view. The scroller position in the scroll track indicates where you are in relation to the beginning or end of the window content. Additionally, the scroller length indicates how much of the total content the window can display at once. The shorter the scroller is, the less you can see without scrolling. The scroller is normally blue. The scroll bar controls do not appear if scrolling would not bring anything else into view.

✦ **Resize control.** Drag to adjust the size of the window.

 Note   The color of the Close, Minimize, Zoom, and Scroller controls may be gray instead of red, yellow, green, and blue. You set the color by using the General pane of System Preferences application, as described in Chapter 15.

You won't find all the window controls on every kind of window. For example, document windows have all or most of the available controls, dialogs generally have fewer window controls available, and alerts have fewer still.

Using Classic window controls

Windows in the Classic environment have most of the same controls as the Aqua windows, but Classic window controls have different appearances and locations. Figure 2-14 shows examples of Classic window controls.

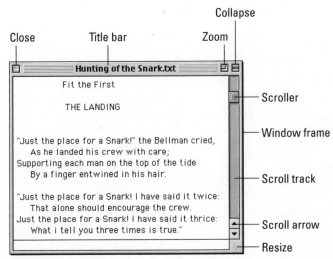

Figure 2-14: Classic windows have many controls.

The Classic window controls have these effects:

✦ **Title bar.** Drag to move the window. Double-clicking the title bar may collapse or expand the window the same as the collapse box described below.

✦ **Close box.** Click to make the window go away. Pressing Option and clicking may close all windows in the same application.

✦ **Zoom box.** Click to make the window as large as it needs to be to show all its contents, up to the size of the screen. (A zoomed window usually leaves a margin on the right side of the screen.) Click again to make the window resume its previous size and location.

✦ **Collapse box.** Click to hide all but the window's title bar, or if the window is collapsed, click to show the entire window. Pressing Option and clicking may collapse (or expand) all windows in the same application.

✦ **Scroll arrows, scroller, and scroll track.** Click a scroll arrow to move the window's contents a little; press an arrow to move smoothly; click the scroll track above or below the scroller to move in chunks; drag the scroller to bring another part of the window's contents into view quickly. The scroll bar controls do not appear if scrolling would not bring anything else into view.

✦ **Resize control.** Drag to adjust the size of the window.

✦ **Window frame.** Drag to move the window.

As with the Aqua windows, you won't find all the window controls on every Classic window. Document windows have all or most of the available controls, movable dialogs have fewer controls, and immovable dialogs have no controls built into their borders.

Interacting with windows

When more than one standard window is open, only one window is considered active, meaning that you can interact with all the items in it. You may be able to interact with some window controls and other items in inactive windows, but you can't interact with everything in inactive windows, especially in inactive Classic windows.

Recognizing the active window

You can tell the active window because it is in front of inactive windows. Therefore, the active window overlaps all other windows except palettes belonging to the same application as the active window. (Palettes float in a layer above the active window.) In addition, the active window is conspicuous because the controls of inactive Aqua windows are dim, and the controls of inactive Classic windows actually disappear. Figure 2-15 shows active and inactive windows.

Figure 2-15: The active window is in front of inactive windows, and its controls are more conspicuous (especially when you see the windows in color).

Making another window active

You can make any visible window the active window by clicking any visible part of it. Making a window active brings it in front of the window that was previously active. If the new active window belongs to an application with palettes, they all come to the front, as well. When you make a Classic window active, all other windows belonging to the same application move in front of the previous active window. To make all the windows of a Mac OS X application come forward together, click the application's icon in the Dock, which we cover later in this chapter.

Note   If an alert or a dialog other than a sheet is displayed, you may need to dismiss it (by clicking its OK button or Cancel button) before you can make another window active in the same application program.

Interacting with inactive windows

If you want to interact with something in an inactive window, you can always click the window to make it active and then click again to interact with the object of your desire in the window. In some cases, you don't have to click twice to interact with items in an inactive window. For instance, you can operate the Close, Minimize, and

Zoom buttons in most inactive Aqua windows. Clicking the Zoom button of an inactive window changes the window's size. In addition, some applications bring a window to the front when you click the window's Zoom button. The Finder does not behave this way; a Finder window that's in the background stays in the background when you click the window's Zoom button. If you think about what the Close and Minimize buttons do, you can see why clicking one of these in an inactive window does not bring the window to the front. The ability to interact directly with an item in an inactive window is called *click-through*.

Some items in inactive Aqua windows respond when you interact with them, while other items in the same windows don't respond. A responsive window control in an inactive Aqua window becomes more pronounced when the mouse pointer passes over it. A responsive item labeled with text or a symbol (such as an arrow) is supposed to have a dark label to indicate that it is enabled. An unresponsive item is supposed to have a dim label to indicate that it is disabled. However, Mac OS X applications don't follow these rules uniformly. You will have to learn by trial and error which items are responsive in inactive windows. These visual distinctions don't apply to inactive Classic windows, which generally don't have responsive items anyway. Figure 2-16 illustrates the difference between responsive and unresponsive items in inactive Aqua windows.

Window Tricks

You can move and minimize most inactive windows without bringing them to the front. The following window tricks work even on windows that don't have visible controls, as is the case with all inactive Classic windows:

✦ To move an inactive window, press ⌘ while dragging the window's title bar. Alternatively, you can ⌘-drag the frame of an inactive window to move the window.

✦ To collapse all windows that belong to the same application as the active window, press Option while clicking the active window's minimize button. For Classic windows, Option-click the collapse box of any window that belongs to the same application as the active window. In some cases, you get the same effect by pressing Option and ⌘ while double-clicking the title bar of any window that belongs to the same Mac OS X or Classic application as the active window.

✦ To collapse or expand an inactive window, press ⌘ while double-clicking its title bar.

Note that with inactive Classic windows, these tricks work only if the active window belongs to the same application as the inactive window you want to affect. If the active window is an Aqua window, then applying these tricks to any inactive Classic window brings the Classic window to the front.

If the tricks that involve double-clicking don't work with Classic windows, then you need to change a setting in the Options pane of the Classic environment's Appearance control panel, as described in Chapter 15.

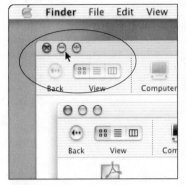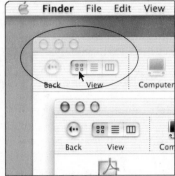

Figure 2-16: As the pointer passes over items in an Aqua background window, responsive items become more pronounced (left), but unresponsive items don't (right).

Operating Buttons and Other Controls

Inside many windows are a variety of controls that you operate by clicking or dragging with the mouse. Examples include push buttons with text or picture labels, checkboxes, radio buttons, sliders, little arrows for increasing or decreasing numeric values, disclosure triangles, scrolling lists, and tabs. These controls are available in the Mac OS X Aqua environment and the Classic environment, with some cosmetic differences.

Using push buttons

A *push button* causes an action to take place when clicked. A label on the button indicates the action that the button performs. The label may be text or graphic. Push buttons with text labels are generally rectangular with rounded ends. Buttons with graphic labels may be any shape. Figure 2-17 illustrates push buttons.

Using standard OK and Cancel buttons

Many dialogs have buttons labeled OK and Cancel. Clicking OK accepts all the settings and entries in the dialog. Clicking Cancel rejects any changes you may have made in the dialog and restores all settings and entries to their state before the dialog appeared. A shortcut for clicking the Cancel button is pressing the Escape key (the Escape key labeled esc) or pressing the ⌘ and Period (.) keys in combination.

Recognizing the default button

One button in an Aqua dialog, alert, or sheet may pulsate, going from light gray to a darker color (initially blue, but you can change colors as described in Chapter 15). The other buttons are all light gray. This is the *default button*. In the Classic environment, the default button has a heavy border and does not pulsate.

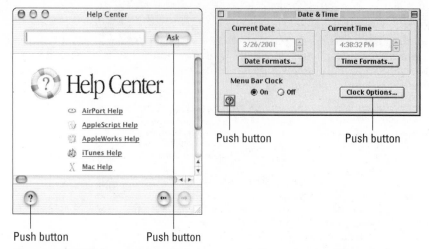

Push button   Push button

Push button   Push button

Figure 2-17: Click a push button in an Aqua (left) or Classic (right) window to cause an action to take place.

The default button represents the action that you most often want to take. However, if the most common action is dangerous, then a button representing a safer action may be the default button. As a shortcut for clicking the default button, you can press the Return key or the Enter key.

Using radio buttons

Radio buttons let you select one setting from a group. They're called radio buttons because they work like the station presets on a car radio. Just as you can select only one radio station at a time, you can select only one radio button from a group. To select a radio button, click it. The selected radio button is darker than its unselected neighbors. Figure 2-18 illustrates radio buttons.

Figure 2-18: Click a radio button in an Aqua (left) or Classic (right) window to select one setting from a group.

Using checkboxes

A *checkbox* lets you turn a setting on or off. When a setting is on (or selected), a check mark appears in the checkbox. When a setting is off (or deselected), the checkbox is empty. When a setting is partly on and partly off because it indicates the state of more than one thing, such as the format of a range of text, a dash appears in the checkbox. Unlike radio buttons, checkboxes are not mutually exclusive. You can turn on checkboxes in any combination. Clicking a checkbox reverses its state. Figure 2-19 shows examples of checkboxes.

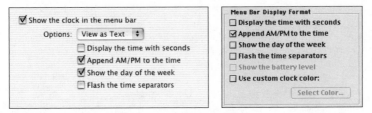

Figure 2-19: Click checkboxes in Aqua (left) and Classic (right) windows to turn settings on and off individually.

Using bevel buttons

A *bevel button* has a beveled edge that gives it a three-dimensional look, and it bears a label that indicates its function. Bevel buttons mimic the function and behavior of other items: push buttons, radio buttons, checkboxes, or pop-up menus. A bevel button can be labeled with text, a graphic, or both. Figure 2-20 illustrates bevel buttons.

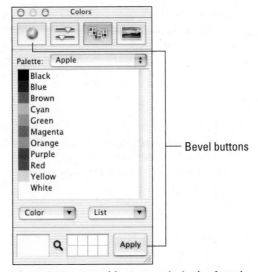

Figure 2-20: Bevel buttons mimic the function and behavior of push buttons, radio buttons, and other types of controls.

Using sliders

A *slider* consists of a track that displays a range of values or magnitudes and the slider itself, also known as the *thumb*, which indicates the current setting. You can change the setting by dragging the slider. An Aqua slider is a dark color (initially blue, but you can change colors as described in Chapter 15). Figure 2-21 shows examples of sliders.

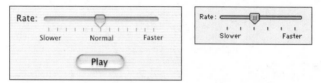

Figure 2-21: Drag a slider in an Aqua (left) or Classic (right) window to change a setting across a range of values.

Using little arrows

Little arrows, which point in opposite directions, let you raise or lower a value incrementally. Clicking an arrow changes the value one increment at a time. Pressing an arrow continuously changes the value until it reaches the end of its range. Figure 2-22 illustrates little arrows.

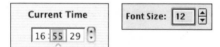

Figure 2-22: Click or press a little arrow in an Aqua (left) or Classic (right) window to change a value incrementally.

Using disclosure triangles

A *disclosure triangle* controls how much detail you see in a window. When the window is displaying minimal detail, clicking a disclosure triangle reveals additional detail and may automatically enlarge the window to accommodate it. Clicking the same triangle again hides detail and may automatically shrink the window to fit. Figure 2-23 shows an example of disclosure triangles.

Using scrolling lists

A *scrolling list* displays a list of values in a box with an adjacent scroll bar. If there are more values than can be displayed at once, the scroll bar becomes active and you can use it to see other values in the list. Clicking a listed item selects it. You may be able to select multiple items by pressing Shift or ⌘ while clicking. Figure 2-24 illustrates scrolling lists.

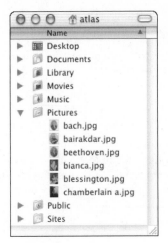

Figure 2-23: Click a disclosure triangle to adjust the amount of detail shown.

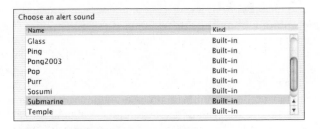

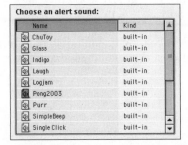

Figure 2-24: Scroll a list to see an item you want and then click to select it (Shift-click or ⌘-click to select multiple items) in an Aqua (top) or Classic (bottom) window.

Using tabs

Tabs in Mac OS windows look like the tabs on dividers used in card files and ring binders, and they have a similar function. They divide the contents of a window into discrete pages or sections, with each tab connected to one section of window content. Apple calls each tabbed section a *pane*, but this term is not commonly used (at least not yet). You can see only one pane at a time, and you switch to a different pane by clicking its tab. Figure 2-25 shows an example of tabs.

Figure 2-25: Click a tab to see what's in its pane.

Working with Icons

Icons are small pictures used to represent many objects in the Mac OS. You work with the objects by manipulating their representative icons. For example, you work with the applications, documents, folders, and disks in your computer by manipulating icons on the computer screen. This section explains what the look of an icon tells you about it and how you use icons.

Recognizing different types of icons

Mac OS X icons have a different look from icons in previous Mac OS versions. They are typically larger and much more photo-realistic. Unlike the fixed-size icons in previous Mac OS versions, Mac OS X icons can be arbitrarily sized up to 128 x 128 pixels. (A *pixel*, or picture element, is equivalent to a single dot on the screen. These dots make up all the text and graphics that appear on your computer's screen.) In some contexts, you decide how large you want Mac OS X to display icons. In other contexts, Mac OS X scales icons to fit the available space. Icons designed for earlier versions of the Mac OS may appear somewhat jagged or grainy when they are scaled larger than their fixed dimensions, which are usually 32 x 32 pixels.

An icon's basic appearance often gives you some idea of what kind of item it represents. You can usually identify icons for applications, documents, and folders by common characteristics of each type.

Identifying application icons

Application icons come in three basic varieties:

✦ **Regular Mac OS X applications.** Icons of regular Mac OS X applications have several distinctive characteristics. An application icon depicts the kind of information it creates or views, such as pictures, notes, or a particular type of document. Application icons usually include a tool that suggests the type of task the application helps you perform, such as a pen for writing or a pair of glasses for viewing. Mac OS X application icons may be drawn in a perspective that makes them look like objects sitting on the desk in front of you. Figure 2-26 shows several Mac OS X application icons.

✦ **Mac OS X utilities.** The icon of a utility application communicates the auxiliary function it performs. This genre of icons uses color sparingly; they are predominantly shades of gray. Utility icons may be drawn in a perspective that makes them look like objects on a shelf at your eye level. Figure 2-27 shows some icons of Mac OS X utilities.

✦ **Classic applications.** Icons of Classic applications generally have much simpler designs than Mac OS X application icons. Many Classic application icons are based on a diamond shape, which was the original standard for Mac applications.

Figure 2-26: Icons of Mac OS X applications depict the kind of information the application creates or views and what you can do with it.

Figure 2-27: A utility application's icon in Mac OS X depicts the auxiliary function that the utility performs.

Identifying document icons

Icons that look like a sheet of paper with a dog-eared corner generally represent document files, which can contain the text, pictures, sounds, and other kinds of data stored on your computer. The kind of data in a document may be depicted in its icon. In addition, a document icon may indicate which application created it by including a derivative of the application's icon. Figure 2-28 shows several document icons.

Figure 2-28: Document icons represent files that contain text, picture, or other data.

Identifying folder icons

Icons that look like folders represent the folders in which programs, documents, and other items are organized on your disks. A folder with a special purpose may incorporate an image that indicates the particular kind of items the folder contains. Figure 2-29 shows some folder icons.

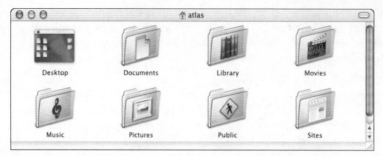

Figure 2-29: Folder icons may indicate the kind of items inside.

Selecting icons

The look of an icon has no bearing on how you use it. Everyone who uses a Mac quickly learns to select icons by clicking, but even some seasoned veterans don't know that you can select more than one icon at a time. In addition, you can select icons individually by typing instead of clicking.

When you select an icon, the Mac OS highlights it by making it darker. Figure 2-30 shows an example of an icon that is highlighted and one that isn't.

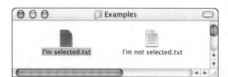

Figure 2-30: Mac OS X highlights the selected icon by making it darker.

Selecting multiple icons by clicking

Ordinarily, clicking an icon selects it (highlights it) and deselects the icon that was highlighted. After selecting the first icon, you can select a group of icons in the same window by pressing the ⌘ key while clicking each icon in turn. At any time, you can deselect a selected icon by holding down the ⌘ key and clicking it again.

In a window where icons are displayed in a list, you can select a whole range of icons with two clicks. First, you click one icon to select it; then you press Shift while clicking another icon to select it and all the icons between it and the first icon you selected.

Note The effect of the Shift key on selecting multiple icons is different in Mac OS X than in earlier versions of the Mac OS. In earlier versions, Shift-clicking icons in a list has the effect that ⌘-clicking icons has in Mac OS X.

Selecting multiple icons by dragging

In addition to selecting multiple icons by clicking with the ⌘ or Shift keys, you can select adjacent icons by dragging the mouse pointer across them. As you drag, the Mac OS displays a shaded rectangle, called a *selection rectangle*, and every icon it touches or encloses is selected. Icons are highlighted one-by-one as you drag over them, not en masse after you stop dragging. All icons must be in a single window. Figure 2-31 is an example of selecting several icons with a selection rectangle.

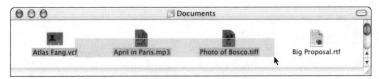

Figure 2-31: Drag across adjacent icons to select all of them.

You can combine dragging with the use of the ⌘ key. Pressing ⌘ while dragging a selection rectangle across unselected icons adds the enclosed icons to the current selection. Conversely, pressing ⌘ while dragging a selection rectangle across selected icons deselects the enclosed group without deselecting other icons (if any).

Selecting by typing

When you know the name of an icon that you want to select but aren't sure where it is in a window, you can quickly select it by typing. Typing may be faster than clicking if the icon you want to select requires lots of scrolling to bring it into view.

To select an icon in the active window by typing, simply type the first part of its name. You need to type only enough of the name to identify the icon you want uniquely. In a window in which every icon has a completely different name, for example, you need to type only the first letter of a name to select an icon. By contrast, in a folder where every icon begins with Mac, you have to type those three letters plus enough additional letters to single out the icon you want. When selecting by typing, capitalization doesn't matter.

While typing, pressing an arrow key selects the icon nearest the currently selected icon in the direction that the arrow key points. In a window where icons are not displayed in a list, pressing Tab selects the next icon alphabetically and Shift-Tab selects the previous icon alphabetically. Table 2-1 summarizes keyboard selection techniques.

Table 2-1 Selecting Icons by Typing	
To Select This	*Do This*
An icon	Type the icon's partial or full name.
Next icon up	Press Up Arrow (↑).
Next icon down	Press Down Arrow (↓).
Next icon alphabetically*	Press Tab.
Previous icon alphabetically*	Press Shift-Tab.

*Applies only to a window where icons are not displayed in a list.

Looking at the Dock

The Dock, arguably the single most noticeable new feature in Mac OS X, gives you immediate access to the applications, documents, and folders that you use most. If you're familiar with previous Mac OS versions, you probably realize that the Dock takes over most of the functions handled in Mac OS 9 and earlier — and still handled in the Classic environment — by the Apple menu, the Application menu, the Application Switcher window, and the Launcher control panel. Figure 2-32 illustrates the Dock.

Moving, hiding, and showing the Dock

The Dock initially appears at the bottom of the screen at all times. You can move the Dock to the left side or the right side of the screen. To change the Dock position, choose Position on Left or Position on Right from the Dock submenu of the Apple menu.

You can also change a setting to have the Dock hide until you move the mouse pointer to the edge of the screen. To make this change, choose Turn Hiding On from the Dock submenu of the Apple menu. If this setting is turned on, the Dock remains visible only while the pointer is in it. When you move the pointer away from the Dock, the Dock hides automatically. The Dock reappears when you move the pointer to the edge of the screen where the Dock is hiding.

Figure 2-32: The Dock contains icons for frequently used applications, files, minimized windows, and so forth.

Going over the Dock

The Dock contains an initial set of icons, which you can rearrange to suit your needs. (We explain how to add, remove, and move Dock icons in Chapter 4.) The initial set of Dock icons includes the following:

✦ **Finder.** An application for managing the files and folders stored on your computer, always at the left end of the Dock

✦ **Mail.** An application for sending and receiving e-mail

✦ **iChat.** An instant messaging (IM) client compatible with AOL's AIM client

✦ **Address Book.** A contact list for people, business, and so on, integrated with Apple's Mail application and the rest of Mac OS

✦ **Microsoft Internet Explorer.** An application for browsing the Internet

✦ **iTunes.** An application for playing, organizing, and recording digital music from CDs, MP3 files, and Internet radio

✦ **iPhoto.** An application for transferring and organizing photos from digital still cameras

✦ **iMovie.** An application for working with digital video

✦ **Sherlock.** An application for searching your computer, your network, and the Internet

✦ **QuickTime Player.** An application for viewing digital movies

✦ **System Preferences.** An application for customizing Mac OS X on your computer

✦ **Apple – Mac OS X.** A link to the Mac OS X page on Apple's Web site

✦ **Trash.** A container for discarding files and folders that you no longer need

More icons are added to the Dock automatically as you use your computer. When you open an application, its icon bounces up and down in the Dock and remains there while the application is open. (Chapter 5 explains how to open applications.) In addition, when you minimize an Aqua window (by clicking its Minimize button, described earlier), it shrinks to the size of an icon and appears in the Dock. A window shrinks to the Dock with a wavering visual effect that Apple likens to a genie going into a bottle, or the application can shrink in a linear scale progression. You can change the visual effect by choosing Dock Preferences from the Dock submenu of the Apple menu, as described in Chapter 4.

Appreciating Dock niceties

The Dock is divided into two sections, separated by a thin vertical line. The items to the left of the line are applications. The right section contains everything else, such as minimized windows, files, and folders. As new applications are opened, they appear in the Dock to the left of the vertical line (between the System Preferences and Apple – Mac OS X icons). New documents and windows minimized to the Dock appear between the Apple – Mac OS X and the Trash icons.

The icons of items in the Dock sometimes provide feedback. For example, an application that is currently open has a small upward-pointing triangle underneath it. Another example: The Mail icon indicates the number of new messages waiting for you.

Identifying Dock icons

When you move the mouse pointer to a Dock icon, the icon's name appears above it. Clicking a Dock icon opens it. When you click a minimized window in the Dock, the window emerges and becomes full-sized again.

If the Dock fills up with icons, they shrink in size. With many small icons in the Dock, you can't easily tell what each icon represents. In such cases, you can drag the mouse pointer across the Dock to see each icon's name in turn. For even more help identifying small Dock icons, you can change a setting so that the Dock magnifies the icons near the pointer. Figure 2-33 illustrates the Dock's magnification feature.

Figure 2-33: The Dock can magnify icons near the pointer to help you identify them.

Sleeping, Shutting Down, or Logging Out

When you are ready to finish a session with your computer, you need to do one of the following:

✦ Make the computer sleep to save energy.

✦ Log out so someone else can log in and use the computer (assuming the computer is configured for multiple users).

✦ Restart the computer for various reasons.

✦ Shut down the computer properly.

Sometimes, you may want to have just the Classic environment sleep, stop, or restart. This section explains how to do these things.

Caution   If you shut down your Mac improperly, for example by disconnecting the power, you risk damaging files stored on it. Such damage may be minor and not readily apparent, but an accumulation of minor damage may lead to mysterious, serious problems later. You can find some maintenance procedures in Chapter 25.

Making the computer sleep (and wake up)

If you're not going to use your computer for a while, you can save energy and reduce wear and tear on the computer by making it sleep. When you're ready to use your computer again, you can wake it quickly. Waking from sleep is much faster than starting up.

Note   If you're a computer veteran, you may be accustomed to shutting down your computer because you want to begin your next session with a clean slate by starting up anew. You should not need to regularly shut down and start up Mac OS X because its Unix foundation operates much more cleanly than Mac OS 9 and earlier. However, some maintenance operations may not happen according to schedule if you have your computer sleep every night, as we explain in Chapter 25.

Going to sleep

To make your computer sleep, do one of the following:

✦ If you have a PowerBook or iBook, close the lid.

✦ Choose Sleep from the Apple menu.

✦ If your keyboard has a Power key, press it and then press the S key or click the Sleep button in the resulting dialog, which is shown in Figure 2-33.

✦ If your keyboard has an Eject key, you can shut down by pressing the Option Command-Eject combination.

✦ If your keyboard has an △ key, press Control-△ and then press the S key or click the Sleep button in the resulting dialog, shown in Figure 2-34.

✦ If you have an iMac with a slot-loading CD-ROM or DVD-ROM drive, Apple Cinema display, or Apple Studio LCD display, press its power button. Note that an iMac with a tray-loading CD-ROM drive will shut down rather than sleep when its power button is pressed.

✦ Configure your computer to sleep automatically after a period of inactivity by using the Energy Saver pane of System Preferences, as described in Chapter 15.

Note   Some Power Mac G4 models can't be put to sleep if a PCI card is installed. When this is the case, the Apple menu's Sleep command is dim. You can still configure the computer to sleep when it's idle.

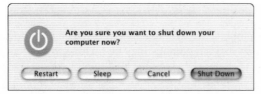

Figure 2-34: An alert appears when you press the power key on some keyboards, the Control and △ keys on some other keyboards, or the power button on some Apple displays.

Waking up

To make your computer wake up from sleep, do one of the following:

- ✦ If you have a PowerBook or iBook, open its lid (this action doesn't wake all PowerBook models).
- ✦ Press any key on the keyboard.
- ✦ Click the mouse.
- ✦ Shout, "Wake up!" into the computer's microphone (just kidding).

Logging out of Mac OS X

You can log out of Mac OS X so that someone else can log in or so that you can log in again, possibly with a different user account name. To log out, choose Log Out from the Apple menu. A dialog appears in which you must confirm or cancel your intention to log out. Figure 2-35 shows this dialog.

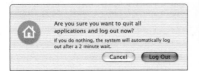

Figure 2-35: After choosing Log Out from the Apple menu, you must confirm or cancel your intention to log out.

If you click Log Out in the dialog, Mac OS X instructs all open applications to quit. If any open application has a document with unsaved changes, it asks whether you want to save the changes before quitting. After all applications have quit, the login window appears, as previously shown in Figure 2-2.

The login window appears after you log out even if your computer is configured to log in automatically. In this case, you can have the computer log in automatically by clicking the Restart button in the login window.

Tip   You can configure your computer so that the Restart and Shut Down buttons don't work in the login window. This makes it more difficult, although not impossible, for someone to restart the computer with Mac OS 9 or a CD, which may allow them to access your Mac OS X files. We explain how to disable these buttons in Chapter 15.

Restarting the computer

You need to restart your computer far less often with Mac OS X because it doesn't crash as often as earlier Mac OS versions. Nevertheless, you may need to restart your computer after installing new software or to get the computer to recognize a new device that you have connected.

Use any of the following methods to restart your computer:

✦ Choose Restart from the Apple menu.

✦ If your keyboard has a Power key, press it; then press the R key or click the Restart button in the dialog that appears, which was previously shown in Figure 2-34.

✦ If your keyboard has an △ key, press Control-△ and then press the R key or click the Restart button in the dialog that appears, which was previously shown in Figure 2-34.

✦ Log out and then click the Restart button in the login window.

With any of these methods, Mac OS X tells all open applications to quit. Any open application that has a document with unsaved changes will ask whether you want to save the changes before quitting. After all applications have quit, the computer shuts down and then automatically starts up as described at the beginning of this chapter.

Shutting down the computer

Although you can leave the computer running indefinitely and just make it sleep when no one is using it, you can also shut it down. Shutting down saves more energy than sleeping.

You can use any of these methods to shut down:

✦ Choose Shut Down from the Apple menu.

✦ If your keyboard has a Power key, press it and then press the Enter key or click the Shut Down button in the dialog that appears, which was previously shown in Figure 2-34.

✦ If your keyboard has an △ key, press Control-△ and then press the Enter key or click the Shut Down button in the dialog that appears (previously shown in Figure 2-34).

✦ If you have an iMac with a tray-loading CD-ROM drive (not a slot-loading drive), press the power button on the computer.

✦ Log out and then click the Shut Down button in the login window.

When you shut down your computer, Mac OS X tells all open applications to quit. If an open application has a document with unsaved changes, it asks whether you want to save the changes before quitting. After all applications have quit, the computer shuts off its power.

Having the Classic Environment Sleep, Stop, or Restart

If the Classic environment is running on your computer, you can have it sleep, stop, or restart independently of Mac OS X and Mac OS X applications.

✦ The Classic environment sleeps to reduce its use of your computer, thereby improving the performance of Mac OS X applications that are running. The Classic environment is preset to sleep when no Classic applications have been open for five minutes. You can change this interval.

✦ Stopping the Classic environment reduces its use of your computer's processor and RAM to nothing. (The Mac OS 9 operating system used by the Classic environment still occupies space on your hard disk.)

✦ Restarting the Classic environment after a Classic application quits unexpectedly or develops a serious problem makes the Classic environment much more reliable.

You stop the Classic environment, restart it, or change the waiting time for Classic sleep in the Classic pane of System Preferences. You can find more information in Chapter 15.

Summary

Here's what you know after reading this chapter:

✦ When you start up your computer, it loads Mac OS X into its memory from disk.

✦ During startup, Mac OS X goes through a login procedure in an effort to keep unauthorized people from using the computer. The login procedure is mandatory but can be automated.

✦ Mac OS X can be configured to start the Classic environment automatically after login.

✦ Menus present lists of commands or attributes for you to choose from. Menus almost always appear in the menu bar at the top of the screen. Elsewhere, distinctive arrows indicate pop-up menus, and Control-clicking an item may display a contextual menu for it.

✦ Mac OS X has several types of Aqua windows: regular windows, dialogs, sheets, alerts, and palettes. The Classic environment has all these window types except sheets.

✦ Aqua and Classic windows have controls for moving, closing, minimizing, zooming, scrolling, and resizing.

✦ One window is active, and you can interact with all items in it. You may also be able to interact with some items in inactive windows.

✦ Inside many windows are a variety of controls that you operate by clicking or dragging with the mouse. These controls include push buttons, radio buttons, checkboxes, bevel buttons, sliders, little arrows, disclosure triangles, scrolling lists, and tabs.

✦ Icons represent applications, documents, folders, disks, and other items in your computer. An icon's basic appearance tells you which type of item it represents.

✦ You select an icon by clicking it. You can select multiple icons by ⌘-clicking, Shift-clicking, and dragging.

✦ The Dock at the bottom or side of the screen contains icons of items you use often. You can rearrange the Dock's initial set of icons to suit your needs.

✦ When you are ready to finish a session with your computer, you need to make it sleep, log out of Mac OS X, restart the computer, or shut it down. You can also have the Classic environment sleep, stop, or restart independently of Mac OS X applications that are running.

✦   ✦   ✦

Managing Your Workspace

Ask a hundred Macintosh users to name the application program they use most often and only a few would come up with the correct answer: the Finder. People don't think of the Finder as a program they use or need to learn to use. In fact, it is a very rich application program that is included with Mac OS X for managing the contents of your computer.

This chapter explains some simple ways in which you can use the Finder to view the variety of objects that your computer contains. The chapter describes the objects that you see and manipulate while using the Finder. The chapter tells you how these objects appear in Finder windows and how you can change the view presented in any Finder window. Finally, this chapter explains how to use Finder windows to browse disks, folders, and the files they contain.

This chapter covers only Finder basics. Other Finder operations are covered in Chapters 4 and 5. Chapter 4 describes how to customize the Finder toolbar and set view options for Finder windows. Chapter 4 also explains how to change the picture displayed on the Desktop and customize the Dock. In addition, Chapter 4 tells you how to create folders, move and copy files, make aliases, and work with disks. Chapter 5 describes how to open document and application files with the Finder.

Recognizing Objects in Your Workspace

Your computer contains a variety of objects that you can manage and use. These objects are part of your *workspace* on the computer, and they include a hard drive, folders, application programs, documents, aliases, and other files. Besides the hard drive, your computer may also have an optical drive for CDs or DVDs. You work with all these objects in the Finder. You can see these objects as icons in Finder windows, and you can manipulate the icons to work with the objects that they represent. Your computer workspace also includes a special container for objects that you want to remove from the computer. This container is the Trash, and it's part of the Dock in Mac OS X. (In Mac OS 9 and earlier, the Trash is part of the Finder.) The Dock is also part of your workspace, as is the menu bar. Figure 3-1 shows what a typical Mac OS X workspace looks like initially.

In the remainder of this section, we discuss what the various objects in your workspace are and for what you might use them. We don't discuss the Dock and the menu bar here, because we covered both of them in Chapter 2. *How* to use the objects in your workspace is covered later in this chapter and in Chapter 4.

Finder windows

The Finder is a special application. Unlike most other applications, you don't have to do anything to make it start running. The Finder starts running automatically when you log in and keeps running until you log out. The Finder's icon is always at the end of the Dock. If the Dock is at the bottom of the screen, the Finder's icon is at the far left end of the Dock. If the Dock is on the side of the screen, the Finder's icon is at the top of the Dock. Clicking the Finder's icon in the Dock brings your Finder windows to the front so you can work in them. If you don't currently have any Finder windows, clicking the Finder's icon in the Dock creates a new Finder window, as shown previously in Figure 3-1. We cover the basics of using Finder windows later in this chapter; customizing them is discussed in Chapter 4.

The Desktop

The vast expanse of swirling blue that's displayed behind Finder windows and behind the Dock is called the *Desktop.* The Desktop is part of the Finder and for historical reasons is sometimes referred to as the Finder. Actually, the Desktop is only part of the Finder.

The Desktop normally displays an icon for the computer's hard drive. If the computer has more than one hard drive, or if the hard drive is divided into multiple volumes (as described in Chapter 4), you see an icon for each hard drive volume. You also see an icon for a CD or DVD that's inserted in the computer. In addition, an icon appears on your Desktop for each file server your computer is connected to, if any. If your computer has Mac OS 9 installed for the Classic environment, the Desktop normally has an icon that represents the Mac OS 9 Desktop. All these different icons normally appear on the Desktop, but you can suppress them by changing settings in Finder Preferences (as described in Chapter 4).

In addition, you can put other icons on the Desktop. Anything you put on your Desktop is kept in a special folder named Desktop. Mac OS X keeps your Desktop's contents and appearance separate from other people who log in with other user account names. Each user account has its own Desktop folder. We cover how to put icons on the Desktop, change the picture displayed on the Desktop, and customize other aspects of the Desktop in Chapter 4.

The Desktop folder has a distinctive icon, and you can see the contents of your Desktop folder in a Finder window while still seeing the contents of your Desktop on the Desktop proper. (We cover how to open a folder to see its contents later in this chapter.) Figure 3-2 shows an example of the Desktop folder icon and the Desktop folder contents in a Finder window.

Note Although the icons of hard drives, CDs, and other disk volumes may appear on the Desktop, your Desktop folder does not contain these items. The icons of disk volumes appear on the Desktop because the Finder displays them there together with items from your Desktop folder.

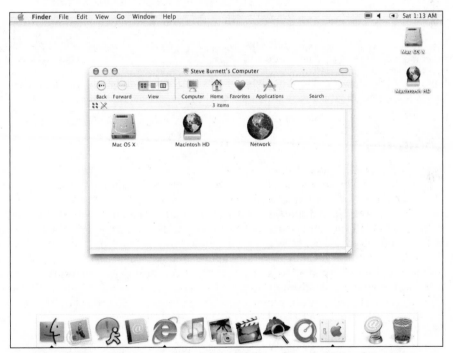

Figure 3-1: Your Mac OS X workspace includes a variety of objects that you can manage with the Finder.

Figure 3-2: Each user account has its own private Desktop, and items you put on your Desktop are kept in your Desktop folder.

Computer

The Desktop is part of the hierarchy into which your computer workspace is organized. The root level or nexus of your hierarchical workspace is called *Computer*. If you display the Computer level in a Finder window, you see icons for the disk volumes that are available on your computer. You also see the Network icon; if you log in to your computer with a user account from a network server, the Network icon provides a gateway to files and folders located on the network server. To see the Computer level of your workspace, shown previously in Figure 3-1, choose Computer from the Go menu or click the Computer button in the toolbar at the top of a Finder window.

Trash

At the opposite end of the Dock from the Finder icon, you see an icon resembling a wire-mesh wastepaper basket. This is the Trash — the receptacle into which you place things you want to be rid of. Any of your computer's files or folders that you place in the Trash stays there until you empty the Trash. Chapter 4 explains several methods for placing files and folders in the Trash, removing items from the Trash, and emptying the Trash.

Applications

Applications are the programs you use to do your work or have fun. In Mac OS X, the standard location for applications is in a folder named Applications. You can see the contents of the Applications folder by choosing Applications from the Go menu or by clicking the Applications button in the toolbar at the top of a Finder window. The contents of the Applications folder are available to all users of your Mac OS X system. Figure 3-3 shows the initial contents of the Applications folder.

Figure 3-3: The Applications folder includes a number of useful applications, some of which are in the AppleScript and Utilities folders.

A number of useful applications are installed with Mac OS X. Some of these applications are in the AppleScript folder or the Utilities folder, which are inside the Applications folder. Table 3-1 lists the applications provided with Mac OS X 10.1 and identifies the applications that are normally located in an interior folder of the Applications folder. The contents of your Applications folder may be different, because Apple adds and subtracts from the bundled software as time passes, and someone else who uses your computer may install additional applications.

Table 3-1
Included Applications

Name	Folder	Brief Description
Acrobat Reader	Applications	Adobe's standard viewer for PDF files.
Address Book	Applications	Lets you manage an address (postal and e-mail) and phone book. Integrated with LDAP (Lightweight Directory Access Protocol) directory searches and linked to Mail (see later in this table).
Calculator	Applications	A very basic calculator, controlled from the keypad or mouse.
Chess	Applications	A graphical front end for GNU Chess, a pretty decent chess program with multiple difficulty settings and both 2-D and 3-D views.
Clock	Applications	Displays either an analog or digital clock — can be in a floating window or in the Dock. Because all it does is display the time, it is not terribly useful unless you turn the menu-bar clock off.
iChat	Applications	Instant messaging (IM) client.
iDVD	Applications	Used to burn DVDs in Macs equipped with a SuperDrive.
Image Capture	Applications	Download photos from compatible (USB) digital cameras. Comes with a series of AppleScripts to automatically reformat and arrange pictures.
iMovie	Applications	Digital video editing application.
Internet Connect	Applications	Manage PPP application for dial-up Internet connections.
Internet Explorer	Applications	Microsoft's Web browser.
iPhoto	Applications	Still video editing and cataloging application.
iTunes	Applications	Play songs from audio CDs, MP3 files, and Internet radio stations. Burn recordable CDs on Macs equipped with CDRW drives.
Mail	Applications	Flexible e-mail application. Supports multiple accounts and personalities; links to Address Book.
Preview	Applications	View graphic and PDF files. Also used to access print preview from applications.

Name	Folder	Brief Description
QuickTime Player	Applications	Apple's application to play, create, and edit multimedia files.
Sherlock	Applications	Searches the Internet for you.
Stickies	Applications	Create and manage notes windows.
System Preferences	Applications	Control Panel application for your System Preference settings.
TextEdit	Applications	Styled text editor – a mini-word processor.
Script Editor	AppleScript	Record, create, and edit AppleScript (and other OSA scripting system) files.
AirPort Admin Utility	Utilities	Change individual settings of an AirPort base station device, including settings that aren't changed by the AirPort Setup Assistant application (described next).
AirPort Setup Assistant	Utilities	Guides you through providing an AirPort base station device with the settings it needs to get a wireless AirPort network connected to the Internet.
Apple System Profiler	Utilities	Utility to report how your hardware is configured and what software you have installed. This is a handy diagnostic tool when tracking down hardware and software problems.
Audio MIDI Setup	Utilities	Central control for routing audio and MIDI.
Bluetooth File Exchange	Utilities	Bluetooth short-range wireless data transfer utility.
ColorSync Utility	Utilities	Verifies and repairs ColorSync ICC (International Color Consortium) profiles. These profiles are used to synchronize color input and output between various device types (monitors, scanners, printers, and the like).
Console	Utilities	Presents a window to the Unix console log for your session, letting you see messages from Mac OS X and applications. This tool is primarily useful only to programmers and system administrators. Remember that underlying everything you do in Mac OS X, you are really running a Unix system.

Continued

Table 3-1 *(continued)*

Name	Folder	Brief Description
CPU Monitor	Utilities	Small utility to graphically depict how busy your computer's processor is.
DigitalColor Meter	Utilities	Presents the RGB (or other) color information for the pixels under the pointer.
Directory Access	Utilities	Set up the LDAP services and authentication protocols used by Directory Services and Mac OS X.
Disk Copy	Utilities	Creates and mounts disk image files. Disk images are a common distribution format for new software from Apple and other companies.
Disk Utility	Utilities	Used to verify, repair, and format disk volumes.
Display Calibrator	Utilities	Use this to calibrate your display, creating a custom ColorSync profile for use by ColorSync-aware programs.
Grab	Utilities	Used to take screen pictures, either of the entire screen or a selection.
Installer	Utilities	Used by Apple and some software developers to install new software and updates to your computer.
Key Caps	Utilities	Shows what characters each key or key combination produces in any installed font.
Keychain Access	Utilities	Used to store and retrieve your user IDs and passwords for files, remote sites, servers, and so forth.
NetInfo Manager	Utilities	Used to administer a NetInfo server configuration.
Network Utility	Utilities	A collection of network and Internet utility programs.
ODBC Administrator	Utilities	ODBC (Open Database Connectivity) configuration.
Print Center	Utilities	Configure, register, and monitor printers.
ProcessViewer	Utilities	Lists all programs and system services running, who's running them, and how much CPU time and memory they're consuming.
StuffIt Expander	Utilities	Freeware utility that will expand StuffIt and Zip archives, as well as a number of other formats.
Terminal	Utilities	This is your window into the Unix command line environment. See Chapter 27 for further information.

Documents

With many applications, you work with information in *documents*. Depending on the capabilities of an application, you may be able to use it to view, create, modify, print, and perform other actions on the information in documents. A document may contain one type of information or a combination of information types. Many applications specialize in documents that contain one type of information, such as words, pictures, numbers, databases, music, and movies. Some applications let you work with documents containing several types of information.

The information in a document is stored in a document file. The file may be located on your computer's hard drive or on a CD or disk that you can remove from your computer. A document file may also be located on the Internet or on a file server on your local network. We explain more about working with documents in Chapter 5, and about working with files on your network or the Internet in Chapter 10.

Home Folder

Mac OS X provides every user account with a *home folder* for storing document files. Your home folder's name is the short name of your user account. You can see your home folder's contents by choosing Home from the Go menu or by clicking the Home button in the toolbar at the top of a Finder window. Figure 3-4 shows the initial contents of a home folder.

Figure 3-4: Every user account has a home folder, and it initially contains other folders for organizing documents.

Your home folder initially contains a number of other folders for organizing documents files according to the type of information they contain. These folders have special icons, which you can see in Figure 3-4. You can add other folders and remove folders, and we describe how in Chapter 4. Here are the standard folders in a home folder:

✦ **Desktop.** Contains items that appear on your Desktop.

✦ **Documents.** Meant to contain any kind of document, especially documents that don't match any other folder in the home folder.

✦ **Library.** Meant to contain files used by applications specific to the user.

✦ **Movies.** Meant to contain digital motion video. (Chapter 15 covers viewing and creating digital video.)

✦ **Music.** Meant to contain digital audio. (Chapter 14 covers playing and creating digital audio.)

✦ **Pictures.** Meant to contain digital still video. (Chapter 14 covers playing and creating digital audio.)

✦ **Public.** Meant to contain documents and folders that you want to make available to other users of your computer and users of other computers on your local network. (Chapter 19 explains how to share the contents of your Public folder.)

✦ **Sites.** Contains files for a Web site that you can host on your computer. (Chapter 20 explains how to host your own Web site.)

Most of the folders in your home folder are available only to you (or to someone who logs in to your computer with your account name). Except for the Public folder and the Sites folder, the folders in your home folder are protected so that other users who log in with different account names can't see the folder contents. You can change the protection on any folder in your home folder so that other users have access to its contents. We explain how to change folder protection in Chapter 4.

iDisk

In addition to storing documents in your home folder, you can keep them on the Internet in a private storage area called an *iDisk*. Apple provides your iDisk storage area on one of its Internet file servers. Apple also specially designed the iDisk to integrate with Mac OS X and Mac OS 9. An iDisk contains folders for organizing documents; these folders have the names as the folders as your home folder. An iDisk also has a folder named Software, which contains additional applications and other software that you can copy to your computer. Because it's on the Internet, you can access your iDisk from any Mac with Mac OS X or Mac OS 9.

To use an iDisk, you must have a .Mac account with Apple, and you must configure Mac OS X to use your .Mac account. You have an opportunity to configure Mac OS X to use your .Mac account during the initial setup process that occurs when you install Mac OS X or first start up a new Mac with Mac OS X preinstalled. You can also sign up for a .Mac account during the initial setup process if you don't already have an account. As of this writing, Apple includes a free trial membership with new Macintoshes. If you don't configure Mac OS X for your .Mac account during the initial setup process, you can do so later. Chapter 10 explains how to sign up for a .Mac account and configure Mac OS X to use it.

Aliases

Sometimes you want a file or folder to be in more than one place. For example, you may want to keep your document files organized by putting them in folders and putting those folders in other folders. The trouble is, when you want to see a document, you end up digging through folders to find the document file you want to see. Aliases cut through the organizational red tape. Think of an alias as a stand-in or an agent for a real application, document, folder, or disk. You can place aliases in any handy location, such as on the Desktop or in the Dock.

Aliases even look a lot like the items they represent. An alias usually has the same icon as the item it represents, except that the alias icon has a small curved arrow superimposed to indicate that it is an alias. The name of an alias is usually the same as the item it represents, in some cases with the word *alias* added. You can change the name of an alias and give it a custom icon; Chapter 4 explains how to make these changes for any item. Figure 3-5 shows an alias and the item it represents.

Figure 3-5: An alias looks a lot like the item it represents.

Like the documents, applications, and other files on your disks and hard drives, aliases are files containing information — the information in an alias is just a different kind of information. Whereas a document contains text, pictures, or other data, and an application file contains code and resources, an alias contains a pointer to another file, folder, or disk.

Mac OS X uses that pointer information to locate the alias's *original item*. This process is called *resolving* an alias. Mac OS X can successfully resolve an alias, even if you rename the original item or move it to a different folder. However, the connection between an alias and its original item does break if the original item no longer exists. For example, an alias breaks if you move its original item to the Trash and empty the Trash.

Note   An alias of an item on a CD or other removable disk breaks if the CD or removable disk that contains the original item is removed from the computer. This fragile behavior occurs in Mac OS X versions 10.1 and earlier but does not occur in Mac OS 9 and earlier. A future update of Mac OS X may make aliases of items on CDs and other removable disks as robust as such aliases are in Mac OS 9. (If you use an alias of an item on a CD or removable disk in Mac OS 9 and the CD or removable disk is not in the computer, an alert tells you the name of the missing CD or removable disk and asks you to insert it.)

When you perform certain actions with an alias, Mac OS X resolves the alias and uses the original item instead. These actions include opening the alias and dragging another icon to an alias. When you perform certain other actions with an alias, Mac OS X does not resolve the alias, but acts directly on the alias itself. These actions include renaming, moving, copying, and deleting an alias. We cover working with aliases in detail when we delve into working with files and folders later in this chapter and in Chapters 4 and 5.

Other files

Besides aliases, documents, and applications, Mac OS X provides a plethora of other files, many of which you may never use, at least knowingly. For example, you don't directly use the thousands of files that are used by Mac OS X and the Unix kernel (also known as Darwin) beneath it to manage your Mac and its networking and to present the Aqua interface. These files reside in a special folder named System, which is located on the Mac OS X startup disk. This System folder also contains the files for the Unix command-line shell and all the Unix tools that go with it, in case you ever find the need or desire to use Unix commands in the Terminal application, as described in Chapter 26.

Viewing Finder Windows

In the Finder windows we've seen so far — the windows showing your home folder, the Applications folder, and your Desktop folder — the files and folders in the window are displayed as icons. Rather than viewing the items in a Finder window as icons, you can view the contents as an ordered list of item names and other details, or you can view contents in columns, as shown in Figure 3-6.

Using Finder window controls

Regardless of a Finder window's view format, it has all the standard window controls that we covered in Chapter 2. You can use these controls to close, minimize, zoom, and resize the window. You can move the window by dragging its title bar. You can scroll or resize the window to see more of its contents. You can show or hide the toolbar at the top of the window by clicking the lozenge-shaped toolbar button in the upper-right corner of the window. Figures 3-7 identify the controls in Finder windows and show a Finder window with and without its toolbar.

A Finder toolbar contains useful buttons for choosing a view format and switching the window to a different folder, as described in the rest of this chapter. You can customize the toolbar by adding and removing buttons, and we explain how in Chapter 4.

Figure 3-6: A Finder window may display its contents as icons, in a list, or in columnar format.

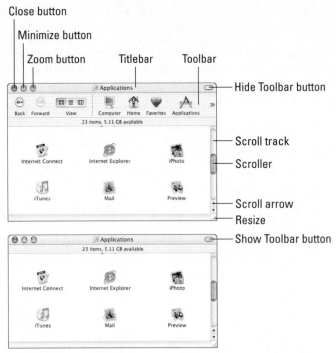

Figure 3-7: A Finder window displaying the optional toolbar and with its toolbar hidden.

Several of the Finder window controls have equivalent menu commands and keyboard shortcuts, as follows:

Close button	File⇨Close	⌘-W
Minimize button	Window⇨Minimize Window	⌘-M
Zoom button	Window⇨Zoom Window	
Toolbar button	View⇨Show Toolbar	⌘-B
Toolbar button	View⇨Hide Toolbar	⌘-B

Choosing a view

You can choose your view format for the active Finder window in one of two ways.

✦ Choose a view format from the Finder's View menu—As Icons, As List, or As Columns.

✦ Click the appropriate part of the View button in the window's toolbar. Click the left part of the button to view as icons, the middle part to view as a list, or the right part to view as columns.

Working in an icon view

The icon view is the original Finder view, dating back to the very first Macs shipped in 1984. Since then, this view has been enhanced in many small ways, but it is fundamentally the same view. You select an icon by clicking it, typing the first part of its name, pressing Tab or Shift-Tab, or pressing arrow keys. You can select multiple icons by dragging across them or by ⌘-clicking or Shift-clicking each icon in turn.

If the icons in an icon view are in disarray, you can have the Finder align them in neat rows and columns. You clean up the active window by choosing View➪Clean Up. You can clean up individual icons by holding down the ⌘ key while dragging them singly or in groups. Figure 3-8 shows a Finder window before and after being cleaned up.

You can also have the Finder alphabetize the icons and align them in rows and columns. Do this by choosing View➪Arrange by Name. Figure 3-9 shows a Finder window before and after being arranged by icon name.

The Finder can keep the icons in a window arranged for you. You set up automatic icon arrangement in the Finder's View Options window as described in Chapter 4.

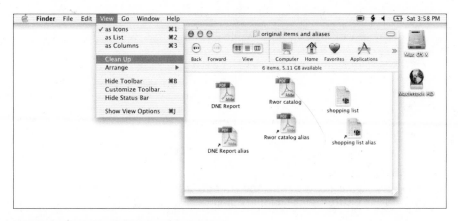

Figure 3-8: A Finder window before and after the icons are arranged neatly.

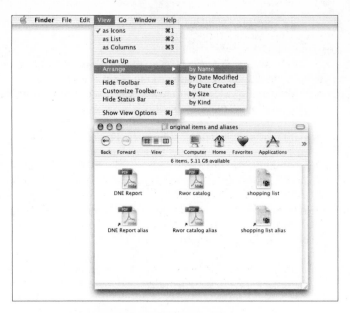

Figure 3-9 A Finder window before and after the icons are arranged alphabetically.

Working in a list view

List views can pack a lot of information in a window, and you can use that information to organize the list view. You can sort the list by any of the column headings at the top of the view. You can see the contents of enclosed folders in an indented outline format. Also, you can simultaneously select items contained in more than one enclosed folder.

Changing the sort order

When you initially view a window as a list, the items are arranged alphabetically by name. You can sort the list in a different order by clicking one of the column headings near the top of the window. For example, to list the items in the order in which they were last modified, click the Date Modified heading.

A quick glance at the column headings tells you the sort order. The dark heading indicates the sort order in a Finder window. You can reverse the sort order by clicking the heading again. An arrowhead at the right end of the heading indicates the sort direction.

Rearranging and resizing columns

The columns of a list view are adjustable in a Finder window. You can change the size of a column by moving the mouse pointer to the right edge of the column heading. The pointer is in the right place for resizing a column when the pointer looks like a sideways pointing arrow. Then press the mouse button and drag left or right. Figure 3-10 is an example of resizing a column in a list view.

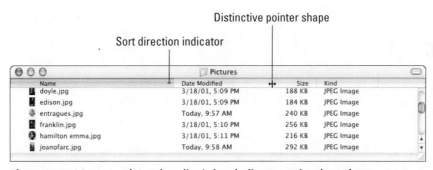

Figure 3-10: Drag a column heading's borderline to resize the column.

 Tip
You don't have to widen a column in a list view just to read one long name. You can display the entire name in a help tag by pointing at the name and waiting a few seconds. If you can't wait, point at the name and press Option to see the help tag immediately.

You can also change the order of columns. Simply drag the column heading to the left or right. As you drag, the pointer looks like a hand and you see a pale image of the column you are moving. You can't move the Name column. Figure 3-11 is an example of rearranging columns.

Expanding and collapsing folders

The Finder displays list views in an indented outline format. The levels of indentation in the outline show how folders are nested. The indented outline provides a graphical representation of a folder's organization. You can look through and reorganize several folders all in one window. Figure 3-12 shows an example of a list view with both expanded and collapsed folders.

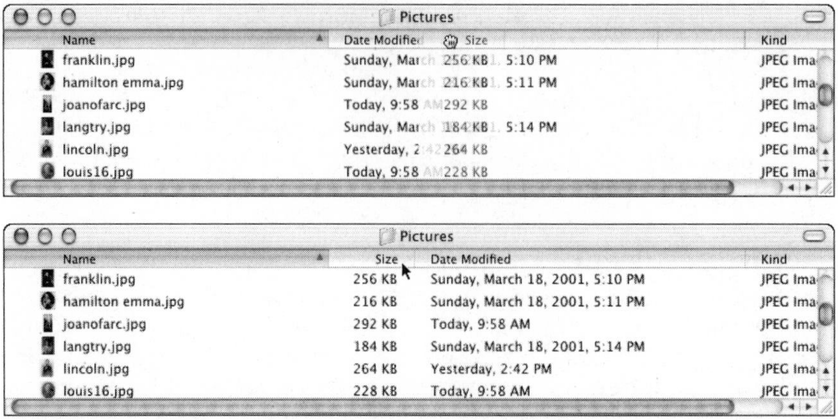

Figure 3-11: Drag a column heading to move the column.

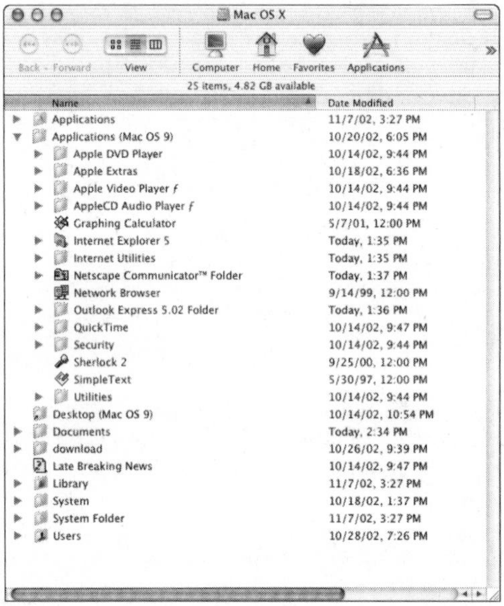

Figure 3-12: A list view with expanded and collapsed folders.

Disclosure triangles next to folder names tell you whether the folders are expanded or collapsed. If a triangle points to the right, the folder next to it is collapsed, and you cannot see its contents. If the triangle points down, the folder is expanded, and below the folder name, you can see a list of the items in the folder.

To expand a folder, click the triangle to the left of the folder's icon. When you expand a folder, Finder remembers whether folders nested within it were previously expanded or collapsed and restores each to its former state. Figure 3-13 shows a folder before and after expanding it.

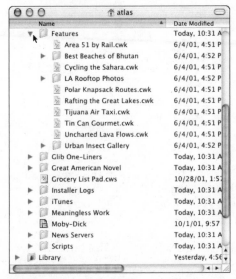

Click to reveal the contents in the folder.

Figure 3-13: Click a right-pointing triangle (Documents on the top) to expand a folder and display its contents (bottom).

To collapse a folder, click the down-pointing triangle to the left of the folder's icon. It returns to the right-pointing orientation, and the contents are no longer displayed.

To collapse a folder and any open subfolders within it, press Option while clicking the disclosure triangle of the outer folder. To expand a folder and all the subfolders within it, press Option while clicking the disclosure triangle.

Tip   If you have a folder or multiple folders selected, you can press ⌘-→ to expand them or ⌘-Option-→ to expand them and all their nested subfolders. To collapse folders from the keyboard, ⌘-← collapses the outline to that level.

Selecting from multiple folders

After expanding several folders in a list view, you can select items from more than one of the expanded folders. To select an additional item, press ⌘ while clicking it. If you want to select consecutive items, drag a selection rectangle across the consecutive items or select the first item and Shift-click the last item. If you need to deselect a few items, ⌘-click each item. Figure 3-14 shows a list view with items selected from two folders.

Name	Date Modified	Size	Kind
▼ 📁 Features	Today, 12:01 PM	--	Folder
📄 Area 51 by Rail.cwk	6/4/01, 4:51 PM	24 KB	com.a...ument
▼ 📁 Best Beaches of Bhutan	Today, 12:02 PM	--	Folder
📄 Best Beach...Bhutan.cwk	6/4/01, 4:51 PM	24 KB	com.a...ument
▶ 📁 Bhutan Pictures	Today, 12:02 PM	--	Folder
📄 Cycling the Sahara.cwk	6/4/01, 4:51 PM	24 KB	com.a...ument
▼ 📁 LA Rooftop Photos	6/4/01, 4:52 PM	--	Folder
📄 Polar Knapsack Routes.cwk	6/4/01, 4:51 PM	24 KB	com.a...ument
📄 Rafting the Great Lakes.cwk	6/4/01, 4:51 PM	24 KB	com.a...ument
📄 Tijuana Air Taxi.cwk	6/4/01, 4:51 PM	24 KB	com.a...ument
📄 Tin Can Gourmet.cwk	6/4/01, 4:51 PM	24 KB	com.a...ument
📄 Uncharted Lava Flows.cwk	6/4/01, 4:51 PM	24 KB	com.a...ument
▶ 📁 Urban Insect Gallery	6/4/01, 4:52 PM	--	Folder
▶ 📁 Glib One-Liners	Today, 10:31 AM	--	Folder
▶ 📁 Great American Novel	Today, 10:31 AM	--	Folder
📄 Grocery List Pad.cws	10/28/01, 1:57 AM	292 KB	com.a...plate

Figure 3-14: In a list view, you can select items from multiple folders.

Selected items remain selected if you expand other folders in the same window. Selected items also remain selected if you collapse folders in the same window, except that any selected items in a folder you collapse are no longer selected.

Working in a column view

Like list views, column views pack a lot of information into one window. This view's heritage is the NeXT browser view, and it first appeared on the Mac in the shareware utility, Greg's Browser, back in 1989. Understanding the column view and becoming comfortable with its use is fairly important because you see column views in the dialogs for opening and saving documents within applications (as explained in Chapter 5).

A column view shows a folder and its contents in the same window. When you select a folder in a column view, that folder's contents appear in the next column to the right. When you select an alias of a folder, Mac OS X resolves the alias and the Finder displays the original folder's contents in the next column to the right. When you select a file, its icon or a preview of its contents appears in the next column to the right. Whether you see a file's icon or a preview of its contents depends on the type of file. For an application, you always see an icon and some facts about the application. For some types of documents that contain text or graphics, you see a preview. Figure 3-15 shows a column view with a preview of a graphics document.

Figure 3-15: A column view shows the folder structure on a disk and may show a preview of the selected file.

A column view differs markedly from an icon view or a list view in how much of your folder structure you can see. Where an icon view shows only one folder and a list view shows one folder plus the folders it contains, every column view can show any part of the folder structure on any disk that's available on your computer. By scrolling a column view to the left, you can traverse the folder hierarchy to the Computer level. By scrolling to the right, you can traverse the folder hierarchy the other direction until you reach the currently selected folder or file.

Unlike list or icon views, you have no control over the sorting order in a column view. Items in each column are always listed alphabetically. (Actually, the order of items is based on the character-set ordering established for your system and language.)

What you gain with a column view is rapid browsing of the folder structure on a disk and a large preview of a selected document or application. What you lose is rapid manipulation of files, such as moving them from one branch of the folder structure to another or selecting files from multiple folders at one time.

Selecting multiple items

You can select multiple consecutive items in a single folder by clicking the first one and Shift-clicking the last one. Selecting nonconsecutive items is accomplished via ⌘-clicking the items. When multiple items are selected, no preview shows, nor do selected folders expand in the next column.

Resizing columns

Column width is adjustable in a column view. You can adjust the widths of all columns uniformly or the width of a single column, as follows:

✦ To resize all columns uniformly, drag the handle at the bottom of any column divider to the right or left.

✦ To resize one column, press Option while dragging the handle at the bottom of the column divider on the right side of the column.

Browsing Folders and Disks

The main thing all three Finder views have in common is that their primary function is to enable you to navigate the folder structure of your disks and open applications and documents. In the remainder of this chapter, we investigate ways you can navigate through your folders to locate a document or application that you want to use. Then in Chapter 5 we explain how to open and work with applications and documents.

Opening folders and disks

One way to navigate the folder structure of your disks is by opening disk and folders. You can open any disk or folder that you can see in a Finder window or on the Desktop. When you open a disk or a folder, you see its contents in a Finder window. If these contents include folders, you can open one of them to see its contents in a Finder window. By opening folders within folders, you make your way through the folder structure. If you open the right sequence of folders, eventually you open the folder that contains a document or application that you're looking for.

To open a disk or folder that you have located in a Finder window or on the Desktop, you can use any of these methods:

✦ Double-click the icon or the name of the item.

✦ Click the item's icon to select it, and then choose File➪Open.

✦ Click the item's icon to select it, and then press ⌘-O.

✦ Control-click the item's icon to display its contextual menu, and then choose Open from the contextual menu.

All these methods for opening items work in any Finder window viewed as icons or columns. The methods also work for opening items on the Desktop (which is always viewed as icons).

Note
In a list view of Mac OS X 10.1.1 and earlier, you must first click an item to select it before you can display its contextual menu by Control-clicking the item.

When you open a folder, its contents may appear in the same Finder window or a new Finder window. A folder opens in the same Finder window if the window's toolbar is showing. If you hide the toolbar in a Finder window before double-clicking a folder in the window, the folder's contents are displayed in a new Finder window. You can reverse these two rules by pressing the ⌘ key while opening a folder. For example, if you ⌘-double-click a folder in a Finder window whose toolbar is showing, the folder's contents appear in a new Finder window. You can also change a Finder preference setting to make the Finder normally display a new window when you open a folder; we cover setting Finder preferences in Chapter 4.

Opening the alias of a folder or disk has exactly the same effect as opening the folder or disk that the alias represents. If you open an alias of a folder or disk, Mac OS X resolves the alias and the Finder displays the contents of the original folder or disk.

Navigating a list view

You don't have to open disks or folders to navigate your folder structure in a Finder window viewed as a list. A list view provides the additional technique of expanding the outline as described earlier in this chapter. Instead of opening a folder or disk that you see in a list view, you can see the contents of a disk or folder by clicking the disclosure triangle next to its icon.

Navigating a column view

You also don't need to open a folder or disk to navigate your folder structure in a column view. Instead of opening a folder or a disk that you see in a column view, you can merely click the icon or name of the folder or disk. Upon selecting a folder or disk, its contents appear in the column to the right of the selected item. If you select an alias of a folder or disk in a column view, the contents of the original folder or disk appear in the next column.

Scroll the window horizontally to navigate through your folder structure. Scroll left to move closer to the disks and other volumes on your computer. Scroll right to move closer to the selected file or folder.

Previewing files in a column view

One of the column view's nicest features is that, when you select certain types of document files, you see a preview of that document's contents in the rightmost column. Previews display for several types of documents, including plain text, PDF, sound, movie, and graphics files. For a document with multiple pages, the preview shows the first page. The preview for a sound or movie appears with a small QuickTime controller, which you use to hear the sound or see the movie. We cover QuickTime extensively in Chapters 13 and 14. For now, just know that you can click the Play button at the left end of the controller to play the movie or sound preview. The small Play button looks like a right-pointing arrowhead, as shown in Figure 3-16.

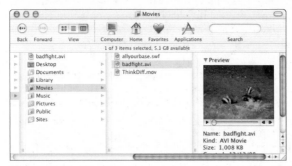

Figure 3-16: Preview your movie, sound, graphics, and text files in a Finder window viewed as columns.

Note   Preparing the preview for a long PDF document or even a very large plain text document can take a long time and cause the Mac to be unresponsive. To guard against extreme delays, the Finder doesn't show a preview for text and multiple-page PDF documents larger than about 500K.

Finding your path

As noted earlier, a column view gives you a quick look at the path through the folder structure from the Computer level to the item or items displayed in the right-most column. You don't have to be in a column view to obtain this path information, though. At the top of a Finder window, you see an icon for the folder you're in, accompanied by its name. By pressing the ⌘ key and clicking the name, a menu will pop up, showing the hierarchy of folders traversed to get back to the Computer level. The current folder is at the top of the pop-up menu and the Computer level is at the bottom, as shown in Figure 3-17.

Figure 3-17: See the path through your folder structure by ⌘-clicking the title of a Finder window.

Creating a new Finder window

Mac OS X gives you a few ways to create new Finder windows:

✦ Choose File⇨New Finder Window.

✦ Press ⌘-N.

✦ Open a folder from a Finder window whose toolbar is hidden.

✦ Press ⌘ while opening a folder from a Finder whose toolbar is showing.

✦ Click the Finder icon in the Dock if no Finder window is currently displayed, not counting minimized Finder windows in the Dock.

For experienced Mac users, the second option is going to require considerable retraining. Since the beginning of the Mac OS, ⌘-N has been the keystroke to create a new folder. (The shortcut for creating a new folder in Mac OS X is ⌘-Shift-N.) Because ⌘-N tells applications to create a new window (so long as the application's authors follow Apple's Human Interface Guidelines, available from www1.fatbrain.com/documentation/apple), this new mapping is more consistent and will probably be easier for new Mac users; however, old habits are hard to break.

Using the Window menu

When you have multiple Finder windows displayed and want to use one in particular, figuring out which of them is the one you want can often be difficult. Tediously moving windows around and bringing them to the front one after another was your only recourse prior to Mac OS 9. In Mac OS X, the Finder sports a Window menu that lists all of the Finder windows by name. You can quickly bring a particular Finder window to the front by choosing it from the Window menu. Figure 3-18 shows an example of the Finder's Window menu.

Figure 3-18: Bring a Finder window to the front by choosing it from the Window menu.

In Mac OS X, Finder windows can become intermingled with windows belonging to other applications. This window behavior is another change for experienced Mac users to get used to. In Mac OS 9 and earlier, all of one application's windows comprise a group or layer that is separate from the window layer of every other application. The window layers never mix in Mac OS 9 because clicking a window belonging to an application brings its entire layer of windows to the front. In contrast, clicking a window belonging to a Mac OS X application brings just that one window to the front. If you click Finder windows alternately with windows belonging to other Mac OS X applications, the windows end up stacked in the order you clicked them regardless of application, as shown in Figure 3-19.

Bringing just the clicked window forward is a consistent and flexible behavior, but there are times when you will want the traditional behavior. This is the raison d'être of Bring All to Front in the Window menu. Choose Window⇨Bring All to Front, and all the Finder windows will now be in front of other applications' windows, while retaining their own front-to-back ordering. Choosing Window⇨Bring All to Front does not bring any minimized windows to the front; they stay in the Dock. Let us hope that developers of other Mac OS X applications follow the Finder's lead.

Tip   You can also bring all of the Finder's windows to the front by clicking the Finder's icon in the Dock. To bring all Finder windows to the front while hiding all other windows, ⌘-Option-click the Finder's icon in the Dock.

Figure 3-19: Finder windows can become intermingled with windows belonging to other Mac OS X applications.

Using the Go menu

Brand new to the Mac OS X Finder is the Go menu. Consolidated in this one menu are many of the built-in navigational aids that are located in the Apple menu of Mac OS 9. The Go menu has some new navigation methods as well.

Several items in the Go menu are the names of folders you've already encountered as buttons in the Finder window toolbar. Choose Computer, Home, iDisk, or Applications from the Go menu to display the contents of the corresponding folder in the front Finder window. (If no Finder window is currently displayed, a new Finder window appears.) All of these Go menu items have handy keyboard shortcuts. Computer is ⌘-Option-C, Home is ⌘-Option-H, iDisk is ⌘-Option-I, and Applications is ⌘-Option-A. Figure 3-20 shows the Go menu.

Favorites

The Favorites submenu of the Go menu lists items that you identify as your favorites. The keyboard shortcut for Go To Favorites is ⌘-Option-F. Choosing an item from the Favorites submenu opens the item. If the item is a folder or a disk, its contents appear in the front Finder window. (A new Finder window appears if none is currently displayed.)

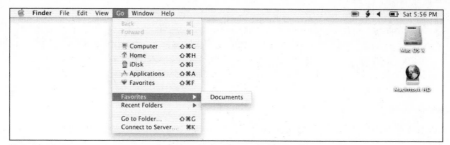

Figure 3-20: Go just about anywhere with the Go menu.

The Favorites folder contains an alias for every item listed in the Favorites submenu (except the first item). Initially, the Favorites submenu lists only your Documents folder, and your Favorites folder contains only an alias of your Documents folder. Chapter 4 explains how to add and remove items in the Favorites submenu.

Recent Folders

The Recent Folders submenu of the Go menu lists the last 10 folders that you displayed in the Finder. This submenu is similar in concept to the Recent Items menu in the Apple menu, which lists applications and documents that you have recently used. Unlike the Apple⇨Recent Items submenu, the Go⇨Recent Folders submenu doesn't have a menu choice for clearing the current list of recent folders. (The Apple⇨Recent Items submenu is described in more detail in Chapter 5.)

Go To Folder

If you know the exact name and path to the folder you want (and you type well), choose Go⇨Go To Folder (or press the keyboard shortcut ⌘-~). The Finder displays a dialog in which you type the path and name of the folder desired. This is far from the traditional Macintosh graphical interface, but it is one near and dear to the hearts of folks coming from Unix and MS-DOS. To be honest, one of your authors uses it fairly often when navigating through folders with lots of files in them.

A complete path to a folder begins with a slash character (/) and is followed by the names of every folder from the outermost folder to the folder that you want to open, with an additional / between folder names. For example, /Applications/ Utilities is the path to the Utilities folder of the Applications folder.

If you don't start the pathname with a /, the Finder looks for a *relative path,* one which starts in the current folder. For example, if the Applications folder is open in the front Finder window, you can open the Utilities folder by typing just Utilities in the Go To Folder dialog.

Tip   Unix pathname shortcuts all work in the Go To Folder dialog. For example, if you're in a folder on another volume and wish to be in the Sites folder of your home folder, just press ⌘-~ to display the Go To Folder dialog and type ~/Sites to be transported. Similarly, to get to the Public folder of another user named spenser, you would type ~spenser/Public. See Chapter 26 for more on Unix.

Back

If you want the front Finder window to go back to the folder or disk that it last displayed, choose Go➪Back (or press ⌘-[). You can continue going back by choosing Go➪Back again. When the front Finder window can't go back any more because it is displaying the first folder or disk that it ever displayed, the Back item is disabled (dim) in the Go menu. The Back item in the Go menu is equivalent to the Back button in the Finder window toolbar.

Connect To Server

The Go menu's final choice provides access to file servers, either on your own network or on the Internet. Choosing Go➪Connect to Server displays a dialog in which you specify the server that you want to connect to. The Connect to Server dialog provides a pop-up menu of recent and favorite servers, in addition to servers on your local network. The disclosure button hides or shows the network browser pane, where you can select a network in the left column and a server on that network in the right column. Instead of choosing a server from the network browser or the pop-up menu, you can type the server's URL or IP address in the Address text box. We discuss the Connect to Server dialog in much more detail in Chapter 10. Figure 3-21 shows an example of the Connect to Server dialog and its pop-up menu.

Figure 3-21: Browse the network to choose a server, or enter its address.

Summary

This chapter presented you with an introduction to the Finder, your window into the contents of your Mac. After reading this chapter, you know how to do the following:

✦ Recognize Finder windows, the Desktop, the Computer level, the Trash, applications, documents, your home folder, your iDisk, and aliases.

✦ View any Finder window as icons, a list, or columns.

✦ Work in an icon view, a list view, and a column view.

✦ Browse folders and disks in your Finder windows.

✦ Navigate your folder structure by opening disks and folders in sequence.

✦ Navigate a list view and a column view.

✦ See previews in a column view.

✦ Find the path through your folder structure to the folder currently displayed in a Finder window.

✦ Create a new Finder window.

✦ Bring a Finder window to the front with the Window menu.

✦ Display the Computer level, your home folder, your iDisk, or the Applications folder in the front Finder window.

✦ Open an item you have designated as a favorite.

✦ Open one of the 10 folders that you most recently displayed in a Finder window.

✦ Go back to the folder last displayed in the front Finder window.

✦ Connect to a file server.

To learn more about using the Finder and the Dock, proceed to Chapter 4.

✦   ✦   ✦

Enhancing Your Workspace

Y ou got an introduction to the Mac OS X Finder and
Desktop in Chapter 3. Now you're going to find out how
to customize Finder windows, the Desktop, and the Dock to
suit *your* tastes and to improve your enjoyment and productivity. In this chapter, you learn what the optional status bar in
Finder windows can tell you about folders and disks. You find
out how to customize the toolbar in Finder windows. You
learn how to set view options that affect the look of each
Finder window and how to change the picture on the Desktop.
You also investigate ways to get the most from the Dock.

In addition, this chapter describes techniques for working
with files, folders, aliases, and disks. These techniques
include creating folders and moving, copying, and deleting
files and folders. You learn how to make aliases hop — create
them, change them, fix them if they break, and more. You
also learn how to remove, mount, and erase disks and other
volumes.

Finally, this chapter explains how to see and change detailed
information about files, folders, and volumes in the Finder's
Info window. Here you can rename, lock or unlock, apply a
custom icon, and attach comments to an item. You can also
set the application to open a document and set a folder's
access privileges.

Tuning Finder Windows

You already know how to view a Finder window as icons, a
list, or columns. You also know how to clean up an icon view
and change the sorting of a list view. In addition, you know
how to show and hide the toolbar at the top of any Finder window. We covered all these operations in the Chapter 3. These
are only some of the ways you can customize Finder windows.

Other methods for tuning Finder windows include showing and hiding a status bar in every window and customizing the toolbar that appears in every window. These methods are covered in this section.

Showing and hiding the status bar

The Finder can display a status bar at the top of every Finder window. To show the status bar in every Finder window, choose View⇪Show Status Bar. This menu command then changes to Hide Status Bar, and choosing it does what you expect. The status bar appears directly below the toolbar or below the title bar if the toolbar is hidden. Depending on what is in a particular Finder window, its status bar may report some or all of the following information, as shown in Figure 4-1:

✦ **Number of items in the window.** Does not include items inside folders that are in the window except for folders that are expanded in a list view.

✦ **Space available for additional items.** This is the amount of unused storage space on the disk or other volume that contains the folder whose contents appear in the window. The space available is omitted in a window that shows the Computer level.

✦ **Restricted access privileges.** If you do not have Write privileges for the folder, disk, or other item whose contents appear in the window, a small icon that looks like a crossed-out pencil appears near the left end of the Status bar.

✦ **Automatic icon arrangement.** If the window is an icon view and is set up for automatic icon arrangement, an icon at the left end of the status bar indicates the type of arrangement. An icon that looks like a grid means icons always snap to an invisible grid. An icon that depicts four tiny aligned icons means icons in the window are kept arranged by name or another criterion. We describe how to set up automatic icon arrangement later in this chapter under "Setting View Options."

Customizing a Finder window toolbar

As you can see in Figure 4-1, the default toolbar consists of a number of buttons with their names beneath them: Back, Forward, View, Computer, Home, Favorites, and Applications. You can customize the toolbar to meet your needs. Apple enables you to add other buttons, and you can arrange them any way you want. You can also set the toolbar to display buttons as named icons, icons without names, or names alone. To make these changes, choose View⇪Customize Toolbar. The active Finder window changes to display the Customize Toolbar dialog box shown in Figure 4-2.

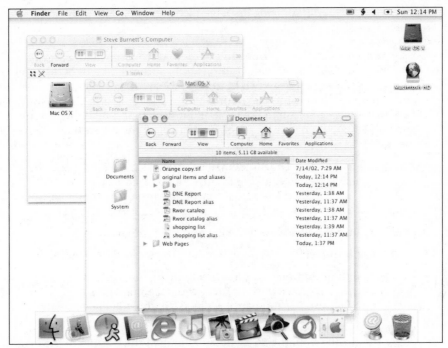

Figure 4-1: You can display a status bar at the top of every Finder window.

Figure 4-2: Add, remove, and rearrange buttons in a Finder window's toolbar by using the Customize Toolbar dialog box.

With the Customize Toolbar dialog displayed, change the toolbar by doing the following:

✦ **Add buttons.** Drag buttons to the toolbar from the main part of the dialog. You don't have to add buttons only at the right end of the toolbar. If you drag a button between two buttons in the toolbar, they move apart to make room for the button you're dragging. If the toolbar is full of buttons and you drag another button to the toolbar, buttons that don't fit on the toolbar appear in a pop-up menu. To see this menu, click the arrow that appears at the right end of the toolbar.

✦ **Add icons as buttons.** Drag folders, files, or disks from Finder windows to the toolbar. The items that you drag to the toolbar become buttons there. For example, if you create a folder for a particular project within your Documents folder, drag its icon to the toolbar to make it accessible with a single click.

✦ **Remove buttons.** Drag buttons away from the toolbar.

✦ **Rearrange buttons.** Drag buttons to different places on the toolbar.

✦ **Revert to default buttons.** If you've customized the toolbar and want to get back to the default set of buttons, drag the boxed default set from the lower part of the dialog to the toolbar to replace whatever is currently there.

✦ **Change toolbar mode.** Show items as icons with names, icons only, or names only by choosing from the Show pop-up menu at the bottom of the dialog. Figure 4-3 shows the three toolbar modes.

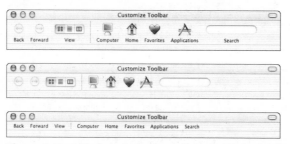

Figure 4-3: A Finder window's toolbar displaying both icons and text (top), only icons without text (middle), and only text (bottom).

Note Although you can add folders to the toolbar, the Dock is usually a better place for folders. As we discuss later in this chapter, a folder icon in the Dock has a hierarchical menu that provides access to anything in the folder or the folders within it.

Tip Clicking a folder button in the toolbar opens the folder in the same window as the toolbar. If you ⌘-click a folder button in the toolbar, the folder opens in a new Finder window.

Setting View Options

The Finder in Mac OS X provides still more ways to tweak the basic icon and list views. In this section, we discuss the adjustments you can make to icon and list views in the View Options window, which you display by choosing View⇨Show View Options. The options in this window are different for icon view and list view, as shown in Figures 4-4.

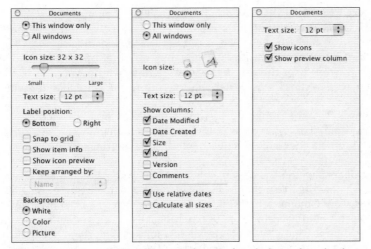

Figure 4-4: View options for a Finder window in icon view (top), list view (middle), and column view (bottom).

The View Options window displays the settings of the folder, disk, or other item whose name appears in the title bar of the active Finder window. To reinforce this fact, the same name appears in the title bar of the View Options window. If you make another Finder window active (bring it to the front), the View Options window changes to show settings for the item named in this Finder window's title. Therefore, you can only see the View Options settings for one folder at a time.

The View Options settings don't really apply to the active Finder window. The View Options settings actually apply to the folder, disk, or other item whose name appears in the title bar of the active Finder window. The settings for the folder shown in a Finder window remain when you close the window. If you open the same folder in another Finder window later, the Finder uses the folder's established View Options settings. (You can alter this behavior by changing an option in Finder Preferences, as described later in this chapter.) If a background Finder window is displaying the contents of the same folder as the active Finder window, then both windows have the same title and changes you make to the View Options settings affect both windows.

Using global or individual view options

Each folder can be displayed in a Finder window according to global View Options settings or the folder's individual View Options settings. The option at the top of the View Options window determines which settings the displayed folder in the active Finder window uses.

✦ **This window only.** The folder displayed in the active Finder window uses its individual View Options settings.

✦ **All windows.** The folder displayed in the active Finder window uses the global View Options settings.

The wording of these settings is a bit misleading. Like all other options in the View Options window, the option at the top of the View Options window applies to the folder that's displayed in the active Finder window, not to the actual Finder window.

The Finder keeps track of the option at the top of the View Options window separately for icon view and list view. For example, a folder's list view can use global settings while the same folder's icon view uses individual settings.

Note   If the View Options window is closed, some changes you make in a Finder window affect whether the folder that is displayed in the window is set to use global or individual View Options settings. If you rearrange or resize columns in a list view, the folder is automatically set to use individual View Options settings for list view. When you open the View Options window for this folder, you see that the option at the top of the window has been set to "This window only."

Setting global or individual view options

The option at the top of the View Options window also determines whether changes you make to the View Options settings affect one folder or many, as follows:

✦ **This window only.** Changes you make in the View Options window affect only the folder displayed in the active Finder window.

✦ **Global.** Changes you make in the View Options window affect all folders that use the global View Options settings.

 Tip   Get in the habit of double-checking the option at the top of the View Options window before you change any settings in the window. Unless you're sure that you want to change the global settings many folders use, set the option at the top of the View Options window to "This window only."

Setting list view options

For a list view, you can set the icon size and select which of seven optional columns you want shown. By selecting just the columns you need to see in a window, you can see most or all columns without scrolling the window. Of course, you can make more columns fit in a window by widening the window or reducing column widths, as described in Chapter 3.

A list view always includes the Name column. The columns that you can show or hide are the following:

✦ Date Modified (selected by default)

✦ Date Created

✦ Size (selected by default)

✦ Kind (selected by default)

✦ Label

✦ Version

✦ Comments

Note   Although the Mac OS X Finder can display a Labels column, you can't set an item's label with the Mac OS X Finder. If you select the Labels column, it displays the label name that was assigned to an item under Mac OS 9 or earlier.

Another option for list views determines whether the Finder displays relative dates — yesterday, today, tomorrow — rather than the actual month, day, and year. For dates other than yesterday, today, and tomorrow, the Finder uses the date and time formats that are set in the International pane of System Preferences (as described in Chapter 15). The column width determines whether the Finder uses the long date format or short date format from System Preferences. For example, a standard-width column that shows Tue, Jan 2, 2001 12:00 PM would show 1/2/01 12:00 PM in a narrower column or Tuesday, January 2, 2001 12:00 PM in a wider column.

You can also set an option to have the Finder calculate folder sizes and display them in a list view. Folder size calculation takes place in the background, while you're doing other things, and folder sizes are slow to appear.

The last option for list views determines whether normal (small) icons or large icons precede the names in list views.

Setting icon view options

In a Finder window set to icon view, you can set the icon size, text size, automatic arrangement of icons, item info, item preview, and background color or picture.

Changing the icon size in an icon view

To change the icon size in an icon view, use the Icon Size slider in the View Options window. If you set the slider for the smallest size, the icon's name displays next to the icon rather than below it. The icons of most Mac OS X applications and their documents are designed to look great at any size. The icons of Classic applications and their documents don't look as good at larger sizes, because Classic icons were not designed for Mac OS X's huge sizes. Classic icons look best at either the smallest size or at standard size, which is one hatch-mark to the left of the smallest size on the Icon Size slider. Figure 4-5 illustrates the minimum, standard, and maximum sizes icons available in icon views.

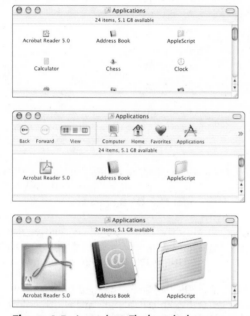

Figure 4-5: Icons in a Finder window at minimum (16 x 16 pixels) size (top), at standard (32 x 32 pixels) size (middle), and at maximum (126 x 128 pixels) size (bottom).

Changing the icon arrangement in icon view

The Icon Arrangement setting in the View Options window determines whether the Finder automatically aligns icons in an icon view. You can select one of the following three settings:

✦ **None.** Icon placement is random. The Finder does not enforce any icon alignment. There is not a specific checkbox for this setting, just deselect the positioning checkboxes.

✦ **Snap to grid.** The Finder automatically aligns each icon on an invisible grid. The grid button (shown earlier) displays at the top of the window in the upper left-hand corner.

✦ **Keep arranged by.** The Finder aligns icons on an invisible grid and places them in order according to the setting of the pop-up menu in the View Options window. A drop-down menu offers the options to arrange the icons by Name, Date Modified, Date Created, Size, or Kind.

You can also select whether to Show Item Info. This option displays the number of items within a folder as text beneath the folder.

Changing the background in icon view

In addition to specifying icon size and arrangement, you can specify the background for a folder displayed in an icon view. Here are your options:

✦ **White.** The standard white appears in the background behind your icons.

✦ **Color.** Makes the background a solid color, which you can specify by following these steps:

1. **After selecting the Color setting, click the small swatch of the currently selected color that appears in the View Options window.** This action displays the standard Mac OS X Color Picker window, shown in Figure 4-6.

2. **Across the top of the Color Picker window, select the type of color picker you want to use.** You can select from a Color Wheel (the default option), Color Sliders, Color Palettes, Image Palettes, and Crayons.

3. **Pick the background color you want.** Depending on the type of color picker you selected, you pick a color by clicking a color wheel, adjusting sliders, typing numbers, or clicking a color swatch. For example, the Crayons color picker has swatches that look like crayons. The Color Wheel picker has a color wheel that you can use to specify hue angle (dominant color) and saturation (amount of color) and a slider that you can use to specify a lightness value (closeness to black or white).

4. **Click OK.**

✦ **Picture.** Makes the background a picture, which you can specify by following these steps:

1. **After selecting the Picture setting, click the Select button that appears in the View Options window.** The Select A Picture dialog box appears, shown in Figure 4-7.

2. **In the Select A Picture dialog box, select a graphics file that contains an appropriate picture and click Select.** This dialog box is like the column view of a Finder window. When you select a graphics file, a preview of it appears in the dialog box. (This dialog box is a standard Open dialog box, which we cover in more detail in Chapter 5.)

Figure 4-6: Set a background color in the Color Picker.

Figure 4-7: Select a graphics file to use as a background picture for an icon view.

Customizing the Desktop

Now that you've seen how to customize the appearance of Finder windows, the obvious question to ask is, "How do I customize the Finder Desktop?" After all, the Finder Desktop is always present, and it is an obvious candidate for customization. The answer is twofold. Use the View Options window to change icon size and automatic arrangement. Use the Desktop pane of System Preferences to change the Desktop background.

Changing Desktop icon size and arrangement

The View Options window can show settings for the Desktop as well as for a Finder window. If you choose View➪Show View Options and then click the Desktop, the Desktop becomes active and its settings appear in the View Options window. The title of the View Options window even changes to Desktop. The Desktop is always in icon view, and it has the same options for icon size and icon arrangement as any icon view. For more specific information on these options, refer back to the coverage of setting icon view options earlier in this chapter. Figure 4-8 shows the View Options window with the Desktop active.

Figure 4-8: Set the size and automatic arrangement of Desktop icons in the View Options window.

However, the View Options window does not display options for the Desktop background as it does for an icon view of a Finder window. You set the Desktop background by using the System Preferences application, as explained in the following section.

Changing the Desktop background

When it comes to the overall appearance of the screen, nothing has more impact than changing the Desktop background. You can cover the Desktop with a solid color or a picture by choosing an image file as follows:

1. **Click the System Preferences icon in the Dock.** The System Preferences window appears, showing buttons for different types of settings.

2. **In System Preferences, click the Desktop button or choose View⇨Desktop.** The System Preferences window changes to show the settings for changing the Desktop background, as shown in Figure 4-9.

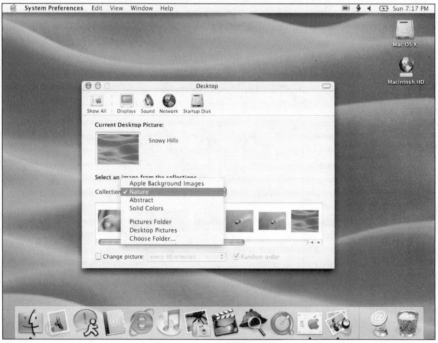

Figure 4-9: Set the Desktop background in the Desktop pane of System Preferences.

3. **Select an image.** Here are some techniques for selecting an image:

   • **If you see an image you like at the bottom of the window, click the image.**

   • **Use the scroll bar to see more images in the current collection.**

- **See a different set of images by choosing one from the Collection pop-up menu.** Your choices include Apple Background Images, Nature, Abstract, and Solid Colors. The collection of images appears at the bottom of the window.

- **See images from your Pictures folder by choosing Pictures Folder from the Collection pop-up menu.** If the Pictures folder of your home folder contains any images, they appear at the bottom of the window.

- **See images from any folder by choosing Choose Folder from the Collection pop-up menu.** A dialog appears. This dialog is like a column view of a Finder window. In this dialog, select the folder you want and click the Open button. Images from the selected folder appear at the bottom of the window.

4. **Choose System Prefs⇨Quit System Preferences when you are satisfied with the Desktop background.** The Desktop Preferences window goes away, and you are back in the Finder.

Setting Finder Preferences

The Finder has a number of preference settings that affect the appearance of icons on the Desktop, behavior of Finder windows, emptying the Trash, and showing extensions on the names of files. You change these preference settings by choosing Finder⇨Preferences. The Finder Preferences window appears, as shown in Figure 4-10.

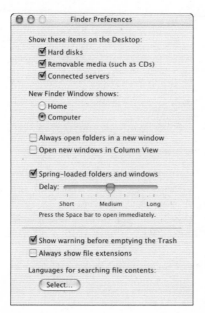

Figure 4-10: The Finder's preference settings affect Desktop icons, Finder windows, the Trash, and file extensions.

Options in Finder Preferences have the following effects:

✦ **Show these items on the Desktop.** Select the types of items that you want the Finder to display on your Desktop. These items are displayed together with items located in the Desktop folder of your home folder. All items appear at the Computer level of your workspace regardless of the settings here.

✦ **New Finder Window shows.** Select what you want to see when you create a new Finder window — the contents of your home folder or the Computer level of your folder structure.

✦ **Always open folders in a new window.** Select this option to reverse the Mac OS X Finder's habit of displaying a folder's contents in the very window that displayed the folder's icon when you opened the folder. This makes the Mac OS X Finder spawn windows in the same way as the Mac OS 9 Finder.

✦ **Open new windows in Column View.** Select this option, and the Finder opens new windows in column view.

✦ **Spring-loaded folders and windows.** If you drag an icon over a closed folder, the folder will automatically open after a delay. This delayed opening is called spring-loading. This slider sets the time delay between your dragging an icon over a folder and that folder springing open. If you set the delay too long and you want a folder to open immediately, drag the icon over the folder, then press the Space bar on the keyboard.

✦ **Show warning before emptying the Trash.** Deselect this option if you want the Finder to empty the Trash without first having you confirm the action. If this option is off, the Finder also deletes locked items from the Trash without any warning.

✦ **Always show file extensions.** Select this option if you want to see name extensions (suffixes) for all files that have them. This option overrides all settings that individually hide the extensions of particular files. We cover name extensions in more detail and explain how to hide them for individual files later in this chapter.

Using the Dock

If Steve Jobs's keynote addresses are any indication, he considers the Dock to be the coolest feature in Mac OS X. His opinion is open to debate, with strong arguments on both sides. However, the Dock is definitely new, flexible, and eye-catching, and it packs some hidden power. By the way, the Dock is also translucent and colorless. Whatever is behind the Dock shows through. Most people assume that the Dock's color is light blue because the standard Desktop picture is blue.

Adding Dock icons

Add any icon to the Dock by dragging it to the Dock and place it where you want it, with the restriction that applications must be placed on the same side of the separator line as the Finder, and everything else must be placed on the other side of the line. Placing an application's icon in the Dock gives you one-click access to the application regardless of what application is currently active. When you place a document's icon in the Dock, it is available to you at all times, just like application icons.

Using pop-up Dock menus

The real convenience and power come when you place a folder or disk icon in the Dock. Of course, you can click it to display its contents in a new Finder window. But if you click and hold (or Control-click) a folder icon in the Dock, you see a hierarchical menu that enables you to traverse the folder structure and open anything it contains. A folder's pop-up Dock menu also contains a Show in Finder command. Choose Show in Finder to see the folder in a Finder window. Figure 4-11 shows an example of a folder's pop-up Dock menu.

Figure 4-11: Get to any part of a folder when its icon is in the Dock.

Removing Dock icons

Removing an item from the Dock is also extremely simple. Drag the icon out of the Dock, let go, and it disappears in a puff of smoke. You can't remove the Finder or the Trash from the Dock.

Moving icons in the Dock

You can rearrange icons in the Dock by dragging them to different positions. As you drag an icon across the Dock, the other icons move apart to make room for the icon you're dragging. You can place the icon you're dragging in any space that opens up by releasing the mouse button.

Open applications in the Dock

Every application that is currently open has its icon in the Dock. If an application is open, a small marker appears below the application's icon in the Dock. When you click and hold (or Control-click) the icon of an open application in the Dock, a pop-up menu appears, giving you application-specific choices. For example, the Finder's pop-up Dock menu presents a list of available windows, and you can choose one to bring it to the front. This menu isn't a great benefit when you're already working in the Finder, because its Window menu does the same job and is more convenient. But the Finder's pop-up Dock menu is a great way to bring up a particular Finder window while you're working in another application. Other applications list different items in their pop-up Dock menus. Figure 4-12 shows an example of the Finder's pop-up Dock menu, displaying the open windows that can be brought to the front by selecting from the pop-up menu. If there are no windows open on the Desktop, the Finder pop-up menu displays "No windows."

Figure 4-12: The pop-up Dock menu of an open application may include items that are specific to the application.

Minimized windows in the Dock

When you minimize a window by clicking its Minimize button, you have a live miniature of the window in the Dock. Whatever was displayed in that window is also displayed, but reduced in size, in the minimized window. Furthermore, the window belongs to an application that is still running (albeit in the background), and the application can continue updating the minimized window in the Dock. For example, Apple loves to demonstrate this capability by playing miniature

QuickTime movies in the Dock. (Chapter 13 describes how to play QuickTime movies.) However, few applications are programmed to update minimized windows in the Dock.

Control-click (or click and hold) a minimized window, and its pop-up Dock menu informs you that you are clicking a minimized window rather than an icon. Clicking a minimized window icon in the Dock restores the window to full size.

Resizing the Dock

Not only does the Dock resize automatically as items are added to or removed from it, but you can resize the Dock (and the icons in it) yourself. To do this, move the pointer to the vertical line that separates application icons from folder and document icons. When the pointer changes to look like a two-headed arrow, drag down to make the Dock smaller or up to make the Dock larger. You can also resize the Dock by changing a setting in Dock Preferences, as described shortly. Figure 4-13 and illustrates the difference between a large and a small Dock.

Figure 4-13: The Dock at maximum size, filling the width of the screen (top), the Dock at minimum size (bottom).

Tip   You can scale the Dock up or down incrementally, so that the icon size is always a multiple of 16 pixels, by pressing Option while you drag the separator line.

Setting the Dock position and hiding

The Dock can be at the bottom of the screen or at either side. The bottom of the screen is longer than the sides and has room for more Dock icons. But the Dock can get in your way more at the bottom than on a side. At the bottom of the screen, the Dock interferes with making windows the full height of the screen to minimize vertical scrolling. The Dock is least obtrusive on the right side of the screen, because most applications display windows aligned with the left side of the screen.

You can make the Dock stay out of your way altogether by having it hide until you move the pointer to the edge of the screen. The disadvantage to Dock hiding is that it makes the Dock less convenient. You have to wait for the Dock to appear. The wait is brief, only a second or so, but it is long enough to become aggravating. On a small or low-resolution screen, you may want to consider trading convenience for room on the Desktop.

Set the Dock position and hiding by choosing appropriate commands from the Dock submenu of the Apple menu. Alternatively, you can use the Dock's contextual menu, which you display by Control-clicking the separator line in the Dock, as shown in Figure 4-14.

Figure 4-14: Experiment with Dock size, position, and hiding to find a combination that works best for you.

Setting Dock magnification

If you make the Dock very small, icons in it become hard to recognize. The Dock can magnify icons near the pointer so they are easier to recognize. To make this happen, choose Apple➪Dock➪Turn Magnification On. Alternatively, you can Control-click the Dock's separator line to display its contextual menu, and choose Turn Magnification On. When magnification is turned on, the menu commands change to Turn Magnification Off.

Choosing a visual effect

When you minimize a window, the Dock normally shows a visual effect that resembles a genie being sucked into a bottle.

The genie-in-a-bottle visual effect that occurs when you minimize a window is pretty amazing. After a while, you may get tired of it and wish the window would just minimize more quickly. Beginning with Mac OS X 10.1, you can choose the Scale Effect. It's simpler than the Genie Effect — the window gradually gets smaller as it minimizes — and it is a bit faster. You can set the visual effect by Control-clicking the separator line in the Dock and then choosing from the contextual menu that appears.

Setting Dock preferences

All of the Dock changes that you can make with the Dock's contextual menu and the Dock submenu of the Apple menu can also be made in the Dock pane of System Preferences. Here's the procedure:

1. **Choose Apple⇨Dock⇨Dock Preferences.** The Dock pane of System Preferences appears, as shown in Figure 4-15.

2. **In Dock Preferences, change the settings as desired.** For guidance on specific settings, refer to the previous discussions in this chapter.

3. **Choose System Prefs⇨Quit System Prefs.** The Dock Preferences window goes away, and you are back in the Finder.

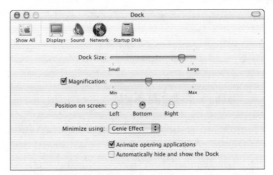

Figure 4-15: Change Dock size, magnification, hiding, position, and visual effect in the Dock pane of System Preferences.

Desktop Keyboard Shortcuts

The Mac OS X Finder provides a number of keyboard shortcuts that aren't listed in any of the menus. The following table lists actions available from the keyboard.

Keystroke	Action
⌘-↑	Move up a level to the folder containing the currently displayed folder
⌘-Option-↑	Move up a level and close the current window
⌘-↓	Open the selected folder or file
⌘-Option-↓	Open the selected folder or file and close the current window
⌘-Shift-↑	Select the Desktop
Tab	Select the next icon alphabetically
Shift-Tab	Select the previous icon alphabetically
↓	Select the icon beneath the currently selected icon
↑	Select the icon above the currently selected icon
→	Select the icon to the right of the currently selected icon
←	Select the icon to the left of the currently selected icon
⌘-Tab	Cycle through the active applications
⌘-Shift-Tab	Cycle through the active applications in the reverse order
any character	Select the first icon whose name starts with that character or the first icon alphabetically after that character if no icon's name starts with the typed character

Working with Files and Folders

There is more to do with the Finder other than fiddling with the way you view the content of folders and disks. Here are some of the things you do with the Finder:

✦ Rename files and folders.

✦ Create new folders for organizing your files.

✦ Move files into different folders.

✦ Make copies of files and folders.

✦ Delete files and folders that you don't want.

Renaming items

Clicking a file or a folder highlights the item's icon and its name but does not select the name for editing. This behavior protects your files and folders from being accidentally renamed by your cat walking across your keyboard (which has actually happened). Before you can edit a file or folder name, you must select the name for editing. Then you can replace, delete, or insert text in the name. While editing a name, you can also use the Undo, Cut, Copy, and Paste commands in the Edit menu, which we discuss later in this chapter.

Mac OS X permits file and folder names to be 255 characters in length, as opposed to the 31-character limit on names in Mac OS 9 and earlier. However, Mac OS X imposes the 31-character limit for files and folders that are located on a disk that has the Mac OS Standard format (also known as HFS). The higher limit applies to disks that use the Mac OS Extended format (also known as HFS Plus) or the UFS format (Unix File System). Your Mac OS X startup disk uses Mac OS Extended or UFS, and the disk that has Mac OS 9 installed for the Classic environment uses Mac OS Extended. You can learn the format of a disk by using the Finder's Info window, which is covered at the end of this chapter.

Note Be aware that names longer than 31 characters are not fully visible if you restart in Mac OS 9, nor are they recognized by Classic applications. In either case, a long file name is displayed as a 31-character name by truncating the long name and adding a serial number to the end. Therefore, if you're going to use a file in a Classic application or after restarting with Mac OS 9, you should probably keep the file's name to 31 characters or less.

Selecting a name for editing

To rename a folder, file, or other item, you must explicitly select its name. Use either of these methods:

✦ In an icon view or a column view, select the icon that you want to rename (for example, by clicking the icon), wait briefly, and then click the name to select it.

✦ In a list view, click the name that you want to change, wait briefly, and the name is selected automatically.

An icon whose name is selected for editing has a distinctive look: The icon is highlighted as usual, and the name has a box around it. The box does not appear unless the name is selected for editing. Figure 4-16 shows an icon with its name selected and another icon with its name not selected.

Figure 4-16: A boxed icon name is ready for editing (left), but a highlighted icon isn't (right).

Note   Some item names cannot be selected for editing. You can't rename such an item because it is locked or you don't have Write privileges for the item. You may be able to unlock the item, but you probably can't give yourself Write privileges. We discuss locking, unlocking, and privileges in detail later in this chapter.

Changing all or part of an item name

Right after you select an item name, the whole name is selected. With the whole name selected, you can replace it completely by typing a new name. If you just want to change part of the name, you can select that part and replace or delete it. You can also select an insertion point and type additional text. Figure 4-17 shows one icon name entirely selected, another name partially selected, and an insertion point in a third name.

Figure 4-17: Select all of an icon name (left), part of an icon name (middle), or an insertion point (right).

To replace or delete part of an item name, do the following:

1. **Select the name for editing.** Use any of the methods just described.

2. **Position the pointer where you want to begin selecting in the name.** When the pointer is over the selected text, it should be shaped like the letter I.

3. **Hold down the mouse button and drag the pointer to select part of the name.** As you drag, Mac OS X highlights the text you are selecting.

   To select one word, you can double-click the word instead of dragging across it.

4. **Release the mouse button to stop selecting.**

5. **Type a replacement for the selected part of the name or press Delete to remove the selected text.**

6. **Press Return to end your editing.** Alternatively, you can click outside the name that you're editing.

To insert text in an item name, follow these steps:

1. **Select the name for editing.** Use any of the methods just described.

2. **Position the pointer where you want to make an insertion.** When the pointer is over the selected text, it should be shaped like the letter I.

3. **Click to place an insertion point.** A thin flashing line marks the position of the insertion point.

4. **Type your insertion.**

5. **Press Return to end your editing.** Alternatively, you can click outside the name that you're editing.

When selecting part of an icon name or an insertion point in the name, be sure to wait until the selection box appears around the name. The Finder may think that you're double-clicking an icon and open it if you click the name and then immediately click, double-click, or drag in the name to select part of it. (Opening icons is discussed in greater depth in Chapter 5.)

> **Note** Icon names can't include colons because the Mac OS uses colons internally to specify the path through your folder structure to a file. A pathname consists of a disk name, a succession of folder names, and a filename, with a colon after each name except the last name. For example, the pathname `Mac OS HD:Applications:Chess` specifies the location of the Chess application on a startup disk named Mac OS HD. Putting a colon in a filename would interfere with the scheme for specifying paths, so the Finder won't let you do it.

Using Cut, Copy, and Paste commands

While editing a name, you can use the Cut, Copy, and Paste commands in the Edit menu. To copy all or part of an icon name, select the part that you want to copy and choose Copy from the Edit menu. The Copy command places the selected text on the Clipboard, which is an internal holding area. Then you can paste what you copied by selecting all or part of another icon's name and choosing Paste from the Edit menu. At this point you can make changes to the name that you pasted; you must make changes if the icon whose name you're working on is the same as that of another icon in the same folder. Whatever you copied remains on the Clipboard until you use the Copy command or the Cut command. The Cut command works like the Copy command, but Cut also removes the selected text while placing it on the Clipboard.

Selecting Text with the Keyboard

With an icon name selected for editing, you can move the insertion point or change the selection by pressing the arrow keys.

↑	Moves the insertion point to the beginning of the name
↓	Moves the insertion point to the end of the name
→	Moves the insertion point to the right
←	Moves the insertion point to the left
Shift-→	Selects more (or less) of the name to the right
Shift-←	Selects more (or less) of the name to the left

Whether Shift-→ and Shift-← selects more or less depends on the direction that you dragged when you initially selected part of the name.

Using the Undo command

After editing an icon name, you can undo your changes by choosing Undo from the Edit menu. The Undo command usually works while you are editing a name, and it always works after you finish editing a name (by pressing Return).

Creating a new folder

Create a new folder by using the New Folder command in the File menu (⌘-Shift-N). The new folder is created in the active Finder window or on the Desktop if no Finder window is visible. Therefore, to create a folder inside another folder, you must first open the existing folder. If the folder is already open but its window is covered by another window, bring the window you want forward by clicking it. You can also bring the window to the front by choosing it from the Window menu or by choosing the window from the Finder's pop-up Dock menu. (To use this menu, Control-click the Finder icon in the Dock.)

When you create a new folder, the Finder gives it a generic name and selects the name to make renaming easy. To rename the new folder, just type the name you want it to have. Your typing replaces the preselected name.

If you want to create a folder on the Desktop, you don't have to close or minimize all Finder windows. To create a folder on the Desktop, click the startup disk icon (or any other icon on the Desktop) to make the Desktop active. Then choose File⇨New Folder (⌘-Shift-N) to create a new folder.

Tip   A quick way to create a new folder on the Desktop or in a background window is to Control-click the place where you want the new folder and choose New Folder from the contextual menu that pops-up. You can do this one-handed if you have a two-button mouse; just right-click to get the contextual menu.

If you create a folder in the wrong place, don't sweat it. You can move it as described next.

Moving items

To move an item to a different folder on the same disk, drag it to the window or icon of the destination folder. Similarly, you can move an item to the Desktop by dragging it from its current location to any place on the Desktop.

To drag an item, position the pointer over it, press the mouse button, and continue pressing as you move the mouse. The pointer moves across the screen and drags the item with it. Release the mouse button when the item is positioned over the destination folder icon or window. When you position your item over a folder icon, the Finder highlights the destination icon by making it darker. When you drag an item over a Finder window, the Finder highlights the window by drawing a heavy border inside the window frame. The highlight visually confirms your target.

You can drag an item by its icon or its name. In a list view, you can also drag an item by any text on the same line as the item's icon, such as its modification date or kind.

Tip   If you're working in a list view and want to move an item from an enclosed folder to the main level of the window, just drag the item to the column header.

 If a folder or disk is open, you can move it by dragging the small *proxy icon* in the title bar of its window. To drag a proxy icon, you must place the pointer over it and hold down the mouse button for a second before dragging the icon away. Proxy icons are handy when you want to move a folder that's open. Even if you can't see the folder's regular icon, you can move the folder by dragging its proxy icon to another folder's icon, a Finder window, the Desktop, or the Dock. If you change your mind about the drag or realize that you've accidentally selected and dragged the wrong icon, the Mac OS X Finder also lets you undo a move by immediately choosing Edit➪Undo or pressing ⌘-Z.

Undo in the Finder

The Mac OS X Finder lets you undo far more operations than any previous Finder. Not only can you undo renaming a file, you can now undo moving an item (including moving it to the Trash), copying an item, or duplicating an item. You still can't undo emptying the Trash, creating a new folder, or making an alias.

Places You Cannot Create New Folders

You cannot create a new folder inside some folders because you do not have Write privileges for all folders. For example, you cannot create a new folder in the System folder, the Users folder, or another user's home folder. These folders are off limits to protect their contents. We discuss privileges in more detail later in this chapter.

If you do not have Write privileges for the folder that's displayed in the active Finder window, the New Folder command is disabled (dim) in the File menu and is not included at all in the window's contextual menu. The easiest way to keep an eye on your Write privileges is to have the Finder window status bar showing (choose View⇨Show Status Bar). If you see an icon that looks like a pencil with a line through it at the left end of the status bar, you don't have Write privileges for the folder displayed in the window.

Copying items

To copy an item to another folder on the same disk, press Option while you drag the item to the destination folder. The pointer has a little plus sign (+) to remind you that you're making a copy when you Option-drag.

The Finder always copies an item when you drag it to a folder that's on another disk. Again, the Finder displays a little plus sign (+) on the pointer when you position an item over a folder of a different disk. When you drag an item to another folder, the Finder figures out whether the destination folder is on the same disk as the source folder or not. If so, the Finder moves the items you're dragging to the destination folder. If not, the Finder copies the items you're dragging.

When you copy an item to a folder that already contains an item by the same name, an alert asks whether you want to replace the item at the destination. If you copy a group of items and more than one of them has the same name as items at the destination, you are alerted one by one for each of the duplicates. Figure 4-18 shows an example of the alert the Finder displays to verify replacement.

Figure 4-18: The Mac OS X Finder lets you decide whether to replace existing files of the same name.

Note

Being able to decide on a file-by-file basis when there are name conflicts and still continue the copy or move is a big improvement from Mac OS 9. However, one loss of information occurs — unlike the Mac OS 9 Finder, the Mac OS X Finder does not tell you which of the files is newer.

Duplicating an item

You can duplicate an item in the same folder by selecting it and choosing Duplicate from the File menu. If the item is a folder, the duplicate contains duplicates of everything in the original folder. You can also duplicate an item by Option-dragging it to another place in the same window. One more way to duplicate an item: choose Duplicate from the contextual menu that pops up when you Control-click the item.

The Finder constructs the name of a duplicate item by adding the word *copy* to the name. Additional copies of the same item also have a serial number added. If the name doesn't have an extension, the word *copy* and the serial number appear at the end of the name. If the name does have an extension, the word *copy* and the serial number appear before the extension. For example the first duplicate of a folder named Untitled Folder is Untitled Folder copy, but the first duplicate of a file named Readme.txt is Readme copy.txt.

I'm Sorry, I Can't Do That

Mac OS X doesn't permit you to move or copy some items. For example, you can't move or copy your items into another user's home folder. Conversely, you can't move items that belong to other users into any of your folders, although you may be able to copy other users' items into your folders.

The Finder won't let you move an item from its current location unless you have Write privileges for the item. If you try to move an item for which you don't have Write privileges but do have Read privileges, the Finder makes a copy of the item instead. If you don't have Write or Read privileges for an item, the Finder doesn't let you move or copy the item.

Regardless of your Write privileges for an item that you want to move or copy, you must also have Write privileges for the destination folder. If you try to move or copy an item to a folder for which you don't have Write privileges, the Finder displays an alert, saying the destination folder cannot be modified.

We cover privileges at the end of this chapter.

Deleting items

Deleting files and folders is a two-step process. First, you need to move them to the Trash and then you need to empty the Trash. Before emptying the Trash, you can open it and remove items from it.

Moving items to the Trash

Move one or more items to the Trash by using one of the following four ways:

✦ Drag the items to the Trash icon in the Dock.

✦ Select the items and choose Finder⇨Move To Trash.

✦ Select the items and press ⌘-Delete (which is the keyboard shortcut for choosing Finder⇨Move to Trash).

✦ Control-click an item, or select several items and Control-click one of them, and then choose Move To Trash from the contextual menu that appears.

Viewing and removing Trash contents

You can see the contents of the Trash by clicking the Trash icon in the Dock. The Trash contents appear in a Finder window. You can remove items from the Trash by dragging them out of this Finder window and placing them in another folder or on the Desktop. (As you observed in Chapter 3, the items you put on the Mac OS X Desktop are actually located in the Desktop folder of your home folder.)

Note   When you view the Trash contents, you see only items that you have moved to the Trash since you last emptied it. If other people use your computer with different login accounts, you do not see items that they have moved to the Trash. Mac OS X keeps a separate Trash for each user.

Emptying the Trash

Empty the Trash by using one of the following methods:

✦ Choose Finder⇨Empty Trash.

✦ Press ⌘-Shift-Delete.

✦ Control-click the Trash icon (or click it and hold) and when the pop-up Dock menu appears, choose Empty Trash.

In the first two methods, the Finder displays a warning, asking if you really want to permanently delete the items that are in the Trash. If you use the pop-up Dock menu, the Trash is emptied without warning. Figure 4-19 shows the warning.

Tip   If you find the Trash warning annoying, you can eliminate it by changing a setting in Finder Preferences, as described earlier. The warning also does not appear if you press ⌘-Shift-Option-Delete.

Figure 4-19: If you choose File⇨Empty Trash or press ⌘-Shift-Delete, the Finder confirms that you really want to empty the Trash.

Working with Aliases

In some ways, aliases act like the files or folders they represent. In other ways, aliases act like the independent files they actually are. Accordingly, you use many of the same techniques when working with aliases that you do when working with files and folders, although some differences do exist. In this section, we cover the following techniques for working with aliases:

✦ Making aliases

✦ Renaming aliases

✦ Dragging items to aliases of folders

✦ Moving, copying, or deleting an alias

✦ Fixing broken aliases

Making an alias

You can make aliases for files, folders, and disks. You can make more than one alias for the same original item and put each alias in a different location.

Making an alias is a simple procedure. Do one of the following:

✦ **Select an item and then choose File⇨Make Alias or press ⌘-L.** (Mac OS X has a different keyboard shortcut than Mac OS 9 and earlier.)

✦ **Control-click an item to pop up its contextual menu and choose Make Alias from there.**

✦   **Press ⌘-Option while dragging an item to the place where you want an alias of it.** You can start pressing ⌘-Option any time while dragging, but you must hold down the keys while you release the mouse button to make an alias. While you press ⌘-Option, the pointer acquires a small right-pointing arrow in addition to its normal large left-pointing arrow.

An alias has the same icon as the original item, except that the icon has a small curved arrow superimposed to indicate it is an alias. The alias also inherits the name of the original item. If the alias and the original item are in the same folder, the Finder adds the word *alias* to the alias name. The Finder also adds a serial number as needed to prevent a new alias from having the same name as another alias in the same folder. The word *alias* is omitted when you make an alias by ⌘-dragging the original item to another folder. Figure 4-20 illustrates making an alias.

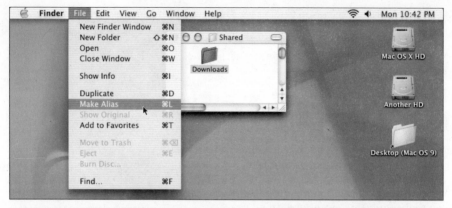

Figure 4-20: The Make Alias command (top) creates an alias that looks a lot like the original item (bottom).

Tip   The proxy icons in Finder window title bars can be very handy for making aliases. Just press ⌘-Option while dragging the proxy icon to make an alias of the original folder or disk that the proxy icon represents.

Renaming an alias

Immediately after you create an alias, its name is selected for editing. You can change the name by typing a replacement or by using the other name-editing techniques described earlier in this chapter. For example, you may want to remove the word *alias* from an alias name so the alias has the same name as its original item.

An alias can have exactly the same name as its original item as long as they are in different folders. If an alias is in the same folder as its original item, move the alias somewhere else before you try to make the alias's name the same as the original item's name. Of course, an alias and its original can be in the same folder if their names are very similar but not identical. For example, the alias name could have an extra blank space at the end of its name.

Removing the Word *alias*

To remove the word *alias* quickly from an alias's name, try this:

1. **Select the name for editing.** (For example, select the alias and then press Return to select its name.)

2. **With the name selected for editing, double-click the word *alias* in the name.** Don't double-click too soon, because the Finder will open the alias's original item, as described in Chapter 5.

3. **Press Delete twice.** The first time deletes the selected word *alias,* and the second time deletes the space before that word.

4. **Press Return to end editing.**

Dragging items to an alias of a folder

If you drag an item to an alias of a folder, Mac OS X resolves the alias and the Finder puts the dragged item into the original folder. In other words, dragging an item to an alias of a folder has the same effect as dragging the item to the original folder. The reverse is not true. When you drag an alias, Mac OS X does not resolve the alias. Dragging an alias to a folder moves just the alias.

Moving, copying, and deleting an alias

After you make an alias, you can manipulate it as you would any other item. You can move it, copy it, and delete it.

✦ If you move an alias to a different folder, its original item is not affected. Only the alias is moved.

✦ If you move an alias to another folder, the alias still knows where to find its original item.

✦ If you make copies of an alias, all the copies of the alias refer to the same original item. Even copies of an alias that you place on another disk will find the original item on the original disk.

✦ If you delete an alias, its original item is not deleted.

Finding an original item

You can find an alias's original item by choosing File⇨Show Original (⌘-R). The Show Original command displays a Finder window that contains the original item, scrolls the original item into view, and selects it.

Fixing broken aliases

If you try to show an alias's original item but the original item has been deleted, the Finder tells you that the original item can't be found. You may get the same result if you try to use a broken alias in some other way, such as trying to open the alias of a folder that has been deleted. Figure 4-21 shows the alert that you see in the Finder if Mac OS X can't resolve an alias.

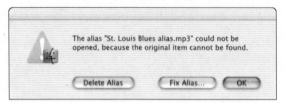

The alias "St. Louis Blues alias.mp3" could not be opened, because the original item cannot be found.

Delete Alias   Fix Alias...   OK

Figure 4-21: The Finder displays an alert when it can't find an alias's original item.

Note   You may not get the alert shown in Figure 4-21 if you try to use a broken alias in an application other than the Finder. In a Classic application, the alert you see when you try to use a broken alias looks different and in some cases does not name the alias or allow you to fix the alias. In a Mac OS X application, the alert you see may simply state the item could not be opened.

The Finder's alert has a Delete Alias button and a Fix Alias button. Clicking Delete Alias moves the alias to the Trash. Clicking Fix Alias displays a Fix Alias dialog in which you can choose a new original for the alias. This dialog is like the column view of a Finder window. In this dialog, select a file or folder to be the new original item and click the Choose button. Figure 4-22 shows the Fix Alias dialog in which you choose a new alias.

```
                        Fix Alias

Choose the item that you want alias "St. Louis Blues alias.mp3" to open.

         From:  Music

  April in Paris.mp3
  St. Louis Blues.mp3


                                          MP3


Go to:

Add to Favorites            Cancel      Choose
```

Figure 4-22: Choose a new original for a broken alias.

Working with Favorites

One way Mac OS X uses aliases is to keep track of folders and files that you designate to be your Favorites. Toward this end, Mac OS X has already created a special Favorites folder in which to keep aliases of your favorite items. Your Favorites folder is located in the Library folder of you home folder.

Nothing prevents you from putting original items in your Favorites folder, but putting aliases there usually works out better. From an organizational standpoint, it makes sense to keep applications in your Applications folder and documents in your Documents folder or some folder inside it. Instead of putting original applications and documents in your Favorites folder, you can put aliases. Actually, you may want to make favorites of the folders in which you keep your documents, rather than making favorites of individual documents. By making favorites of folders that you use frequently, you can more easily get to the folders when you want to save or open documents in them. Mac OS X starts you along this track by putting an alias of your Documents folder into your Favorites folder.

Making Favorites

The Finder provides a couple of methods that streamline making a Favorite of files and folders. You don't have to open your Favorites folder and drag aliases of files and folders into it.

To make Favorites, do any of the following:

✦ **Select one or more files and folders and choose File⇨Add To Favorites (⌘-T).** The Finder immediately makes an alias of every selected item and puts the aliases in your Favorites folder.

✦ 💜 **Press ⌘-Option and drag an item to the Favorites button in a Finder window toolbar.** This action makes an alias of the item you're dragging and puts it in your Favorites folder.

Deleting Favorites

Because Favorites are just aliases, you delete them like any other file.

1. **Open your Favorites folder.** You can do this by clicking the Favorites button in a Finder window toolbar or by choosing View⇨Favorites⇨Go To Favorites.

2. **Move the favorites that you want to delete to the Trash.** Use any of the four methods described earlier in this chapter; for example, drag the favorites to the Trash icon in the Dock.

Deleting an alias doesn't delete the original file or folder. However, if any favorite is not an alias — its icon does not have a small curved arrow in the lower-left corner — you may not want to move it to the Trash. The Favorites folder shouldn't contain any original files or folders unless you put them there. If your Favorites folder does have an original file or folder that you don't want to be a favorite any more, yet you don't want to delete the item, move the item from your Favorites folder to another folder.

Working with Disks and Other Volumes

When you click the Computer button in a Finder window toolbar, you see all the disks and other volumes available on your computer. In Unixspeak, these volumes are called *mount-points,* for historical reasons having to do with mounting large spools of data tape.

Looking at drives, partitions, and volumes

The simplest example of a volume is a disk, such as your internal hard drive, a Zip disk, or a CD-ROM. However, a disk can be *partitioned* so that it contains two or more volumes. A partitioned disk is like a duplex or apartment building; one building holds two or more separate residences, and one disk can have two or more independent volumes. In many of the figures in this book, you see two disk icons on the Desktop. These two icons actually represent two volumes on a Mac's internal hard drive. (One of your authors named the volumes OSX and OS9.1; the other author named the volumes Mac OS X and Another HD.) If you want to partition your hard drive into multiple volumes, you use the Disk Utility application as described in Chapter 22.

Similarly, a mounted disk image is a volume. Apple and many software developers distribute software updates (and sometimes entire software products) in a disk image file. You mount disk image files and make your own disk image files with the Disk Copy application, which is also described in Chapter 22.

File servers and iDisks are also volumes. We explain how to access these volumes in Chapter 10.

Mac OS X represents each type of volume with a distinctive icon. For example, hard drives and partitions have an icon that looks like an internal hard drive. Figure 4-23 shows several different volume icons.

As mentioned earlier in this chapter (in "Setting Finder Preferences"), you decide whether volume icons show on your Desktop or not. The default is to show them on your Desktop.

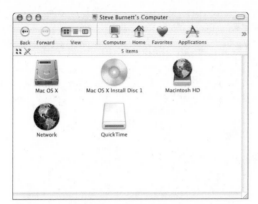

Figure 4-23: Various types of volumes have different icons.

Ejecting removable disks

Remove disk icons by *unmounting* (also known as *ejecting*) the disk. Although ejecting really only applies to removable disks, such as Zip disks or CDs, the same term is used throughout the Mac OS for consistency. Eject a volume by using one of the following methods:

✦ Drag the volume's icon to the Eject button in the Dock. (The Trash icon changes to an Eject icon when you're dragging a volume icon.)

✦ Control-click the volume's icon, either in the Computer window or on the Desktop, and choose Eject from the contextual menu.

✦ Select the volume's icon and choose File⇨Eject (⌘-E).

✦ Select the volume's icon and press the Eject key on your keyboard (if it has one).

If the volume isn't in use (*in use* refers to open files), the Finder removes it from the Desktop and the Computer window. Because the System volume (the one containing Mac OS X) is in use, you cannot ever eject it.

Removable disks, such as Zips and CDs, are remounted by inserting them back in their drives. Disk images are remounted by double-clicking the images and allowing the Disk Copy application to mount them. Hard drives and partitions can be remounted by logging out and logging back in to Mac OS X or by using the Disk Utility application.

Erasing volumes

Sometimes, particularly with removable disks like Zip disks, you need to return a disk to its "as new" condition so that you can reuse it. This process is called *initializing* or *erasing* a disk. You accomplish this with the Disk Utility application. The procedure is described in Chapter 22.

Using the Info Window

Mac OS X keeps a great deal of detailed information about your files, folders, and disks beyond what's available in regular Finder windows. A time may come when you want to see or change some of this information. The Finder enables you to do so in its Info window. You can see the Info window by choosing File⇨Show Info. Figure 4-24 shows some of the information you can see in the Info window.

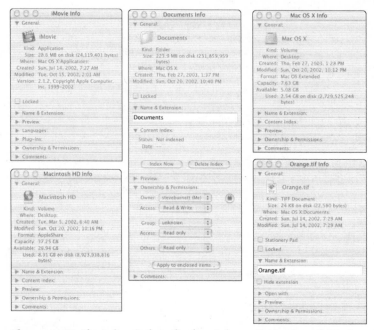

Figure 4-24: The Info window displays information not available in Finder windows.

The Info window displays information about the file, folder, or disk that is currently selected in the Finder. With the Info window displayed, you see information about a different item by selecting the item in a Finder window or on the Desktop. When you select a different item, its information appears in the Info window. If you select several items, the Info window displays a summary of the selection.

For most items, the Info window displays a lot of information, usually too much information to fit in the window at once. Therefore the Info window presents its information in several categories. You choose the category you want to see from a pop-up menu near the top of the Info window.

Some categories are present for all items, but other categories are present only for certain kinds of items. For example, the General, Name & Extension, Preview, Ownership & Permissions, and Comments categories are available for every file, folder, and disk.

In some categories, the details you see also depend on the kind of item that's currently selected in the Finder. For example, the General category includes kind, size, location, creation date, and modification date for all documents, applications, and folders, but only applications have version information. Some information you can change, but some you can only look at.

In this section, we're not going to examine every bit of information that appears in the Info window. (Phew!) We're going to look at how you can use the Info window to make the following changes:

- ✦ Lock a file
- ✦ Change an item's name
- ✦ Hide an item's name extension
- ✦ Attach comments to an item
- ✦ Apply a custom icon to an item
- ✦ Remove an item's custom icon
- ✦ Set the application that opens a document
- ✦ Select a new original item for an alias
- ✦ Set access privileges for an item
- ✦ Select Mac OS X or Classic for an application

Tip Unlike Mac OS 9 and earlier, in which you could see separate Info windows for multiple files simultaneously, Mac OS X shows only one Info window. On the one hand, you can no longer easily compare the information of two files side by side. On the other hand, you can quickly see the information for several items in succession without rummaging through a clutter of Info windows. Here's how: With the Info window showing, use the arrows keys to march through a list view or column view, or click items one after the other in any view.

Locking or unlocking an item

 You can use the Info window to lock files individually so that they can't be changed. After locking a file, you can open the file and copy it, but you can't change its name or its contents. In addition, the Finder does not let you move locked files into the Trash. You can tell a file is locked by the small, lock-shaped badge on its icon. Lock a file by following these steps:

1. **Select the file that you want to lock.** Information for the selected item appears in the Info window.

2. **Select the Locked option in the Info window.** The Locked option appears at the bottom of the Info window. You can't change an item's Locked option if you're not the item's owner.

Renaming an item

The name of the item that's currently selected in the Finder appears at the top of the Info window. (Only the first part of the name appears if it is very long.) However, you can't edit the name at the top of the Info window. You can edit the name in the Info window by following these steps:

1. **Select the item that you want to rename.** Information for the selected item appears in the Info window.

2. **Select the right-pointing triangle to the left of Name and Extension to open the Name & Extension section.** The Name & Extension section will display the name and extension of the item, as shown in Figure 4-25.

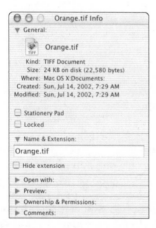

Figure 4-25: Rename an item and hide its extension by choosing Name & Extension from the Info window.

3. **Edit the item name in the text box.** You can edit the name by inserting, replacing, and deleting text in the text box as described earlier for editing an item name in a Finder window. For example, if you select the entire name, you can simply type a replacement for it. You can't change the name if the item is locked or if you don't have Write privileges for the item.

Tip

To select the entire name in the Info window, choose Edit⇨Select All (⌘-A).

When editing a name in the Info window, do not change or delete the extension — the letters preceded by a period at the end of the name. If you remove or change the extension, you may be unable to open the file or it may open with the wrong application. Not all files have an extension, but if a file has an extension leave it alone.

Hiding the name extension

In Mac OS X, some files must have a name extension to identify the type of file. The extension is several letters that follow a period at the end of the name. For example, the three-letter extension txt denotes a file that contains plain text.

The extension can be hidden on a file-by-file basis to make Mac OS X appear more like Mac OS 9 and earlier. Here's the procedure:

1. **Select the file whose name extension you want to hide.** Information for the selected item appears in the Info window.

2. **Select the right-pointing triangle to the left of Name and Extension to open the Name & Extension section.** The Name & Extension section displays the name and extension of the item. Figure 4-25 shows the Hide extension option.

3. **Select the option labeled Hide extension.** This option can't be changed if the item doesn't have an extension that Mac OS X recognizes. You can't change this option if the item is locked or if you don't have Write privileges for the item.

Historically, Mac OS files have not needed name extensions because they have always had internal codes that identified not only the type of file but also the application that created it. Many applications still create files with these internal codes, and for these files a name extension is not required. If a file has the internal codes, the Finder recognizes them and uses them to determine which icon to display for the file, which application should open the file (the creator application), and which other applications can open the file (compatible applications).

Mac OS X changes everything because it does not require applications to have internal codes that identify file type and creator application. Instead, files can now depend entirely on name extensions to identify file type. Relying on name extensions is arguably an inferior method because it makes names more complicated and makes editing names trickier. Moreover, a name extension doesn't identify a creator application, only a file type. Hiding the name extension is a compromise that makes the name simpler and easier to edit.

Attaching comments

You can attach notes or comments to folders and files by using the Info window as follows:

1. **Select the file or folder to which you want to attach comments.** Information for the selected item appears in the Info window.

2. **Select the right-pointing triangle to the left of Comments to open the Comments section.** A text box for comments appears at the bottom of the Info window, as shown in Figure 4-26.

3. **Type anything you want in the text box provided for comments.** Although the window has no scroll bar to see lengthy comments, you can scroll through the comments by pressing the arrow keys or by dragging the pointer past the borders of the entry box. You can't change the comments if the item is locked or you don't have Write privileges for the item.

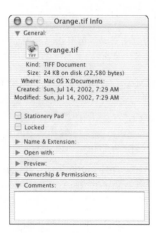

Figure 4-26: Enter comments for a file or folder by opening the Comments section of the Info window.

Applying a custom icon

If you don't want all of your folder icons to look the same, or if you don't like the default icons provided by applications for either the application itself or the documents they create, you can (on a file-by-file basis) attach custom icons of your choosing to those files through the Info window.

To attach a custom icon, follow these steps:

1. **Copy an image that you want to use as an icon.** You can do this by opening an image file and choosing Edit⇨Copy (⌘-C). This command puts a copy of the picture on the Clipboard.

   Mac OS X supports icons up to 128 x 128 pixels in size, a 16-fold increase in area from the 32 x 32 pixels supported in Mac OS 9 and earlier. Therefore, try to copy a square image that is as close as possible to 128 x 128 pixels. If the image is larger, the Finder scales it down.

2. **In the Finder, make sure that the Info window is showing and select the file or folder whose icon you want to replace.** The selected item's icon appears in the General section of the Info window.

3. **In the General section of the Info window, click the icon to select it.** When the icon is selected, a border appears around it. You can't select the icon if the item is locked or you don't have Write privileges for the item.

4. **Choose Edit⇨Paste (⌘-V).** The Finder pastes the image from the Clipboard into the item's icon, as shown in Figure 4-27.

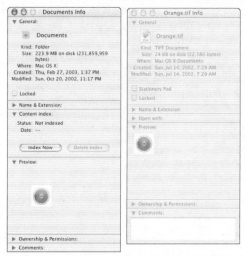

Figure 4-27: After copying an image, you can paste it as a custom icon in the Info window.

Removing a custom icon

You can remove a custom icon as follows:

1. **Select the file or folder whose custom icon you want to remove.** The selected item's icon appears in the corner of the Info window.

2. **In the General section of the Info window, click the icon to select it.** You can't select the icon if the item is locked or you don't have Write privileges for the item.

3. **Press the Delete key.** The custom icon disappears and the standard icon for the selected file or folder returns.

Setting the application to open a document

In the Info window for a document, you can specify which application should open this particular document. In addition, you can specify that the same application be used to open other documents of the same type. Here's the procedure:

1. **Select the document that you want to assign to a different application.** Information for the selected document appears in the Info window.

2. **Select the right-pointing triangle to the left of Open with to open the Open with section.** The application that's currently assigned to open the document is identified in the Info window, as shown in Figure 4-28.

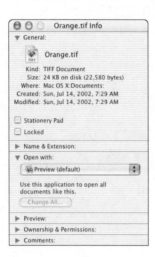

Figure 4-28: The Info window shows which application is assigned to open the selected document.

3. **Click the icon for the currently assigned application, and choose an application from the pop-up menu that appears.** This pop-up menu lists all the applications that claim to open type of file currently selected. The last choice on this menu is Other. Choose Other to specify an application that's not listed but is one you know opens the document in question. You can't change the application if the document is locked or if you don't have Write privileges for the item. Figure 4-29 shows an example of the pop-up menu that lists alternate applications.

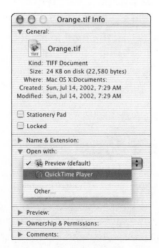

Figure 4-29: Choose an application to open the document that's shown in the Info window.

4. **If you want to use the chosen application to open all documents of the same type as the document shown in the Info window, click the Change All button.** This button is disabled if you did not choose a different application in Step 3.

Selecting a new original for an alias

Instead of throwing away an obsolete or broken alias and making a new one, you can recycle the old alias by assigning it a new original item. Frankly, creating a new alias and discarding an old one is easier than assigning the old one a new original item, and recycling old aliases has no positive environmental impact. Nevertheless, you may have an alias on which you have lavished great attention — fancy custom icon, elaborate comments, clever name — and repurposing such a work of art may be easier than recreating it. Perhaps you have an alias in your Favorites folder that refers to a project folder buried inside your Documents folder, and you want to keep using the same alias when you move on to a new project folder. Whatever your reason for taking advantage of the power that the Info window grants you to redirect an alias, here is the procedure for doing the deed:

1. **Select the alias to which you want to assign a new original item.** A Select New Original button appears in the General section of the Info window. This button is disabled if the alias is locked or you don't have Write privileges for the alias.

2. **Click the Select New Original button.** The Fix Alias dialog box appears. This dialog box is like the column view of a Finder window and is shown previously in Figure 4-15.

3. **In the Fix Alias dialog, select a file or folder to be the new original item and click the Choose button.**

Setting access privileges

The Info window includes several options to provide protection for your files, folders, and volumes.

✦ You can lock them so that they can't be changed, assuming that you have the privileges to do so. We covered locking and unlocking items earlier in this chapter.

✦ You can set access privileges, which control who has access to your items and what level of access they.

✦ You can set an option telling Mac OS X to ignore privilege restrictions on a disk or other volume. To set this option, you must know the name and password of an administrator account.

The option to ignore privileges isn't available for your System volume — the one from which you start up Mac OS X. Security and reliability issues make this a wise limitation. Operating with access privileges ignored amounts to operating as the

System Administrator (root user) and can lead to all kinds of accidental if not malicious trouble, as we explain in Chapters 16 and 26. For example, necessary support files could be accidentally deleted or overwritten, rendering your system unusable.

Understanding access privileges

Some of the files and folders on your computer's hard disk belong to you, and you control whether other people who use your computer with different login accounts can see and change the items that you own. You control access to a file or folder by changing its privilege settings.

You own the following items, and you can change their privilege settings:

 ✦ Your home folder and its initial contents

 ✦ Files and folders that you put in your home folder

 ✦ Files and folders that you put in the Shared folder

 ✦ Files and folders that you put in another user's Public folder.

If you have an administrator account, you own the following additional items, and you can change their privilege settings:

 ✦ Files and folders that you put in the Applications folder

 ✦ Files and folders that you put in the main Library folder

Similarly, some files and folders belong to other users. They change privilege settings to control whether you can see and change the items that belong to them.

Besides the items that belong to you and other users, many files and folders belong to the system. No one who logs in with an ordinary user account or an administrator account can change privileges of items that belong to the system. (If you want to risk damaging your system, you can change privilege settings of system-owned items by logging in as the System Administrator, a technique discussed in Chapter 16.)

Changing access privileges

You change privileges of a folder or file in the Finder's Info window, as shown in Figure 4-30, by following these steps:

 1. **Select the file or folder whose privileges you want to change.** Information for the selected item appears in the Info window.

 2. **In the Info window, select the right-pointing triangle to the left of Ownership & Permissions to open the Ownership & Permissions section.** The privilege settings for the selected item appear in the Info window.

3. **If your account name appears as Owner, you can change the privileges granted to the three user levels.** You must be the owner of an item to change its privileges. Table 4-1 explains the various privileges you can grant for each of the following user levels:

- **Owner.** Specifies what you (the owner) can do with the item.

- **Group.** Specifies what members of the named group can do with the item. The wheel and admin groups include all administrator accounts. The staff group includes all user accounts.

- **Everyone.** Specifies what users who are not members of the named group can do with the item.

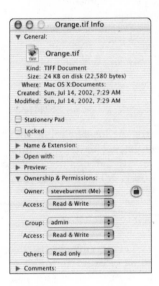

Figure 4-30: Change privilege settings for a folder or file by choosing Privileges from the Info window's pop-up menu.

Note   Owner privileges must be at least as broad as those for Everyone. Group privileges must also be at least as broad as those for Everyone. For example, if Everyone has Read & Write privileges, then all levels must be set to Read & Write. If you run afoul of these rules, Mac OS X automatically increases the privilege settings at higher levels.

Table 4-1
Privilege Settings for Files and Folders

Setting	Privileges Granted for a File	Privileges Granted for a Folder
Read & Write	Open the file. Copy the file. Change, move, and delete the file.	Open the folder. Copy the folder. See enclosed files and folders. Create, change, move, and delete enclosed files and folders.
Read only	Open the file. Copy the file.	Open the folder. Copy the folder. See enclosed files and folders.
Write only	Not applicable.	Drag items into the folder. Save files in the folder.
None	None	None

Note To establish Write-only access to a folder, it must be inside a folder that has Read or Read & Write privileges. For example, your Public folder has Read-only privileges for Everyone. Inside the Read-only Public folder is a folder named Drop Box, which has Write-only privileges for Everyone. Other users couldn't access your Drop Box folder at all if you put it inside a folder with Write-only privileges.

Ignoring privileges

Before you set the option to have Mac OS X ignore all privilege settings on a disk or other volume so that you can move, delete, rename, or add to a folder or file, stop. Ask yourself: Can what you do now harm another user's files or jeopardize the integrity of the system?

If you're absolutely positive that you want to ignore privileges on a volume, select its icon. The option for ignoring privileges appears in the Info window when you choose Privileges from the Info window's pop-up menu. If you select this option, a dialog appears in which you must enter the name and password of an administrator account.

Caution For everyday operations, leave the option to ignore privileges turned off. If you leave this option turned on, you may one day accidentally delete, move, or modify the wrong file or folder.

Selecting Mac OS X or Classic for an application

Some applications can be opened as Mac OS X applications or as Classic applications. This kind of application normally opens as a Mac OS X application, but you can set it to open in the Classic environment. (These applications are all built on the Carbon framework, but not all Carbon applications offer a choice of environment.) To set an application to open as a Classic application, do the following:

1. **Select the application whose environment you want to set.** Information for the selected item appears in the Info window.

2. **Select the option labeled "Open in the Classic environment."** If the application is one that can open as a Mac OS X application or a Classic application, you see an option labeled "Open in the Classic environment." If this option is missing, the application can operate only in one environment (or you haven't yet chosen General Information from the pop-up menu). Figure 4-31 shows the option for setting an application to open in the Classic environment.

   Select the option if you want the application to open as a Classic application, or deselect the option if you want the application to open as a Mac OS X application.

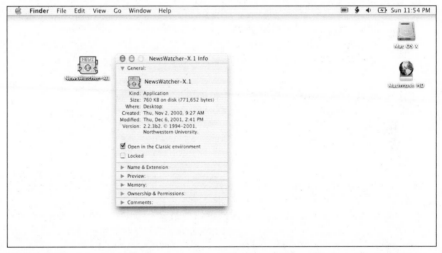

Figure 4-31: Some applications can be set to open in the Classic environment (or not) by choosing General Information from the Info window's pop-up menu.

Summary

In this chapter, you learned how to modify the behavior and appearance of your Finder windows and the Dock. You also saw how to rename, move, copy, and delete items in the Finder as well as work with disks and other volumes. In addition, you learned how to work with aliases and favorites. Finally, you saw how to use the Info window to set access privileges, lock and unlock items,rename a file, hide a name extension, attach comments, apply a custom icon, change the original item of an alias, choose the application that opens a document, and set some applications to open in the Classic environment.

✦   ✦   ✦

Working with Applications and Documents

You found out just how nifty the Finder is in the last two chapters, but you can spend only so much time browsing and organizing files and folders. Pretty soon it's time to get some real work or play done. When that time comes, you need to open some applications and documents. Applications provide the tools to do your work or have your fun. Documents are the result of doing the work or having the fun.

In this chapter we take a quick look at the different types of applications you can use in Mac OS X, and then we explore how you open applications to start using them. We also talk about opening documents with the Finder and with other applications that are open. We discuss how to manage having several applications open at the same time. Then we delve into some basic methods of editing documents — copy-and-paste, drag-and-drop. We cover the ways you can create new documents and save the documents you have created or changed. Finally, we describe how to quit using applications that you're finished with.

This chapter covers general techniques that apply to almost all applications and documents. Other chapters get specific about particular applications that are included with Mac OS X. You can find out where we cover each application by scanning the table of contents or checking the index.

Looking at Mac OS X Applications

With Mac OS X, you use applications built on three different frameworks named Cocoa, Carbon, and Classic. The diversity of these frameworks reflects the parentage of Mac OS X: the traditional Mac OS wedded with NeXT's Unix genealogy. The frameworks exist because each enables an important type of applications to work with Mac OS X.

This state of bliss did not always exist. For many years, Apple wanted to move to a completely new Mac OS like Mac OS X, but couldn't. On the one hand, Apple couldn't orphan the applications upon which Mac users had come to rely. On the other hand, Apple could not get enough application developers to agree to completely rewrite all their software for a new Mac OS that required them to use development tools and programming languages not in common use.

Regardless of the merits of the two programming languages best supported by these new development tools, Objective C and Java, neither is used for such mainstream applications as Microsoft Office, Adobe Photoshop, Macromedia Flash, Internet Explorer, Netscape Communicator/Navigator, and so forth. The developers of these applications were unwilling to invest time, manpower, and money to rewrite these from the ground up for a new Mac OS and then commit to maintaining the new Mac OS version in parallel with a Microsoft Windows version written in a different programming language. Doing this would wipe out a major strength of these applications, namely that each application's Mac OS and Windows versions share a great deal of program code. Typically, only about 20 percent of the application needs to be written specifically for Mac OS or Windows; the rest is shared.

Apple has addressed these concerns in Mac OS X. Developers have a choice. They can update their existing applications to benefit from the new Mac OS X features. They can develop innovative applications by using the new development tools. They can also do nothing, at least for a while, because most existing Mac OS 9 applications still work in Mac OS X just like they do in Mac OS 9.

Some may quibble as to whether there are two, three, four, or even more types of Mac OS X applications. The conservative, literal quibblers say that there are two application types: *Cocoa* and *Carbon*. Most of the rest say that there are three — including *Classic* as the third type. Some split the Cocoa family into Objective C and Java. Finally, some include BSD Unix command-line applications as another variety. In this chapter, we discuss the following types of applications that you can use in Mac OS X:

✦ *Cocoa applications* are programs written from the ground up by using the new development tools provided by Mac OS X; these Cocoa applications require Mac OS X to run. No one really expects to make Windows versions of Cocoa applications.

✦ *Carbon applications* are programs having their genesis in the Mac applications that have been around a while. Carbon applications can run in Mac OS 8.1–9.2.2 (with the addition of the CarbonLib system extension) in addition to Mac OS X.

✦ *Classic applications* are applications originally made for Mac OS 9 or earlier. Classic applications run in the Classic environment of Mac OS X, an emulator of sorts, known also simply as Classic. Most, but not all, Mac OS 9-compatible applications work well in the Classic environment. Those applications that require extensions (not the shared library kind) may be either fully or partially incompatible.

Cocoa and Carbon applications all benefit from the major new features of Mac OS X, including protected memory, preemptive multitasking, multithreading, and built-in multiprocessor support. Classic applications cannot benefit from these Mac OS X features, although the Classic environment (as a Mac OS X application) does. Thus, if something crashes inside the Classic environment and results in the crash of Classic, your other Mac OS X applications continue to run (or, at least, they should).

Classic applications suffer from an additional handicap. After you log in to Mac OS X, you can use Cocoa and Carbon applications right away. Before you can use any Classic applications, you have to wait for the Classic environment to start up. This takes about as long as starting up Mac OS 9. (Classic startup actually looks like Mac OS 9 starting up in a window.) If you have your System Preferences set to start Classic automatically at login (as described in Chapter 15), your login process takes longer to complete. In any event, Mac OS X operation with Classic running is less responsive than otherwise because Classic steals a lot of memory and processor cycles as it runs.

Understanding Packages

Although all Mac OS X applications appear in the Finder as a single icon, many of them actually consist of a collection of folders and files. Examples of such applications are as close as your Applications folder. Almost every application included with Mac OS X in the Applications folder and the Utilities folder is one of these application packages. These compound applications are variously known as *packages, bundles,* or *application wrappers.* The terms are synonymous. Put simply, a package is a structured collection of files and folders that looks to users like a single file.

In Mac OS X, application packages have the name extension `.app`. You don't ordinarily see this name extension because Mac OS X hides it. You can see this extension in the Finder's Info window. (Choose View➪Show Info and then choose Name & Extension from the Info window's pop-up menu.) In Mac OS 9, packages are identified by an internal code that tells the Mac OS 9 Finder to display the package as if it were a single file.

Packages can be stored on volumes that have the UFS format as well as on volumes that have the Mac OS Extended format (also known as HFS Plus). Thus they are considerably more flexible than traditional Mac applications, which aren't packages. An application that isn't a package generally has a two-part file and extensive Finder information, with the part known as the resource fork being equivalent to an application package's Resources folder. The problem with two-fork files with extensive Finder information is that they must be stored on volumes that have the Mac OS Extended format. The traditional two-forked applications can't be stored on volumes that use the UFS format (Unix File System). Because of this, Apple hopes to wean application developers away from the use of resource forks, and packages are the means to do so.

When you double-click an application package, say Preview, it opens and runs; however, Preview is not a single file. You can see what we mean if you Control-click the Preview icon in the Finder and choose Show Package Contents from the contextual menu. Doing this presents a Finder window with a folder icon named Contents. Opening the Contents folder, you see it contains a Resources folder, and opening the Resources folder reveals the various files and folders containing the resources used by Preview, as shown in the following figure.

Continued

Continued

The Mac OS folder of the Contents folder contains the file that actually runs when you double-click the application icon in the Finder. The PkgInfo file contains the Type and Creator information so familiar to experienced Mac users. The really interesting file is the one named Info.plist in the Contents folder — it is an *XML* (eXtensible Markup Language) property list, hence, the extension `.plist`. This property list includes much of the information traditionally found in Macintosh application resource forks, such as type, creator, version string, short version string, and language.

For Cocoa applications, the resource folder contains a number of files ending in `.nib` — these are NeXT Interface Builder files. NIB files contain the interface description information (such as window dimensions, buttons, and the like) in a classes `.nib` file and the actual binary data in an objects `.nib` file.

You also see a file called COPYING — that's just a license file from an organization named *GNU* (Gnu's Not Unix), which is required to be included with any code distributed based upon their libraries and tools, such as the libraries and Objective C compiler that NeXT brought to the party.

Opening Applications and Documents

You open an application when you want to work with it. This action is also called *launching* an application. You open a document when you want to view or edit its contents. For example, you can open TextEdit when you want to view, edit, or create a text document. (You can also work with text documents by opening a variety of other applications.) Numerous ways to open applications, documents, and other types of files and folders are available. This section discusses a variety of ways to open applications and documents.

Opening items with the Finder

The methods presented in Chapter 3 for opening folders in the Finder can also be used for opening an application or document with the Finder:

✦ Double-click the program or document icon that you want to open.

✦ Select the application or document that you want to open and then choose File⇨Open (⌘-O).

✦ Control-click the item that you want to open and choose Open from the contextual menu that appears.

Opening a document by using any of these methods automatically opens an application to handle the document. The Finder determines which application handles the document, opens that application, and then tells that application to open the document. As you can see, double-clicking a document starts quite a chain of events.

Suppose that you want to open multiple documents. No problem! Just select them all and then double-click one of them or use the Open command. If the documents are handled by different applications, the Finder opens each application and tells it which documents to open.

One noticeable difference exists between opening multiple Mac OS X applications and opening multiple Classic applications. When you open several Classic documents and applications, the Finder tells the Classic environment to open them, and Classic opens each application in turn — when the first Classic application has opened, the next one opens, and so forth. In contrast, Mac OS X applications open concurrently — each Mac OS X application starts opening before the previous Mac OS X applications have completed opening.

Opening a document with another compatible application

Instead of opening an application with the application that usually handles it, you can open it with any compatible application. For example, the Preview application can open documents that are usually handled by Adobe Acrobat.

To open a document with any compatible application, drag the document icon onto the icon of the application that you want to use. For example, if you have a Web page you saved from Internet Explorer that you want to edit in TextEdit, drag the document icon onto the TextEdit icon (or onto an alias to TextEdit).

In most cases, if the application is compatible with the document, the application's icon becomes highlighted. Release the mouse button while the application icon is highlighted, and the application opens the document. If the application is not already open, the Finder opens it automatically. If an application can't open a document you drag to it, nothing happens — no highlighting, no opening. Figure 5-1 shows how an application icon looks if it can open a document that you drag to it.

 Note   Some applications can't really open certain documents with which they appear to be compatible. For example, TextEdit tries to open a picture or movie file that you drag to the TextEdit icon, but displays a window full of gibberish instead of a picture or a movie. This happens because TextEdit interprets the picture or movie data as if it were text characters, and displays this "text." Ironically, TextEdit can display pictures and movies that are included in document files that are saved by TextEdit.

Figure 5-1: When you drag a document to a compatible application, the application's icon becomes highlighted.

Opening items in the Dock

As discussed in Chapter 4, you can place icons of frequently used documents in the Dock and click the icon in the Dock to open the document. You can also place your Favorites or Documents folder in the Dock; then click and hold on the icon in the Dock to produce a menu of files and folders you can traverse to find the item you want to open, as shown in Figure 5-2.

Figure 5-2: Open items with icons in the Dock and items listed in the pop-up menu of folders in the Dock.

You can also open a document by dragging its icon to a compatible application that is in the Dock. The application's Dock icon becomes highlighted, and you can let go. If the application is running, it opens the document. If the application is not open, the application opens and then opens the document.

Opening documents within an application

You can also open documents from within an application by choosing Open from that application's File menu. Choosing File⇨Open displays an Open dialog. This dialog enables you to go through your folders and select a file that you want to open. Three different versions of the Open dialog exist:

✦ Mac OS X applications all use one version of the Open dialog.

✦ Some Classic applications use an Open dialog that's been around since System 7. (It's pretty similar to the original Open dialog used in the very first Mac OS.)

✦ Newer Classic applications use an Open dialog known as Navigation Services.

Mac OS X Open dialog

When you choose File⇨Open in a Mac OS X application, you see an Open dialog reminiscent of the Finder's column view, as shown in Figure 5-3.

You can use the file browser to navigate through your folders to find the item you want to open, just as you do in the Finder's column view. Each column shows the contents of a folder, and clicking a folder causes its contents to appear in the next column to the right. You can scroll left to see folders closer to the Computer level or scroll right to see the currently selected folder.

You can quickly go to a file or a folder in an Open dialog's file browser if you can see the file or folder outside the dialog on the Desktop or in a Finder window. All you do is drag the file or folder to the dialog.

Initially the Open dialog shows two columns, but you can widen the dialog to see more columns. Drag the resize control at the lower-right corner to make the dialog larger or smaller.

You can move the Open dialog to see items under it. Move the dialog by dragging its title bar.

Figure 5-3: In Mac OS X applications, the Open dialog is like a column view in the Finder.

If you like to type and you can remember the full path to the file you seek, you can type the path in the Go to text box and click Open (or press Return) to open the file. Similarly, if you don't recall the file's exact name but do recall the full path to the file's folder, you can type the path in the Go to text box and press Return to have the Open dialog position there.

The Open dialog has three buttons at the bottom of the dialog:

✦ **Add to Favorites button.** Creates a new shortcut in your Favorites list for the selected folder or file.

✦ **Cancel button.** Dismisses the dialog without opening anything.

✦ **Open button.** Tells the application to open the selected file. This is the default button, so pressing Return is the equivalent of clicking Open.

Unfortunately, the name of the folder shortcut created in the Favorites list is the name of the folder, so you can't create Favorites in this way for two folders (in different locations) that have the same name; if you try to do this, Mac OS X asks whether you want the new Favorite to replace the old one.

Tip If you want to keep the old Favorite and add this new Favorite that has the same name, switch to the Finder, click Favorites in your Finder window toolbar, and rename the existing shortcut — it's just an alias.

Applications may customize the Open dialog by placing their own controls near the bottom of the dialog. As the example shown in Figure 5-3 shows, TextEdit adds a pop-up menu for choosing a text encoding method and a checkbox for ignoring rich text formatting when it opens the document you select.

To open a document, you select it in the list and click the Open button. Alternatively, you can double-click the document in the list or click it and press Return or Enter.

Classic Open dialog

If you choose File➪Open in a Classic application, you are presented with one of two dialogs — either the "old" Open dialog or the Navigation Services Open dialog, which made its debut with Mac OS 8.5. These dialogs are shown in Figures 5-4 and 5-5.

Figure 5-4: A Classic application may use a standard Open dialog window.

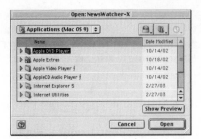

Figure 5-5: A Classic application may use a Navigation Services dialog window.

An Open dialog shows items from the Desktop, from the main level of one disk, or from one folder at a time in a scrolling list. The Open dialog also has buttons and a pop-up menu for opening disks, folders, and, ultimately, the document you want. In some applications, the Open dialog includes a place to display a preview of the document that's currently selected in the dialog. Each application can also add its own unique controls to assist in opening documents. You can't move an Open dialog on the screen, you can't change its size, and you can't switch to another Classic application (as described later in this chapter) while an Open dialog is displayed. (You can switch to another Mac OS X application.)

Classic Navigation Services dialog

Classic's Navigation Services dialog does the same job as the Open dialog but eliminates many of its shortcomings. The scrolling list of files, called the *browser,* looks and operates a lot like the list view of the Finder. You see the icon, name, and modification date of every item in the folder or disk volume named at the top of the list. For each listed item, the modification date automatically reduces from the longest date format (Monday, January 1, 2002) to the shortest format (1/1/02), depending on the space available. You can click the column headings to sort the list by name or date. You can also reverse the sort order by clicking the triangular sort-direction indicator at the right end of the headings (above the scroll bar).

Next to each folder and disk volume icon is a disclosure triangle. Clicking this triangle expands the folder or volume to display the items inside it.

As you can tell from the presence of a title bar, the Navigation Services dialog is movable. You can drag it by its title bar or its frame. In addition, you can switch to another open application (including the Finder) while the Navigation Services dialog is displayed.

Look closely at the bottom-right corner of a Navigation Services dialog. The textured area there is a size box that you can drag to resize the dialog.

You may occasionally encounter a Navigation Services dialog that you can't move or resize. If this happens, the application program you are using is restricting the Navigation Services dialog because the application can't handle the screen updating that would be required if you were to move or resize the dialog.

Opening a document in Classic

You open a document that's listed in a Classic Open or Navigation Services dialog by selecting it (clicking it once) and clicking the Open button. In some cases, especially in Navigation Services dialogs, the Open button may have a different name, such as Choose or Select. You can also double-click a document to open it. Either way, the dialog goes away, and the document appears in a window.

You can select more than one document in a Navigation Services dialog if the application program you're using enables this. To select additional documents, Shift-click them. You can even select multiple items from different folders. To select additional items in another folder, click the folder's disclosure triangle to expand the folder, and then Shift-click the items in it that you want to open.

If you realize while double-clicking an item in a Classic Open or Navigation Services dialog that you are pointing at the wrong item, you can cancel the operation as long as you have not released the mouse button. To cancel, hold down the mouse button on the second click and drag the pointer outside the dialog before releasing the mouse button.

Instead of canceling a double-click in a Classic Open dialog, you can continue pressing the mouse button and drag the pointer to the item that you want to open. When you release the mouse button, the currently selected item opens. This trick does not work in a Navigation Services dialog, which lets you do other things by dragging items (more on this subject shortly).

Opening a folder in Classic

The only way to see documents in a folder that's listed in a Classic Open dialog, and one of the ways to see documents in a Navigation Services dialog, is to open the folder. To open a folder, either select it and click the Open button or double-click it. When you open a folder, its contents take over the scrolling list, and its name appears at the top of the list. The other way to see a folder's contents in a Navigation Services dialog is to click the folder's disclosure triangle so that it points down. This method doesn't make the folder's contents take over the scrolling list or change the name above it.

The pop-up menu above the scrolling list in a Classic Open or Navigation Services dialog identifies the folder whose contents you see in the scrolling list. You can use the pop-up menu to go back through the folder layers toward the Desktop. At the bottom of the pop-up menu is the Desktop, and just above it is the disk that contains the folder that you currently see in the dialog. Choosing an item from the pop-up menu takes you to that item and displays its contents in the dialog. As a shortcut in the Open dialog, you can move back one folder to the folder that contains the currently listed folder by clicking the name of the disk where it is displayed above the Eject button in the dialog. This shortcut is not available in a Navigation Services dialog.

You can quickly show a folder's contents in a Navigation Services dialog if you can see the folder's icon outside the dialog on the Desktop or in a Finder window. All you do is drag the folder icon to the dialog. This shortcut does not work in a Classic Open dialog.

Changing disks in Classic

If you use more than one disk, you may want to see folders and files from a different disk in a Classic Open or Navigation Services dialog. You can do this by showing the Desktop in the dialog and opening the disk there. One way to show the Desktop in the dialog is to choose it from the pop-up menu above the scrolling list in the dialog. You can also show the Desktop in an Open dialog by clicking the Desktop button. A Navigation Services dialog has no Desktop button; instead, you use the Shortcuts button as described next.

You can eject a CD-ROM, DVD-ROM, floppy disk, or other removable disk in an Open or Navigation Services dialog. When you insert a different disk, you see its contents in the Open or Navigation Services dialog. To eject a disk from an Open dialog, click the Eject button. In a Navigation Services dialog, use the Shortcuts menu (described next) to eject a disk. You don't have to go to the Desktop before ejecting a disk in either kind of dialog.

Navigation Services' Shortcuts, Favorites, and Recent menus

At the top of a Navigation Services dialog are three picture buttons that can speed your way through the dialog. Each of these buttons displays a pop-up menu when you click the button. Figure 5-6 shows examples of these menus.

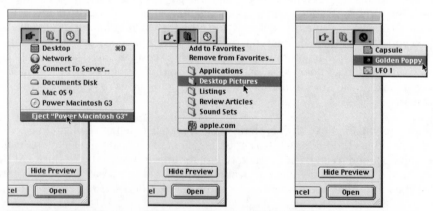

Figure 5-6: The Shortcuts (left), Favorites (middle), and Recent (right) pop-up menus speed your way through a Navigation Services dialog.

The *Shortcuts* button looks like a hard disk icon with a globe behind it and displays a menu that lists every disk volume that has an icon on the Desktop. Choosing a disk from this menu displays the disk's contents in the dialog. The Shortcuts menu gives you easy access to the Desktop, your local drives, your iDisk, your local network, and file servers. In addition, the Shortcuts menu has an Eject command for every removable disk that you're currently using.

The *Favorites* button looks like a folder with a bookmark ribbon on it and displays a menu of your favorite files, folders, and volumes, based on the contents of the Favorites folder in the System Folder used by Classic. (The application you're using can filter out all but the kind of items — file types and folders — you're opening.) Choosing an item from the Favorites menu displays it in the Navigation Services dialog. The Favorites menu also includes commands for adding and removing items on the menu. You can add an item by selecting it in the Navigation Services dialog and choosing Add to Favorites from the Favorites menu. As a shortcut, you can simply drag the item from the scrolling list in the Navigation Services dialog to the Favorites button. You can remove items by choosing Remove From Favorites on the Favorites menu. This action displays a scrolling list of your favorites in a dialog — select one or more on the list (Shift-click or ⌘-click to select multiple items) and click Remove. Your favorite items are also available in the Classic Apple menu.

The *Recent* button looks like a clock face and displays a menu of documents that you recently opened. Choosing an item from this menu displays it in the Navigation Services dialog. In some applications, the Recent menu also lists folders and volumes that you recently opened. Furthermore, the application that you're using can restrict the Recent menu to showing only the kind of item (for example, folders, Word documents, or graphic files) that you're opening. Navigation Services keeps track of recent items by storing aliases of them in a folder inside the Navigation Services folder in the Preferences folder, which is in the Mac OS 9 System Folder used by Classic. (For details on aliases, see Chapters 3 and 4.)

Navigating Classic Open and Navigation Services dialogs by keyboard

You can move through folders and open items by using the keyboard as well as the mouse. In a Classic Open or Navigation Services dialog, typing an item's full name or the first few characters of it selects the item. For example, pressing *M* selects the first item that begins with the letter *M* or *m*. Typing several letters quickly specifies a longer name to be selected, but pausing between keys starts the selection process all over again. The Key Repeat Rate setting in the Keyboard pane of System Preferences (described in Chapter 15) determines how long you must pause to make a fresh start. After you have selected an item in an Open or Navigation Services dialog (by any means), pressing Return or Enter opens the item. These dialogs recognize many other keyboard shortcuts. Table 5-1 has the details.

Table 5-1
**Keyboard Shortcuts for the Classic Open
and Navigation Services Dialogs**

Objective	Keystroke
Select a listed document, folder, or disk	Type the item's full or partial name
Scroll up in the list of items	Up arrow (↑)
Scroll down in the list of items	Down arrow (↓)
Open the selected item	Return, Enter, ⌘-down arrow (↓), or ⌘-O
Open the enclosing folder or disk	⌘-up arrow (↑)
Expand the selected folder	⌘-right arrow (→)*
Collapse the selected folder	⌘-left arrow (←)*
Go to the next disk	⌘-right arrow (→)**
Go to the previous disk	⌘-left arrow (←)**
Go to the Desktop	⌘-Shift-up arrow (↑) or ⌘-D
Eject the current disk	⌘-E**
Eject the floppy disk in drive 1	⌘-Shift-1
Eject the floppy disk in drive 2	⌘-Shift-2
Click the Open button	Return or Enter
Click the Cancel button	Escape or ⌘-period(.)
Show the original of an alias (instead of opening it)	Option-⌘-O*, Option-double-click, or Option-click Open button

*Works in Navigation Services dialog but not in Open dialog.

**Works in Open dialog but not in Navigation Services dialog.

Opening items at login

If you want to have an application, document, or anything else open every time you log in, Mac OS X makes that easy for you. The Login pane of the System Preferences application has a list of items that open automatically right after you log in. To change the list, you must first open the Login pane of System Preferences. You can do this as follows:

1. **Open the System Preferences application.** One way you can do this is by clicking the System Preferences icon in the Dock.

2. **Click the Login Items button in the System Preferences window.** The Login Items window appears. The list of login items appears, initially empty and ready for you to make changes. Figure 5-7 shows a Login Preferences window where Grab starts up automatically but is hidden, and Mail opens automatically and is visible.

You can change the Login Items list as follows:

✦ **To add items:** Follow these steps:

1. **Click the Add button.** An Open dialog appears in which you select one or more items that you want added.

2. **In the Open dialog, select one or more items that you want to add.** Click once to select one item; Shift-click to select adjacent items; and ⌘-click to select nonadjacent items.

3. **Click Open to add the selected item or items to the Login Items list.** If you change your mind, click Cancel to dismiss the dialog without adding any items.

✦ **To remove an item:** Select it in the list and click the Remove button.

✦ **To rearrange the order in which listed items open during login:** Drag items up or down in the list.

✦ **To hide an item automatically when it opens during login:** Click the Hide checkbox next to the application name in the list. A hidden item stays open but doesn't take up any screen space.

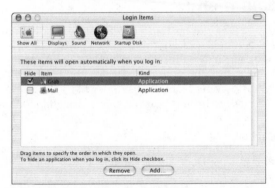

Figure 5-7: Change the list of items opened during login by clicking the Login Items tab in the Login Preferences window.

Note

If you add a Classic application or document to the Login Items list, the Classic environment starts up automatically and then the Classic application or document opens. You can have the Classic environment start automatically when you log in. Set this up in the Classic pane of System Preferences, as described in Chapter 15.

Opening items at logout

Mac OS X provides no explicit mechanism for opening applications or documents on logout. Since, however, Mac OS X is a Unix system underneath its pretty façade, the capability of setting such preferences in your shell's logout script exists; however, that discussion is beyond the scope of this book.

Tip   You can place aliases to Mac OS X applications in your Classic environment's Shutdown Items folder to force them to open when you quit from Classic by logging out.

Opening items at Classic startup or shutdown

You can also make Classic applications or their documents open automatically when Classic starts up or shuts down by placing those items (actually, aliases to the items are a better choice) in the Startup Items and Shutdown Items folders of the Mac OS 9 System Folder used by Classic. Why, you may ask, would I want to open an application or document when I'm shutting down? Consider, as a possibility, running a backup script to copy files that were changed in the last 24 hours from your Documents folder to a Zip disk or just playing a sound that says, "See you next time."

Note   Applications open before documents, which open before aliases. Within those groups, items open in alphabetic order.

Opening with the Apple menu

In Mac OS 9 and earlier (at least, Mac OS from System 7 onward), the Apple menu is a launching pad for applications, documents, or anything else that you can open with the Finder. Any item you choose from the Classic Apple menu opens as if you double-clicked it in the Finder. You can add items to the Classic Apple menu by placing them, or aliases of them, in the Apple Menu Items folder of the System Folder used by Classic. To remove an item from the Apple menu, drag its icon out of the Apple Menu Items folder.

With Mac OS X, the Dock serves this purpose. Drag items you want to have available at a single click into the Dock, and the Dock keeps them available until you drag them out and make them go "poof."

One remnant of the Classic Apple menu functionality remains in Mac OS X — Recent Items — in a slightly improved state. Choosing Apple⇨Recent Items displays a submenu with labeled sections for Applications and Documents. The Recent Items submenu enables you to easily reopen an application or document that you used recently. Suppose, for example, that you recently quit from the Grab application. Rather than opening the Applications folder, then opening the Utilities folder, and finally opening Grab again, you merely choose Apple⇨Recent Items⇨Grab, and the application reopens.

While useful for applications, Apple⇨Recent Items is even more desirable for reopening documents because you are far more likely to have them distributed throughout a hierarchy of folders. Navigating your folder structure to reopen a document that you recently used takes much longer than choosing the document from the Recent Items submenu.

The Recent Items submenu in Mac OS X keeps track of 5 to 50 recent applications and 5 to 50 recent documents. You can change the numbers of items tracked in the General pane of System Preferences, as described in Chapter 15.

In the Mac OS X Apple menu, the Recent Items submenu has an additional and a very handy menu choice: Clear Recent Items. This choice empties out the Recent Items submenu but doesn't affect the actual items that were listed.

Managing Multiple Open Applications

With every version of the Mac OS since System 7 (and even versions of System 6, if you had the MultiFinder option enabled), you can have more than one application open simultaneously, assuming that you have enough memory available. Mac OS X takes that capability to new heights, removing most of the restrictions based on available memory. When an application is open in Mac OS X, the Finder is open in the background, and you can switch to the Finder without quitting the application you were just using.

This ability to have multiple applications open simultaneously is called *multitasking*. In Mac OS 9 and earlier, this multitasking is *cooperative,* meaning that the various open applications have to voluntarily take turns using the computer's processor, memory, and other hardware. Mac OS X has *preemptive* multitasking, which means that Mac OS X parcels out chunks of time to the various open applications.

Multitasking is convenient but can be disorienting. For example, a stray mouse click may make another open program active, bringing its window to the front and covering the windows of the program you were using. If this happens unexpectedly, you may think that the program you're using has crashed when it is actually open and well in the background. You must get used to having multiple layers of open programs like piles of paper on a desk. Fortunately, you can hide application layers on the Mac — unlike layers of paper on your desk — as discussed later in this section.

No matter how many applications you have open, only one has control of the menu bar. The application currently in control is called the *active application*.

Switching programs

When you have more than one application open, you can switch to another application by clicking its icon in the Dock. You can also switch to another application by clicking any of its windows. If you're using a Classic application, you can also switch to another application by choosing it from the Classic Application menu at the right end of the menu bar.

When you switch to another application, its menus take over the menu bar. If it's a Mac OS X application, its name appears as the title of the application menu, which is next to the Apple menu. If a Classic application is active, its icon and possibly its name appear as the title of the Classic Application menu, which is at the right end of the menu bar. All the menus between the Apple menu and the Help menu (if present) belong to the active application.

If you switch applications by clicking an application icon in the Dock, all of the application's windows come forward as a group. (Windows that are minimized in the Dock remain there.) If you're a Mac OS 9 veteran, this layered window behavior is what you expect.

If you switch to a Mac OS X application by clicking one of its windows, only that window comes forward. Other windows belonging to the same application remain where they are. You can bring them all to the front by clicking the application's icon in the Dock or by choosing Window➪Bring All to Front. (Some applications don't have this menu command.) For Mac OS 9 veterans, this window behavior will take some getting used to.

Classic applications follow Mac OS 9 rules. If you switch to a Classic application by clicking one of its windows, all of the Classic application's windows come forward together. Only the windows of the one Classic application come forward. Other open Classic applications stay where they are.

Reducing window clutter

With many applications open, the screen quickly becomes a visual Tower of Babel. You can eliminate the clutter by choosing the Hide Others from the application menu. This command hides the windows of all applications except the currently active one. You can hide the active application's windows and simultaneously switch to the most recently active application by choosing Hide *Application* (where *Application* is the name of the active application) from the application menu. To make the windows of all applications visible, choose Show All from the application menu.

Tip   A quick way to hide all background applications is to ⌘-Option-click the active application's icon in the Dock. If you ⌘-Option-click another application's icon in the Dock, it becomes active and all other applications' windows are hidden. To hide the active application while switching to another application, Option-click the other application's icon in the Dock or option-click a window belonging to the other application.

Attending to background applications

If a Mac OS X application that's open in the background needs your attention, its icon starts jumping completely out of the Dock. The icon jumps far enough that you can see it even if the Dock is hidden. To find out what has made the application so excited, click its icon in the Dock. When the application's windows come forward, look for an alert or a dialog that you need to attend to. Figure 5-8 shows an example of an application jumping for attention.

Figure 5-8: When an application's icon jumps out of the Dock, the application needs your attention.

Moving Document Contents Around

While a document is open, you can generally move its contents to different locations within the same document or other documents. The traditional method to move contents is via the Edit menu's Copy, Cut, and Paste commands. Most programs also let you drag content from one place to another or, by holding down the Option key while dragging, copy the content from one spot to another.

Copy, Cut, and Paste

One of the first things a Mac user learns is to use the Cut, Copy, and Paste commands in an application's Edit menu to transfer data from one place to another within a document or between documents. The first thing you do is select the data you wish to move. Next, you choose Edit⇨Cut (if you wish to move the original data) or Edit⇨Copy (if you wish to move a copy of the data). Either of these actions places the data on the *Clipboard,* a storage area for data being moved. Next, you select the location where you wish the data placed. Finally, you choose Edit⇨Paste to put it there.

Pasting does not remove the data from the Clipboard. The data remains there until you use Cut or Copy again to place new content on the Clipboard or you log out.

You can Cut, Copy, and Paste within a single document, between multiple documents of a single application, or between the documents of different applications. This technique rapidly becomes second nature, especially after you start using the keyboard shortcuts: ⌘-X for Cut, ⌘-C for Copy, and ⌘-V for Paste.

Drag and Drop

The Mac OS provides a more direct way to copy text, graphics, and other material within a document, between documents, and between programs. This capability, called *drag-and-drop editing,* works only with programs that are designed to take advantage of it. Fortunately for you, this includes most Mac OS X applications that open documents.

To move material within a document, open the document and select the text, graphic, or other data you wish to move. Then, position the mouse pointer over the selected material, press the mouse button and drag the selected material to its new location. As you drag, a lightened, ghostlike version of the selected material follows the pointer, and if you're dragging text, an insertion point shows where the material appears after you stop dragging. If you want to copy rather than move the material, press Option before releasing the mouse button. Figure 5-9 shows some text being moved within a TextEdit document.

Figure 5-9: With drag-and-drop editing, you can move data within a document.

Tip   If you have trouble dragging selected material from a window, try holding down the mouse button a moment longer before you start to drag.

To copy material between documents, first open both documents and position them so that you can see the source material and the place where you want to drop a copy of it. Select the text, graphic, or other source material and then drag the selected material to the place in the second document where you want the copy. As you drag, an outline of the selected material follows the mouse pointer. When the pointer enters the destination window, a border appears around the content area of the window; and if you're dragging text, an insertion point shows where the copy appears when you stop dragging. Note that you do not have to press Option to make a copy when dragging between documents. You can use the same method to copy between two documents in the same application or between documents or windows in different applications. The only requirement is that the destination window be capable of handling the type of material you are dragging. Figure 5-10 shows some text being copied from a TextEdit window into a Stickies note.

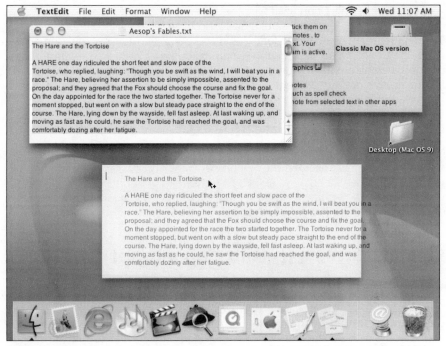

Figure 5-10: With drag-and-drop editing, you can move text, images, and other material between windows.

Some people prefer drag-and-drop to cut-and-paste editing because they find it easier to use. Drag-and-drop editing has one clear advantage: It doesn't wipe out the contents of the Clipboard, so it's a good method to use when the Clipboard contains important material that you're not ready to replace.

Clipping files

You can also drag selected material from a document to the Desktop or to a folder, where the Finder creates a clipping file that contains a copy of the dragged material. You can open a clipping file to see it in the Finder, but you can't select anything in a clipping file. You can copy the contents of a clipping file to a document by dragging the clipping-file icon to the open document's window.

Clipping files can contain text, pictures, QuickTime movies, or sound, but a single clipping file can contain only one type of data.

You can use a clipping file over and over. For example, you can keep clippings that contain your letterhead, the company logo, a list of your e-mail addresses, and any other element that you use frequently.

Creating Documents

You won't always be opening documents that already exist. Sometimes you need to create new ones. Many application programs automatically create a brand-new, untitled document when you double-click the application icon. Most applications let you create a new document any time you want one by choosing File⇨New.

Creating copies of documents

You can also create a document by making a copy of an existing document. This method is especially useful if the existing document contains something you want to include in a new document, such as a letterhead or some boilerplate text. To make a copy of a document, use the Finder's Duplicate command or one of the other methods described in Chapter 4.

Creating documents with stationery pads

Rather than duplicating a document each time you want a copy of it, you can make it a stationery pad. When you open a stationery pad, you get a new document with a preset format and contents. It's like tearing a sheet off an endless pad of preprinted stationery (hence the name). Some stationery pads have a distinctive icon that looks like a stack of documents and indicates which application opens the stationery pad. Other stationery pads have blank document icons or icons indistinguishable from those of standard documents.

Some applications allow you to save an ordinary document as a stationery pad — some call it a template — and we explain how in the next section. Anyway, you can convert any document into a stationery pad in the Finder's Info window, as shown in Figure 5-11, by following these steps:

1. **In the Finder, select the document you want to make into a stationery pad.**

2. **Choose File⇨Get Info (⌘-I).** This command brings up the Info window.

3. **Select the Stationery Pad checkbox.**

Figure 5-11: You can make a stationery pad in the Finder's Info window.

What happens when you open a stationery pad depends on whether the application that opens it knows the difference between stationery pads and regular documents. If the application knows about stationery pads, it always creates a new untitled document with the format and content of the stationery pad. If the application doesn't know about stationery pads, the Finder should create a new document by making a copy from the stationery pad and having the application open the copy.

Saving Documents

After creating a new document or making changes to a document you opened, you need to save the document on disk so that the changes persist. Make sure that the document's window is active (in front of other document windows) and choose File⇨Save or File⇨Save As. For a new document, either of these commands displays a dialog in which you name the document and select the folder where you want it saved. For a previously saved document, the Save command does not bring up a dialog; the application automatically saves the changed document in place of the previously saved document. The Save As command always brings up a dialog so that you can save a copy of a previously saved document.

The Save dialog has a simple form and an expanded form. The expanded form shows a file browser like the one in an Open dialog. You switch between the simple form and the expanded form by clicking the disclosure button, which is next to the pop-up menu labeled Where. The expanded Save dialog has buttons that enable you to create a new folder or place a selected folder in your Favorites list. Figure 5-12 shows an example of a simple Save dialog and an expanded Save dialog.

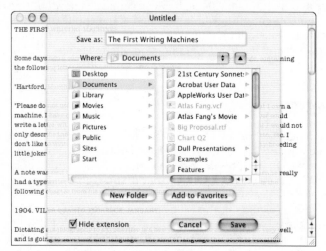

Figure 5-12: Click the disclosure button to switch between the simple Save dialog (first image) and the expanded Save dialog (second image).

A Save dialog has a pop-up menu giving you the choice of the current folder, the Desktop, your home folder, and a hierarchical menu to your iDisk. This pop-up menu also lists folders you have added to your Favorites, and the menu lists recently used folders. In addition, the Save dialog has a text box where you enter the name for the document. The Save dialog may have an option for hiding the name extension, and the dialog may have other controls for setting document format options.

The file browser of the Save dialog works like a column view in the Finder. Each column shows the contents of a folder, and clicking a folder causes its contents to appear in the next column to the right. You can scroll left to see folders closer to the Computer level or scroll right to see the currently selected folder.

You can quickly go to a file or a folder in a Save dialog's file browser if you can see the file or folder outside the dialog on the Desktop or in a Finder window. All you do is drag the file or folder to the dialog.

The Save dialog is also resizable. Drag the resize control at the lower-right corner to make the dialog larger or smaller.

In some applications, the Save dialog is a sheet that's attached to the window of the document being saved. In other applications the Save dialog is independent, and you can move it by dragging its title bar.

Tip Some Mac OS X applications indicate that a document has unsaved changes by displaying a small dot at the center of the document window's Close button. (Applications built on the Cocoa framework do this.)

Specifying a name and location

The first time you save a document, and every time you use the Save As command, you need to type a name for the document in the space provided in the dialog. You also need to specify where you want the document saved. To do that, select a folder or the Desktop in the pop-up menu; or you can use the file browser to navigate to the desired location.

Tip While you are entering a name for the document to save in a Save dialog, the Cut, Copy, and Paste commands are available from the Edit menu. This means that you can copy a name for a document from within the document before choosing the Save command, and then you can paste the copied name into the dialog. When pasting a document name, only the first 31 characters are used for applications which have not been updated for long file name support, and up to 255 characters are used for those which have been updated; the rest are omitted. You can also use the keyboard equivalents: ⌘-X for Cut, ⌘-C for Copy, and ⌘-V for Paste.

Saving a stationery pad

In many applications, you can designate in the Save dialog whether to save a document as a stationery pad or as a regular document. Some applications offer this choice with two radio buttons; one labeled with a regular document icon, and the other labeled with a stationery pad icon. Other applications offer many document format options, including stationery or template, in a pop-up menu in the dialog. Figure 5-13 shows an AppleWorks Save dialog with Document and Template radio buttons — you click Template if you wish the document saved as a stationery pad.

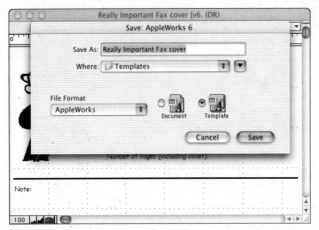

Figure 5-13: Some applications let you save a document as a stationery pad, also called a template.

Quitting Applications

Mac OS X provides a number of ways to quit from a running program. Some are for normal situations; others are for use when a program stops responding.

Using the application's Quit command

Every application menu has a Quit command at the bottom, with a standard keyboard equivalent of ⌘-Q. Using the Quit command is the preferred method for quitting from an application. When you choose this command, the application asks whether to save each unsaved document, as shown in Figure 5-14, before closing that document's window. This is the same dialog that you see if you click the Close button of an unsaved document's window. In this dialog, the Save and Don't Save buttons are self-explanatory. The Cancel button tells the application that you've changed your mind about quitting. If you click Cancel, the application doesn't quit and the document it was asking you about saving remains in the forefront.

Quitting with a pop-up Dock menu

You can also quit an application by Control-clicking (or clicking and holding) its icon in the Dock. When the pop-up Dock menu appears, choose Quit from it. This method is handy for quitting an application that's open in the background, because you can quit the background application without making it active.

If you quit an application in this manner, the application's icon may start jumping out of the Dock. This behavior indicates that the application needs your attention. It probably wants to ask you what to do about documents with unsaved changes.

Figure 5-14: You're asked to save open documents when you quit an application.

Quitting by logging out, shutting down, or restarting

Another way is to quit all open applications is by choosing Apple⇨Log Out (⌘-Shift-Q) or Apple⇨Shut Down or Apple⇨Restart. Choose any of these commands, and you are asked whether you really wish to quit from all open applications. If you answer affirmatively, each application quits in turn, asking what to do about unsaved changes as shown in Figure 5-14. Again, canceling the save in any document's Close dialog cancels the logout, restart, or shutdown.

Forcing an application to quit

Inevitably, occasions arise when an application stops responding to input, preventing you from quitting. Mac OS X gives you a number of ways to force the offending application to quit. Choosing Apple⇨Force Quit or pressing ⌘-Option-Esc presents the window shown in Figure 5-15. Select the unresponsive application in the Force Quit Applications window and click the Force Quit button.

Alternatively, you could launch the Process Viewer utility, which is located in the Utilities folder of the Applications folder (path /Applications/Utilities). Process Viewer presents the Process Listing window shown in Figure 5-16. Select the process you wish to terminate and choose Processes⇨Quit Process (⌘-Shift-Q). Selecting this method bypasses any save dialogs, and unsaved changes are lost.

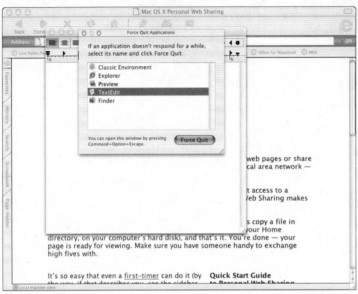

Figure 5-15: Select a runaway application you wish to have quit.

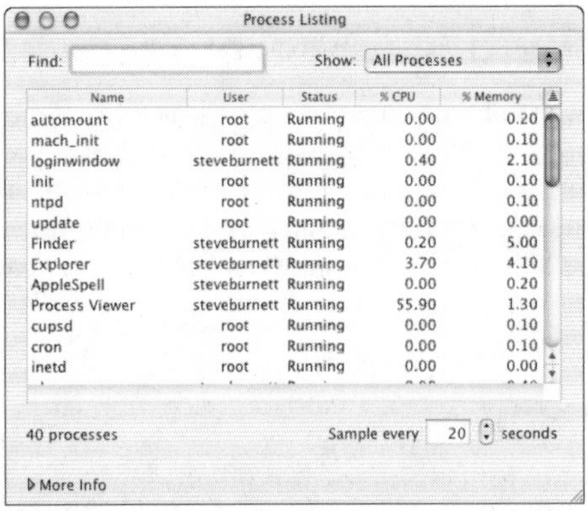

Figure 5-16: The Process Listing window provides the opportunity to view allocation of system resources.

Summary

In this chapter, you learned how to do the following:

✦ Open applications with the Finder, Dock, and Apple menu.

✦ Open documents from the Open dialog in applications.

✦ Open applications and documents at login and when the Classic environment starts.

✦ Manage having several applications open simultaneously.

✦ Edit documents with copy-and-paste and drag-and-drop editing.

✦ Create new documents, copies of documents, and stationery pads.

✦ Save documents with the Save dialog.

✦ Quit applications and force unresponsive applications to quit.

✦　　✦　　✦

Going on the Internet

The Internet is an amazing resource for work, play, education, or hobbies. The Internet gives you access to an incredible variety of information and entertainment resources, from online newspapers and encyclopedias to the latest research data to stage and film reviews, and much more. Electronic mail (e-mail) connects people all around the world, bringing words from far away lands to your screen just seconds after they're sent. Mac OS X makes it easy to get on the Internet; it includes a setup assistant to get you connected easily and many applications that help you surf the Net.

Setting Up an Internet Connection

Before you can tap the wealth of information and services on the Internet, you need to make sure that your computer is set up to make an Internet connection. Therefore, you must have an account with an Internet provider, and your computer must be set up to use this account.

You can obtain an Internet account by signing up with an Internet Service Provider (ISP). As its name suggests, an ISP is a company that provides Internet access. ISPs generally charge a monthly fee for you to access the Internet via modem, ISDN, cable modem, or DSL.

You can sign up for a free trial ISP account during the initial setup of Mac OS X, as described in Appendix A. You can also readily find ISP services advertised in your local newspaper, the Yellow Pages, and on television, or ask your friends and family for recommendations. You can always switch to a different ISP if you find a deal you like better later. However, if you do change ISPs, you may have to change your e-mail address and have to notify all your e-mail correspondents of your new address. If you receive lots of e-mail, you may need to keep your old account open for a while so that you don't miss any e-mail from people who don't send to your new address right away.

Instead of signing up with an ISP, you may be able to get Internet access at home by going through your workplace or school. Check with the network administrator to see if your workplace or school has a modem pool that you can dial into or if they can provide you with an ISDN or DSL connection.

If you're using a computer at work and your computer is connected to a local network, chances are you have Internet access via the local network. In this case your network administrator should be able to help you set up the Internet on your computer.

You can also set up a local network at home or in a small office and use it to share a single ISP account. This approach is especially effective with a cable modem or DSL account, because one of these accounts has enough capacity for several people to send and receive e-mail and browse the Web.

Setting up your computer for the Internet

To help you configure your computer for an Internet connection, Mac OS X includes a Setup Assistant application that leads you through a series of decisions and questions to gather your Internet information. This Setup Assistant runs automatically after installation of Mac OS X. Therefore, your computer is probably already set up for an Internet connection. (You can find full details on installation and initial setup in Appendix A.)

Because the Setup Assistant allows you to skip its Internet setup steps, your computer may not be configured for an Internet connection. If your computer isn't set up for an Internet connection, you need to take care of it now. Unfortunately, you can't use the Setup Assistant because it only works immediately after Mac OS X installation. Instead, you must change settings in the Internet pane of the System Preferences application as described in Chapter 15 and change settings in the Network pane of System Preferences as described in Chapter 18.

Checking your Internet connection

If you're not sure whether your computer is configured for an Internet connection, you can check it fairly easily. If your computer uses a modem, AirPort, or ISDN to connect to the Internet, you can check the connection by using the Internet Connect application. You can also use this same application to check the setup of a DSL or other connection that uses PPPoE. If your computer has a cable modem, DSL (without PPPoE), or local network connection, you can check it by using the Apple-Mac OS X icon in the Dock.

Types of Internet Connections

By using Mac OS X, you can connect to the Internet via regular modem, cable modem, DSL, local network, AirPort, or ISDN. These connections differ in many ways. DSL and cable modem connections are significantly faster than ISDN and regular modem connections. What's more, DSL and cable modem connections give you constant access to the Internet; you can get your e-mail, browse the Web, and use other Internet applications immediately and continually after starting up your computer. Some DSL accounts use a technology called PPPoE (PPP over Ethernet) to require that you begin an Internet session by logging in with a name and password, but Mac OS X can automate a PPPoE login.

Modem and ISDN connections are not intended to provide continuous access to the Internet. You must start an Internet session by having your computer make a new modem or ISDN connection and disconnect to stop the session. Although Mac OS X can automate making a connection, you still have to wait 15 to 30 seconds for a modem connection to take place (2 to 4 seconds for an ISDN connection). The difference between making a modem connection and having a continuous DSL or cable modem connection is like the difference between making a trip to the library for a book and having the book you want already on your desk.

Regular modem and ISDN connections do have a couple of advantages. For one, your computer's security is not at risk from an Internet intrusion while it is disconnected from the Internet. Additionally, a portable computer with a modem can connect to the Internet almost anywhere you find a telephone line. With DSL, cable modem, and ISDN connections you must have a special line and equipment installed. Last but not least, a regular modem account costs less than the others.

Rather than connecting directly to the Internet using one of the means already discussed, your computer may connect by way of a local Ethernet network or an AirPort network. The local network or the AirPort network's base station has its own Internet connection, which may be via cable modem, DSL, regular modem, ISDN, or a more esoteric means. The local Ethernet network or the AirPort network can share its Internet connection with multiple computers on the network.

Checking a connection via regular modem, AirPort, ISDN, or PPPoE

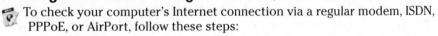 To check your computer's Internet connection via a regular modem, ISDN, PPPoE, or AirPort, follow these steps:

1. **Open the Internet Connect application.** You can open Internet Connect by double-clicking its icon in the Application folder. Internet Connect displays a connection window. This window is shown in Figure 6-1, which appears in the next section.

   If your connection window shows only configuration and status information, click the arrow button next to the Configuration pop-up menu to expand the window.

2. **Set the Configuration pop-up menu for the connection you want to test.** To test a connection via your internal modem, set it to Internal Modem (obviously). For a PPPoE connection, set it to Built-In Ethernet. For a connection via a USB device, set the pop-up menu accordingly. The pop-up menu lists only the connection alternatives that are available on your computer.

If you set the Configuration pop-up menu to Internal Modem, Built-In Ethernet, or an external USB modem, then your computer has been set up for an Internet connection if the name setting is not blank. You can try out the connection as described in the next section.

If the name setting is blank, your computer is not set up for a modem, ISDN, or PPPoE connection. You can find instructions for completing the setup in Chapter 18.

The settings for service provider and alternate number are optional and can be blank. If the telephone number setting or the password setting is blank, you have to fill in the blanks before connecting.

If you set the Configuration pop-up menu to AirPort, check the Base Station ID setting. Unless this setting is Not Available, your computer is ready to access the Internet via AirPort. If this setting is Not Available, then the AirPort base station may be out of range or not configured correctly. AirPort base station configuration is covered in Chapter 18.

Note   If you are connected to the AirPort base station but still cannot reach the Internet, it is possible the base station is on the local network, and the connection from the local network to the Internet is down. Contact the person responsible for the network if this is the case.

If the connection you need is missing — for example, your computer connects via DSL with PPPoE but the pop-up menu does not include an Ethernet choice — then settings in the Network Preferences may be incomplete or incorrect. These settings should have been configured during the initial setup procedure that follows installing Mac OS X. We explain how to configure these settings in Chapter 18.

Checking a connection via cable modem, DSL, or local network

 To check your computer's Internet connection via cable modem, DSL, or a local network, follow these steps:

1. **Click the Apple - Mac OS X icon in the Dock.** This icon looks like an at sign (@) with a spring under it. If someone has removed this icon from the Dock, choose Apple⇨Get Mac OS X Software instead. The Internet Explorer application opens and tries to display a page from the Apple Web site.

2. **Click No if the Internet Explorer displays a message asking if you want to make it your default Web browser.** If the Apple Web page appears, your computer's Internet connection is set up and working.

If the browser displays a message that says the specified server could not be found, your computer is not correctly set up for an Internet connection. You can find instructions for completing the setup in Chapter 18.

Accessing Internet Services

Setting up your computer to connect to the Internet makes it ready to access e-mail, Web pages, and other Internet services. If you have a continuous connection to the Internet, then you can skip the rest of this section and access Internet services at any time by using the applications described in subsequent sections of this chapter. You have a continuous connection to the Internet if you connect via cable modem, DSL without PPPoE, or a local network. An AirPort base station can also provide a continuous connection.

If you don't have a continuous connection, then you must have your computer establish a connection with your Internet provider. You don't have a continuous connection to the Internet if you connect via regular modem, ISDN, or DSL with PPPoE. An AirPort base station can also provide a connection that is not continuous. In any of these cases, you can connect manually by using the Internet Connect application. You can also use menu bar icons to connect manually via regular modem, ISDN, or PPPoE. Instead of connecting manually, you can configure Mac OS X to connect automatically when you use an application that accesses Internet services.

When you finish using Internet services, you can disconnect from your Internet provider. You may want to disconnect if your Internet provider charges for the amount of time you are connected or the phone company charges for the time you use the phone line. You have to disconnect if you need to use the phone line or the modem for something else. You can configure Mac OS X to disconnect automatically after the Internet connection has been idle for a period of time. (You don't need to disconnect if you access Internet services via cable modem, local network, or DSL without PPPoE.)

Connecting manually with Internet Connect

You can connect manually by using the Internet Connect application. You can use this application to dial your ISP via modem or ISDN, establish a PPP connection over Ethernet (PPPoE), or have your AirPort base station establish a connection. For a modem or ISDN connection, Internet Connect makes a telephone call to your Internet provider and provides your account name and password. For a PPPoE connection, Internet Connect doesn't make a phone call, but it must provide your account name and password. For an AirPort connection, the AirPort base station provides the account name and password as needed.

To make an Internet connection manually by using Internet Connect, follow these steps.

1. **Open the Internet Connect application.** You can open Internet Connect by double-clicking its icon in the Application folder. Internet Connect displays a connection window. If your connection window shows only configuration and status information, click the arrow button next to the Configuration pop-up menu to expand the window. Figure 6-1 shows examples of expanded connections windows.

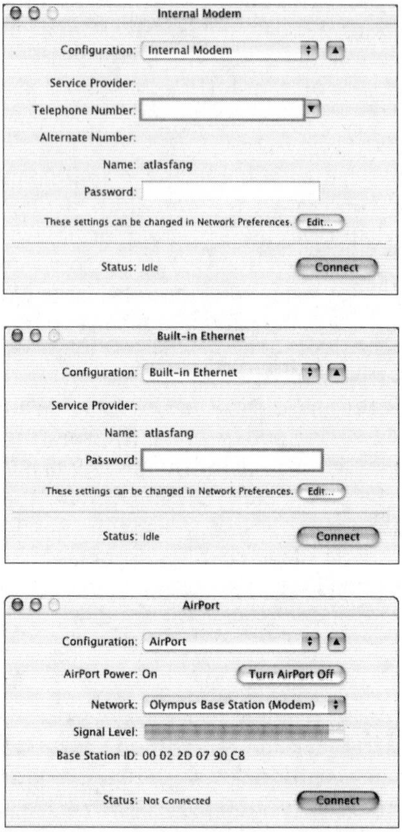

Figure 6-1: A modem or ISDN connection (top) or PPPoE connection (middle) must be configured with at least an account name, and an AirPort connection (bottom) must have a Base Station ID other than Not Available.

2. **Choose the connection you want to make from the Configuration pop-up menu.** To make a connection, select one of the following:

   - Internal modem connection, choose Internal Modem.

   - PPPoE connection, choose Built-In Ethernet (or another Ethernet port, if your computer uses one for its Internet connection).

   - AirPort connection, choose AirPort.

   - USB device connection, choose accordingly.

   The pop-up menu lists only the connection alternatives that are available on your computer. We explain how to configure your computer for various types of Internet connection in Chapter 18.

3. **Do one of the following:**

   - If you're connecting via modem, ISDN, or PPPoE and the Name or Password settings are blank, fill them in. If the Telephone Number setting is blank, enter it. (Telephone Number is not present for a PPPoE configuration.) The Service Provider setting can be blank, as can the Alternate Number (if present).

     If your connection window shows only the Configuration and Status information, you can expand the window to see the other settings by clicking the arrow button next to the Configuration pop-up menu.

   - If you're connecting via AirPort and the Network setting indicates no AirPort network is selected, choose one from the Network pop-up menu. (Be sure to choose a network with an AirPort base station.) If the network you choose requires a password, a dialog appears in which you must enter the password.

     If the AirPort network you want to use is not listed in the Network pop-up menu and you know the network's exact name and password, choose Other from the pop-up menu to display a dialog in which you enter the name and password.

4. **When all settings are complete, click the Connect button.** Watch the Status area at the bottom of the window for messages about the progress of the connection. While the connection is in progress, you can stop it by clicking the Cancel button (which replaces the Connect button). When the connection is made, Internet Connect displays connection information at the bottom of the connection window. The status information may be simply the word Connected, or it may be more elaborate, as shown in Figure 6-2.

   If you are connecting via AirPort and Internet Connect has no Connect button, then your AirPort base station has a continuous connection to the Internet. In this case, you do not need to have the base station make a manual connection.

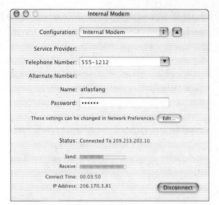

Figure 6-2: Internet Connect displays information about an active modem connection at the bottom of the connection window.

Connecting manually with menu bar icons

You can connect manually by using the Modem icon, AirPort icon, or the PPPoE icon in the menu bar. If the Modem icon, AirPort icon, or PPPoE icon isn't visible in the menu bar, you can make it appear by changing a setting in Internet Connect or the Network pane of System Preferences.

Connecting manually with the Modem icon

If your computer connects to the Internet via regular modem or ISDN and you can see the Modem icon in the menu bar, you can use the icon to make a connection manually. Simply click the Modem icon to display its menu, and choose Connect from this menu. If a dialog appears asking for your password, type the password for your Internet account. This dialog does not appear if your password is saved in the PPP settings of the Network pane of System Preferences, as described in Chapter 18. Figure 6-3 shows the dialog that requests entry of your Internet account password.

Figure 6-3: You may have to enter your Internet account password when connecting manually.

To see messages about the progress of the connection, click the Modem icon and look at the top of the icon's menu. The status message at the top of the menu is not updated.

When you use the Modem icon to connect, Mac OS X gets the necessary connection information from the PPP settings in the Network pane of System Preferences. This information includes the telephone number of your Internet service provider, your Internet account name, and your password for this account. The phone number and account name must be correct—they can't be blank—in Network Preferences for the connection to succeed. The password can be blank in Network Preferences, in which case the dialog shown in Figure 6-3 appears when you connect.

If you cannot connect manually by using the Modem icon, settings in the Network Preferences may be incomplete or incorrect. We explain how to configure these settings in Chapter 18.

Connecting manually with the PPPoE icon

⟨⋯⟩ If your computer connects to the Internet via DSL with PPPoE and you can see the PPPoE icon in the menu bar, you can make a manual connection by using this icon. To do this, click the icon to display its menu, and choose Connect from this menu. If a dialog appears asking for your password, type the password for your Internet account. This dialog does not appear if your password is saved in the PPPoE settings of the Network pane of System Preferences as described in Chapter 18. The dialog that requests your password is shown in Figure 6-3.

To see messages about the progress of the connection, click the PPPoE icon and look at the top of the icon's menu.

When you use the PPPoE icon to connect, Mac OS X gets the necessary connection information from the PPPoE settings in the Network pane of System Preferences. This information includes your Internet account name and password. The account name must be correct—not blank—in Network Preferences for the connection to succeed. The password can be blank in Network Preferences, in which case the dialog shown in Figure 6-3 appears when you connect.

If you cannot connect manually by using the PPPoE icon, settings in the Network Preferences may be incomplete or incorrect. We explain how to configure these settings in Chapter 18.

Showing and hiding the Modem, PPPoE, and AirPort icons

You can show and hide the Modem, PPPoE, and AirPort icons separately in the menu bar. The settings that control the visibility of these icons are in the Internet Connect application and in the Network pane of System Preferences. We explain how to change Network Preferences settings in Chapter 18. To change these settings in Internet Connect, do the following:

1. **Open the Internet Connect application.** You can open Internet Connect by double-clicking its icon in the Application folder. Internet Connect displays a connection window, previously shown in Figure 6-1.

2. **From the Configuration pop-up menu, choose the connection whose icon you want to show or hide.** To show or hide the Modem icon, choose Internal Modem or any other modem connection. To show or hide the PPPoE icon, choose Built-in Ethernet or any other Ethernet connection. (If the pop-up menu does not include any Ethernet connections, Mac OS X is not configured for a PPPoE connection. We explain how to configure a PPPoE connection in Chapter 18.) To show or hide the AirPort icon, choose AirPort.

3. **Select the checkbox to show or hide the menu bar icon.** This checkbox is labeled Show modem status in menu bar, Show PPPoE status in menu bar, or Show AirPort status in menu bar depending on the type of connection. For Modem or PPPoE connections, the checkbox is below the Password setting. For AirPort connections, the checkbox is below the Network pop-up menu.

Connecting automatically

You can have Mac OS X automatically connect via modem, AirPort, ISDN, or PPPoE whenever you open an application that requires an Internet connection. For example, when you open Internet Explorer and it looks for a Web page, Mac OS X will make the connection automatically; then Internet Explorer can go to the Web page.

Note
Sometimes an automatic connection takes a long time to complete. The Web browser or other application that you're using to access the Internet may stop waiting for the connection; it *times out* and displays an alert. In many cases the wording of this alert is vague, technical, or misleading. Dismiss the alert and try again. Your second attempt to access a Web page or otherwise access the Internet via an automatic modem, AirPort, ISDN, or PPPoE connection will usually be successful. If the alert appears again, you need to troubleshoot your Internet connection.

Setting up an automatic Internet connection via AirPort

You can set Mac OS X to connect automatically to the Internet via AirPort by following these steps:

1. **Open the Internet Connect application and choose AirPort from the Configuration pop-up menu.**

2. **If the Network setting indicates no AirPort network is selected, choose one from the Network pop-up menu.** (Be sure to choose a network with an AirPort base station.) If the network you choose requires a password, a dialog appears in which you must enter the password.

   If the AirPort network you want to use is not listed in the Network pop-up menu and you know the network's exact name and password, choose Other from the pop-up menu to display a dialog in which you enter the name and password.

   If the AirPort base station does not connect automatically, you must configure it as described in Chapter 18.

Setting up an automatic Internet connection via modem or ISDN

You can set Mac OS X to connect automatically to the Internet via modem or ISDN by following these steps:

1. **Display the Network pane of the System Preferences application**. You can do this by choosing Apple⇨Location⇨Network Preferences.

2. **Choose Internal Modem or the appropriate external device from the Configure pop-up menu and then click the PPP tab.** Figure 6-4 shows the Internal Modem PPP settings.

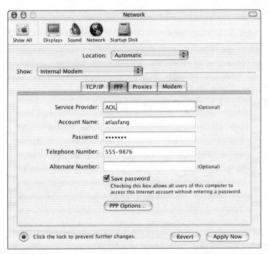

Figure 6-4: Set up an automatic Internet connection via modem or ISDN in the Network pane of System Preferences.

3. **Click the PPP Options button.**

4. **In the dialog that appears, select "Connect automatically when needed."** Figure 6-5 shows this dialog.

Setting up an automatic Internet connection via PPPoE

You can set up Mac OS X to connect automatically to the Internet via DSL with PPPoE by following these steps:

1. **Display the Network pane of the System Preferences application.** You can do this by choosing Apple⇨Location ⇨Network Preferences.

2. **Choose Built-in Ethernet from the Configure pop-up menu and then click the PPPoE tab**. If your computer connects to the Internet via a different Ethernet port, choose it instead. Figure 6-6 shows the Built-In Ethernet PPPoE settings.

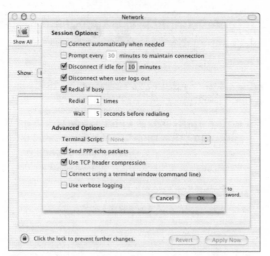

Figure 6-5: The first option in the PPP Options dialog controls automatic Internet connections via modem or ISDN.

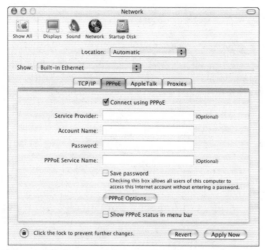

Figure 6-6: Set up an automatic Internet connection via PPPoE in the Network pane of System Preferences.

3. Select "Connect using PPPoE" at the top of the PPPoE panel.

4. Click the PPPoE Options button.

5. In the dialog that appears, select "Connect automatically when needed."
   Figure 6-7 shows this dialog.

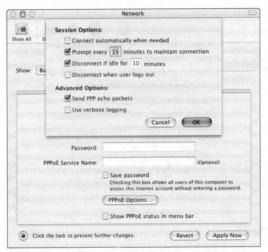

Figure 6-7: The first option in the PPPoE Options dialog controls automatic Internet connections via PPPoE.

Disconnecting

An Internet connection made via modem, AirPort (without a continuous Internet connection), ISDN, or PPPoE can be ended at any time. You can use the Internet Connect application to end any of these types of Internet connection. You can also use the Modem menu bar icon to end a modem or ISDN connection, and you can use the PPPoE menu bar icon to end a PPPoE connection. You can also configure Mac OS X to end a modem, ISDN, or PPPoE connection automatically.

As mentioned earlier, if your computer connects to the Internet connection via cable modem, DSL without PPPoE, AirPort, or local network, you generally don't disconnect your computer from the Internet. You can turn off these connections by changing advanced settings in the Network pane of System preferences. We explain how in Chapter 18.

Disconnecting with Internet Connect

To end a connection with Internet Connect, click the Disconnect button in Internet Connect's connection window, previously shown in Figure 6-1. Your modem or ISDN equipment hangs up. If you connect via AirPort but don't see a Disconnect button in Internet Connect's window, you have a continuous connection. To disconnect this type of AirPort connection, you can turn off the AirPort card as described in Chapter 18.

Disconnecting with the Modem icon

If your computer connects to the Internet via regular modem or ISDN and you can see the Modem icon in the menu bar, you can use the icon to end the current connection. Simply click the Modem icon to display its menu and choose Disconnect from this menu. Your modem or ISDN equipment hangs up.

Disconnecting with the PPPoE icon

If your computer connects to the Internet via DSL with PPPoE and you can see the PPPoE icon in the menu bar, you can end the current connection by using this icon. To do this, click the icon to display its menu and choose Disconnect from this menu.

Disconnecting with the AirPort icon

If your computer connects to the Internet via AirPort and you can see the AirPort icon in the menu bar, you can end the current connection by using this icon. To do this, click the icon to display its menu and choose Disconnect from this menu.

Disconnecting automatically

If your computer connects to the Internet via regular modem, ISDN, or PPPoE, you can configure Mac OS X to end the connection automatically. You can set it to disconnect after a period of specified inactivity. You can have it prompt you periodically with a dialog and disconnect if you fail to respond to the dialog (because you have left your computer and forgotten to disconnect manually). In addition, you can set it to disconnect when you log out of Mac OS X. You set up these options in the Network pane of System Preferences. For a modem or ISDN connection, follow the procedure described earlier for setting up an automatic connection via modem or ISDN, but set the second, third, and fourth options to your liking in the PPP Options dialog, shown previously in Figure 6-5. For a PPPoE connection, follow the procedure described earlier for setting up an automatic connection via PPPoE, but set the second, third, and fourth options to your liking in the PPPoE Options dialog, shown previously in Figure 6-7.

Browsing the World Wide Web

The World Wide Web is the breakthrough technology that shook the Internet to public prominence, so much so that many people think that the Web is the Internet. However, the Web is just one of the many services available over the Internet. It happens to be the most interesting because it lets you easily access text and pictures from places all over the world.

You access the Web with a program called a *Web browser*. One of the most popular Web browsers, Microsoft Internet Explorer, is installed with Mac OS X. Several other browsers also work with Mac OS X, and you can learn more about them and even obtain installation software for them by viewing their Web sites with Internet Explorer. One of the most popular Web browsers of all time, Netscape Navigator, is available alone or as part of Netscape Communicator, which also handles e-mail, from Netscape (www.netscape.com). A Mac OS X browser named Fizzilla, which is based on the same program code as Netscape Communicator 6, is available from the Mozilla Organization (www.mozilla.org/ports/fizzilla/). Another Mac OS X Aqua browser is OmniWeb from the Omni Group (www.omnigroup.com). You can have more than one Web browser application installed on your computer, and you can use them interchangeably.

Understanding Web terminology

To use the Web, it helps to know a bit of its terminology. Web browser programs display information in *Web pages*, which can contain text, pictures, and animation as well as audio and video clips. The machines that store all of this information and that serve it to you on request are called *Web servers*. On a Web page, the underlined text usually indicates one or more *links,* which are also known as hyperlinks. Clicking a link takes you to another Web page. The intriguing thing about a link is that it can take you to a Web page on the same Web server or a page on any other Web server on the planet. So, it's possible to click your way around the world and not even know it!

Using Internet Explorer

You can open Internet Explorer by clicking its icon in the Dock. When Internet Explorer opens, it displays a browser window and goes to a Web page that has been previously designated as the home page. With Mac OS X, the home page is initially set to the Apple Live Home page.

Changing the home page

You can change the home page setting to a different Web page or to no page at all. To do this, follow these steps:

Selecting a Default Web Browser

The first time you open Internet Explorer, it asks if you want to make it your default browser. If you answer yes, then Mac OS X opens Internet Explorer whenever you do something in another application that leads to a Web page. For example, you might click a link in the Sherlock application that leads to a Web page. Sherlock tells your default Web browser to go to the link you clicked.

Internet Explorer wants to be your default Web browser.

Selecting Internet Explorer as your default browser is not a permanent decision. You can make a different application your default Web browser at any time. To change the default browser, follow these steps:

1. **Open the System Preferences application by clicking its icon in the Dock.**

2. **Click the Internet button in the System Preferences window.**

3. **Click the Web tab to display the Web preference settings.**

4. **Choose a Web browser from the Default Web Browser pop-up menu.** If this menu does not include the application you want to make your default browser, choose Select from this menu to display a dialog in which you can select any application on your computer. (Don't bother selecting anything other than a Web browser application.)

Note that changing the default browser isn't 100 percent effective because some applications always send Web page links to Internet Explorer, ignoring the default browser setting in the Internet pane of System Preferences.

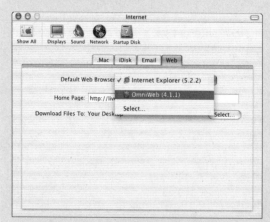

Change the default Web browser in the Internet pane of System Preferences.

1. **In Internet Explorer, choose Preferences from the Explorer menu and then click Browser Display on the left side of the Preferences dialog.**

2. **In the Home Page section on the right side of the dialog, change the Address setting to the address of the page that you want to be the home page, or click Use None for no home page.**

3. **Click OK to make your change effective.** Figure 6-8 shows the Browser Display section of Internet Explorer's Preferences dialog.

Figure 6-8: Change various aspects of browser behavior in the Browser Display section of Internet Explorer's Preferences dialog.

Going beyond the home page

From the home page, you can go to other places on the Web by clicking a link on the page. Underlined text on the page is usually a link. Graphics on the page can also be links. To determine whether something is a link on a Web page, move the mouse over the area; if the pointer turns from an arrow to a pointing hand, it's a link.

Clicking links is a good way to browse the Web, but you should also know how to use the browser's other navigation features, which include toolbar buttons, location or address box, Favorites menu (Bookmarks menu in some browsers), Go menu, and multiple browser windows. Internet Explorer also has Favorites buttons and a tabbed Explorer bar.

Navigating with toolbars

The toolbars at the top of the browser window contain a set of buttons that you can use to navigate the Web. These navigation buttons help you move from one page to the next, move to your home page, or get around the Web page that you're currently viewing. Each browser has several different toolbars. Internet Explorer has a Button bar, Address bar, Favorites bar, Explorer bar, and Status bar. Figure 6-9 shows the initial configuration of toolbars in Internet Explorer 5.1.

Figure 6-9: The standard toolbars in Microsoft Internet Explorer help you get around the Web.

Button bar

The Button bar in Internet Explorer contains an assortment of buttons for navigating the Web and buttons for other tasks such as printing. Here's what the basic navigation buttons do:

✦ **Back.** Takes you to the page you were just viewing. You can keep clicking the Back button to go to previous pages. Doing so is useful when you're browsing and want to get back to a place that you want to read again. In Internet Explorer 5.1, a pop-up menu of recently visited Web pages appears when you click the Back button and hold down the mouse button.

✦ **Forward.** Returns you to a subsequent page after you've used the Back button. If you've clicked the Back button to go back several pages, click and hold the Forward button to see a pop-up menu of recently visited Web pages. Most times, this button is grayed out (which means it's unavailable) because you are at the front of your browsing session.

✦ **Stop.** Tells the browser to stop loading a page and to display as much of the page as it has loaded.

✦ **Refresh.** Tells the browser to get the current Web page from the Internet again and redisplay it. This reloading is useful with pages that have constantly changing content, such as online news.

✦ **Home.** Takes you back to the home page — the page that loads automatically when the browser starts up. (If you changed Internet Explorer's Preferences to specify no home page as described earlier in this chapter, this button is inactive.)

✦ **AutoFill.** Attempts to fill out a form on the current page by using information from Internet Explorer's Preferences settings. To set up this information, choose Explorer⇨Preferences and click AutoFill Profile on the left side of the Preferences dialog.

✦ **Print.** Prints the current Web page on the printer you have selected. Be aware that many Web pages are wider or taller than a sheet of paper, so one Web page may print on several sheets of paper. You may be able to make a Web page fit on one sheet of paper by using the Print Preview command (choose File⇨Print Preview) to change the page orientation or reduction factor.

✦ **Mail.** Opens the default e-mail application (covered later in this chapter). Click and hold the Mail button to pop up a menu of e-mail tasks, such as Read Mail or New Message.

Address bar

Below the navigation buttons is a box labeled Address. You can use it to identify the address, or URL, of the current page and to enter the URL of a page you want to see. To see a page whose address you know, click the old address to select it, type the new address, and press Return or Enter. You can also select all or part of the address and choose Edit⇨Copy to copy it to the Clipboard.

When you type a URL in the address box or location box, you don't have to type in the entire URL of a site you want to visit. For starters, you can omit the `http://` part of the URL because, if the address you type begins with `www`, the browser assumes it and puts it in for you when you press Return. Additionally, as you type a URL, the browser attempts to complete it by using the addresses from recently visited sites or your Favorites list.

Tip You can turn off the automatic completion of URLs by choosing Explorer⇨ Preferences, clicking Browser Display on the left side of the Preferences dialog and clearing the Use Address AutoComplete checkbox. Figure 6-8, shown previously, illustrates this setting.

Understanding URLs

You've probably seen Web addresses in advertisements—they're the ones that look like www.paramount.com. These Web addresses are one example of a type of address called a *URL*, which stands for Uniform Resource Locator. The nice part about URLs is that they can point you directly to any Web page or to any file on an FTP site. In fact, you can find a URL for everything that you can get to on the Internet.

A URL begins with a code that specifies a kind of Internet protocol. (Protocols also exist for local networking protocols, such as afp:// for AppleTalk Filing Protocol.) The remainder of the URL specifies a location in terms of a server or account name, a *domain name* (the name of the organization or company that owns the server), and, in some cases, a file directory. In the http://www.paramount.com example, http:// specifies that the address is for a Web page, www is the name of a computer that serves Web pages, and paramount.com is the domain name.

Favorites bar

The Favorites bar enables you to create one-click shortcuts to your favorite Web sites. The Favorites bar comes configured with a selection of Web sites, and you can modify it. You can add the current Web page to the Favorites toolbar by dragging the @ symbol from the Address bar to the Favorites toolbar. You can also drag a link from the browser window to the Favorites toolbar. To remove a shortcut from the Favorites toolbar, just drag it to the Trash icon in the Dock.

Status bar

The status bar, located at the very bottom of the browser window, shows useful information as you are viewing a Web page. While a page is loading, the status bar displays its size and gauges how long it will take to load. After a page has loaded, the status bar shows the URL of a link if you leave the pointer over it briefly without clicking.

Explorer bar

Internet Explorer displays its tabbed Explorer bar along the left edge of a browser window. The Explorer bar has five labeled tabs and an unlabeled button above the tabs. Click a tab to see what it contains and then click it again to collapse the tab against the left side of the window. Here's what the tabs do:

   ✦ **Favorites tab.** Contains a list of Web pages that you have added to the Favorites menu, as described later in this chapter. Click a listed page to see it.

   ✦ **History tab.** Lists the last 300 addresses that you visited, organized chronologically. Click a link to go to that page again. You can change the number of addresses that are remembered by choosing Explorer⇨Preferences and clicking Advanced on the left side of the Preferences dialog.

✦ **Search tab.** Provides a portal to many kinds of searches, including Web pages, people's addresses, and even dictionaries.

✦ **Scrapbook.** Maintains copies of Web pages you have previously viewed and added to an Internet scrapbook. Click the Add button on this tab to put the page you're currently viewing in the scrapbook for future reference. Click a listed page to see the scrapbook copy.

✦ **Page Holder.** Makes it easier to explore many links from a single page by keeping that page on the page holder tab. Click the Add button on this tab to hold the current page on the tab. Then click a link on the held page to see the linked page in the main part of the browser window.

Tip

If the Explorer bar is expanded, you can resize it. Start by placing the pointer over the gray border that's immediately to the left of the Explorer bar's five tabs. When the pointer shape changes to two small arrows pointing left and right, you can drag right or left to make the Explorer bar wider or narrower.

Customizing toolbars

Toolbar buttons are very useful; however, they take up a fair amount of space. You can make the buttons smaller by eliminating their icons and displaying just their text labels or vice versa. Make this change by choosing Explorer⇨Preferences, clicking Browser Display on the left side of the Preferences dialog and then choosing your preferred settings from the Toolbar Settings pop-up menu on the right side of the dialog. Figure 6-9 illustrates this setting.

Adding and removing buttons

You can also customize which buttons appear on the Button bar by choosing Customize Toolbars... from the View menu. Explorer fills the browser window with buttons that you can drag to the Button bar. You can remove a button from the Button bar by pressing ⌘ while dragging the button to the Trash icon in the Dock.

Hiding and showing toolbars

You can hide any toolbar or show a hidden toolbar by choosing the toolbar from the View menu. To hide all the toolbars at the top of the window, either choose View⇨Collapse Toolbars or click the unlabeled arrow button located immediately above the tabbed Explorer bar. When you hide the toolbars in this manner, small versions of the basic navigation buttons—Back, Forward, Stop, and Refresh—appear in a column at the left edge of the window. To show all the toolbars again, choose View⇨Expand Toolbars or click the unlabeled button again. Figure 6-10 shows a browser window with all toolbars hidden.

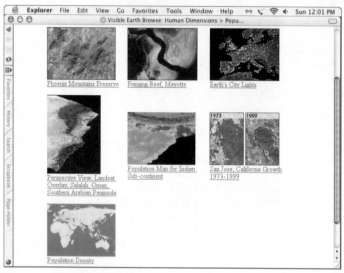

Figure 6-10: Hide all toolbars to significantly increase the space available for viewing a Web page.

Navigating with bookmarks and the Favorites menu

Rather than remembering the URL for a page, you can add a *bookmark* for it to Internet Explorer's Favorites menu. A bookmark keeps track of the URL and the name of a Web page.

Creating a bookmark

To create a bookmark for the current Web page, choose Add Page to Favorites from the Favorites menu. The browser adds the name of the page to the bottom of the menu. You can go back to that Web page later by choosing its name from the Favorites menu.

Organizing the Favorites menu

If your Favorites menu gets messy, you can organize it. Start by clicking the Favorites tab on the Explorer bar to see the contents of the Favorites menu as a list. Then do any of the following:

✦ Rearrange bookmarks, folders, and divider lines by dragging them to other places in the list.

✦ Drag bookmarks into a listed folder to make them appear in the corresponding submenu of the Favorites menu.

✦ Click the disclosure triangle next to a folder in the list to show or hide bookmarks in the folder.

✦ Create a new folder or divider line by clicking the Organize button on the Favorites tab and choosing New Folder or New Divider from the menu that pops up.

✦ Remove a bookmark, folder, or divider by dragging it from the list to the Trash icon in the Dock.

Navigating with the Go menu

The Go menu in Internet Explorer keeps a list of the recently visited pages. To go back to a page, choose it from the Go menu.

Opening multiple browser windows

You can have more than one browser window open at a time. This feature is useful because you may want to read one page while another page loads from the Internet. Browser windows are independent, and you can have as many Web pages open as your computer has the memory to handle. To open another browser window, choose File⇨New Window. Be aware that opening multiple windows increases the memory requirements of the browser and could make it more likely to quit unexpectedly.

You can also open a link in a new window by Control-clicking or clicking and holding a link and then choosing from the contextual menu that pops up. Internet Explorer's Page Holder tab, described earlier, may help you avoid using multiple windows by allowing you to hold onto a page while visiting its links consecutively. However, the Page Holder doesn't work well with some pages that list the results of searching a Web site. In such cases, use the contextual menu to open a new window for a link you want to visit.

Searching the Internet

As mentioned previously, you can search for specific information on the Web by clicking the Search tab in the Internet Explorer's Explorer bar. The Search tab actually acts as an agent for many individual Internet search sites, which are also known as *search engines*. You can directly use any search site by typing its URL in the Web browser's Address bar. Here are the URLs of several popular Web search sites:

✦ Google — www.google.com

✦ Teoma — www.teoma.com

✦ Vivísimo — www.vivisimo.com

✦ WiseNut — www.wisenut.com

✦ Daypop — www.daypop.com

✦ Yahoo!—`www.yahoo.com`

✦ Excite—`www.excite.com`

✦ InfoSeek—`infoseek.go.com`

✦ Lycos—`www.lycos.com`

✦ AltaVista—`www.altavista.com`

✦ Northern Light—`www.northernlight.com`

✦ Ask Jeeves—`www.ask.com`

Each Internet search site has a unique index of the Web, so an identical search at each site produces different results. The most comprehensive search entails using several search sites, which is what the Internet Explorer's Search tab does.

In Mac OS X, you can also conduct a comprehensive search of the Web with Sherlock. Sherlock is discussed in Chapter 7.

How Search Sites Work

The explosion in the number and popularity of Web pages has spawned a corresponding increase in the number of search sites. These sites use different methods for collecting and displaying pages. Sites such as Yahoo! are primarily directories; Yahoo! lists Web sites, organized hierarchically by category, that have been submitted by Web site developers and manually reviewed by Yahoo!'s staff. Other popular search sites, such as Google and AltaVista, use *robots* or *spiders* to automatically crawl through the Web and gather information, which is collected in a database and made available for searching via keywords or phrases. Many robot-driven sites also feature part of their database of Web sites in directory-style lists of links, for those users who prefer browsing rather than searching on keywords. The directory-style sites take advantage of the automated sites' technology as well. As of this writing, if a search turns up nothing in Yahoo!'s categories, Yahoo! automatically forwards the search to Google.

All Web sites need to pay the bills, and search sites are no exception. In addition to the usual banner advertisements, many search sites are becoming *portals*, which provide not only search functionality but links to online shopping, weather, news, and just about any other kind of information they think you might need. The search sites partner with other providers, such as online bookstores, allowing you to continue your search for information or products at that provider's site.

Don't be disappointed if a favorite site of yours doesn't show up in searches. It takes awhile for automated robots to crawl through the billions of pages on the Web, and directory sites make editorial decisions about which sites to include.

Sending and Receiving E-mail

Although not as flashy as the Web, electronic mail is the most popular reason people use the Internet. E-mail lets you communicate with people all over the world. Unlike regular mail, your correspondents can be reading your messages within minutes after you send them, no matter whether the recipients are across the street or halfway around the world.

Using the Mail application

Mac OS X includes an e-mail application simply named Mail, and it has an icon in the Dock for easy one-click access. With Mail you can check mail from multiple Internet e-mail accounts, send and receive messages formatted with styled text and embedded pictures, and set up rules to automatically filter your mail based on content.

Setting up e-mail information and preferences

Before Mail can send and receive e-mail for you, it must know your e-mail address, password, and other information. You may have entered all the necessary information as part of Mac OS X's initial setup procedure (fully described in Appendix A). If not, then the first time you open Mail, it displays a dialog in which you can enter the necessary information. Figure 6-11 shows this dialog.

Figure 6-11: If needed e-mail information is missing, Mail asks you for it.

Selecting an E-Mail Application

Although Mac OS X includes the Mail application, you don't have to use it. You may prefer to stick with another e-mail application that you're already using, or your company may require that you use a particular application. You may be able to use one of the many Mac OS 9 e-mail applications in the Mac OS X Classic environment. These include Eudora Pro 5.0 from Qualcomm (www.eudora.com) and Entourage:Mac from Microsoft (www.microsoft.com/mac). You can upgrade to a Mac OS X e-mail application when Eudora Pro 5.1, Entourage for Mac OS X, and other upgrades become available.

If you don't want to use Mail regularly, you can add another e-mail application's icon to the Dock for easy access. You can also set this application to be the default e-mail application on the Email tab of the Internet pane of System Preferences. The default e-mail application is opened when you click an e-mail link in Sherlock, Internet Explorer, and other applications.

Here's the e-mail information that Mail needs so it can send and receive your e-mail:

✦ **E-mail Address.** The address where people send you e-mail, for example atlasfang@mac.com.

✦ **Incoming Mail Server.** The Internet name for the computer from which Mail receives your e-mail, for example mail.mac.com.

✦ **Mail Server Type.** Is determined by the provider of your e-mail account, as explained in the sidebar "POP versus IMAP E-mail."

✦ **User Account ID.** This item is usually the first part of your e-mail address (the part before the @ symbol).

✦ **Password.** This item is optional here. If you omit the password here, you must enter it every time you open Mail. But you are less likely to forget it if you need to check your mail from another computer and no one else will be able to get your e-mail if you let them use your Mac OS X account.

✦ **Outgoing (SMTP) Mail Server.** The Internet name for the computer to which Mail sends your e-mail, for example smtp.mac.com.

If you don't know the information that Mail needs, check with your Internet service provider or other organization that provides your e-mail service, such as Apple's iTools for a .Mac e-mail account.

After Mail opens, you can specify additional e-mail information and you can set up additional e-mail accounts. You do this by choosing Mail➪Preferences and clicking the Accounts button in the Preferences window. The additional information you can specify includes your full name, which appears in e-mail you send, and an SMTP user ID and password, which your e-mail provider may require to be different from your main user account ID and password.

The Preferences window includes many other settings. For example, you can create a signature to append to messages you send, and define rules that process your incoming mail. You can always return to preference settings to tweak the settings later by choosing Mail⇨Preferences.

Using Mail's viewer window

After your e-mail information is set up, Mail displays a viewer window. It has a tool-bar at the top, a list of messages below them, and a message preview area at the bottom. A panel on the right side of the window lists mailboxes, which contain your messages. Figure 6-12 shows a viewer window and mailbox panel.

To see a list of messages in any mailbox, select the mailbox by clicking its name in the mailbox panel. If you see only the message "No mailbox is selected" in the bottom part of a viewer window, you need to select a mailbox in the mailbox panel. If you don't see an Inbox and other individual mailboxes for an account that's listed in the mailbox panel, you probably need to click the disclosure triangle located to the left of the account name in the panel. Clicking a disclosure triangle in the mailbox panel alternately shows and hides the contents of the account that's adjacent to the triangle.

POP versus IMAP E-Mail

The provider of your e-mail account may let you set it up as a POP account or an IMAP account. With a POP account (Post Office Protocol), you transfer (download) your incoming messages from the POP server on the provider's computer to the Mail application's database on your computer's hard drive. Normally, your messages are deleted from the server after they have been transferred to your computer. You can keep your messages on the server as well as on your computer by changing a preference setting in Mail and some other e-mail client applications. Because the messages are still on the server, you can get them again from another computer (perhaps while traveling). However, you have a limit to the amount of space your messages can occupy on the provider's server. Therefore, make sure that after transferring messages to your computer, Mail periodically deletes the trans-ferred messages from the server.

With an IMAP account (Internet Message Access Protocol), Mail and most other e-mail applications transfer only the header information (such as sender, subject, date, and size) from your incoming messages to your computer. Then you preview the message headers to decide which messages to transfer in full to your computer. Moreover, you can preview the same messages on more than one computer because your incoming messages normally remain on the provider's server until you delete their headers. An IMAP account is very con-venient if you need to check your e-mail while away from your main computer, because you see the same mail wherever you go.

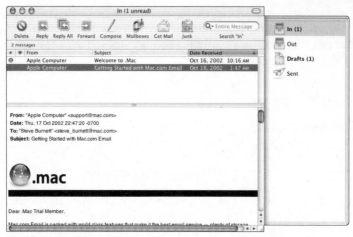

Figure 6-12: See a list of mailboxes, a list of messages in the selected mailbox, and a preview of the selected message in Mail's viewer window.

You can work with the messages listed in a viewer window as follows:

✦ **Preview a listed message.** Click the message in the list.

✦ **Select messages in the list.** Click any information listed for a message. ⌘-click additional messages to select them also, or Shift-click to select a range of messages.

✦ **List only selected messages.** Choose View➪Focus On Selected Messages.

✦ **Search the messages.** Type in the toolbar's Search box and use the adjacent pop-up menu to specify which part of each message to search. If Mail finds messages that meet your search criteria, it lists only those messages.

✦ **Resize the list and preview areas.** Drag the divider bar at the bottom of the list up or down.

✦ **Hide or show the message preview area.** Double-click the divider bar at the bottom of the list.

✦ **Sort the list by a column.** Click a column heading. The heading becomes highlighted to indicate that it is the sort key. Click the highlighted column heading to switch between forward and reverse sort order. Alternatively, you can choose a sort column and direction from the Sort submenu of the View menu.

✦ **Rearrange columns.** Drag a column heading left or right to move the column.

✦ **Resize columns.** Drag a column heading's right borderline left or right to make the column narrower or wider.

✦ **Show or hide columns.** In the View menu, choose the appropriate command to show or hide the Number, Flags, Contents, or Message Sizes columns. The Read Status, From, and Date & Time columns always appear.

✦ **See more or fewer columns at once.** Click the window's Zoom button or resize the window.

Receiving mail

To get your mail, click the Get Mail button at the top of the viewer window (or choose Mailbox⇨Get New Mail). If you want to monitor the progress, choose Window⇨Activity Viewer. You can also have Mail check for new mail automatically by setting how often you want this to happen in the Accounts section of Mail's Preferences dialog.

The number of unread messages appears in parentheses next to the mailbox name in the mailbox panel. Unread messages are marked with a bullet in the list of messages below the buttons in a viewer window. The number of unread messages also appears superimposed on the Mail icon in the Dock.

You can read a message in the preview area at the bottom of a viewer window, but you won't have to scroll as much if you open the message in its own window. To read a message in its own window, double-click it in the list of messages. Figure 6-13 is an example of an e-mail message window.

Figure 6-13: You can read an e-mail message in its own window.

Composing messages

Mail gives you several options for dealing with your e-mail correspondence. You can reply to messages you receive, forward them to other people, or compose new messages.

Replying to messages

To reply to a message you are reading, click the Reply button or the Reply All button at the top of the window. Reply and Reply All both create a new message. Reply addresses the new message only to the sender, and Reply All addresses the new message to the sender and everyone else who received the original message. Instead of clicking these buttons, you can choose equivalent commands from the Message menu.

The new message appears in a separate window. It has the same subject as the original message, except that the reply subject is prefixed with *Re:* The body of the reply includes the text of the original message.

Type your reply message above the original message, and click the Send button (or choose Message⇨Send Message) to send your message flying to its destination. Figure 6-14 shows a reply message in progress.

Figure 6-14: You can reply to a message you have received.

Note   When replying to a message, especially a long one, it's generally considered good *netiquette* (etiquette on the Internet) to trim the text of the original message down to the essentials. You can adjust how the text from the original message appears in the Fonts & Colors section of Mail's Preferences dialog.

Forwarding messages

To forward a message you are reading, click the Forward button at the top of the window (or choose Message➪Forward Message). The original message appears in a new window, with the subject prefixed by *Fwd:* You need to supply the e-mail address of the person to whom you are forwarding the message. You may want to add some introductory text above the forwarded message. Click the Send button (or choose Message➪Send Message) to send the message on its way.

Composing new messages

To compose a new message, click the Compose button at the top of a viewer window or choose File➪New Compose Window. Type each recipient's e-mail address separated by commas on the To line. On the Cc (carbon copy) line, add any additional recipients who should receive a copy of the message (but aren't necessarily expected to reply). Type a subject on the Subject line and type the message in the bottom pane. If you want to get fancy, you can select different text styles, colors, and fonts from the Format menu. When you're done, click Send.

You can add a recipient to a Favorites list for future quick access by clicking the Favorites button and then typing the e-mail address, or you can click the Address button to look up recipients by using the Address Book application.

 Tip Mail remembers the addresses of people to whom you have recently sent e-mail. When you start to type an address on the To line, Mail autocompletes the address for you or provides a drop-down list if more than one address matches what you're typing. If you don't want to use Mail's suggested address, just type over it.

 Note By default, Mail uses Rich Text Format (RTF) to compose messages so that you can send messages with styled text and inset pictures. Not all e-mail programs can read this format, however. To change the format of an individual message, choose Make Plain Text from the Format menu when you are composing the message. If you know most of the people you send e-mail to use e-mail programs that don't support formatted messages, you may want to change your preferred message format to plain text. Choose Mail➪Preferences, click Composing, and choose Plain Text from the Default message format pop-up menu.

Using the Address Book

The Mail application is linked to the Address Book application, which you can use to store frequently used e-mail addresses and related contact information (such as phone numbers and birthdays). You can open the Address Book by choosing Addresses from the Window menu or by clicking the Address button in a message composition window. The Address Book can contain individual contacts, also know as virtual address cards (V-cards), and groups of contacts. Figure 6-15 shows how contacts appear in the main Address Book window.

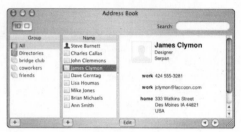

Figure 6-15: Use the Address Book application to store e-mail addresses and other contact information.

Using the main Address Book window

The main Address Book window displays three columns. The first column shows the directories and groups defined in the Address Book. The second column shows the names in the selected group, one name per line. The third column shows the card selected in the second column. You can work with contacts in the Address Book window as follows:

✦ **Select contacts in the list.** Click the name or any other information listed for a contact to select the card. ⌘-click additional contacts to select them also, or Shift-click to select a range of contacts. If you select one contact, its basic information appears in the third column of the Address Book window.

✦ **View the list by group.** Choose a group from the Group column.

✦ **Filter the list.** Type in the Search box. The Address Book looks for the search text in the information listed for each contact and hides all contacts whose listed information doesn't include the search text. In other words, the Address Book lists only address cards that have the search text in at least one column in the list.

✦ **Resize columns.** Drag a column heading's right borderline left or right to make the column narrower or wider.

✦ **Add columns.** In the Available Fields submenu of the View menu, choose any item that doesn't have a check mark to add the corresponding column.

✦ **Remove columns.** In the Available Fields submenu of the View menu, choose any item that has a check mark to remove the corresponding column.

✦ **See more or fewer columns at once.** Click the window's Zoom button or resize the window.

The Address Book's Preferences window shown in Figure 6-16 displays options for display order, sort order, address format, font size, and vCard format. The vCard format is a common standard used in many applications and uses, from mail programs to PDAs such as Palm Pilots and Handspring Visors, and many newer models of cellular phones.

Modifying Toolbars in Mail

Many windows in the Mail application have toolbars, and these toolbars normally have buttons and other items displayed as icons with names. You can hide a toolbar or modify it in other ways by using the toolbar's contextual menu or a toolbar item's contextual menu. (You can display the toolbar's contextual menu by Control-clicking the toolbar, and you can display a toolbar item's contextual menu by Control-clicking the item.) You can modify the toolbars in Mail as follows:

✦ **Hide the toolbar, or show it if it is hidden.** Click the lozenge-shaped toolbar button in the upper-right corner of the window.

✦ **Show items as icons with names, icons only, or names only.** Choose the style you want from the toolbar's contextual menu, or ⌘-click the lozenge-shaped toolbar button one, two, or three times.

✦ **Add items.** Choose Customize Toolbar from the toolbar's contextual menu, or ⌘-Option-click the lozenge-shaped toolbar button. Either action displays a dialog that contains items you can drag into the toolbar.

Continued

Continued

✦ **Remove items.** Choose Remove Item from the button's contextual menu. Alternatively, ⌘-drag an item away from the toolbar to see it vanish in a puff of smoke. If the Customize Toolbar dialog is displayed (as described above for adding buttons), you don't have to press ⌘ to drag an item away from the toolbar.

✦ **Move items.** ⌘-drag an item right or left to a different place on the toolbar. If the Customize Toolbar dialog is displayed (as described above for adding buttons), you don't have to press ⌘ to drag an item to another place on the toolbar.

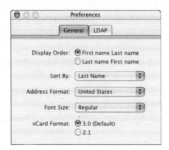

Figure 6-16: Use the Address Book Preferences window to set display formats and options for the address cards.

Creating a new contact

To add a new contact to the Address Book, click the Add New Person (+) button at the bottom of the names column of the Address Book window (or choose File➪New). A window appears in which you can enter the new contact's information. Enter a name, e-mail address, and phone number. If desired, click on the card name in the Names column and drag it to a group in the Groups column to add the card to that group. You can add a picture by dragging a picture file to the square box at the top of the card in the display column. Press the Tab key to move between the fields to enter more information such as postal address and additional phone numbers. You can also rename the label for a field on a card. For example, you might want to label a telephone number as "front desk," or an address as "warehouse" or "beach house." To rename a label, click on the pair of small triangles between the label and the field to display a pop-up menu. Choose Custom . . . from the pop-up menu and a window will appear prompting you to Add a new custom label. Enter the new label and then click OK. When you're done entering information, click Save. Figure 6-17 shows an example of the window for entering a new contact.

Figure 6-17: Enter contact information in a new card in the third column of the Address Book window.

Editing a contact

You can edit an existing contact's information by selecting the card in the Names column, then clicking the Edit button below the display of the card in the third column.

Creating groups

After you add a few contacts to the Address Book, you can create groups to make mailing to several people at once easier. To add a new group, do either of the following:

✦ Choose File⇨New Group.

✦ In the main Address Book window, select some contacts that you want to be in the new group, and then choose File⇨New Group From Selection.

Either of these actions displays a new Group Name in the Group column. The Group Name for the new group is already selected, so you can simply type the name for the new group and then press Return on the keyboard. In this window, type a name and description for the group. You can remove a contact from the group by selecting it in the group window and pressing Delete. You can add contacts to a group by selecting them in the Names column and dragging the selected names to the group. To drag a contact successfully, position the mouse pointer over the contact's icon in the Names list, hold down the mouse button for a couple of seconds, and then drag. As you drag, a small address card icon follows the pointer. Figure 6-18 shows an example of dragging a contact from the Names column to a group.

Figure 6-18: Enter group information in a separate window.

Back in the Mail program, you can send to all of a group's members simply by typing the name of the group on the To line of a message you're composing.

Finding e-mail addresses in LDAP directories

You can also use the Address Book to look on the Internet for a person's e-mail address and phone number. Start by clicking the Directory icon in the Group column of the Address Book window. Any LDAP directories you have entered will show in the Names column, which changed its name to Directories when you selected the Directories icon. Enter the name or other information you have in the Search field in the upper-right corner of the Address Book window to search for that person or company. Figure 6-19 shows the Directories view of the Address Book window.

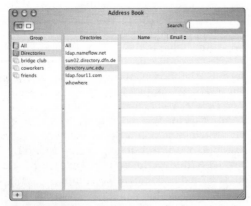

Figure 6-19: Use the Address Book to look up e-mail addresses and phone numbers in LDAP directories.

The Address Book looks up address information on LDAP (Lightweight Directory Access Protocol) servers, which are located on host computers on the Internet, and perhaps on your own organization's local network. You can add and remove LDAP servers in the Address Book Preferences.

If the LDAP search doesn't find many exact matches for the criteria you specify, the results of the search will include close matches.

To add an address from the resulting list to an Address Book, drag the icon from the leftmost column of the LDAP Directory Search window into the list of names in the main Address Book window.

Note   The LDAP directory search feature works in Mac OS X 10.0.4, but does not work in Mac OS X 10.1. The Directory button is present by default in the Address Book toolbar of Mac OS X.10.0, but you must add the Directory button in the Address Book toolbar of Mac OS X 10.1 (as described in the previous sidebar). However, the Directory button is dim in Mac OS X 10.1. An update of Mac OS X 10.1 may restore the LDAP directory search feature.

Sending e-mail attachments

In addition to text messages, you can send files with your e-mail messages. Documents, archives of multiple files (created using DropStuff from Aladdin Systems at www.aladdinsys.com, for instance), and other programs and files can be sent as attachments to an e-mail message by using special protocols. Sending files as attachments can be useful if you'd like to send an AppleWorks document to a friend or colleague, for example, or even if you'd care to send a shareware or freeware application to an e-mail recipient.

Adding an attachment in Mail is simple; just look for the paper clip. With new e-mail (or reply e-mail) open in its window, click the Attach button in the toolbar. In the dialog that appears, select the file you want to attach, and click Open. To attach multiple files, hold down Shift while selecting each one before clicking Open. You can attach additional files by clicking the Attach button again.

Your attachment is represented in your message by an icon. If you select a picture to attach, that picture may be embedded in the body of your message. When you send the e-mail message, attachments and embedded pictures go with it.

Note   It's generally considered good netiquette to send an attachment only to recipients who expect it or would want it. In particular, a large attachment can tie up the computer of a recipient who has a modem or other relatively slow Internet connection; if you send a large attachment without permission, you may upset the recipient.

Receiving attachments

When you receive a message containing an attachment, you see the icon of the attachment in the body of the message. If the attachment is a multimedia file (picture, sound or video clip), you may see it embedded in the body of the message, depending on the format of the attached file. Double-click the attachment icon to open the attached file. You can also drag an attachment icon or embedded picture from the body of the e-mail message to the Desktop or a Finder window; the picture becomes the icon of the corresponding attached file. Figure 6-20 shows an attachment icon in an e-mail message.

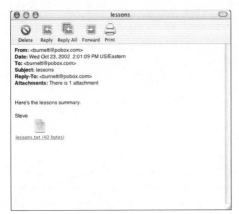

Figure 6-20: Icons in your e-mail messages represent attachments.

Caution   Use extreme caution when opening attachments from unknown sources. Many e-mail users have become unwitting carriers of viruses that destroy data and copy themselves across the network to other users' machines. While most of these viruses have primarily affected Windows users, it pays to be careful no matter which operating system you are using. You can learn more about protecting against viruses in Chapter 25.

Participating in Newsgroups

In addition to e-mail and the Web, Usenet is another part of the Internet. You can think of Usenet as a worldwide bulletin board system, where people from everywhere can post messages and join discussions about subjects that interest them. Each subject is called a newsgroup. More than 25,000 newsgroups cover virtually every subject imaginable. To find a newsgroup that interests you, you have to know a little about the structure of newsgroup names. A newsgroup name has several parts separated by periods. The first part specifies the general subject, the next part narrows the subject, and subsequent parts narrow the subject still further. Table 6-1 shows the most common top-level newsgroup names, and Table 6-2 shows examples of full names of newsgroups.

Table 6-1
Common Top-Level Newsgroup Names

Identifier	Included Subjects
alt	Subjects that don't fit into one of the other official categories
biz	Business
comp	Computers
misc	Miscellaneous subjects
news	News and other topical information
rec	Recreational hobbies and arts
sci	Scientific
soc	Social
talk	Debates

Table 6-2
Sample Full Names of Newsgroups

Newsgroup Name	Subject
alt.tv.simpsons	Adventures in Springfield
comp.sys.mac.advocacy	Let's hear it for the Mac
rec.sport.triathlon	For the Iron man in all of us
sci.med.nutrition	Scrutinize your diet here

Choosing a Newsreader

You can find the newsgroup of your dreams using a variety of programs. Two Mac OS X newsreaders are NewsWatcher-X, available at www.electricfish.com, and Thoth, available at www.thothsw.com. Figures 6-21 and 6-22 show these applications in action.

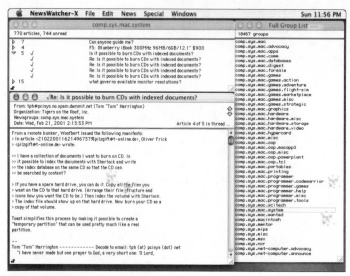

Figure 6-21: Use NewsWatcher-X to find and discuss topics that interest you.

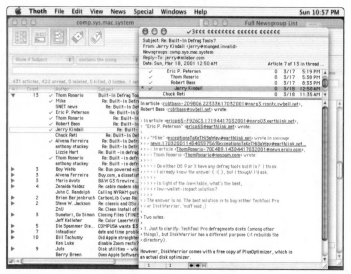

Figure 6-22: Use Thoth to participate in newsgroup discussions.

Several Classic applications are available for news reading as well. Outlook Express is a popular integrated e-mail and news client that is available from Microsoft and also has many useful tools for newsgroup reading. Netscape Communicator also has a built-in newsreader.

Tip   You can also browse and search newsgroups from your Web browser by going to the Google Groups site (`http://groups.google.com`).

Summary

Mac OS X makes it easy to harness the incredible power of the Internet.

✦ Getting on the Internet with Mac OS X is pretty simple. All it takes is a quick walk through the initial Mac OS X Setup Assistant.

✦ If you skip the Internet setup steps in the Setup Assistant, you have to use the Internet and Network panes of the System Preferences application.

✦ After you've set up an Internet connection via cable modem, DSL, local network, or AirPort wireless, you're ready to browse the Web, get your e-mail, and use other Internet services.

✦ If you connect to the Internet via a regular modem, ISDN, or PPPoE, you must make a connection to your Internet provider. You can have Mac OS X make the connection automatically.

✦ Mac OS X includes Internet Explorer for browsing the Web. Other browser applications are also available.

✦ Mac OS X also includes an e-mail application named Mail, which you can use to send, receive, and organize your e-mail messages. Mail coordinates with the included Address Book application, which stores e-mail addresses and other contact information.

✦ You can get on the Usenet and participate in the thousands of discussion groups that are available on nearly any topic imaginable. Two newsreader applications for Mac OS X are NewsWatcher-X and Thoth.

✦   ✦   ✦

Searching with Find and Sherlock

Mac OS X includes two powerful tools to search for information: the Find command and the Sherlock application. Find searches for files or folders on your disks, and Sherlock searches the Internet for information. In either case, a search can be extremely simple or very sophisticated. For example, Find can simply search for file by name, or it can search by a complex combination of over a dozen other attributes, such as date, size, and kind. Find can also search for text inside documents. When it comes to searching the Internet, Sherlock can search one site or a group of related sites, such as popular Web search engines (About, Lycos, LookSmart, and so on), people-search sites, reference sites, auction sites, and many others. This chapter explains the uses of the Find command and Sherlock.

Searching for Files and Folders

No matter how carefully you organize your folders and disks, the time will come when you can't find a file or folder without a lot of digging through layers of folders. The Find command fetches lost or buried items with less effort. Using Find, you can search by name, text content, or a combination of name, content, and other criteria, such as file size or modification date. You determine which folders and volumes (disks) Find searches. When a search ends, Find displays a list of the files, folders, and volumes that match your search criteria. You can do a lot with items on this list, including see folder locations, open them, and put them in the Trash.

Searching by name

Searching for files, folders, and volumes by name is a simple matter. You specify the name or part of the name you want to find and where you want Find to look for it. There are two ways to search using Find — by using the stand-alone Find window and by using the Search field in Finder window toolbars. To see a Find window, as shown in Figure 7-1, click in the desktop or on the Finder icon to switch the active application to the Finder and then use the File➪Find command. The keyboard shortcut for Find is ⌘-F to open the Find window.

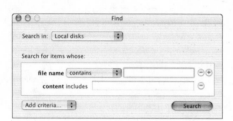

Figure 7-1: Use the Find command to search for files on volumes attached to your computer.

In Mac OS 10.2, every Finder window has a built-in Search command, as shown in Figure 7-2, which works as a simple Find window without as many options. If the toolbar is hidden, show the toolbar by clicking the lozenge-shaped button in the upper-right corner of the window. If the window is not wide enough to display the Search field in the toolbar, click the double-arrowhead at the right end of the toolbar and select Search from the pop-up menu, as shown in Figure 7-3, to display the Find window shown in Figure 7-1.

Figure 7-2: Every Finder window includes a Search field in the toolbar.

Figure 7-3: Narrow Finder windows place the Search command in a pop-up menu on the right side of the toolbar.

To use the Find window to search for files, follow these steps:

1. **Open the Find window.**

2. **In the text box, enter the name or part of the name that you want to find.**
   To enter text in the text box, you can click inside the box or press Tab as needed to place an insertion point in the box. If the box already contains text from a previous search request, pressing Tab selects this text so that you can replace it simply by typing.

   It doesn't matter how you capitalize the name or partial name that you type. Find considers the lowercase and uppercase forms of letters to be the same; *ReadMe* is the same as *readme, Readme,* or *README.*

3. **Click the Search button or press Return to begin the search.**

Looking at found items

When Find finishes searching, it shows the list of items it found, as shown in Figure 7-4. Find also counts the number of items it found and displays the total in the horizontal bar, just below the list of found items. If Find doesn't find any items that match the name you specify, the message "No items were found" appears in the horizontal bar.

You can scroll through the list of found items to see if it includes the file or folder you are seeking. If you see a likely item, click it once to see its folder location appear in the information area at the bottom of the Search Results window. Double-click any item in the list of searchable sources or any item in the information area to open the item. If you double-click a folder, a new Finder window opens to display the folder's contents. If you double-click an application, it opens. If you double-click a document file, the associated application opens and displays the document contents in a window.

You can do other things with files and folders in the found items list, such as find other items that are similar to one of the found items. We discuss these options later in this chapter.

Stopping a search

If you happen to specify a search that takes a long time and you don't want to wait any more, you can stop the search by clicking the small x button just below the lozenge-shaped toolbar button in the upper-right of the Search Results window. If you stop a search in progress, Find does not display a list of items it found before you stopped the search.

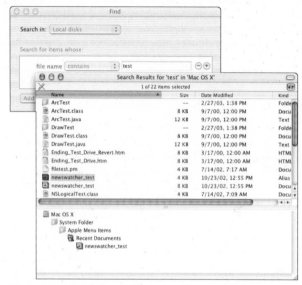

Figure 7-4: Search results display in a separate Search Results window.

Revising or repeating a search

If you want to repeat a search and possibly revise the name to search for or the sources to search, click the Find window behind the Search Results window to bring the Find window to the front. To expand your search, shorten the name entered in Find's text box or turn on more searchable sources. To narrow your search, lengthen the name to search for or turn off some sources.

Searching in Particular Folders

Initially, the Find command is set to search "Everywhere," which includes your home folder and the storage volumes connected to your computer, such as its internal hard drive, CD-ROM, and external disks connected to the computer's ports. You may be searching entire disks when all you need to search is a folder or two.

Adding a folder to the Find command

If you'd like to search only in particular folders (including these folders' enclosed folders and files) you can add these folders to the list of searchable sources in the Find command. Then you can turn on only the particular folders in the list that you want to search. If you turn on only one folder, Find searches only that folder. If you turn on multiple folders in the list of searchable sources, Find searches all of the folders.

Note When Find searches a folder, it must visit each item that the folder contains. When searching an entire volume, Find can quickly search a catalog of the volume's contents instead. Although an individual folder takes longer to search, you may not notice, unless the folder contains many items. The catalog is not something you can normally see; Mac OS X maintains it and makes it invisible to people using the computer.

To add a folder to the list of searchable sources, follow these steps:

1. **Open the Find window, shown in Figure 7-1.**

2. **Choose "Specific places" from the pop-up menu, as shown in Figure 7-5.**

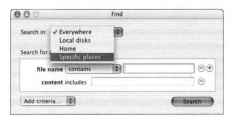

Figure 7-5: Choose "Specific places" from the Search In pop-up menu of the Find window.

3. **Click the Add button to the right of the Search In pop-up menu to show the Choose a Folder window in Figure 7-6.** As a shortcut, you can double-click the folder that you want to add.

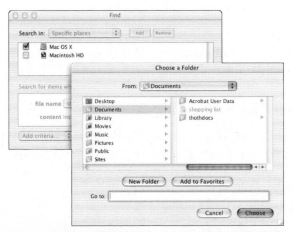

Figure 7-6: Select the folder you want to add to Find's list of searchable sources and then click Choose.

Removing a folder from the Find command preferences

Not only can you add folders to the Find window's list of sources, but you can also remove folders from the list as well. To remove a folder from the list of searchable sources:

1. **Select one or more folders in the Find window's list of sources.** To select a folder, click its icon or name. Find highlights the folder's name and icon to indicate that it is selected. (The checkbox in the On column does not indicate whether a folder is selected for this purpose.)

   To select an additional folder, ⌘-click its icon or name. To select a range of folders, click the first one and then Shift-click the last one. You can also select a range of folders by dragging across their icons or names.

2. **Click the Remove button.** The selected folders are removed immediately. If you accidentally remove a folder, you can add it to the list again as described earlier.

Searching for Text in Files

Instead of searching for files by name, you can search the text contents of your document files. Find has the ability to look inside certain kinds of documents and search them for keywords. Therefore, you don't have to laboriously open and search files one by one for the text information you want. By using Find, you can quickly and easily find the files that contain the information you seek. In addition, you can use Find to find a file when you don't remember its name but do remember what it contains.

What can Find search?

By necessity, Find can only search documents that contain text, and it can't get into every kind of document that contains text. In general, you'll have success searching the following kinds of documents:

✦ **Plain text documents,** like those you can edit in the TextEdit application

✦ **HTML documents,** which are plain text documents with codes that are used to create Web pages

✦ **PDF files** (Adobe's Portable Document Format)

✦ **Microsoft Word documents**

✦ **AppleWorks word processing documents**

✦ **WordPerfect documents**

✦ **E-mail** stored by Eudora, Outlook Express, and some other e-mail applications

In addition to searching document contents for key words, Find also searches file, folder, and disk names for the same keywords.

Note   When searching the text contents of HTML and PDF documents, Find intelligently ignores the text formatting commands that occur naturally throughout these documents. Special Text Extractor plug-in files make this possible. These plug-in files are in the PlugIns folder at `/System/Library/Find/PlugIns/`.

Specifying contents to find

Generally, you get the best results when searching by contents if you specify the least common keywords that you think will be in the documents that you want to find. If instead you specify common words that occur in many of your documents, the results of your search by contents will be a long list of mostly extraneous documents. To find the fewest extraneous documents, try to think of one or two unusual words that occur in only the documents that you want to find, and have Find search for those unusual words.

To search by contents, follow these steps:

1. **Open the Find window shown in Figure 7-1.**

2. **In the "content includes" text box, enter the keywords that you want to find as shown in Figure 7-7.** To enter text, the text box must be selected. If necessary, you can accomplish this by clicking inside the box or pressing Tab as needed to place an insertion point in the box. If the box already contains text from a previous search request, pressing Tab selects this text so that you can replace it simply by typing.

   It doesn't matter how you capitalize keywords. Find considers the lowercase and uppercase forms of letters to be the same; for example, *iMac* is the same as *imac, Imac,* or *IMAC.*

3. **Click the Search button or press Return to begin the search.**

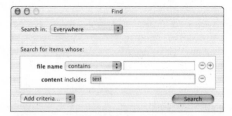

Figure 7-7: The Find window can search contents of several types of files in volumes of the computer that have been indexed.

Note   Find can search document contents only in folders and volumes (disks) that have been indexed.

Looking at found documents

When Find finishes searching by contents, it displays a list of the documents it found. Find also counts the number of documents it found and displays the total number below the list of found documents. If Find doesn't find any documents that match the keywords you specify, it displays a message to that effect.

Ranking the relevance of found documents

Find lists the found documents according to their relevance. A document's relevance is determined by how often the keywords occur in it and how close together they are in it. The more often the keywords occur and the closer their proximity, the higher the document's relevance. This method of evaluating relevance is not always 100 percent accurate. The document you're looking for may not have the very highest relevance. Even so, the document you want probably will be nearer the top of the list than the bottom. Find indicates the degree of each found document's relevance with the length of a bar in the list of found documents. The longer the bar, the more relevant Find judges a document to be. Figure 7-8 shows how Find ranks found documents by relevance when it displays the results of searching by contents.

Doing more with found documents

Aside from the relevance ranking, the list of found documents that results from a search by contents is similar to the list of found items that results from a search by name. If you click a listed document once, its folder location appears in the information area at the bottom of the Find window. Double-clicking a document opens it. You can discover what else you can do with files and folders in the found documents list, such as finding similar documents, later in this chapter.

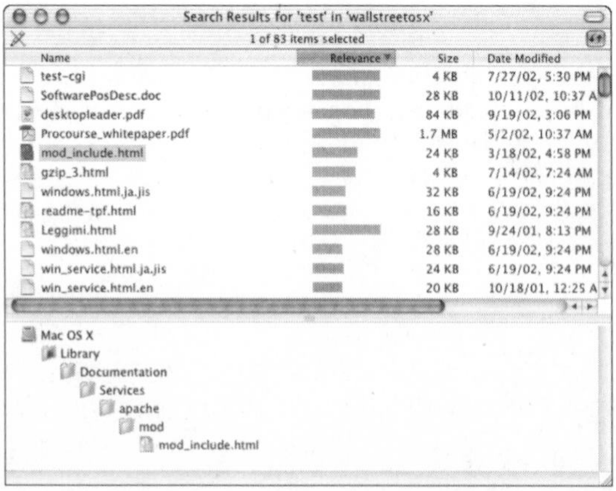

Figure 7-8: After searching by contents, Find ranks found documents by their relevance to the keywords.

Indexing folders

Searching the contents of documents seems almost magical, but isn't. It requires some advanced preparation. Before Find can search document contents, it must index them. The Finder can create an index for each folder that you add to its list of searchable sources (as described earlier in this chapter). It stores each folder's index in an invisible file inside the folder. This file contains a database of words from the documents in the folder.

Given an index database, the Finder can determine whether the words in your search request exist in the indexed files by quickly searching the database. This search happens quickly because the database is much smaller than the aggregate length of the files it indexes. In addition, searching the index database is faster because the words in it are arranged in order. The first time you search a volume that is not indexed, Find begins by creating an index for that volume then searching the index. Therefore, your first search of a new volume will take longer than any subsequent searches.

> **Note** The Finder indexes only the first 2,000 unique words of each document to keep the index database file from becoming too large and bogging down searching by contents. Therefore, the Finder does not index all the words in a document that contains more than 2,000 unique words. The closer a unique word is to the end of such a long document, the less likely the Finder is to include it in the index. If the Finder doesn't index some words in a long document due to this limitation, you won't be able to find that document by searching for those words.

Creating indexes

The Finder initially indexes your home folder, and it automatically indexes other folders when you add them to the list of searchable sources. You can also have Find index some volumes, such as removable disks and network volumes, but it doesn't index entire volumes automatically. The Finder cannot index all folders and volumes.

> **Note** Actually, the Finder does not prepare content indexes. It hands off this task to an application named ContentIndexing. ContentIndexing hides while it is operating and quits automatically when it finishes indexing. If you want to see ContentIndexing at work, open the Process Viewer application (in the Utilities folder) while the Finder is reporting that indexing is under way, and look for ContentIndexing in Process Viewer's list of running processes.

What can and can't be indexed

The folders and volumes you index can be located on your computer, another computer on your network, or a network file server. To index a folder, you must have the privilege to save items in it.

Cross-Reference   For more information about using folders from file servers and other computers on your network, see Chapter 10.

Find cannot index some types of folders and volumes because it cannot write (save) their index files. As you may expect, Find cannot write an index file on a write-protected disk, such as a CD-ROM or a locked Zip disk. What's more, Find cannot index a folder for which you do not have the "write" privilege, which is the privilege to make changes. Many such folders are on your Mac OS X startup disk. It's also common not to have write privileges for folders from network file servers and other computers on your network.

Note   Although you can't create an index on an existing CD-ROM, you may have CD-ROMs that are indexed. The index for such a CD-ROM was created in advance and recorded as part of the CD-ROM's contents. If you have a CD-R or CD-RW recorder, also known as a CD burner, you can provide a Find index for it by creating an index of the folder or disk whose contents will be recorded on the CD.

Tip   You may be able to index a folder that Find says can't be indexed. Try logging in as a user who has administrator privileges and indexing again. If you still can't index the folder, log in as the root user (System Administrator) and try again. Note that Find maintains separate lists of searchable sources for each user. So any folders you add while logged in as one user you will have to add again after logging in as another user. We cover administrator and root user privileges in Chapter 16.

Updating indexes

The Finder updates indexes every time you search that folder or volume. Updating an index generally takes much less time than creating the index initially.

Find determines which indexes to update by going through the list of searchable sources. An index becomes out of date when you change the contents of an indexed document, add documents to an indexed folder or volume, or remove documents from an indexed folder or volume. Find can't search a folder accurately by contents if the folder's index is out-of-date. The more outdated an index is, the less accurate the search will be.

Manually updating or creating an index

You can manually update the index for any indexable folder or volume listed in the Files channel, or you can create the index for an indexable folder or volume that doesn't have one. Follow these steps to start indexing manually:

1. **Select the item you want to index by clicking its icon or name in a Finder window.**

2. **Choose File⇨Get Info.** The Get Info window appears as shown in Figure 7-9.

Figure 7-9: Indexes can be updated using the Content Index pane of the Get Info window.

3. **Click the disclosure triangle to the right of Content Index to show the Content Index pane of the Get Info window**. The Content Index pane displays.

4. **Click the Index Now button.** The index for the volume, folder, or disk is updated.

Indexing in the background

Indexing a folder or volume that contains many documents may take many minutes or even hours. You can let the Finder continue indexing in the background while you use the computer for other tasks. This background indexing is usually unobtrusive thanks to Mac OS X's preemptive multitasking.

Adjusting indexing speed and disk use

The speed at which the Finder creates and updates indexes depends on the number of languages it uses. The amount of disk space required for index files also depends on the number of languages. Fewer languages yield faster and smaller indexes.

To select which languages Find uses, follow these steps:

1. **Choose Finder⇨Preferences to display the Preferences dialog, shown in Figure 7-10.**

2. **Click the Languages button at the bottom of the Finder Preferences window to display the Languages dialog and then select the languages that you want the Finder to use when it creates and updates indexes.** Figure 7-10 shows the Languages dialog.

Figure 7-10: Make indexing faster or slower and make indexes smaller or larger, by selecting fewer or more languages.

Deleting indexes

If you want to create a completely new index for a folder that already has one, you can delete the existing index. It's a good idea to delete a folder's existing index and create a new one if you make major changes to the folder or if you notice Sherlock becoming noticeably slower at searching the folder by contents. Follow these steps to delete an index:

1. **Select the item you want to index by clicking its icon or name in a Finder window.**

2. **Choose File⇨Get Info. The Get Info window appears, as shown in Figure 7-9.**

3. **Click the disclosure triangle to the right of Content Index to show the Content Index pane of the Get Info window**. The Content Index pane displays.

4. **Click the Delete Index button.**

5. **Click OK when asked to confirm that you really want to delete.**

Searching by Multiple File Attributes

Sometimes you can't find what you're looking for by searching the text contents or the names of files, folders, and volumes. You may need to take into account such other attributes as the age, size, or kind of item you're looking for. Under these circumstances, you need to perform a custom search in the Find window.

Performing a custom search

To perform a custom search, open the Find window, as shown in Figure 7-1, and click the Add criteria pop-up menu, as shown in Figure 7-11.

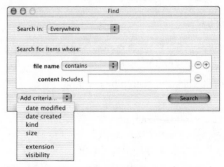

Figure 7-11: Adding criteria to the Find window can narrow the search results to more precise results.

Select the criteria you want to add to the Find window to add them. You can add several kinds of additional criteria as shown in Figure 7-12. To remove an item, click the minus button to the right of the field. If a field has a plus sign in a button to the right of the field, clicking the button adds another search criteria field of the same kind. Figure 7-12 shows examples of these additional search criteria and controls.

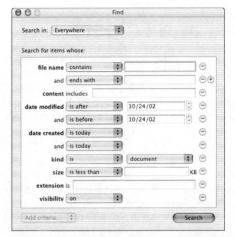

Figure 7-12: Adding criteria to the Find window can narrow the search results to more precise results.

Table 7-1 explains the additional criteria usable for searching.

	Table 7-1
	Settings for Find's More Search Options
Attribute	**What Find Looks For**
file name	A file, folder, or volume whose name contains/starts with/ends with/is/is not/doesn't contain the text you enter
content includes	Text within documents, like the search by contents we described earlier
date created	A file, folder, or volume whose creation date is/is before/is after/is not; is today; is within 1/2/3 days of; is within 1/2/3 weeks of; is within 1/2/3/6 months of the date you enter
date modified	A file, folder, or volume whose modification date is/is before/is after; is today; is within 1/2/3 days of; is within 1/2/3 weeks of; is within 1/2/3/6 months of the date you enter
size	A file whose size is less than/is greater than the number of KB you enter (1024KB = 1MB)
kind	A file whose kind is/is not alias/application/document /folder /audio/image/movie
extension	A file whose extension is the character set you enter
(visibility) is	A file or folder that is invisible/visible

Working with Found Files and Folders

When a search of the volumes on your computer ends, Find displays a list of files, folders, and disks that match your search criteria in a Search Results window, as shown in Figure 7-4. This list of found items appears in a separate window from the Find window, and you can go back to the Find window to change your search criteria. Each search appears in a separate Search Results window. You can rearrange the Search Results list as described earlier in this chapter, and you can work with the listed items in many ways.

Obviously, you can browse the list of found items for items that particularly interest you. Less obviously, you can see the volume and folders in which a found item is located, and you can copy the name of a found item to the Clipboard. You can move or copy found items to any Finder window or the Desktop, make aliases of found items, and move found items to the Trash.

In addition, you can open found items or the folders that enclose them. If a found item is a document, you can print it. If a found item is an alias, you can show its original in a Finder window. With some types of found files, you can have Find find similar files. This section describes how to do all these things.

Seeing the path to a found item

You can see the path to a found item through the hierarchy of its enclosing folders. Simply select the item in the list of found items and look at the information area below the list of found items, as shown previously in Figure 7-4.

Copying the name of a found item

You can copy the name of a found item by selecting it in the bottom section of the Find window (which displays the path) and choosing Edit⇨Copy. Then you can insert the name in the TextEdit application or anywhere else you can edit text by going to that application and then choosing Edit⇨Paste.

Moving or copying a found item

You can move a found item by dragging it from the list of found items to a Finder window, the Desktop, or a folder icon in either of these places. If you want to copy an item instead of moving it, simply press the Option key while you drag it from Find's list of found items. You don't need to press Option if the place you're dragging an item is on a different volume than the item's current location. Items are always copied, not moved, when you drag them to a different volume.

If you change your mind about moving or copying a folder while in the midst of dragging it, you can cancel the operation by dragging to the menu bar and releasing the mouse button. Alternatively, you can drag the folder back where it came from or to the title bar of Find's window, but the menu bar is an easier target to hit. If you change your mind after you've dragged it, you can undo the move by choosing Edit ⇨ Undo Move of "file name" — Find supplies the file name to help you remember what you just did — or the keyboard shortcut ⌘-Z.

If you can't move or copy any items to a particular folder, then you may not have the privilege to make changes to that folder. If you can't move or copy one particular item to any folder, you do not have privileges to change that item or the folder it's in. Either your privileges for the item don't allow moving it from its folder or your privileges for the folder don't allow moving anything out of it. (We covered the effect of privileges on moving and copying in Chapter 4.)

Tip   Instead of moving, copying, or performing another operation on found items one at a time, select multiple items and act on them all at once. Click one item to select it and then ⌘-click each additional item that you want to select. Select a range of items by dragging across them or by clicking the first item and then Shift-clicking the last one.

Making an alias of a found item

You can make an alias of a found item by pressing the Option and ⌘ keys while you drag it from Find's list of found items to a Finder window or the Desktop.

Opening a found item

You can open a found item by double-clicking it or by selecting it and choosing File⇨Open Item. The item you open can be in the list of found items or it can be in the hierarchical path displayed at the bottom of the Find window. Opening a folder displays its contents in a Finder window. Opening a document file opens the associated application and displays the document contents in a window.

Tip   While opening a found item from a Find window, you can simultaneously close the Find window by holding down the Option key as you double-click or choosing File⇨Open Item.

Opening a found item's enclosing folder

You can open the folder that encloses a found item by selecting the found item and choosing File⇨Open Enclosing Folder. A Finder window opens, showing the found item selected among the other contents of the enclosing folder.

Moving a found item to the Trash

You can move a found item to the Trash by dragging it from the list of found items to the Trash icon in the Dock or by selecting the item and choosing File⇨Move to Trash.

Seeing the original of an alias

You can see the original of an alias in the list of found items by selecting the alias and choosing File⇨Get Info. A Get Info window opens for the alias, with the path to the original shown in the General pane of the Get Info window.

Searching the Internet

Due to its immense size, searching the Internet can be a real chore. Search engines and directories abound—AltaVista, Ask Jeeves, Excite, Google, HotBot, LookSmart, Lycos, and Yahoo! are just a few—but you often have to search several of them to find what you want. With Sherlock, you can conduct a search of many sites at once. Sherlock searches multiple Web sites simultaneously and displays the combined results in its window. You can see a brief summary of any found site in the Sherlock window, and with one or two clicks in Sherlock, you can have your Web browser go to a found site.

Sherlock gains access to each Web site through a plug-in file created by Apple, other companies, or individuals. These plug-ins make it possible for Sherlock to search not only Web search engines, such as those mentioned in the previous paragraph, but other searchable Web sites including Amazon, eBay, and other e-commerce sites. News sites and Web magazines also supply Sherlock plug-ins that enable you to search their sites with Sherlock.

Each Sherlock plug-in appears as a search site in a Sherlock channel. Sherlock initially has several Internet channels, with each channel containing a different category of search sites. Besides the basic Internet channel for search engines and directories, Sherlock has channels for picture searches, stocks, movies, yellow pages, eBay, flights, dictionary, translation, and Apple's AppleCare Web sites. You can reorganize and add your own channels.

Note   To use any of Sherlock's Internet channels, you need a connection to the Internet. If your computer uses a modem to connect to the Internet, you should make sure that your computer is set to dial up and make a connection automatically or that a connection is already made before you start an Internet search in Sherlock. Chapter 6 tells you how to make an Internet connection with a modem. If you didn't set up your computer for an Internet connection during the initial Mac OS X setup procedure, as described in Appendix A, see Chapter 18 to find out how to set up a connection now.

Opening Sherlock

To begin your search, you can open Sherlock and display its main window by using two different methods. You can

✦ **Open Sherlock from the Dock.** You can open Sherlock and display its window by clicking the Sherlock icon in the Dock at the bottom of the screen. This action opens the Sherlock application, displaying its window. Of course, you won't be able to open Sherlock from the Dock if someone has removed its icon. (Removing and adding items to the Dock is mentioned in Chapter 4.) Figure 7-13 shows the Sherlock icon in the Dock and in a Finder window.

✦ **Open Sherlock from a Finder window.** You can also open Sherlock by double-clicking its icon wherever it appears in a Finder window or even on the Desktop, if someone has put it there. For example, normally a Sherlock icon is in your Applications folder, which you can open by clicking the Applications button at the top of a Finder window.

Exploring the Sherlock Window

Sherlock for Mac OS X does not have the brushed aluminum window of Sherlock 2 in Mac OS 9. Instead, Sherlock for Mac OS X has a normal Aqua window. (Sherlock 2's brushed aluminum window received much criticism because it lacked window controls for zooming and minimizing the window.) Figure 7-14 gives you a look at the Sherlock window in Mac OS X.

Figure 7-13: Open Sherlock by clicking or double-clicking its icon.

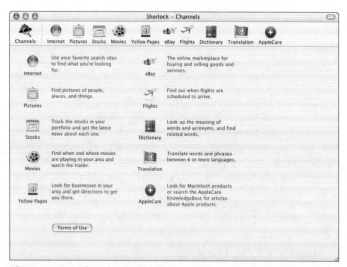

Figure 7-14: The Sherlock window has separate areas for the following (top to bottom): channel selection, search criteria, information area, and viewing more information about a selected source.

The channel to search

At the top of the Sherlock window are several channel buttons, which enable you to switch between different types of searches. Each channel button specifies the type of information you can search for, including files and folders, Web pages, products, people, or news. Each channel also specifies a group of sources you can search, and in this regard, most channels are actually groups of Internet sites.

You change search channels by clicking a channel button. When you do, Sherlock reconfigures its window to list the channel's searchable sources across the bottom of the window and to display appropriate search criteria for the type of information that the channel can search for. Sherlock shows which channel is currently selected by adding the channel name to the title of the Sherlock window.

Tip   Clicking the icons for one of the channel's searchable sources on the bottom edge of the Sherlock window causes the URL for that source to load in your default Web browser.

What to search for

Below the channel buttons is a text box in which you enter a search request. The search request consists of words that you want Sherlock to search for. To enter your search request in this text box, click inside it and begin typing. You can also press Tab; however, you may need to press Tab more than once to select this text box and see an insertion point blinking there. To further indicate when the text box is selected, Sherlock highlights it by drawing a dark gray border around it. Figure 7-15 shows a search request being entered in the text box.

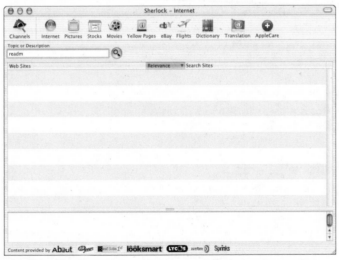

Figure 7-15: The text box and any options below it specify what to search for.

Below the text box for entering a search request, you may see options for additional search criteria. The combination of options — in fact, whether there are any options — depends on the type of search.

The Search and Back buttons

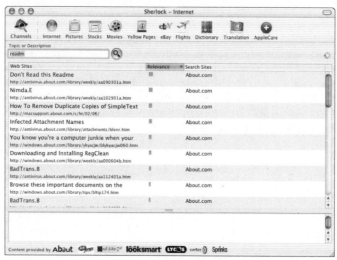

The large round Search button, which is labeled with a picture of a magnifying glass, starts a search and can stop a search that is under way. When the Search button is colored green, clicking it starts a search. When the Search button is colored red, a search is under way and clicking the button stops the search.

The list area

In the middle of its window is the list area. After a search, Sherlock places the list of items it has found in this area. We explore what you can do with found items later in this chapter. Figure 7-16 shows an example list of found items.

Figure 7-16: After a successful search, Sherlock displays a list of found items in the middle of its window.

Rearranging Sherlock's list area

Whether you see a list of found items or a list of searchable sources, you can rearrange the list in several ways. You can

✦ **Resize the list.** Drag the grip in the bar that separates the list from the information area to change the relative height of the list area and the information area below it. Resizing the Sherlock window also changes the size of the information area.

✦ **Sort the list.** Click the heading of the column by which you want Sherlock to sort the list. Sherlock highlights the column heading.

✦ **Reverse the sort order.** Click the column heading that is currently highlighted to change from a descending order to an ascending order or vice versa. The arrow next to this column heading points down for a descending sort or up for an ascending sort.

✦ **Move a column.** Drag the column's heading left or right to move the column. While you drag a column heading, the mouse pointer looks like a clutching hand.

✦ **Resize a column.** Drag the borderline on the right side of a column's heading to resize the column. The mouse pointer looks like a two-headed arrow when you place it over the borderline.

Tip   You can't remove a column from a list of found items, but you can effectively hide it. Simply resize the column to its minimum width and move it to the right side of the list.

The information area

The bottom part of the Sherlock window displays information about whatever is selected in the list above it. For example, if you select an Internet site from the list of searchable sources, information about that site is displayed. (Information is not available for all Internet sites.) The information area may be blank if nothing is selected in the list. Figure 7-17 shows an example of the information area with a found item selected in the search area.

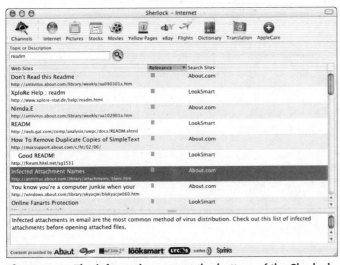

Figure 7-17: The information area at the bottom of the Sherlock window tells you more about the item selected in the list above it.

Searching Web pages

When you switch Sherlock to the Internet channel, Sherlock reconfigures its window to accommodate the different requirements of an Internet search. Figures 7-16 and 7-17 showed Sherlock set to the Internet channel.

Searching the Internet channel

1. **Click the Internet channel button if it's not already selected.**

2. **In the text box, enter one or more words that describe the information you want to find.**

   To enter text, the text box must be selected. If necessary, you can accomplish this by clicking inside the box or pressing Tab as needed to place an insertion point in the box. If the box already contains text from a previous search request, pressing Tab selects this text so that you can replace it simply by typing.

   The search request you enter will be interpreted differently by various Web search engines, directories, and other Internet search sites. Sherlock will not attempt to revise or adjust your request to accommodate these different interpretations. In general, you can simply enter a series of words that you think may generate results, such as *Olympic bobsled trials* or *outdoor camping*. You can also try interposing words that express a logical relationship, such as *and, or,* and *not.* You have to experiment with different combinations of words to see what generates the best results with different Internet search sites.

3. **Click the Search button or press Return to begin the search.**

Getting Better Web Search Results

The way you phrase your request when searching the Internet can profoundly affect the results. Each search engine, directory, and other site that you search on the Internet may take into account word order, punctuation, capitalization, and logical relationships, such as *and, or,* and *not.* Making matters even more complicated, the various search sites do not all follow the same rules for evaluating a search request. Nevertheless, these general guidelines can help you phrase your request so that your Internet searches in Sherlock turn up the results you want:

✦ **Word order.** Try putting the most important words first, even if you have to enter them in an unnatural order. Many search engines, directories, and other search sites consider the order of words in your request when determining how well each Web page matches your request. For example, you may get better results with *Stooges Three* than with *Three Stooges.*

✦ **Logical relationships.** Use the words *and, or,* and *not* to express logical relationships between words and phrases as follows:

- **and** before a word means that you want information that includes the word between two words means that you want only information that contains both the words.

- **or** between two words means that you want information that contains either one or both of the words.

- **not** or **-** (a minus sign) before a word means that you want information that does not include the word.

For example, searching for *Aztec and Toltec* finds information that includes both terms. If you search for *Aztec or Toltec,* you'll get a lot more results because your results will include information that contains either term. Search for *Aztec not Toltec* and you'll get results that include the first term but don't include the second term. Most Internet search engines and directories recognize logical relationships expressed by *and, or,* and *not.*

✦ **Commas.** Try using commas between words and phrases. Although many search engines, directories, and other search sites don't require commas, some work better if you separate each keyword or phrase with a comma. A comma has generally the same effect as the word *or,* but commas cause some search sites to consider a Web page to better match your request when the site contains more of the words or phrases in your request.

✦ **Capitalization.** Some search engines, directories, and other search sites notice whether you capitalize words. If you don't capitalize, they ignore capitalization while searching; if you do capitalize, they look for the same capitalization as yours.

✦ **Quotation marks.** Some search sites prefer that you put phrases or proper names between quotation marks, such as "tape recorder" or "Huckleberry Finn." Additionally, some search sites find variations of unquoted words but not of quoted words. For example, searching these sites for *international* finds variations including intern, national, internationals, and so on; searching these sites for "international" finds only the literal quoted word.

Looking at Internet search results

Sherlock begins displaying the results of searching the Internet channel as soon as it receives them from any of the search sites. As other search sites return their results, Sherlock merges them in the list area in the middle of its window. For each Web page that matches your search request, Sherlock displays an icon indicating the search site that found the page together with the page's name, relevance to your search request, and Web site. You can rearrange the list of results as described earlier.

You can see a summary of any listed Web page by clicking its icon, name, or site. The summary appears in the information area below the list of results. The summary is provided by the search site, and its composition varies from one search site to the next. Figure 7-18 shows an example of the list of results from an Internet search.

Seeing a listed Web page

You can see all of a Web page that appears in Sherlock's list of results by doing either of the following:

✦ Double-click the name of a listed Web page that you want to see.

✦ Drag the name of a listed Web page to a Web browser window.

Whichever method you use, Sherlock sends the page's Web address to your Web browser, which takes over and attempts to load the page via your Internet connection.

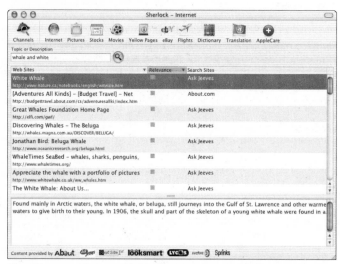

Figure 7-18: After searching the Internet channel, Sherlock lists the Web pages that each of your search sites matched to your search request, and displays a summary of the page that's currently selected in the list.

Copying a listed Web page's summary

You can copy part of the summary that's listed in the search results by selecting the Web page, clicking in the information area of the Sherlock window, and choosing Edit⇨Select All, then Edit⇨Copy. Sherlock places about 140 characters of the summary onto the Clipboard. Then you can go to TextEdit or any other application that lets you edit text and insert the partial summary by choosing Edit⇨Paste.

Copying a listed Web page's address

You can copy the address of a Web page by selecting the page in the list of search results and dragging the Web page listing from the middle of Sherlock's window to the window of a text document or other place where you can edit text. Dragging a Web page listing from Sherlock inserts the page's address, not its name.

Saving a link to a listed Web page

 If you'd like to create a file that links to one of the Web pages from Sherlock's list of Internet search results so that you can see the page later, drag the page's name from Sherlock's list to any Finder window, the Desktop, or a folder icon in either of these places. This causes the Finder to create an Internet Location file, which you can open any time you want to see the Web page. You can recognize an Internet Location file by its distinctive icon.

Cross-Reference You'll find more information about Internet Location files in Chapter 10.

Searching other Internet channels

Besides the basic Internet channel for searching the Web, Sherlock has several other predefined Internet channels. You can switch to any of the following Internet channels by clicking a button at the top of the Sherlock window: Pictures, Stocks, Movies, Yellow Pages, eBay, Flights, Dictionary, Translation, and AppleCare. These channels are described in the following paragraphs.

Pictures channel

The Pictures channel includes search sites for finding pictures on the Internet. To use it, enter a subject you want to find pictures of in the text box, and click the Search button. To see the Internet address of a found picture, click the picture once to select the picture. The Internet address shows in the bottom edge of Sherlock window. Double-clicking a picture sends the Internet address to your Web browser.

Stocks channel

The Stocks channel provides the ability to track stocks you are interested in. You can see a close-to-real-time price (delayed 15 minutes), see a summary of recent news headlines if any exist for the company, and view a graph of the stock's performance over time. If you select a news article in the news pane, a link will appear in the information area at the bottom of the window. Clicking that link shows the story in the Web browser. To add a new stock to the list, enter the company's name or stock abbreviation in the search field and click the magnifying glass to start the search. A view of the Stocks channel is shown in Figure 7-19.

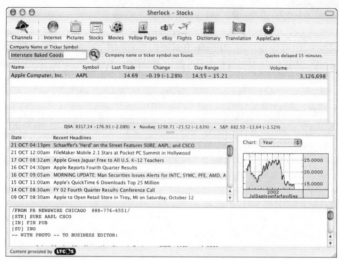

Figure 7-19: Use the Stocks channel to track stocks of interest.

Movies channel

The Movies channel has movie, theater, and showtime information provided by moviefone. To use this channel, choose to organize either by movies or theaters, enter a zip code and choose a date from the pop-up menu on the right, then press Return. When the list of movies appears, choose the movie you are interested in and the middle pane will show the theaters the movie is playing at. Choose a theater to see the showtimes for the selected date. The results include movie name, theater, showtimes, summary, poster, and the movie trailer, as shown in Figure 7-20.

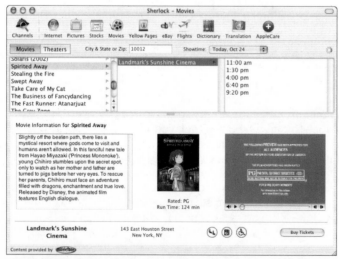

Figure 7-20: When Sherlock searches the Movies channel, the results include dates, times, and movie previews.

Yellow Pages channel

The Yellow Pages channel provides address, telephone, driving information, and maps for businesses. Enter a city and state or zip code and a business name you're looking for, use, and click the Search button. The result lists the name, telephone number, address, and distance as well as driving directions and a map from your specified location for each that matches your search request. A view of the Sherlock Yellow Pages channel is shown in Figure 7-21.

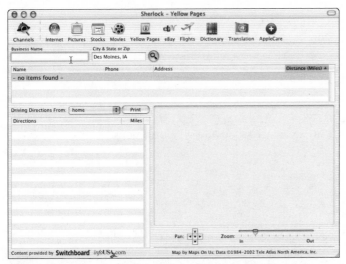

Figure 7-21: Use the Yellow Pages channel to find businesses of interest and their locations.

eBay channel

The eBay channel can be used to shop and to bid on auctions, just as though you were using a Web browser. You can track auctions through Sherlock. A view of the Sherlock eBay channel is shown in Figure 7-22.

Flights channel

The Flights channel lets you search for information on flight status of current flights. You can search either for a specific flight by airline and number, or you can search with departure and arrival city. When you find the flight you are interested in, click it and view its arrival or departure status and other information, as shown in Figure 7-23.

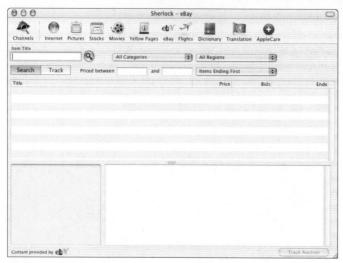

Figure 7-22: Use the eBay channel to shop and bid on auctions.

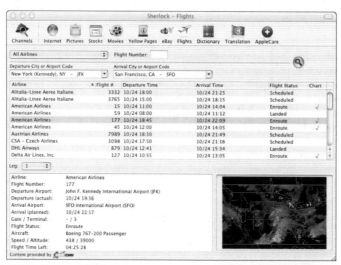

Figure 7-23: Use the Flights channel to search for information on current flight status.

Dictionary channel

The Dictionary channel lets you search for information on words as well as acronyms and the names of famous people. To use the Dictionary channel, enter a word, name, acronym, or term in the text field then click the Search button. Synonyms, definitions, and other information will appear as shown in Figure 7-24.

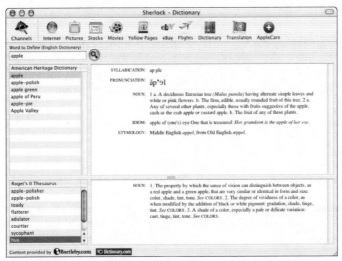

Figure 7-24: Use the Dictionary channel to search for information on words, acronyms, and famous names.

Translation channel

The Translation channel lets you search for information on flight status of current flights. Enter the text you wish to translate from in the top field labeled Original Text, select a to and from language pair from the pop-up menu, then click the Translate button. An example is shown in Figure 7-25.

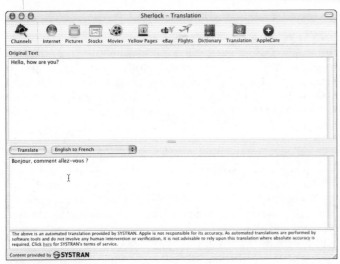

Figure 7-25: Use the Translation channel to translate text to and from languages.

AppleCare channel

 The AppleCare channel lets you search Apple's Knowledge Base of information on Apple hardware and software. Enter a topic or description of the item or issue in the text field in the upper-left and click the Search button. Knowledge Base articles appear in the main field. Clicking a Document title shows the article in the information area at the bottom of the Sherlock window. An example is shown in Figure 7-26.

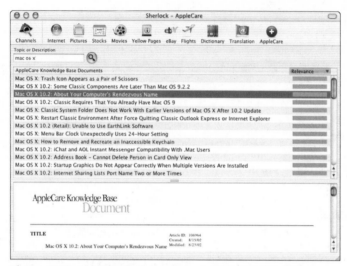

Figure 7-26: Use Sherlock to access Apple's helpful online Knowledge Base articles.

Modifying Sherlock Channels

The predefined Internet, Pictures, Stocks, Movies, Yellow Pages, eBay, Flights, Dictionary, Translation, and AppleCare channels may be all you need but if not, you can add to and reorganize these 10 channels. You can add new channels for Internet search sites, and you can delete the channels you add. You can customize the look of the Sherlock toolbar and adjust the Sherlock Preferences.

Note   Sherlock repairs and updates its standard Internet channels periodically, and in so doing could undo changes you have made to the configuration of the standard channels. Every time you open Sherlock, it verifies that each standard channel exists and has its standard search sites. If channels or search sites are missing, it restores them from the Internet. In addition, Sherlock periodically checks the Internet for newer versions of standard search sites and channels, and it automatically updates your system as needed. If you move search sites out of a standard channel or remove a standard channel altogether, Sherlock's automatic update and repair mechanisms will eventually restore the standard search sites and channels you moved or removed.

Adding a channel to Sherlock

Adding a new channel to Sherlock is a simple task, once you find a Web site that provides a channel for the version of Sherlock that ships with Mac OS 10.2. When you find a Web site with a Sherlock 3.5 and above compatible channel, click the link on the Web site for the channel, and the new channel should appear in the Sherlock toolbar.

Deleting a channel

If you want to delete a channel, choose View➪Customize Toolbar to show the customizing toolbar pane. Click the channel you want to remove from the toolbar and drag it into the customizing pane. The channel icon will vanish in a small puff of smoke. Figure 7-27 shows the Sherlock customizing toolbars pane.

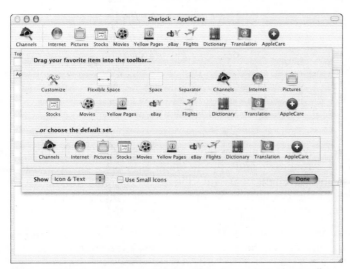

Figure 7-27: Rearrange and delete the channels in the toolbar.

Rearranging and replacing channels

The channel buttons at the top of the Sherlock window are not permanently fixed in their initial positions. You can move them around, and you can replace one channel with another.

To move a channel button, simply open the Customizing Toolbars and drag a channel icon to the right or left in the toolbar until it is where you want it to be, then release it. The other icons will reorder themselves to fit the space.

Editing preferences

Sherlock can be configured to better suit your needs. The four areas of preferences that can be set are Locations, Countries, Subscriptions, and Security. To set preferences for Sherlock, follow these steps:

1. **Open Sherlock if it hasn't been opened already.**

2. **Choose File⇨Preferences to open the Sherlock Preferences window.** It should appear with the Locations tab selected, as shown in Figure 7-28.

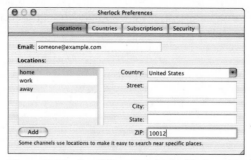

Figure 7-28: Set different geographic locations for Sherlock to use as a starting point in the Locations tab.

3. **Enter as much information as you feel useful to Sherlock to use.** For example, if you are new to a town and are unfamiliar with the local area, the full street address and zip might be useful to help the map function of the Yellow Pages find driving directions for you, or the zip code alone might be enough to find showtimes for movies in your area.

4. **Click the Countries tab to change the Preferences window as shown in Figure 7-29.** To turn on a channel for a country, click the country name to select it, then click the Turn On button to turn on the channels for that country. If the selected country's channel is turned on, the button will display Turn Off.

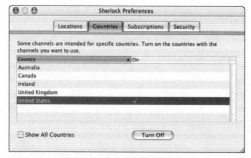

Figure 7-29: The Countries tab helps the Sherlock channels deliver the correct information.

5. **Click the Subscriptions tab to change the Preferences window as shown in Figure 7-30.** To add a channel, click the Add button, then enter the URL into the sheet and click Add. To unsubscribe from a channel or to remove that channel, select the channel in the Subscriptions list and click the Remove or Unsubscribe buttons.

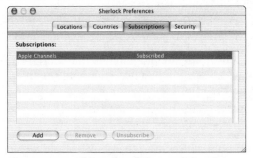

Figure 7-30: The Subscriptions tab is where to add new channels, and unsubscribe or remove unwanted channels.

6. **Click the Security tab to change the Preferences window as shown in Figure 7-31.** On this tab, you can add sites with permissions to upload new sites in their channels, and control the acceptance or rejection of cookies.

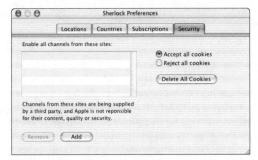

Figure 7-31: The Security tab is used to set cookie permissions for sites in channels.

Making Multiple Searches

Sherlock can have a number of searches set up at the same time, each in a separate window. You can switch to a different Sherlock window or create a new window whenever Sherlock is not in the midst of conducting a search. Each window can have a different search that is completed or is in the process of being set up. To create a new Sherlock window, choose File⇨New Window.

Summary

Here's what you should know after reading this chapter:

✦ Use Find to search files and folders on volumes and disks attached to your computer. Use Sherlock to search the Internet for other information.

✦ Use the Find command to search by name, text content, or a combination of name, content, and other criteria such as file size or modification date. You determine which folders and volumes Find searches. When a search ends, Find displays a list of the files, folders, and volumes that match your search criteria. You can do a lot with items on this list, including see their locations, open the items, and put them in the Trash.

✦ Before Find can search file contents, it must index them. You can manually start indexing a given folder or volume.

✦ You can open the Sherlock application from the Dock or from a Finder window.

✦ You switch channels by clicking channel buttons at the top of the Sherlock window.

✦ You enter the words that you want Sherlock to search for in the text box below the channel buttons.

✦ The Search button to the right of the text box starts a search and can stop a search that is under way.

✦ In the middle of its window, Sherlock lists items it has found. You can resize these lists, sort them in a different order, and move and resize their columns.

✦ The bottom part of the Sherlock window displays information about whatever is selected in the list above it.

✦ Sherlock has 10 standard channels for searching the Internet — Internet, Pictures, Stocks, Movies, Yellow Pages, eBay, Flights, Dictionary, Translation, and AppleCare — and you can add more. Each channel lets you search multiple Web search engines, directories, and other search sites all at once. Sherlock displays the combined results of the simultaneous searches in its window. You can see a brief summary of any found site in the Sherlock window, and with one or two clicks in Sherlock, you can have your Web browser go to a found site.

✦ You can move and copy Internet search sites between channels, add your own search sites, rearrange the channels, and add your own channels.

✦ Each Internet search site in a Sherlock channel corresponds to a search site plug-in file. Sherlock includes a number of search site plug-ins, and you can get more from various Web sites.

✦ Sherlock can have a number of searches going at the same time, each in a separate window.

✦   ✦   ✦

Getting Help

If you have a question about something displayed on your computer or if you aren't sure how to accomplish a task, the Mac OS may be able to provide on-screen help. Mac OS X displays several types of help. One type of help briefly describes objects when you point at them with the mouse. A much more extensive type of help explains how to perform common tasks, and you read and interact with this type of help like you browse Web pages. Another type of help, which is used only by some Classic applications, interactively guides you step-by-step through tasks. In addition to the help information included with the Mac OS, many applications also provide on-screen help.

Displaying Help Tags

You can get immediate information about some objects on the screen by displaying their *help tags*. If an object has a help tag, it automatically appears near the mouse pointer when you position the pointer over the object and wait a few seconds. You can recognize a help tag by its distinctive small yellow box, which contains a very short description of the object under the pointer. If no such box appears when you hover the pointer over an object on-screen, the object has no help tag. You do not have to click anything or press any keys to make a help tag appear. Figure 8-1 shows an example help tag.

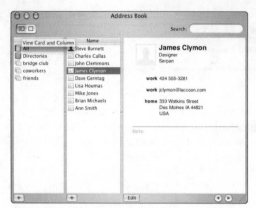

Figure 8-1: A help tag provides a description
of the object in a Mac OS X application.

Mac OS X provides help tag capability, but not all objects have help tags.
Commonplace objects, such as window controls and scroll bars, have no help tags.
Menus and menu items never have help tags. Buttons and other objects have help
tags only if the application that they are part of provides descriptions to be displayed inside the help tags. Classic applications cannot provide help tags at all, and
many Mac OS X applications do not provide any help tags.

If you have used Balloon Help in Mac OS 9 or earlier, you probably realize that the Mac
OS X help tags replace Balloon Help. On the downside, help tags provide much less
helpful information than Balloon Help. On the upside, help tags are less intrusive and
don't need to be turned on and off. Balloon Help is still available for Classic applications, as described in "Using Balloon Help for Classic Applications" later in this chapter.

Using the Help Menu and Help Buttons

Help tags aside, the Mac OS provides on-screen help through the Help menu and
Help buttons. The Help menu lists the kinds of help available in the application you
are currently using. The kind of help that you get varies from application to application. Some Mac OS X applications provide help through the Help Viewer. Some
Classic applications provide help through Apple Guide. Other applications have
their own means of providing on-screen help. We cover the different on-screen help
systems in more detail later in this chapter. Figure 8-2 is an example of the Help
menu in Mac OS X.

Figure 8-2: Get help on-screen with the Help menu.

Tip You can always get general help by going to the Finder application and then choosing from the Help menu.

Using a Mac OS X Help button

As a convenience, some windows include a Help button that you can click to get help specifically for that window. In Mac OS X windows, the Help button is a round button with a distinctive question mark on it. Clicking a Mac OS X Help button opens the Help Viewer application and displays a relevant help article or a list of relevant articles.

Using a Classic Help button

In Classic windows, the Help button is a square button with a distinctive question mark on it. Clicking a Classic Help button may provide help through the Help Viewer application or through Apple Guide.

Browsing and Searching Help Viewer Articles

When you need more information than help tags provide, use the Help Viewer application to find and read short how-to articles. In the Help Viewer, help is available by browsing a table of contents or by searching for words that describe the help you need. Some of the articles you read have links that you click to see related material. These links work just like Web links, although you don't need to know how to use the Web to use the Help Viewer.

The Help Viewer is the main source of general how-to help for Mac OS X. It also provides separate sections of specialized help on Apple technologies, such as AppleScript and QuickTime. In addition, some applications add their own sections of specialized help to the Help Viewer. All the available help sections are listed in an overall table of contents in the Help Viewer, as explained in the following paragraphs.

Displaying the Help Viewer

You display on-screen help in the Help Viewer application by choosing a command from the Help menu or clicking a Help button. The application you're using determines what you see in the Help Viewer. You may see an overall table of help contents, a list of help topics, a list of help article titles, or a single help article.

Displaying general Mac help topics

While using the Finder, you can have the Help Viewer application display a list of general Mac help topics. Follow these steps:

1. **If you're not currently using the Finder, switch to it.** For example, click any Finder window or click the Finder icon at the end of the Dock.

2. **Choose Help⇨Mac Help to display a list of Mac Help topics in the Help Viewer, as shown in Figure 8-3.**

Figure 8-3: The Mac Help section in the Help Viewer application lists general Mac help topics.

Displaying Help Viewer sections

The Help Viewer application has a table of contents called Help Center, and it lists the major sections of help available. To view the list of help sections, click the Help Center button in the upper-left corner of the Help Viewer window. You may see just the help sections included with Mac OS X, or you may see additional sections included with other software. Figure 8-4 shows an example of the Help Center list.

Displaying help for the active application

If the application you're using provides on-screen help via the Help Viewer, you can generally display this help by choosing a command from the Help menu. For example, while using Sherlock choose Help⇨Sherlock Help to display a list of Sherlock-related topics in the Help Viewer, as shown in Figure 8-5.

Figure 8-4: When the Help Viewer application displays the Help Center, you see a list of available help sections.

If the window you're working in has a Help button, clicking it may display a relevant help article or a list of articles. For example, while setting up the Print dialog of a Mac OS X application, click the Help button to display an article about choosing printing options.

Figure 8-5: Opening the Help Viewer from Sherlock shows Sherlock-specific help. The Help Center is always available by clicking the Help Center button.

Mac OS X Help Viewer versus Classic Help Viewer

If you use Classic applications, your Mac has a Classic version of the Help Viewer as well as a Mac OX version. If either version is open, it tries to display help for both Mac OS X applications and Classic applications. The Mac OS X version of the Help Viewer doesn't display help correctly for some Classic applications. What's worse, the Classic version of the Help Viewer doesn't display help correctly for most Mac OS X applications. Therefore, you should quit the Classic version of the Help Viewer before displaying help for a Mac OS X application. It's also a good idea, although not as crucial, to quit the Mac OS X version of the Help Viewer before displaying help for a Classic application.

You can tell whether either version of the Help Viewer is open by looking for its icon in the Dock. The Mac OS X Help Viewer's icon looks like a life preserver. The Classic Help Viewer's icon looks like a large blue question mark inside a gray diamond. As usual, you know the application is open if a black marker appears below its icon in the Dock.

Browsing Help Viewer links

If you've used a Web browser, you should be familiar with the way the Help Viewer works. The blue underlined words in Help Viewer are links that you can click to see related material. For example, if you choose Mac Help from the Help menu and then click an underlined help topic, you see a list of relevant article titles. Clicking an underlined article title displays the article in the Help Viewer. Articles themselves may also contain underlined links. Figure 8-6 shows an example of searching for the words "keychain" and "password" with the second link selected, and Figure 8-7 shows that help article.

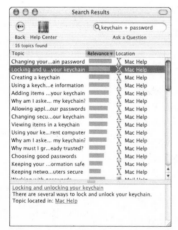

Figure 8-6: Click an underlined link to see related material in the Help Viewer.

Figure 8-7: A Help article may contain links and commands.

Where the Help Viewer links may take you

Links in articles take you to many places inside and outside the Help Viewer. If the author of the help article writes clearly, you should have a good idea about where the link takes you. The possibilities include the following:

✦ A link may show you another article in the Help Viewer window.

✦ An **"Open . . ." link** probably opens the application that the article describes.

✦ A **"Tell me more" link** displays a list of articles that are related to the current article.

✦ A **More link** at the bottom of a list of article titles takes you to a continuation of the list.

✦ A **"Go to the website" link** shows you a related Web site in your Web browser. Other links may also go to Web sites, which is especially likely if the link includes an Internet address or is near an Internet address in the help article. However, clicking an Internet address that is not underlined in a help article does nothing. Text that is not underlined is not a link in the Help Viewer.

✦ A link may also display interactive, step-by-step help in an Apple Guide window (described in "Following Apple Guide Interactive Help for Classic Applications" later in this chapter).

Tip   Links visited since you opened the Help Viewer are green instead of blue.

Retrieving Help from the Internet

Sometimes the Help Viewer retrieves help articles from the Internet. For example, an application may initially have only its most popular help articles installed on your computer and keep less commonly read articles on the Internet. If you click a link to an article that's on the Internet, the Help Viewer automatically caches it on your computer. If you later want to read an article that the Help Viewer has already retrieved from the Internet, the Help Viewer displays the cached article from your computer. If the article was retrieved more than three days earlier, the Help Viewer checks the Internet for a newer version. Of course the Help Viewer can retrieve articles from the Internet only if your computer has an Internet connection. If your computer has a dial-up connection to the Internet or you must go through an authentication procedure to make an Internet connection, the Help Viewer displays a dialog asking whether you want to make the connection.

If your computer isn't connected to the Internet and the Help Viewer needs to retrieve an article, you must approve the connection.

Browsing with Help Viewer buttons

Besides clicking links, you can go places in the Help Viewer by clicking buttons.

✦ Click the left-arrow button to go back to the previous page in the Help Viewer.

✦ After going back, click the right-arrow button to go forward.

✦ Click the Help button to open the Help Center and see its list of help sections.

Searching Help Viewer

If you're looking for help on a specific subject and don't want to browse through links until you find it, use the Help Viewer to search all of the articles for the help you need. In the "Ask a Question" text box at the top of the Help Viewer window, type some words that describe the help you need and then press the Return key on your keyboard. When typing words to search for, you can include special characters to describe the help you need more precisely. Table 8-1 describes these special characters. Figure 8-6 shows an example of a search in the Help Viewer.

Tip   If your search words don't turn up the help articles you want, try different forms of the words you used or use the thesaurus for another name of your topic. The Help Viewer looks up your search words in an index of help articles. The index is prepared by using Sherlock technology, which we covered in Chapter 7.

Table 8-1			
Special Characters for Help Viewer Searching			
Character	*Meaning*	*Search Example*	*Search Results*
+	and	desktop + Finder	This example finds articles that include both "desktop" and "Finder."
|	or	desktop | Finder	This example finds articles that include either "desktop" or "Finder."
!	not	desktop ! Finder	This example finds articles that include "desktop" but exclude "Finder."
( )	grouping	picture + (Finder | desktop)	This example finds articles that include "picture" and either "desktop" or "Finder."

Using Balloon Help for Classic Applications

When you are working in a Classic application and need immediate information about objects that you see on-screen, turn on Classic *Balloon Help*. With Balloon Help on, you position the pointer over an object and a concise description of it appears in a cartoon-style balloon. The balloon points to the object and tells you what the object is, what it does, what happens when you click it, or some portion of this information. You do not have to press any keys or click anything to make Help Balloons appear. Figure 8-8 is an example of Balloon Help within a Classic Application.

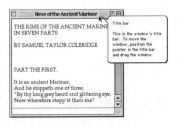

Figure 8-8: A Help Balloon describes the object under the pointer in a Classic application.

The Classic environment provides Balloon Help capability, but not all objects have Help Balloons. Many applications provide no Balloon Help at all.

Turning Balloon Help on and off

You turn on Balloon Help by choosing Show Balloons from the Help menu. That command changes to Hide Balloons. Choosing it again turns off Balloon Help. You can display Balloon Help by pressing a combination of keys if you install the shareware program Helium from Tiger Technologies (www.tigertechnologies.com), described in Chapter 23.

Working with Balloon Help on

Everything works normally when Balloon Help is on. Using Balloon Help does not put the Mac in help-only mode. It's similar to someone standing over your shoulder and describing on-screen objects to you.

Help Balloons appear whether you press the mouse button or not. You click, double-click, and otherwise use applications normally, except that you may perceive a slight delay as Help Balloons come and go when you move the pointer slowly across items that have Balloon Help descriptions.

The object that a Help Balloon describes may be large or small and individual or collective. For example, the Close box in the active window's title bar has its own Help Balloon. In contrast, an inactive window has one balloon for the whole window. Sometimes a Help Balloon describes a group of items. For example, one balloon tells you about all the scrolling controls in a scroll bar. Figure 8-9 shows the Help Balloons for a Close box and a scroll bar.

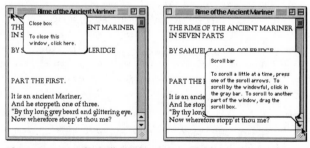

Figure 8-9: Help Balloons vary in scope.

What Balloon Help knows

Balloon Help knows about all standard objects in Classic windows and menus, including the following:

✦ Classic windows in general

✦ The Classic Help menu

✦ The Classic Apple and Application menus (which are described in Chapter 5)

✦ Standard parts of the Classic Open, Save, and Navigation Services dialogs (all of which are described in Chapter 5)

✦ The Classic Page Setup and Print dialogs (which are described in Chapter 9)

Balloon Help cannot describe a specific Classic application's menu commands, window contents, dialogs, and so on unless the application's developer or publisher has included the necessary information. For example, Apple has provided complete Balloon Help for many of its Classic accessory and utility programs.

Balloon Help is not available at all in Mac OS X applications. Instead, Mac OS X offers help tags (which are covered in "Displaying Help Tags" at the beginning of this chapter).

Following Apple Guide Interactive Help for Classic Applications

Apple Guide is another form of how-to help that is available for some Classic applications. Apple Guide shows and tells you how to get things done while you actually do them. Step-by-step instructions appear in a guide window, which floats above all other windows. As you move from step to step, Apple Guide may coach you by marking an object on-screen with a circle, arrow, or underline. Figure 8-10 is an example of an Apple Guide instruction and coaching mark.

Notice that the Apple Guide window has a Zoom box and a Collapse box. Use these controls to temporarily shrink the window so that you can see what's underneath it. Then use the boxes again to restore the window.

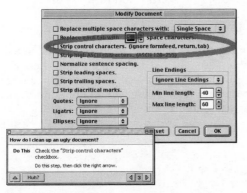

Figure 8-10: Apple Guide displays step-by-step instructions in a floating window and draws coaching marks to point out objects on-screen.

Displaying Apple Guide

An Apple Guide window may appear when you do any of the following:

✦ Choose a command from the Classic Help menu

✦ Click a Help button in a Classic window

Of course neither of these actions displays an Apple Guide window in a Classic application that doesn't provide Apple Guide help. Therefore, in some Classic applications, these actions display another type of on-screen help. If an Apple Guide window appears, it may list topics that you can browse, or it may begin step-by-step instructions for a specific task. Each Classic application that provides Apple Guide help determines the content and organization of the help. The Classic application determines what you first see in the Apple Guide window. For example, while you are using the Classic Tex-Edit Plus application, you can choose Tex-Edit Plus Guide from the Help menu to display an Apple Guide topics window for Tex-Edit Plus. (Tex-Edit Plus is shareware from Trans-Tex Software, `http://nearside.com/ trans-tex/`.)

Using an Apple Guide topics window

For many applications, Apple Guide first displays a topics window. A title at the top of the window tells you what software the help covers. For example, SimpleText Guide covers only topics related to SimpleText.

An Apple Guide topics window generally includes the following three large buttons, which you click to choose how you want to find help:

✦ **Topics button.** Displays a list of topics for you to scan.

✦ **Index button.** Displays an index of keywords for you to browse.

✦ **Look For button.** Allows you to search for keywords in the Help index.

Scanning Apple Guide topics

To see a list of help topics and a list of tasks and terms, follow these steps:

1. **Click the Topics button at the top of the Apple Guide topics window.**

2. **Click a topic on the left side of the topics window to display a list of specific tasks and terms on the right side.** If the list on the right includes headings in bold, you can show and hide individual tasks or terms under the heading by clicking the disclosure triangle next to the heading. Figure 8-11 shows an example of Apple Guide topics, tasks, and terms.

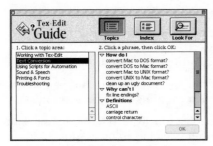

Figure 8-11: Click the Topics button
to see a list of topics in Apple Guide.

Browsing an Apple Guide index

You can browse an Apple Guide index by following these steps:

1. **Click the Index button at the top of an Apple Guide topics window.** Apple
   Guide displays an alphabetical list of key terms used in the guide.

2. **Do any of the following:**

   • **Scroll through the index with the scroll bar.**

   • **Scroll the index to entries starting with a particular letter of the alpha-
     bet by dragging the pointer at the top of the index list to that letter or
     by simply clicking that letter.** You can't see all 26 letters of the alphabet
     at the top of the index list, but you can see more by clicking and
     dragging the pointer slightly past the last letter that you can see.

3. **Click an entry in the index to display a list of tasks in which that entry
   appears.** Figure 8-12 shows an example of an Apple Guide index.

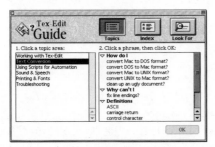

Figure 8-12: Click the Index button
to see an index in Apple Guide.

Searching Apple Guide for keywords

You can have Apple Guide look for words that you specify; follow these steps:

1. **Click Look For at the top of an Apple Guide topics window.**

2. **On the left side of the window, click the arrow button and type a keyword or two that describe the step-by-step instructions that you want to see.**

3. **Click Search (or press Return) to see a list of relevant tasks on the right side of the window.** Figure 8-13 is an example of searching Apple Guide for a keyword.

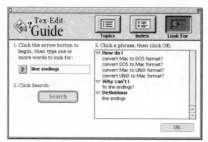

Figure 8-13: Click the Look For button to search for help in Apple Guide.

Following step-by-step instructions

When you double-click an item on the right side of the Apple Guide topics window (or select the item and click OK), the topics window goes away. Another Guide window appears with an introduction to the task or a definition of the term you selected in the topics window. Figure 8-14 is an example of the step-by-step window.

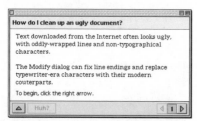

Figure 8-14: The first Apple Guide step describes the task or defines the term.

Read the information in the Guide window and follow any instructions it gives you. To go to the next step in a multiple-step task, click the right-pointing arrow at the bottom right of the Guide window. To back up one step, click the left-pointing arrow.

If you decide that you have selected the wrong task or term, return to the topics window by clicking the Topics button at the bottom of the Guide window. The Topics button may be labeled with an up-pointing arrow, a question mark, or the word *Topics*. You can also put away Apple Guide altogether by closing all guide windows.

At each new step, the guide may draw a circle, line, or arrow on-screen to point out a menu title or other object that you must use to complete the step. These coaching marks appear in red or another color. If the step calls for you to choose from a menu, Apple Guide colors and underlines the menu item you should choose, as well.

If the Guide window mentions something you don't understand, try clicking the Huh? button at the bottom of the Guide window for clarification. (This button may be labeled I'm Stuck.) Clicking this button brings up another Guide window that may contain a definition of a term or begin step-by-step instructions for accomplishing a task related to the task you initially chose. For example, clicking Huh? in Step 3 of the task "How do I clean up an ugly document?" in the Text-Edit Plus Guide displays a definition for control character. The Huh? button is dimmed when additional information is not available.

If you work ahead of the step currently displayed in the Guide window, Apple Guide can adjust to catch up. When you click the right-pointing arrow to go to the next step, Apple Guide skips ahead to the next step that matches your location in the task.

While you're following the steps in Apple Guide, you can still use your computer normally. If the Guide window is in your way, drag it somewhere else or click its Zoom box to make it smaller; click again to make it larger. Collapse a Guide window into its title bar by clicking its Collapse box.

If you have not properly completed a step when you click the right-pointing arrow at the bottom of the Guide window, Apple Guide explains what you need to do to get back on track.

Exploring Other Avenues of Help

Many applications add how-to help, on-screen reference material, or other items to the Help menu. For example, many applications published by Adobe, FileMaker, and Microsoft list on-screen help commands in the Help menu. The help may appear in the Help Viewer or in your Web browser. Some applications use other help systems to display their on-screen help. For instructions on an application's own help system, check the documentation that came with the application.

You can find additional help on the Web for your Macintosh computer, Mac OS X, popular applications, and add-on hardware. Check the following sites:

✦ **AppleCare Service and Support** at www.apple.com/support/

✦ **AppleCare Knowledge Base** at http://kbase.info.apple.com/

✦ **Apple Manuals** at www.info.apple.com/manuals/manuals.taf

✦ **Apple Mac OS X Support** at www.info.apple.com/usen/macosx/

✦ **MacFixIt** at www.macfixit.com

✦ **MacInTouch** at www.macintouch.com

✦ **The Web site of the company** that makes the software or hardware for which you need help

Summary

Here's what you should know after reading this chapter:

✦ Mac OS X displays on-screen help in the form of help tags and Help Viewer articles. For Classic applications, Mac OS X displays Help Viewer articles, Help Balloons, and Apple Guide instructions.

✦ If an object has a help tag, you view it by positioning the mouse pointer on the object and waiting a few seconds. A help tag appears in a small yellow box and succinctly describes the object under the pointer.

✦ The Help Viewer application displays short how-to articles, and you can display them by choosing items from the Help menu or by clicking a Help button in a window that has one.

✦ Some Help Viewer articles include links that you click to see related articles, open related applications, or connect to an Internet site.

✦ You can search all Help Viewer articles for words you specify, optionally using the special characters +, |, !, and () to pinpoint what you want to find.

✦ Balloon Help briefly describes the object under the mouse pointer in some Classic applications, using cartoon-like dialog balloons. You turn Balloon Help on and off by choosing commands from the Help menu in these Classic applications.

✦ In the Classic environment, Apple Guide shows and tells you how to complete a task as you do it. As you follow instructions displayed in a floating guide window, coaching marks call your attention to menus, buttons, and other objects that you need to use.

✦ Some applications use help systems not provided by Mac OS X, but most still list commands for getting help in the Help menu.

✦   ✦   ✦

At Work with Mac OS X

Printing Documents

Regardless of what type printer you use, almost every application manages the printer and the printing process in the same manner. Mac OS X enforces this consistency by offering complete printing services to applications. All applications employ the same software components to prepare page descriptions for printing and to communicate with the printer. These components are called printer drivers, and Mac OS X comes with drivers for common USB printers from Canon, Epson, and Hewlett-Packard, in addition to a variety of Ethernet-connected printers, in the Printers folder of the main Library folder on your startup disk (path /Library/Printers).

If you have one of the supplied USB printers connected, Mac OS X recognizes it automatically, and that printer is set as the default choice in the Print dialog box.

Note Because you can choose from all available printers in the Print dialog box's pop-up menu, the Chooser and Desktop Printers available under Mac OS 9 are not present in Mac OS X. You would, however, still use the Chooser to designate printers for the Classic environment, and they will require their own printer drivers in the Extensions folder of Classic's System Folder.

One thing you notice about the Mac OS X Finder is that it does not include a Print command in its File menu (or any other menu). If you wish to print a Finder window or the Desktop, you take a picture of the screen using the Grab utility and print that from within Grab or Preview. The real loss of convenience is that you can no longer select a group of icons and choose Print, expecting each document's application to launch, present its Print dialog box, and initiate printing, nor can you drag icons to a chosen printer icon and expect them to print.

These losses in convenience are balanced (or outweighed) by the fact that you can now choose any available printer right in the Print dialog box, preview any print job, and save the job as a PDF file.

Printer Setup

Mac OS X supplies a collection of print drivers for popular USB printers from Canon, Epson, and Hewlett-Packard — though far from an exhaustive list. These vendors are making printer drivers available as they are completed. If your printer is not on this list, you can probably find its driver at its manufacturer's Web site. Additionally, Mac OS X recognizes a wide variety of PostScript printers connected via AppleTalk or via an IP network.

All of these printer drivers are located in the main Library folder of your startup disk (path /Library/Printers), grouped into folders for each manufacturer and with *PPD* (PostScript Printer Description) files and plug-ins folders for PostScript printers.

Managing Your Available Printers List

Assuming that you don't have a local USB printer recognized by Mac OS X the first time you print, the Print dialog box says No Printer Selected in the Printer pop-up menu, as shown in Figure 9-1. Proceed as follows:

Figure 9-1: Uh-oh! No printer selected, you need to add one.

1. **Select Edit Printer List... from the Printer pop-up menu to present the Print Center utility's window, as shown in Figure 9-2.** Various printers, such as the HP LaserJet shown in Figure 9-3, are recognized automatically.

Figure 9-2: The Print Center window in Mac OS X

2. **Click the Add button to display the available printers, as shown in Figure 9-3.**

Figure 9-3: Your list of printers — click Add to add another printer to the list.

3. **From the top pop-up menu, select**

• **USB,** if you have a USB printer attached.

• **Directory Services,** if you have a Rendezvous-equipped printer attached to the network. Rendezvous is a networking protocol that provides automatic discovery and connection of Rendezvous-aware applications and devices. As of this writing, Epson, Hewlett-Packard, and Lexmark are adding Rendezvous to newer printers. The Rendezvous dialog box is shown in Figure 9-4.

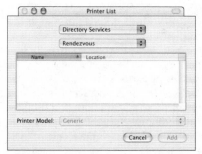

Figure 9-4: Choose Directory Services from the pop-up menu to add a Rendezvous-equipped printer.

- **AppleTalk,** if you wish to select a printer on your local Ethernet network, illustrated in Figure 9-3.

- **IP Printing,** if you wish to connect to a printer on the Internet or through a DNS (Domain Name Server). You will need an IP address or network name of the printer. Figure 9-5 shows the IP Printing window.

Figure 9-5: Choose IP Printing from the pop-up menu to connect to a printer via DNS.

4. Click the Add button to add the printer to your available printer list.

To remove a printer, just select the printer you want to delete in the Print Center's list and click the Delete button.

Overview of Printers

Network, serial, and USB; PostScript and non-PostScript; inkjet, laser, dye sublimation, dot matrix, and impact — all ways to categorize printers. And there are overlaps among these categories. For example, just because many PostScript printers are networked laser printers doesn't mean that a USB inkjet printer isn't networked or is PostScript. Also, just because Macs do not have parallel ports but many popular printers (for Windows) require a parallel connection doesn't preclude use of a Windows printer by a Mac. USB-to-parallel converter cables exist to make these printers available for use with a Mac, if the printer driver is available for Mac.

First things first: a networked printer is a printer accessed via a network connection such as Ethernet. Networked printers are shared by computers on the network and are further broken down into two categories — AppleTalk and remote printers. AppleTalk is usually used for printers such as LaserWriters and LaserJets on a local network. You can print to remote printers by entering an IP address or DNS name. USB printers are typically physically connected to your Mac or to a USB hub, which is connected to your Mac. USB printers are dedicated printers in the sense that the only Mac that "sees" them is the one to which they're connected. The USB printer sharing that's available in Mac OS 9 is not available (yet) in Mac OS X. Serial printers are "dinosaurs" in the sense that they are being replaced by USB and, thus, very few Mac OS X-capable computers even have serial ports anymore.

PostScript is a *page description language* (PDL) developed by Adobe Systems. The language has operators, variables, and commands that control precise shape and placement information for everything that gets drawn on a page, not just the fonts, although they are the most obvious example people see. A PostScript printer has a *raster image processor* (RIP), which translates the PostScript code into a *raster image* (set of discrete dots) that represents the data on the printed page at the current printer resolution. Thus, a one-inch line that is 1/6 of an inch thick is translated into 15,000 dots at 300 dpi, and into 240,000 dots at 1200 dpi. Because the RIP is an embedded computer requiring its own memory, you typically find PostScript printers to be more expensive than non-PostScript printers (not to mention the fee charged by Adobe to the printer manufacturer for using their RIP). Although more common on laser printers, you can also find PostScript inkjet printers and dye-sublimation printers.

Inkjet printers produce their output by spraying streams of ink through tiny nozzles onto the paper, transparency, or other media. Laser printers use heat to affix tiny particles of toner to the output medium. Dye-sublimation printers melt wax (like what is found in crayons) onto the page.

The least expensive printer type, at least initially, is the inkjet. If, however, you're going to be producing a lot of output you'll find that the cost of consumables (ink cartridges) is fairly high. A single cartridge typically lasts about 500 pages and costs approximately $20 (some less, some more). In contrast, a fairly typical laser printer produces about 4,000 pages from one toner cartridge that costs approximately $100. The vast majority of current inkjet printers produce photo-realistic color output, but producing photo-quality images requires a color cartridge in addition to the black ink cartridge. Of course, the amount of ink expended to produce an 8x10 color photograph exhausts the cartridge very quickly as well. (I usually get about 25 full-page photos per color cartridge.) Color laser printers also exist, but they are significantly more expensive. If you don't have a need for color output and you're going to be producing a lot of printouts, an inexpensive laser printer is probably more economical; however, if you need color, the inkjet is your best bet. If you can afford both, having both a laser printer and an inkjet available serves you well for all purposes.

Laser printers require different paper trays for different paper sizes, another expense and another item to store. With an inkjet, you just adjust the paper guides. Some current laser printers also have an optional attachment to produce *duplex* print—printing on both sides of the page without you having to flip the pages.

Basic Printing

After Mac OS X recognizes your printers, printing is quite straightforward. No longer do you need to work with different-looking Page Setup and Print dialog boxes for every printer type. Furthermore, because the Mac OS X graphics engine, Quartz, uses PDF as its underlying format, you can print any file to PDF format just like the documents and forms from so many corporate Web sites.

The first step toward printing your document is to establish the page parameters. In Mac OS, this is handled through the Page Setup dialog box. (Windows users are accustomed to seeing it called Printer Setup.)

Page Setup attributes

The Page Setup dialog box is where you determine the size paper to print on, whether you are going to print *portrait* (taller than wide) or *landscape* (wider than tall), the direction the paper feeds, and whether your document is going to reduce or enlarge the media before printing. All of these options are called *page attributes* and are available in a handy screen for one-stop shopping, as shown in Figure 9-6.

The Settings pop-up menu has another choice, Summary. Summary is a textual consolidation of the various choices made under Page Attributes. The Summary pane is handy when you have made a lot of changes in different panes and want to verify the settings without having to go through the panes one at a time.

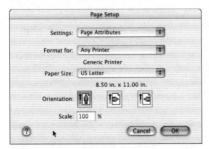

Figure 9-6: General document printing parameters are set in the Page Setup dialog box.

Applications use the information from Page Setup to establish default margins and where page breaks occur.

When you select Page Attributes from the Settings pop-up menu, the following options appear:

✦ **Format for.** Enables you to select a specific printer to format a document or a generic printer. A generic printer has a limited set of capabilities — essentially those that would be available on any printer. When you choose a specific printer, its printer type is displayed beneath the pop-up menu.

✦ **Paper Size.** Enables you to select from the various paper sizes. A generic printer supports only US Letter, US Legal, A4, and B5 paper sizes, but specific printers will generally support a wider range, possibly including such things as #10 envelopes or 3 x 5-inch index cards. The physical dimensions of the paper size are displayed below the Paper Size pop-up, as shown in Figure 9-6.

✦ **Orientation.** Determines whether the top of the printed page is on the short edge of the paper (portrait), the bottom of the long edge (landscape), or the top of the long edge (also landscape).

✦ **Scale.** Reduces or enlarges the printed image according to the percentage you enter. Full size is 100%. Because the page image is rendered in resolution-independent PDF, you don't have rigid minimum and maximum values imposed for scale. As a rule of thumb, however, you should keep in mind the physical limitations of your printer and the resolutions it can print.

Setting Print options

Choosing Print from an application's File menu (probable keyboard shortcut is ⌘-P) produces a dialog box like the one displayed in Figure 9-7. Choosing from the unlabeled pop-up menu changes what is displayed in the lower part of the dialog box. The choices in this pop-up menu vary depending on the printer chosen in the Printer pop-up menu. The following selections are likely to be present, in addition to a number of application-specific and printer-specific choices:

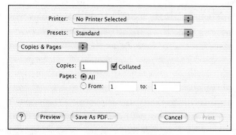

Figure 9-7: Use the Print dialog box to specify what pages you want printed and how you want them printed.

✦ **Copies & Pages.** Shown in Figure 9-7. You can specify the number of copies you want to print and if you want to collate them, how you want it done — one full copy, followed by the next or all the copies of each page to print together. You also can specify whether you want all pages of the document printed or just a specific range. Note that the numbers in the Page boxes are not the numbers you give the pages in the document, but rather the physical enumeration of pages. For example, if the first page of your document is numbered 23 (maybe it's Chapter 2 of your opus), for the purposes of the Print dialog box, that is page 1. If you want, you can specify just the starting page in the first box and leave the second box blank to print from that page to the end of the document or just the ending page in the second box (leaving the first box blank) to print from page 1 to that point.

✦ **Layout.** Layout, as shown in Figure 9-8, allows you to specify how many pages you want to print per sheet of paper from the Pages per Sheet pop-up menu. This is usually referred to as *N-up* printing. If you choose more than one page per sheet, the print driver automatically scales the pages to fit. Use the Layout Direction buttons to specify where the pages print on each sheet and the border pop-up menu provides the ability to specify a border to print around each page (even if it is one per sheet). The large diagram at the left of the dialog box depicts your choices.

✦ **Save As....** Nifty feature that saves and names the group of settings currently in place. To save the current settings for the print job, click the Presets pop-up menu and choose Save As... You can use the Rename command on the Presets pop-up menu to rename a saved print job setting later if you think of something more appropriate. In future print sessions, that choice appears in the Presets pop-up menu at the top of the Print dialog box.

The Preview button creates a temporary PDF file, which is then opened in the Preview utility for your perusal. If you like, you can save the file from within Preview as either a TIFF or PDF file.

Instead of printing to a printer, the Save as PDF... button allows you to save the document as a PDF. Click the Save as PDF... button to show a Save to File window shown in Figure 9-9, which you use to choose where on the computer to save the PDF.

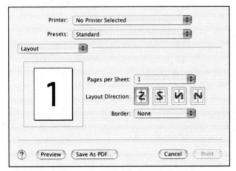

Figure 9-8: N-up printing is quick and easy with the Print dialog box in Mac OS X.

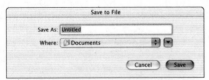

Figure 9-9: Use the Save to File window to save the PDF of your document to your computer.

Managing a Printer's Jobs

The Print Center application is your headquarters for managing each printer's print queue. Open the Print Center (located in the Utilities folder of the Applications folder) and either double-click in the printer list the printer whose queue you want to manage or select the printer and choose Printers⇨Show Jobs (⌘-O) to open a window for that printer's queue, as shown in Figure 9-10.

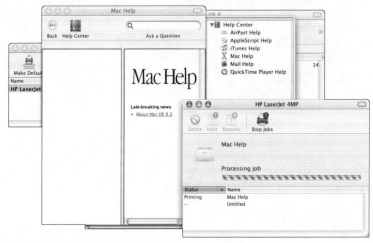

Figure 9-10: Use the Print Center to check the status of a print queue.

Working with Print Jobs

As mentioned earlier, under Setting Print Options, preview any print job by clicking the Preview button in the Print dialog box. When you do so, a temporary file is created and then opened in the Preview application, as shown in Figure 9-11.

This preview is fully formatted as it will appear when your printer finishes processing. Apple's ColorSync technology matches the color profile of your selected printer to your monitor so that you can see how the colors appear (assuming that your ink cartridges or toner cartridges are working as they should). Preview's default is to scale each page to fit on-screen (⌘-=). Select Preview from its Display menu to show pages in their actual size (⌘-A), zoom in (⌘-↑), or zoom out (⌘-↓). You can also turn text anti-aliasing on or off in the File⇨Preferences window (the default setting for anti-aliasing is on).

Note   To make things perfectly clear, each page is fully formatted as it appears in the printout. N-up printing puts multiple pages on a single sheet of paper. N-up layout is *not* reproduced in the preview.

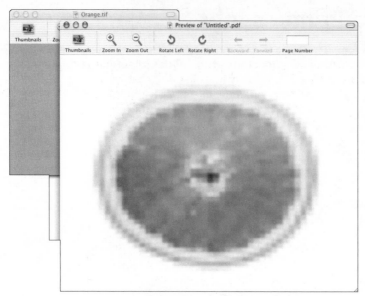

Figure 9-11: The Print dialog box provides true WYSIWYG.

More Print Options

As we mentioned earlier in this chapter, different printers and applications offer additional choices in the Print dialog box's unlabeled pop-up menu. Some more common features offered by common Epson printers include the following:

✦ **Print Settings.** Where you tell the printer driver whether to print in color or black and white, what type of media (paper, film, or transparencies) is being used, and whether to emphasize speed or quality.

✦ **Advanced Settings.** Includes some of the same options as Print Settings (media, color v. black and white, and quality) in addition to Halftoning control, Microweave on or off, and whether to print mirrored (Flip Horizontal).

✦ **Color Management.** Where you specify whether to use ColorSync or to use Color Controls. Selecting the Color Controls radio button makes color controls visible in the window, as shown in Figure 9-12.

✦ **Summary.** Displays a textual accumulation of your settings from all the different panels available.

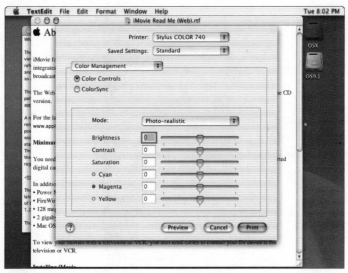

Figure 9-12: Take control of the finest details of your color ink usage.

A LaserWriter driver offers at least the following additional choices:

✦ **Paper Feed.** Enables you to specify the location from where the paper feeds. Set the pages to come from the same source or click the First page from the radio button to choose a specific source for the first page as well as a source for the remaining pages.

✦ **Error Handling.** Enables you to specify whether or not you want a detailed report of any PostScript errors. You can also specify whether to switch trays if one runs out of paper and the printer has more than one tray available.

✦ **Summary.** Provides a textual accumulation of your settings from all the different panels.

Applications often have at least one application-specific menu choice. As an example, BBEdit, a popular text editor among programmers and Web page designers, includes the ability to specify whether to use the font displayed in the document or substitute another font, turn fractional widths (automatic kerning) on, or click the Options button to display the dialog box shown in Figure 9-13.

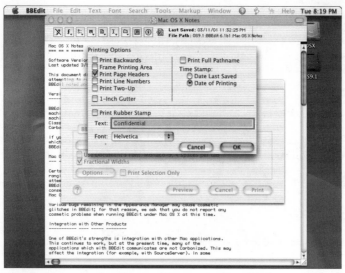

Figure 9-13: BBEdit offers a wide range of application-specific options.

Printing from Classic Applications

Classic applications do not have access to Mac OS X printer drivers or their range of options, such as outputting PDF or previewing your output. Classic applications use the printer drivers available in the Extensions folder of the Classic environment's System Folder. The general procedures for printing, however, are the same in Classic applications as in Mac OS X applications.

As recently as 10.1, no serial printer drivers were available for Mac OS X, including all the venerable StyleWriter printers. Serial printer support has improved significantly since 10.1, though. The Classic environment's System Folder is chock-full of drivers for no-longer manufactured Apple printers. Significantly, though, only a couple of computers qualified to use Mac OS X even have serial ports (in particular the Beige G3), so unless you've added a serial card, that won't be much of an issue. And because your machine is that old, you are already familiar with printing to your printer via Mac OS 9.

This section is geared toward printing from Classic applications for users without that experience. In particular, it covers printing to networked printers because there are far more variations than we could possibly hope to cover in this space. Coverage for USB printers is brief—install your printer driver (if it's not already there) into the Extensions folder of Classic's System Folder using whatever installer your printer manufacturer includes.

Start a Classic application so that you have the Classic menu bar showing and choose Apple⇨Chooser. The left side of the Chooser window displays an icon for each Classic printer driver. After you select your printer driver on the left, the right side of the Chooser window displays a list of available printers or ports. You select the printer you want to use or the port to which the printer is connected. After selecting a printer, close the Chooser. Then, in your various Classic applications, make your Page Setup and Print selections.

Printing to a networked printer from Classic

Networked printers recognized by the Classic environment are PostScript printers, and they use the LaserWriter 8 printer driver. The group of PostScript printers includes all Apple LaserWriters with PostScript, as well as the vast majority of PostScript printers from other manufacturers such as HP, Lexmark, and Tektronix.

To select your default printer, follow these steps:

1. **Launch the Classic application you want to use so that the Classic menu bar is at the top of your screen.**

2. **Choose Apple⇨Chooser.**

3. **Click the LaserWriter 8 driver.** A list of printers appears on the right.

4. **Select your desired printer.**

5. **Close the Chooser.**

Fortunately, the Apple LaserWriter 8 Print dialog box is almost as smart as the Mac OS X Print dialog box. While it won't list all your printers in the Printer pop-up menu, it does list all your available LaserWriter-compatible printers, so you can switch between the LaserWriter-compatible printers there.

Setting LaserWriter 8 Page Setup options

Selecting the Page Setup command for a printer using LaserWriter 8 presents a dialog box with settings for Page Attributes, which is very similar in function to the Mac OS X version in its choices although it looks different (Figure 9-14).

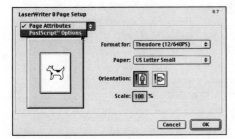

Figure 9-14: Choose a group of options for LaserWriter 8 Page Setup.

The Page Attributes options are almost identical to the Mac OS X choices, with the following exceptions:

✦ Orientation provides only two choices—portrait or landscape. You cannot specify the leading edge for landscape documents.

✦ Generic Printer is not available as a choice.

✦ Scaling is limited to a range of 25% to 400%.

Due to Classic's less-capable graphics engine and font support, you have fewer PostScript options than in OS X, as shown in Figure 9-15.

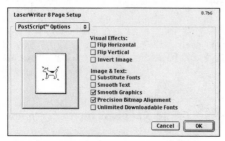

Figure 9-15: Set PostScript Options for LaserWriter 8 Page Setup.

✦ **Flip Horizontal/Flip Vertical.** This option creates mirror images of your document. Your selected option appears in the illustration in the dialog box. Flip Horizontal flips the image right to left, which is useful if you are creating a film image on a Linotronic imagesetter for a transparency or if the pages have to be emulsion side down.

✦ **Invert Image.** This option makes all the black parts of a page print white, and vice versa. You probably won't have much use for this parlor trick unless you create film negatives on a slide printer that has no method of its own for creating negative images.

✦ **Substitute Fonts.** This option substitutes PostScript fonts for any fixed-sized screen fonts for which no PostScript or TrueType equivalent is available (as described in Chapter 12). For example, Geneva becomes Helvetica, Monaco becomes Courier, and New York becomes Times. The one drawback of font substitution is that although the variable-size font is substituted for its fixed-sized cousin, the spacing of letters and words on a line does not change, and the printed results often are remarkably ugly. For the best results, do not use fixed-size fonts that lack TrueType or PostScript equivalents, and leave the Substitute Fonts option off.

✦ **Smooth Text.** This option smoothes the jagged edges of fixed sizes that have no matching PostScript fonts or TrueType fonts. For best results, avoid such fonts, and leave the Smooth Text option off.

✦ **Smooth Graphics.** This option smoothes the jagged edges of bitmap graphic images created with painting programs. Smoothing improves some images, but blurs the detail out of others. Try printing with Smooth Graphics set both ways, and go with the one that looks best to you. This option has no effect on graphics created with drawing programs, such as FreeHand and Illustrator.

✦ **Precision Bitmap Alignment.** This option reduces the entire printed image to avoid minor distortions in bitmap graphics. The distortions occur because of the nature of the dot density of bitmap graphics. For example, 72 dpi (dots-per-inch), the standard screen-image size, does not divide evenly into 300 dpi, 400 dpi, or 600 dpi (the dot density of many laser printers). When you print to a 300-dpi printer, for example, turning on this option reduces page images by 4 percent, effectively printing them at 288 dpi (an even multiple of 72 dpi). The reductions align the bitmaps properly to produce crisper output.

✦ **Unlimited Downloadable Fonts.** This option enables you to use more fonts than your printer's memory can hold at one time. The printing software is able to do this by removing fonts from the printer's memory after they are used, making way for other fonts. Be aware that the constant downloading and flushing of font files takes time and, thus, slows printing. EPS (Encapsulated PostScript) graphics using fonts that are not present elsewhere on the page do not print correctly because the printer substitutes Courier for those orphan fonts. If you see Courier in a graphic where you did not want it, make sure that this option is turned off.

Setting LaserWriter 8 Print options

When you choose the Print command for a printer that uses the LaserWriter 8 driver, you see a dialog box with settings for the number of copies, page numbers to print, paper source, output destination, and more. You switch among several groups of options by choosing a group from the unlabeled pop-up menu near the top of the dialog box. Figure 9-16 illustrates the pop-up menu for switching among groups of options in the Print dialog box for LaserWriter 8.

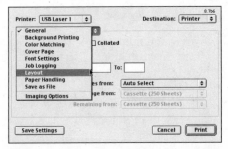

Figure 9-16: You can choose from among many options for LaserWriter 8 printing.

You'll notice that these print settings are almost identical to the choices described earlier for AppleTalk printers under Mac OS X. The differences are as follows:

✦ **Destination pop-up menu.** This menu enables you to choose whether your output is sent to the printer or saved to disk. The ability to select the print job's destination is similar in concept to the Output Options choice under Mac OS X, with the exception that the default save format is PostScript rather than PDF, and that a variety of options is available in the Save as File panel. If you have the Acrobat Distiller software installed, you can select Acrobat PDF as the output format on the Save as File panel.

✦ **Save Settings.** This feature applies only to the current printer and does not allow you to name the set. The last-used settings become the default settings for that printer.

✦ **Background Printing.** This feature enables you to determine whether printing should function as a multitasking operation or whether all other Classic activity should be subordinate to the printing task.

✦ **Cover Page.** This feature enables you to direct the printer to produce a cover page and, if so, whether it should print before or after the document. The cover page reports the document name, your user name, and when it was printed.

✦ **Font Settings.** This option enables you to annotate your PostScript output with comments where font changes are made. It also lets you specify which fonts are downloaded.

✦ **Job Logging.** This feature is the equivalent of the Error Handling choice under Mac OS X.

Unfortunately, because you do not see Desktop Printers while Classic is running and further that the Classic Finder's menu bar never appears, you don't really have any tools for managing the Classic print queue.

Managing the Classic Printing Queue

You can use the PrintMonitor application to view and manage the queue of waiting print requests for some printers that don't have desktop icons. The PrintMonitor application handles printing of waiting print requests while you continue working with other applications. PrintMonitor opens in the background automatically whenever there are print requests in the PrintMonitor Documents folder (inside the System Folder), deletes each print request that it prints, and quits automatically when the PrintMonitor Documents folder is empty.

Some printers made by companies other than Apple come with their own applications for managing the queue of waiting print requests. For instructions on using one of these applications, check the documentation that came with your printer.

Viewing the print queue

While PrintMonitor is open in the background, you can make it the active application by clicking its icon in the Dock. You also can open it at any time by double-clicking its icon, which is located in the Extensions folder of Classic's System Folder. Making PrintMonitor active or opening it displays its window. The PrintMonitor window identifies the print request that is printing, lists the print requests waiting to be printed, and displays the status of the current print request. Figure 9-17 shows the PrintMonitor window.

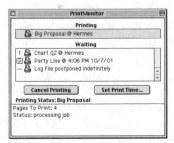

Figure 9-17: View queued print requests from Classic applications in the PrintMonitor window.

PrintMonitor automatically hides its window when you switch to another application, but PrintMonitor remains open in the background as long as it has print requests to process.

Changing the printing order

PrintMonitor ordinarily processes print requests in chronological order, oldest first. You can change the order by dragging print requests in the PrintMonitor window. You drag a print request by its icon, not by its name or sequence number.

Scheduling printing requests

You can schedule when PrintMonitor will process a print request, or you can postpone a print request indefinitely. First, select the print request you want to schedule (by clicking it) in the PrintMonitor window. You can select the print request being printed or any print request waiting to be printed. Then click Set Print Time. Figure 9-18 shows the dialog in which you set a time and date for processing a print request or postpone it indefinitely.

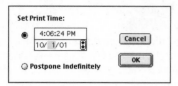

Figure 9-18: Schedule a
specific time for a print request.

A print request scheduled for later printing appears in PrintMonitor's waiting list
with an alarm-clock icon in place of a sequence number. A print request postponed
indefinitely appears in the waiting list with a dash in place of a sequence number,
and it will not be printed until you schedule a print time for it.

Stopping and starting printing

You can suspend all background printing by choosing Stop Printing from
PrintMonitor's File menu. Before PrintMonitor stops printing, it finishes the print
request that it is currently printing. To resume printing, choose Resume Printing
from the File menu.

Setting PrintMonitor preferences

PrintMonitor can notify you when something happens that requires your attention
during background printing. For example, PrintMonitor can notify you when you
need to manually feed paper for background printing. An alert box, a blinking
PrintMonitor icon in the Classic menu bar, or both, can notify you. To specify how
you want to be notified, you use the Preferences command in PrintMonitor's File
menu. Note that if you turn off notification of manual paper feed and forget to feed
paper when the printer needs it, the printer eventually cancels the print request
automatically. Figure 9-19 shows the Preferences dialog box for PrintMonitor.

Figure 9-19: Set PrintMonitor
preferences.

You can also use the Preferences command to specify how you want to be notified about printing errors, such as PrintMonitor not being able to locate a printer that is supposed to print a print request. PrintMonitor can just display a diamond symbol next to its name in the Application menu at the right end of the menu bar, or it can display the symbol and blink its icon in the menu bar, or it can do both of those things plus display an alert. You can turn off everything except the diamond in the Application menu.

Note   Regardless of the notification settings that you make in PrintMonitor's Preferences dialog box, you are always notified that PrintMonitor requires your attention by the PrintMonitor icon bouncing high out of the Dock.

Summary

In this chapter, you've seen how to designate which printers you use in both Mac OS X and Classic. You've also seen how to view and manage their print queues using Print Center in Mac OS X and PrintMonitor in Classic. Other topics covered include creating PDF files rather than a hard-copy printout and previewing your print job as well as a comparison of different printer categories.

✦   ✦   ✦

Accessing Files Via Local Network and Internet

Even though you may own some books and videos, you probably augment your reading and viewing with books borrowed from a library or videos rented from a nearby video store. Similarly, you can work with more files than you have on your computer's disks by sharing files from other users on a network or by downloading files from sources around the world via the Internet.

In this chapter, you learn how to store and share files on an iDisk via the Internet. You also learn how to use files and storage space on file servers located on your local network. In addition, this chapter tells you how to obtain files from the Internet by using a Web browser or an FTP client application.

If your computer isn't already on a network, Chapter 18 explains how to set up your own local network. Chapter 19 describes how you configure Mac OS X for file sharing, and Chapter 20 explains how to allow access to some of your files via FTP or Web pages.

Storing and Sharing Files on an iDisk

An iDisk is one of the major benefits of a .Mac account, the other major iTools benefit being the handy mac.com e-mail account that we introduced in Chapter 6. An iDisk provides 20MB or more of storage space remotely located on an Apple file server. Your computer connects to an iDisk via the

Internet. You can copy files to and from an iDisk, and you can open files directly from an iDisk. You can also share pictures, music, movies, a Web site, and other kinds of files from your iDisk with anyone who has a Web browser on any kind of computer.

Note   If that 20MB iDisk with the free trial membership isn't enough storage space for you, Apple will allocate more space (up to 1GB) for an annual fee of about $50 per 100MB. Visit www.mac.com for more information.

All you need to use an iDisk in Mac OS X is the Finder, which is specially designed to work with an iDisk. This section explains how to sign up for a .Mac account and configure Mac OS X to use it. In addition, this section describes how you connect to an iDisk, work with an iDisk in the Finder, and share files from the iDisk.

Signing up for a .Mac account

The question of signing up for a free trial .Mac account arises during the initial setup process that follows installation of Mac OS X. If you already have a .Mac account at that time, the Setup Assistant program offers to configure Mac OS X to use your account. If you don't already have a .Mac account, the Setup Assistant offers to create one on the spot.

If you haven't already created a .Mac account or if you'd like another .Mac account, you can easily create one now. To do this, perform the following steps:

1. **Start System Preferences.** You can do this by choosing Apple⇨System Preferences or by clicking the System Preferences Dock icon.

2. **Click the Internet button or choose View⇨Internet.**

3. **Click the .Mac tab, and then click the Sign Up button**.

4. **When your Web browser opens and displays the .Mac page, fill in the information requested there, as shown in Figure 10-1.** This page's format could change slightly, but should look very much like what you see here.

5. **Submit the form.**

You are informed if your account request was accepted. If you failed to provide some required information, you are asked to resubmit the form with the missing information included. Another possible reason for a rejected request is if your selected member name is already in use. If that problem arises, you are asked to try a different member name, and .Mac suggests some variations of the one you originally proposed.

After your account exists, you're informed that a copy of your signup information is sent to your new e-mail account, as well. See Chapter 6 for a discussion of using Mail to access your .Mac e-mail. Following that, you are asked whether you want to send announcement iCards (electronic greeting cards) to people informing them of your new e-mail address.

Figure 10-1: Apple's form to create a .Mac account

(Web page courtesy of Apple Computer, Inc.)

Configuring Mac OS X for your .Mac account

When you get a new .Mac account, you can configure Mac OS X to use this particular .Mac account in the Finder and the Mail application. Configuring Mac OS X to use a .Mac account enables you to connect easily to this account's iDisk in the Finder. Configuring Mac OS X to use a .Mac account also sets up the Mail application to use the account for e-mail. To configure Mac OS X for a .Mac account, follow these steps:

1. **Start System Preferences.** Either choose Apple⇨System Preferences or click the System Preferences icon in the Dock.

2. **Click the Internet button or choose View⇨Internet.**

3. **Click the .Mac tab, and then enter your .Mac member name and password.**

Connecting to iDisks with Mac OS X

After configuring Mac OS X for your .Mac account, you can connect to your iDisk with the Finder. You can connect to another iDisk if you know the name and password of the corresponding .Mac account. You can also connect to an iDisk with a Web browser. In addition, you can connect to iDisks by using aliases or Favorites that you have created.

Connecting to your iDisk with the Finder

If you have configured Mac OS X with your .Mac member name and password, you can connect to your iDisk in the Finder by doing either of the following:

✦ Choose Go⇨iDisk or press ⌘-Option-I.

✦ 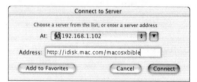 Click the iDisk button in the toolbar of any Finder window. If the iDisk button is not present, you can add it by customizing the toolbar as described in Chapter 4.

Connecting to another iDisk with the Finder

If you have an additional .Mac account, you can connect to this account's iDisk by using the Finder's Connect To Server command. You can also use this command to connect to someone else's iDisk if you know the .Mac member name and password. In either case, proceed as follows:

1. **In the Finder, choose Go⇨Connect To Server.**

2. **Enter the iDisk address in the Address box of the Connect To Server dialog.** This address has the form `http://idisk.mac.com/dotmacname`. Substitute the actual .Mac member name for *dotmacname*. Figure 10-2 shows an example iDisk address entered in the Connect To Server dialog.

3. **In the next dialog, enter the .Mac member name and password, and then click OK.** Figure 10-3 shows the dialog in which you enter the .Mac account information.

Figure 10-2: Enter the Internet address of an iDisk that you want to use.

Figure 10-3: Enter the .Mac member name and password for an iDisk that you want to use.

Connecting to an iDisk with a Web browser

Although the Finder is the most convenient means of connecting to an iDisk, you can also connect by using a Web browser. In the Web browser, go to the .Mac page of the Apple Web site (`www.mac.com`). Click the iDisk link, sign in with your .Mac member name and password, and then click the Open Your Disk button. Your iDisk appears in the Finder.

Connecting to an iDisk with an alias or Favorite

While connected to an iDisk, you can create an alias or Favorite of the iDisk, as described in Chapter 4. After creating an alias of an iDisk, you can connect to the iDisk again by double-clicking its alias. After making a Favorite of an iDisk, you can connect to the iDisk again by choosing it from the Favorites submenu of the Go menu. In either case, you have to enter the .Mac member name and password as shown previously in Figure 10-3.

Viewing an iDisk

If you double-click an iDisk, it opens and you see a regular Finder window containing several folders, some of which have the same names as the standard folders of your home folder. You also see a document that you can open to read what Apple has to say about iDisks. You may notice that items appear slowly in an iDisk window. The iDisk performance is limited by the speed of your Internet connection. However, Mac OS X improves subsequent performance of the iDisk by caching a directory of the iDisk contents. Figure 10-4 shows the folders of an iDisk.

Figure 10-4: See and work with an iDisk in a Finder window.

Copying items to and from an iDisk

You can copy files and folders to and from an iDisk just as you would copy files to and from any other disk. For example, you can copy an item by dragging it from one Finder window that shows your home folder to another Finder window that shows a folder on an iDisk. Be prepared for the copying to take a while. Copying to or from an iDisk goes only at the speed of your Internet connection, which is far slower than the speed of your computer's hard drive or CD-ROM drive.

Opening files

Rather than copy files from an iDisk and then open the copies from your home folder, you can open files directly from an iDisk. An iDisk is just another disk, and files on it can be opened using the usual methods for opening files from your home folder. Opening a file from an iDisk takes longer than opening the same file from your hard drive because the file contents are transferred at the speed of your Internet connection. Therefore you should avoid opening applications or large documents directly from an iDisk. Figure 10-5 shows a document file being opened directly from an iDisk.

Getting software from an iDisk

One folder in every iDisk, the Software folder, doesn't actually take up any of the 20MB allotted to the iDisk. The Software folder works like an alias, giving you access to a number of applications from Apple and third-party software developers, which you may find useful. The exciting part of the Software folder is that some of this software is specifically for Mac OS X users. Because the contents of this folder are constantly changing, we're not going to enumerate the files in it. Just remember that it is a handy place to look for software — from games to productivity tools. To use an application from the Software folder, copy the application's disk image or installer file to your Applications folder or your home folder. Then double-click the copied file to install the software.

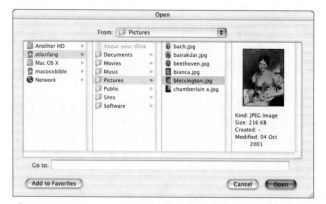

Figure 10-5: You can open files directly from an iDisk.

Caution   Be aware that many of the applications from the Software folder are without any warranty of fitness and can even be preliminary or limited versions of commercial products. Read the accompanying documentation files before installing the application.

Creating a Web site on an iDisk

You can create a Web site in the Sites folder of your iDisk by using the HomePage part of the .Mac Web site. You can also use Web authoring applications, such as BBEdit (BareBones Software, www.barebones.com), GoLive (Adobe Systems, www.adobe.com), or Dreamweaver (Macromedia, www.macromedia.com) to create files for the Sites folder of your iDisk. All the files comprising your Web site go into the Sites folder.

Anyone can visit the Web site by pointing a Web browser at http://homepage. mac.com/*dotmacname*, where your .Mac member name replaces *dotmacname* in the URL.

Sharing files from your iDisk

The Public folder of your iDisk is interesting because it enables you to share files with other Internet users. Anything you place in this folder is automatically available to any Mac user who has a .Mac account and knows your .Mac member name. Other Mac users can see and copy files from the Public folder of your iDisk. Only you can change the contents of your Public folder. Conversely, you can see and copy, but can't change, files in the Public folder of anyone else's iDisk. Mac users access someone else's iDisk Public folders as follows:

✦ Anyone using Mac OS X 10.1 can see and copy files in an iDisk Public folder by choosing Connect to Server from the Finder's Go menu and entering the address http://idisk.mac.com/*dotmacname*/Public where *dotmacname* is the .Mac member name.

Note　No one needs to know your .Mac password to access the Public folder of your iDisk. All anyone needs to know is your .Mac member name.

✦ Additionally, you can make your iDisk Public folder available to anyone who is using a Web browser on any kind of computer. You do this by using the HomePage part of the .Mac Web site to create your own File Sharing Web page. You must have something in your iDisk Public Folder to share before you start to create the File Sharing page.

To create your iDisk File Sharing page, proceed as follows:

1. **Use a Web browser to navigate to the main .Mac page at** www.mac.com **and log in.**

2. **On the page that appears, click the HomePage icon at the top of the page.**

3. **Click a tab in the left column to choose a category and then click on a theme in that category to choose it.** Choosing a theme is shown in Figures 10-6 and 10-7. For this example, click on the left-side tab *Newsletter*.

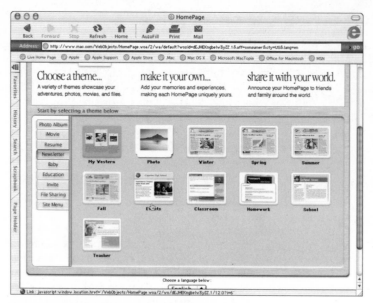

Figure 10-6: Choose a category of themes.
(Web page courtesy of Apple Computer, Inc.)

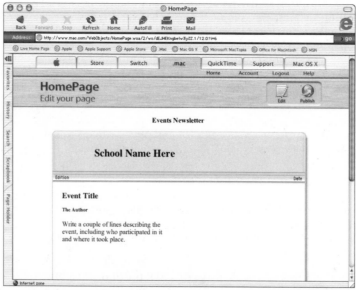

Figure 10-7: Select a theme and color scheme for your sharing page.
(Web page courtesy of Apple Computer, Inc.)

4. **Click a theme.** For this example, click the Newsletter theme. Selecting a theme results in displaying a template page, as shown in Figure 10-8.

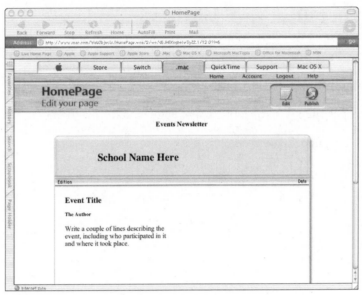

Figure 10-8: Customize the page name and labels.
(Web page courtesy of Apple Computer, Inc.)

5. **Click the Edit button to customize the name and the display information.**
   Edit the text in the various text boxes to provide the information you want to present.

6. **Click Preview to see what the page will look like or click Publish to finalize the operation and make the page available to others.** If you click Preview and don't like what you see, you can return to Step 5.

Using your iDisk with Mac OS 9

Even if you normally use Mac OS X, you may occasionally need to use your iDisk on a Mac OS 9 computer. With Mac OS 9, you can connect to your iDisk by using the Chooser or the Network Browser.

✦ In the Chooser, click the AppleShare icon and then click the Server IP Address button. Next enter `idisk.mac.com` as the server address. Then enter the .Mac member name and password.

✦ In the Network Browser, choose Connect to iDisk from the Shortcuts pop-up menu, or choose Connect To Server from the Shortcuts pop-up menu and enter `idisk.mac.com` as the server address. Then enter the .Mac member name and password.

Using your iDisk with Microsoft Windows

If you're not near a Mac and need a file from your iDisk, you can open your iDisk on a computer with Microsoft Windows XP, Windows ME, Windows 98, or Windows 2000.

✦ In Windows XP, open My Network Places and under Network Tasks, click Add a network place. The Add Network Place Wizard leads you through the process of creating a shortcut to a Web Folder. As the location of the Web Folder, enter http://idisk.Mac.com/*itoolsname* where *itoolsname* is your .Mac member name.

✦ In Windows ME or Windows 98, double-click the My Computer icon, double-click the Web Folders icon, and double-click Add Web Folder. As the location to add, enter http://idisk.Mac.com/*itoolsname* where *itoolsname* is your .Mac member name.

✦ In Windows 2000, open My Computer, choose Map Network Drive from the Tools menu, and click "Web folder or FTP site." As the location to add, enter http://idisk.Mac.com/*itoolsname* where *itoolsname* is your .Mac member name.

Disconnecting an iDisk

When you finish using an iDisk, you can disconnect it by dragging its icon to the Trash. When you drag an iDisk in Mac OS X, the Trash icon changes to look like an Eject symbol (triangle with a line below it) and its name changes to Disconnect. Disconnecting an iDisk removes it from the Finder.

You can leave an iDisk connected as long as you like. Connection time is unlimited in Mac OS X. (In Mac OS 9, connection time is limited to one hour, or 30 minutes of inactivity.)

Connecting to File Servers

If your computer is connected to a network, you may be able to work with files and use storage space located on other network computers. Because these computers provide files and storage space, they are known as *file servers.* A file server may be a computer that no one uses for personal work because it is dedicated to providing network services. A file server can also be someone's personal computer that is set up to share its files with other network computers.

To use either kind of file server (dedicated server or a file sharing computer), all you need is the Finder. With the Finder, you can connect to a file server, mount server volumes, see your access privileges on the server volumes, and copy files.

You can also use the Finder to open files from a server, or you can open server files directly in other applications. When you're finished using a server, you use the Finder to disconnect it.

All these aspects of using file servers are covered in this section. As we mentioned at the beginning of the chapter, Chapter 18 has information on creating a local network, and Chapter 19 has information on setting up your Mac to share its files.

Connecting with the Go menu

As mentioned in Chapter 3, the Finder's Go menu includes a choice to Connect To Server (⌘-K). Choosing Go⇨Connect To Server presents (surprise) the Connect to Server dialog. This dialog may be collapsed or expanded — to hide or show a list of networks and file servers — by clicking the disclosure button next to the At pop-up menu. When the dialog is expanded, you can drag its resize control to see more or fewer columns of the central list. Figure 10-9 shows both states of the Connect To Server dialog.

Note
You may think that the Network icon at the Computer level in the Finder would be your path to servers on the network. That assumption is correct only if your network has a NetInfo server and a network administrator has configured your computer to use it. Otherwise, you use the Connect To Server dialog.

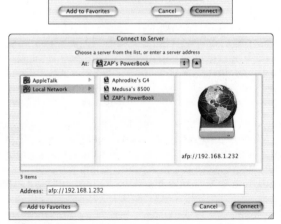

Figure 10-9: Connect to a file server or a file sharing Mac by using the Connect To Server dialog.

Connecting to AppleTalk File Servers

Mac OS X normally uses the TCP/IP protocol to communicate with AppleShare file servers and file sharing computers. However, many AppleShare file servers still use the AppleTalk protocol that was the standard for Mac file servers during the 15 years prior to Mac OS X. Beginning with Mac OS X version 10.1, Mac OS X can use both TCP/IP and AppleTalk for file servers and file sharing. But Mac OS X does not use AppleTalk unless it was activated when your computer was set up for a network. If you don't see AppleTalk listed above Local Network in the Connect To Server dialog, then you need to activate AppleTalk before you can connect to file servers and file sharing computers that use it. You make AppleTalk active in the Network pane of System Preferences, as described in Chapter 18.

The AppleTalk address of a file server is different from a TCP/IP address, because AppleTalk identifies file servers by name. If a file server's AppleTalk name includes spaces or symbols, these elements have to be encoded in the Address box of the Connect To Server dialog. For example, the AppleTalk address of a file server whose name is Aphrodite's G4 would appear as `afp:/at/Aphrodite%d5s%20G4` in the Address box. The code `%d5` stands for an apostrophe, and the code `%20` stands for a space. (These codes are based on ASCII code of the character, expressed as a hexadecimal number.)

Note that the AppleTalk address of an AppleShare file server or file sharing computer begins with `afp:/` protocol identifier. This is similar to the `afp://` protocol identifier that begins the TCP/IP address of an AppleShare file server. However, the AppleTalk address has only one slash after the colon.

Besides the disclosure button and the obvious Cancel and Connect buttons, the Connect To Server dialog includes the following items:

✦ **At pop-up menu.** Lists file servers (both dedicated servers and file sharing computers) that you have used recently and file servers that you have made favorites. Choose a file server from this pop-up menu to connect to the server. If this pop-up menu includes any favorite servers, it also includes a Remove From Favorites choice. Choosing Remove From Favorites displays a dialog in which you can select one or more favorite servers and remove them as favorites.

✦ **List of networks and file servers.** The left column lists networks that may have file servers that Mac OS can connect to. If you select a network on the left, a list of file servers (both dedicated servers and file sharing computers) appears on the right. The list of servers may take a little while to appear, depending on the characteristics of the network. This list appears only in the expanded dialog.

Note   If your Mac has file sharing turned on, you see your Mac listed as one of the file servers on the network.

✦ **Address box.** Displays the address of the file server that's currently selected in the At pop-up menu or in the list of file servers. The first part of the address, `afp://`, designates the AppleShare file protocol. Mac OS file sharing and Mac file servers commonly use this protocol to communicate with computers wanting file service.

You can also enter an address directly in this box. For example, entering `afp://192.168.1.33` would connect you to the file server (or file sharing computer) whose IP address is 192.168.1.33.

✦ **Add to Favorites.** Click this button to make the currently selected file server a favorite.

Identifying yourself to the file server

After selecting a file server and clicking Connect in the Connect To Server dialog, an unnamed dialog appears in which you identify yourself as a guest or a registered user of the file server. Figure 10-10 shows an example of this identification dialog.

Figure 10-10: Establish your identity as a guest or registered user of a file server.

To connect as a registered user, select the Registered User option and enter your registered name and password in the dialog. The owner of the file server that you want to access must have assigned this name and password. If your own computer is set up as a file server (using file sharing, as described in Chapter 19) and you're connecting to it from another computer, enter your account name and password. When you enter your password, you must type it exactly right, including uppercase and lowercase letters (it's case-sensitive). Then click OK.

If you're not a registered user and the Guest option isn't disabled (grayed out), you can connect to the file server without entering a name and password. However, guests usually have far fewer privileges on a file server than registered users. If the Guest option is disabled, guests are not permitted to access the file server. If you don't have a registered name and password for the file server, ask its owner to give you one.

Connecting to AppleTalk-TCP/IP File Servers

Some file servers can communicate using AppleTalk and TCP/IP. You see these dual-protocol file servers listed in two places in the Connect To Server dialog. When you select AppleTalk in this dialog's list of networks, you see the dual-protocol file servers listed among the AppleTalk file servers. Likewise when you select TCP/IP in the list of networks, you see the dual-protocol file servers listed among the TCP/IP file servers.

If the same file server appears in the AppleTalk list and the TCP/IP list, you should select the file server in the TCP/IP list. The TCP/IP protocol is faster than the AppleTalk protocol.

For best performance, a file server that can use TCP/IP should be configured to use this protocol in addition to or instead of AppleTalk. For example, a Mac OS 9 computer with file sharing turned on normally uses AppleTalk but can be configured to also use TCP/IP. To configure a Mac OS 9 computer for TCP/IP file sharing, open its File Sharing control panel and turn on the option labeled "Enable File Sharing clients to connect over TCP/IP" as shown in the following figure.

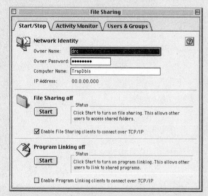

Set Mac OS 9 file sharing to use TCP/IP
in the File Sharing control panel.

On a related note, a Mac OS X computer can launch applications that are located on a Mac OS 9 computer that has both file sharing and program linking turned on. The applications run in the Classic environment. For best performance, you should configure Mac OS 9 to use TCP/IP for program linking. You do this in the File Sharing control shown here by turning on the option labeled "Enable Program Linking clients to connect over TCP/IP."

Setting preferences for file server connections

While identifying yourself as a registered user or guest, you can change some preference settings for the file server connection. You may also be able to change your password for the server. You make these changes by clicking the Options button in the identification dialog shown in Figure 10-10. Clicking this button presents another dialog in which you can specify how your password is transmitted. You can also decide whether you want the password added to your Keychain, which saves you the trouble of entering them every time you connect to the server. (The Keychain is discussed in detail later in this chapter.) If you click the Save Preferences button, the current settings become the default settings for future file server connections. If you click the Change Password button, yet another dialog appears in which you make the change. Click OK to return to the identification dialog. Figure 10-11 shows the preference settings dialog.

Figure 10-11: Set preferences for a file server connection.

Selecting network volumes

When you connect to a server, you see another dialog. This dialog tells you the name of the server to which you're connecting and the various volumes on that server that you can mount, as shown in Figure 10-12.

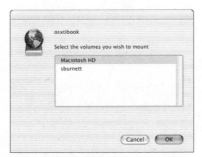

Figure 10-12: Select the volumes you want to mount from the file server.

Connecting as a registered user gives you the choice of any folders or volumes to which you have access as one of the following:

✦ Any folders or volumes to which the owner or a member of the access group has access

✦ Any folders or volumes to which everybody else has access

✦ The Public folders of all other accounts on that Mac OS X machine

If the server allows Guest access and you choose to connect as a Guest, you get to choose from the Public folders, and any folders and volumes to which everybody else has access are enabled. Refer to Chapter 4 for more discussion of access privileges, which are set in the Finder's Info window.

Connecting with an alias or Favorite

After mounting a server volume, you can make an alias of the volume or add it to your Favorites. If you expect to use a server volume in the future, making it a Favorite or creating an alias streamlines the connection and mounting process. Opening an alias or a favorite skips the Connect To Server dialog and takes you straight to the server identification dialog shown previously in Figure 10-10. What's more, you can connect to a server and mount a volume by selecting its alias or Favorite in an Open dialog or a Save dialog. However, when you select an alias or Favorite of a server volume in an Open dialog or a Save dialog, the server identification dialog may not appear on top of the Open or Save dialog. If this happens, you hear the system alert sound when you click anywhere in the Open or Save dialogs. To work around this situation, drag the Open dialog or Save dialog to the bottom of the screen, revealing the server identification dialog behind it.

To add a server to your Favorites, select its icon and choose File⇨Add To Favorites (⌘-T). To create an alias, select the icon and choose File⇨Make Alias (⌘-L) or Control-click the icon and choose Make Alias from the contextual menu.

Connecting to Microsoft Windows File Servers

In a world dominated by Microsoft Windows (at least on the computing front), being able to access files on a Windows file server is important. Beginning with Mac OS X version 10.1, you can use the Connect To Server dialog to connect to Microsoft Windows file servers. These include Windows NT file servers, Windows 2000 file servers, and Windows 98 computers with file sharing turned on.

In Mac OS X 10.1, Windows file servers don't appear in the list of networks and file servers that's displayed in the middle of the expanded Connect To Server dialog. You have to enter the file server's address in the Address box. The address of a Windows file server has the form `smb://server/share/` where `server` is the name or IP address of the file server and `share` is the name of the volume or folder that you want to connect to. For example, the address `smb://192.168.1.2/Public/` would connect to the Public folder of the Windows file server whose IP address is 192.168.1.2. If you use a file server's name instead of its IP address, you may need to type the name in all capital letters.

After entering the address of a Windows file server and clicking Connect in the Connect To Server dialog, another dialog appears in which you specify your workgroup or domain, username, and password on the Windows file server, as shown in the following figure.

Identify yourself when connecting
to a Windows file server.

If any problems occur that prevent connecting to a Windows file server, an alert appears saying no file services are available at the address you specified. This message may indeed mean the Windows file server is not available. The message also occurs if you simply mistype the address, workgroup, username, or password. Note that Mac OS X 10.1 can't connect to a Windows file server if the server name or share name includes any spaces, even if you encode them as %20.

To simplify future connections to a Windows file server, enter its address in the Connect To Server dialog and click Add to Favorites. Next time you want to connect to the same file server, you can choose it from the At pop-up menu and avoid retyping the address.

For a different experience connecting to Windows file servers, you can try the DAVE 4 software from Thursby Systems (www.thursby.com). Other products enable Mac OS 9 to access Windows file servers, including MacSOHO from Thursby and DoubleTalk from Connectix Corporation (www.connectix.com).

Yet another alternative is to install software on the Windows computer to make it an AppleShare file server. If you do this, the Windows computer appears in the list of servers together with Mac file servers and Mac OS file sharing computers. One product that provides AppleShare service in Windows is PC MACLAN from Miramar Systems (www.miramarsys.com).

Recognizing your access privileges

Just as you can recognize your access privileges to folders on your Mac in the Finder, the same indicators are present for server volumes and the folders they contain. The symbols for each type of privilege and description of access are as follows:

✦ **Read Only.** A small icon that looks like a pencil with a line through it appears in the Status Bar for a folder or volume where you can see the contents but may not change them.

✦ **No Access.** A folder icon with a circled red minus sign in the lower-right corner is a volume or folder that you cannot open or otherwise manipulate.

✦ **Write-only access.** A circled blue down arrow in the lower-right corner marks a *drop box* folder. You can put files into a drop box, but you cannot open it.

Figure 10-13 shows examples of these folder icons and the read-only indicator in the Status Bar.

Figure 10-13: Special folder icons and an icon in the status bar indicate your access privileges.

Transferring network files

When you're working with files that reside on other computers on the network, you are limited by the speed of the network for every read and write operation. Working with files on your local disk is much faster.

Because Mac OS X treats mounted server volumes as though they are local disks, you can drag files to or from a server volume to copy them.

Opening network files

Because Mac OS X treats mounted server volumes exactly as though they are local disks, you can navigate to them in an Open dialog, as shown in Figure 10-14, and open them. Similarly, you can save to the network server in a Save dialog.

Figure 10-14: Open a file from a server just as though it is a local disk.

Disconnecting from network volumes and servers

 When you finish using a network volume, you can remove it from the Finder by using any of the following methods:

✦ Drag the volume's icon to the Disconnect icon in the Dock. (The Trash icon changes to a Disconnect icon when you're dragging a network volume.)

✦ Control-click the volume's icon and choose Eject from the contextual menu.

✦ Select the volume's icon and choose File⇨Eject (⌘-E).

Removing a network volume from the Finder is also known as *unmounting* (not dismounting) the volume.

Disconnecting from a network file server involves no more than removing all that server's volumes from the Finder.

Using the Keychain

Virtually every file server to which you connect, some of the Web sites you visit, and a number of network services you invoke require you to identify yourself with a name and a password. These combinations of name and password are called *access keys.* or just *keys* for short. If other people can guess your keys easily, the main reason for having keys — security — is subverted. Similarly, if you use the same key for multiple accounts, anyone who obtains the key to one account can access the rest of your accounts — again, not a good thing. The difficulty with using multiple keys is the inconvenience of having to remember multiple not-easily-guessed keys and further, to remember which keys go with which account.

Apple developed a *keychain* technology to help you keep track of your various account names and passwords. In fact, the keychain can automatically provide your name and password as needed. Apple first introduced the concept of a keychain with System 7 Pro's AOCE (Apple Open Collaborative Environment), also known as PowerTalk, a decade ago. Because AOCE's acceptance was less than inspiring, even the well-liked pieces, such as the keychain, were not widely used. PowerTalk disappeared from Apple System Software releases after System 7.5.5. Apple revived the keychain in Mac OS 9 and, because it didn't bring with it the overhead and clumsiness of AOCE, many more users started taking advantage of it. Now, with Mac OS X, the keychain continues to be even better integrated with Mac OS and its software.

You can use keychains to hold passwords for applications, Web sites, and servers. When you launch the application or connect to the server or Web site, your keychain supplies the password so that you don't have to type it — providing that you are using keychain-aware software.

Note   It is really somewhat sad that Microsoft did not make Internet Explorer 5.2, the version included with Mac OS X 10.2, keychain-savvy. Instead, Internet Explorer uses its own mechanism for storing and retrieving passwords — one neither as secure nor as easy to use as Apple's keychain.

Initially, Mac OS X creates a default keychain, whose name is the same as your login account's short name, and a password that matches your login password. When you log in to Mac OS X, this keychain is automatically unlocked for you. You're not limited to just this one keychain, though. You can create multiple keychains to store password information for different purposes if you desire. One reason to create multiple keychains is if you wish to segregate some groups of keys from the rest and not have all your keys accessible at the same time. You may not want your spouse to know your keys for certain FTP sites, but might also need to make the keys for other sites available.

Copying a keychain to another computer

If you want to use a keychain from your computer on another Mac OS X computer, you simply copy the keychain file. The usual location for keychain files is the Keychains folder in the Library folder of your home folder (path ~/Library/Keychains). You can copy a keychain to a Zip disk or other media, and then to another Mac OS X computer. The steps are as follows:

1. **Copy your keychain to a location (such as a removable disk) that you can access from the other computer.**

2. **Open Keychain Access on the other computer (in the Utilities folder of its Applications folder).**

3. **Choose Edit⇨Keychain List.**

4. **Click Add and select your keychain.**

Creating a keychain

If you want to create additional keychains, you do so with the Keychain Access application, which is in the Utilities folder of your Applications folder. Launch Keychain Access and choose File⇨New⇨New Keychain. In the regular Save dialog that appears, enter a name for your new keychain, select a location for it, and click the Save button. Figure 10-15 shows the Save dialog for creating a keychain.

Figure 10-15: Name the keychain you're creating.

After a moment, the New Keychain Passphrase dialog appears. Decide on a password or phrase that you want to unlock the keychain, and enter it in both text boxes. The passphrase can be up to 255 characters in length and is case-sensitive. As with all passwords, this should be something that you can remember and that you can type "blind" but will not be easily guessed by others. Click the disclosure triangle labeled Details to see the location of the keychain and the identity of the application that is creating it. Figure 10-16 shows the New Keychain Passphrase dialog.

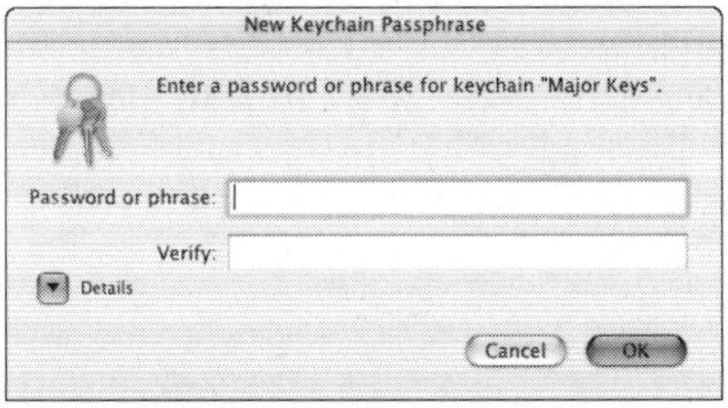

Figure 10-16: Enter the passphrase for your new keychain twice.

Adding an item to your keychain

After you enter the identical passphrase twice and clicked OK, Keychain Access displays your new keychain's window. Initially, it is empty.

To add items to your keychain, select File⇨New⇨New Password Item to show the New Password Item dialog (Figure 10-17). Click the Show Typing checkbox to see what characters you're typing in the Password textbox, rather than the bullet characters normally displayed. When you're done, click Add. Keychain Access presents a dialog asking for the passphrase to the keychain to which you're adding this item.

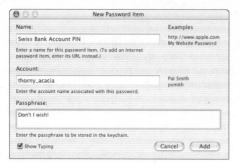

Figure 10-17: Specify access information and name the item you're adding in the New Password Item dialog.

Tip

If you want the keychain whose window is in front to be your default keychain (the one automatically unlocked when you log in to Mac OS X), choose File➪Make *"keychain name"* Default.

Locking and unlocking your keychain

When a keychain is unlocked, all items in it are available to keychain-aware applications; however, if the keychain is locked, the items are unavailable until you unlock the keychain by entering the passphrase when prompted.

Locking a keychain is simple. In the keychain's window in Keychain Access, click the Lock button. When the keychain is locked, the detail information is hidden and the button's name changes to Unlock. You can also lock a keychain by choosing File➪Lock *"keychain name"* (⌘-L) and can lock all keychains by choosing File➪Lock All Keychains.

Managing keychain items

After adding items to your keychain, you need to consider keeping them up-to-date. For example, periodically changing your passwords is considered good practice for security reasons. Alternatively, you may want to remove keys to file servers or Web sites that no longer exist.

Removing a keychain item is easy. In the Keychain Access window, select the item you want to delete and click the Remove button.

As in the Finder, Keychain Access enables you to view information for keychain items. Select the item and view its information in the bottom of the Keychain window. The two tabs show Attributes (Figure 10-18) and Access Control (Figure 10-19).

Figure 10-18: The Attributes tab of Keychain Access shows general information about a selected keychain item.

Attributes tab

In the Attributes tab, you can click the Show Passphrase button to see the item's password. In this pane, you are also shown the kind of item it is (application, Internet, AppleShare, and so on), where it is located, to which account it belongs, when it was created, and when last modified. You also are presented with a Comments text box where you can enter information about the item (such as a URL for named Web server items). If the item mounts a file server or makes an Internet connection, a Go There button appears to the right of the Show Passphrase button.

Figure 10-19: The Access Control tab of Keychain Access allows different levels of security for keychain items in the same keychain.

Access Control tab

In the Access Control tab, you find an option labeled "Always allow access to this item." If this option is not selected, you are always prompted for confirmation, including prompting for your keychain password, on any attempt to access this item. You can specify applications that always have access to this keychain item by adding the applications to the list in the "Always allow access by these applications" pane. Then set the approved applications using the Add and Remove buttons.

Changing keychain settings

You can set conditions under which your keychain automatically locks, and you can change the password for a keychain by choosing Edit⇨"*keychain name*" Settings.

In the Change "*keychain name*" Settings dialog (Figure 10-20), select the first option to set a timespan before the keychain automatically locks. Select the second option to automatically lock the keychain when the system goes to sleep. Clicking the Change Password button presents a dialog identical to the one shown previously in Figure 10-16 where you set the passphrase for a new keychain.

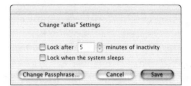

Figure 10-20: Control the settings for automatically locking a keychain or change a keychain's password in this dialog.

Downloading Files from the Internet

In addition to using files from file servers and iDisks, you can obtain useful (and sometimes, absolutely frivolous) files on the Internet from other computers all over the world. The process of copying files from the Internet to your computer is called *downloading*. Similarly, if you send a file from your computer, you are *uploading* the file.

On the Internet, files are commonly sent using a protocol called *File Transfer Protocol* (FTP). A computer can make files available using this protocol by running a type of program called an *FTP server*. This term also refers to the combination of the server program and the computer that's running it. You may sometimes hear people refer to an *FTP site*, which is a collection of files on an FTP server that are available for downloading. An FTP site has the same function on the Internet as a file server on your network.

To receive or send files using this protocol, you use software called an *FTP client* on your computer. The FTP client connects your computer to an FTP server and handles downloading and uploading (receiving and sending) the files. An FTP client has the same function on an FTP site as Finder has with a file server or an iDisk.

Most Web browsers include FTP functionality, so if you encounter an FTP link to a file while browsing the Web, you don't have to use another application to download the file. For the occasional file, a Web browser's capabilities are more than adequate. If you have occasion to download many files from an FTP server, a dedicated FTP client application is a good investment. Similarly, the dedicated clients are much better if you want to upload files to an FTP server.

Getting ready to download

Before you can download a file, you have to know where it is and what protocol is needed to access it. This is where the URL comes in — URLs specify both the protocol and the location. Further, you should specify where you want the downloaded files saved. Some applications use the download location specified in the Internet pane of System Preferences, while other applications have their own settings.

Setting a download location with Internet Preferences

One place to make this specification is in the Internet pane of System Preferences. Proceed as follows:

1. **In System Preferences, click the Internet button or choose View⇨ Internet.** You see the Internet pane of System Preferences, shown in Figure 10-21.

2. **Click the Web tab and then specify the path to the folder where you want downloaded files to go.** You can do this by clicking the Select button, and then in the dialog that appears, navigating to the desired folder and clicking the Select button in the dialog. The path to the folder that you selected appears in the Internet Preferences window in the box labeled Download Files To. Alternatively, you can type a path directly into this box.

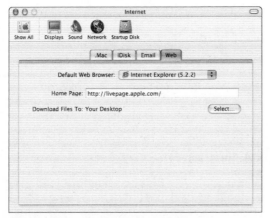

Figure 10-21: Specify the folder you prefer for downloaded files by using the Internet pane of System Preferences.

Setting a download folder for Internet Explorer

Unfortunately, the settings in Internet Preferences are ignored by many Web browsers, notably Internet Explorer 5.2, which is included with Mac OS X 10.2. To specify the folder where you want Internet Explorer to download files, follow these steps:

1. **In Internet Explorer, choose Preferences from the Explorer menu and then click Download Options on the left side of the Preferences dialog.** Figure 10-22 shows the Browser Display section of Internet Explorer's Preferences dialog.

2. **Click Change Location and then select folder where you want Internet Explorer to put downloaded files.**

3. **Click OK to make your change effective.**

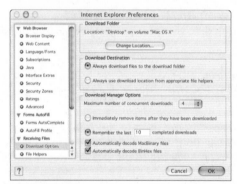

Figure 10-22: Internet Explorer 5.2 has its own setting for the folder where downloaded files go.

Setting a download location for other applications

Other applications ignore the settings in the Internet pane of System Preferences, and they have their own preference settings for download locations. If you want to change these download locations, you must change each application's preferences settings separately. Use the procedure just described for Internet Explorer for guidance.

Downloading with a Web browser

As you browse the Web, you see links to files that you can download. When you come across a link to an interesting file, click the link. The Web browser starts file transfer while displaying the progress in a file-transfer status window. Figure 10-23 shows an example of such a transfer in Internet Explorer.

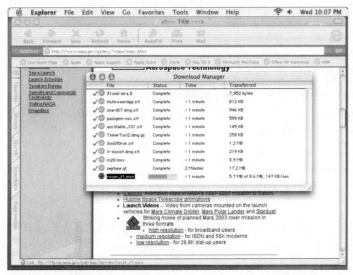

Figure 10-23: Internet Explorer's Download Manager window shows downloading progress.

Transferring files with an FTP client application

When you download files with a Web browser, you have to click a different link for each file you download. Further, most Web browsers cannot upload files to an FTP server. The FTP client applications come into play here. Three of the most popular FTP client applications are Fetch, Interarchy, and Transmit.

Downloading with Interarchy

Interarchy is a terrific Internet tool by Peter N. Lewis — Australian Mac wizard. It has been known, in previous incarnations, as Anarchie and Anarchie Pro. Interarchy is $45 from Stairways Software (www.stairways.com).

Handling not only FTP but also HTTP transfers, Interarchy starts you out with the control window shown at the bottom left of the screen in Figure 10-24. Clicking FTP presents the FTP dialog shown in the upper left of the screen. Stairways (Interarchy's distributor) even provides a set of Bookmarks to commonly used Mac Web sites and allows you to add your favorite sites, displayable in the Bookmarks window (Home⇨List Bookmarks).

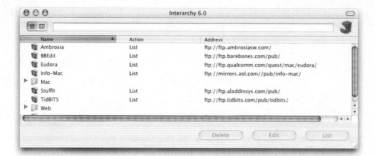

Figure 10-24: Interarchy has a straightforward basic interface with some presupplied bookmarks to get you started.

After you enter your FTP information in the FTP dialog, click the List button (use the Save button to add it as a bookmark). Interarchy connects to your FTP server and displays a window listing all the files and directories immediately accessible. This window works very much like a Finder window in that you can drag items to or from, initiate transfers, and open directories and access their contents (just double-click the folder icons). Indicative of Interarchy's origins "down under," the pointer changes to a hopping kangaroo, rather than the traditional spinning wheel to indicate when the application is busy.

Downloading with Fetch

One of the first FTP clients for the Mac, Fetch was developed by Dartmouth University. Now Fetch Softworks (www.fetchsoftworks.com) owns the application and has enhanced Fetch to Version 4.0.1 for Mac OS X 10.1. Fetch costs $25.

After specifying the FTP server and your login information in the initial window, Fetch presents a window, such as the one shown in Figure 10-25. Double-click a folder in the list to display its contents and then use the pop-up menu at the top of the window to move back up the folder hierarchy.

To download files, you can either double-click them or select one (or more) and click the Get button. Use the Put Files button to specify the files you want to upload to the current folder.

Alternatively, you can download files by dragging them from the list to a folder on your disk or to the Desktop. Similarly, you can upload files by dragging them from the Finder to the Fetch window's list.

Fetch lets you maintain a list of shortcuts to frequently visited sites. In addition, Fetch lets you use the Mac OS X keychain to automatically provide your name and password for any FTP site.

Figure 10-25: Download files from a Fetch window by dragging them to the Finder.

Downloading with Transmit

Formerly known as Transit, Transmit (from Panic Software, www.panic.com) is a $24.95 FTP client application. Opening Transmit presents a window with a Fetch-like view of your Mac on the left and a login pane on the right. After you connect to an FTP server, the login pane is replaced by another Fetch-like view — this time of the FTP server, as shown in Figure 10-26. Drag files and folders from one pane to the other to transfer files. Progress is displayed at the bottom of the window and, if you want more information, click the disclosure triangle to show more information about the file being transferred, the connection, and host. Drag items to the wastebasket icon to remove them.

Using the Terminal application

If you don't want to use a graphical FTP client, you do have an FTP capability provided in Mac OS X's Unix underpinnings. You can use the FTP command on the Unix command line in the Terminal application. See Chapter 26 for more information on Terminal and Unix.

Figure 10-26: Drag and drop between panes of a Transmit window to transfer files via FTP.

The FTP command is a fully functional FTP client, but detailing its options and syntax are something beyond the scope of this discussion. You can read about the FTP command in its online documentation, which is part of the *man pages* Unix documentation included with Mac OS X. (We cover man pages in Chapter 26.)

Decoding and decompressing files

Generally, files downloaded from the Internet require conversion to a format that your Mac can utilize. This file conversion is necessary for several reasons. For one, Mac OS files can have two parts, called *forks,* plus Finder information that must all be combined into a one-part file for transfer over the Internet, which can't handle two-part files. In addition, *binary* files — pictures, formatted text, music, movies, and application programs, and all others except plain text — are encoded as plain text files on some FTP and Web servers.

The most common encoding used for Mac files is called *BinHex* (short for Binary to Hexadecimal). Other encodings include *uuencode* (Unix-to-Unix encoding) and *mime* (Multipurpose Internet Mail Extensions), also known as Base 64. All encodings increase the amount of data being transferred because they have to represent strings of bits by using a set of printable characters — usually about 64 characters.

In addition to being encoded, which increases the size, most files that you download from the Internet will also be compressed, which decreases the size. Another benefit of compressing files is that multiple files can be compressed into one *archive* file. Archiving files makes transmission easier (only one file to transfer) and guarantees that all the related files will be kept together.

You can use many compression methods. The most common Mac compression method is the one used by the StuffIt products from Aladdin Systems (www. aladdinsys.com). In fact, Aladdin has released StuffIt for Microsoft Windows as well; however, ZIP is the entrenched compression standard for Windows, although RAR is making inroads. For Unix, compress and gzip are the two dominant compression methods.

Using decoding and decompression utilities

When you receive a file that has been encoded and possibly compressed as well, software on your computer must decode and decompress the file before you can use it. First, the software decodes the BinHex or otherwise encoded file and saves a decoded version of the file. Then the software decompresses this file and saves yet another file. The last file is the one you can actually use. You can end up with two or three files: the encoded version (typically with an extension of .hqx or .bin), the compressed version (usually with the extension .sit or .sea), and the binary file. You'll probably want to throw away the encoded and compressed versions after you have the decoded binary file.

The application programs that handle decoding and decompressing are sometimes called *helper* applications because they work in conjunction with FTP clients, Web browsers, and other Internet applications that receive and send files on the Internet. The Web browser or FTP client inspects a downloaded file's extension and tells the appropriate helper application to decode or decompress a file. The helper opens (usually in the background), does its job, and quits. Often, you won't even be aware that the process has taken place.

StuffIt Expander

A helper application that comes with Mac OS X can handle virtually all of your decoding and decompressing needs. This free application is called StuffIt Expander from Aladdin Systems. StuffIt Expander can decode and decompress most Mac files you find on the Internet. It can decode BinHex (.hqx, .hcx, or .hex) or MacBinary (.bin) files, and it can decompress StuffIt (.sit), gzip (.gz), Compact Pro (.cpt), and ZIP (.zip) files. StuffIt Expander is easy to use; if your Internet applications don't open it automatically as needed, you can simply drag downloaded files to the StuffIt Expander icon. You can also set StuffIt Expander preferences to automatically decode and decompress all files that show up in a particular folder that you choose.

What's really great about the StuffIt Expander package is that it operates transparently. When you click an FTP link in your Web browser, the browser downloads the file from the FTP server and then hands off the file to StuffIt Expander, which decodes the file (converting it back into a binary file), decompresses the file further if necessary, and automatically quits. StuffIt Expander can also handle batches of files to be decoded and decompressed at the same time, and (if you prefer) it's smart enough to automatically delete the BinHex-encoded files after it finishes decoding them.

Instead of using the ZIP format, you can compress by using the StuffIt format that's commonly used on Macs. You can compress files in this format with the DropStuff program that's part of the StuffIt Lite package from Aladdin. PC users who want to expand your compressed files need the Windows version of the StuffIt Expander program, which is free from Aladdin Systems.

ZipIt

If you need to compress files that you want to send to a Windows PC on the Internet, you have two choices. If you want to compress files by using the ZIP method, which is the standard method on PCs, you can run the ZipIt program on your Mac or you can use the DropZip program, which is part of the StuffIt Lite package from Aladdin (`www.aladdinsys.com`). ZipIt can also decompress ZIP files on your Mac. ZipIt is shareware. (Others are available as well, including PKZip Mac, MacZip, and UnZip for Mac, all available from popular download servers, such as `www.download.com` on the Web.)

Compress and gzip

You also have the Unix compress and gzip programs available from the Unix command line in your Terminal application.

Summary

In this chapter, you read about creating a .Mac account and using an iDisk, which provides 20MB or more of storage space remotely located on an Apple file server. Your computer connects to an iDisk via the Internet. You can copy files to and from an iDisk, and you can open files directly from an iDisk. You can also share pictures, music, movies, a Web site, and other kinds of files from your iDisk with anyone who has a Web browser on any kind of computer. All you need to use an iDisk in Mac OS X is the Finder, which is specially designed to work with an iDisk.

This chapter also showed you how to connect to and work with files and use storage space located on file servers on your local network. The file servers can be dedicated file servers, or they can be personal computers using Mac OS file sharing. The basic means of connecting to file servers and file sharing computers is the Finder's Connect To Server dialog. To determine your access privileges to a folder, you can look at the folder's icon, open it, and look for a small icon in the Status Bar of its window. This chapter also discussed transferring and opening files on the network. In addition, you learned how to disconnect from shared folders and disks.

You can use the Mac OS X keychain to automatically provide your name and password when you connect to a file server. And you can streamline subsequent connections to a file server by opening an alias of it or of any item in it.

Besides working with file servers on your local network, you can download and upload files on the Internet. This chapter told you about downloading with a Web browser or an FTP client. After the files are downloaded, they will probably need to be decoded and decompressed so that you can use them.

✦   ✦   ✦

Harnessing Standard Services

In the old days, users frequently desired to use the spell checker they were accustomed to in one application when using another application, and they were frustrated that they could not do so. Each application provided its own solution for such common tasks as spell checking, sending e-mail, or annotating the open document. Apple attempted to address this need with the technology known as OpenDoc, but it was never really accepted in the marketplace. Apple dropped the technology in 1996-1997. Mac OS X provides a more general facility to achieve the goal, and that is the Services submenu of the application menu.

The Services menu allows applications to offer their capabilities to other applications. These *client* applications don't have to know what is being offered ahead of time. The Services menu works quite simply. You select some data in an application, such as the string of text, "We're coming to visit on Sunday." Then you choose a command from an application listed in the Services submenu, such as the Mail command's Mail Text option and the command is executed on the selection, invoking Mail to create a new mail message with "We're coming to visit on Sunday," already placed in the message body. Similarly, in TextEdit you could invoke the Grab service's Selection option to allow you to select a part of the screen to be inserted as an image in your TextEdit document.

Using Services often seems as though you're copying data from one application and pasting it into another, the latter of which modifies the data and copies the result back into the original application. For example, select a folder in the Finder and choose a StuffIt Service that compresses the folder and puts it into an archive. This archive is placed back in the same place as the original folder. However, this action can be one-way as well. For example, select a name in a word processing document and then select a Service that looks up the name by using an LDAP (Lightweight Directory Access Protocol) server, starts your e-mail application, and opens a new message window with the found e-mail address after the To: line.

Several applications included with Mac OS X provide services. This chapter describes the services provided by the Finder, Grab, Mail, Stickies, Speech, Summarize, and Text Edit.

The Finder

The Finder application provides three services to other applications, Open, Reveal, and Show Info, as shown in Figure 11-1.

Figure 11-1: Use the Finder to Open, Reveal, and Show Info.

✦ **Open.** Opens the file with its default application, opens a selected folder or volume and displays the contents in a Finder window, or starts an application. Essentially, the Open command in a menu acts the same way as a double-click on the item's icon. If you type the path to a folder in a text file, highlight the pathname and select Services➪File➪Open, the folder will open in a new Finder window.

✦ **Reveal.** Reveals a Finder window and selects the item.

✦ **Show Info.** Displays the Show Info window for the selected item.

Grab

Apple has long made it easy to take "snapshots" of your Mac screen and parts thereof. Mac OS X provides this capability via the Grab utility. Some of the nicer aspects of the Classic screen capture, such as capturing just a single window, are missing in Mac OS X; however, Grab balances that deficiency by providing Timed Screen captures and by providing the dimensions of an image being created from a selection.

Grab lends its services to other applications, allowing you to take a snapshot of the entire screen, a selection, or a timed screen shot, as shown in Figure 11-2.

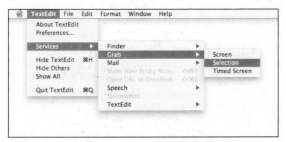

Figure 11-2: Grab Services include full screen, screen selection, and timed full-screen captures.

For example, while working in TextEdit you can choose TextEdit⇨Services⇨ Grab⇨Screen and a full-screen picture would be inserted in your TextEdit document at the current insertion point. Figure 11-3 shows a partial screen capture inserted into a Text Edit document.

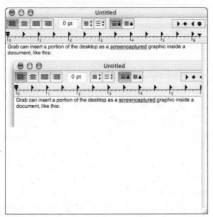

Figure 11-3: Grab can capture only a portion of the screen if desired.

Screen capture without Grab

Beginning with Mac OS X Version 10.1, you can capture the full screen or a selected area without using the Grab utility. The following keystrokes do the trick:

✦ ⌘-Shift-3 captures the full screen.

✦ ⌘-Shift-4 provides a crosshairs pointer to select the area you want captured.

With either keystroke, the screen shot is saved as a TIFF picture file on the Desktop.

Screen capture in the Classic environment

From the very first days of the Mac in 1984, you could take a screen shot by pressing ⌘-Shift-3. In those early days, the image resulted in a MacPaint file reflecting the 512-x-384-pixel screen. Similarly, ⌘-Shift-4 sent that screen image directly to your ImageWriter dot-matrix printer. As display and printer technology advanced, so did these built-in *FKEY* resources (it stood for Function KEY, before there were specific Fn keys on a Mac keyboard).

In the Classic environment, Mac OS 9 provides several ways to capture a screen shot, including the following:

✦ ⌘-Shift-3 takes a picture of the full Mac screen.

✦ ⌘-Shift-4 provides a crosshair cursor to take a picture of a selection.

✦ ⌘-Shift-CapsLock-4 provides a shutter icon to take a picture of a given window by clicking in it.

Screen captures taken with these keystrokes in the Classic environment are stored at the top level of your Classic startup disk (or folder) by the name Picture *n*, where *n* increases by one for each one taken. These files are in PICT format and have the Classic application SimpleText set as their creator application.

Clicking in a Mac OS X window or on the Desktop switches you out of the Classic environment without taking the screenshot. Therefore, you can't (for example) take a shot of a Mac OS X window by using ⌘-Shift-CapsLock-4 while in a Classic application and clicking in a Mac OS X window.

One of the more frequent uses of ⌘-Shift-4 under Mac OS 9 was to select an icon-sized image to use as a custom icon or to insert such an image in a document. ⌘-Shift-4, and its Grab equivalent, are unnecessary in Mac OS X. Just drag the icon into a TextEdit document, and you have the icon saved in your text.

Note   There is an exception to the above drag-the-icon method. If the file is a graphic file, such as a PICT, JPEG, TIFF, or GIF file, the image in the dragged file is dropped into the document rather than the icon. Go back to the selection method and use Grab if you need the icon of a graphic file.

Mail

The Mail application supplied by Mac OS X provides services to a variety of other applications. A typical use of the Mail service is as follows:

1. **Select a name or e-mail address in the body of your TextEdit document (or other word processor — it has to support Services).**

2. **Select Services⇨Mail⇨Send To from the application menu.** The Mac OS X Mail application opens with a new e-mail message addressed as you specified, shown in Figure 11-4.

Be aware that the Mail⇨Send To service does not check for a valid e-mail address or name. It merely takes the text you provide and places that text into the To: field of a new mail message. Note that the Mail⇨Send To service breaks the text into strings of less than 256 characters if it is too long.

Similarly, select a block of text, an image, or other material and choose Services⇨ Mail⇨Send Selection from the application menu to create a new e-mail message in Mail with the selected text or image in the body of the e-mail message, as shown in Figure 11-5.

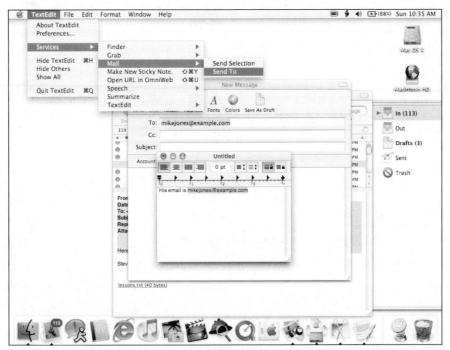

Figure 11-4: Use Mail's Send To service to create a mail message addressed to the selected name.

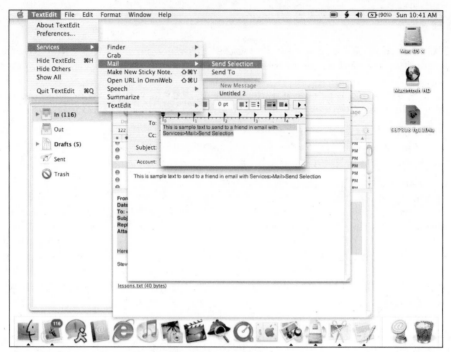

Figure 11-5: Use Mail's Send Selection service (top) to make an e-mail message from selected text and other media (bottom).

Mail also provides the service of mailing a file. To use this service, simply select a file or an entire folder in the Finder and then choose the Finder⇨Services⇨ Mail⇨Send File command, as shown in Figure 11-6. This command will not be visible in the Finder unless a file is elected.

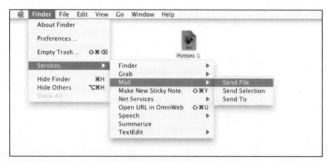

Figure 11-6: Use Mail's Send File service to make an e-mail message from a selected file or folder.

Stickies

For those fans of Post-It Notes and their electronic counterpart, Stickies, Mac OS X Stickies registers as a service. Any selected text in an application that supports services can be made into a Sticky by choosing Services➪Make Sticky (⌘-Shift-Y) from the application menu. Stickies is launched, if it isn't already, and a new Sticky containing your selected text (up to the maximum size of a Sticky) appears, as shown in Figure 11-7.

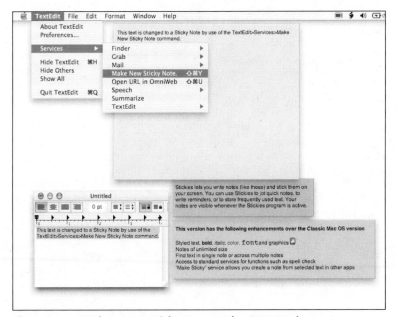

Figure 11-7: Make a new Sticky Note on the OS X Desktop.

Note   Although Stickies can contain graphics in Mac OS X, the service ignores any graphics within the selection when it creates the Sticky.

Being a good Mac OS X citizen, Stickies supports services, as well. If you have a Sticky open, you can choose from any of the supported services.

Speech

Any text selected in an OS X file can be sent to the Speech service and can be read aloud, by selecting the text and choosing the Services➪Start Speaking Text command as shown in Figure 11-8. To quit, use the Services➪Stop Speaking command. To change the settings for Speech, use the Speech pane in System Preferences. System Preferences are covered in more detail in Chapter 15.

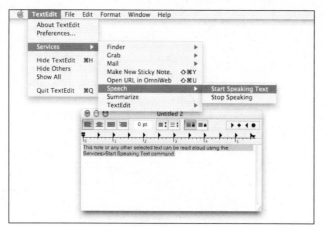

Figure 11-8: Use Speech's Start Speaking Text command to read text, notes, or e-mail aloud.

Summarize

A service that's available beginning with Mac OS X Version 10.1 takes currently selected text and quickly summarizes it by extracting key sentences. This service is unusual because it's provided by an application that you don't use otherwise. The service is called Summarize, and it's provided by the Summary Service application. To use this service, you select some text in a document and choose Services⇨ Summarize from the application menu. The Summary Service application opens, prepares a summary of the selected text, and displays the summary in a window. Figure 11-9 shows an example of the Summarize service.

Tip   If you select some text but the Summarize choice is disabled (dim) in the Services submenu, the Summarize service is not available in the application you're using. You can summarize the selected text by copying it to a document in the TextEdit application. Then select the text in the TextEdit document and choose TextEdit⇨ Services⇨Summarize.

When the summary window appears in the Summary Service application, you can save the summary as a text document by choosing File⇨Save As. In addition, you can edit the summary by using the Edit menu and other regular text editing methods. You can even check the spelling in the summary by choosing Edit⇨Spelling or Edit⇨Check Spelling.

Note   You won't find the Summary Service application in your Applications folder. It's buried in the Library folder of the folder named System.

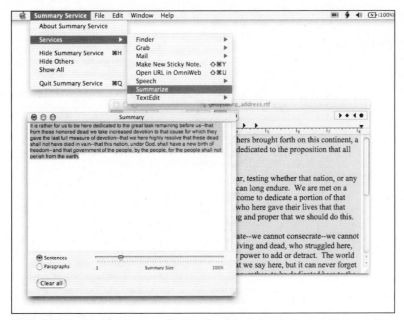

Figure 11-9: Use the Summarize service to prepare a summary of selected text.

TextEdit

The TextEdit application, the versatile text editor and word processor included with Mac OS X (covered in more detail in Chapter 22), provides two services:

✦ Open a file by name

✦ Create a new file containing selected text, pictures, and so forth

To open a file by name, as shown in Figure 11-10, you select text that specifies a full path to the file and then choose Services⇨TextEdit⇨Open File from the application menu. If the file cannot be found, an error message appears stating that the file could not be opened; however, the error message doesn't tell you why the attempt failed.

You can also select a block of text and other media. Then choose Services⇨ TextEdit⇨Open Selection from the application menu to create a new TextEdit document using the selected media, as shown in Figure 11-11. Because both text and other media are combined, you can edit the result. This service is a useful adjunct to clipping files.

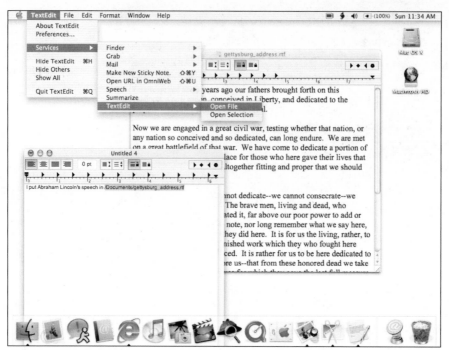

Figure 11-10: Open a file in TextEdit by selecting a full path and using the Services menu.

Other Services

Other applications that you install may provide additional services. For example, the OmniWeb application (www.omnigroup.com) provides a service that tries to open a Web page using selected text as a URL. In Figure 11-1 at the beginning of this chapter, you can see the Open URL in OmniWeb command, which was added to Services when the third-party OmniWeb Web browser was installed on this particular OS X installation.

Services provided by a newly installed application may not become available until the next time you log in.

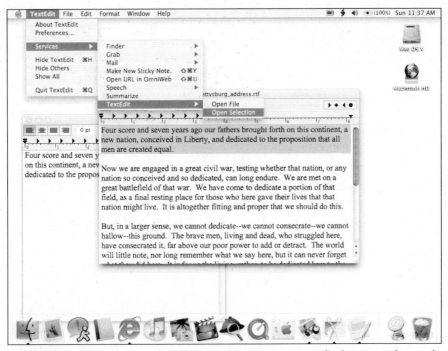

Figure 11-11: Use the Services menu (top) to create a TextEdit document from selected text and other media (bottom).

Summary

In this chapter, you learned that some Mac OS X applications support a Services submenu in their application menu and some (maybe even the same ones) are available to use as services. You've also seen that some of the applications and utilities shipped with Mac OS X are both service providers and service clients. Refer to Chapter 22 for more information on the applications and utilities that come with Mac OS X.

✦   ✦   ✦

Taking Charge of Fonts

With the original Mac OS font technology, text looked great when displayed or printed as long as you stuck to a half-dozen font sizes—usually 9, 10, 12, 14, 18, and 24 points—these were called *bitmap fonts* because they were painted representations of the character sets. Apple's TrueType font technology, a standard part of Mac OS 9 and earlier (introduced in System 6.0.8) and adopted by Microsoft as the standard font format for their Windows operating system, makes odd sizes and big sizes, such as 11, 13, 36, 100, and 197 points look just as good as prebuilt sizes. PostScript fonts (originated at Adobe Systems) are generally used in professional settings to get the highest print quality. Fairly new on the scene are OpenType fonts—a joint venture by Adobe and Microsoft to codify, in a single file, all the information for a font. Whatever your project, though, you can easily set up Mac OS X to make fonts look good.

Understanding Typography

Regardless of the font technology (see "Introducing Font Technologies" later in this chapter), the primary goal is the clear presentation of text. From the careful printing of medieval scribes through Gutenberg's early printing press to modern printing technologies, clear and attractive text has been the goal.

Typesetting purists cringe when they hear computer users discuss fonts, because we computer users don't distinguish between font and face. Similarly, we seem to be oblivious to the distinction between italic and oblique style. To purists, a font is a typeface at a given size. For example, Times-Roman 12 Bold Oblique is a *font*, Times-Roman Bold Oblique is a *typeface*, and Times-Roman is a type *family*.

Early typefaces, classified as *Oldstyle*, were developed primarily during the late fifteenth century and into the early eighteenth century. These typefaces are distinguished by curves that stress to the left and by noncontrasting stroke weights. Some examples of *Oldstyle* faces are Bembo, Garamond, and Minion.

Traditional typefaces found their heyday during the eighteenth century. They exhibit more stroke contrast than Oldstyle faces, sharper serifs, and vertically stressed curves. Times, Stone Serif, and Baskerville are representative of Traditional faces.

Modern faces first appeared in the late eighteenth century and were considered to be quite radical in their design. Sharp contrast in stroke weight, ranging from hairlines to bold and strong vertical stress is typical in a Modern typeface. Some examples of Modern faces include Bodoni and Melior.

Slab serif typefaces made their appearance in the early nineteenth century and were originally called *Antiques* and are occasionally referred to as *Egyptian*. The strokes are usually of equal weight throughout, with nontapering serifs and a vertical emphasis. Common typewriter fonts, such as American Typewriter and Memphis fall into this category.

William Caslon introduced *Gothic* faces in 1916. Gothic faces are sans serif with little contrast in their stroke weights. Similarly, they seldom have true italic versions, utilizing an *oblique* (slanted) variation. Helvetica, Arial, and Stone Sans are common examples.

Script (also called *cursive* or *brush*) faces resemble handwriting. Some have their characters connecting; others don't. The only feature script faces have in common is that they appear to have been handwritten rather than drawn or printed. Brush Script, Mistral, and Zapf Chancery are examples of this type.

Other, less common groups of faces are *Display* (too ornate to be used for large bodies of text), *Blackletter* (typical of faces emulating the printing of scribes in the Middle Ages), *Polyglot* (non-Roman foreign language fonts, such as Cyrillic, Arabic, and Kanji), and *Pi* (pictorial fonts).

Introducing Mac Font Technologies

As mentioned earlier, a number of font technologies have made their appearance in the Mac OS. Most technologies are supported in Mac OS X (QuickDraw GX fonts being a partial exception). Mac OS X displays and prints text in four types of fonts:

- ✦ Bitmap
- ✦ TrueType
- ✦ PostScript
- ✦ OpenType

Bitmap fonts

Bitmap fonts (sometimes referred to as *fixed-size* fonts) are the original fonts used on the very first Macs in 1984. Each bitmap font contains an exact, dot-for-dot picture of each character (letter, digit, or symbol) in the font. Figure 12-1 shows the dots in an enlarged view of two characters of a bitmap font.

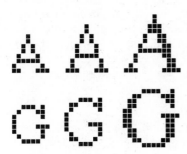

Figure 12-1: Bitmap fonts contain dot-for-dot pictures of characters. (Times capital A and G at 12, 14, and 18-point sizes enlarged to show detail.)

Each bitmap font looks great in one size only, so bitmap fonts usually are installed in sets. A typical set includes 9-, 10-, 12-, 14-, 18-, and 24-point font sizes. If you need text in a size for which no bitmap font is installed, the Mac OS must scale a bitmap font's character bitmaps up or down to the size you want. The results are mis-shapen or blocky, as shown in Figure 12-2.

Times 9. ABCD EFG HIJKL MNO PQRSTUV WX YZ abcdefghijklmno pqrstuvwxyz 123
Times 10. ABCDEFGHIJKLMNOPQRSTUVWXYZabcdefghijklmnopqrstu
Times 11. ABCDEFGHIJKLMNOPQRSTUV WXY Zabcdefghijklmn
Times 12. ABCDEFGHIJKLMNOPQRSTUV WXY Zabcdefghij
Times 13. ABCDEFGHIJKLMNOPQRSTUVWXY Zabcde
Times 14. ABCDEFGHIJKLMNOPQRSTUVWXY Za
Times 16. ABCDEFGHIJKLMNOPQRSUVW
Times 18. ABCDEFGHIJKLMNOPQRST
Times 20. ABCDEFGHIJKLMNOPQ
Times 24. ABCDEFGHIJKLM
Times 30. ABCDEFGHIJ

Figure 12-2: Bitmap fonts look best at installed sizes — note the blockiness of the 20- and 30-point font sizes. (Enlarged to show detail.)

TrueType fonts

TrueType is a variable-size font technology. Instead of fixed-size bitmaps, TrueType fonts use curves and straight lines to outline each character's shape. Because TrueType fonts are based on outlines, they sometimes are called *outline fonts*. Figure 12-3 is the outline of an example TrueType letter.

Figure 12-3: TrueType fonts are based on outlines. (Times capital G shown.)

TrueType fonts look good at all sizes. They work with all Mac OS applications and all types of printers, including PostScript printers. The Mac OS smoothly scales a TrueType font's character outlines to any size on a display screen and on printers of any resolution, all with equally good results. The Mac OS also lets you mix TrueType fonts with bitmap and PostScript fonts. Figure 12-4 is an example of TrueType font scaling.

Times 9. ABCD EFG HIJKL MNO PQRSTUV WX YZ abcdefghijklmnopqrstuvwxye 123
Times 10. ABCDEFGHIJKLMNOPQRSTUVWXYZabcdefghijklmnopqrstu
Times 11. ABCDEFGHIJKLMNOPQRSTUVWXYZabcdefghijklmn
Times 12. ABCDEFGHIJKLMNOPQRSTUVWXYZabcdefghij
Times 13. ABCDEFGHIJKLMNOPQRSTUV WXYZabode
Times 14. ABCDEFGHIJKLMNOPQRSTUVWXYZa
Times 16. ABCDEFGHIJKLMNOPQRSUVW
Times 18. ABCDEFGHIJKLMNOPQRST
Times 20. ABCDEFGHIJKLMNOPQ
Times 24. ABCDEFGHIJKLM
Times 30. ABCDEFGHIJ

Figure 12-4: TrueType fonts scale smoothly to all sizes and resolutions. (Enlarged to show detail.)

Mac OS X can recognize both traditional Mac TrueType files and font suitcases, which are folder-like containers of traditional Mac font files. Because traditional Mac font files have two forks (parts), called the data fork and the resource fork, these font files and font suitcases must be stored on disks or other volumes that have the Mac OS Extended format (also known as HFS Plus). Mac OS X also recognizes Windows TrueType font files, which have the filename extension of .ttf or .ttc. Windows files don't have two forks, so the data fork and resource fork are combined in a Windows TrueType file. Additionally, Mac OS X recognizes Mac TrueType font files that have the file name extension of .dfont. These files contain only a data fork (no resource fork), making the .dfont files usable even on a UFS-formatted volume.

Tip

Look closely at some text in a TrueType font and at the same text in an equivalent bitmap font. You can see differences in letter shape, width, and height that may affect text spacing. The TrueType fonts match the PostScript fonts used in printers better than bitmap fonts do. Bitmap fonts display faster, however, and many of them look better on-screen in sizes smaller than 18 points.

PostScript fonts

PostScript fonts were the first to look great at any size and any resolution. They use an outline font technology invented by Adobe Systems. PostScript is similar to

TrueType but differs from TrueType in how PostScript mathematically specifies font outlines and how it adjusts the outlines for small font sizes and low resolutions.

Note TrueType was developed initially as a response to the closed nature of PostScript fonts and the exceedingly high license fees charged by Adobe to include a PostScript rendering engine in LaserWriters. Adobe responded to this assault on the turf it controlled by disclosing the Type 1 definition, allowing competition in the marketplace for PostScript fonts.

Unlike bitmap and TrueType fonts, which each resides within a single file, Type 1 Postscript fonts have two files that must be properly installed for the font to function properly. Each PostScript font has a screen font file and its associated printer font file. Although a PostScript screen font appears in font menus and on-screen correctly without its associated printer font installed, the font does not print correctly. In addition, a font does not appear in a font menu, nor does text previously formatted with that font appear correctly on-screen without its associated screen font installed. This is true whether ATM is being used or not.

PostScript fonts are divided into two main categories, imaginatively called Type 1 and Type 3. Most PostScript fonts that you see are Type 1, because they yield better results at small font sizes and low resolutions. Although Type 1 fonts generally look better, Type 3 fonts are more elaborate. The characters in Type 3 fonts have variable stroke weights, and are filled with something other than a solid color, such as shades of gray or blends that go from white to black. Mac OS X does not provide support for Type 3 fonts.

PostScript fonts were originally designed for printing on LaserWriters and other PostScript output devices. In Mac OS 9, and hence in the Classic environment, Adobe Type Manager (ATM) software smoothly scales PostScript fonts to any size for non-PostScript printers and the display screen. With ATM and PostScript fonts, you didn't need a set of bitmap or TrueType fonts for the screen display. Just one bitmap size will suffice. ATM is included on the Mac OS 9 CD that comes with Mac OS X. Look in the Adobe Software folder and you will find ATM(r) 4.6.

Mac OS X, on the other hand, includes built-in support for Type 1 fonts in three variations:

✦ Screen font files, optionally in a font suitcase, plus corresponding PostScript Type 1 outline fonts

✦ QuickDraw GX-enabled font suitcase

✦ QuickDraw GX-enabled MultiMaster font suitcase

TrueType fonts cannot replace PostScript fonts for a number of reasons. For one, PostScript fonts include in the font a lot of information — kerning information and hints that help the font look better at different sizes — that TrueType fonts do not. Additionally, PostScript offers more than outline fonts. It's a *page description language* that precisely specifies the location and other characteristics of every text and graphic item on the page. For just PostScript's font capabilities, though, the OpenType font format was developed.

OpenType fonts

Adobe and Microsoft worked jointly to create the OpenType font format. An extension of the TrueType font format, the OpenType font format supports PostScript font data in the same file with TrueType font data. OpenType fonts and the operating system services that support them provide users with a simple way to install and use fonts, whether the fonts contain TrueType outlines or PostScript outlines.

The OpenType font format addresses the following goals:

✦ Broader multiplatform support

✦ Better support for international character sets

✦ Better protection for font data

✦ Smaller file sizes to make font distribution more efficient

✦ Broader support for advanced typographic control

OpenType fonts are also referred to as TrueType Open v.2.0 fonts because they use the TrueType font file format (which the Mac OS identifies internally as 'sfnt'). PostScript data included in OpenType fonts may be directly rasterized or converted to the TrueType outline format for rendering, depending on which rasterizers have been installed in the host operating system. But the user model is the same: OpenType fonts just work. Users do not need to be aware of the type of outline data in OpenType fonts. And font creators can use whichever outline format they feel provides the best set of features for their work, without worrying about limiting a font's usability.

OpenType fonts enable font creators to design better international and high-end typographic fonts by including OpenType Layout tables. These tables contain information on glyph (character) substitution, glyph positioning, justification, and baseline positioning, which enables text-processing applications to improve text layout, making minute adjustments to the kerning and tracking.

Additionally, OpenType fonts enable the handling of large glyph sets by using Unicode encoding. Unicode allows broad international support, as well as support for typographic glyph variants.

With ATM 4.6, partial OpenType support now extends to Mac OS 8.1 and later. OpenType fonts are not recognized by earlier versions of ATM and, even with ATM 4.6 installed, may not be compatible with or recognized by various older applications.

In Mac OS X, OpenType fonts typically have a file name extension of .otf.

Installing Fonts

In the beginning, there were font suitcases and a utility called the Font/DA Mover, which many users found very confusing. At that time, fonts were installed only in the main System file. In addition to confusing users, these modifications to an active System file led to frequent System corruption. The advent of System 7 had fonts sitting loose in the System Folder. Although this location was a big improvement in ease of use and stability, it made an absolute mess of the System Folder. System 7.1 brought the Fonts folder within the System Folder, and organization improved markedly.

This situation remains in Mac OS 9, and hence in the Classic environment, with minor variations such as how many font suitcases can be open at a time. In the Classic environment, most fonts are in the Fonts folder of the Mac OS 9 System Folder, but some may be found in the System Folder itself. Fonts may also be installed directly in the System file, although this practice is uncommon in Mac OS 9.

Mac OS X, however, brings a whole new approach. First, Mac OS X has no System Folder, as such. Second, Mac OS X is a multiuser operating system, and different users may want or need different font sets.

Fonts required by Mac OS X are installed in the Fonts folder of the Library folder in the folder named System (path /System/Library/Fonts). The contents of this Fonts folder are available to all users and should not be altered.

Additional fonts for all users should be installed in the Fonts folder of the main Library folder (path /Library/Fonts). To install fonts in this folder, you must log in to Mac OS X with the name and password of an administrator account, such as the account created during initial setup of Mac OS X.

Each Mac OS X user account also has a Fonts folder in the Library folder of its home folder (path ~/Library/Fonts). You can install fonts for your use by dragging them into the Fonts folder of your Library folder. Fonts in your Fonts folder will not be available to (or bother) other users of your computer. Conversely, other fonts in other users' Fonts folders are not available to you.

Note

In Mac OS X, you must place font files in a Fonts folder. Or, if the fonts come with an installer program, run the installer to put the fonts where they belong. The Mac OS X Finder does not automatically route font files into a Fonts folder if you drag them to a Library folder icon or a System Folder icon, unlike Mac OS 9 which does route font files dragged to the System Folder.

After installing new fonts in a Fonts folder, you may not have access to them until you quit the application in which you wish to use the font and relaunch the application.

Understanding Font Priorities

When multiple versions of a particular font are installed — bitmap, TrueType, and PostScript — Mac OS 9 and earlier have a confusing priority scheme as to which version is used. Dependencies are based on the type of output device (screen or printer).

With Mac OS X, this scheme is no longer an issue. With Quartz (PDF) imaging both on-screen and to output devices, whichever font you choose is the one that is rasterized by Quartz.

This straightforward scheme does have an exception. When you use a Classic application, fonts installed in your Mac OS 9 System Folder (or managed by a Classic font management utility) are used rather than the fonts installed for Mac OS X, and Classic chooses the font based upon what you're doing, as described next.

Displaying fonts on-screen in Classic

For screen display, Classic first tries to find a bitmap font in the exact size needed. If it can't find that, it looks for a TrueType version of the font that it can scale to the needed size. If no TrueType version is installed, Classic then tries to have ATM, if installed, scale a PostScript font to the needed size. ATM Deluxe can even use Adobe Multiple Master fonts to display temporary substitutes that closely match PostScript fonts not installed on your computer. If no other font is available, Classic scales the best available bitmap font.

When both bitmap and TrueType versions of the same font are present, Classic always derives styled fonts from the bitmap version, even if a styled TrueType version is installed. For example, if you have a bitmap 12-point Times plain and a TrueType Times italic installed (but no bitmap 12-point Times italic), Classic derives a 12-point Times italic by slanting the bitmap 12-point Times.

Individual applications can tell Classic to ignore bitmap fonts if a TrueType equivalent is available and current versions of many popular applications work just this way, telling Classic to ignore bitmap fonts. You may be able to turn this behavior on and off in some of your Classic applications. Check each Classic application's preference settings for a preference that tells the application that you prefer outline fonts. A decision to ignore bitmap fonts in one Classic application does not affect other applications — Classic always prefers bitmap fonts, unless an application specifically overrides it.

Printing fonts on PostScript printers

When choosing among bitmap, TrueType, or PostScript versions of the same font for printing on a PostScript printer, Classic looks first for a PostScript font from the printer's ROM, RAM, or hard drive (if any). If the printer doesn't have the PostScript font, Classic tries to download (copy) it from the various places in the Mac OS 9

System Folder: the Fonts folder, the Extensions folder, or the System Folder itself. Failing that, Classic then tries to use a TrueType font. As a last resort, Classic uses a bitmap font.

If Classic can find no PostScript equivalent for a TrueType font, it sends the TrueType font to the printer before sending the document to be printed. If the printer is one that can't handle TrueType fonts, Classic converts the TrueType font to PostScript, with some loss of quality at small point sizes, and sends that. Either way, sending fonts causes a significant delay on many printers. If you use TrueType-only fonts with a PostScript printer that has its own hard drive or a large amount of memory, you may be able to reduce printing time by downloading (sending) the TrueType fonts to the printer in advance of printing documents. Fonts you download to a printer's hard drive remain there unless you remove them. Fonts you download to a printer's memory remain there until you turn off the printer, or, in some cases, until someone else prints on the printer with a different version of printer software than you use.

Printing fonts on a non-PostScript device

On a printer or other device that doesn't have PostScript, Classic tries to use TrueType fonts. If your Mac OS 9 System Folder doesn't have a needed TrueType font but does have ATM installed, Classic looks for a PostScript version of the font. If neither type of outline font is available, Classic uses a bitmap font.

If you print on a non-PostScript printer, such as a Hewlett-Packard DeskJet or Epson Stylus and have both bitmap and TrueType fonts installed, text may not look quite the same on-screen as it does on paper. Character shapes may be different. More importantly, the spacing of words in the line may not match. When this happens, Classic has used a bitmap font for display (at 72 dots-per-inch) and a TrueType font for printing (at a higher resolution). You can fix the problem by removing the bitmap font from the Fonts folder of the Mac OS 9 System Folder, or perhaps from the System file there. In some Classic applications, you may also be able to set an option that tells Mac OS 9 to ignore bitmap fonts.

Managing Fonts for Mac OS X Applications

Mac OS X provides a new method for selecting the font family, typeface, and size that you want used in a document. Instead of or in addition to traditional Font and Size menus, some Mac OS X applications now display the Mac OS X Font Panel for setting font specifications. The Font Panel also helps you organize your fonts.

Mac OS X 10.2 also provides a font smoothing setting that affects all displayed fonts in Mac OS X applications.

Setting font family, typeface, and size

Mac OS X provides a major new interface to Mac font management — the Font Panel. With the now-familiar multicolumn browser for selecting your fonts, you construct fonts (in the typographer's sense) for use. You select a font family in one column, a typeface in the next column, and a size in the next column. Depending upon the application, you find the Font Panel (possibly under a different name), in the application's Format menu or Text menu — wherever you actually find fonts listed. Some Mac OS X applications do not use the Font Panel. Figure 12-5 shows the Font Panel.

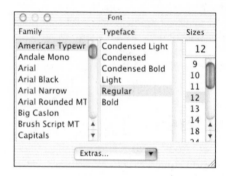

Figure 12-5: Specify the font by choosing family, typeface, and size in the Mac OS X Font Panel.

One downside to the Font Panel is that it doesn't provide a preview, so you can't see how a font looks. This, in our opinion, is a significant oversight, which will shortly be addressed by Apple or an ambitious third-party developer. If you want to see how a font appears, use the Key Caps utility application and choose the family and face from the Font menu — those families having multiple faces provide a submenu so that you may choose which family you want to use.

Organizing Mac OS X fonts

With the introduction of *collections* as a grouping tool, so that you can create sets of fonts you use for particular purposes, you eliminate the need for many third-party utilities designed to help the Classic application users organize their fonts. You see a column of font collections when you enlarge the Font Panel by clicking its Zoom button or dragging its Resize control. Figure 12-6 shows font collections in an enlarged Font Panel.

Mac OS X comes with five preassembled font collections:

✦ Classic

✦ Fun

✦ Modern

✦ PDF

✦ Web

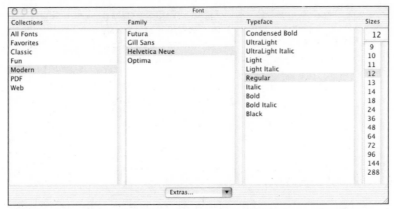

Figure 12-6: Enlarge the Font Panel to see available font collections.

You can add, delete, and rename collections and the families within them by choosing Edit Collections from the Extras pop-up menu at the bottom of the Font panel. When you do this, the Font Panel becomes the Font – Collections panel shown in Figure 12-7.

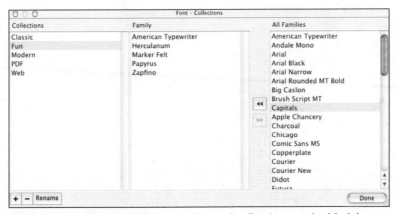

Figure 12-7: Move families into and out of collections and add, delete, or rename collections.

Setting Font Panel options

You can also specify which sizes are displayed in the Sizes list of the Font Panel and whether that list is presented as a list or a slider by choosing Edit Sizes from the Extras pop-up menu. When you do this, the Font Panel becomes the Font – Sizes panel shown in Figure 12-8.

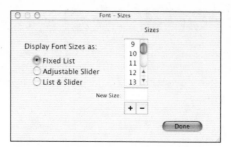

Figure 12-8: Specify how you select sizes and which sizes are shown by using the Font-Sizes panel.

Setting text smoothing for Mac OS X

Mac OS X smoothes text on-screen by blending jagged edges with the background color. This process is called *anti-aliasing*. Beginning with Mac OS X Version 10.1, you can specify the smallest font size that you want smoothed in Mac OS X applications. You can also specify the style of font smoothing you want to use, from Light, Medium (described as best for flat panel monitors), Strong, and Standard (described as best for CRT monitors).You change these settings with pop-up menus at the bottom of the General pane of System Preferences, as shown in Figure 12-9.

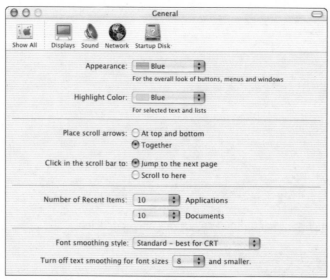

Figure 12-9: Adjust text smoothing for Mac OS X applications by using the General pane of System Preferences.

Setting Font Options for Classic Applications

Although Classic handles font display and printing automatically, you can set a few options that affect how fonts look. You can set a font-smoothing option in the Appearance control panel, for example. If you use ATM with Classic, you can adjust how it scales PostScript fonts.

Font smoothing

Font smoothing for Classic applications is independent of Mac OS X text smoothing. You can turn Classic font smoothing on or off in the Font section of the Appearance control panel. When font smoothing is turned on, you can also specify the smallest font size that you want smoothed. Since smaller fonts can become blurry and harder to read when smoothed, you can set the smallest font size to be smoothed in windows. Classic anti-aliases all TrueType fonts this size or larger on monitors set to display at least 256 colors or grays. Classic does not anti-alias any fixed size (bitmap) fonts. ATM, as described next, handles anti-aliasing of PostScript fonts. Figure 12-10 shows the font smoothing options in the Appearance control panel.

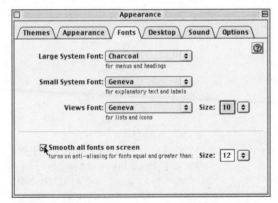

Figure 12-10: Set font-smoothing options for Classic applications by using the Appearance control panel.

Adobe Type Manager (ATM) options

You can set several options that affect how the optional Adobe Type Manager (ATM) software scales PostScript fonts for Classic applications. The ATM font smoothing appears on-screen and on printers that don't use PostScript. In addition, you can set options that affect ATM's performance. You make these settings in the ATM control panel. Figure 12-11 shows the ATM control panel.

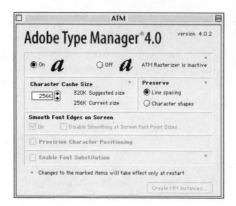

Figure 12-11: Set smoothing and performance options for PostScript fonts in Classic applications by using the ATM control panel.

Note

Adobe Type Manager is required only if you're using PostScript fonts and want to see them rendered properly on a non-PostScript device (such as your screen or most inkjet printers). If you don't find ATM in your Classic Control Panels menu, you can find it on the Mac OS 9 installation CD. Note that ATM Version 4.5.2 or higher is required with Classic — other versions crash and keep Classic from starting if installed. The ATM Deluxe control panel also crashes Classic if it hasn't been updated to Version 4.5.2 or higher. At the time we write this, ATM 4.6 is the version included on the Mac OS 9 CD.

Character Cache Size option

The Character Cache Size option affects performance. If applications seem to scroll more slowly with ATM turned on, try increasing this size.

Preserve option

The Preserve option determines whether ATM preserves line spacing or character shapes when it scales text. Preserving line spacing keeps line breaks and page breaks from changing with and without ATM, but this setting may clip the bottoms of some letters and vertically compress some accented capital letters. Preserving character shapes reduces the clipping but may change line breaks. The clipping occurs only on-screen and on output devices that don't use PostScript. No clipping occurs on a PostScript printer.

Smooth Font Edges on Screen option

The Smooth Font Edges on Screen option smoothes font edges on-screen in the same way the Appearance control panel does — by blending their jagged edges with the background color. Whereas Appearance works with all TrueType fonts, ATM works on Type 1 PostScript fonts. ATM can anti-alias color text only when the monitor is set to display thousands or millions of colors. If the monitor is set to display 256 colors, ATM can anti-alias only black-and-white text.

Precision Character Positioning option

The Precision Character Positioning option displays more accurate spacing, especially at small font sizes. Turning on this option causes ATM to calculate character positions on a fractional pixel basis, which may slow text display of some documents on slower computers.

Other ATM features

The version of ATM included with Mac OS 9 does not have all the features of ATM Deluxe. ATM Deluxe can create substitute fonts dynamically when you open a Classic document that contains fonts your system doesn't have. This font substitution feature preserves line breaks in documents but only approximates the look of missing fonts. Other ATM Deluxe features facilitate reviewing, organizing, adding, and removing large numbers of Classic fonts as well as diagnosing some font problems. Adobe sells ATM Deluxe separately (www.adobe.com).

ATM 4.6 or later provides support for OpenType fonts, although not all Classic applications recognize OpenType fonts even with ATM 4.6 installed (most will).

Summary

In this chapter, you learned that fixed-size (bitmap) fonts look good only at installed sizes, but that the Mac OS can smoothly scale TrueType, PostScript, and OpenType fonts to any size for the display screen or any type of printer. With the addition of Adobe Type Manager (ATM) software, PostScript fonts also look good on the display screen and non-PostScript printers when you use Classic applications.

You also learned that all three types of fonts are kept in the Fonts folder of the main Library folder (path /Library/Fonts) or, for fonts available to just one user, in Fonts folder of the Library folder in that user's home folder (path ~/Library/Fonts). You can add and remove fonts by dragging their icons to and from these Fonts folders, although you need to log in with the name and password of an administrator account to install in the Fonts folder of the main Library folder. If you use ATM with Classic, you can adjust how ATM scales PostScript fonts.

In addition, this chapter explained how Mac OS 9 chooses between bitmap, TrueType, and PostScript versions of the same font in Classic applications. The priorities are different for the display screen, PostScript printers, and non-PostScript printers.

This chapter also described the Font Panel, which provides a new method for selecting the font family, typeface, and size in some Mac OS X applications. The Font Panel also helps you organize your fonts.

In this chapter, you also read that Mac OS X 10.2 provides font-smoothing settings that affect all displayed fonts in Mac OS X applications. This setting is in the General pane of System Preferences.

Finally, this chapter told you how to adjust smoothing of TrueType fonts displayed in Classic applications by using the Appearance control panel. You can also set smoothing and performance options for PostScript fonts in Classic applications by using the ATM control panel.

✦   ✦   ✦

Viewing and Editing Video

Apple and Mac OS X give you many ways to enjoy video. Apple's QuickTime technology enables you to watch digital movies, including MPEG video. With QuickTime VR, you can view virtual reality panoramas and objects interactively. Basic QuickTime support, including the Player application, is included with Mac OS X. For a $30 upgrade fee, Apple will send you a registration key to unlock QuickTime Pro functionality.

If your computer has a DVD-ROM or DVD-R drive, you can play back DVD-encoded movies. If you have FireWire ports, you can use iMovie to view and edit digital video from a digital camcorder and then record the edited video back to the camcorder or create QuickTime movies for distribution to colleagues, friends, and relatives. This chapter explains how to use all of this video software.

If your computer has a TV tuner expansion card, you need to restart with Mac OS 9 to use the Apple Video Player application to view videos from video equipment, such as a camcorder, VCR, or television and to capture that video input digitally on disk until an equivalent application becomes available for Mac OS X.

Introducing QuickTime Movies

Apple's QuickTime software enables your computer to work with data that changes over time, or *time-based data*, such as motion pictures with sound. In other words, it lets you store and watch movies on your computer. In fact, every Macintosh computer that's qualified to use Mac OS X can play QuickTime movies (and so can most other Macintosh and Windows computers). QuickTime doesn't require any special equipment, although faster computers generally play movies more smoothly than slower computers.

Apple's QuickTime software not only makes it possible to play movies on your computer, QuickTime makes movies ubiquitous! You don't need a special application to watch QuickTime movies. Most applications let you copy and paste movies as easily as you copy and paste graphics, and you can play a QuickTime movie wherever you encounter one. For starters, you can watch QuickTime movies from AppleWorks 6. Figure 13-1 is an example of a QuickTime movie in an AppleWorks window.

Figure 13-1: You can watch a QuickTime movie in AppleWorks and other applications.

QuickTime movies are more than a motion picture and a soundtrack. QuickTime expands the definition of *movie* considerably to include all kinds of interesting data that change or move over time. With the latest version of QuickTime, movies can include any combination of the following:

✦ **Motion pictures.** What you watch on TV or at the movies.

✦ **Digitized sound recordings.** Music and other sounds that play in CD-quality sound (44.1kHz, 18-bit stereo).

✦ **Synthesized music.** Based on the MIDI (Musical Instrument Digital Interface) standard, that takes far less disk space to store than digitized sound, yet sounds realistic and plays in CD-quality.

✦ **Text.** For closed-caption viewing, karaoke sing-a-longs, or text-based searches of movie content.

✦ **Sprites.** Sprites are graphic objects that move independently, like actors moving on a stage with a motion-picture backdrop.

✦ **MPEG.** Movies that use the common MPEG-1 and new MPEG-4 video and audio standards. MPEG-2 playback is an additional component available for a small fee.

✦ **AVI.** Movies that are common on Windows. The file type actually covers a broad range of movie codecs. (Although not all varieties of AVI are currently supported by QuickTime — for example, Intel has not ported the Indeo 2.63 codec to the Mac.)

✦ **Graphics.** QuickTime 6 includes support for Macromedia Flash 5 and JPEG 2000.

✦ **Panoramas and objects.** Permits viewing objects in 360 degrees using QuickTime VR methods.

✦ **Timecode information.** Displays elapsed hours, minutes, seconds, and frames at the bottom of a playing movie.

✦ **Functional information.** Information that tells QuickTime how other tracks interact.

What's in a movie

The motion pictures, sound, and other types of time-based data in a QuickTime movie exist in separate tracks. A simple movie may consist of one video track and one sound track. A more complex movie may have several video tracks, several audio tracks, and closed-caption text tracks for text subtitles. Each video track could be designed for playback with a specified number of available colors (for example, 256 colors, thousands of colors, or millions of colors), each audio track could provide dialog in a different language (English, Spanish, Japanese, and so on), and each closed-caption text track could provide subtitles in a different language.

If a QuickTime movie contains MIDI-synthesized music, sprites, or a QuickTime VR scene or object, then each item is in a separate track. QuickTime takes care of synchronizing all tracks so that they play at the proper time.

QuickTime magic

A computer shouldn't be capable of playing digital movies any more than a bumblebee should be able to fly. Without compression, a single full-screen color picture in a 640 x 480 window takes about a megabyte of disk space. To show 30 pictures, or frames, per second, which is what you see on TV, a computer has to store, retrieve, and display close to 30MB per second. Only the fastest computers and hard disk drives are that fast. Even if you have such a computer, storage space is still a problem for movies. For example, a one-minute digital video clip requires over 200MB of disk space.

QuickTime uses every trick in the book to play movies. Most movies are smaller than the full 640 x 480 pixels available for digital video. In QuickTime's early days, when PowerPC processors didn't exist and single-speed CD-ROM drives were state-of-the-art, QuickTime movies were the size of a large postage stamp (160 x 120 pixels). Today, quarter-screen movies (320 x 240 pixels) play back smoothly from a CD-ROM, and fast Macintosh computers can play full-screen (640 x 480) movies from a hard disk or streaming from the Internet via a broadband connection with relative ease.

Note   If you minimize a QuickTime Movie Player window into the Dock while a movie is playing, it continues to play—in miniature—in the Dock's minimized window representation.

QuickTime movies may play back fewer frames per second than TV or movies. You see 30 *fps* (frames per second) on television or videotape in the United States and other countries that use the NTSC standard (25 fps in Europe and other places that use the PAL or SECAM standards). By comparison, many QuickTime movies are designed to play at 10 or 15 fps from a CD-ROM.

Showing small pictures at slow frame rates reduces the amount of data to be stored, retrieved, and displayed, but not nearly enough. So QuickTime compresses movies, largely by throwing out the redundant parts. Built-in and add-on *codecs*, or *compressor/decompressor,* software performs the compression. These special algorithms come in various formats, generally offering different trade-offs between picture quality and the amount of data required for a movie. A compressed movie contains less data to store on disk. Just as importantly, a compressed movie contains less data to be transferred each second from that hard disk, CD-ROM, or the Internet to the screen.

Getting QuickTime software

You get the basic QuickTime software as a part of the standard installation of Mac OS X. You can upgrade to QuickTime Pro, unleashing many additional editing features, for $29.95 by phone (1–888–295–0648) or from Apple's QuickTime site on the Web (www.apple.com/quicktime/). In some cases, you can get a free upgrade to QuickTime Pro when you purchase a retail version of the Mac OS or various software packages, such as Final Cut Pro.

Note   If you are upgrading to Mac OS X and had previously upgraded to QuickTime 5 Pro after October 12, 2000, you can enter your QuickTime Pro registration information in the Registration window opened by choosing QuickTime Player⇨Preferences and then choosing Registration from the pop-up menu.

Compressed Images

QuickTime not only handles time-based and interactive media, but it also extends the Macintosh PICT graphics format, which is the standard graphics format in Mac OS 9 and earlier, to handle compressed still images and image previews. An application that recognizes QuickTime can compress a graphic image by using any QuickTime-compatible software or hardware compressor that is available on your computer. All applications that can open uncompressed PICT images are also capable of opening compressed PICT images. QuickTime automatically decompresses a compressed PICT image without requiring changes to the application program.

What's in QuickTime Pro?

What do you get when you plunk down $29.95 to upgrade from the basic edition of QuickTime to QuickTime Pro? The upgrade enables the PictureViewer Pro application to save still images (in BMP, JPEG, Photoshop, PICT, or QuickTime Image format). The upgrade similarly enables the QuickTime plug-in for Web browsers to save movies from the Web.

Moreover, the upgrade brings many improvements to the QuickTime Player application. Here's some of what QuickTime Player Pro can do that the basic QuickTime Player cannot:

✦ Create new movies

✦ Open a sequence of still images as a movie (a slide show)

✦ Import and export to and from a large number of additional video formats

✦ Export sound tracks to several additional sound formats

✦ Apply video and audio compression

✦ Edit movies by drag-and-drop editing and with Cut, Copy, and Paste commands

✦ Extract individual tracks from a movie

✦ Show and set the movie poster frame

✦ Present a movie centered on a black screen

✦ Play a movie at full-screen size

✦ Play a movie in a continuous loop

✦ Play only the selected part of a movie

✦ Adjust the size and orientation of each video track in the movie frame

✦ Show and set the following additional movie, video track, and sound track information

For more detailed information on the differences between QuickTime 6 and QuickTime Pro, visit Apple's QuickTime Pro Web site at http://www.apple.com/quicktime/upgrade/.

Playing QuickTime Movies

QuickTime makes it possible to play movies in all kinds of applications and it establishes standard methods for controlling playback in all applications. You can use a standard QuickTime movie controller and other standard methods for controlling playback when the controller is absent. The QuickTime Player application included with QuickTime has additional features used to play movies. If you play movies that contain MIDI-synthesized music, you may be able to affect how they sound by setting some options in the QuickTime Settings control panel.

Using the QuickTime movie controller

You usually control playback of a QuickTime movie in an application other than QuickTime Player with a standard collection of buttons and sliders along the bottom edge of the movie. With this controller, you can play, stop, browse, or step through the movie. If the movie has a soundtrack, you can use the controller to adjust the sound level. The controller also gauges where the current scene is in relation to the beginning and end of the movie. By pressing certain keys while operating the controller, you can turn the sound on and off, copy and paste parts of the movie, play in reverse, change the playback rate, and more. Figure 13-2 illustrates the functions of a standard QuickTime movie controller for a music file. (Some applications have variants of the standard controller and may put the controller in a palette that floats above the document window.)

Figure 13-2: Use controls below a movie file to play, pause, browse, or step through it and adjust its sound volume. *(Image courtesy of NASA)*

Playing and pausing

To start a movie playing, click the Play button. This button has a right-pointing triangle like the play button on a tape recorder or VCR. While a movie is playing, this button becomes a pause button (with two vertical lines on it).

Stepping forward and backward

The two arrow buttons to the right of the play bar step backward and forward at the rate of one frame per click. The step buttons have different effects on movies that don't have frames. For example, in a movie that has only sound or music tracks, each click of a step button skips ahead or back a quarter of a second.

Tip Holding the step buttons down makes the file fast forward and rewind. If you hold the step buttons down while a movie is playing, you speed up the audio (or play it backward) as well.

Going to another part of the movie

The gray play bar in the middle of the movie controller shows the position of the currently playing frame relative to the beginning and end of the movie. To go to a different place in the movie, you can drag the playhead in the play bar or simply click the play bar (at or near the location of the movie segment that you want to see).

QuickTime Controller Shortcuts

The QuickTime movie controller responds to all kinds of keyboard shortcuts. Pressing Return or Spacebar alternately starts and pauses play forward. Pressing ⌘-Period (.) also pauses playing. You can press ⌘-Right Arrow (→) to play forward and ⌘-Left Arrow (←) to play backward. Press the Right Arrow (→) to step forward and the Left Arrow (←) to step backward. To raise or lower the sound level, press the Up Arrow (↑) or the Down Arrow (↓). Shift-Up Arrow (↑) raises the sound level beyond its normal maximum.

You can also go immediately to the beginning or end of the movie. To go to the beginning, Option-click the backward-step button. To go to the end, Option-click the forward-step button.

Adjusting the sound

To adjust the sound level, use the button labeled with the speaker. Click and hold down this button to pop up a slider (shown in Figure 13-2) that you can use to raise or lower the sound level. You can turn the sound off and on by Option-clicking the speaker button. You can set the sound level to up to three times louder than its normal maximum by holding down Shift while adjusting the level with the slider. If the speaker button is absent, the movie has no sound.

Changing playback direction and speed

To play the movie backward, ⌘-click the backward-step button. In some applications, you can Control-click either step button to reveal a jog shuttle that controls the direction and playback rate. Dragging the jog shuttle to the right gradually increases the forward playback rate from below normal to twice normal speed. Dragging the jog shuttle to the left has the same effect on playback speed, but makes the movie play backward.

Choosing a chapter

A text area appears to the left of the step buttons in the movie controller for some movies. This chapter list button lets you go to predetermined points in the movie, in the same way that index tabs let you turn to sections of a binder. Pressing the chapter list button pops up a menu of chapter titles and choosing a chapter title takes you quickly to the corresponding part of the movie. If the chapter list button is absent, either the movie window is too small to show the chapter list or the movie has no defined chapters.

Playing movies without controllers

Applications may display movies without controllers. In this case, a badge in the lower-left corner of the movie distinguishes it from a still graphic. To play a movie that has a badge and no controller, double-click the movie. If you press Shift while double-clicking the movie, it plays backward. Clicking a playing movie stops it. You can also display a standard movie controller by clicking the badge. Figure 13-3 shows a QuickTime movie with a badge.

Figure 13-3: A badge identifies a movie without a controller.

Note   Badge is a term for a distinguishing mark superimposed on an icon or image to indicate that it isn't a standard icon or image — such as the little arrow to indicate an alias icon. In Figure 13-3, the badge is the little film strip image at the lower left of the picture of Spenser.

Viewing with QuickTime Player

Although you don't need a special application to view QuickTime movies, QuickTime includes one called QuickTime Player. With the QuickTime Player menu commands, you have more control than in some other applications over playing a movie. In some cases, however, you have less control over a movie. That's because the QuickTime Player application sports a sleek interface that has traded some features to look more like a consumer device. So, although some of the controls are more like those found on a VCR, for example, QuickTime Player lacks some of the controls that you have in other applications, such as AppleWorks 6.

First, look at QuickTime Player's controls and how they differ from the standard QuickTime controls. Then look at some of the additional features that the QuickTime Player Pro application offers. Some commands are not available in the basic edition of QuickTime Player, which comes with the free version of QuickTime. These commands become available when you upgrade to QuickTime Pro. The following descriptions of QuickTime Player commands indicate the QuickTime Player versions in which the described command is available.

Using QuickTime Player controls

When you open a movie in the QuickTime Player application, you find a number of slight differences from the QuickTime controls found in other applications, as Figure 13-4 shows.

Figure 13-4: QuickTime Player has the usual controls for movie playback.

Most of the differences in QuickTime Player controls are cosmetic. The play bar and playhead are located above the play/pause and step controls, which are larger in QuickTime Player than in the QuickTime controller of other applications. QuickTime Player has separate controls for going to the start or end of the movie, and it has a TV button for accessing QuickTime TV channels, which we discuss later in this chapter. QuickTime Player also displays some extra information, including the elapsed time display to the right of the play bar and the audio equalizer display to the left of the play bar. A few features are missing. For example, you can't ⌘-click the step buttons to bring up a shuttle jog control.

Tip　　After clicking the TV button to see QuickTime TV channels, you can return to the QuickTime movie that was previously displayed in the window by clicking the TV button again.

In addition to the clearly visible volume control, QuickTime Player has several hidden audio controls. To reveal the hidden controls—Balance, Bass, and Treble—choose Movie⇨Show Sound Controls or simply click the audio equalizer at the right end of the play bar. See Figure 13-5.

Tip

You can change the volume quickly by clicking in the slider track instead of dragging the slider. For example, to set full volume, click at the right end of the slider track. When the Balance, Bass, and Treble controls are showing, you can drag the mouse over the settings instead of clicking the plus and minus buttons. To raise the sound level beyond its normal maximum, press Shift-Up Arrow (↑).

Figure 13-5: QuickTime Player has hidden audio controls.

Using QuickTime Player Favorites

QuickTime Player can keep track of your favorite movies to make playing them more convenient. You designate which movies are your Favorites, and then you can play one by choosing it from a menu or clicking an item in a list window as shown in Figure 13-6.

To see a list of your favorite movies in a window choose Favorites⇨Show Favorites. The Favorites window is empty until you add movies as Favorites. To make a movie a Favorite, drag its movie file from the Finder to the Favorites window. You can drag several movie files at the same time to make Favorites of them all. You can make a Favorite of a movie that's open in QuickTime Player by bringing the movie to the front and choosing Favorites⇨Add Movie As Favorite.

To play a favorite movie, click its icon in the favorites window or choose it from the Favorites submenu.

You can rearrange the Favorites window by dragging icons to different positions in the window. You can remove a Favorite by Control-clicking its icon in the favorites window and choosing Delete Favorite from the contextual menu that appears.

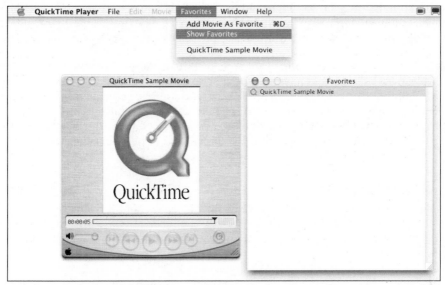

Figure 13-6: QuickTime Player can display your favorite movies in list form, and clicking an icon opens the movie.

Using controls within movies

For the most part, you'll probably confine your mouse clicks to the QuickTime Player controls. Occasionally, you may find it useful to actually click inside the movie window. For example, QuickTime can display Macromedia Flash documents, which may include buttons and links that can be clicked in the movie window. If you're viewing an image (especially one that's available via a streaming QuickTime connection over the Internet), you may be able to click a button or link in the QuickTime Player movie window.

Changing the QuickTime Player window size

Unlike many other applications that can show QuickTime movies, the QuickTime Player application displays QuickTime movies in windows with resize controls. If you resize a movie window, QuickTime resizes the movie to fill the window. A resized movie generally plays less smoothly if you change its proportions. As a precautionary measure, QuickTime normally forces movie windows to maintain their original proportions. To resize without this constraint, press Shift while dragging the resize control.

A movie looks best at an even multiple of its original size, such as half-size or double size. QuickTime Player constrains a movie to an optimal multiple of its original size if you press Option while dragging the movie window's resize control. To quickly change a window to the nearest even multiple of its original size, Option-click its resize control.

In addition to dragging a movie window's size box, you can use QuickTime Player menu commands to resize it. The basic edition of QuickTime Player has Half Size, Double Size, and Normal Size commands as well as a Fill Screen command.

In addition, people may confuse Fill Screen with Full Screen here — Fill Screen will always have the controller, whereas Full Screen does not. Full Screen is a Present Movie option that turns your entire screen into a movie screen, with all controls, the Player, and the menu bar hidden. The movie plays in Full Screen just as if someone were projecting it onto your display. Fill Screen, on the other hand, simply increases the size of the QuickTime Player window to fill either the height or width of the screen, not counting the menu bar.

Presenting a movie

Instead of displaying a movie in a window, you can present it centered on a completely black screen. In QuickTime Player Pro, choose Movie ➪ Present Movie (⌘-M). (The Present Movie command is not available in the basic edition of QuickTime Player.)

The Present Movie command displays a dialog in which you can set the movie size and specify whether you want to play the movie normally or in slide show fashion (one frame at a time, for example). If your computer has more than one display, this dialog lets you select the display on which you want the movie presented. Setting a movie's presentation size in this dialog to Double or Full Screen usually produces better results than resizing the movie manually before presenting it.

To stop a movie presentation, click the mouse button. With a slide show presentation, clicking the mouse button advances to the next movie frame; double-clicking goes back one frame. Pressing Esc or ⌘-period stops a slide show presentation.

Searching for a text track

While viewing a movie that contains a text track, you can search for specific text in the movie. In QuickTime Player Pro, choose Edit ➪ Find (⌘-F) — if there are no text tracks, Find is disabled (grayed-out). (Text searching is not available in the basic edition of QuickTime Player.)

The Find command displays a dialog in which you search forward or backward to find text. If QuickTime Player finds the text you're looking for, it immediately shows the corresponding part of the movie and highlights the found text. You can search for another occurrence of the same text by choosing Find Again from the Edit menu. Figure 13-7 shows an example of a movie with found text highlighted.

Choosing a language

QuickTime movies can have sound tracks in several languages. To select the language you want to hear, choose Movie ➪ Choose Language. QuickTime Player displays a dialog that lists the available languages. If the Choose Language command is disabled (grayed out), the movie doesn't have sound tracks in multiple languages.

Figure 13-7: Find text in a movie's text track.

Playing continuously (looping)

You can set QuickTime Player Pro to play a QuickTime movie in a continuous loop, either always playing forward or playing alternately forward and backward. Choose Loop or Loop Back and Forth from the Movie menu. (These commands are not available in the basic edition of QuickTime Player.)

Selecting part of a movie and playing it

In QuickTime Player Pro, you can select part of a movie and then play only the selected part. (You can't select part of a movie in the basic edition of QuickTime Player.)

To select part of a movie while playing that part, follow these steps:

1. **Drag both of the selection triangles to the far-left edge of the play bar (see Figure 13-8).**

2. **Move the playhead to the place in the movie where you want to begin selecting.**

3. **Shift-click the play button to start the movie and begin selecting the movie segment.**

4. **Release Shift to end the selection and stop playing.** The selected part of the movie appears gray in the play bar. Figure 13-8 shows a movie that has been partly selected.

Figure 13-8: Selecting part of a movie with the Shift key or selection triangles makes part of the play bar turn gray.

To select part of a movie without playing it, use these steps:

1. **Drag the left selection triangle to the first frame you'd like to select.**

2. **Drag the right selection triangle to the last frame you'd like to select.**

3. **Adjust the selection by doing either of the following:**

   • Drag a selection triangle.

   • Click a selection triangle; then use the Left (←) and Right (→) Arrow keys to adjust the selection frame by frame.

To play the selected part of a movie, follow these steps:

1. **Choose Movie⇨Play Selection Only (⌘-T).**

2. **Click the Play button.** When a check mark is next to Play Selection Only in the Movie menu, all the movie controls and QuickTime Player commands apply only to the selected part. For example, the Loop command causes only the selected part to play continuously, and the first-frame and last-frame buttons go to the beginning and end of the selection.

To cancel a selection: Drag both selection arrows to the far-left side of the play bar.

Playing every frame

In QuickTime Player Pro, you can prevent QuickTime from dropping any video frames to keep the video and audio tracks synchronized. If you want to see every frame, even if it means playing the movie more slowly and without sound, choose Movie⇨Play All Frames. (The Play All Frames command is not available in the basic edition of QuickTime Player and is disabled if there is no video track.)

Playing all movies

You can have QuickTime Player Pro play all movies that are currently open by choosing Movie⇨Play All Movies. (This command is not available in the basic edition of QuickTime Player.)

Saving QuickTime Movies from a Web Browser

When you view a QuickTime movie in a Web browser window, the movie is downloaded from Internet but is not saved permanently on your hard drive. You may be able to save the movie from the Web browser as a movie file on your hard drive so that you can watch the movie again in QuickTime Player without downloading the movie again. You can save a QuickTime movie from a Web browser only if you have QuickTime Pro and only if the author of the movie allows saving the movie.

To save a QuickTime movie that's displayed in a Web browser, Control-click the movie and choose Save As QuickTime Movie from the contextual menu that appears. You can also make the contextual menu appear by clicking a movie in the browser window and holding the mouse button down for a few seconds. (The Save As QuickTime Movie choice does not appear in the contextual menu if you do not have QuickTime Pro or the author of the movie does not allow saving the movie.)

Watching Streaming QuickTime Media

QuickTime 4.0 introduced a new technology to the world of QuickTime — *streaming media*. QuickTime 6, the version included with Mac OS X 10.2, has significantly improved the performance of streaming media. With streaming media, QuickTime movie files (whether they contain video, audio, text, or other elements) are sent over the Internet a piece at a time. Those pieces are reassembled in QuickTime Player and played back almost as quickly as the data arrives over the Internet. In this way, movies can be viewed (or listened to) more quickly over the Internet. Likewise, live events can be displayed in real time over the Web.

Tip For optimum streaming, QuickTime Player consults the settings on the Connection tab in your QuickTime System Preferences. Make sure these settings match the speed of your connection so that you get better playback from streaming movies.

With some streaming media movies, you can pause, play, and move back and forth within the movie file by using the play bar or the forward and reverse controls. In others, especially live events, you won't have as much control — pausing and playing again takes you to the current moment in the live event instead of picking up where you left off.

QuickTime streaming media uses an Internet protocol known as RTP (real-time transport protocol). RTP is similar to the familiar HTTP protocol used for Web pages, but RTP is designed specifically for the special requirements of streaming media. With RTP, movies are not downloaded to your computer. Instead a continuous data stream is sent to your computer, and QuickTime plays it immediately.

QuickTime movies can also be sent to your computer via the HTTP or FTP protocols. With HTTP or FTP, the entire movie is downloaded to your computer. (If you don't have QuickTime Pro, the movie may be downloaded to a temporary file that is deleted automatically.) You don't necessarily have to wait for the entire movie to finish downloading before it begins playing. Many QuickTime movies use a technology called *fast start* or *progressive download.* In practice, fast-start movies may seem like streaming video. In fact, QuickTime begins playing the first part of the movie while it continues to download the remainder.

Interacting with QuickTime VR Images

You can do more with QuickTime than play linear movies. Apple's QuickTime VR software lets you explore places as if you were really there and examine objects as if they were with you. When you view a QuickTime VR panorama of a place, you can look up, look down, turn around, zoom in to see detail, and zoom out for a broader view. When you view a QuickTime VR object, you can manipulate it to see a different view of it. As you explore a panorama, you can move from it into a neighboring panorama or to an object in it. For example, you could move from one room to another room and then examine an object there.

You can interact with a QuickTime VR panorama or object from any application in which you can view a linear QuickTime movie. You can use QuickTime Player, a Web browser, TextEdit, AppleWorks, or any other application that can play QuickTime movies.

When you view a QuickTime VR panorama or object, a QuickTime VR controller sometimes appears at the bottom of the window. It's in the same place as the controller for a regular QuickTime movie (especially those viewed with the conventional controller in applications like AppleWorks). As with regular QuickTime movies, the QuickTime VR controller in QuickTime Player looks different than the VR controller in other applications. The cosmetic differences don't affect the functions of the controller buttons.

Actually, you don't use the QuickTime VR controller as the primary means of inter-acting with a QuickTime VR image. You simply drag the mouse pointer to explore a QuickTime VR panorama or investigate a QuickTime VR object. The remainder of this section describes how to use the mouse pointer and the VR controller to inter-act with a QuickTime VR image.

Exploring VR panoramas

➡ ⬅ To look around a QuickTime VR panorama, you click the picture and drag left, right, up, or down. The picture moves in the direction that you
⬆ ⬇ drag, and the pointer changes shape to indicate the direction of movement. Figure 13-9 shows a QuickTime VR panorama being moved to the left.

Figure 13-9: When you pan a QuickTime VR panorama, the pointer indicates the direction of movement.

Investigating VR objects

To manipulate a QuickTime VR object, you drag it left, right, up, or down. As you drag, the object, or some part of it, moves. For example, it may turn around so that you can see all sides of it, or it may open and close. The author of the VR picture determines the effect.

When viewing a QuickTime VR object, you can also place the pointer near an inside edge of the VR window and press the mouse button to move the object continu-ously. Figure 13-10 shows several views of QuickTime VR object.

Figure 13-10: Drag a QuickTime VR object in any direction to see another view of the object.

(Images courtesy of John Greenleigh/Flipside Studios.)

Revealing the VR controller

When you view a QuickTime VR image in a Web browser window, the VR controller may not appear at the bottom of the image. If you have QuickTime Pro, you can view the VR image with a VR controller by saving the VR image as a QuickTime movie file on your hard drive and opening the movie file in QuickTime Player. The method for saving a VR image is the same as the method described earlier for saving a regular QuickTime movie. To recap: Control-click the movie or click the movie and hold the mouse button until the contextual menu appears, and choose Save As QuickTime Movie from the contextual menu. (The Save As QuickTime Movie choice does not appear in the contextual menu if you do not have QuickTime Pro or the author of the VR image does not allow saving it.)

Zooming in and out

While viewing a QuickTime VR panorama or object, you can zoom in or out.

+ **To zoom in:** Click the VR controller button that looks like a plus sign or press the Control key.

+ **To zoom out:** Click the button that looks like a minus sign or press the Shift key.

As you zoom in on a VR object, it eventually becomes too large to see all at once in the QuickTime VR window. You may be able to view another part of a zoomed-in VR object by clicking the controller button labeled with a four-way arrow and then dragging the object or by pressing Option while dragging. Either way, the object holds its pose as it moves around in the window. To resume normal operation, click the button again or release the Option key. (You don't need to use the four-way drag button or the Option key with a VR panorama, which you can pan just by dragging across it.)

Interacting with hot spots

A QuickTime VR panorama or object can contain hot spots. You click these areas of the picture to cause some action to occur. Typically, the action involves going to another panorama or object. A hot spot can trigger another kind of action, such as displaying text in the empty area of the VR controller or taking you to a Web page.

Hot spots are normally unmarked. One way to find them is to move the pointer around the panorama or object. When the pointer is over a hot spot, the pointer's shape changes. A variety of different pointer shapes may indicate a hot spot. One common shape is a large white arrow pointing up.

You can also have QuickTime VR show the hot spots in the picture. To highlight the hot spots with shaded rectangles, click the VR controller button labeled with an up arrow and question mark. If you double-click this button, it stays down and you can see all hot spots as you drag the pointer to move the picture. Figure 13-11 is an example of an outlined hot spot in a QuickTime VR panorama.

Figure 13-11: Hot spots are revealed in a QuickTime VR panorama (the highlighted area).

If clicking a hot spot takes you to another panorama or object, you can go back to your previous location by clicking the back button, which is labeled with a left arrow in the VR controller. If you've progressed through several hot spots, you can retrace your steps by clicking the back button repeatedly.

Making a QuickTime Slide Show

Telling a story or delivering a message through a sequence of pictures—as they say, a picture is worth a thousand words—is a very common use of computers. Major applications, such as Microsoft's PowerPoint, are devoted to this task. An entire module of AppleWorks 6 is also dedicated to this task, as are some capabilities outside the AppleWorks 6 Presentation module. Presenting slide shows from images on your disks is also a major feature of such applications as GraphicConverter and iView Multimedia.

QuickTime allows you to create slide shows from images on your disk, as well. But, and this is a big but, QuickTime combines them into a platform-independent file that you can view on any computer with QuickTime support. Being able to present the file on just about any computer via QuickTime is so useful that Microsoft included saving a presentation as a QuickTime file as one of the major new features in PowerPoint 2001.

Of course, going to the effort of importing multiple image files, placing and orienting them just so, and then saving the result as a QuickTime file in PowerPoint seems like an awful lot of effort. QuickTime Pro makes the task a whole lot easier, as follows:

1. **Collect the image files you want in your slide show in a single folder.**

2. **Give them a common name followed by a sequential number, such as appear in Figure 13-12.**

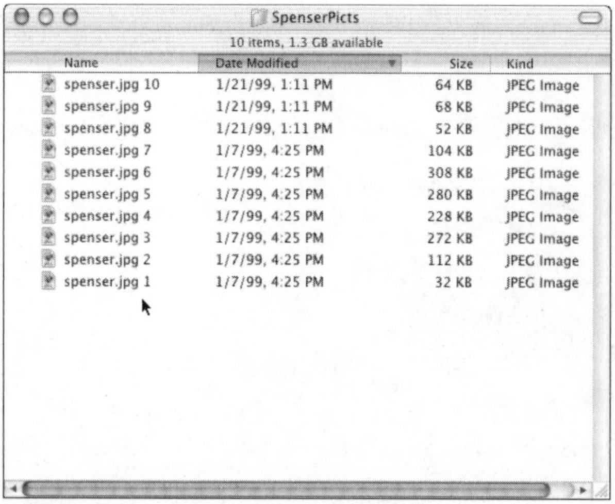

Figure 13-12: Give all the files you want in your slide show the same name, but followed by sequential numbers for the order in which you want them to appear.

3. **In QuickTime Player, choose File⇨Open Image Sequence and select the first file in your sequence of pictures, as shown in Figure 13-13.**

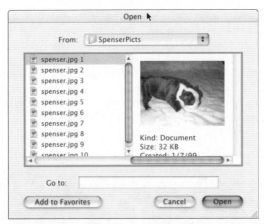

Figure 13-13: Select the first file you want to have appear in your slide show, QuickTime will do the rest.

4. **Choose a Frame rate in the Image Sequence Settings dialog that appears, as shown in Figure 13-14.** The default of 15 frames per second is useful for animations, but you will probably want something a bit slower for a slide show.

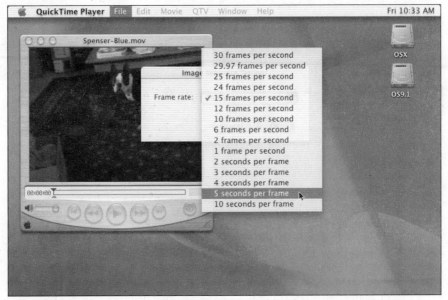

Figure 13-14: Tell QuickTime how long you want each frame to stay on screen.

QuickTime Player Pro then creates a movie, showing each picture in sequence. If you want to save this QuickTime movie, choose File➪Save As and then name the movie in the Save dialog that appears, shown in Figure 13-15. The default radio button selection, Save normally (allowing dependencies), requires you to transport the folder of images along with the QuickTime movie. We recommend, unless you're always going to show the slide show from the machine on which you created it, that you make the movie self-contained (as shown in the figure) to avoid having a piece or pieces missing when you make your presentation.

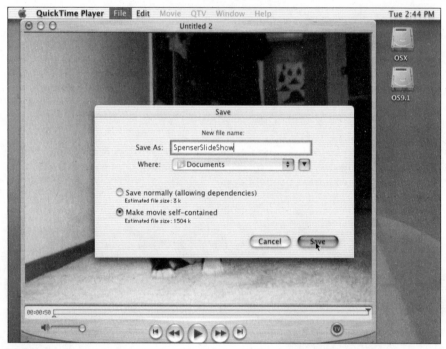

Figure 13-15: Save your movie with pointers to the original files or as a self-contained entity.

Note   Slide shows are most effective when all the images are the same size and orientation.

Caution   If the audio sequence is longer than your slide show, its play is sped up to fit the length of your show; conversely, if it is shorter than your slide show, the clip is slowed down to fit the slide show's length. You should choose a clip as close in length to that of your slide show as possible. You can find the length required by choosing Movie➪Get Movie Properties (⌘-J) and choosing Time from the right-hand pop-up menu.

Basic QuickTime Movie Editing

As is usually the case if you want to use QuickTime for much more than a viewer, editing your QuickTime movies and tracks requires an update to QuickTime Pro. One of the first changes you may notice if you've upgraded to QuickTime Pro is that the play bar has two markers at the bottom — you use these to mark the beginning and end of a selection as shown earlier in Figure 13-6. Another change is that the Edit menu has added a slew of extra options, including the ability to Delete Tracks, Extract Tracks, and more. The Movie menu has added a Present Movie option so that you can have your QuickTime movie take over the whole screen.

The selection markers and additional Edit menu options give you the tools to do a significant amount of editing — either to create a new movie or to modify an existing movie. With these options you can add, eliminate, and rearrange scenes and then save the movie under the same or a new name.

Fine-tuning a selection

Of course, you can drag the selection triangles to the point where you want them. However, this sort of gross movement tends to make positioning on a particular frame of your movie somewhat difficult. Use the drag technique to get the triangle into the general vicinity of the frame, then click a selection triangle and press the Left- or Right-Arrow keys to move the selection triangle one frame in that direction or hold down the appropriate arrow key to move the selection triangle in that direction in slow motion.

Working with selections

After you've made your selection, you can play just the selection by choosing Movie⇨Play Selection Only (⌘-T). You can even drag the picture from the movie screen to the Desktop or a Finder window to create a movie clipping — just double-click it to view the clip.

You can cut, copy, or clear the contents of a selection using the corresponding Edit menu commands or trim everything but the selection from the movie by choosing Edit⇨Trim.

To paste a cut or copied selection in another location within your movie (or even in a different movie), position the playhead where you want the insertion to occur and choose Edit⇨Paste (⌘-V). The pasted information appears, and the selection markers show you where it begins and ends.

Tip   A quick way to add a title or silent-movie style text block is to paste text in at the current frame. This inserts a two-second block of white text against a black background — QuickTime makes use of any font and style information that was with the text on the clipboard. This also works to insert still pictures. You can even drag text files directly to the QuickTime Player screen to get the two-second inserts.

These editing techniques work with all editable QuickTime movies — even sound files such as AIFF.

Note Some media types, such as MPEG-1 files, which are playable in QuickTime Player, are not editable with these tools. If the movie is in one of these non-editable formats, all the Edit menu choices are disabled.

Adding a Sound Track to Your Movie

By using QuickTime Player Pro's editing capabilities, you can add an audio (sound) track to your movie before saving it. Import the audio file to a new movie and copy the desired portion (or all of it) to the Clipboard. Now, select the slide show movie and choose Edit⇨Add Scaled.

Adding QuickTime Text Tracks

QuickTime lets you include multiple tracks in a single movie. One of these track types is the *text track*. Text can be used for credits, subtitles, title screens, or teleprompter text.

You can create text tracks very easily in any word-processor or editor that allows you to save as plain text (sometimes called *ASCII* text). If you use TextEdit, be sure to choose Format⇨Make Plain Text (⌘-Shift-T). To create a text track, follow these steps:

1. **Create and save your plain text file.**

2. **Copy the text to the Clipboard.**

3. **In QuickTime Player Pro, position the playhead where you want the track to begin.**

4. **Choose Edit⇨Add (⌘-Option-V) to position the text file at that point, overlaying the image.** The default duration for a text track inserted in this manner is two seconds. If you want a different duration, make a selection covering the duration and choose Edit⇨Add Scaled (⌘-Option-V). The text track is added with each paragraph of your text file covering its own sequence of frames.

Occasionally, you might want something other than white text on a black background. You might want different colors to better coordinate with the movie frames. To adjust the text color, proceed as follows:

1. **Choose Movie⇨Get Movie Properties (⌘-J) to open the Properties window for your movie.**

2. **From the pop-up menu on the left, choose the text track.**

3. **From the pop-up menu on the right, choose Graphics Mode.**

Applying QuickTime Effects

Concealed in the Export dialog (File⇨Export, ⌘-E), QuickTime Pro includes a number of *filters* (special effects) that you can apply to your movie. You find these filters by first setting the Export dialog's Export pop-up menu to Movie to QuickTime Movie, next clicking the Options button in the Export dialog and then clicking the Filter button in the Movie Settings dialog that appears. See Figure 13-16 for both the Movie Settings dialog and the Choose Video Filter dialog.

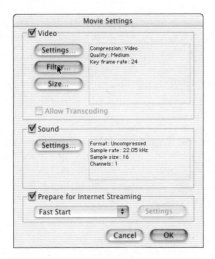

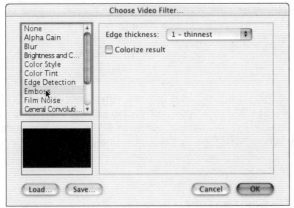

Figure 13-16: You can apply video special effects to a movie as you export it.

QuickTime Pro even enables you to save filter settings for later use via the Save and Load buttons in the Choose Video Filter dialog. Unfortunately, you can only apply one filter to a movie on export. Therefore, if you want to accumulate effects, you need to export with one effect, load that movie, and apply another effect when exporting it, and so on—cumbersome, but possible.

The available filters (13 of them) let you adjust brightness, color, and contrast; apply blurs or sharpen, add film noise (simulating scratches and dust) or a lens flare (similar to what happens when you have the sun in front of you reflecting off the lens).

Working with iMovie 2

For visually oriented people, probably the biggest "WOW-factor" application to hit the Mac since the original MacPaint in 1984 was iMovie. While you may or may not find iMovie 2 on your Mac OS X CD (depending upon when you bought it and whether it came bundled with your Mac), Apple has iMovie 2 for Mac OS X available for free download via your iDisk. The iMovie application is included in a default installation of OS X 10.2.

With iMovie 2 and a compatible digital camcorder, you can create digital video at least the equal of many B-movies and approaching some substantial films in quality. We can't give a full course on the use of iMovie 2 in the space available here, but we show you the basics. For more thorough coverage, we would recommend Todd Stauffer's *iMovie 2 For Dummies*.

Getting started with iMovie 2

When you launch iMovie 2, its window takes over your whole screen. If your Dock isn't hidden, we recommend that you turn on Dock hiding by choosing Apple⇨Dock⇨Turn Hiding On (⌘-Option-D). Click the New Project button, name your project in the Create New Project dialog, and you are ready to start, as shown in Figure 13-17.

Tip   The higher the screen resolution, the easier it is to work with iMovie. Although you can operate in iMovie at 800 x 600 resolution, as shown in Figure 13-17, by dint of much scrolling, we recommend that you operate at 1024 x 768 or greater resolution. (Of course, we recommend that for Mac OS X, in general.)

iMovie's three main panes are the following:

✦ **Monitor:** Where you watch and edit clips

✦ **Shelf:** Where you store clips and apply effects to them

✦ **Clip and timeline viewers:** Where you arrange clips and construct your movie

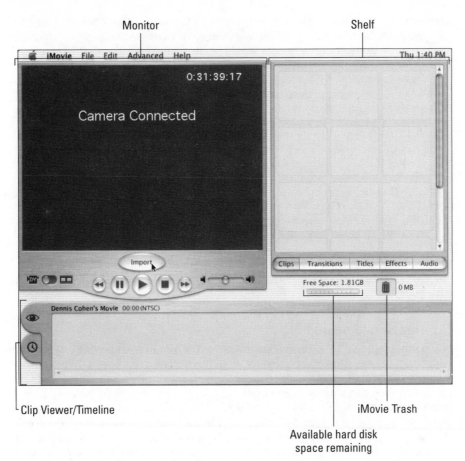

Monitor   Shelf

Clip Viewer/Timeline   iMovie Trash

Available hard disk
space remaining

Figure 13-17: iMovie 2's window takes the whole screen and has a number of panes in it.

The monitor

You use the monitor to view clips or the entire movie, edit clips, and switch between camera and view modes. When a camera is connected, as shown in Figure 13-17, iMovie tells you your location within the tape.

Note

Time in iMovie is measured in hours, minutes, seconds, and frames. If you are using NTSC video (the standard within the United States and Canada), there are 30 frames (really 29.97) per second of video. If your video format is PAL (Europe and most of Asia), there are 25 frames per second.

The buttons along the bottom of the monitor vary depending upon whether the toggle switch to the left of the buttons is in the camera or editing position. In camera mode, the buttons are Reverse, Pause, Play, Stop, and Fast Forward. The Import button tells iMovie to start the camera playing and to import the video coming over the FireWire cable.

When you're in editing mode, the buttons are reverse, go to beginning, play/pause, present full screen, and fast-forward.

The shelf

When you import clips from your camera, each individual clip first appears on the shelf. New clips start at scene breaks (where your camera stopped and restarted recording), where you stop and then restart importing, and when the clip gets to 2GB in length (a little over nine minutes).

When you click one of the buttons at the bottom of the shelf, its appearance changes to show controls for adding transitions, titles, special effects, and working with audio.

The Transitions panel

When you click the Transitions button at the bottom of the shelf, the Transitions panel appears, as shown in Figure 13-18. In it, you see a list of possible transitions, including their names and a small green button with one or two arrowheads on it. Transition buttons with one arrow act on a single clip, and indicates whether it occurs at the beginning (for example, a Fade In) or the end (for example, a Fade Out). Two arrowheads indicate that the transition occurs at the end of one clip and the beginning of the next, for example a Cross Dissolve. In addition to the transitions and effects included with iMovie, you can obtain more from Apple's iMovie Web pages (www.apple.com/imovie) or by purchasing collections from a third-party such as GeeThree (www.geethree.com).

Figure 13-18: You select a transition here, and it will preview in the small pane at the upper right.

These transitions affect the clips selected in the clip viewer. In most cases, you can also control the speed (duration) of the transition, as well as the direction in which it moves.

After you have created the transition you want in the Transitions panel, make the clip viewer (covered later) active and drag the icon for the desired transition from the Transitions panel to the clip it affects (or between the two clips) in the clip viewer. When the appropriate spacing appears in the clip viewer, release the mouse button. This will apply the transition you created. Until you do this, you're just experimenting.

The Titles panel

Similar to the Transitions panel, the Titles panel lets you create titles and credits to show in your iMovie. If you find the little Preview pane in the Titles panel too small, you can click the Preview button and watch your credits in the monitor, as shown in Figure 13-19.

Figure 13-19: You can preview your credits or titles in the monitor if you wish.

As you can see in Figure 13-19, 800 x 600 resolution significantly truncates the display areas for the Title panel's lists, showing only three of the more than a dozen title effects available and only two of the lines of the displayed text.

The Title panel gives you control over direction, duration (speed), text color, font, and font size. The Over Black checkbox lets you specify that the text appears over a black background. iMovie creates a clip with a black background for you to insert in your clip viewer rather than overlaying it on a selected clip. The QT Margins checkbox tells iMovie to keep the text within a TV set's viewable area so that nothing gets cropped if you play it on a television set. TV sets operate in an overscan mode, in that there is more of the picture than is displayed on the screen.

The Effects panel

Special effects are applied to clips. You can select from seven included effects (more are available for download or purchase, as described earlier), each of which has its own set of parameters and controls. With effects, you can change the colors, contrast, and brightness of your clips. You can also create interesting effects, such as a fade from sepia to the normal coloration of your video to give that effect so often seen in movies and on television. The Effects panel is shown in Figure 13-20.

Figure 13-20: Set effects options, preview the effects, and apply effects in the Effects panel.

If you want the effect to apply to the entire clip, both the Effect In and Effect Out sliders should be set to 0:00. If, however, you want the effect to gradually take place, set the sliders appropriately — remember that Effect Out is measured backwards from the end of the clip.

One example of using these staged effects is to go from a sepia-toned still frame to full-color live action (as was done so well in the classic movie, *The Sting*), as follows:

1. **Place a sepia-toned still image of the first frame of your clip just before the clip.**

2. **Select the Sepia Tone effect.**

3. **Move the Effect Out slider to the left to mark the point where you want the effect to end (almost to the beginning of the clip).** By putting the still clip at the end and using the Effect In slider, you could also dissolve to a sepia-tone still.

The Audio panel

The Audio panel is where you add sound effects to your movie. You can simply drag one of the sounds from the list (shown in Figure 13-21) to one of the audio tracks in the timeline viewer.

You can use the Record Voice button (and your Mac's microphone) to create narrative to do voice-overs during your movie. Similarly, the Record Music button enables you to capture music from a CD. When an audio CD is inserted in your CD or DVD drive, a list of tracks appears in this section's list box. Select the one you want to import, click the Record Music button, and iMovie converts the track to an AIFF file and imports it onto the lower audio track of your timeline viewer.

Figure 13-21: Add sound effects, narrative, or a background score using the Audio panel.

The clip and timeline viewers

The wide pane with two tabs at the bottom of your iMovie screen houses the clip viewer (the tab with the eyeball) and the timeline viewer (the tab with the clock face).

You can drag clips and transitions from the shelf to either the clip viewer or timeline viewer, but much of your editing (particularly cut and paste) will probably be easier in the clip viewer. The timeline viewer is handy for editing individual tracks of your movie—you have a video track and two audio tracks, as shown in Figure 13-22.

Figure 13-22: You can edit individual tracks in the timeline viewer.

Tip
You can extract the audio portion of your video clip onto one of the timeline viewer's audio tracks by choosing Advanced⬧Extract Audio (⌘-J). Then, you can turn the volume for the original video track off or down low using the volume control at the bottom of the viewer and move the audio tracks around to give effects similar to those of a television news broadcast where you continue to hear the newscaster speak while you're being shown footage taken in the field.

Editing your movie clips

The monitor provides a playhead and two selection triangles, identical in function to those described earlier in the discussion of QuickTime Pro. iMovie shows you a lot more, though, when you drag the playhead — the video in the monitor fast-forwards and reverses so that you can see exactly where you are at any time. This technique of dragging the playhead is called *scrubbing*. You can also position the playhead to any point by clicking on that point in the timeline viewer. Just as in QuickTime Player Pro, you can advance or reverse a frame at a time by using the arrow keys — ← to go back a frame and → to go forward a frame. Holding down the Shift key when pressing the Left- or Right-Arrow keys moves you 10 frames at a time.

The selection triangles are called *crop markers* in iMovie. Just as with the playhead, you can move the crop markers by clicking on them and then using the arrow keys. You can then choose Edit⇨Clear to remove the selected portion of the clip or Edit⇨Crop (⌘-K) to remove everything but the selected portion from the clip.

> **Tip**
>
> If you want to remove crop markers, just click on the clip's icon on the shelf. This immediately clears all crop markers. Additionally, until you empty iMovie's Trash, you can recover deleted material by repeatedly choosing Edit⇨Undo until you get back to where you wanted to be.

Saving your iMovie

Generally, you want to save your iMovie, either back to the camera to play on a TV or to QuickTime so that you can put it on the Web, send it in an e-mail, or burn it to a CD. If your Mac has the Apple SuperDisk DVD drive or a compatible product, you can also include your iMovie on a DVD that you create with the iDVD 2 application from Apple (www.apple.com/idvd/). All of these actions are initiated by choosing File⇨Export Movie (⌘-E) and then choosing from the Export pop-up menu shown in Figure 13-23.

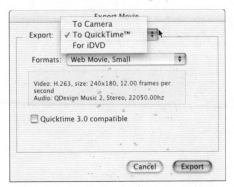

Figure 13-23: Choose how you want to save your movie in the Export Movie dialog.

Configuring and Updating QuickTime

QuickTime is highly configurable to suit your situation and use. This section will cover some of the settings you can adjust in QuickTime. To begin with, click on the System Preferences icon in the Dock to open System Preferences, as shown in Figure 13-24.

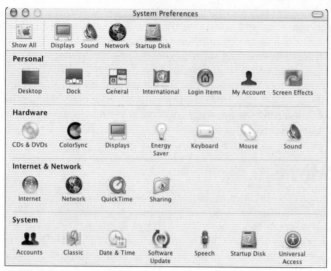

Figure 13-24: Access QuickTime Preferences within System Preferences.

Click on the QuickTime icon, found in the Internet & Network section of System Preferences, to open the QuickTime pane shown in Figure 13-25.

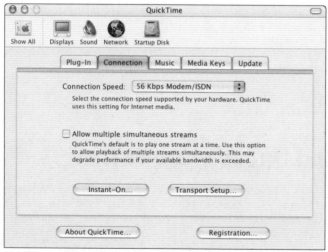

Figure 13-25: The QuickTime pane shows the Connection tab by default.

Set your system's connection speed with the pop-up menu so that QuickTime knows how fast to request data and at what rate to display the audio or video so as to avoid creating gaps while you wait for the next part of the data to download. If you have a fast connection, you may select the "Allow multiple simultaneous streams" checkbox, or click the Instant-On... button to shorten the wait at the beginning.

In the Plug-Ins tab (Figure 13-26), you can use the checkboxes to choose whether or not to play a movie automatically, to save a movie in the web browser's disk cache, and to enable kiosk mode, which reduces the amount of control someone has available. If you click on the MIME settings... button you see the MIME sheet shown in Figure 13-27.

Click the Update tab to view the information shown in Figure 13-28.

Figure 13-26: Use the Plug-In tab to alter QuickTime's behavior within a Web browser.

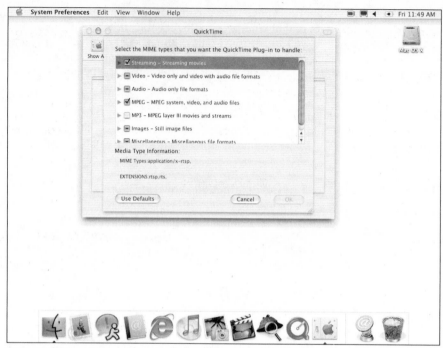

Figure 13-27: Choose the types of media formats QuickTime handles in a Web browser with the MIME sheet of the Plug-Ins tab.

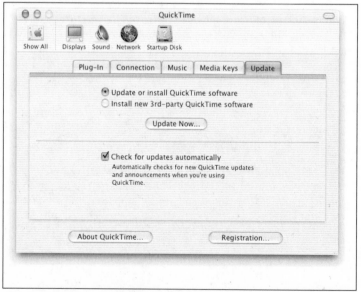

Figure 13-28: Use the Update tab to find and install new QuickTime components and applications.

If you click the Update Now... button on the Update tab, QuickTime checks for new codecs and other QuickTime software. This QuickTime update feature is separate from the Software Update in System Preferences for OS X.

With a QuickTime Player window open, choose the command QuickTime Player⇨Preferences⇨Player Preferences as shown in Figure 13-29. The Player Preferences window appears as shown in Figure 13-30.

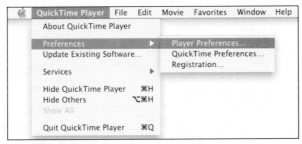

Figure 13-29: Choose the Player Preferences command to show the window for the QuickTime Player Preferences.

Figure 13-30: Set the behavior of the QuickTime Player application in Player Preferences.

Summary

In this chapter, you've seen how to use Apple's QuickTime technologies to play, edit, and create movies, and to set preferences for both QuickTime as part of OS X and the QuickTime Player application. You've also seen how to use iMovie 2 to create movies from digital video cameras and save them to QuickTime or back to the camera.

✦   ✦   ✦

Playing and Recording Audio

Apple wants the Mac to be your digital hub — whether it is video, audio, or text. In Chapter 13, you discovered that QuickTime provides a rich environment for handling all sorts of media, and that iMovie is a great tool for creating video files. Of course, you can play digitized music and sounds in QuickTime Player; however, you can only play one song at a time, and QuickTime Player doesn't have all the bells and whistles that audioholics want, such as playlists and a database of the audio files available.

Working with iTunes

The free iTunes application enables you to burn CDs, which makes purchasing third-party software tools less necessary if all you want to burn are audio CDs. In addition to *ripping* (recording audio CDs and encoding them in MP3, AIFF, or WAV format) audio from CDs, iTunes also writes audio CDs from MP3 collections called *playlists,* by using a compatible CD-RW drive. Additionally, you can download MP3 files to a variety of MP3 players, such as the Nomad and the Rio and play streaming audio from a huge assortment of Internet radio stations.

Playing MP3 and CD audio with iTunes

The iTunes window, as shown in Figure 14-1, is divided into panes. The tall, slender pane on the left of the window is the *Source* pane. In the Source pane, you determine from where you select your audio. You can make audio selections from your iTunes Library, Internet radio, a mounted audio CD, a connected MP3 player, or a playlist.

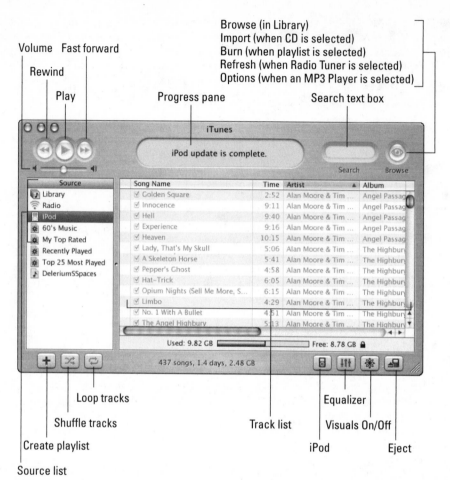

Figure 14-1: The iTunes window offers multiple sources for your listening pleasure.

Playing songs

To play songs, you can do the following:

  ✦ Double-click the song.

  ✦ Select the song and press Return or Enter.

  ✦ Select the song and click the Play button.

You can also move between adjacent songs by using one of the following methods:

  ✦ Press ⌘-← (previous song) and ⌘-→ (next song).

  ✦ Choose Controls➪Previous Song or Controls➪Next Song.

When a song is playing, iTunes displays your choice of a progress bar or equalizer display. The progress bar is shown in Figure 14-2 — you can position or reposition playing to any point in a song by dragging the progress bar playhead (the diamond) to the desired location. To view the equalizer display in this area, all you need to do is click the little arrowhead to which the arrow pointer is pointing in the figure.

Figure 14-2: The iTunes progress bar lets you position the playhead anywhere within a song if you only wish to listen to a part of the tune or if you wish to replay a passage.

In Figure 14-2, you see the song title displayed at the top of the progress area. Click this line of text to switch between song title, artist, and album name. Over time, this information automatically cycles between the three possibilities.

Note iTunes takes title, artist, and album information from what are called ID3 tags — textual information stored within an MP3 file. A number of other fields are also described by ID3 tags, which are discussed later in this chapter.

Below the title-artist-album line is the timeline, which you can also click, switching between Total Time, Elapsed Time, and Remaining Time.

For the audiophiles amongst our readership, the equalizer display gives you an amusing light show depicting what is happening on the two output channels (left and right speakers). If you hear an imbalance in the sound, you can utilize it to see if your problem is because of one of your speakers or if the recording is unbalanced. You can adjust the equalization with the Equalizer window. The button to display the Equalizer was shown in Figure 14-1. Clicking the Equalizer button shows the Equalizer window shown in Figure 14-3. Clicking the pop-up menu shows a wide range of preset equalization options.

Tip Clicking the iTunes window zoom button (+) reduces the window to just the controls at the top left and the progress area. Further, the buttons are now positioned vertically at the left edge of the window with close (X) on top, minimize to dock (–) in the middle, and zoom (+) on the bottom. Clicking zoom again pops you back to the original size, which is a handy way to keep the window around in an unobtrusive manner.

Managing your iTunes Library

The *iTunes Library* is the collection of all the MP3 songs you've played in iTunes (less those you've deleted from the iTunes Library), plus all those you've added using File⇨Add to iTunes Library or by using the Import button when a CD is selected. The iTunes feature adds the song to your iTunes Library whether you've double-clicked an MP3 file on your Desktop or in a Finder window or imported it from an audio CD. If you look in your home folder's Documents folder, you see an iTunes folder. This folder contains a database file, which keeps information on the 32,000 songs that iTunes can handle. This iTunes folder also contains an iTunes Music folder, and inside it are more folders that contain the songs in your iTunes Library. The folders inside the iTunes Music folder are named for performers, and each performer's folder contains folders with the names of album titles.

If you download MP3 files from the Internet, you can add them to your iTunes Library by performing the following steps:

1. **Choose File⇨Add to Library.**

2. **Locate the item (folder or file) you want to add.**

3. **Click the Choose button.**

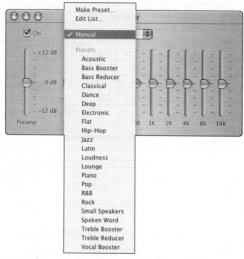

Figure 14-3: The iTunes Equalizer window adjusts balance of audio ranges.

Listening to Internet Radio

iTunes supports an ever-changing and growing list of Internet radio stations, divided into categories, as shown in Figure 14-4. Just click the disclosure triangle next to the genre of interest and then select the radio station of interest. You need to have an active Internet connection first as iTunes doesn't make one for you. Of course, if you have an always-on broadband connection, such as a T1, DSL, or cable modem connection, remembering to make an Internet connection isn't a problem. (Chapter 6 explains how to make an Internet connection.)

Figure 14-4: You probably can't receive as many radio stations on a real radio, and these stations are all nicely sorted by genre.

Tip

Select stations where the Bit Rate field is lower than your connection speed. For example, if your modem cannot actually get a 56K connection, then you should avoid 56kbps streams.

Downloading to digital MP3 players

Well on their way to taking the place of the Walkman and its clones from the portable music market, digital MP3 players are well supported by iTunes. As long as your MP3 player is on the list of supported devices (see Apple's iTunes Web page because this list grows constantly), you can hook it up by using the supplied USB cable and have it show up in your source list. Select your MP3 player in the source list and see its contents, from which you can delete or add items. Adding items to your MP3 player is very simple — just select the songs you want to add from the iTunes Library or a playlist and then drag the songs to the MP3 player in the source list. A screen shot of adding songs to a Diamond Rio in the source list is shown in Figure 14-5. You cannot play items on the MP3 player in iTunes or move items from the MP3 player to iTunes.

Figure 14-5: Adding a group of songs to Diamond Rio is just a matter of dragging their names to the Rio in the source list.

Using Apple's iPod MP3 player

The iPod MP3 player is tightly integrated with iTunes. If an iPod is connected to a Firewire-equipped Macintosh and the iPod is selected in the Source list of iTunes, an iPod window appears, as shown in Figure 14-1, and the Eject button becomes an Eject iPod button. Clicking the iPod button displays the iPod Preferences window, shown in Figure 14-6.

Figure 14-6: Use the iPod Preferences window to change how iTunes and an iPod work together.

Making use of playlists

The playlist is a powerful and useful feature in iTunes. A *playlist* is like a folder containing aliases to your audio songs. You can create a playlist by clicking the "Create a playlist" button (the plus sign button in Figure 14-1) and then naming it in the source list. Playlists let you group songs that you like to hear together and put them in the order you want to hear them. Just select them from the iTunes Library and drag them to the playlist group in the source list.

Note   An alternate and often easier method of creating a playlist involves selecting the songs in the iTunes Library list and choosing File⇨New Playlist from Selection (⌘-Shift-N). iTunes creates a new playlist entry with the name selected for your editing pleasure. When you then select the playlist, the selected songs are displayed in the song list window. Doing this is a great way to create a playlist containing songs by a particular artist.

Clicking the Shuffle button, the Playlist button with the crossed arrows, you can randomize the order of items in a playlist. Clicking it again reverts you to the original order. You can also click the Repeat button to *loop* a playlist.

You can also work with subsets of a playlist without creating a new playlist just by deselecting the boxes next to the names of the songs you don't want played.

If you want your playlist to open in its own window, just double-click the playlist's icon. To delete a playlist, for example after burning your own CD of it (see the next topic), just click the playlist's icon to select it and press Delete or choose Edit⇨Clear.

Smart Playlists are a new feature of iTunes in version 3 and up. With Smart Playlists, you can have iTunes automatically create and update playlists as you add and remove music from your iTunes Library.

Recording your own audio CDs

Possibly the most useful feature of a playlist is that it, combined with a compatible CD-RW drive, lets you write audio CDs suitable for use in most standard CD players. Just create your playlist by dragging the songs into the order you want them to appear, checking the time at the bottom of the window to make sure that your material fits on a CD (usually either 74 minutes or 80 minutes), and clicking the Burn CD aperture in the upper-right corner of the window. iTunes asks you to insert a recordable CD into your CD burner and then to click the Burn CD button. At that point, just sit back and relax while iTunes creates your CD. You can listen to music while iTunes burns the CD. The burning process is shown in Figure 14-7.

Note   You can set iTunes to automatically start whenever a blank CD or DVD is inserted into the drive with the CDs and DVDs pane of System Preferences, covered in Chapter 15.

Figure 14-7: iTunes creates audio CDs for you from your MP3 playlists, if you have a compatible CD burner.

Although you can record to a CD-R or a CD-RW and have no difficulties reading the disc on your computer, your experiences using such discs in commercial audio CD players can vary widely. Many standard CD players, especially those made more than two or three years ago, have problems reading CD-R media. Even more have difficulty with CD-RW media. The reasons for these difficulties are rooted in the methods used to record the data on the different media. Standard CDs have physical pits in an aluminum (or other metallic) surface, below the transparent layer encasing the metallic disc. A player's laser detects those deviations in the surface to read the stored data. A CD-R emulates this pitting with charged layers of a photosensitive dye. A CD-RW emulates this pitting with a chemical compound, which crystallizes when heated to the correct temperature, but returns to its liquid state when heated even more and then allowed to cool. In any event, the lasers in many older CD players do not operate at a wavelength that allows them to read CD-R or CD-RW media. Before purchasing a CD player, check to see whether its specifications are CD-R compatible.

Blank CD-R media typically has two sizes listed—one in minutes and one in megabytes. The two most common sizes are 74 min/640 MB and 80 min/700 MB. When you're recording audio to a CD, only look at the time figure. The megabytes figure refers to data CDs.

Note Another type of CD player can play both audio CDs and what are called MP3 CDs. These MP3 CDs are actually data discs, which are written in a format known as ISO 9660 and can contain literally hundreds of MP3 files. iTunes cannot create these CDs, but you can burn them if you purchase a third-party CD burning software package, such as the award-winning Roxio Toast 5 Titanium (www.roxio.com). You can also use this software to create VideoCDs and data discs in a variety of formats. And, if you have the right hardware, you can burn DVDs as well.

Working with iTunes song and album information

The iTunes window (refer to Figure 14-1) has a large pane dedicated to displaying information about the songs in the currently selected source — playlist, audio CD, MP3 player, or iTunes Library. By choosing Edit⇨View Options, you can control which of the 13 tag fields defined in the ID3 standard are displayed.

With the exception of the song field, which iTunes keeps on the left, you can rearrange the order of the other columns by dragging a column header over another column header. The column with the dark header is the column by which the display is sorted. The small arrow at the right of the selected column header indicates whether it is an ascending (A-Z) or descending (Z-A) sort, and you can reverse the order by clicking the header.

Looking up album information

The *i* in iTunes stands for the Internet. Not only can it stream radio from the Internet, but it can make use of the CDDB (Compact Disc Data Base) at www.gracenote.com to look up information about your CDs, retrieve song names, album title, artist information, and other pertinent information.

If you select the Connect To Internet When Needed box in your iTunes Preferences (on the General tab), iTunes automatically connects to the Internet when you insert an audio CD. If you want iTunes to check manually, choose Advanced⇨Get CD Track Names.

Note The information in the CDDB has been submitted by various people and sometimes more than one person submits album information for a CD, resulting in slightly different entries (spelling differences and the like) for the same CD. CDs are recognized by the number of songs and the respective lengths of those songs. Thus, if two different CDs have the same number of songs and each corresponding song is the same length, you may have to choose the appropriate entry. As an experiment, one of your authors burned his own CD, which was a compilation of songs from various CDs in his collection with lengths that matched a specific CD. Yes, this author has a perverse sense of humor. The CDDB, as expected, misrecognized the compilation CD. It's a useful tool, but it isn't infallible.

Entering song information manually

You can enter or edit song information manually by using in-place editing or a dialog for songs that are on your hard disk. You can even edit song information for songs on CD-ROMs and other locked sources. iTunes holds the information you enter in its database, overriding any information previously obtained from the Internet. Naturally, iTunes can't change the song information on the CD-ROM or other locked source itself. You may have some songs stored in locations that prevent you from editing their information. Songs on noneditable media, such as CD-ROMs, are not editable in this way because iTunes cannot write the information back to the read-only media. For example, you can't edit the information of songs that are located in a folder to which you have read-only access, such as the Public folder of someone else's home folder.

In-place editing is a straightforward Macintosh editing operation. Just click to select the record; then click in the text field to select it and start typing. To avoid the typing hassle, you can select a song and choose File➪Get Info (⌘-I) to display the Song Information dialog, as shown in Figure 14-8. You can change the title in the text box at the top; all other information is located on the Tags tab. You can navigate to adjacent songs by using the Prev Song and Next Song buttons.

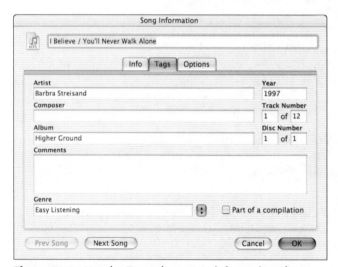

Figure 14-8: Use the Tags tab to enter information about a song.

Watching iTunes visual effects

If you find the iTunes song lists boring while you're listening to your favorite tunes or a book on disk, you can replace the window's contents with iTunes Visual Effects. These effects are often reminiscent (at least to us) of the strobe-light effects shown in the movies of the 1960s.

Special iTunes Symbols

iTunes employs some graphic symbols for specific purposes. The following table describes the ones you're most likely to encounter and gives a description of what they mean.

Moving waveform	Indicates the song is being currently being imported
Circled exclamation point	Indicates the song can't be located
Speaker	Indicates the song being played

You start and stop the show by clicking the Visuals On/Off button, which is located in the lower-right corner of the iTunes window (review Figure 14-1). Alternatively, you can choose Visuals⇨Turn Visual On or Visuals⇨Turn Visual Off (⌘-T). You can also use the Visuals menu to set the size of the visual effects show. Three sizes are available for show within the iTunes window (Small, Medium, and Large) as well as a Full Screen (⌘-F) mode.

Pressing the I key while the effects are on displays information about the song, which gradually fades out. Pressing ? presents a list of some of the key options. This list is not comprehensive—maybe that's why it's called *Basic* Visualizer Help. Some other keys that affect the Visualizer are Q, W, A, S, Z, and X—all of which switch among the effects being used. The first two cycle forward and backward through the lists of first effects, the next two through the list of secondary effects, and the last two through the list of tertiary effects.

Managing a music library

The iTunes Library is a database and a database isn't very useful if you can't browse it, search it, filter it, edit records in it, delete records, or produce reports. Although iTunes isn't exactly a FileMaker Pro for music, it meets the basic requirements.

Searching your iTunes Library

As we described earlier, you have control over which columns are displayed and how the song list is sorted. The Search area at the top of the window (see in Figure 14-1) acts as a filter. Any text you enter there limits the songs presented in the song list area to those that contain the text in one of the displayed columns.

When the iTunes Library is selected in the Source pane, a Browse button appears in the upper-right corner of the iTunes window (where the Burn button is for a Playlist). Clicking the Browse button reveals extra filtering control lists, as shown in Figure 14-9.

Note   For the Genre column to appear, you must select the Show Genre When Browsing checkbox on the iTunes Preferences General tab.

Figure 14-9: Click the Browse button to filter by genre, artist, or album.

Making a choice in one list restricts the choices to only those for the given selection in lists to the right. For example, selecting Comedy under Genre narrows the choices in Artist to only those artists who have songs with Comedy in the Genre tag field. If you select an artist, only the albums for that artist are listed in the Albums column. For this reason, filling in the ID3 Tags is very important if you want to browse your iTunes Library effectively. Only the genres, artists, and albums you have in your iTunes database appear in the various lists. We discuss ID3 tags in more detail shortly.

Removing songs from your iTunes Library

Removing a song from your iTunes Library is simplicity itself. All you need to do is select the song in the Library's song list and press the Delete or Clear key. Doing so does not remove the song from your disk, though.

If you want to remove the song from both the disk and the Library, the easiest method is to perform the following:

1. **Select the song in the Library's song list.**

2. **Control-click it and choose Show Song File from the contextual menu to display the file in a Finder window.**

3. **Now, just drag the file into the Trash (⌘-Delete).**

4. **Return to iTunes and press the Delete key with the song highlighted.**

Where to Find MP3s

Where, you may wonder, do I obtain MP3 files, especially now that they're not freely available through Napster? Have no fear—you can obtain MP3 files from numerous places.

One easy way to obtain MP3 files is to make them yourself from your own audio CDs. Just insert the CD and import the songs by selecting the CD in the source list and clicking the Import button. iTunes begins importing your songs as MP3 files. You can set the quality of your MP3 file on the iTunes Preferences dialog's Importing tab, as shown in the figure below. You also can choose to import the song as an AIFF file if you want to write it back out to another CD without any loss of quality. Similarly, you can save it as a WAV file, the Windows world equivalent of AIFF. The higher the quality setting, the more space your MP3 files take on the disc and in memory. If you experience ragged-sounding MP3s from files you import, you may want to deselect the Play Songs While Importing checkbox. This is an acknowledged problem with early releases of iTunes and Mac OS X, and the problem could persist on slower computers with updated iTunes and Mac OS X.

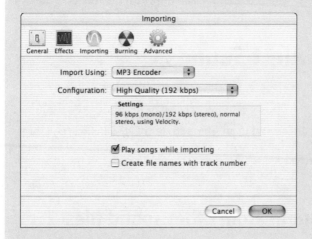

More music is available from Apple's iTunes Web pages and numerous other Web sites around the Internet. Use Sherlock on a search site, such as Google.com, to locate them.

Additionally, you can use Internet newsgroups in the alt hierarchy. If you fire up a newsreader (such as Thoth, described in Chapter 6) and check out the newsgroups whose names start with alt.binaries.sound.mp3, you'll find numerous choices with literally hundreds of MP3s per day being posted in each group. If you thought Napster ripped off the recording industry (pun intended), it didn't hold a candle to the music fans populating these groups. To learn about the protocols and customs of these eclectic groups, refer to the Frequently Asked Questions (FAQ) document at the MP3 FAQ Web site (www.mp3-faq.org)—be forewarned that the majority of the people contributing to and using these groups use Microsoft Windows, not Mac OS X, and that discussions and recommendations are biased in that direction.

Managing ID3 tags

As they say in sports, *no pain, no gain*. This saying is certainly true when it comes to gaining information from your database. If you don't go to the pain of entering the tag data, you won't have the advantages that accrue from searching for the information.

If no tag data exists, as is all-too-often the case with music obtained over the Internet, iTunes displays the file name in place of the title information and the other fields are blank. Enter the song information manually, as described earlier in this chapter.

The ID3 Tag format has gone through a number of versions, and each is slightly different from its predecessors. iTunes can convert the data format between the different versions of ID3 when you select songs and choose Advanced⇨Convert ID3 Tags. If you're going to exchange MP3 files with Windows users, you should be aware that many of the Windows users are using MP3 player software that does not handle ID3 version 2 tags well, and you may want to convert to an appropriate Version 1 variant.

Recording System Alert Sounds

Mac OS X stores system alert sounds in much the same manner that it stores fonts. Alert sounds that are available to all users are stored in an Alerts folder nested inside the main Library folder, at path /Library/Audio/Sounds/Alerts. Sounds that are available to an individual user are stored in an Alerts folder nested inside the Library folder of the user's home folder, at path ~/Library/Audio/Sounds/Alerts. The alert sounds included with Mac OS X are stored in the Sounds folder of the Library folder that's in the folder named System (path /System/Library/Sounds).

Converting alert sounds from other sound files

Alert sounds are stored as AIFF files, which usually have the file name extension .aif. You can create AIFF files from almost any audio file that QuickTime recognizes by using QuickTime Player Pro and exporting to AIFF or by extracting the data from an audio CD by using QuickTime Player or iMovie.

Recording your own sounds

iMovie is also a great tool for recording your voice or other special effects by using the Audio effects panel and its Record Voice button (see Chapter 13). Of course, you need a microphone-equipped Mac to record your voice. Audio songs created in iMovie in this manner are found in the movie's Media folder with a name like Voice 01.

To save this sound as an AIFF file, suitable for use as an alert sound, proceed as follows:

1. **Open the iMovie voice track in QuickTime Player Pro.**

2. **Choose File⇨Export.**

3. **Choose Sound to AIFF from the Export pop-up menu.**

4. **Make sure that the name in the Save As text box is what you desire, editing if necessary, and choosing your destination from the Where pop-up menu.**

5. **Click Save.**

Until the introduction of the Power Mac G4 with digital audio in January 2001, you could count on having an audio-in jack on your Mac. In this jack, you plugged in a microphone, because the Mac didn't have one built-in (some models, such as the iMac, do and some don't) or because you wanted to use a higher-quality microphone than the built-in microphone. This jack was actually more than just a microphone jack, although that was how it was labeled. It was a *line-in* jack, which means that you could plug in external audio devices, such as an amplifier, and record what came over the line — a very handy way to digitize old analog recordings, such as the tape recording of a meeting or baby's first words. Some OS X applications can use the line-in jack, but at this time you may have to use Classic or restart with Mac OS 9 to take advantage of this jack.

Creating Login Sounds

Because Mac OS X is a multiuser system, you can't play a startup sound and a shutdown sound as you can with Mac OS 9. You can, however, create a sound file and have it play when you log in to Mac OS X. You make sound files play during login by adding them to the list of login items the Login pane of System Preferences, as described in Chapter 15.

If you add an MP3 file as a login item, iTunes opens when you log in and plays the MP3 file. If you add an AIFF sound file as a login item, QuickTime Player opens the sound but does not necessarily play the sound automatically. To have QuickTime Player play the sound automatically, you must make sure that your QuickTime Player preferences are set to play movies automatically when opened. (QuickTime Player considers the AIFF sound to be a sound-only movie.)

Adding an MP3 file or AIFF file as a login item has the unfortunate side effect of leaving iTunes or QuickTime Player open after playing the sound. A more thorough solution would be to create an AppleScript application that opens the sound file, plays the sound, and then quits the application that played the sound (iTunes or QuickTime Player). Make this AppleScript application a login item instead of the sound file. (Chapter 21 explains how to make an AppleScript application.)

Summary

In this chapter, you learned how to use iTunes to play your CDs and other audio files, download music to an MP3 player, listen to Internet radio, manage your database of music, build and manage playlists, and create your own audio CDs. You also learned about MP3 format versus AIFF and WAV. In addition, you can now create and add alert and login sounds.

✦   ✦   ✦

Setting System Preferences

Your computer is highly configurable. Numerous settings let you adjust various aspects of its operation, including the keyboard and mouse sensitivity, the screen resolution and color depth, the way the computer uses energy, and the alert sound you hear.

Where to Find Preference Settings

You inspect and change the settings just mentioned and many, many more with the System Preferences application. The settings in System Preferences apply to all of Mac OS X and the applications you use with it. In addition to System Preferences, a number of the Mac OS 9 control panels' settings apply to Classic applications (but not to Mac OS X applications). Each Mac OS X application and Classic application can also have its own preferences settings.

Preference panes

Because System Preferences encompasses so many preference settings, the settings are grouped and each group appears in a separate pane. This chapter covers most of the System Preferences panes, but some panes are covered in other chapters. Table 15-1 specifies where each System Preferences pane is covered in this book.

Table 15-1
Coverage of System Preferences

System Preferences Pane	Covered in
Accounts	Various sections of Chapter 16
CDs and DVDs	"Sound Settings" in this chapter
Classic	"Classic Startup Settings" in this chapter
ColorSync	"Color Matching Settings" in this chapter
Date & Time	"Date, Time, and Location Settings" in this chapter
Desktop	"Customizing the Desktop" in Chapter 4
Displays	"Display Settings" in this chapter
Dock	"Using the Dock" in Chapter 4
Energy Saver	"Energy Saver Settings" in this chapter
General	"General Appearance and Behavior" in this chapter
International	"Language and Regional Preferences" in this chapter
Internet	"Internet Settings" in this chapter
Keyboard	"Adjusting the Keyboard, Mouse, or Trackpad" in this chapter
Login Items	"Login and Startup Settings" in this chapter and various sections of Chapters 2 and 16
Mouse	"Adjusting the Keyboard, Mouse, or Trackpad" in this chapter
My Account	Various sections of Chapter 16
Network	Various sections of Chapter 18
QuickTime	Various sections of Chapter 13
Screen Effects	"Display Settings" in this chapter
Sharing	Various sections of Chapters 19 and 20
Software Update	"Software Update Settings" in this chapter
Sound	"Sound Settings" in this chapter
Speech	Various sections of Chapter 17
Startup Disk	"Login and Startup Settings" in this chapter
Universal Access	"Adjusting the Keyboard, Mouse, or Trackpad" in this chapter

Classic control panels

The settings in System Preferences also affect the Classic environment and Classic applications. In effect, System Preferences replaces many of the control panels that are used for preference settings in Mac OS 9. Only about a third of the Mac OS 9 control panels are actually useful in the Classic environment. The obsolete control panels are present in case you want to start up your computer with the same Mac OS 9 that you use for the Classic environment. Table 15-2 specifies which control panels are still useful and where each one is covered in this book. Table 15-3 specifies which Mac OS 9 control panels are obsolete in the Classic environment and what to use instead in Mac OS X.

 Note   The Mac OS 9 control panels have no affect on Mac OS X applications, including the Finder.

Table 15-2
Coverage of Classic Control Panels

Mac OS 9 Control Panel	Covered in
Appearance	"General Appearance and Behavior" in this chapter
Apple Menu Options	"General Appearance and Behavior" in this chapter
AppleTalk	"Configuring AppleTalk for Classic applications" in Chapter 18
Date & Time	"Date, Time, and Time Zone Settings" and "Language and Regional Preferences" in this chapter
Easy Access	"Adjusting the Keyboard, Mouse, or Trackpad" in this chapter
Extensions Manager	"Classic Startup Settings" in this chapter
General Controls	"General Appearance and Behavior" in this chapter
Keyboard	"Adjusting the Keyboard, Mouse, or Trackpad" in this chapter
Mouse	"Adjusting the Keyboard, Mouse, or Trackpad" in this chapter
Numbers	"Language and Regional Preferences" in this chapter
Software Update	"Software Update Settings" in this chapter
Sound	"Sound Settings" in this chapter
Speech	Various sections of Chapter 17
Text	"Language and Regional Preferences" in this chapter

Table 15-3
Obsolete Control Panels in Classic Environment

Mac OS 9 Control Panel	Mac OS X Replacement
ColorSync	ColorSync pane of System Preferences
Control Strip	Icon menus in the menu bar and some Dock icons
DialAssist	No equivalent in Mac OS X
Energy Saver	Energy Saver pane of System Preferences
File Sharing	Sharing pane of System Preferences
Infrared	No equivalent in Mac OS X
Internet	Internet pane of System Preferences
Keychain Access	Keychain Access application
Launcher	Dock
Location Manager	No equivalent in Mac OS X, although you can change network locations with the Apple menu (see Chapter 18)
Map	Date & Time pane of System Preferences
Memory	Not needed in Mac OS X
Modem	Network pane of System Preferences
Monitors	Displays pane of System Preferences
Multiple Users	Users pane of System Preferences
Password Security	Login pane of System Preferences
PowerBook SCSI Disk Mode	No equivalent control panel in Mac OS X. The replacement functionality, Firewire Target Disk Mode, does not need an ID# to be set. To boot a Firewire-equipped Mac as an external Firewire hard disk, connect the Firewire ports of two Macs together and reboot the one you want to use as an external disk while holding the T key down. The Firewire icon should appear on the screen within a couple of seconds, and the Mac's hard disk should mount on the other system's Desktop immediately. When you're done, dismount the Firewire disk, then disconnect the Firewire cable and reboot the Mac.
Remote Access	Internet Connect utility (and the Network pane of System Preferences)
Startup Disk	Startup Disk pane of System Preferences
TCP/IP	Network pane of System Preferences

Mac OS 9 Control Panel	Mac OS X Replacement
Trackpad	Mouse pane of System Preferences
USB Printer Sharing	Not available in Mac OS X
Web Sharing	Sharing pane of System Preferences

Application preferences

Each application you use may have its own preference settings apart from System Preferences and Classic control panels. In general, you display an application's preferences by choosing its Preferences menu command. The Preferences command is customarily in the application menu of a Mac OS X application. In a Classic application, the usual place for a Preferences command is the Edit menu. However, some applications put the Preferences command in a different menu and may even use a different name for the menu command. Consult the application documentation for specific information.

Using System Preferences

This section describes the scope of Preference Settings, how to open System Preferences, display a pane whose settings you want to see or change, configure the System Preferences toolbar, and deal with locked settings in System Preferences.

Scope of preference settings

Because Mac OS X is designed for more than one person to use it on the same computer, it keeps many preference settings separately for each user. This means that many of the changes you make in System Preferences don't affect anyone else who logs in to your computer with a different name and password. The same is true of preference settings that you change in Mac OS X applications.

Although many Mac OS X preference settings are yours alone, everyone who uses your computer shares settings in the following panes:

- ✦ **Date & Time.** All users share the same settings except the menu bar clock settings.
- ✦ **Displays.** All users share the same settings.
- ✦ **Energy Saver.** All users share the same settings.
- ✦ **Network.** All users share the same settings.
- ✦ **Sharing.** All users share the same settings.
- ✦ **Startup Disk.** All users share the same settings.
- ✦ **Users.** All users share the same settings.

Note   Preference settings that you change in Classic control panels and applications are another story. The Classic environment is not inherently a multiuser environment. Changes you make to preference settings in Classic control panels and applications affect everyone who uses your computer.

Opening System Preferences

From reading other chapters, you probably already know that you can open System Preferences by clicking its icon in the Dock or by choosing System Preferences from the Apple menu. When System Preferences opens, it displays a window that shows buttons for the different panes of settings. Beginning with Mac OS X 10.1, the buttons are logically arranged by function, as shown in Figure 15-1.

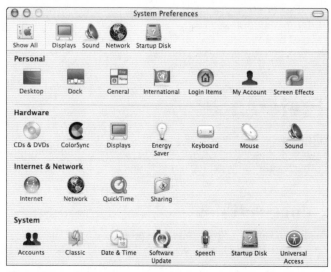

Figure 15-1: When System Preferences opens, its window displays buttons for all available panes of settings.

Each button in the System Preferences window corresponds to a pane of preference settings. To see a pane, click its button or choose the pane by name from the View menu. The System Preferences window changes to show the settings for the pane whose button you clicked, and the title of the window changes to the name of the pane. If you want to return to the display of buttons for all panes, click the Show All button in the upper-left corner of the window or choose View⇨Show All.

Configuring the System Preferences toolbar

No matter which pane of preference settings it is currently displaying, the System Preferences application can display a toolbar at the top of its window. The toolbar contains buttons for frequently used System Preferences panes. You can customize the toolbar so that it contains the buttons that you use most often. In addition, you can hide the toolbar or set it to display buttons as named icons, icons without names, or names alone. You configure the System Preferences toolbar as follows:

 ✦ **Hide or show toolbar:** Hide the toolbar, or show it if it is hidden, by clicking the lozenge-shaped toolbar button in the upper right corner of the window. Alternatively, choose View⇨Hide Toolbar or View⇨Show Toolbar.

✦ **Change toolbar mode:** Show items as icons with names, icons only, or names only, as well as large or small versions, by ⌘-clicking the lozenge-shaped toolbar button one to five times.

  • Start with the default view, with icons and names.

  • One ⌘-click shrinks the icons and names to a smaller size.

  • A second ⌘-click restores the icons to the original (large) size, but removes the names.

  • A third ⌘-click shrinks the icon-only view to the smaller icon size.

  • A fourth ⌘-click returns the names at their original (large) size, but deletes the icons.

  • A fifth ⌘-click shrinks the name-only view.

  • A sixth ⌘-click returns to the original (large) size icons and names view. Figure 15-2 shows the three primary (icons and names, icons only, names only) toolbar modes.

✦ **To add buttons:** Drag buttons to the toolbar from the main part of the window. You don't have to add buttons only at the right end of the toolbar. If you drag a button between two buttons in the toolbar, they move apart to make room for the button you're dragging. If the toolbar is full of buttons and you drag another button to the toolbar, buttons that don't fit on the toolbar appear in a pop-up menu. To see this menu, click the arrow that appears at the right end of the toolbar.

✦ **To rearrange buttons:** Drag buttons to different places on the toolbar.

✦ **To remove buttons:** Drag buttons away from the toolbar. Removing a button from the toolbar does not remove it from the System Preferences window. You can't remove the Show All button from its special place at the left end of the System Preferences toolbar.

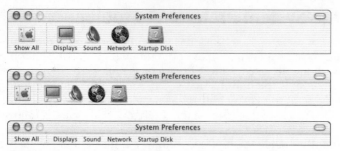

Figure 15-2: Change the toolbar mode in System Preferences by ⌘-clicking the toolbar button.

Unlocking preference settings

The settings in some panes of System Preferences may be locked. You can tell whether settings are locked in two ways.

✦ The locked settings are dim (displayed in gray text rather than black text).

✦ The security button near the bottom-left corner of the window appears locked.

Table 15-4 lists the system settings that can be locked.

Table 15-4
Preference Settings That Can Be Locked

System Preferences Pane	Settings That Can Be Locked
Date & Time	All settings except the menu bar clock settings
Energy Saver	All settings
Login Items	All login window settings but not the list of login items
Network	All settings except choosing a different location
Sharing	All settings
Startup Disk	System Folder selected for startup
Accounts	All settings except current user's password and password hint

To change locked settings, you need to know the name and password of an administrator account. The first user account created for your computer is an administrator account. This is the account created during the initial setup of Mac OS X. You can find more information on administrator accounts in Chapter 16. To unlock preference settings, follow these steps:

1. **Click the locked security button.**

2. **In the dialog that appears, enter the name and password of an administrator account.** Your account name is preentered in this dialog, so if you are logged in as an administrator, you can simply enter your password. If you are logged in as an ordinary user, you have to enter the password and also change the name. Figure 15-3 shows the dialog in which you enter the name and password to unlock preference settings.

3. **Click OK.**

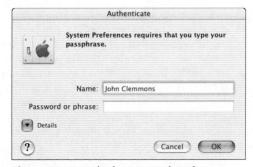

Figure 15-3: Unlock protected preference settings by entering the name and password of an administrator account.

Note If your computer has only one administrator account and you have forgotten its password, you can reset the password by using the Mac OS X installation CD, as described in Chapter 16.

Using Classic Control Panels

All control panels that you use for setting preferences for the Classic environment are separate applications. These applications are located in the Control Panels folder of the System Folder that's used for starting the Classic environment on your computer. In addition, these applications are normally listed in a submenu of the Classic Apple menu.

You can open the Classic control panel in two ways:

✦ You can open a Classic control panel by double-clicking its icon in a Finder window. If the Classic environment is not currently running, Mac OS X starts it automatically before opening the control panel.

✦ If a Classic application is already open, switch to the Classic application and choose the control panel that you want to open from the Control Panels submenu of the Classic Apple menu.

Besides affecting the Classic environment, changes that you make with control panels are also in effect if you start up your computer with the same Mac OS 9 that you use for Classic. In fact, you can make a few changes that are not apparent in the Classic environment but are apparent when you start up with Mac OS 9. We discuss specifics about these changes later in this chapter.

Adjusting the Keyboard, Mouse, or Trackpad

Although you may think of Mac OS X as something you look at, you also touch it by means of the keyboard, mouse, or trackpad. The behavior of the keyboard, mouse, or trackpad is adjustable to allow for differences among users. If you have trouble double-clicking or feel that the mouse pointer moves too slowly or too quickly, you can adjust the mouse or trackpad sensitivity. Likewise, if you end up typing characters repeatedly when you mean to type them only once, adjust the keyboard sensitivity. You adjust the sensitivity of the keyboard, mouse, or trackpad by using the Keyboard and Mouse panes of System Preferences. Some settings in Keyboard Preferences and Mouse Preferences govern Classic applications as well as Mac OS X applications. For other keyboard and mouse settings, you use the Keyboard and Mouse control panels. The control panel settings are in effect only when you use a Classic application.

Instead of operating menus, toolbars, the Dock, and various controls by using the mouse, Mac OS X lets you use the keyboard. The settings for full keyboard access are in the Keyboard pane of System Preferences.

If you have difficulty typing, moving the mouse, or clicking the mouse button, you can set up alternative methods of using them. These alternatives are especially helpful for people with disabilities. You configure these alternatives by using the Universal Access pane of System Preferences.

Keyboard Preferences

The Keyboard pane of System Preferences has settings for keyboard sensitivity and full keyboard access.

Settings tab

When you press almost any key on the keyboard and hold it down, the computer types that character repeatedly as long as you keep the key pressed. (The ⌘, Option, Control, Caps Lock, and Esc keys don't repeat.) In the Keyboard pane of System Preferences, click the Settings tab to change how quickly the characters repeat and how long you must hold down a key before the repeat feature kicks in. If you find repeating keys annoying rather than handy, disable the repeat by setting the Delay Until Repeat control to Off. Figure 15-4 shows the settings you see when you click the Settings tab in Keyboard Preferences.

Figure 15-4: Set keyboard sensitivity in Keyboard Preferences.

Full Keyboard Access tab

Mac OS X introduces full keyboard access. Normally full keyboard access is turned off. When you turn on full keyboard access, you can use the keyboard to select an icon in the Dock or a button in a Finder toolbar. You can also use the keyboard to operate menus in the Finder and some other applications. In addition, you can use the keyboard to operate push buttons, checkboxes, radio buttons, sliders, and other controls in some windows and dialogs. Some Mac OS X applications respond more completely to full keyboard access than others. Classic applications don't respond to keyboard access methods at all.

Click the Full Keyboard Access tab in Keyboard Preferences to change how Mac OS X responds to keyboard control of the menu bar, the Dock, toolbars, and buttons and other controls in windows and dialogs. You can turn full keyboard access on and off, and you can designate which key combinations switch the focus of the keyboard. Figure 15-5 shows the settings for full keyboard access in Keyboard Preferences.

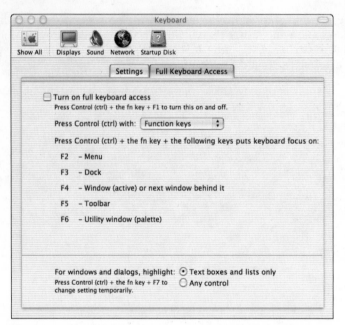

Figure 15-5: Set full keyboard access in Keyboard Preferences.

Note   After you turn on full keyboard access, you may need to quit a Mac OS X application and open it again before it responds to keyboard control.

While full keyboard access is turned on, you press certain keys to focus the keyboard on the menu bar, the Dock, the active window's toolbar, a palette, a window, or a dialog. You can choose which keys change the focus of the keyboard by using the pop-up menu labeled "Press Control (ctrl) with." (This pop-up menu is in Keyboard Preferences.) You can choose to use the Control key in combination with certain function keys, certain letter keys, or other keys that you specify. Table 15-5 lists the keystrokes that determine the focus of full keyboard access.

You press other keys to highlight one of the items on which the keyboard is currently focused, such as a menu item, an icon in the Dock, a toolbar button, or a control setting in a dialog. The highlighted item has a dark border. You press yet another key to select the highlighted item or take another action. Table 15-6 lists the key combinations that highlight items, select items, and take other actions.

Table 15-5
Changing the Focus of Full Keyboard Access

Action	Use Control key with*		
	Function Keys	*Letter Keys*	*Custom Keys*
Full keyboard access on or off	Control-F1	Control-F1	Control-F1
Focus on menu bar	Control-F2	Control-m	Control-*custom key*
Focus on Dock	Control-F3	Control-d	Control-*custom key*
Focus on toolbar	Control-F5	Control-t	Control-*custom key*
Focus on a palette (utility window) and then on each palette in turn	Control-F6	Control-u	Control-*custom key*
Cancel current focus on menu bar, Dock, toolbar, or palette, and focus on active window or dialog	Esc	Esc	Esc
Focus on next window of the same application	⌘-'	⌘-'	⌘-'

*Choose Function key, Letter keys, or Custom keys (and specify which custom keys) in Keyboard Preferences.

Table 15-6
Highlighting and Taking Action with Full Keyboard Access

Action	Keystroke
Highlight the next icon, button, menu, or control	Tab
Highlight the previous icon, button, menu, or control	Shift-Tab
Highlight the next control when a text box is selected	Control-Tab
Highlight a control next to a text box	Control-arrow keys
Highlight the next menu item, tab, item in a list, or radio button	Arrow keys
Move slider	Arrow keys
Restrict highlighting in the current window to text boxes and lists, or allow highlighting of any control in the current window	Control-F7
Select the highlighted item, or deselect it if it is already selected	Space bar
Click the default (pulsating) button or the default action in a dialog	Return or Enter
Click the Cancel button in a dialog	Esc
Close menu without selecting highlighted item	Esc
Cancel menu bar, Dock, or toolbar highlight	Esc

Mouse Preferences

You can change the way Mac OS X responds to your manipulation of your computer's mouse or trackpad by setting options in the Mouse pane of System Preferences. The trackpad options are available only on a PowerBook or iBook computer. Figure 15-6 shows Mouse Preferences.

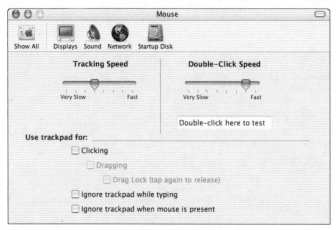

Figure 15-6: Set mouse (first image) or trackpad (second image) sensitivity in Mouse Preferences.

The settings in Mouse Preferences have the following effects:

✦ **Tracking Speed.** Determines how fast the pointer moves as you glide the mouse or trackpad. You may want to adjust the tracking speed if you change the display resolution. For example, if you change from the display resolution from 1024 x 768 to 800 x 600 pixels, you may want a slower tracking speed because the pointer has a shorter distance across the display screen. This setting affects both Mac OS X and Classic applications.

✦ **Double-Click Speed.** Determines how quickly you must double-click for Mac OS X to perceive your two clicks as one double-click rather than two separate, unrelated clicks. This setting affects only Mac OS X applications. To set the double-click speed for Classic applications, use the Mouse control panel as described later.

✦ **Clicking and Dragging.** If you select Clicking, you can click by tapping on the trackpad as well as by pressing the trackpad button. If you select Dragging, you can drag without pressing the mouse button.

To drag an object when both of these settings are turned on, follow these steps.

1. **Begin to double-tap the object, but don't lift your finger on the second tap.**

2. **Move your finger across the trackpad to drag the object across the screen.** If your finger reaches the edge of the trackpad and you need to drag further, you can lift your finger briefly, put it down again on the opposite edge of the trackpad, and continue dragging.

3. **Dragging ends when you keep your finger off the trackpad for a few seconds, unless you select the Drag Lock checkbox.** With this setting on, you can leave your finger off the trackpad indefinitely, and you stop dragging an object by tapping the trackpad again.

✦ **Ignore trackpad while typing.** If you sometimes brush the trackpad while typing, your typing may not go where you intended unless you turn on this setting.

✦ **Ignore trackpad when mouse is present.** If selected while a mouse is plugged in, this option disables the trackpad completely.

Universal Access Preferences

In the Universal Access pane of System Preferences, you can adjust the display and behavior of OS X for different needs of sight and sound, as well as set up alternative methods of using the keyboard and mouse in Mac OS X and Classic applications. *Mouse Keys* lets you use the numeric keypad portion of the keyboard to move the pointer on the screen and to click as if you were using the mouse button. *Sticky Keys* lets you type combination keystrokes such as ⌘-O one key at a time. The Universal Access pane was introduced with Mac OS X 10.1. All four tabs of the Universal Access pane show the same three checkboxes at the bottom of the window:

✦ **Allow Universal Access Shortcuts.** Several of the Universal Access options can be turned on and off by use of keyboard shortcuts. Selecting this box uses those keyboard combinations for these purposes.

✦ **Enable access for assistive devices.** Enables OS X to work with equipment such as a screen reader.

✦ **Enable text-to-speech for Universal Access preference[CS1]s.** Placing the mouse cursor over labels and options in the Universal Access window will cause OS X Speech to read that option aloud.

The first two checkboxes are cleared by default, but the third option is selected by default. These three checkboxes are shown at the bottom of Figures 15-7, 15-8, 15-9, and 15-10.

Seeing tab of Universal Access Preferences

The Seeing tab of the Universal Access System Preferences provides options to benefit people with different vision-oriented limitations. You can turn Zoom on and off, reverse the display to show white on black text instead of black on white, and set the display to grayscale.

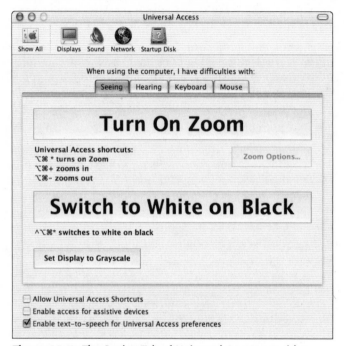

Figure 15-7: The Seeing Tab of Universal Access provides vision-oriented display options.

Hearing tab of Universal Access Preferences

The Hearing tab of the Universal Access System Preferences offers a full-screen flash option as a substitute for alert sounds, provides a test of the flash screen substitute, and provides a button to open the Sound System Preferences to adjust the sound volume.

Keyboard tab of Universal Access Preferences

Click the Keyboard tab in Universal Access Preferences to set up the Sticky Keys feature for Mac OS X and Classic applications. If you turn on this feature, you can type a combination of modifier keys — ⌘, Shift, Option, or Control — one key at a time. For example, you can type ⌘-Shift-S (the standard keyboard shortcut for File⇨Save As) by pressing ⌘, then Shift, and then S. Figure 15-9 shows the settings you see when you click the Keyboard tab in Universal Access Preferences.

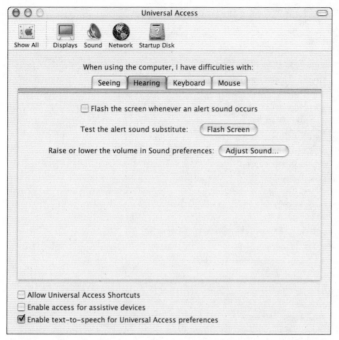

Figure 15-8: The Hearing tab of Universal Access provides hearing-oriented display options.

Besides turning Sticky Keys on or off in the Keyboard tab of Universal Access Preferences, you can set an option to hear a beep (not the system alert sound) when you press a modifier key. You can also set an option to see the symbols of modifier keys superimposed on the screen. If the option to use keyboard shortcuts is turned on at the top of Universal Access Preferences, you can turn Sticky Keys on or off by pressing Shift five times in succession.

When Sticky Keys is on and the option to show modifier keys on-screen is also on, pressing a modifier key causes the key's symbol to be superimposed on the screen. Press another modifier key and its symbol is superimposed as well. Press the same modifier key a second time and its symbol is removed. Press any other key to have it combined with the modifier keys whose symbols are currently superimposed on the screen. Press Esc to cancel all the modifier keys whose symbols are currently superimposed on the screen.

A button near the bottom of the Universal Access Keyboard tab acts as a shortcut to open the Keyboard System Preferences window to adjust the key repeat delay time.

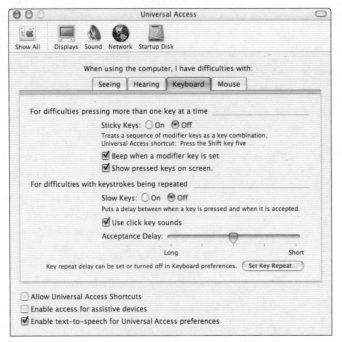

Figure 15-9: Set up sequential typing of combination keystrokes by clicking the Keyboard tab in Universal Access Preferences.

Mouse tab of Universal Access Preferences

Click the Mouse tab in Universal Access Preferences to set up the Mouse Keys feature. If you turn on this feature, you can click, drag, and move the pointer with the numeric keypad instead of the mouse or trackpad. Figure 15-10 shows the settings you see when you click the Mouse tab in Universal Access Preferences.

Tip   Mouse Keys is very handy for moving graphic objects precisely. For this use, try setting the Initial Delay to Short.

The Mouse tab has the following settings:

    ✦ **On and Off.** If the option to use keyboard shortcuts is selected at the top of Universal Access Preferences, you can turn Mouse Keys on or off by pressing the Option key five times.

    ✦ **Initial Delay.** Determines how long you must hold down a keypad key before the pointer starts responding. As long as you keep pressing keypad keys to control the pointer, the delay does not recur. The delay occurs only with the first keypress after a period during which you have not used the keypad for pointer control.

✦ **Maximum Speed.** Determines how fast the pointer gets going if you keep holding down a key. You have better control with a slow speed, but moving the pointer across the screen takes longer.

When Mouse Keys is on, the 5 key in the keypad acts like a mouse button. Press once to click; press twice to double-click. The eight keys around 5 move the pointer left, right, up, down, and diagonally. Pressing 0 locks the mouse button down until you press the period key in the keypad. You do not have to hold down 0 like you hold down the actual mouse button.

Tip   If the pointer seems unresponsive, make the Initial Delay shorter and the Maximum Speed faster in Universal Access Preferences. Conversely, if you feel like you don't have enough control over the pointer, make the Initial Delay longer and the Maximum Speed slower.

A button near the bottom opens the Keyboard System Preferences as a shortcut for turning on full keyboard access.

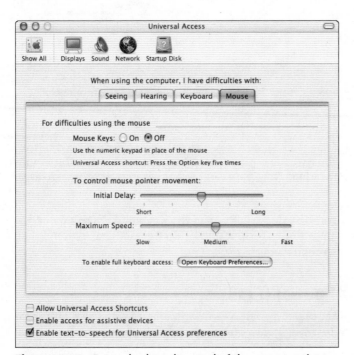

Figure 15-10: Set up keyboard control of the mouse pointer by clicking the Mouse tab in Universal Access Preferences.

Keyboard control panel (Classic)

You can use the Keyboard control panel to assign functions to the F1 through F12 keys in the Classic environment. On iBook and some PowerBook models, you can assign functions only to the F5 through F11 keys. The function key assignments do not work in Mac OS X applications, including the Finder. Click the Function Keys button in the Keyboard control panel to display the dialog in which you set function key assignments, as shown in Figure 15-11.

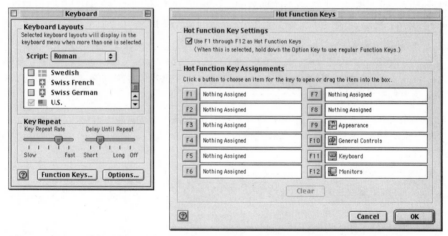

Figure 15-11: The Keyboard control panel governs function key assignments for Classic applications.

The Keyboard control panel also enables you to choose a keyboard layout for Classic applications. You use this option when you want to type in a different language in a Classic application. The Keyboard Layout settings are covered later in this chapter.

The function key assignments that you make in the Keyboard control panel have no effect on Mac OS X applications. The function key assignments work only when a Classic application is the active application.

Mouse control panel (Classic)

You can use the Mouse control panel to set the double-click speed for Classic applications. Figure 15-12 shows the Mouse control panel.

The double-click speed is the only setting in the Mouse control panel that affects Classic applications. (All settings in the Mouse control panel take effect if you start up the computer with Mac OS 9.) None of the settings in this control panel has any effect in Mac OS X applications.

Figure 15-12: The Mouse control panel governs the double-click speed for Classic applications.

General Appearance and Behavior

If you don't like the general appearance and behavior of Mac OS X, you can change how it uses color to highlight menus, controls, and text. You can also change how windows scroll when you click in their scroll bars. You make these changes in the General pane of System Preferences.

You have more control over the appearance and behavior of the Classic environment. Using the Appearance control panel, you can change colors, fonts and font characteristics, sound effects, scroll bar behavior, and window behavior.

What's more, you can use the General Controls control panel to change a number of other settings that affect Classic applications. By using the Apple Menu Options control panel, you can change how the Classic Apple menu works.

General Preferences

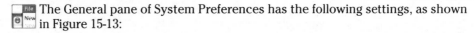 The General pane of System Preferences has the following settings, as shown in Figure 15-13:

- ✦ **Appearance.** No doubt you've noticed a lot of blue highlights in Mac OS X menus and controls, not to mention the red, yellow, and green window controls that flash when you pass the mouse pointer over them. If you find these colors distracting or just don't like all that blue, you can change all these colors to shades of gray.

- ✦ **Highlight color.** You can also choose the color that highlights selected text and items in lists in Mac OS X applications.

- ✦ **Place scroll arrows.** With this setting, you specify whether one scroll arrow appears at each end of a scroll bar or both scroll arrows appear together at one end a scroll bar.

- ✦ **Click in the scroll bar to.** This setting specifies what normally happens when you click a scroll track above or below the scroller. You can have this action scroll one page or scroll to where you clicked the scroll track.

✦ **Number of recent items.** You can set how many recently used items are listed in the Recent Items submenu of the Apple menu. Set a number of recent applications and a number of recent documents. Each number can be 5, 10, 15, 20, 30, or 50.

✦ **Font smoothing style.** This pop-up menu specifies the style of text smoothing OS X uses, from Standard (recommended as best for CRT displays), to Light, Medium (recommended as best for flat panel displays), and Strong.

✦ **Turn off text smoothing for font sizes.** This setting specifies the font size above which Mac OS X smoothes text.

Tip   To temporarily reverse what happens when you click a scroll track above or below the scroller, press Option while clicking the scroll track.

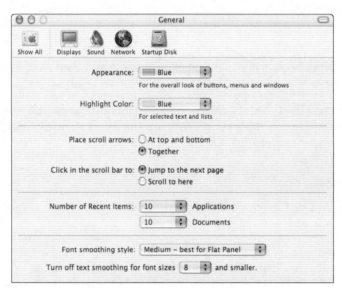

Figure 15-13: Set several options that affect general appearance and behavior in Mac OS X by using General Preferences.

Note   Settings in the General pane of System Preferences do not affect the Classic environment. For Classic, use the Appearance control panel, described next.

Setting Font Smoothing

The point of font smoothing is to improve the looks of text displayed on-screen. Font smoothing works by blending the edges of text with the background, a technique known as *anti-aliasing*. Because of the way Mac OS X handles fonts, the best choice for text smoothing is 8. Here's why. Mac OS X displays text using the TrueType version of a font even if a bitmap version of the font is installed on your computer. Unfortunately, without text smoothing the TrueType versions of fonts rarely look as good as bitmap fonts in font sizes below 12 points (10 points with some fonts). Furthermore, Mac OS X displays text using fractional font widths, meaning some characters are a certain number of pixels plus a fraction of a pixel in width. It's not possible to display a fraction of a pixel, but with text smoothing Mac OS X approximates fractional pixels by using gray pixels. Without text smoothing, Mac OS X rounds off fractional pixels resulting in too much space between some characters and too little space between others.

Appearance control panel (Classic)

The Appearance control panel has a variety of settings that affect the appearance and behavior of Classic applications. The Appearance control panel also has many settings that do not affect the Classic environment but do take effect if you restart your computer with Mac OS 9. Naturally, none of the settings in the Appearance control panel has any effect on Mac OS X applications. The Appearance control panel has the following tabs, which are described next:

✦ Themes

✦ Appearance

✦ Fonts

✦ Desktop

✦ Sound

✦ Options

Themes tab

Click the Themes tab of the Appearance control panel to switch all the Appearance control panel's settings at once to any of several combinations (called *themes*) that have been previously set up and saved by name. You can choose from among several preconfigured themes, and you can save your own additional themes. Switching to a different theme may change some settings that don't affect the Classic environment, but do take effect if you restart your computer with Mac OS 9. Figure 15-14 shows the Themes tab of the Appearance control panel.

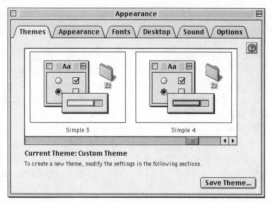

Figure 15-14: The Themes tab of the Appearance
control panel lets you switch all the control
panel's settings at once in the Classic environment.

If you click Save Theme, the Appearance control panel displays a dialog in which
you can type a name for the theme you're creating. You can change the name of any
theme that you created by selecting its preview and choosing Theme Name from
the Edit menu. You can't change the names of preconfigured themes.

To remove a theme, select its preview in the Appearance control panel and choose
Clear from the Edit menu.

Appearance tab

The Appearance tab of the Appearance control panel has three settings. They are
shown in Figure 15-15 and have the following effects:

✦ **Appearance.** In theory, you can change this setting to give the Classic environment a different overall look than the gray *platinum appearance* it inherits
from Mac OS 9 and its predecessors. In reality, Apple has never released any
alternate appearances, making the Appearance option irrelevant.

✦ **Highlight Color.** Determines the color used to highlight text that you select in
Classic applications.

✦ **Variation.** Determines the color used to highlight Classic menus and controls.

Fonts tab

In the Fonts tab of the Appearance control panel, you can set the font used for
menus, window titles, button names, and some text in dialogs. You can also turn
font smoothing on or off, and set a minimum font size for smoothing. Two settings,
Small System Font and Views Font, have no effect in the Classic environment but
take effect if you restart your computer with Mac OS 9. Figure 15-16 shows the
Fonts tab of the Appearance control panel.

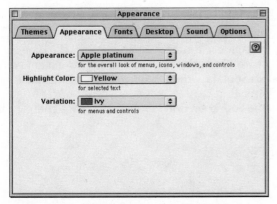

Figure 15-15: The Appearance tab of the Appearance control panel sets highlight colors for text, menus, and controls in Classic applications.

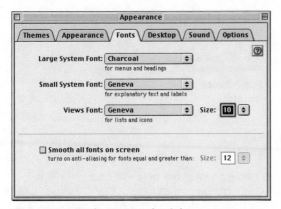

Figure 15-16: The Fonts tab of the Appearance control panel sets the menu font and controls font smoothing in Classic applications.

In the Classic environment, font smoothing makes some fonts look better but others look worse. For instance, font smoothing improves three of the choices for large system font: Capitals, Textile, and Sand. The other choices look blurry with font smoothing. Another problem with font smoothing is that it may make small font sizes blurry. In this case, increase the Size setting.

Desktop tab

The Desktop tab of the Appearance control panel affects the look of the Desktop if you start up the computer with Mac OS 9. These settings have no effect in Mac OS X or the Classic environment. Instead, use the Desktop pane of System Preferences, as described in Chapter 4.

Sound tab

Click the Sound tab of the Appearance control panel to set sound effects that can play in Classic applications. You can choose a sound set and specify the types of actions that you want sound effects to accompany. The Classic environment comes with only one sound set—Platinum Sounds. Other sound sets are available on the Internet, for example from David Kha at http://hometown.aol.com/zephcetloa/index.html. Figure 15-17 shows the Sound section of the Appearance control panel.

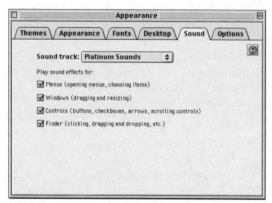

Figure 15-17: The Sound tab of the Appearance control panel sets sound effects for various actions in Classic applications.

Options tab

Click the Options tab of the Appearance control panel to determine how scroll bars work in Classic applications and whether you can minimize Classic windows by double-clicking their title bars. If the Smart Scrolling option is selected, as it is by default, both up and down scroll arrows appear at only one end of the scroll bar. In addition, the length of the scroll box indicates how much you can see without scrolling. The longer the scroll box, the more you can see without scrolling. If you deselect Smart Scrolling, the up arrow appears at one end of the scroll bar, the down arrow appears at the other end, and the scroll box has a fixed length. Figure 15-18 shows the Options tab of the Appearances control panel.

Tip   Classic scroll bars are actually more configurable than the Smart Scrolling option suggests. With a utility application, such as Smart Scroll by Marc Moini (www.marcmoini.com), you can have one scroll arrow at each end of the scroll bar, both arrows at one end, or both at both ends. You can also turn proportional scroll boxes on or off independent of the scroll arrow setting.

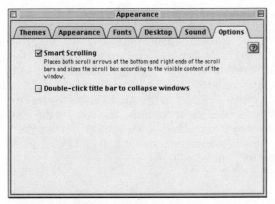

Figure 15-18: The Options tab of the Appearance control panel sets up scroll bars and collapsing windows in Classic applications.

General Controls control panel (Classic)

The General Controls control panel has four miscellaneous settings that affect the Classic environment. One setting controls whether the Launcher control panel opens automatically when the Classic environment starts up. Two other settings regulate the blinking rates for the text insertion point and menus. Another setting determines which folder you see first in a dialog for opening or saving a document in a Classic application. The two dim settings are always turned on and can't be changed in the Classic environment. Figure 15-19 shows the settings in the General Controls control panel.

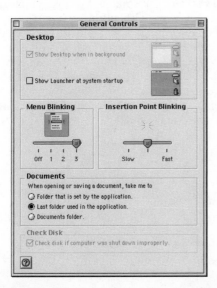

Figure 15-19: The General Controls control panel has miscellaneous settings that affect Classic applications.

Apple Menu Options control panel (Classic)

Settings in the Apple Menu Options control panel determine whether the Apple menu in the Classic environment has submenus and remembers recently used items. If the Submenus option is turned on and you highlight a folder in the Classic Apple menu, then a submenu lists the contents of the folder. Turning on the option to remember recently used items creates folders in the Apple menu for tracking the documents, applications, and servers used most recently. You can set the number of documents, applications, and servers to track. If you want to suppress the tracking of one type of item, set the number to be remembered to 0 (zero). Figure 15-20 shows the Apple Menu Items control panel.

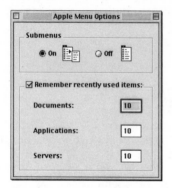

Figure 15-20: The Apple Menu Options control panel governs submenus and recently used items in the Apple menu of the Classic environment.

Display Settings

If you stare at your display screen for hours on end (like many of us do), you want the view to be crisp and easy on the eyes. If you work with color, you want your screen to display colors as accurately and consistently as possible. If you work with more than one display screen on your computer, you need to have control over how the two work together. If your display is not a flat-panel type, you can set up a screen saver to protect the display against image burn-in.

Toward these goals, you can adjust your display by using the Displays and Screen Saver panes of System Preferences. You can also make quick adjustments with the Displays menu icon.

Displays Preferences

The Displays pane of System Preferences has tabs that you click to access its settings. Your Displays Preferences may have some or all of the following tabs and settings:

✦ **Displays.** Settings for screen resolution, number of colors, refresh rate, contrast, and brightness

✦ **Color.** Settings for selecting a color profile and calibrating your display

✦ **Geometry.** Settings for adjusting the shape and position of the screen image (not present for all makes and models of displays)

✦ **Arrange.** Settings for adjusting how multiple screens work together (present only if you have more than one display and your computer can work with them independently)

Display tab of Displays Preferences

Click the Display tab in Displays Preferences to adjust the resolution, number of colors, refresh rate, contrast, or brightness of your display. You can also change a setting to show or hide the Displays icon in the menu bar. Some settings are not available with some types of displays. For example, no contrast setting for the LCDs (liquid crystal displays) is used in PowerBooks, iBooks, and flat-panel displays. Figure 15-21 shows the settings you may see when you click the Display tab in Displays Preferences.

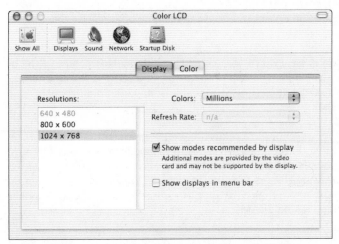

Figure 15-21: Set screen resolution, number of colors, refresh rate, contrast, and brightness by clicking the Display tab of Displays Preferences.

Nonrecommended display modes

Some choices of settings for resolution, colors, and refresh rate are dim to indicate they are not recommended. If you want to choose one of these, deselect the checkbox labeled "Show modes recommended by display." If you choose a nonrecommended mode, an alert appears in which you must click the Confirm button to retain the mode. If you do not click Confirm within 10 seconds, Mac OS X automatically reverts to the previous mode. This automatic reversion is necessary because some nonrecommended modes may cause the display to show a distorted or black image, which prevents you from reverting to the previous mode by yourself.

Resolution and colors

The two most basic display settings are resolution and number of colors. *Resolution* is the size of the rectangular screen image — the number of pixels (picture elements or dots) wide by the number of pixels high. The number of colors, often called *color depth,* is the number of different colors that can be displayed for each pixel of the screen image. Color depth is sometimes referred to as *bit depth*, which is a measure of the amount of memory it takes to store each pixel (more colors require more bits of memory per pixel).

The higher the number of colors, the more realistic the screen image can look. However, increasing the number of colors doesn't necessarily make the screen display better, because the picture displayed on-screen may not make use of all of the available colors. For example, a black-and-white photograph is still black, white, and shades of gray when displayed on a screen capable of displaying millions of colors per pixel.

You have two practical choices of color depth in Mac OS X: thousands or millions of colors per pixel. Mac OS X can't accurately render its Aqua interface with a lower color depth. However, some old Classic applications may be programmed to require a color depth of 256 colors.

The settings for resolution depend on the capabilities of the display and the computer's video card, but in general range from 800 x 600 pixels (the size of the original iBook display) up to 1600 x 1024 pixels (the size of a 22-inch Apple Cinema Display). Some displays can show only one resolution, while most recent displays can show multiple resolutions.

Resolution and number of colors are related because increasing either requires more video memory. If you increase the resolution, Mac OS X may have to automatically reduce the number of colors. Conversely, you may be able to set a higher number of colors by decreasing the resolution. On early 233MHz iMac and beige Power Mac G3 models, you can make higher resolutions and numbers of colors available by installing more video RAM (VRAM).

Refresh rate

The significance of the refresh rate setting gets into the mechanics of displaying an image on the screen. The video card sends the screen image to the display one thin line of pixels at a time. After the video card sends the last line, it starts over again with the first line. The refresh rate is a measure of how fast the video card sends lines of the screen image to the display. A higher refresh rate means the entire screen image gets redisplayed more often. The refresh rate is of concern on a display with a CRT (cathode ray tube, or picture tube). If the refresh rate is below about 75 Hertz, the CRT's glowing phosphors may fade perceptibly before they are refreshed. Your eyes perceive this as a flickering of the video image, and the flickering can lead to eye fatigue and headache. A display with an LCD (liquid crystal display) doesn't flicker regardless of the refresh rate.

Each make and model of display has certain combinations of resolution and refresh rate that produce a clear, bright image with minimum flicker. If you set the refresh rate to a value that is not recommended for the display, the image probably is distorted or dark.

Color tab of Displays Preferences

Click the Color tab in Displays Preferences to select a color profile for your display or to calibrate the display, creating a new color profile for it. Figure 15-22 shows the settings you see when you click the Color tab in Displays Preferences.

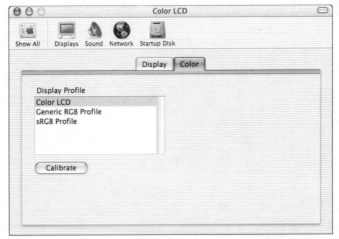

Figure 15-22: Set the display's color profile or calibrate the display by clicking the Color tab of Displays Preferences.

You can create a custom profile for your display and your viewing preferences by clicking the Calibrate button in the Color pane of Displays Preferences. A custom profile accounts for your display's age and individual manufacturing variations. What's more, you can configure custom profiles for different resolutions, white points, and gamma corrections. With most displays, clicking the Calibrate button opens the Display Calibrator Assistant. The Calibrator walks you through the process that calibrates your display and creates a new ColorSync profile. The Display Calibrator Assistant is covered in Chapter 22.

Note   The Calibrate button does not open the Display Calibrator Assistant under certain conditions. The Calibrate button may open another calibration application that has been installed on your computer and probably works with a special display calibration device. In addition, the Calibrate button may be replaced altogether by a Recalibrate button if you have an Apple ColorSync display, AppleVision display, or 21-inch Apple Studio Display. In these cases, clicking Recalibrate activates the self-calibrating hardware built into these displays.

Geometry tab of Displays Preferences

With some displays, such as the built-in display of an iMac, Displays Preferences has a Geometry tab that you can click to adjust the shape and position of the screen image. You can expand the display area, so that less black border is visible. You can also change the pincushion (how concave the sides of the picture are) and the rotation of the display. Figure 15-23 shows the settings you see when you click the Geometry tab in Displays Preferences on an iMac.

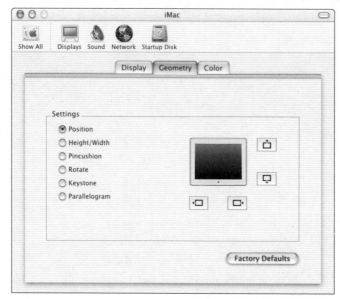

Figure 15-23: Adjust the shape and position of the screen image by clicking the Geometry tab of Displays Preferences.

When you click one of the geometry settings, buttons appear next to the small screen in the Displays Preferences window. Clicking these buttons adjusts the image size or shape as indicated by the graphic labels on the buttons. You can also make adjustments by dragging edges or the center of the small screen; the shape of the pointer tells you which way to drag. If you wreak havoc on your display by experimenting with the geometry settings, click the Recall Factory Settings button to returns the settings to their presets.

Arrange tab of Displays Preferences

If your computer has two displays or more, you may be able to arrange how they work together. In one arrangement, called *display mirroring* or *video mirroring,* the second display shows exactly the same image as the first display. The other arrangement treats each display as part of an extended Desktop — as you move the pointer across the Desktop, it goes from one display to the next. Some Mac models, such as the iMac DV, can use two displays only for display mirroring, not for an extended Desktop.

If your computer gives you a choice between display mirroring and an extended Desktop, Displays Preferences has an Arrange tab that you can click to set the arrangement you want. Figure 15-24 shows the settings you see when you click the Arrange tab in Displays Preferences.

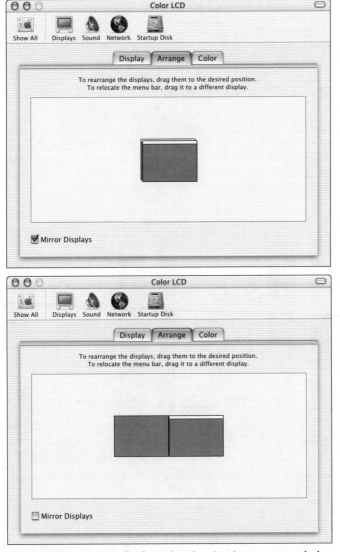

Figure 15-24: Set up display mirroring (top) or an extended Desktop (bottom) with two or more displays by clicking the Arrange tab of Displays Preferences.

You can change the relative positions of the displays in an extended Desktop by dragging the small screens in Displays Preferences. You can set which display has the menu bar by dragging the little menu bar to the appropriate small screen in Displays Preferences. When you have two or more displays in an extended Desktop, Displays Preferences has a separate window on each display. Each window has a Display tab, Color tab, and other tabs for adjusting the display where the window is located. Only one of the windows has an Arrange tab.

Note   To turn on the display mirroring setting, both displays must be set to the same resolution and number of colors.

Display settings in the menu bar

Besides using the Displays pane of System Preferences to adjust your display, you can also use the Displays icon in the menu bar. Click the Displays icon to see a menu of available screen resolutions and numbers of colors. This menu lists all your displays and has a command for turning mirroring on or off. The menu also has a command for opening the Displays pane of System Preferences. Figure 15-25 shows some of the forms that the Displays menu can take.

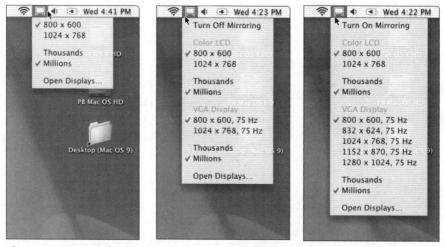

Figure 15-25: Use the Displays icon to turn off display mirroring or set the screen resolution and number of colors for one display or more.

If the menu bar does not already contain the Displays icon, you can add it by changing a setting in Displays Preferences. This setting was shown previously in Figure 15-21.

Tip You can move the Displays icon by pressing the ⌘ key and dragging the icon. Drag the icon left or right to change its position relative to other icons on the right side of the menu bar. Drag the icon off the menu bar to make it vanish in a puff of smoke.

Screen Effects Preferences

If you leave an unchanging image on your display for a long time, a vestige of the image may be visible after something happens to change the display. This phenomenon, called screen *burn-in,* is temporary on an LCD screen but can be permanent on a CRT screen. You can prevent burn-in by using a *screen saver,* which automatically presents a constantly changing animation or slide show whenever the computer is idle for a period of time.

Mac OS X has a screen saver that you set up in the Screen Effects pane of System Preferences. This pane has the following tabs and settings:

✦ **Screen Effects.** Sets the animation or slide show to be presented and shows a preview of it.

✦ **Activation.** Sets the amount of idle time before the screen saver's presentation begins and determines whether you have to enter your password when the screen saver wakes.

✦ **Hot Corners.** Designates corners of the screen that either start the screen saver or prevent it from starting when you move the mouse into the designated corners.

Screen Effects tab of Screen Saver Preferences

To adjust what is displayed while your computer is idle, click the Screen Effects tab in Screen Effects Preferences and change the settings shown in Figure 15-26 as follows:

✦ **Screen Effects.** From the list of available animations and slide shows, select the one that you want to have displayed while your computer is idle. A preview of the current selection appears in the Preview window.

✦ **Test.** Click the Test button to find out whether the selected animation or slide show looks good and performs well at full size.

✦ **Configure.** Set options for the selected animation or slide show by clicking the Configure button. This button is dim if the current selection has no options.

Paradoxically, using a screen saver with an LCD screen does not prolong its life. The major factor affecting the life of an LCD screen is its backlight, which grows steadily dimmer with use. While the screen saver is running, the backlight is on and growing dimmer bit by bit. The best way to prolong the life of an LCD screen is to have it turned off after a period of inactivity. You can set this up in the Energy Saver pane of System Preferences, as described later in this chapter.

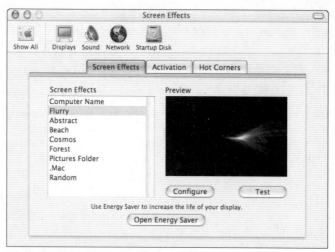

Figure 15-26: Select, test, and configure an animation or slide show to be displayed while the computer is idle by clicking the Screen Effects tab in Screen Effects Preferences.

Activation tab of Screen Effects Preferences

To adjust how and when the screen saver is activated, click the Activation tab in Screen Saver Preferences and change the settings shown in Figure 15-27 as follows:

✦ **Time until screen effect starts.** Specifies the amount of idle time that will elapse before the screen effect starts its presentation. If you want to deactivate the screen effect, set the time interval to Never.

✦ **Password to use when waking the screen effect.** Specifies whether or not you want the screen effect to ask for your password when it wakes. The screen effect wakes in response to mouse or keyboard activity.

Hot Corners tab of Screen Effects Preferences

To set up screen corners as triggers for the screen saver, click the Hot Corners tab in Screen Effects Preferences. You can change what the screen effect does when the mouse pointer enters a corner of the screen by clicking the corresponding checkbox in the Hot Corners tab. These checkboxes, which are shown in Figure 15-28, indicate the effect of each screen corner as follows:

✦ **Check mark.** Indicates this corner starts the screen saver.

✦ **Minus sign.** Indicates this corner prevents the screen saver from starting.

✦ **Empty.** Indicates this corner neither starts nor stops the screen saver.

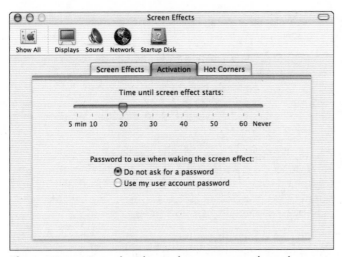

Figure 15-27: Set a time lag and your password requirements for the screen saver by clicking the Activation tab in Screen Effects Preferences.

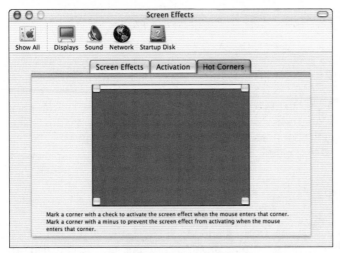

Figure 15-28: Set up screen corners to start the screen effect or prevent it from starting by clicking the Hot Corners tab in Screen Effect Preferences.

Sleep Is Better Than a Screen Saver

A screen saver has the benefit of preventing screen burn-in and can be mildly entertaining. What can be wrong with that picture? Plenty, if the screen you're saving happens to belong to a PowerBook or iBook that you operate on battery power. You see, the screen saver forces the battery-powered display to remain on — presumably while you are not using the computer — draining the battery at a rapid clip. Save the battery by having the display go to sleep.

Batteries aren't an issue if your display is plugged in, but a screen saver has other drawbacks. If the display has an LCD screen, a screen saver keeps its backlight turned on. The backlight gets dimmer with use and eventually goes out altogether. Replacing the backlight is an expensive proposition; not like changing a light bulb. (Insert your favorite light-bulb joke here.) Save the backlight by having the display go to sleep.

Finally, there is the green factor. Leaving the display turned on so that it can show a screen saver to no one while you're away uses electricity, quite a bit of it in the case of a CRT display. Generating the electricity creates pollution and probably contributes to global warming. Give the planet a small break by having the display go to sleep or by turning it off.

As a compromise, you can set your display to go to sleep five or ten minutes after the screen saver kicks in. To have your screen go to sleep, use the Energy Saver pane of System Preferences as described later in this chapter.

Sound Settings

You can make a few adjustments to the sounds your computer makes. You can adjust the alert sound and other sound settings for Mac OS X applications in the Sound pane of System Preferences. You can set the alert sound and its volume for Classic applications in the Sound control panel.

Sound Preferences

The Sound pane of System Preferences has three tabs that you click to access its settings, Sound Effects, Output, and Input. No matter which tab you click, you can adjust the main system volume or mute it altogether. You can also turn on an option to adjust the volume from the Sound icon in the menu bar. You can see the sound volume and Sound icon settings in Figure 15-29.

Sound Effects tab of Sound Preferences

Click the Sound Effects tab in Sound Preferences to select an alert sound and set its volume to be as loud as or quieter than other sounds. You can also choose the device you want used for alert sounds if your computer has more than one audio output device. The alert sound settings affect only Mac OS X applications. (For Classic alert sound settings, use the Sound control panel.) Figure 15-29 shows the sound effects settings in Sound Preferences.

Figure 15-29: Adjust volume and balance controls and select an alert sound by clicking the Alerts tab in Sound Preferences.

You can add more alert sounds by placing sound files of the AIFF format in the Sounds folder inside your home folder's Library folder. If System Preferences is open when you add or remove sounds from your Sounds folder, you must quit System Preferences and open it again to see the effect of your changes.

If you log in as an administrator, you can also install sounds that all users can see. These sounds go in the Sounds folder in your main Library folder. If the main Library folder doesn't have a Sounds folder, you can create one.

Output tab of Sound Preferences

Click the Output tab in Sound Preferences to choose the audio device you want used for sound output and set the stereo channel balance for the device. Figure 15-30 shows the sound output settings in Sound Preferences.

Input tab of Sound Preferences

Click the Input tab in Sound Preferences to choose the audio device you want used for sound input and set the input volume for the device. Figure 15-31 shows the sound input settings in Sound Preferences.

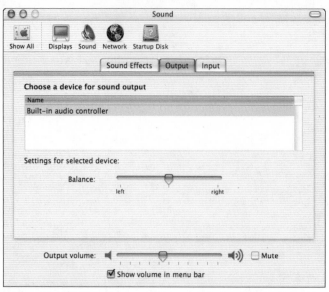

Figure 15-30: Choose an audio output device and set its stereo balance by clicking the Output tab in Sound Preferences.

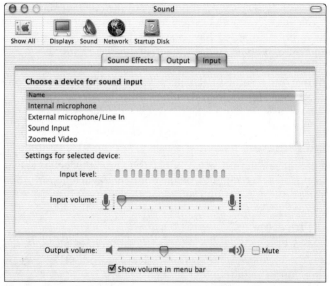

Figure 15-31: Choose an audio input device and set its input volume by clicking the Input tab in Sound Preferences.

Sound level in the menu bar

Besides adjusting the main system volume level in the Sound pane of System Preferences, you can also use the Sound icon in the menu bar. Click the Sound icon to see a volume control, as shown in Figure 15-32.

Figure 15-32: Use the Sound icon to adjust the main volume level.

Tip

You can move the Sound icon by pressing the ⌘ key and dragging the icon. Drag the icon left or right to change its position relative to other icons on the right side of the menu bar. Drag the icon off the menu bar to make it vanish in a puff of smoke.

Sound control panel (Classic)

 The alert sound settings for Classic applications are in the Sound control panel. You can select an alert sound from a list in the control panel. You can also adjust the alert volume or mute it. None of the other settings in the Sound control panel has any effect in the Classic environment. (For overall volume and balance controls and for Mac OS X alert sound settings, use the Sound pane of System Preferences.) Figure 15-33 shows the Sound control panel settings for alert sounds.

You can add more alert sounds for the Classic environment, but you have to restart your computer with Mac OS 9 to do it. These alert sounds must be System 7 Sound format, and they go into the System file of the System Folder used for the Classic environment. You can't open this System file with Mac OS X's Finder, but you can open it with the Finder after starting up with Mac OS 9.

Tip You can add and remove sounds from the System file used by the Classic environment without restarting your computer with Mac OS 9 if you can use another computer with Mac OS 9 on your network. First you stop the Classic environment and start file sharing on your computer. Then go to the other computer and connect to your computer. From the other computer, open your computer's System file and move sound files in or out as you like. Close the System file and disconnect from your computer. When you return to your computer, you can start the Classic environment and it uses the modified System file. (You can find more information on file sharing in Chapter 19 and on connecting to another network computer in Chapter 10.)

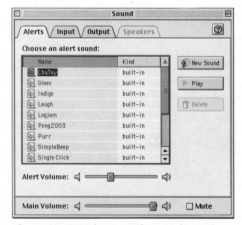

Figure 15-33: The Sound control panel sets the alert sound and its volume for Classic applications.

CDs and DVDs Preferences

In 10.2, a new control panel was introduced that provides customization of OS X's response to CDs and DVDs. You can set an application to start, a script to run, or simply to ignore the newly inserted disc. Figure 15-34 shows the CDs and DVDs panel.

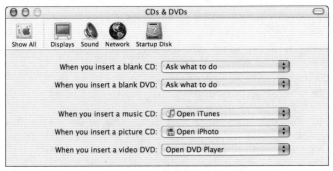

Figure 15-34: The CDs & DVDs panel.

Energy Saver Settings

All Macs capable of using Mac OS X can save energy while they are inactive by automatically going into sleep mode. In sleep mode, the computer uses very little power. A typical Desktop computer uses between 15 and 30 watts while in sleep mode, and a display made after the middle of 1999 uses between 8 and 15 watts while sleeping. These numbers are based on the requirements for complying with the U.S Environmental Protection Agency's Energy Star program. Most Macs that can use Mac OS X comply with the Energy Star requirements, and all Apple displays made since the middle of July 1999 comply.

Naturally you can save even more energy by switching off your display when you leave your computer for a while. (You cannot switch off an Apple display that has the ADC connector without shutting down the computer.) Shutting down your computer would conserve even more energy, but having your computer sleep has advantages, too. The sleep state keeps applications and documents open so that when you wake the computer, you can start work from where you left off.

Energy Saver Preferences

The Energy Saver pane of System Preferences has two tabs—Sleep and Options. Their controls and settings let you determine when your computer sleeps and wakes. If your computer is a PowerBook or iBook, you can also set an option to show the battery status in the menu bar. The battery status option is not present on a Desktop Mac.

Sleep tab of Energy Saver Preferences

Click the Sleep tab in Energy Saver Preferences to adjust how much energy your computer saves by setting how long it remains inactive before going to sleep. You can set separate sleep timings for the whole system and the display, and choose whether or not to put the hard disk to sleep when possible. Figure 15-35 shows the sleep settings in Energy Saver Preferences.

Note   Installing a PCI card may prevent a Power Mac from going to sleep according to the timing for system sleep as set in Energy Saver Preferences. This behavior depends on the particular make and model of the PCI card. Some cards can be upgraded to eliminate this behavior. Even if the system can't sleep, you can still use set separate timings for display sleep and hard disk sleep.

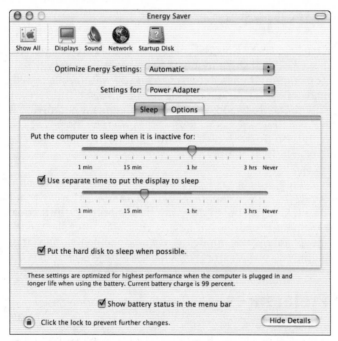

Figure 15-35: Use Energy Saver Preferences to specify when your system, display, and hard disk should begin sleep mode automatically.

Options tab of Energy Saver Preferences

Click the Options tab of Energy Saver Preferences to set options that determine when your computer wakes from sleep. Figure 15-36 shows the settings that you see when you click the Options tab in Energy Saver Preferences.

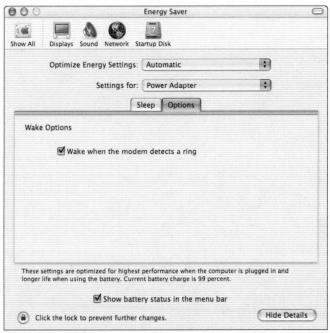

Figure 15-36: Set options for waking from sleep and showing the Battery status icon by clicking the Options tab in Energy Saver Preferences.

Energy Saver has a number of new settings in 10.2 intended to help portable (PowerBook and iBook) users. These options are available from the pop-up menu at the top of the window, as shown in Figure 15-37. As an example, the Presentations setting ensures the display will not black out and sleep, whether or not the PowerBook is using a power adaptor or is on battery.

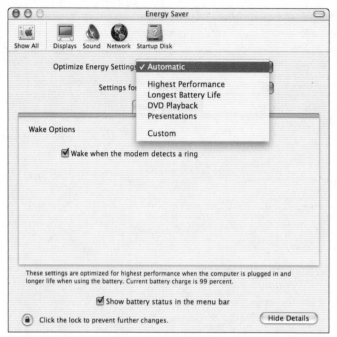

Figure 15-37: Set options for portables in Energy Saver Preferences.

Starting sleep manually

Although Mac OS X puts your computer to sleep after a period of inactivity, you gain additional energy savings by putting it to sleep manually if you know you won't use it for a while. Some of the following methods may work on your computer:

✦ Choose Sleep from the Apple menu. (The Sleep command is dim on a Power Mac with a PCI card that prevents system sleep.)

✦ Press the Power key on a keyboard that has one. On an Apple Pro keyboard, which has no power key, press the Control and Eject keys at the same time. (The Eject key is in the upper-right corner of the numeric keypad.) After pressing Power or Control-Eject, a dialog appears asking whether you want to restart, sleep, cancel, or shut down. Click Sleep or press the S key.

✦ On a PowerBook or iBook, close the lid.

✦ On newer Mac models — such as a Power Mac G4, a Power Mac G4 Cube, or an iMac with slot-loading optical disc drive — press the power button on the computer.

✦ On newer Apple displays — such as an Apple Studio Display with LCD screen and USB ports or an Apple Cinema Display — press the power button on the display. (On other Apple displays, pressing the power button simply turns off the display.)

Waking up your computer

To make your Mac wake up, try the following methods:

✦ Click the mouse button.

✦ Press any key on the keyboard (the Caps Lock and function keys may not work for this purpose).

✦ Open a PowerBook or iBook.

Battery status in the menu bar

If the Battery icon is showing in the menu bar, you can use it to monitor the condition of your computer's battery. The appearance of the Battery icon itself indicates whether the computer is using or recharging the battery, and how much battery capacity remains, as detailed in Table 15-7.

Besides indicating the battery condition graphically, the Battery icon can report the battery condition in words. You can see this information by clicking the Battery icon and looking at the top of the menu that appears. If the computer is using the battery, the first item in the Battery menu reports the hours and minutes of life remaining. If the computer is charging the battery, the menu reports the hours and minutes until the battery is fully charged. You can show the hours and minutes or an equivalent percentage in the menu bar by choosing from the Show submenu of the Battery menu.

Table 15-7 Battery Icon Appearance	
Battery Icon	**Meaning**
[battery icon]	Battery fully charged and computer operating on AC power
[battery icon]	Battery charging and computer operating on AC power
[battery icon]	Battery in use and partly depleted
[battery icon]	No battery; computer operating on AC power

Tip

You can move the Battery status icon by pressing the ⌘ key and dragging the icon. Drag the icon left or right to change its position relative to other icons on the right side of the menu bar. Drag the icon off the menu bar to make it vanish in a puff of smoke.

Login and Startup Settings

The process of starting up your computer is pretty straightforward, and so is the login process. Yet, you can change some aspects of startup and login. You make these changes in the Startup Disk and Login panes of System Preferences.

Startup Disk Preferences

 Besides Mac OS X, your computer may have other Mac OS versions installed. For example, it's quite likely that Mac OS 9.1 or later is installed for the Classic environment. You can restart your computer with another Mac OS version as long as its System Folder includes all the files necessary for startup. You may have alternate Mac OS System Folders on one disk volume or different volumes. You can select any of the eligible System Folders in the Startup Disk pane of System Preferences, or choose the Network Startup option to search for a network volume to start up from, as shown in Figure 15-38.

Figure 15-38: Startup Disk Preferences specifies which Mac OS System Folder is used the next time your computer starts up.

Note

Startup Disk Preferences sometimes scans your hard disk or disks for eligible System Folders. While it does this, it may dim some of the System Folder icons. You can't select a System Folder icon while it is dim. Wait a minute or so and all the icons should become available.

After selecting a System Folder for startup, you can restart with it right away by clicking the Restart button in Startup Disk Preferences. If you don't want to restart yet, you can close the Startup Disk Preferences window, quit System Preferences, or switch to another application. Whether you click Restart or not, an alert appears asking you to confirm that you want to change the System Folder for the next startup.

Login Preferences

Mac OS X requires everyone to log in with a name and password, although the login process can happen automatically during startup. The three panes covered in this section are Accounts and Login Items.

Accounts

The Accounts pane of System Preferences (Figure 15-39) is used to add, edit, and delete users, to set limits on the capabilities of the users, to set automatic login, and to set login options. We cover the Accounts pane in more detail in Chapter 16. To set a user to automatically log in, select the user in the list, then click the Set Auto Login... button. A dialog will display prompting for that user's password.

Figure 15-39: Set a specific user to automatically login in the Accounts window.

To edit a user, select the user's name in the list and click the Edit User button. A window will appear as shown in Figure 15-40 where the user's password, icon, and other features can be changed. You will need to enter that user's password before you can edit their account information.

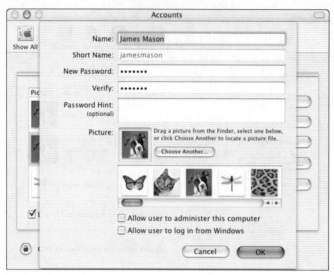

Figure 15-40: Edit a user's information in the Accounts window.

Login Options tab of Accounts

Click the Login Options tab in Accounts to configure the window used for logging in manually. The Login Options settings are shown in Figure 15-41 and have the following effects:

✦ **Display Login Window as.** Select the first option, "Name and password," if you want to require that users type an account name as well as the password in the login window. Select the second option, "List of users," if you want users to be able to select an account name from a list. The second option is more convenient but less secure than the first option. (See Chapter 16 for more information on multiple users.)

✦ **Hide Restart and Shut Down buttons.** Selecting this option makes it harder for someone to circumvent the Mac OS X file and folder protections by restarting from a Mac OS 9 CD.

✦ **Show password hint after 3 attempts to enter a password.** Selecting this option makes it easier for someone to guess a password.

Note   You create a password hint in the Accounts pane of System Preferences. Early versions of Login Preferences incorrectly state that you do this in "the Password pane" (which does not exist).

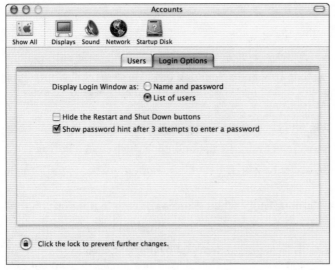

Figure 15-41: Set login options in the Login Options tab of the Accounts window.

Login Items

Click the Login Items icon in System Preferences to set up a list of applications and documents to be opened automatically when you log in. You can add, remove, rearrange, and hide items in the list. You can't add folders to the list. Figure 15-42 shows an example of the list you can configure.

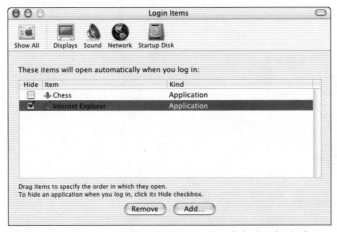

Figure 15-42: Set up a list of items opened during login by clicking the Login Items icon of System Preferences.

Change the Login Items list as follows:

✦ **To add items:** Follow these steps:

1. Click the Add button.

2. In the dialog that appears, select one or more items. Click once to select one item; Shift-click to select adjacent items; and ⌘-click to select nonadjacent items.

3. Click Open to add the selected item or items to the login items list.

✦ **To remove an item:** Select it in the list and click the Remove button.

✦ **To rearrange the order in which listed items open during login:** Drag items up or down in the list.

✦ **To hide an item automatically when it opens during login:** Turn on the Hide setting in the list.

Tip

You can also add items to the Login Items list by dragging their icons from Finder windows or the Desktop to the Login Items list. For example, drag an MP3 file to the list to have it played when you log in.

Note

If you set an application or a document as a login item and it requires a password to open, it does not open during login. Its icon appears in the Dock, and you must click the icon and enter the password to open the item. Examples of such items include e-mail applications and encrypted documents.

My Account

The My Accounts pane (Figure 15-43) of System Preferences is used to set and change your own password, to choose or change your login icon, and to edit your Address Book card in the Address Book application. To change your password, click the Change... button. A dialog will display prompting for that user's password.

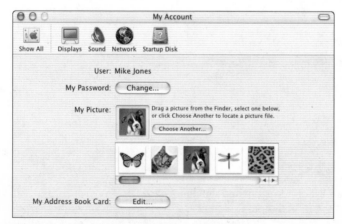

Figure 15-43: Change your password and login icon in the My Accounts pane of System Preferences.

Why Login Items No Longer Open Automatically

If you make an item a login item and later move the item to a different folder, the item will no longer open automatically during login. For example, if you make an MP3 file from your Music folder a login item and later move the MP3 file to a new folder within the Music folder, the MP3 will no longer open and play during startup. Moreover, a login item breaks if you so much as move or rename any folder in the login item's path. For example, if you make a document a login item and them move the folder that contains the document from your home folder to the Documents folder within your home folder, the document will no longer open during login. This problem occurs because Mac OS X keeps track of login items by pathname rather than alias.

To work around this problem, remove the nonfunctional item from the Login Items list in System Preferences, and then add the item back.

Classic Startup Settings

The Classic environment starts up automatically when you open a Classic application, but you can also have it start as soon as you log in. In addition, you can start Classic manually, restart it, and force it to quit. If you have Mac OS 9.1 or later installed on more than one disk volume, you can specify which to use for the Classic environment. You do all this and more in the Classic pane of System Preferences.

As the Classic environment starts up, a number of files are loaded that extend the capabilities of Mac OS 9 in the Classic environment. You can individually deactivate these files, commonly called *extensions* or *startup files,* with the Extensions Manager control panel. You may want to deactivate extensions to reduce the amount of memory required by Mac OS 9 in the Classic environment, improve its performance, or troubleshoot Classic problems.

Classic Preferences

The Classic pane of System Preferences has three tabs: Start/Stop, Advanced, and Memory/Versions. Their controls and settings let you take charge of when and how the Classic environment starts and stops.

Start/Stop tab of Classic Preferences

Click the Start/Stop tab in Classic Preferences when you want to start the Classic environment manually, stop it, restart it, or force it to quit. You can select the startup volume for Classic, if you have Mac OS 9.1 or later installed on more than one volume. If you would rather not wait for Classic to start up when you open a Classic application, turn on the setting to have Classic start up on login. Figure 15-44 shows all the buttons and settings in the Start/Stop tab of Classic Preferences.

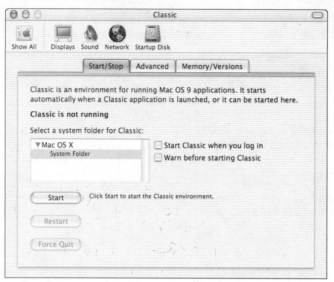

Figure 15-44: Manually control Classic and configure basic settings for starting it automatically.

Having the Classic environment start up right away when you log in has pros and cons. To the good, you don't have to wait while Classic starts up when you open a Classic application. But unless you have a fairly fast computer, you may find it gets unacceptably sluggish while Classic is starting up.

You can click the Stop button or the Restart button with impunity. Before Classic stops, you have a chance to save every open Classic document that has unsaved changes. Clicking these buttons is like shutting down or restarting a computer with Mac OS 9.

Caution

Forcing the Classic environment to quit is a drastic measure equivalent to pulling the power cord on a computer with Mac OS 9. You do not have an opportunity to save changes in Classic documents that are open. Before forcing Classic to quit, try clicking the Stop button in Classic Preferences. If that doesn't stop Classic, then switch to each Classic application that is open and try to quit it by choosing File⇨Quit. You should consider clicking Force Quit in Classic Preferences only after attempting to quit each open Classic application properly.

Advanced tab of Classic Preferences

Click the Advanced tab in Classic Preferences when you want to start Classic (or restart it, if it's already running) with special conditions imposed. In the Advanced tab, you can also adjust Classic sleep and rebuild the Classic desktop database file. Figure 15-45 shows the buttons and settings in the Advanced tab of Classic Preferences.

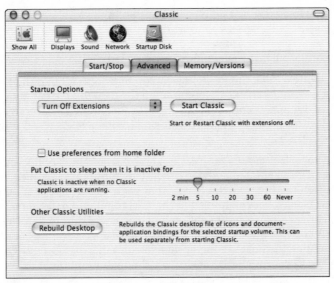

Figure 15-45: Configure special Classic startup conditions, adjust Classic sleep, and rebuild the Classic desktop file in the Advanced tab of Classic Preferences.

The Advanced tab has the following three sections of settings:

✦ **Startup Options.** Choose one of the following special startup conditions from the pop-up menu and then click a button to start or restart the Classic environment:

- **Turn Off Extensions.** Starts Mac OS 9 for the Classic environment with all extensions temporarily deactivated. This condition makes Classic start up very rapidly, but features provided by extensions are not available. (This choice has the same effect as starting up a computer with Mac OS 9 while holding down the Shift key.)

- **Open Extensions Manager.** Opens the Extensions Manager control panel while starting up the Classic environment. You can use Extensions Manager to activate and deactivate extensions individually. (This choice has the same effect as starting up a computer with Mac OS 9 while holding down the spacebar.)

✦ **Use Key Combination.** Starts up Mac OS 9 for the Classic environment as if you were holding down up to five keys. The point of this is that some extensions work differently when certain keys are held down during startup. You specify which keys to "hold down" by typing them while the pop-up menu in the Advanced pane is set to Use Key Combination. The keys you type are listed below the pop-up menu. You can clear the list by pressing Clear on the numeric keypad.

✦ **Put Classic to sleep when it is inactive for.** Set the timing for Classic sleep mode. When Classic goes into sleep mode, it uses very little of the computer's memory or processing power. However, opening a Classic application may take longer when Classic is in sleep mode.

✦ **Other Classic Utilities.** Click the Rebuild Desktop button to rebuild the Classic environment's desktop database file. Rebuilding the desktop file can fix problems with Classic document and application icons losing their distinctive appearance and with Classic documents refusing to open when you double-click their icons in the Finder.

The Classic desktop file contains information about what kinds of documents each Classic application creates and can open. This file also has copies of the distinctive icon for every type of document that each Classic application can create. The Mac OS uses information from the desktop file to determine which icon to display for each Classic application and document and to determine which Classic application should open a document that you double-click in the Finder. Rebuilding the desktop file updates it with information newly extracted from the Classic applications installed on your computer.

Memory/Versions tab of Classic Preferences

Click the Memory/Versions tab in Classic Preferences when you want to see more detailed information on the Classic environment running, as shown in Figure 15-46.

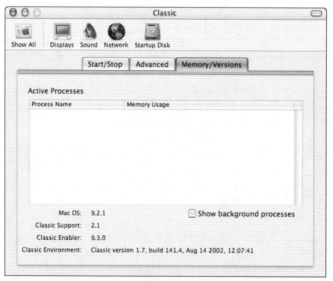

Figure 15-46: View version, memory use, and processes of the Classic environment in the Memory/Versions tab of Classic Preferences.

Extensions Manager control panel (Classic)

The Extensions Manager control panel can individually deactivate extensions and other startup files in the Mac OS 9 System Folder and in its Control Panels, Extensions, Startup Items, and Shutdown Items folders. The Extensions Manager window has a scrolling list of these items. For each listed item, the Extensions Manager displays its status (on or off), name, size, version, and the package it was installed with. You can also display each item's type and creator codes by selecting options with the Preferences command (in the Edit menu). Figure 15-47 is an example of the Extensions Manager.

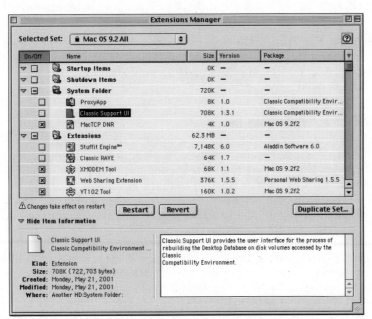

Figure 15-47: Deactivate and activate Classic startup items with the Extensions Manager control panel.

Reorganizing the Extensions Manager list

You can reorganize the Extensions Manager list as follows:

✦ View items grouped by the folders they're in, grouped by the package they were installed with, or ungrouped. Choose a view from the View menu.

✦ Collapse and expand a group by clicking the disclosure triangle next to the group name or by double-clicking the name.

✦ Sort the list within each group by clicking any column heading to set the sort order.

✦ Adjust the widths of the Name and Package columns by dragging the right boundary line of the Name column heading or the left boundary line of the Package column heading. (You can't adjust the other column widths.)

Seeing detailed information about an item

You can view the detailed information about an item two ways:

✦ See more information about an item by clicking the item's name to select it and then clicking the disclosure triangle labeled Show Item Information at the bottom-left corner of the Extensions Manager window.

✦ Open the folder that contains an item by clicking the item's name to select it and then choosing Find Item from Extensions Manager's Edit menu. (The Get Info command in Extension Manager's Edit menu does not work in the Classic environment.)

Activating and deactivating items

You deactivate or activate an extension or other item by selecting or deselecting the checkbox next to the item's name. Activating or deactivating a group affects all the items in the group. You can save the current configuration of the Extensions Manager as a named set by choosing New Set from the File menu. Your named sets appear in the Selected Set pop-up menu in alphabetical order, and choosing a set from that pop-up menu changes Extensions Manager to the configuration saved for that set.

Changes you make to the status of any items take place when you restart the Classic environment (or when you restart the computer with Mac OS 9). To restart Classic immediately, click the Restart button in Extensions Manager. To restart Classic after quitting Extensions Manager, open the Classic pane of System Preferences and click the Restart button there. To cancel the changes you've made, click Revert in the Extensions Manager window.

Note   Deactivating startup items removes features from the Classic environment. If you remove startup items that are required for the Classic environment, Mac OS X notices they are missing the next time you start Classic and displays an alert in the Classic startup window offering to replace the missing items.

Extensions Manager puts items that you deactivate into special folders inside the Mac OS 9 System Folder as follows:

✦ Deactivated items from the Extensions folder go into the Extensions (Disabled) folder.

✦ Deactivated control panels go into the Control Panels (Disabled) folder.

✦ Deactivated items from the System Folder go into the System Extensions (Disabled) folder.

Using preconfigured sets of extensions

Extensions Manager comes with two preconfigured sets of extensions: Mac OS 9.1 All and Mac OS 9.1 Base. (The version number is higher if you are using Mac OS 9.2.1 or later for the Classic environment.) These sets are locked so that you can't change them.

You may think that Extensions Manager's preconfigured, locked sets would keep all the items turned on that are required for the Classic environment. This is the case with Mac OS 9.2.1, but not with Mac OS 9.1. In Mac OS 9.1, both the All and the Base sets turn off some essential items.

If you want to use one of the preconfigured Mac OS 9.1 extension sets when starting the Classic environment, you need to make a copy of the set and make sure that it has all items turned on that are required for the Classic environment. You can use Extensions Manager to determine which of the items that Classic requires are turned off when you choose Mac OS 9.1 All or Mac OS 9.1 Base. Follow these steps:

1. **Choose Mac OS 9.1 All or Mac OS 9.1 Base from the Selected Set pop-up menu.**

2. **Choose File⇨Duplicate Set.** Extensions Manager makes a copy of the set.

3. **Choose View⇨As Items and click the On/Off column heading**. This sorts the startup items by their on/off condition so that all items that are turned off are listed together.

4. **Scroll the list looking for items that are turned off and have Classic in the name or Classic Compatibility Environment in the Package column.**

5. **Make sure all the Classic items are turned on, and then use this set instead of the original locked set when you start the Classic environment.**

Color Matching Settings

The way we use digital equipment to produce color output has an inherent problem. Displays, scanners, digital cameras, and so on create color with light, whereas any tangible output that you create (from color laser printouts to four-color offset lithography) creates colors with pigment. These two different methods create slightly (or sometimes vastly) different sets of colors. What's more, each individual device has a specific range of colors that it can reproduce.

The ColorSync software in Mac OS X can improve color accuracy by matching a color profile for your display to color profiles for printers, scanners, digital cameras, and other color equipment you use. Each profile specifies the range of colors that a particular type of display can show, printer can print, scanner can scan, and so on. The ColorSync software uses the profiles to adjust colors so that they look as alike as possible on all compatible equipment.

ColorSync Preferences

C You can set up ColorSync for your working environment by changing settings in the ColorSync pane of System Preferences. You probably don't need to change these settings unless you are a graphic arts professional.

The ColorSync settings specify default profiles for embedding in documents you create. In addition, you can specify a color matching method (CMM).

For ColorSync to do its job, you need to use it in all stages of image creation, editing, and output. Besides specifying profiles in ColorSync Preferences, you need to specify ColorSync color matching when you print a color document. In addition, take advantage of any ColorSync options that are available in application programs you use for scanning, image creation, image editing, page layout, and printing. For specific instructions on setting up color management in a particular product, consult the product's documentation.

The ColorSync software in Mac OS X includes generic profiles and profiles for several Apple displays. Profiles for other devices come with the devices themselves or are available from the companies that make the devices. You can create a custom ColorSync profile for your display as described earlier in this chapter under "Display Settings."

Default ColorSync profiles for documents

You choose default profiles for your new documents by clicking the Default Profiles tab in the ColorSync panel. The RGB, CMYK, Gray, or Lab default profile you select is embedded in new documents you create unless the software that creates the documents specifies another profile. A default profile is also used for documents you open that don't have embedded profiles. The type of document determines which of the default profiles is used. Figure 15-48 shows the settings for default document profiles in the ColorSync panel.

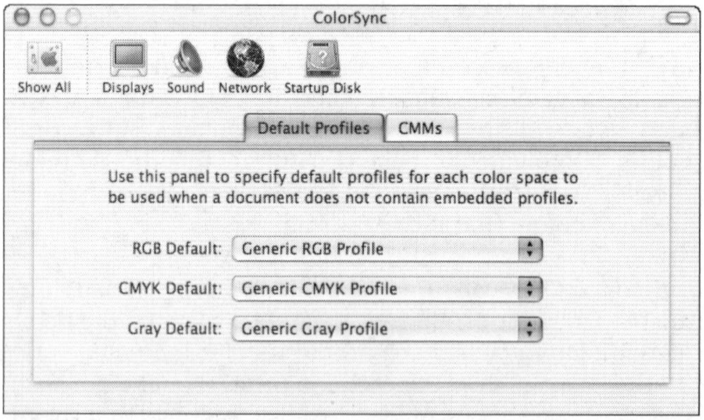

Figure 15-48: Specify profiles for documents that don't get profiles from the software that creates them in the Default Profiles tab of ColorSync Preferences.

ColorSync color matching methods

If your computer has an alternate color matching method installed, you can choose to use it instead of the Apple CMM. You change the color matching method by clicking the CMMs tab in the ColorSync panel, shown in Figure 15-49.

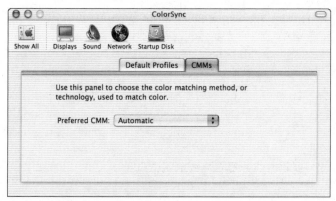

Figure 15-49: Specify preferred color matching method in the CMMs tab of the ColorSync panel.

Internet Settings

Mac OS X keeps track of preference settings commonly used by all kinds of Internet applications. For example, your e-mail reader certainly needs to know your e-mail address, but so do your Web browser, FTP application, and newsgroup reader. The makers of some Internet applications use Mac OS X's Internet preference settings so that you don't have to enter or change these settings repeatedly in each application.

You set commonly used preferences for the Internet in the Internet panel of System Preferences. Your Internet applications may also let you change some of the same preference settings. For example, you can change your e-mail password in your e-mail application or Internet Preferences. The most recent change takes precedence.

The Internet pane of System Preferences organizes its settings by category:

   ✦ .Mac

   ✦ iDisk

   ✦ Email

   ✦ Web

   ✦ News

To see and change the settings for a category, click its tab in Internet Preferences.

.Mac tab of Internet Preferences

Click the .Mac tab in Internet Preferences to enter your .Mac member name and password. If you don't already have an .Mac account, you can click a button to sign up for a free trial membership, or pay for one. Mac OS X is tightly integrated with .Mac and it's easy to set up the Mail application to handle your .Mac e-mail account. In addition, the Finder makes it easy to connect to the your iDisk that's included with your .Mac account. You can copy files to and from your iDisk as easily as with any network disk. The iDisk is a convenient place to store and share files on the Internet, or set up a small Web site. It's also a convenient source of free and demonstration software for Mac OS X and the Classic environment. Figure 15-50 shows the .Mac tab in Internet Preferences.

Figure 15-50: Specify your .Mac account name and password or get an account by clicking the .Mac tab of Internet Preferences.

iDisk tab of the Internet Preferences

As your iDisk is part of your .Mac account, you'll want to have entered your .Mac account name and password in the fields on the .Mac tab of the Internet panel shown in Figure 15-50. If you have an active Internet connection, when you click the iDisk tab of Internet Preferences you see the information shown in Figure 15-51. On this tab you can see how much of your available iDisk space you've used, and the settings for the public part of your iDisk folder (whether to allow others to upload to your iDisk, and whether to require a password to access the public part of your iDisk).

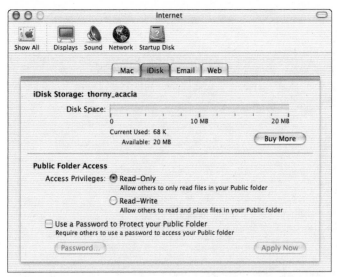

Figure 15-51: Set settings for your .Mac iDisk by clicking the iDisk tab of Internet Preferences.

Email tab of Internet Preferences

Click the Email tab in Internet Preferences to enter the details of your e-mail account. If you have more than one e-mail account, enter the details of your most public account here. If you have a .Mac account, you can turn on a setting so that all the details of your .Mac e-mail account are entered for you. You can also choose the e-mail application you prefer to use. This application is the one that opens and creates a new e-mail message when you click a link. Figure 15-52 shows the details you enter for your e-mail account in the Email tab of Internet Preferences.

After changing the default e-mail reader setting in Internet Preferences, you may need to log out of Mac OS X or restart your computer for the change to take effect. The default e-mail reader specified in Internet Preferences is the application that opens to create a new e-mail message when you open an Internet location file for an e-mail address. In addition, some applications that let you click links to the Internet have the default e-mail reader create a new message when you click a link to an e-mail address. Internet location files and links to e-mail addresses have URLs that begin with `mailto:`.

Figure 15-52: Enter the details of your e-mail account by clicking the Email tab of Internet Preferences.

Web tab of Internet Preferences

Click the Web tab of Internet Preferences to specify the Web browser that you prefer to use. You can also see settings for the home page, search page, and download folder that you wish Web browsers would use. Who knows, maybe some day Internet Explorer, OmniWeb, and other Web browsers will actually use these settings. Figure 15-53 shows the settings you can make in the Web tab of Internet Preferences.

After changing the default Web browser setting in Internet Preferences, you may need to log out of Mac OS X or restart your computer for the change to take effect. The default Web browser specified in Internet Preferences is the application that opens to display a Web page when you open an Internet location file for a Web page. In addition, some applications that let you click links to Web pages have the default Web browser display a Web page whose link you click. For example, the Help Viewer application included with Mac OS X 10.1 honors the default Web browser setting. Internet location files and links to Web pages have URLs that begins with `http://` or `https://`.

Tip   If you want to make sure that your preferences for home page, search page, and download folder are honored, set them with the Preferences command in the application menu of your Web browser.

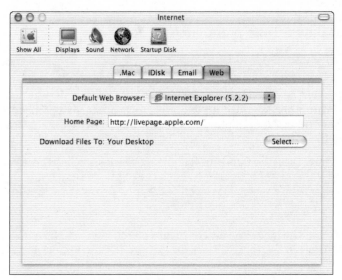

Figure 15-53: The settings you make in the Web tab of Internet Preferences may be overridden by preference settings in your Web browser.

Date, Time, and Time Zone Settings

In addition to displaying a clock on your menu bar, your computer uses date and time information for a variety of operations. For example, your computer uses date and time information to provide files with creation and modification dates and to time-stamp e-mail. You can adjust most of your computer's clock and calendar settings in the Date & Time pane of System Preferences. The exception is the clock in the Classic menu bar, whose features you configure in the Date & Time control panel.

Date & Time Preferences

The Date & Time panel of System Preferences organizes clock and calendar settings in four tabs:

✦ Date & Time

✦ Time Zone

✦ Network Time

✦ Menu Bar Clock

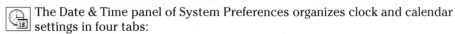

Date & Time tab of Date & Time preferences

Click the Date & Time tab in Date & Time Preferences to set your computer's current date and time.

✦ **To change the Date:** Click the little arrows next to the month and year and click a day in the monthly calendar. If the little arrows are absent, it's because the "Use a network time server" option is selected on the network Time tab shown in Figure 15-56.

✦ **To change the Time:** Drag the hands of the analog clock and click the AM/PM indicator next to this clock. Alternatively, click the digital hour, minute, or second and then either type a new value or click the little arrows next to the digital clock.

You must click Save to put the new time and date into effect. Figure 15-54 shows the clock and calendar settings in the Date & Time tab of Date & Time Preferences.

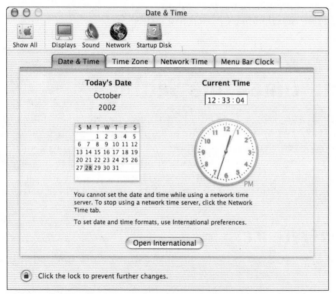

Figure 15-54: Set the computer's date and time by clicking the Date & Time tab of Date & Time Preferences.

Note   If the controls for changing the date and time are missing, you need to click the Network Time tab and then turn off the option labeled Use a network time server.

Time Zone tab of Date & Time Preferences

Click the Time Zone tab in Date & Time Preferences to set your time zone. The pop-up menu lists regions that may have different time zones in the highlighted part of the world. You can click another part of the world to highlight it. If daylight-saving time is in effect for the currently selected time zone, a sunburst graphic appears in the lower-left corner of the map next to the time zone's abbreviation. Figure 15-55 shows the Time Zone tab of Date & Time Preferences.

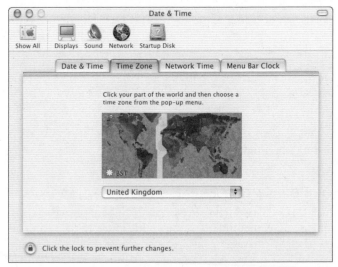

Figure 15-55: Set your time zone in the Time Zone tab of Date & Time Preferences.

Tip Even if you never move your computer, you should set its time zone so that people receiving your e-mail in a different time zone can tell what time you sent the e-mail.

Network Time tab of Date & Time Preferences

Click the Network Time tab in Date & Time Preferences to start or stop synchronizing your computer's clock with a time server on the Internet or your network. If you select the option labeled "Use a network time server," you can choose a time server from the NTP Server drop-down list. Alternatively, you can enter the name or IP address of a computer that provides time synchronization service. Click the Set Time Now button to have Mac OS X update your computer's clock immediately. The Network Time tab of Date & Time Preferences is reflected in Figure 15-56.

Tip Besides the Apple time servers in the NTP Server drop-down list, you can use many public time servers. Check the list on the NTP (network time protocol) Web site at www.eecis.udel.edu/~mills/ntp/servers.htm.

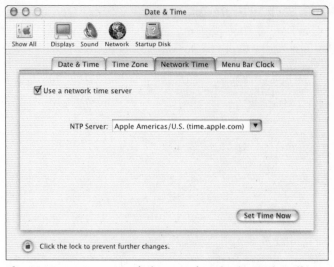

Figure 15-56: Set network time synchronization on or off in the Network Time tab of the Date & Time panel.

Menu Bar Clock tab of Date & Time preferences

Click the Menu Bar Clock tab in Date & Time Preferences to configure the appearance of the clock in the Mac OS X menu bar, as shown in Figure 15-57.

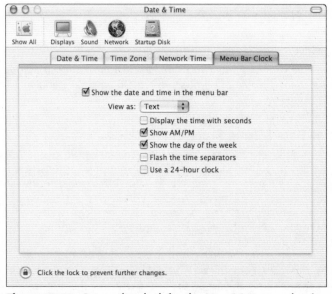

Figure 15-57: Set up the clock for the Mac OS X menu bar in the Menu Bar Clock tab of Date & Time Preferences.

You can see the date by clicking the clock in the menu bar. This action displays a menu with the date at the top of it. In addition, this menu has choices for viewing the clock as an icon or as text and for opening the Date & Time pane of System Preferences.

The menu bar clock initially appears at the right end of the menu bar. You can move it by pressing ⌘ and dragging it. You can remove the menu bar clock by ⌘-dragging it off the menu bar.

Date & Time control panel (Classic)

Although the current time and date that you set in the Date & Time Preferences of Mac OS X also affect the Classic environment, the settings for the clock in the Mac OS X menu bar don't affect the Classic menu bar. You configure the clock for the Classic menu bar in the Date & Time control panel. This control panel also sets standard formats for dates and times in Classic applications, as described next. The Date & Time control panel has an on-off setting for the Classic menu bar clock. Clicking the Clock Options button displays a dialog in which you can set the display format of the clock and set the clock to chime on the hour, half-hour, and quarter-hour. On PowerBook or iBook, you also can turn on or off a battery-level indicator, which appears next to the clock in the menu bar. You can also choose to show the seconds, day, and AM/PM, and you can change the color of the clock, if desired. Figure 15-58 shows the Date & Time control panel and its Clock Options dialog.

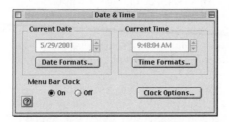

Figure 15-58: Set up the clock for the Classic menu bar in the Date & Time control panel (first image) and its Clock Options dialog (second image).

Language and Regional Preferences

Mac OS X is a multilingual and multiregional operating system. It can display menus, dialogs, and other text in a variety of languages. These include not only languages that use the Roman alphabet, such as English, Spanish, French, and German, but also languages with much larger sets of characters, such as Japanese. Besides accommodating differences in language structure, writing direction, and alphabetical sorting, Mac OS X can also adjust for regional differences in formats for displaying dates, times, numbers, and currency. With Mac OS X, you're not limited to working in one language at a time. You can work in multiple languages and switch languages while you work. However, you may need to install special applications to create documents in different languages.

You switch among the various languages and regional settings separately for Mac OS X applications and Classic applications. For Mac OS X applications, you configure the settings in the International pane of System Preferences. For Classic applications, you configure settings in the Date & Time, Keyboard, Numbers, and Text control panels.

Choosing a language

Some Mac OS X applications are able to display their menus, dialogs, and other text in a number of different languages. Applications with this ability include the Finder and most of the applications preinstalled in the Applications and Utilities folders. You can choose the language you want these Mac OS X applications to use. Your choice does not affect Classic applications. Classic applications are generally localized for one language. To use a Classic application in a different language, you must install a version of the application that is localized for the language you want to use.

To specify the language you prefer to see in menus and dialogs of Mac OS X applications, click the Language tab of International Preferences. The Language tab displays a list of active languages. Each time you open an application, Mac OS X tells it to use the language at the top of the list. If the application doesn't have menus in that language, Mac OS X tells it to use the second language on the list, and so on down the list. Figure 15-59 shows the Language tab of International preferences panel.

You change the language that Mac OS X applications use by rearranging the list of languages in the Languages tab. Drag your first language choice to the top of the list. Drag your second language choice to the second spot on the list and continue in this manner so that the languages are in descending order of preference. Changes you make to the list of languages don't affect applications that are open at the time, including the Finder. Language changes take effect in each application the next time you open it. Language changes take effect in the Finder the next time you log in.

You can add languages to the list and remove them from it. Click the Edit button to see a dialog that lists all installed languages. In this dialog, select the checkbox of each language that you want to appear in the Language tab. You can change the sorting in the dialog by clicking a column heading.

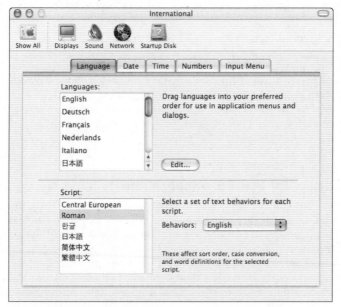

Figure 15-59: Set the language you want for Mac OS X menus and dialogs in the Language tab of International Preferences.

Choosing text behaviors

Languages may use the same script, yet have different rules for alphabetizing, capitalizing, and distinguishing words. In Mac OS X and the Classic environment, this set of rules is called a *text behavior*. You can specify a text behavior separately in Mac OS X and the Classic environment.

Language Script Systems and Keyboard Layouts

The world's languages have many different alphabets and methods of writing (vertical or horizontal, left-to-right, or right-to-left). The software that defines a method of writing is called a language script system, or simply a script. Do not confuse this kind of script with the kind of script you create with AppleScript (as described in Chapter 24).

A language script system specifies which character in the specified language each keystroke produces, as well as how the characters should behave — for example, the direction in which text flows. The script also specifies sort order, number and currency formats, and date and time formats.

Multiple languages can use one language script system. For example, the Roman script is used in most Western languages, such as English, French, Italian, Spanish, and German.

Associated with each language script system are one or more keyboard layouts. A keyboard layout defines the relationship between keys you press and characters entered. For example, the keyboard layout for U.S. English produces a # symbol when you press Shift-3, but the same keystroke produces a £ symbol with the British English keyboard layout.

Choosing text behaviors for Mac OS X applications

You choose a text behavior for Mac OS X applications by clicking the Language tab in International Preferences. In the Language tab, select one of the installed language script systems from the list on the left, and then choose one of the script's regional languages from the adjacent pop-up menu. For example, the Roman script system in Mac OS X has different text behavior rules for Austrian, Brazilian, Canadian French, Catalan, Danish, Dutch, English, Finnish, French, German, Italian, Norwegian, Portuguese, Spanish, and Swedish. The Language tab of International preferences was shown in Figure 15-59.

Choosing text behaviors for Classic applications

You choose a text behavior for Classic applications in the Text control panel. Choose a language script from the Script pop-up menu, and then choose a regional language from the Behavior pop-up menu. Figure 15-60 shows the Text control panel.

Figure 15-60: The Text control panel sets text behavior rules for Classic applications.

Setting date formats

You can set up standard formats for displaying dates. The Finder uses these formats in list views, the Info window, and elsewhere. Other applications may use these formats, or they may have their own preference settings for date formats. You set date formats separately in Mac OS X and the Classic environment.

Setting date formats for Mac OS X applications

You set date formats for Mac OS X applications by clicking the Date tab in International Preferences. You can set the date formats, such as U.S. or British, customarily used in a particular region by choosing them from the pop-up menu at the top of the Date tab. You can also create a custom format by changing individual settings in the Date tab. Figure 15-61 shows the Date tab of International Preferences.

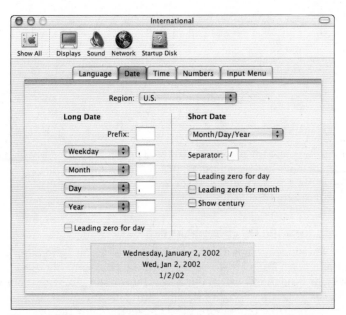

Figure 15-61: Set the date formats for Mac OS X applications in the Date tab of International Preferences.

Setting date formats for Classic applications

You set date formats for Classic applications in the Date & Time control panel. To set the date formats, click the Date Format button. In the dialog that appears, you can choose a region whose customary formats you want to use, or you can create a custom format by changing individual settings. Figure 15-62 shows the Date & Time control panel and its Date Formats dialog.

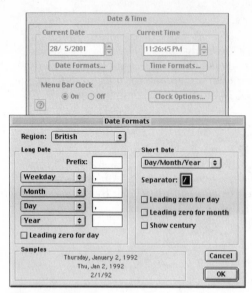

Figure 15-62: The Date & Time control panel sets the standard date formats for Classic applications.

Setting time formats

You can set up standard formats for displaying times. The Finder and many other applications use these formats to display times, but some applications have their own preference settings for time formats. You set time formats separately in Mac OS X and the Classic environment.

Setting time formats for Mac OS X applications

You set time formats for Mac OS X applications by clicking the Time tab in International Preferences. You can set the time formats customarily used in a particular region, such as French or French Canadian, by choosing it from the pop-up menu at the top of the Time tab. You can also create a custom format by changing individual settings in the Time tab. Figure 15-63 shows the Time tab of International Preferences.

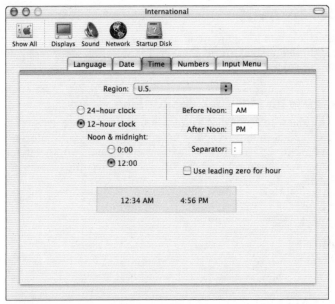

Figure 15-63: Set the time formats for Mac OS X applications in the Time tab of International Preferences.

Setting time formats for Classic applications

You set time formats for Classic applications in the Date & Time control panel. First, you click the Time Formats button. In the dialog that appears, you can choose a region whose customary formats you want to use, or you can create a custom format by changing individual settings. Figure 15-64 shows the Time & Time control panel and its Time Formats dialog.

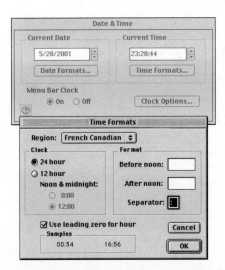

Figure 15-64: The Date & Time control panel sets the standard time formats for Classic applications.

Setting number formats

You can set up standard formats for displaying amounts of currency and other numbers with decimal and thousands separators. You set number formats separately in Mac OS X and the Classic environment.

Setting number formats for Mac OS X applications

You set number formats for Mac OS X applications by clicking the Numbers tab in International Preferences. You can choose a region from the pop-up menu at the top of the Numbers tab to use its customary formats, or specify custom formats by changing individual settings. Figure 15-65 shows the Numbers tab of International Preferences.

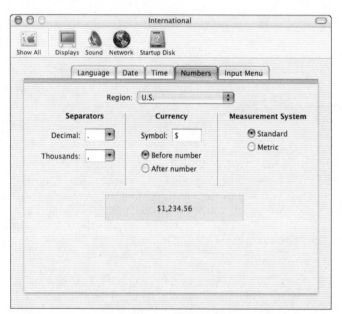

Figure 15-65: Set the numbers formats for Mac OS X applications in the Numbers tab of International Preferences.

Setting number formats for Classic applications

You set number formats for Classic applications in the Numbers control panel. You can choose a preconfigured number format for a region of the world, or you can specify a custom format by entering the punctuation marks to use as separators and the currency symbol. Figure 15-66 shows the Numbers control panel.

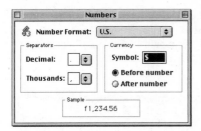

Figure 15-66: The Numbers control panel sets the standard number formats for Classic applications.

Selecting a keyboard layout

Each language has a different keyboard layout. For example, on the keyboard layout for Spanish you can type the letter *n* with a tilde (ñ) by pressing one key instead of the two keys required for the same letter on a U.S. English keyboard layout. In addition, the question mark is in a different location, with an upside-down question mark next to it on the Spanish keyboard layout, and the keys for adding accents to vowels are more accessible. Regions with the same language, such as Australia, Britain, Canada, and the U.S. have different keyboard layouts. You can even find special keyboard layouts for alternate typing methods, such as the Dvorak layout for typing English.

You can compare keyboard layouts by using the Key Caps application (normally located in the Utilities folder). Figure 15-67 compares the U.S. and Spanish keyboard layouts.

Figure 15-67: Compare keyboard layouts by using the Key Caps utility application; shown here are U.S. (top) and Spanish (bottom).

Languages with large character sets augment the keyboard with other methods of inputting characters. For example, Japanese has input methods that involve a control palette, additional windows, and a menu, as shown in Figure 15-68.

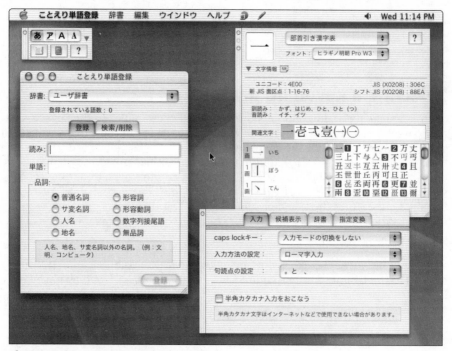

Figure 15-68: Japanese and other languages with many characters have input methods besides a keyboard.

You can switch to a different keyboard layout or input method to facilitate entering or editing text in another language. You can switch keyboard layouts by using several different methods. If you regularly use multiple languages, you can set up a keyboard menu. You can also set up keyboard shortcuts for switching keyboard layouts, and you can have Mac OS X automatically switch the keyboard layout when you select text that uses a different script. For Mac OS X applications, you set up these options using the Input Menu tab of International Preferences. For Classic applications, you set up the keyboard layout options separately by using the Keyboard control panel.

Note   Keep in mind that the key labels printed on your keyboard do not change when you switch keyboard layouts. If you change to a different layout, some keys no longer generate the characters printed on them.

If your computer has more than one language script system, switching keyboard layouts may also change script systems. Each keyboard layout implicitly designates a script system. For example, switching from the U.S. keyboard layout to the Japanese keyboard layout implicitly switches from the Roman script system to the Japanese script system.

Selecting a keyboard layout for Mac OS X applications

You set up a keyboard menu and configure other keyboard options for Mac OS X applications by clicking the Input Menu tab in International Preferences. The Input Menu tab displays a list of available keyboard layouts. Select the checkbox of each keyboard layout that you want to use. You can change the sorting in the list of keyboard layouts by clicking a column heading. Figure 15-69 shows the Input Menu tab of International Preferences.

Figure 15-69: Select keyboard layouts for Mac OS X's Keyboard menu in the Input Menu tab of International Preferences.

If you turn on more than one keyboard layout, a Keyboard menu appears next to the Help menu in Mac OS X's menu bar. The Keyboard menu lists the keyboard layouts that are turned on in the Input Menu tab. You can change the active keyboard layout by choosing a different one from this menu. The last item on the Keyboard menu is Customize Menu, and choosing it displays the Input Menu tab of International Preferences. Figure 15-70 shows an example of the Keyboard menu.

Figure 15-70: Switch Mac OS X's keyboard layout by choosing another one from the Keyboard menu.

If you want to be able to switch keyboard layouts by pressing ⌘-Option-Spacebar or have Mac OS X automatically switch layouts when you select text that uses a different script, click the Options button in the Input Menu tab of International Preferences. This button displays a dialog in which you can set these options on or off. You can always cycle through the language scripts available in Mac OS X by pressing ⌘-Spacebar. Figure 15-71 shows the dialog in which you set the options for switching keyboard layouts.

Selecting a keyboard layout for Classic applications

You set up a keyboard menu and configure other keyboard options for Classic applications in the Keyboard control panel. It lists the keyboard layouts that are available in the Classic environment, and you turn on each one you want to use. Figure 15-72 shows the Keyboard control panel.

A Keyboard menu near the right end of the Classic menu bar lists all the keyboard layouts that are turned on in the Keyboard control panel. You can change the keyboard layout for Classic applications by choosing a different one from this menu. The Classic environment's Keyboard menu looks like the Mac OS X Keyboard menu, previously shown in Figure 15-70.

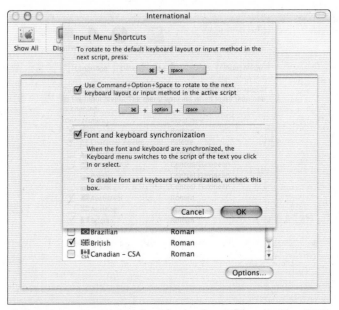

Figure 15-71: Set optional methods of switching the Mac OS X keyboard layout by clicking Options in the Input Menu tab of International Preferences.

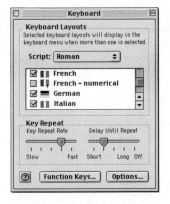

Figure 15-72: The Keyboard control panel specifies which keyboard layouts are listed in the Classic environment's Keyboard menu.

If you want to be able to switch keyboard layouts in Classic applications by pressing ⌘-Option-Spacebar, click the Options button in the Keyboard control panel and turn on the option in the dialog that appears. You can always cycle through the language scripts that are installed in the Classic environment (if more than one script is installed) by pressing ⌘-Spacebar.

Software Update Settings

Apple periodically revises portions of Mac OS X, the applications that come with it, and Mac OS 9 for the Classic environment. You can keep your Mac OS X software up-to-date with the Software Update pane of System Preferences. You can keep your Mac OS 9 software up-to-date with the Software Update control panel. Both the Software Update pane of System Preferences and the Software Update control panel can schedule periodic updates, and you can use them to update manually whenever you like.

Note   Your computer must have an Internet connection to check for updates.

Checking for Mac OS X software updates

In Software Update Preferences, you can schedule a daily, weekly, or monthly check for updates of Mac OS X software. You can also disable scheduled updates. You can begin checking for updates manually at any time by clicking the Update Now button. Figure 15-73 shows the settings and controls for automatic and manual updates in the Software Update pane of System Preferences.

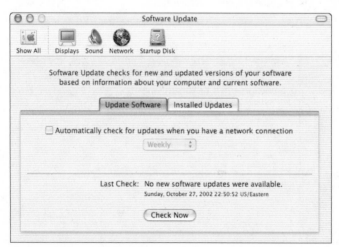

Figure 15-73: Keep Mac OS X software up-to-date with Software Update Preferences.

Installing Mac OS X software updates

Software Update Preferences doesn't actually perform updates. It controls another application, Software Update, which downloads and installs updates. Software Update opens as needed. You don't need to open Software Update from the Finder. (Software Update is buried on your hard disk in the CoreServices folder of the Library folder in the System folder.)

When the time arrives for a scheduled check of available update or you click the Update Now button in Software Update Preferences, the Software Update application opens. (Technically, a part of Software Update named SWUpdateEngine is what opens.) If Software Update finds updates for which your computer is eligible, it lists them in an Install Software window, as shown in Figure 15-74.

Figure 15-74: Select which of the available updates you want to have installed.

To install one or more updates that are listed in the Software Update window, follow these steps:

1. **Indicate which of the listed items you want to have installed by selecting their checkboxes.** You can get more information about a listed item by clicking its name and looking at the bottom of the window. (Some listed updates do not have additional information.)

   Any update that you don't select this time appears again the next time Software Update Preferences checks for updates (unless they have been withdrawn or superseded by other updates).

2. **Click the Install button to install the selected items.** When you do this, an alert may inform you that your computer must be restarted after the update is installed. Some updates don't require a restart, in which case the alert doesn't appear.

3. **If you are logged in as an administrator, you can just enter your password. If you are not logged in as an administrator, you must enter a valid name and password.**

4. **Software Update downloads and installs the software.** While downloading and installing, Software Update displays a progress gauge.

5. **If the update requires a restart, Software Update displays a dialog asking you to click Restart when you're ready to restart your computer.**

Tip

Sometimes one software update must be installed before your computer is eligible for other updates that are available. This is especially likely if you haven't checked for updates in quite a while. To make sure that you're not missing any updates, install all listed updates and again click Update Now in Software Update Preferences. If the list is empty, you know you're completely up-to-date.

If you're interested in seeing what software updates have already been installed on the computer, click the Installed Updates tab of Software Update System Preferences to see the list of installed updates. Figure 15-75 shows the Software Update panel.

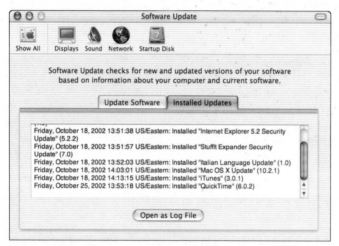

Figure 15-75: Select the Installed Updates tab to see what has already been installed.

Checking for Mac OS 9 software updates

Software Update pane of System Preferences does not monitor for updates to Classic environment software. The Mac OS 9 control panel named Software Update does this. The control panel is simple to use — just open it and click Update Now. A control panel confirms your choice; click OK to continue. If you're connected to the Internet, the control panel will contact Apple's software servers and find out whether there are any updates available for your Mac. If the control panel finds any available updates, it will list them. Place a check mark next to the updates you'd like to download, and then click Install.

You can also schedule updates automatically using the control panel. If you'd like to schedule updates, turn on the option labeled Update software automatically. Now, set a schedule. Click the Set Schedule button to open the Set Schedule dialog. Choose a time of day for the update, and then click the days on which you'd like Software Update to perform its check. When you're done, click OK.

The Software Update control panel has another option if you've enabled scheduled updates: "Ask me before downloading new software." Select this option if you'd like to be notified when new system software is found during a scheduled check.

Note With Mac OS X 10.0.4 and earlier, you can't use the Software Update control panel in the Classic environment. You must restart your computer with Mac OS 9 and then use the Software Update control panel.

Summary

In this chapter, you learned the following:

✦ The settings in System Preferences affect all Mac OS X applications. Many of the settings also affect Classic applications. Settings in a number of Mac OS 9 control panels apply to Classic applications.

✦ Keyboard Preferences and Mouse Preferences set the sensitivity of the keyboard and the mouse or trackpad. You can also set up full keyboard access in Keyboard Preferences. For Classic applications, the Keyboard and Mouse control panels set the function key assignments and double-click speed. You use the keyboard to control the mouse and type combination keystrokes one key at a time by setting up Mouse Keys and Sticky Keys in Universal Access Preferences.

✦ Universal Access provides a set of adjustments for the visibility and hearing of the display and audio of OS X.

✦ In General Preferences, you set colors for highlighting menus, controls, and text. You also set how windows scroll, the number of recently used items that are listed in the Apple menu, and the minimum size for font smoothing. In the Classic environment, the Appearance control panel sets colors, fonts and font characteristics, sound effects, scroll bar behavior, and window behavior. The General Controls and the Apple Menu Options control panels have other settings that affect Classic applications.

✦ In Displays Preferences, you set screen resolution, number of colors, refresh rate, contrast, and brightness. You also select a color profile and calibrate your display. If you have multiple displays, you may be able to adjust how they work together. With some displays, you can adjust the shape and position of the screen image. You can prevent screen burn-in with Screen Effects Preferences.

✦ Sound Preferences sets the overall sound volume, the alert sound, and its volume for Mac OS X applications. For Classic applications, the Sound control panel sets the alert sound and its volume.

✦ Energy Saver Preferences sets timings for sleep mode and options for waking from sleep.

✦ Startup Disk Preferences specifies which Mac OS System Folder is used the next time your computer starts up.

✦ With Accounts, you add and edit users, set up automatic login; and configure the login window.

✦ With Login Items, you set up a list of applications and documents to be opened automatically when you log in.

✦ In Classic Preferences, you can manually control the Classic environment and configure basic and advanced settings for starting it automatically. Use the Extensions Manager control panel to deactivate and activate Classic startup items.

✦ ColorSync Preferences specifies profiles for the equipment you use and for documents that don't get profiles from the software that creates them.

✦ Internet Preferences keeps track of preference settings for iTools, e-mail, Web, and newsgroup applications.

✦ In Date & Time Preferences, you can adjust most of your computer's clock and calendar settings. In the Date & Time control panel, you configure the clock in the Classic menu bar.

✦ International Preferences has settings for language preference, text behavior, date and time formats, number formats, and keyboard layout in Mac OS X applications. Four control panels keep track of these settings for Classic applications: Text, Date & Time, Numbers, and Keyboard.

✦ Software Update Preferences can keep Mac OS X and the applications that come with it up-to-date. You can schedule periodic updates and can update manually whenever you like. Do the same for the Mac OS 9 software used by the Classic environment with the Software Update control panel.

✦   ✦   ✦

Beyond the Basics of Mac OS X

◆ ◆ ◆ ◆

◆ ◆ ◆ ◆

Managing User Accounts and Privileges

Unlike previous Mac OS versions, Mac OS X starts from
the premise that any number of people may use a single
Mac. You begin using the computer by logging in, and then
Mac OS X applications use your personal preference settings.
Your preference settings don't affect other users, and their
settings don't affect you. For example, your changes to the
Dock do not affect its appearance and behavior when someone else logs in. (Some preference settings affect all users.)
Each user also has a home folder in which to save documents.
You have very limited access to other users' home folders,
and they have very limited access to your home folder. Not
only does Mac OS X protect users' home folders and their
contents, it also protects its own folders and their contents.
Mac OS X doesn't normally allow any user to move, remove,
rename, or otherwise change any of the system files or folders. This is very different from Mac OS 9, which allows all normal users full reign over its system files and folders.

You create accounts for the people who use your computer.
Each user account has a unique name and is protected by a
password. You can allow some user accounts to administer
the computer while not allowing other user accounts to
administer. You can also configure Mac OS X to let you use a
special user account that has access to all files and folders.

This chapter discusses the types of user accounts you can set
up and explains how to create and edit user accounts. You
also learn more about how users begin and end sessions with
Mac OS X, and you learn what users share and what's private
for each user. In addition, you learn how to make login manual
or automatic and how each user designates items to be
opened immediately after login. You learn how users change
their passwords and change privileges for their files and folders. Finally, you learn how to enable the special user account
that has unlimited access to files and folders.

Comparing Types of User Accounts

Mac OS X offers two types of accounts for people to use regularly. One type can administer the computer, while the other type cannot. None of these accounts has unlimited access to all files and settings on the computer. For example, these accounts generally do not have access to all files and folders belonging to other accounts. However, someone with an administrator account can enable a special account known as the System Administrator (also known as superuser or root), which has access to all folders and files.

Caution   Although the terms *administrator* and *System Administrator* sound very similar, administrator accounts have much less power than the System Administrator account. In fact, the System Administrator account has so much power that it is dangerous to use regularly. As we explain in the last section of this chapter, you can inadvertently damage your Mac OS X system while using the System Administrator account.

Using an administrator account

Every Mac OS X system has at least one user account for administering the machine. When you use Mac OS X with an *administrator* account, you can change all system preference settings and install software in the main Applications and Library folders, which you see when you open the startup disk's icon (paths /Applications/ and /Library/). As an administrator, you can also create, modify, and delete other user accounts. However, an administrator cannot add anything to or remove anything from another user's folders. Table 16-1 lists system preference settings that can be changed only with an administrator account's name and password.

Table 16-1
Protected Settings That Only Administrators Can Change

System Preferences Pane	Protected Settings
Date & Time	All settings except the menu bar clock settings
Energy Saver	All settings
Login	All login window settings but not the list of login items
Network	All settings except choosing a different location
Sharing	All settings
Software Update	Actual installation of updates (changing of update schedule not protected)
Startup Disk	System Folder selected for startup
Accounts	All settings except current user's password

The owner or primary user of the system usually has an administrator account. One administrator account may be sufficient, or you can set up additional administrator accounts. The advantage to having more administrator accounts is that more people are available to change the settings in Table 16-1 and to install software. Reduced security is a disadvantage to having more administrator accounts. Setting up administrator accounts is like handing out keys to the front door of your home or business. It's more convenient for everyone to have an administrator account on your Mac, but some people may not be knowledgeable or responsible enough to have one.

Situations occur in which you may not have an administrator account for your Mac, even if you're the only person who uses it. For example, in an organization where computers are managed centrally, a computer support specialist may have the only administrator account.

Using an ordinary account

There are many reasons for having ordinary user accounts that don't allow people to administer the computer. Certainly this type of account is fine for people who never need to change the settings listed in Table 16-1 or install software outside their home folders and the Shared folder, which is in the Users folder together with the users' home folders (path /Users/Shared/). This may also be the best type of account for people who need to change protected settings only occasionally. Actually, a reasonable argument can be made for having everyone, you included, regularly use accounts that don't allow administering of the computer.

Tip   For convenient access to applications installed in the Shared folder, put them in a folder that you create inside the Shared folder. For example, create a folder named Shared Applications inside the Shared folder. Then put an alias of the Shared Applications folder in the Applications folder. You need to log in as an administrator to put the alias in the Applications folder, but thereafter anyone can easily use this alias to access applications that are in the Shared Applications folder.

By not using administrator accounts for everyday work, you make the computer more secure. If you have to unlock a setting, you'll be more careful about changing it. What's more, if you leave your computer unattended, someone passing by can't change locked settings.

People who don't have administrator accounts can unlock settings by entering an administrator's name and password. You can even create an administrator account expressly for this purpose. You would give the name and password of this particular administrator account to the ordinary users whom you want to be able to change protected preference settings. No one would actually use the computer with this particular administrator account. This administrator account is something like the restroom key that's attached to a baton and kept behind the counter.

Users don't need an administrator account to install software as long as they don't need to install the software in the Applications folder or main Library folder. All users can install software in their own home folders or the Shared folder.

Tip   To make the computer more secure against tampering by a passerby, set the Screen Saver pane of System Preferences to require the user account password to wake the screen saver. In addition, make the top-right corner of the screen a hot corner for activating the screen saver and get in the habit of slinging the pointer into this corner when you get up from your computer. Chapter 15 explains how to set this up.

Using the System Administrator (root) account

Mac OS X has a System Administrator account, also known by its account name, root; but you may never need to use it. The System Administrator account has complete control over all folders and files on your Mac, including the contents of the normally off-limits folder named System. Naturally, the System Administrator has unrestricted access to all users' folders and files. The freedom the System Administrator has with Mac OS X is similar to what a normal user has with Mac OS 9 or earlier. You sometimes need this much control over the Mac OS 9 system files and folders, but you seldom should need the same amount of control over the Mac OS X system files and folders. Mac OS X is carefully organized so that users shouldn't need to move, delete, rename, or otherwise change the system files and folders that are located in the folder named System and in several hidden folders. All the parts of Mac OS X that users may need to change are located in the main Library folder, where an administrator can change them, or in the Library folder inside each user's home folder, where the user can change them.

You may hear that as the System Administrator you won't be bothered by messages saying you don't have sufficient privileges to save a file, move a folder, rename an icon, and so on. Although annoying, these messages occur to protect Mac OS X from users and users from each other. The System Administrator operates without the safety net that these messages provide. You're better off working as an ordinary user or administrator and changing privileges as needed. If necessary, you can even have Mac OS X ignore privileges. We explain how later in this chapter.

Apple so strongly discourages using the System Administrator account that it's normally disabled in Mac OS X. If you're determined to enable the System Administrator account, you can find out how to do it later in this chapter.

Creating and Editing User Accounts

One user account gets created when you first set up Mac OS X after installing it (or after buying a Mac with it already installed). This original account is an administrator account. Mac OS X uses the original account automatically until you create additional user accounts. You can create more ordinary user accounts and administrator accounts using the original user account. Then anyone using the computer with an administrator account can create, modify, or delete any other user account.

Assigning names and passwords

When you create a user account, you assign it two unique names: a full name and a short name. You also give the account a password. People can use the full name or short name to log in. Mac OS X uses the short name to identify the user on the computer and for the name of the user's home folder. The full name and password can be changed later, but the short name is permanent.

Devising names

When assigning full names and short names, use any naming system that you like. For example, the full name can simply be a user's first and last names, and the short name can be the user's initials, abbreviated first or last name, or combination thereof. The full name can contain spaces and punctuation symbols, for example, John F. Kennedy. The short name is can contain only letters of the alphabet, numbers, and the underscore character (_), for example, jfk or john_k.

Capitalization matters in both full names and short names. For example John F. Kennedy is not the same as john f. kennedy, and jfk is not the same as JFK. Both the long name and the short name must be unique.

 Caution Do not assign anyone the user name "root" (without quotation marks). This name has a special meaning in all operating systems based on Unix, including Mac OS X. If you create a user named "root," problems will result.

Picking secure passwords

Besides the full name and short name, each account has a password. The password can be blank for an ordinary account, but the password cannot be blank for an administrator account. A password can be a secret word, a phrase, or a meaningless string of characters. For best security, a password should not contain words in any dictionary and should contain at least one number or symbol. One approach is to replace the letter O with zero and the letter I with 1, as in Br0wn1e. Another approach is to think of a memorable phrase and use its initials. For example, "The U.S. President lives at 1600 Pennsylvania Avenue" becomes TUSPla1600PA. Note the use of uppercase and lowercase letters in your password, because capitalization matters in passwords. For example, QWIZ and qwiz are not the same password.

Passwords may contain letters, blank spaces, punctuation marks, and special symbols but should not contain colons. Mac OS X recognizes a password with colons under some circumstances but not others.

Creating a user account

If you know the name and password of an administrator account, you create a user account in the Accounts pane of the System Preferences application. You do not need to log in using an administrator account. If you log in as an ordinary user you can unlock the settings in the Accounts pane of System Preferences with an administrator's name and password.

To create a user account, follow these steps:

1. **Open System Preferences and choose View⇨Accounts or click the Accounts button.**

 2. **Unlock the user account settings if they are locked.** The settings are locked if the lock button looks locked and the text next to it says, "Click the lock to make changes."

To unlock the settings, do the following:

1. **Click the lock button at the bottom of the window.**

2. **In the dialog that appears, enter an administrator's name and password, and click OK.** If you entered a valid name and the correct password, you return to the Users window with all settings unlocked.

3. **In the Accounts window, click the New User button to display the New User dialog, shown in Figure 16-1.**

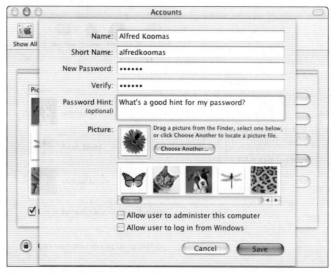

Figure 16-1: Each user account has a name, short name, and login picture.

4. **Enter a full name and a short name.**

5. **Select a login picture.** You can select a login picture any of these ways:

   - Click one of the pictures displayed at the bottom of the dialog.

   - Drag a picture file to the Login Picture well from a Finder window or from the Desktop.

   - Click the Choose button and select a picture file in the Open dialog that appears.

6. **Click in the New Password field and enter a password for the user account.** You may also enter a password hint. The password hint is displayed if the user enters the password incorrectly three times in a row during login. If you enter a hint, make it cryptic enough that other people can't guess the password!

   When you enter the password in the New User dialog, Mac OS X keeps it secret by displaying dots instead of what you actually type. Because you can't visually check that you entered the password correctly, you have to enter it twice. Mac OS compares the two password entries and asks you to reenter them if they are not identical.

7. **Set the option "Allow user to administer this machine."** Select this option only if you want to make this an administrator account. If you want to make this an ordinary account, make sure that the option is turned off.

8. **Set the option "Allow user to log in from Windows."** Select this option if you created the account to share files with Windows File Sharing (SMB/CIFS).

9. **Click Save to create the user account, or click Cancel to not create it after all.** The Login Options tab of the Accounts pane provides some optional settings for login as shown in Figure 16-2.

   - **Display Login Window As.** This option changes the login window from a name and password field, shown in Figure 16-7, to a list of users, shown in 16-5. The list of names option is less secure, because it gives a list of user accounts on the Macintosh.

   - **Hide the Restart and Shut Down Buttons.** Determines whether people can restart or shut down the computer by clicking buttons in the login window. Select this option to make it more difficult for someone to restart the computer by using Mac OS 9, which would allow them to access all Mac OS X files and folders.

   - **Show password hint after three attempts to enter a password.** If you entered a password hint and password hints are currently disabled for the computer, a dialog asks whether you'd like to enable them. Select this option if you want users to see their hints after failing three times to enter the correct password. Make sure that the checkbox for this option is cleared if you don't want hints displayed, making it harder for someone to guess a password.

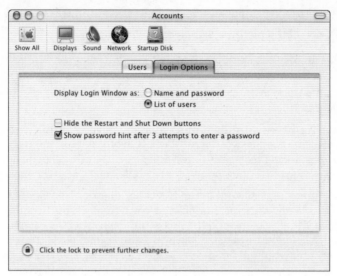

Figure 16-2: The Login Options tab of the Accounts pane offers additional customization of the login process.

Note Creating a new user account does not set it up for e-mail or newsgroup service. And by default the new account's home Web page is set to the Apple Live page (http://livepage.apple.com). To set up e-mail, newsgroup, and Web preferences for a new user account, you must log out of Mac OS X, log in using the new account, and then make the necessary changes in the Internet pane of System Preferences. You may also need to change preference settings in the Mail application or other e-mail application that you use, Internet Explorer or other Web browser, and newsgroup application. Check out Chapter 6 and Chapter 15 for more information.

Editing a user account

Anyone who knows an administrator name and password can edit user accounts in the Accounts pane of System Preferences. It's not necessary to log in using an administrator account. If the settings in the Accounts pane of System Preferences are locked, an ordinary user can unlock them with an administrator's name and password.

To edit a user account, follow these steps:

1. **Open System Preferences and choose View⇨Accounts or click the Accounts button.**

2. **Unlock the user account settings if they are locked.** The settings are locked if the lock button looks locked and the text next to it says, "Click the lock to make changes."

To unlock the settings, do the following:

1. **Click the lock button at the bottom of the window.**

2. **In the dialog that appears, enter an administrator's name and password, and click OK.** If you entered a valid name and the correct password, you return to the Users window with all settings unlocked.

3. **In the list of user account names, select the account you want to change.**

4. **Click the Edit User button and make your changes in the dialog that appears.** The user's account information appears in a dialog like the one previously shown in Figures 16-1 and 16-2. You can edit the full name, password, and password hint. You can also change the setting of the options "Allow user to administer this machine" and "Allow user to log in from Windows." You can't change the short name for the account.

5. **Click OK to accept your changes, or click Cancel to void them.** If you changed the user's password, a dialog appears stating that the user's Keychain password can't be changed to the new account password that you just entered. The existing Keychain password remains in effect until the user logs in (using the new account password) and uses the Accounts pane of System Preferences to change the login password again or uses the Keychain Access application to change only the Keychain password. You can find information on using the Keychain Access application in Chapter 22.

Deleting a user

Someone who knows an administrator name and password can delete user accounts by using the Accounts pane of System Preferences. It's not necessary to log in using an administrator account. An ordinary user can unlock the Delete User capability in the Accounts pane of System Preferences with an administrator's name and password.

There must always be at least one administrator account, so the last remaining administrator account can't be deleted. If the person who is deleting accounts is logged in with an ordinary account, this account can't be deleted either.

When a user account is deleted, its home folder is renamed to end with *Deleted*. This home folder and any other folders that belonged to the deleted user account now belong to an administrator account that was selected during the deletion process. This administrator can examine, move, or back up the contents of the former user's home folder before disposing of the contents.

To delete a user account, use these steps:

1. **Open System Preferences and choose View➪Accounts or click the Accounts button.**

2. **Unlock the user account settings if they are locked.** The settings are locked if the lock button looks locked and the text next to it says Click the lock to make changes.

To unlock the settings, do the following:

1. **Click the lock button at the bottom of the window.**

2. **In the dialog that appears, enter an administrator's name and password, and click OK.** If you entered a valid name and the correct password, you return to the Users window with all settings unlocked.

3. **In the list of user account names, select the account you want to delete, and then click the Delete User button.**

4. **In the confirmation dialog that appears (shown in Figure 16-3), click OK to approve the deletion or click Cancel to not go through with the deletion.**

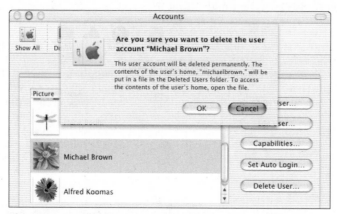

Figure 16-3: Deleting a user account requires a confirmation, and saves that account's information.

Limiting a user's capabilities

You can limit the actions of a user on the computer with the Capabilities sheet shown in Figure 16-4. To limit a user's capabilities, use these steps:

1. **Open System Preferences and choose View⇨Accounts or click the Accounts button.**

2. **Unlock the user account settings if they are locked.** The settings are locked if the lock button looks locked and the text next to it says, "Click the lock to make changes."

To unlock the settings, do the following:

1. **Click the lock button at the bottom of the window.**

2. **In the dialog that appears, enter an administrator's name and password, and click OK.** If you entered a valid name and the correct password, you return to the Users window with all settings unlocked.

3. **In the list of user account names, select the account you want to limit, and then click the Capabilities button.**

4. **Select options from the Capabilities sheet.** You can prevent the user from changing their password, from removing items from the Dock, from burning CDs and DVDs, from opening System Preferences, and limiting the user to only be allowed to run specific applications.

5. **Click OK to accept your changes or click Cancel to void them.**

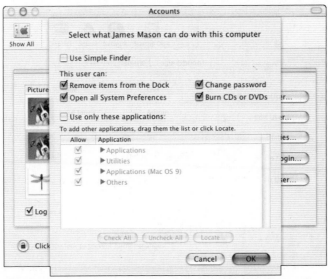

Figure 16-4: A user's activities on the computer may be limited by settings in Capabilities.

Resetting a user's password

If a user can't remember his or her password on your computer, you can log in as an administrator and reset the user's password. If no one can remember the password of any administrator account on your computer, you can reset passwords of ordinary user and administrator accounts by using the Mac OS X installation CD.

Caution

Safeguard your Mac OS X installation CD to prevent someone from using it to gain unrestricted access to your computer.

To reset a password when no administrator account passwords are at hand, follow these steps:

1. **Restart the computer with the Mac OS X installation CD.** Insert the CD and choose Apple⇨Restart.

2. **When you hear the computer's startup chime, hold down the C key until the computer begins starting up from the CD.** You can release the C key when you hear the sounds of activity coming from the CD. After a minute or two, the Installer application opens.

3. **In the Installer, choose Installer⇨Reset Password.** The Password Reset application opens.

4. **At the top of the Password Reset window, select the Mac OS X disk that has a user account whose password needs resetting.**

5. **For each user account whose password needs resetting, do the following:**

   1. **Click the pop-up menu and choose the user account whose password you want to reset.**

   2. **Type a new password in both text boxes and click Save.** If the two entries are not identical, you are asked to reenter them.

   3. **In the dialog that appears, click OK.** The dialog informs you that the password you entered was saved.

6. **When you finish resetting passwords, choose Password Reset⇨Quit Password Reset.** You return to the Installer.

7. **In the Installer, choose Installer⇨Quit Installer.**

8. **In the dialog that appears, click Restart.** The computer restarts.

Getting Along with Multiple Users

When two or more people share a Mac, they take turns using it by logging in and out of Mac OS X. Each user can set up a list of documents and applications to be opened automatically upon login. Each user has a personal home folder, and its contents are normally unavailable to other users, including administrators. In addition, most preference settings that a user changes are personal. Some preference settings are shared by all users. A shared folder is available to all users as well. This section explores these topics in more detail.

Logging in and out

Each user starts a session on the computer by logging in and ends the session by logging out or shutting down. Mac OS X can be configured to log in one particular user account automatically when the computer starts up. Everyone else logs in manually by using the login window. The login window may contain a list of user accounts, or it may contain spaces in which you enter a user account name and password. Figures 16-5 through 16-7 shows the different forms of the login window.

Logging in with a list of user accounts

If the login window contains a name and password field as shown in Figure 16-5, log in to Mac OS X as follows:

1. **Select your account name in the list.** Either click the name in the list or begin typing the name and press Return when the name becomes highlighted.

   If your user account name is not listed, you may be able to log in by typing your complete user account name. To do this, select Other in the list of account names and continue at Step 1 in the next procedure.

2. **In the second login window that appears, type your password.** Figure 16-6 shows the second login window.

3. **Click the Log In button or press Return.** You can start using the computer as soon as you see the menu bar. If the login window shakes back and forth like negative shakes of the head, the password that you entered was not correct for the selected account name. Try entering the password again, or click Go Back to select a different account.

Figure 16-5: If you see this login window, log in by selecting your account name and typing your password in the next login window.

Figure 16-6: After selecting your account name from the list in the previous login window, type your password in this window.

Logging in without a list of user accounts

If the login window contains a name and password field as shown in Figure 16-7, do the following steps:

1. **Enter your account name and password in the spaces provided.** You can enter your full name or your short name. Remember to capitalize the name and password correctly, or Mac OS X won't recognize them.

2. **Press Return or click the Log In button.** If the login window goes away, you can start using the computer as soon as you see the menu bar. If the login window doesn't go away but instead shakes back and forth like someone shaking his head no, Mac OS X did not recognize the name you entered, or the password you entered was not correct for the name you entered. Try again to log in.

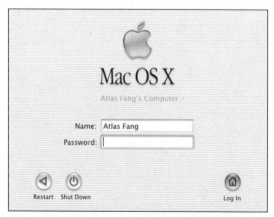

Figure 16-7: If you see this login window, log in by typing your account name and password.

Logging in if you don't see the login window

If someone else has been using the computer or login occurs automatically, you don't see a login window. Your course of action depends on what you see on the display.

✦ **If you see the menu bar, do one of the following:**

  • If you're sure the computer logs in automatically with your account, start using the computer.

  • If you're not sure the computer logs in automatically with your account, log out as described in the next procedure. Then try again to log in.

✦ **If you see a screen saver, wake it and then try logging in again.** Chapter 15 has more information on screen savers.

✦ **If you don't see anything on the display, try the following:**

  • Press any key to wake the computer from sleep mode and then try again to log in. Chapter 15 has more information on sleep mode.

  • Turn on the computer and try again to log in. Chapter 2 explains how to do this.

Logging out

To log out of Mac OS X, follow these steps:

1. **Choose Apple⇨Log Out.** Mac OS X displays an alert asking if you're sure you want to quit all applications and log out now.

2. **Click Log Out and wait until you see the login window.** The more applications you have open when you log out, the longer logging out takes.

Before you see the login window, one or more applications may display alerts asking if you want to save changes to documents. If you click Cancel in any of these alerts, Mac OS X displays another alert naming an application and saying the application canceled the logout operation. Before trying again to log out, you should make sure that all the open documents are saved.

Mac OS X itself cancels the logout if an open application fails to quit. In this case, an alert appears telling you which application has failed to quit. This could happen while the application in question is waiting for you to deal with an unsaved document. You should try quitting the guilty application and then log out again. An application may also fail to quit because it has crashed. The next procedure tells you how to force an unresponsive application to quit.

Shutting down the computer also logs out. Chapter 2 explains how to shut down.

Forcing an unresponsive application to quit

Use these steps to get an application to quit so that you can log out:

1. **Choose Apple⇨Force Quit or press ⌘-Option-Esc.** The Force Quit Applications window appears and lists the applications still open, as shown in Figure 16-8.

Figure 16-8: Force an unresponsive application to quit by selecting it in this window and clicking Force Quit.

2. **Select the unresponsive application in the list and click the Force Quit button.** An alert asks you to confirm that you really want to force the selected application to quit.

3. **Click Cancel if you want to try saving changes and quitting the application normally.** If you click Force Quit in the alert, you lose all unsaved changes in the application's open documents. (Other applications and their documents are not affected.)

4. **When you're finished with the Force Quit Applications window, click its close button.** This window has no Quit command.

Seeing what belongs to each user

After logging in, you can set up Mac OS X the way you like it and know that your settings remain the same the next time you use the computer. Even if other people log in as other users and set up Mac OS X differently, you see your own setup the next time you log in. Mac OS X retains the following items individually for each user account:

✦ Dock configuration

✦ Desktop configuration

✦ Home folder's contents

✦ Trash contents

✦ Favorite items (in the Favorites folder and the Finder's Go menu)

✦ Recent folders in the Finder's Go menu

✦ Recent applications and documents in the Apple menu

✦ Finder preference settings

✦ Finder window configuration: which ones are open, their positions and sizes, their front-to-back ordering, and the global View Options settings (but not a folder's custom view options, if any, or its setting for view as icons or list)

✦ System preference settings in the following panes: Classic, ColorSync, Date & Time's Menu Bar Clock, Desktop, Dock, General, International, Internet, Keyboard, Login Items (but not Login Window), Mouse, QuickTime, Screen Saver, Software Update schedule, Sound, Speech, and Universal Access

✦ Preferences for many Mac OS X applications, including the Address Book database, Mail accounts, and Stickies notes (but not preferences for Classic applications)

In addition, Mac OS X can merge personal fonts and other extras with the fonts and other items that all users share. The following are just some of the personal items that are kept in folders inside the Library folder of each user's home folder:

✦ Audio plug-ins and sounds

✦ Color picker modules

✦ Fonts

✦ Internet search sites for Sherlock

✦ Internet plug-ins for Web browsers and other Internet applications

✦ Keyboard layouts

✦ Printer driver software

✦ Screen saver modules

✦ Sound files for system alerts and other uses of system sounds

✦ Voices for speech synthesis (text-to-speech)

Seeing what users share

Although Mac OS X keeps many settings private for each user, all users do share some items, including the following:

✦ Shared folder (which is inside the Users folder).

✦ Finder window configuration: view as icons or list, and any custom view options set for each folder.

✦ System preference settings in the following panes: Date & Time (except Menu Bar Clock settings); Displays; Energy Saver; Login Window (but not Login Items); Network; Sharing; Startup Disk; Users.

✦ Printers that anyone has added to the Printer List in the Print Monitor application.

✦ Items from folders in the main Library folder or the Library folder that is in the folder named System, including Color Picker modules, ColorSync profiles and scripts, fonts, image capture devices, Internet plug-ins such as QuickTime and iDisk, modem scripts, keyboard layouts, printer driver software, screen saver modules, and voices for speech synthesis.

Making login manual or automatic

On a Mac that people share, it usually makes sense to configure Mac OS X for manual login. Setting up a manual login allows anyone to start up the Mac and log in directly to his or her own user account. If the Mac were configured for automatic login, then everyone who started up the Mac would be logged into the same account automatically. To use their own accounts, they would have to log out and then log in manually using their own account name and password. People may occasionally forget to do this extra work and end up using the automatic login account by mistake.

Automatic login is reasonable if the same person always starts up the computer. This person uses the computer first and logs out, and then someone else can log in manually. This arrangement is perfectly convenient for everyone else since they always have to log in manually anyway. Mac OS X is initially configured to log in automatically using the original administrator account. If automatic login gets turned off, you can turn it back on. You can also change the account used for automatic login.

You configure automatic or manual login in the Accounts pane of System Preferences. You need to be an administrator or know an administrator's name and password.

Setting up your computer for an automatic login

To set automatic login for a given user, use this method:

1. **Open System Preferences and choose View⊃Accounts or click the Accounts button.**

2. **Unlock the user account settings if they are locked.** The settings are locked if the lock button looks locked and the text next to it says, "Click the lock to make changes."

   To unlock the settings, do the following:

   1. **Click the lock button at the bottom of the window.**

   2. **In the dialog that appears, enter an administrator's name and password, and click OK.** If you entered a valid name and the correct password, you return to the Users window with all settings unlocked.

3. **In the list of user account names, select the account you want to change.**

4. **Click the Set Auto Login... button.** A sheet appears with the selected user's name and a password field as shown in Figure 16-9. Enter the user's password and then click the Cancel or OK button as appropriate.

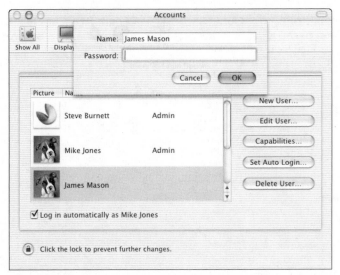

Figure 16-9: Enter a chosen user's name to set the computer to automatically log in as that user.

Setting your computer up for manual login

To set your computer up to require a manual login, follow these steps:

1. **Open System Preferences and choose View⇨Accounts or click the Accounts button.**

2. **In the Accounts window, deselect the checkbox to the left of "Log in automatically as" a user name.**

Selecting applications and documents to open at login

You can set up a list of documents and applications that you want to open automatically when you log in. After logging in, you can change your list in the Login Items pane of System Preferences by adding, removing, and rearranging listed items. You can also designate hidden login items. Each user account has its own private list of login items.

Tip   To have the Classic environment start automatically when you log in, use the Classic pane of System Preferences. You can find detailed instructions in Chapter 15.

Adding login items

To have additional items opened automatically during login, follow these steps:

1. **Open System Preferences and choose View⇨Login Items or click the Login Items button to see a list of items that open automatically when you log in, as shown in Figure 16-10.**

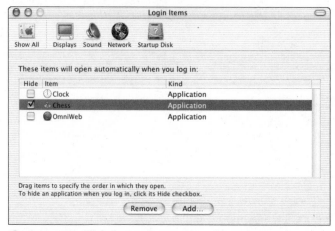

Figure 16-10: Click the Login Items icon in System Preferences to change the list of items that open automatically when the current user logs in.

2. **Click the Add button.**

3. **In the dialog that appears, select one or more items and click the Open button.** Click once to select one item; Shift-click to select adjacent items; and ⌘-click to select nonadjacent items.

Tip   You can also add items to the Login Items list by dragging their icons from Finder windows or the Desktop to the Login Items list. For example, drag an MP3 file to the list to have it played when you log in.

Note   If you set an application or a document as a login item and it requires a password to open, it does not open during login. Its icon appears in the Dock, and you must click the icon and enter the password to open the item. Examples of such items include e-mail applications and encrypted documents.

Note If you make an item a login item and later move the item to a different folder, the item no longer opens automatically during login. For example, if you make an application from the Applications folder a login item and later move the application to a new folder within the Applications folder, the application no longer opens during startup. Moreover, a login item breaks if you so much as move or rename any folder in the login item's path. For example, if you make a document a login item and them move the folder that contains the document from your home folder to the Documents folder within your home folder, the document no longer opens during login. This problem occurs because Mac OS X keeps track of login items by path name rather than alias.

To work around this problem, remove the nonfunctional item from the Login Items pane and then add it back.

Removing login items

To have fewer items opened automatically during login, do the following steps:

1. **Open System Preferences and click the Login Items icon.** (For detailed instructions, see Steps 1 and 2 of the procedure in "Adding login items.")

2. **Select a listed item that you no longer want opened and click the Remove button.**

Rearranging login items

To change the order in which items open automatically during login, use this method:

1. **Open System Preferences and click the Login Items icon.** (For detailed instructions, see Steps 1 and 2 of the procedure in "Adding login items.")

2. **Drag items up or down in the list.**

Designating hidden login items

To have items hide after opening automatically during login hidden, follow these steps:

1. **Open System Preferences and click the Login Items icon.** (For detailed instructions, see Steps 1 and 2 of the procedure in "Adding login items.")

2. **Click to place a check mark in the checkbox next to each listed item than you want to hide.**

Changing your login password

Besides changing your list of login items, you can also change your login password. After logging in, you can change your password in the My Account pane of System Preferences. You don't need an administrator name and password to change your own password. Follow these steps to change your password:

1. **Open System Preferences and choose View⇨My Account or click the My Account button.** The My Account pane appears as shown in Figure 16-11.

2. **Click the Change... button next to Password.** A window will prompt you for your current password, your new password, to reenter your new password to verify it, and for an optional password hint.

3. **When you're done, click the Cancel or OK buttons as appropriate.**

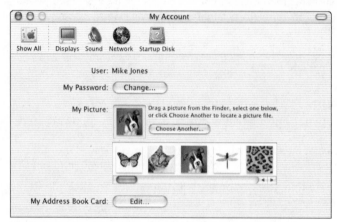

Figure 16-11: Change your own password and login icon, without needing an administrator account, in the My Account pane of System Preferences.

Changing privileges for files and folders

Some of the files and folders on your computer's hard disk belong to your user account, and you control whether other user accounts can see and change the items that your account owns. You control access to a file or folder by changing its privilege settings. Your account owns the following items, and you can change their privilege settings:

✦ Your home folder and its initial contents

✦ Files and folders that you put in your home folder

✦ Files and folders that you put in the Shared folder

✦ Files and folders that you put in another user's Public folder.

If you have an administrator account, it owns the following additional items, and you can change their privilege settings:

✦ Files and folders that you put in the Applications folder

✦ Files and folders that you put in the main Library folder

Similarly, some files and folders belong to other user accounts. People using those accounts change privilege settings to control whether you can see and change the items that belong to them.

Besides the items that belong to user accounts, many files and folders belong to the system. No one who logs in with an ordinary user account or an administrator account can change privileges of items that belong to the system. (You can change privilege settings of system-owned items by logging in as the System Administrator, a technique discussed at the end of this chapter.)

If necessary, you can set an option to have Mac OS X ignore all privilege settings on a disk or other volume. To set this option, you must know the name and password of an administrator account.

Changing privileges

You change privileges of a folder or file in the Finder's Info window, shown in Figure 16-12, by following these steps:

1. **Make the Finder active and choose File⇨Show Info.** One way to make the Finder active is to click its icon at the end of the Dock.

2. **Select the file or folder whose privileges you want to change.** Information for the selected item appears in the Info window.

3. **In the Info window, choose Ownership & Permissions from the pop-up menu.** The privilege settings for the selected item appear in the Info window.

4. **In the Info window's Ownership & Permissions pane, you can change the privileges granted to the three user levels if your account name appears as the owner.** You must be the owner of an item to change its privileges.

   • **Owner.** Specifies what you (the owner) can do with the item.

   • **Group.** Specifies what members of the named group can do with the item. The wheel and admin groups include all administrator accounts. The staff group includes all user accounts.

   • **Everyone.** Specifies what users who are not members of the named group can do with the item.

   Table 16-2 explains the various privileges you can grant for each of the following user levels.

Note   Owner privileges must be at least as broad as those for Everyone. Group privileges must also be at least as broad as those for Everyone. For example, if Everyone has Read & Write privileges, then all levels must be set to Read & Write. If you run afoul of these rules, Mac OS X automatically increases the privilege settings at higher levels.

Figure 16-12: Change privilege settings for a folder or file in the Finder's Info window.

Ignoring privileges

Before you set the option to have Mac OS X ignore all privilege settings on a disk or other volume so that you can move, delete, rename, or add to a folder or file, *stop*. Ask yourself: Can what you do now harm another user's files or jeopardize the integrity of the system?

If you're sure that you want to ignore privileges on a disk or other volume, select its icon. When you have a volume selected, the option for ignoring privileges appears at the bottom of the Privileges pane in the Info window. If you change this option, a dialog appears in which you must enter the name and password of an administrator account.

Note Beginning with Mac OS X version 10.1, you cannot have Mac OS X ignore all privileges on the volume used to start up Mac OS X.

Caution For everyday operations, leave the option to ignore privileges turned off. If you leave this option turned on, you may one day accidentally delete, move, or modify the wrong file or folder.

Table 16-2
Privilege Settings for Files and Folders

Setting	Privileges Granted for a File	Privileges Granted for a Folder
Read & Write	Open the file. Copy the file. Change, move, and delete the file.	Open the folder. Copy the folder. See enclosed files and folders. Create, change, move, and delete enclosed files and folders.
Read only	Open the file. Copy the file.	Open the folder. Copy the folder. See enclosed files and folders.
Write only	Not applicable.	Drag items into the folder. Save files in the folder.
None	None	None

Enabling System Administrator (root) Access

You should avoid using your Mac with the System Administrator account because it bypasses the safeguards that help keep Mac OS X reliable. If you use the System Administrator account, you make Mac OS X susceptible to damage and exploitation. You may cause damage accidentally, or someone may crack your computer and use it to launch attacks on other computers on your local network or the Internet.

Before turning to the System Administrator account, you should try using an administrator account. If you're plagued with messages about insufficient privileges for moving, deleting, or renaming files and folders, try setting Mac OS X to ignore privileges as explained in the previous section.

Use your Mac with the System Administrator account only as a last resort, and then only temporarily. As soon as possible, log out as System Administrator and log in as an administrator or an ordinary user.

You enable System Administrator access with the NetInfo Manager application. You must know the name and password of an administrator account.

 Caution The NetInfo Manager application may look intriguing to you, but do not experiment with it! You may make changes that you regret later. Know what you're doing with NetInfo Manager, and do only what you know.

Enabling System Administrator access

To enable System Administrator access, follow these steps:

1. **Open the NetInfo Manager application.**

2. **Choose Security⇨Authenticate.**

3. **In the dialog that appears, enter the short name and password of an administrator.** You must go through this authentication procedure even if you are currently using the computer with an administrator account.

4. **Choose Security⇨Enable Root User.** If the System Administrator account has never been enabled, an alert appears saying you must now enter a password for the System Administrator account.

   To enter a password for the System Administrator account, follow these steps:

   1. **Click OK to dismiss the alert.**

   2. **In the dialog that appears, enter a secure password and click OK.** The dialog then asks you to enter the password a second time for verification.

   3. **Enter the password a second time and click Verify to put the password into effect or click Cancel to void it.**

   4. **Do the authentication procedure a second time.** Choose Security⇨Authenticate and enter the administrator's short name and password as described in Steps 2 and 3 above.

You can now use the System Administrator account by logging out and then logging in with the name root (all lowercase) and the password you assigned to the System Administrator account.

Note If the login window displays a list of user accounts, the System Administrator account is not included in the list. You must select Other in the list and then enter the System Administrator name and password in the second login window. Other appears in the list of accounts only if the option to include Other User is turned on in the Login pane of System Preferences, as described earlier in this chapter.

Disabling System Administrator access

To disable System Administrator access, follow these steps:

1. **Open the NetInfo Manager application.**

2. **Choose Security⇨Authenticate.** If the Authenticate command does not exist in the Security submenu, first choose Security⇨Deauthenticate.

3. **In the dialog that appears, enter the name and password of an administrator.**

4. **Choose Security⇨Disable Root User.**

Summary

Here's what you learned in this chapter:

✦ If you use Mac OS X with an administrator account, you can change all system preference settings and install software in the Applications folder and main Library folder. An administrator can also create, edit, and delete other users.

✦ If you use Mac OS X with an ordinary account, you can install software in your home folder and the Shared folder. You can change locked settings if you know an administrator name and password.

✦ You create, edit, and delete user accounts in the Users pane of System Preferences. You need an administrator name and password for these tasks.

✦ People take turns using Mac OS X by logging in and out. Login can be automatic for one user, but all others log in manually. You configure this in the Login pane of System Preferences, and you need an administrator name and password to do it.

✦ Users can set up Mac OS X the way they like it and know their settings will be the same the next time they use the computer.

✦ Each user can set up a list of documents and applications to be opened during login. You change this list in the Login pane of System Preferences.

✦ After logging in, you can change your own password. You don't need an administrator password to do this.

✦ You can change the privilege settings of your folders and files by using the Finder's Info window. You can also set an option to have Mac OS X ignore privilege settings on a volume.

✦ You should avoid using your Mac with the System Administrator account because it bypasses the safeguards that help keep Mac OS X reliable.

✦   ✦   ✦

Mastering Speech

Keyboarding and mousing are not particularly natural ways to communicate. For years, computer designers have looked for a more convenient way to operate computers. One of the most compelling ways to work with a computer is simply to talk to it. Present-day Mac OS computers have taken the first steps toward achieving the science fiction of *Star Trek*, when people of the future speak naturally and conversationally with their computers. Macs have been capable of speaking text aloud since 1984, but it wasn't until 1993 that Apple introduced speech recognition.

This chapter describes how to use the text-to-speech and speech recognition capabilities of Mac OS X. The Classic environment has different text-to-speech capabilities, which are also covered in this chapter.

Converting Text to Speech

Your Mac is naturally reticent; you have to do something to make it speak. You can use an application that has commands for speaking the text in a document. You can program the computer to speak. And you can have the computer automatically read out the text of alert messages displayed in the Classic environment.

Regardless of what your computer speaks, it can speak in different voices, and you can generally choose the voice. Your choices include male, female, adult, child, and robotic voices. A few of the voices sing.

This section tells you how to choose a voice for Mac OS X and how to choose a voice for the Classic environment. After selecting the voice you want to hear, you choose among several ways to make your Mac speak. A discussion of speech quality is at the end of the section.

Choosing a voice

Both Mac OS X and the Classic environment have default voices. You can pick the same default voice for Mac OS X and the Classic environment, or you can pick a different default voice for each environment. Each application can use the default voice, pick its own voice, or let you choose a voice for that application's speech. However, not all applications give you a voice choice.

Tip   To set the speaking volume for both Mac OS X voice and the Classic environment, use the Sound icon in the menu bar to change the system volume level. If the Sound icon isn't present, use the Sound pane of System Preferences. (The Classic Sound control panel's settings do not affect the volume in the Classic environment.)

Choosing a voice for Mac OS X

You set the default voice and speaking rate for Mac OS X in the Speech pane of System Preferences. Figure 17-1 shows the Default Voice settings in the Speech Preferences pane.

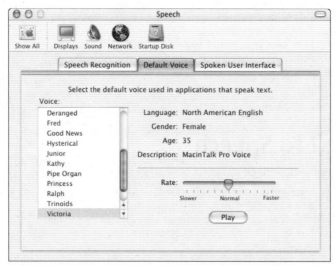

Figure 17-1: Set a speaking voice and speaking rate for Mac OS X in the Speech pane of System Preferences.

To set a voice and a speaking rate for Mac OS X, follow these steps:

1. **Open System Preferences and choose View⇨Speech or click the Speech button.**

2. **Click the Default Voice tab.**

3. **Select any voice from the list on the left side of the Speech preferences pane.** You hear a sample of the voice, and a description of it appears next to the list.

4. **Optionally, change the speaking rate by adjusting the Rate slider.** Each voice has a preset speaking rate. You can hear a sample of the voice at the current rate by clicking the Play button.

Choosing a voice for the Classic environment

You set the voice and a speaking rate for the Classic environment with the Speech control panel. Figure 17-2 shows the Speech control panel's Voice settings.

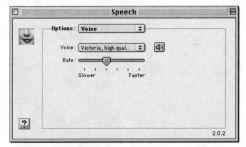

Figure 17-2: Set a speaking voice and speaking rate for the Classic environment in the Speech control panel.

To set a voice and speaking rate for the Classic environment, use these steps:

1. **Open the Speech control panel and choose Voice from the Options pop-up menu.** Recall from earlier chapters that you can open this control panel in several ways, including either of the following:

   • Make a Classic application active and then choose Apple⇨Control Panels⇨Speech.

   • Double-click the Speech control panel's icon, which is located in the Control Panels folder of the System Folder that is used for the Classic environment.

2. **Choose a voice from the Voice pop-up menu.** If you want to hear a sample of the voice, click the button next to the pop-up menu.

3. **Optionally, change the speaking rate by adjusting the Rate slider.** Each voice has a preset speaking rate. If you want to hear a sample of the current rate, click the button next to the Voice pop-up menu.

Choosing an application voice

Applications that speak may use the default voice, or they may let you choose a separate voice for the application. The method for choosing an application's speaking voice varies among applications. For example, in the Classic application SimpleText, you choose a voice from the Voices submenu of the Sound menu. You use quite a different method in Tom Bender's shareware text editor Tex-Edit Plus (www.nearside.com/trans-tex/). In this application, you make voice settings in the Speech pane of the application's Preferences window. Figure 17-3 is an example of SimpleText's Voices submenu.

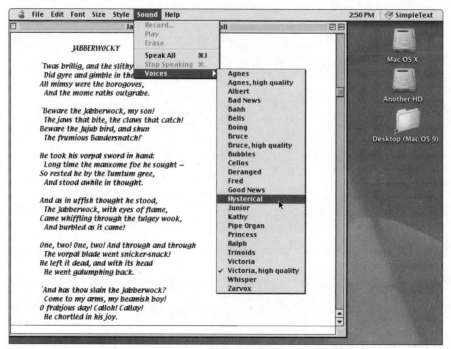

Figure 17-3: Some applications, such as SimpleText, let you choose a speaking voice.

Where voices are installed

Each speaking voice available in Mac OS X applications has a corresponding voice file in one of two Voices folders. The Voices folder that's buried in the folder named System (path /System/Library/Speech/Voices/) contains voice files that are available to everyone who uses your computer. You also have a personal Voices folder inside your home folder's Library folder. If you get additional Mac OS X voices, you can make them available by dragging them to your Voices folder. If your Voices folder contains any voices that you don't want to use, you can remove them. You can't add or remove voice files in the Voices folder within the folder named System. Changes you make to the Voices folder inside your home folder don't affect any other users of your computer.

The Classic environment has a separate set of voice files in another Voices folder; this one is inside the Extensions folder in the Mac OS 9 System Folder used by the Classic environment. These are mostly the same voices that you have in Mac OS X applications, but the Classic environment requires its own voice files. You can remove voices by dragging their files out of this Voices folder. If you obtain additional Mac OS 9 voices from another source, you can make them available by dragging them to the Classic environment's Voices folder. After adding or removing voice files, you must restart the Classic environment for your changes to take effect. Changes you make to the Classic environment's Voices folder affect all users of Classic applications on your computer.

Note　Voice files for Mac OS X are not interchangeable with voice files for the Classic environment. If you find additional voices for Mac OS 9, they won't work in the Voices folder that's inside your Library folder. Likewise, voices for Mac OS X won't work in the Voices folder that's inside the Extensions folder.

Talking Alerts settings

You can use the Speech control panel to set up the manner in which the computer announces alert messages in the Classic environment. Figure 17-4 shows the Speech control panel's Talking Alerts settings.

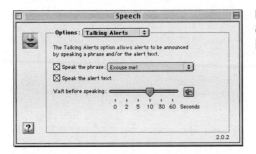

Figure 17-4: Configure the Classic environment's Talking Alerts messages in the Speech control panel.

In the Speech control panel, choose Talking Alerts from the Options pop-up menu. The Talking Alerts settings include the following:

✦ An option that enables the computer to read the text of alert messages aloud.

✦ A slider for adjusting how long the computer waits after it displays an alert message before it speaks.

✦ An option for having the computer speak a phrase, such as "Excuse me!" when it displays an alert.

✦ A button that lets you hear a sample alert using the current settings.

If you choose to have the computer speak a phrase when it displays an alert, you can also choose the phrase that you want to hear from a pop-up menu. The pop-up menu includes a choice that tells the computer to use the next phrase listed in the menu each time it speaks an alert. The pop-up also includes a choice that tells the computer to pick a phrase at random from the list each time it speaks an alert. If you want to add your own phrase, choose Edit Phrase List from the pop-up menu. In the dialog that appears, add, remove, or edit phrases.

If you set the time the computer waits before speaking an alert to more than two seconds, the computer plays the alert sound (a beep or similar sound that is set in the Sound control panel) as soon as it displays an alert and then waits to speak. If you set the time to wait before speaking to less than two seconds, the computer does not play the alert sound before speaking an alert message.

Reading documents aloud

To have your computer speak the text in a document, you need one of the many applications that include commands for speaking. SimpleText is one, and AppleWorks, FileMaker Pro, and Tex-Edit Plus are others. Various applications have different methods for initiating speech. For example, SimpleText has a Speak command in its Sound menu, FileMaker requires a script to be written, and AppleWorks has a Speak Text button that you can add to the Button Bar. Most applications that can speak text speak the currently selected text (the text you have highlighted with your mouse) or all text in the active document if no text is selected.

If you are using an OS X application instead of a Classic application, Speech may be available as a Service. Services are available to OS X applications from the Application menu. An example is shown in Figure 17-5. Services are covered in Chapter 11.

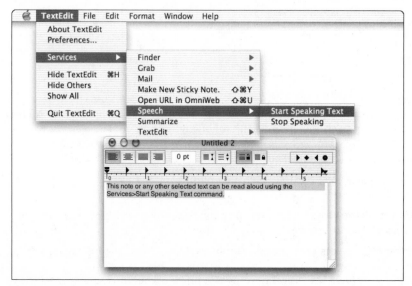

Figure 17-5: Speech is available as a Service to many OS X applications.

Speaking on command

In addition to having documents and alerts read to you, you can program your computer to speak on command. This can be done with AppleScript (which is described in Chapter 21) or with a macro utility, such as QuicKeys from CE Software (www.cesoft.com). The QuicKeys Speak Ease shortcut speaks text entered in its text window or text copied from a document (up to 32K) to the Clipboard. When you type the shortcut's keystroke, the computer speaks the text that you entered or copied. You also can set up a timer so that the computer speaks the text at specified intervals. Figure 17-6 shows the QuicKeys Speak Ease dialog in which you specify a text-to-speech source.

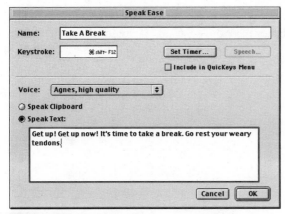

Figure 17-6: Use QuicKeys to program your computer to speak either a message you specify (as shown here) or the Clipboard's current contents.

Sounding natural

Several factors affect how natural computer-generated speech sounds. Clarity of intonation obviously affects how easily you can understand your computer's speech. Less obvious factors include handling contractions, sequencing words idiomatically, avoiding robotic cadence, and generating the sounds of speech.

For natural-sounding speech, the text-to-speech system needs to compensate for idiomatic differences between written and spoken text. This includes expanding contractions, changing word order, and making substitutions. For example, when the system sees $40 billion it should not say, "dollar sign forty billion." The system also has to deal with ambiguous abbreviations, such as "St. Mary's Church is on St. Mary's St."

Making Speech Sound More Natural

The Mac does a pretty good job of speaking text, but you can adjust the cadence and pronunciation of the speech to make it sound more natural. You make these adjustments by adding punctuation and emphasis codes.

When the Mac reads text, it tends to pause less often than a person would. You can make the Mac pause more often by inserting extra commas where you want pauses. For example:

```
You have a lunch date at 12:30, on Tuesday, at the Sam & Ella
Cafe.
```

To insert a brief pause, put single quotation marks around a phrase. For example:

```
Exclusive to the 'Coast Starlight' is the 'Pacific Parlor Car.'
```

Also, the Mac tends to emphasize too many words, making it hard to tell which are important. You can insert the `[[emph -]]` code before a word you want to have less emphasis. This code must have one space before the hyphen, and none anywhere else. Here is an example:

```
The shuttle bus runs every half [[emph -]] hour, on the half
[[emph -]] hour.
```

If you need to add emphasis, insert the `[[emph +]]` code. This code also has one space in it. Here is an example:

```
Food and drink are [[emph +]] not allowed in the museum.
```

Besides saying the right words in the right order, the text-to-speech system has to pronounce them correctly. Consider the different ways *ough* is pronounced in the words *enough*, *ought*, *slough*, *dough*, *through*, and *drought*. Pronunciation also depends on sentence structure, as in "A strong wind can wind a kite string around a tree." Moreover, the system has to avoid putting the emPHASis on the wrong sylLAble. Names pose a special problem because their spelling is even less reliable a guide to pronunciation than ordinary English words.

Getting the words and pronunciation right isn't enough. Without the right cadence, spoken words may sound robotic. Beyond just sounding unnatural, the wrong phrasing may convey the wrong meaning. Compare the meaning of "The dog already ate, Mom" to "The dog already ate Mom."

The most computationally intensive part of speech synthesis is producing the sound of a human voice speaking the text. Each moment of speech requires many mathematical calculations and ample memory. The higher the quality of speech, the greater the computational and memory demands. In other words, a higher-performance computer is capable of higher-quality speech.

After figuring out what words to say, how to pronounce them, and what cadence to apply, the text-to-speech software has to synthesize the actual sounds of speech by using the voice you have chosen. Some voices that come with Mac OS X and the Classic environment are easier to understand than others. The voices that are easier to understand are based on a more sophisticated voice synthesis method known as MacinTalk Pro. The other voices are based on a voice synthesis method called MacinTalk 3.

MacinTalk Pro has three English voices: Agnes, Bruce, and Victoria. All are based on samples of real human speech. To assist with pronunciations, MacinTalk Pro has a dictionary of 65,000 words plus 5,000 common U.S. names. To generate cadence, it uses a sophisticated model of the acoustic structure of human speech that resulted from many years of research.

MacinTalk 3 voices are based on an acoustic model of the human vocal tract. Mac OS X and the Classic environment come with 19 MacinTalk 3 voices, including several novelty voices (robots, talking bubbles, whispering, and singing).

Speech Recognition

Apple made headlines in 1993 when it introduced its speech recognition technology, which was then called Casper. Now the technology enables Mac OS X to take spoken commands from anyone who speaks North American English. You don't have to train the computer to recognize your voice. You just speak normally, without intense pauses, unnatural diction, or special intonation.

English Speech Recognition is designed to understand a few dozen commands for controlling your computer. You can add to and remove some of the commands that the speech recognition system understands, but you can't turn it into a general dictation system. If voice dictation interests you, check out the IBM Via Voice for Macintosh (www.ibm.com/software/speech/mac/) and MacSpeech's iListen (www.macspeech.com).

This section explains how to configure speech recognition and how to speak commands. It tells you how to find out what commands the speech recognition system understands and how to add your own speakable commands.

Note Speech recognition does not work in the Classic environment. Even if you install the Mac OS 9 version of the Apple speech recognition software, which is an optional component, it does not work in the Classic environment. You are not able to set it up in the Classic Speech control panel.

Getting a speech recognition microphone

Speech recognition requires a special microphone. If you use an iMac or PowerBook, the built-in microphone may work for speech recognition. However, the microphone built into some older iMacs and PowerBooks does not work for speech recognition. Apple is characteristically vague about exactly which iMac and PowerBook microphones don't work, so you just have to try your own.

Using a headset

You'll probably get the best results with speech recognition if you use a headset that includes a noise-canceling microphone designed for voice recognition. Many brands and models are available. Some have a standard 3.5mm mini-plug for Macs with microphone jacks, and some have a USB connector for Macs with USB ports. If you don't have any luck with your Mac's built-in microphone, try a headset.

A Mac's microphone jack, also called the sound input port, requires a line-level signal. Headsets designed for the PC market generally produce a weaker, mic-level signal. To use one of these with a Mac, you need an amplifier, such as the NE Mic from Griffin Technology (www.griffintechnology.com).

Using a PlainTalk microphone

Apple also designed a special microphone for speech recognition, and it works with all Macs that can use Mac OS X and have a microphone jack. Called the PlainTalk microphone (Apple part number M7885LL/A or M9060Z/A), it has an unusual shape and a plug that's longer than the normal 3.5mm mini-plug. The tip of the long plug contacts a power source inside the computer, and the microphone uses the power to amplify its signal. The PlainTalk microphone outputs a line-level signal.

The PlainTalk microphone's unusual shape may lead you to use it incorrectly. What looks like the front of the PlainTalk microphone is actually the top. The microphone won't work properly if you hold it in your hand and speak into the broad side that has the most holes. The PlainTalk microphone is designed to sit on top of your monitor with its flat surface down and its small end facing you.

Naturally, Apple's PlainTalk microphone is useless if your Mac doesn't have a microphone jack. In this case, use a microphone with a USB connector or a USB audio adapter, such as the iMic from Griffin Technology (www.griffintechnology.com).

Configuring speech recognition

You configure speech recognition in System Preferences. In Speech Preferences, click the Speech Recognition tab and then click the On/Off tab. Now you can turn speech recognition on and off and specify the kind of feedback you get when you speak commands. You can also click a button to see the contents of the Speakable Items folder, which we cover in more detail later in this chapter. Figure 17-7 shows the On/Off and feedback settings in Speech Preferences.

Turning speech recognition on

When you turn on speech recognition, a round feedback window appears. In addition, the first time you turn on speech recognition, it displays a welcome message that explains how speech recognition works. (You can read this message again by clicking the Helpful Tips button in Speech Preferences.)

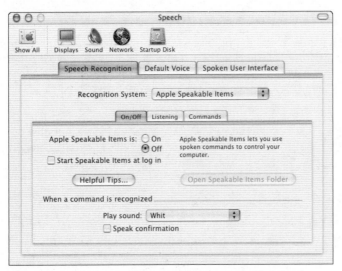

Figure 17-7: Turn speech recognition on and off and set feedback options in the Speech Recognition tab of Speech Preferences.

If you want to have speech recognition turned on automatically every time you log in, select the option labeled "Open Speakable Items at log in." This setting, like all others in the Speech Recognition tab, does not affect other people who log in with different user accounts.

Setting feedback options

Below the On/Off controls in Speech Preferences are settings that affect the feedback you get while using speech recognition. You can turn the Speak confirmation option on or off to control whether the computer speaks its response to your commands in addition to displaying its response in writing.

You can also change the sound that indicates the computer has recognized a spoken command. Choose a sound from the pop-up menu or choose None if you don't want to hear a sound signifying recognition. This pop-up menu lists the sounds from the Sounds folder in the Library folder of the folder named System; the Sounds folder of the main Library folder; and two special sounds, Single Click and Whit, which are part of the speech recognition software. If you put any sounds in the Sounds folder of the Library folder in your home folder, these sounds are not included in the speech feedback pop-up menu.

Looking at the feedback window

The speech feedback window, which appears when you turn on speech recognition, has several unusual attributes. First of all, it's round. It floats above most other windows. What's more, this window has no close button, minimize button, or zoom button. Figure 17-8 shows the speech feedback window in several states.

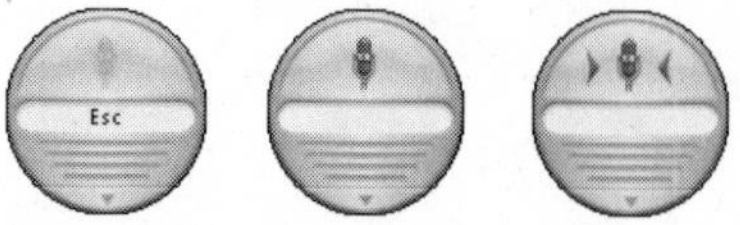

Figure 17-8: A feedback window indicates when speech recognition is idle (left), listening for a command (middle), or hearing a command (right).

Interpreting feedback

The speech feedback window provides the following information about speech recognition:

✦ **Attention mode.** Indicates whether the computer is listening for or recognizing spoken commands, as follows:

- **Not listening for spoken commands.** The small microphone at the top of the feedback window looks dim.

- **Listening for a command.** The small microphone at the top of the feedback window looks dark.

- **Recognizing to a command you are speaking.** You see arrowheads move from the edges of the feedback window toward the microphone picture.

✦ **Listening method.** Indicates how to make the computer listen for spoken commands. You may see the name of a key you must press or a word you must speak to let the computer know that you want it to interpret what you are saying as a command.

✦ **Loudness.** Colored bars on the bottom part of the window theoretically measure the loudness of your voice. In practice, there seems to be no relationship between the indicated loudness level and successful speech recognition. If you see no bars or one blue bar, you're speaking relatively quietly; a blue bar and one or two green bars mean you're speaking louder; and these three bars plus a red bar mean that you're speaking very loudly. Apple recommends you speak loudly enough to keep green bars showing but rarely should the red bar appear.

✦ **Recognition results.** When the computer recognizes a command you have spoken, it displays the recognized command in a help tag above the speech feedback window. The displayed command may not exactly match what you said, because speech recognition interprets what you say with some degree of flexibility. For example, if you say, "Close window," speech recognition probably displays the command it recognized as "Close this window." If speech recognition has a response to your command, it generally displays it in a help tag below the feedback window. Figure 17-9 shows how speech recognition displays the recognized command and its feedback in help tags.

Figure 17-9: Help tags above and below the speech feedback window display the command that the computer recognized and its response, if any.

Using feedback window controls

The only control in the speech feedback window is a pop-up menu, which you can see by clicking the small arrow at the bottom of the window. One menu command opens Speech Preferences, previously shown in Figure 17-7. Another command in the pop-up menu opens a window that lists available speech commands (covered later in the chapter).

You can move the feedback window by clicking it almost anywhere and dragging. You can't drag from the bottom of the window because clicking there makes the pop-up menu appear.

Minimizing the feedback window

Although the speech feedback window has no minimize button, you can minimize it with a spoken command, which is "Minimize speech feedback window." While minimized in the Dock, this window continues to provide most of the same feedback as it does when it is not minimized. While the feedback window is minimized, you don't see help tags containing the recognized command and response. In addition, the window's pop-up menu is not available in the Dock. Figure 17-10 shows the speech feedback window in the Dock.

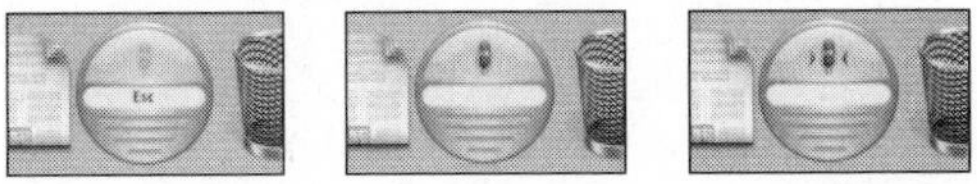

Figure 17-10: While minimized in the Dock, the speech feedback window continues to indicate speech recognition status.

After minimizing the speech feedback window, you can open the window by clicking it in the Dock. You can also open the window by speaking the command, "Open speech feedback window."

Looking at the Speech Commands window

Instead of seeing your spoken command and the computer's response to it displayed briefly in help tags, you can see a list of all your recent spoken commands and the responses to them. The list of commands appears in the Speech Commands window, which also lists the commands you can speak in the current context. You can display this window by choosing Open Speech Commands Window from the pop-up menu at the bottom of the round speech feedback window. You can also open the Speech Commands window with the spoken command, "Open Speech Commands window." Figure 17-11 shows the Speech Commands window when the Finder is the active application.

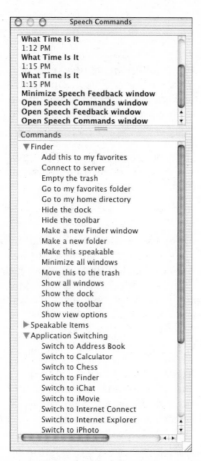

Figure 17-11: The Speech Commands window lists commands you have spoken, responses to them, and commands you can speak.

The commands you have spoken appear at the top of the speech commands window in bold, and any responses appear below each command in plain text. The bottom part of the window displays the commands you can speak in the current context. The list is organized in the following categories:

✦ **Name of current application.** Appears only if the application you're currently using has its own speakable commands.

✦ **Speakable Items.** Includes commands that are available no matter which application you're currently using.

✦ **Applications.** Lists commands for switching to specific applications (switching to an application opens it if necessary).

You can hide or show the commands for a category by clicking the disclosure triangle next to the category name. You can adjust the relative sizes of the top and bottom parts of the speech commands window by dragging the handle located on the bar between the two parts of the window. You find out how to add speakable commands later in this chapter.

Setting the listening method

You don't want the computer listening to every word you say, or it may try to interpret conversational remarks as commands. Two methods control when the computer listens for commands:

✦ **Push-to-talk method.** The most reliable method because the computer listens for commands only when you are pressing a key that you designate.

✦ **Code name method.** The computer listens for its code name and tries to interpret the words that follow it as a command.

Setting the push-to-talk method

You set the listening method in the Speech pane of System Preferences. To set the push-to-talk method and the key that makes speech recognition listen for spoken commands, follow these steps:

1. **In Speech Preferences, click the Speech Recognition tab.** The Speech Recognition settings of Speech Preferences are organized on three tabbed panels, On/Off, Listening, and Commands.

2. **Click the Listening tab.** You see the options for setting the speech recognition listening method. Figure 17-12 shows Speech Preferences set for the push-to-talk method with the Esc key, which is the initial setting.

3. **Set the Listening Method option to Listen only while key is pressed.** This setting means you must hold down the listening key to make speech recognition heed your spoken commands.

4. **If you want to change the listening key, click the Change Key button.** A dialog appears in which you can type the key or combination of keys that you want to use as the listening key. You can use the Esc key, Delete key, any key on the numeric keypad, one of the function keys F5 through F12, or most punctuation keys. You can combine one of these keys with any one or more of the Shift, Option, Control, or ⌘ keys. You can't use letter keys or number keys on the main part of the keyboard.

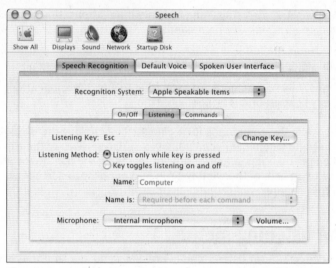

Figure 17-12: Speech recognition set for push-to-talk listening.

Setting the code name method

If you prefer to have the computer listen for a code name that you say before speaking a command, use these steps:

1. **In Speech Preferences, click the Speech Recognition tab.** The Speech Recognition settings of Speech Preferences are organized on three tabbed panels, On/Off, Listening, and Commands.

2. **Click the Listening tab.** You see the options for setting the speech recognition listening method. Figure 17-13 shows Speech Preferences set for the code name method.

3. **Set the Listening Method option to "Key toggles listening on and off."** This setting means pressing the listening key alternately turns listening on and off. Turning listening off puts speech recognition on standby, which may improve the performance of the computer.

4. **If you want to change the listening key, click the Change Key button.** A dialog appears in which you can type the key or combination of keys that you want to use as the key. You can use the Esc key, Delete key, any key on the numeric keypad, one of the function keys F5 through F12, or most punctuation keys. You can combine one of these keys with any one or more of the Shift, Option, Control, or ⌘ keys. You can't use letter keys or number keys on the main part of the keyboard.

5. **Specify a code name.** Type a code name for speech recognition in the text box; the default name is Computer. (Capitalization doesn't matter.) Use the nearby pop-up menu to specify when you must speak the name.

In the pop-up menu that specifies when you must speak the code name, one of the choices makes the code name optional, but not without risk: The computer could interpret something you say in conversation as a voice command.

Other choices in the pop-up menu make the code name optional if you spoke the last command less than 15 seconds ago or 30 seconds ago. The idea is that when you have the computer's attention, you shouldn't have to get its attention immediately following the previous command. You can tell whether you need to speak the code name by looking at the round speech feedback window. If you see the code name displayed in the middle of the feedback window, you have to speak the name before the next command.

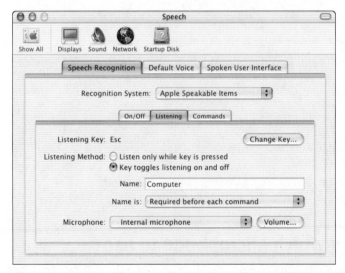

Figure 17-13: Speech recognition set for code name listening.

Specifying what commands to listen for

Speech has commands organized by group. You choose which groups of commands Speech will listen for in the Commands tab of Speech Recognition shown in Figure 17-14. To choose commands by group:

1. **In Speech Preferences, click the Speech Recognition tab.**

2. **Click the Commands tab.**

3. **Click the checkboxes to select and deselect groups of commands.** To activate the Front Windows commands group and the Menu Bar commands group, you must select "Using Assistive Features" in the Universal Access pane of System Preferences. Universal Access was covered in Chapter 15. As you add and remove groups of commands, the groups appear and disappear in the Speech Commands window.

4. **Select or clear the checkbox next to "Require exact wording of Speakable Item command names."** Requiring the speaker to use the exact name of the command improves recognition accuracy and response time. If this is deselected, OS X will attempt to identify a command from more relaxed, casual speech.

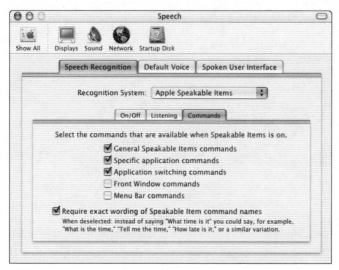

Figure 17-14: Speech recognition organizes commands by group.

Specifying which microphone to use

If your Mac has more than one microphone connected, such as a built-in microphone and an external microphone, you san specify which one you want speech recognition to use. You do this in the Listening settings of Speech Preferences, which are shown in Figure 17-13. Here's the procedure:

1. **In Speech Preferences, click the Speech Recognition tab.**

2. **Click the Listening tab.**

3. **Choose an available microphone from the Microphone pop-up menu.** If your computer has a microphone jack, the pop-up menu includes it as a choice even if no microphone is plugged into the jack.

This method of specifying which microphone to use first appeared in Mac OS X version 10.1. In earlier versions of Mac OS X, the speech recognition software selects a microphone automatically.

Specifying the spoken user interface

Speech can be used in much of OS X's responses to the user. These are configured in the Spoken User Interface tab of the Speech pane in System Preferences, as shown in Figure 17-15. Open System Preferences and then click the Spoken User Interface tab. You can choose what phrase, such as "Alert!" or "Excuse me" to use as a signal phrase. You can edit the list of alert phrases and add your own phrases, too. You can choose a voice just for alert messages that's a different voice than the default voice, the time delay before the alert is spoken. You can also choose to have Speech read text under the mouse cursor as you move the cursor over text.

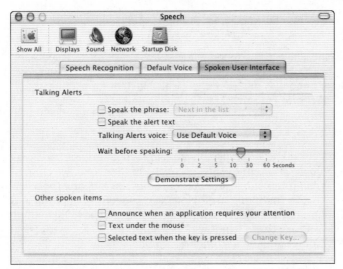

Figure 17-15: Speech recognition organizes commands by group.

Giving spoken commands

After setting up and turning on speech recognition, you are ready to speak commands, and you expect the computer to carry out your order. The recognition feedback window, previously shown in Figure 17-12, tells you whether to use the push-to-talk method or the code name method. You can figure out what to say by looking at the Speech Commands window, previously shown in Figure 17-11.

For best recognition, speak carefully and clearly. Keep your pace and loudness normal. The computer does not understand you if you speak too slowly or loudly. You make yourself harder to understand if you pause between words or speak with exaggerated emphasis. Do pause slightly when saying a command with initials or an acronym, as if you were spelling it out for someone.

Naming Speakable Items

Apple offers a little help when it comes to naming items that you add to the Speakable Items folder. Here are some of Apple's suggestions:

✦ Try to name items so that they don't sound too similar ("Navigator" and "Communicator" are probably better than "Netscape Navigator" and "Netscape Communicator," at least in our experience).

✦ Long command names are more easily recognized.

✦ If you need acronyms or a series of letters in a name, put spaces in between. "Connect using P P P" is better than "Connect using PPP."

✦ Avoid using numerals in your file names. For example, speech recognition doesn't notice the difference between "AppleWorks 5" and "AppleWorks 6."

✦ Make the names of speakable items sound different from each other. If speakable items have names that sound similar, the computer may have trouble distinguishing them. If the computer frequently mistakes one speakable item for another, try changing the name of one or both so that they don't sound alike.

Speech recognition is liberal about the use of *a*, *an*, *the*, *and*, and *or* in spoken commands. For instance, you can say either "Switch to the Finder" or "Switch to Finder." Moreover, you can often substitute *these* for *this*, as in "Copy these to the Clipboard" and "Copy this to the Clipboard." However, speech recognition is not clever enough to act on multiple objects just because you say *these* instead of *this*. For example, if you say, "Close these windows," the computer recognizes the command as "Close this window" and closes only the active window.

The computer is more likely to recognize a phrase that exactly matches a command listed in the Speech Commands window. If the computer has trouble recognizing a spoken command, take the time to look up the command and try saying it exactly as it's listed.

Adding speakable items

You can find out which commands are speakable by looking in the Speech Commands window, but how does the computer know what to list there? The answer is pretty simple: The computer finds speakable commands in the Speakable Items folder. This folder is located in the Speech folder that is in the Library folder in your home folder.

Speech recognition recognizes the names of almost all items in the Speakable Items folder as commands. These commands are generally available in all Mac OS X applications and are listed in the Speakable Items category in the Speech Commands window.

You make the computer understand more spoken commands by adding items to the Speakable Items folder. Anything that you can open in the Finder becomes a speakable command when you add it to the Speakable Items folder.

Adding aliases as speakable items

If you want to open any folders, applications, documents, or any other files by spoken command, simply put aliases of them in the Speakable Items folder. You can change the speakable command that opens an alias by editing the name of the alias. You should remove the word *alias* from any alias names that include it, although speech recognition usually ignores *alias* at the end of a speakable item's name.

When you say the name of an alias that you've added to the Speakable Items folder, the computer opens the original item that the alias points to. For example, if you put an alias of the TextEdit application in the Speakable Items folder, then you can open TextEdit by saying the name of the alias as a spoken command. Generally, you can say just the name of the alias or you can say "open" followed by the alias's name. Saying the word "open" is optional. For example, if you have a speakable alias named "AppleWorks," you can open it by saying either "open AppleWorks" or "AppleWorks." If the computer doesn't respond when you say "open" followed by the name of a speakable item, you can change the item's name so that it begins with "open."

Making an application speakable

In addition to speakable commands that are available in all Mac OS X applications, the speech commands window may list commands specifically for the application you're currently using. For example, when you are using the Finder, the speech commands window lists commands for the Finder, such as "Make a new folder."

Each application with its own speech commands has a folder in the Application Speakable Items folder that is located in the Speakable Items folder. If an application has a folder of speakable commands, the commands are available when the application is the active application. Initially, the Application Speakable Items folder contains folders for the Finder, Internet Explorer, and Mail. You can add folders for more applications. An easy method is to open an application (or make it active, if it's already open) and speak the command, "Make this Application Speakable." Doing so creates an alias for the application in the Speakable Items folder, and it creates a correctly named, empty folder for the application inside the Application Speakable Items folder. Later you can add commands to the application folder, such as commands that you make by using AppleScript.

Note   If you create your own command for a specific application, avoid giving it the same name as an item in the Speakable Items folder. An application-specific command overrides a general command with the same name.

Making speakable commands with AppleScript

To make a multistep, speakable command, use the Script Editor program to create an AppleScript applet that you put in the Speakable Items folder. (An *applet* is a small application, in this case made with AppleScript as described in Chapter 21.) If the speakable command applies to a particular application, put the applet in the application's folder inside the Application Speakable Items folder. The name of the AppleScript applet is the speakable command, and speaking this command opens the AppleScript applet.

With some applications, you can record an AppleScript applet of a procedure while you carry it out. You may also be able to find an existing AppleScript script that you can modify slightly to create the speakable command you need. You can find more information on creating AppleScript applets in Chapter 21.

Summary

After reading this chapter, you know the following about text-to-speech and speech recognition:

✦ You set the default voice and speaking rate for Mac OS X in the Default Voice pane of System Preferences.

✦ You set the voice and set a speaking rate for the Classic environment with the Speech control panel.

✦ An application that speaks may use the default voice or the application may let you choose a different voice.

✦ You can use the Speech control panel to set up the manner in which the computer announces alert messages in the Classic environment.

✦ SimpleText, FileMaker Pro, Tex-Edit Plus, and other applications that include commands for speaking can speak the text in a document.

✦ English Speech Recognition is designed to understand a few dozen commands for controlling your computer.

✦ Speech recognition requires a special microphone, such as a USB headset or the Apple PlainTalk microphone. The built-in microphone works on some iMacs and PowerBooks.

✦ You configure speech recognition in the Speech Recognition tab of Speech Preferences. You can turn it on or off, set feedback options, and set a listening method.

✦ The round speech feedback window indicates whether the computer is listening for spoken commands, how to make it listen, and what it hears while it is listening.

✦ The Speech Command window lists your spoken commands and the computer's responses to them. It also lists the commands you can speak.

✦ You make the computer understand more spoken commands by adding items to the Speakable Items folder. Aliases of folders, applications, documents, and other files become speakable commands that open the aliases' original items.

✦ Each application with its own speech commands has a folder in the Application Speakable Items folder that is inside the Speakable Items folder. You can add items to an application's folder of speakable commands.

✦   ✦   ✦

Setting up a Local Network

I f you have more than one computer in your office or home, you can benefit by connecting them in a network. The idea may seem intimidating, but a simple network is easy to set up and doesn't cost much. Here are some things that you can do with a simple network:

◆ Share one Internet connection among several computers

◆ Share printers

◆ Share files from other computers in your company or home as if their files were on your Desktop, and let other computers share files from your computer

◆ Play games designed for multiple players

◆ Access a central database while other computers do likewise

◆ Maintain a group schedule or calendar

◆ Back up hard disks of all networked computers on a central tape drive

◆ Access your hard disk from a remote location over a telephone line or Internet connection

This chapter focuses on setting up a network so that you can use some of these services. First, the chapter discusses how to get your computer connected to an Ethernet network or an AirPort network. We don't explain how to get connected to a network by modem, because we assume that you already know how to plug a modem into a phone jack. (Hint: It's the same as plugging in a telephone.) The middle sections of this chapter explain how to configure your network connections in the Network pane of System Preferences — also known as Network Preferences — and how to easily switch from one configuration to another by using network locations. The chapter ends by describing how to set up an AirPort base station.

Other chapters describe how to use network services after you set up your network. For information on such Internet services as e-mail and the Web, see Chapter 6. For information on printers and printing, see Chapter 9. For information on accessing shared files, see Chapter 10. For information on sharing your files with other computers, see Chapter 19 and for information on sharing your own Web site or allowing remote access to your computer, see Chapter 20.

Wiring an Ethernet Network

Ethernet is by far the most common wired network used to connect computers. An Ethernet network can include computers using Mac OS X, earlier Mac OS versions, Windows, Unix, and many other operating systems. They can use commonplace application software — for example, e-mail and Web browser applications — to communicate and share services.

All Macs that are qualified for Mac OS X are ready to be connected to an Ethernet network. Older Macs commonly used another type of wiring called LocalTalk, but this type of network can't be used with Mac OS X. A LocalTalk to Ethernet adaptor can enable these older Macs for use on an Ethernet network, though.

The first step in setting up an Ethernet network is to establish lines of communication between the computers and printers that you want on the network. Basically that involves running a cable from each computer, printer, DSL modem or cable modem, and other network device to a central junction box.

Looking at Ethernet cables

Ethernet networks may be wired with several types of cable. The most popular is 10Base-T or 100Base-T cable, also known as *unshielded twisted-pair (UTP)* cable. This type of cable looks like telephone cable and uses RJ-45 connectors that look like big modular phone connectors. Other kinds of cable include Thinnet, thick coax, and fiber-optic Ethernet cables.

Twisted-pair cable is graded according to how well it protects against electrical interference. Category 3 cable is adequate for 10Base-T networks, which have a maximum data transfer rate of 10 Mbps (megabits per second). Category 5 offers more protection, but costs more. The additional cost for Category 5 is insignificant when compared to the cost of installation. Properly installed Category 5 cable can also be used for a faster 100Base-T Ethernet network or even a much faster Gigabit Ethernet network. A 100-BaseT network has a maximum transfer rate of 100 Mbps, and a Gigabit network has a maximum transfer rate of 1000 Mbps.

With Category 5 cable installed properly, you can upgrade a 10Base-T network to 100Base-T or Gigabit without any rewiring. The only caveat is that 100Base-T and Gigabit have more stringent rules about cable installation than 10Base-T. For example, sharp bends are not allowed in 100Base-T and Gigabit cables. Additionally, Gigabit

Token Ring Networks

Besides Ethernet, you can connect Macs by using other types of network wiring, such as Token Ring. Because Mac OS computers don't come with token ring network ports, one must be added in the form of a network adapter card, often called a *network interface card (NIC)*. If your organization has a Token Ring network, you undoubtedly have a network administrator or other expert who has already connected your computer to it or can do so for you. Setting up a Token Ring network is not something that you want to attempt on your own. At any rate, it's outside the scope of this book.

Ethernet requires Category 5 cables that have eight wires (four pairs). Less expensive four-wire (two pair) Category 5 cable works only for 10-BaseT and 100-BaseT.

Looking at Ethernet ports

The computers, printers, and other devices that you want to include in your Ethernet network must each have a built-in Ethernet port or an Ethernet adapter.

Macintosh Ethernet ports

Every Mac qualified to run Mac OS X has a built-in Ethernet port with an RJ-45 connector. Depending on the Mac model, the built-in port may be capable of Gigabit, 100Base-T, and 10Base-T Ethernet; 100Base-T and 10Base-T; or only 10Base-T. Table 18-1 provides the details for Mac OS X-qualified Macs as of Fall 2001.

Table 18-1
Macs with Built-in Ethernet Capabilities

Mac model	Gigabit	100Base-T	10Base-T
iMac - all models		✓	✓
eMac - all models		✓	✓
iBook - all models		✓	✓
PowerBook G4 - Gigabit Ethernet	✓	✓	✓
PowerBook G4		✓	✓
PowerBook G3 Series			✓
PowerBook G3 Series - Bronze keyboard		✓	✓
PowerBook G3 - FireWire		✓	✓

Continued

Table 18-1 (continued)			
Mac model	Gigabit	100Base-T	10Base-T
PowerMac G4 - QuickSilver	✓	✓	✓
Power Mac G4 - 5-Slot, Digital Audio	✓	✓	✓
Power Mac G4 - Gigabit Ethernet	✓	✓	✓
Power Mac G4 - AGP Graphics		✓	✓
Power Mac G4 - PCI Graphics		✓	✓
Macintosh Server G4	✓	✓	✓
Power Mac G4 Cube		✓	✓
Power Macintosh G3 - Blue and White		✓	✓
Power Macintosh G3 - All-In-One			✓
Power Macintosh G3 - Mini Tower			✓
Power Macintosh G3 - Desktop			✓
Power Macintosh G3 - Server			✓

You can add a faster Ethernet port to a Power Mac or PowerBook by installing an Ethernet adapter. An Ethernet adapter for a Power Mac goes in one of its PCI expansion slots. An Ethernet adapter for a PowerBook goes in its PC card slot. After installing an Ethernet adapter, the built-in Ethernet port is still functional.

Printer Ethernet ports

Many printers that are designed to be shared on a network have built-in Ethernet ports. If your printer does not have a built-in Ethernet port, you may be able to install a built-in Ethernet port or to use a separate Ethernet adapter sometimes called a *print server*. Contact the maker of your printer to find out whether either of these options is available for it.

Old printers made for Macintosh networks generally have a different kind of network port known as a LocalTalk port. To use one of these printers on an Ethernet network, you need a LocalTalk-to-10Base-T adapter, such as the EtherMac iPrint LT from Farallon (www.farallon.com).

Making Ethernet connections

In an Ethernet network that uses RJ-45 connectors and twisted-pair cable, you connect the computers by running a cable from each computer to a central connection point known as a *hub* or a *switch*. This is a small box that contains an array of RJ-45

Ethernet ports and some circuitry that enables data to pass from one of its ports to another. The cable from each computer plugs into a separate port on the hub or switch. If you have a printer or other device with an Ethernet port, you run a cable from it to the hub or switch as well.

Comparing hubs and switches

You can use either a hub or a switch in your network, but a switch provides faster connections when more than one computer uses the network at the same time. In a hub, the ports must essentially take turns sending data across a common path. A switch creates separate paths as needed between sending and receiving ports. A hub is like a highway intersection, where cars on each road must take turns going through the intersection. A switch is like a cloverleaf interchange that has flyover ramps connecting the roads.

In some settings, switches are more secure than hubs. A hub provides shared connections, which means the hub broadcasts data from a computer connected to one hub port to all computers connected to other hub ports. If a nefarious hacker can use a computer connected to your hub or surreptitiously connect a laptop to your hub, the hacker can use packet-sniffing software to grab data being sent over the network. A hacker can't monitor all data being sent through a switch because it provides private communications between ports. The security risk of a hub is low in most homes, small offices, and other private settings where hackers can't enter easily and won't find much interesting traffic on the network.

Hubs and switches come in many different sizes, although 4-port, 8-port, and 16-port hubs are the most common. Prices start at about $20 for a generic 4-port 10Base-T hub and go up for more ports and a name brand. 100Base-T hubs cost more than 10Base-T hubs, and switches cost more than hubs.

Connecting hubs and switches

If you use up all the ports on one hub or switch, you can connect another hub or switch to it. You can even use hubs and switches together. Connecting hubs is called *daisy chaining*. Up to four hubs can be daisy-chained with twisted-pair cable. Switches are not subject to this restriction.

Using crossover cables

When connecting two hubs, two switches, or a hub and a switch, you may have to use a specially wired cable called a *crossover cable*. You also may need a crossover cable to connect a cable modem or DSL modem to a hub or switch. The crossover cable has the wires reversed inside one of its plugs. To use a crossover cable, you simply plug each end into a regular port on each device.

You don't need a crossover cable if your hub or switch has an extra port labeled Uplink or a port that you can make into an Uplink port by setting a switch. Plugging a regular cable into an Uplink port has the same effect as using a crossover cable, because the Uplink port's wiring is reversed. Note that if your hub or switch has an extra port labeled Uplink, you probably can't use it and the port next to it at the same time; they're usually one port with two jacks.

Note   A crossover cable looks exactly like a normal Ethernet cable, but using one when you need the other will not work. Attaching a label or keeping the crossover cable where it can't be mixed up with normal Ethernet cables can help.

Connecting a hubless network

You can connect two computers or a computer and one other device in a 10Base-T network without a hub or switch. You simply use a crossover cable to connect the two devices.

Adding an Internet gateway or router

If you want the computers on your local network to share an Internet connection, your network needs an *Internet gateway,* which is also known as an Internet router. An Internet gateway may be software that runs on a computer that's connected to your network, or the gateway may be a specialized piece of hardware. Besides allowing multiple computers to share an Internet connection, most Internet gateways provide a *firewall* that shields the computers on your local network from hackers trying to infiltrate your computers via the Internet.

An Apple AirPort base station can serve as an Internet gateway, as described in the next section. Similarly, the AirPort base station software included with AirPort cards is an Internet gateway. Other Internet gateway software products include Internet Gateway and SurfDoubler from Vicomsoft (www.vicomsoft.com) and IPNetRouter from Sustainable Softworks (www.sustworks.com). At this writing, all these software gateways must run on a Mac with Mac OS 9 or earlier. Sustainable Softworks' IPNetShareX, however, is OS X native. Any computer regardless of operating system—Mac OS X, Microsoft Windows, or Unix—can use the shared Internet connection provided by gateway software that's running on a Mac OS 9 computer.

You may need an Internet gateway even if the computers on your local network do not share an Internet connection. If more than one computer on an Ethernet-based network has a different Internet address provided by your ISP (Internet Service Provider), your network needs a gateway. Without a gateway, all your network traffic flows from one computer up to your ISP and then back down to the other computer. Most DSL and cable modem connections are slower than your local Ethernet network, especially for traffic going from your computers to the ISP. A gateway, either hardware or software, keeps traffic between your computers on your local network. By keeping local network traffic off the Internet link, the gateway can significantly enhance your local network performance.

AirPort and Other IEEE 802.11b Devices

Apple's AirPort products adhere to the computer industry's IEEE 802.11b standard. This means that AirPort networks can include IEEE 802.11b devices not made by Apple. Several companies make 802.11b PC cards and matching PCI adapters that are the equivalent of AirPort cards. These 802.11b products enable older Power Macs and PowerBooks, which can't use AirPort cards, to join an AirPort network. However, Macs with 802.11b cards made by companies other than Apple can't join an AirPort network when started up from Mac OS X 10.0. The AirPort software in early versions of Mac OS X does not include the software drivers to recognize 802.11b cards made by such companies as Lucent, Agere, and Farallon. A future version of Mac OS X may include the necessary software drivers for 802.11b cards not made by Apple.

Establishing an AirPort Network

You don't need Ethernet or any other cumbersome wiring to establish a network with the latest Macs. Recent Power Macs, PowerBooks, iMacs, and iBooks are ready to use Apple's terrific AirPort wireless networking products. AirPort network connections don't require special wiring because they use radio signals to transmit data between machines equipped for wireless networking. Although wireless networking may sound like complicated science fiction, AirPort is actually easier to set up than Ethernet.

A simple AirPort network enables several AirPort-equipped Macs to share files and play multiplayer games, assuming they are within about 150 feet of each other. You equip a Mac for AirPort by installing a small card made by Apple, the AirPort Card (part number M7600LL/B). This card fits a special slot that is present in most recent Mac models. This is the easiest way to share files wirelessly.

For wireless Internet access, you can get a small device made by Apple, the AirPort Base Station (part number M7601LL/B). Alternatively, you can install software on an AirPort-equipped Mac to make it a base station. The base station device or the software base station communicates wirelessly with AirPort-equipped Macs, while also being connected to the Internet. The base station device and software both include an Internet gateway for sharing an Internet connection.

A base station can also bridge the AirPort network and a wired Ethernet network. Then computers connected to AirPort and computers connected to Ethernet can communicate with each other.

This section begins by describing how to install AirPort cards, use Mac OS X to join an existing AirPort network, and monitor an AirPort network connection. Next, this section explains how to create a simple computer-to-computer network (without a base station). Finally, this section tells you how you can turn off the AirPort card with Mac OS X.

Installing AirPort cards

Macs that are ready for AirPort have a built-in antenna and a special slot for Apple's AirPort card, but if your Mac doesn't have one of these cards installed, you may need to obtain one, connect the antenna to it, and install it in the slot. Of course, you don't need to install an AirPort card if you order one with the computer or if someone else already installed a card.

The following Mac models have the necessary antenna and slot for an AirPort card, as of fall 2002:

✦ iBook and iMac with a slot-loading CD or DVD drive (except Indigo iMac with 350MHz processor)

✦ eMac

✦ PowerBook G3 with FireWire ports

✦ PowerBook G4

✦ Power Mac G4 Cube

✦ Power Mac G4 with an AGP graphics slot

Not surprisingly, the procedure for installing an AirPort card is different for each Mac model. Instructions for installing an AirPort card in your computer are in the manual that came with it. You can also find detailed, illustrated instructions for your Mac model on Apple's AirPort support Web site (www.info.apple.com/support/pages.taf?product=airport).

Creating a computer-to-computer AirPort network

If you have two or more computers with AirPort cards installed, you can create an ad hoc wireless network. Apple calls this a *computer-to-computer network.* This network connects the AirPort-equipped computers without an AirPort base station. One computer creates a computer-to-computer network, and other computers within about 150 feet can join it.

Note   Any computer with a wireless card that complies with revision b of the IEEE 802.11 standard should be able to join a computer-to-computer network created by Mac OS X. The IEEE 802.11b standard defines a standard for ad hoc wireless networks called *IBSS* (Independent Basic Service Set), and the Mac OS X AirPort software complies with IBSS. (Version 1.3 and later of the AirPort software used with Mac OS 9 also complies with IBSS.)

Computers connected to an ad hoc wireless network can share files and participate in multiplayer games. They can also access multiuser databases and use other software designed for multiple users.

An ad hoc wireless network does not provide shared Internet access unless one of the computers connected to this network also has an Internet connection and runs Internet gateway software that shares this Internet connection. For example, the AirPort base station software included with AirPort cards is an Internet gateway.

The Internet gateway software can also connect the ad hoc AirPort network to an Ethernet network. This connection enables computers on the wireless network to communicate with computers on the wired network. Of course, the computer that's running the Internet gateway software must be connected to both the AirPort network and the Ethernet network.

To create a computer-to-computer network, follow these steps:

1. **Open the Internet Connect application and choose AirPort from the Configuration pop-up menu.**

2. **Choose Create Network from the Network pop-up menu.** A dialog appears, as shown in Figure 18-1.

Figure 18-1: Create an ad hoc wireless network from any Mac with an AirPort card.

3. **In the dialog, enter a name and a password, change the channel as needed, and click OK.** You must enter a name, but a password is optional. If you leave the password blank, any computer with an AirPort card (or other IEEE 802.11b card) is able to join the network. The network itself has no security, although services on the network may provide their own security. For example, file sharing has security measures, as explained in Chapter 19.

   You may need to change the Channel setting if there are other wireless networks in the vicinity. Each wireless network listed in the Network pop-up menu should use a different channel. When two channels share the same channel, their performance decreases. Because adjacent channels actually overlap, you should leave two unused channel numbers between each used channel for best network performance. Also, because 2.4-GHz cordless telephones use the same frequency range as 802.11b wireless Ethernet devices, they can interfere if they are on the same or a similar channel.

Tip

You can create a computer-to-computer network by using the AirPort status icon in the menu bar. Click this icon to display its menu and choose Create Network from this menu. In the dialog that appears, which is similar to the one shown in Figure 18-1, enter a name, password, and channel number.

Joining an AirPort network

Any Mac with an AirPort card and Mac OS X can join a computer-to-computer AirPort network that's created by another Mac in the vicinity. An AirPort-equipped Mac can also join a network created by an AirPort base station. All available AirPort networks are listed in the Internet Connect application.

Note

An AirPort-equipped Mac with Mac OS X should also be able to join an ad hoc wireless network created by a computer with a wireless card that meets the IBSS standard. Available IBSS wireless networks should be listed together with AirPort networks in the Internet Connect application.

After you have joined an AirPort network, you don't have to rejoin after waking your Mac from sleep, logging out, restarting, or starting up. Although this is convenient, it also poses a security risk. Anyone who logs in after you — even if you restart or shut down — gets on the AirPort network you joined without having to enter the network password (if it has one).

To join an AirPort network, follow these steps:

1. **Open the Internet Connect application and choose AirPort from the Configuration pop-up menu.**

2. **Choose an AirPort network from the Network pop-up menu.**

    If you want to join a *closed network* (a network whose name does not appear in the Network pop-up menu), do the following:

    1. **Choose Other from the Network pop-up menu.**

    2. **Type the network's exact name and password in the dialog that appears.** If the network doesn't have a password, leave the password text box empty.

Tip

You can join an AirPort network (or other IBSS wireless network) by using the AirPort status icon in the menu bar. Just click the icon to display its menu and choose a network from this menu. To join a closed network, choose Other from the AirPort status icon's menu.

Leaving an AirPort network

You can leave an AirPort network by doing any of the following:

✦ Joining another AirPort network.

✦ Turning off the AirPort card as described at the end of this section.

✦ Turning off the AirPort port configuration as described in the section "Configuring Network Ports" later in this chapter.

If all computers leave a wireless computer-to-computer network, including the computer that created the network, it ceases to exist. A wireless computer-to-computer network exists only as long as at least one computer is connected to it. The one computer that remains connected does not have to be the computer that created the computer-to-computer network.

Tip

If you want to leave an AirPort network without joining another and without turning off AirPort, have Mac OS X try to join a nonexistent AirPort network. Begin by choosing Other from Internet Connect's Network pop-up menu or by choosing Other from the AirPort status icon's menu. Then in the dialog that appears, enter a phony AirPort network name and click OK. An alert appears, telling you that an error occurred. This problem is not serious. The computer is now not connected to any AirPort network.

Monitoring an AirPort network connection

You can monitor the status of an AirPort network connection by doing either of the following:

✦ **Look at the AirPort status icon in the menu bar.** If the AirPort status icon is present in the menu bar, the icon's condition indicates the type of wireless network to which the computer is connected — base station, computer-to-computer, or none — and the signal quality of a connection to a base station. Table 18-2 details the states of the AirPort status icon.

✦ **Use Internet Connect.** In the Internet Connect application, choose AirPort from the Configuration pop-up menu. Look at the Signal Level gauge to see the quality of a connection to a wireless base station. (The Signal Level gauge always indicates full strength for a computer-to-computer connection.) Additional status information may be displayed at the bottom of the AirPort connection window, as shown in Figure 18-2.

	Table 18-2	
	States of the AirPort Status Icon	
Icon	**Status**	
	Connected to a wireless base station. More dark bars mean a stronger signal.	
	Connected to a computer-to-computer wireless network.	
	Not connected to any wireless network.	
	AirPort is turned off.	

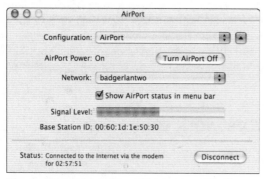

Figure 18-2: The Internet Connect application reports signal strength and other status information in an AirPort connection window.

Turning the AirPort card off and on

Your AirPort card's radio signals may not be allowed, just as cellular telephones may be prohibited, in such places as an airplane or hospital. You can turn off your AirPort card, and later turn it back on, with either of the following methods:

✦ **Use Internet Connect.** In the Internet Connect application, choose New Connection from the File menu to display a new connection window. Then choose AirPort from the Configuration pop-up menu and click the Turn AirPort Off button or the Turn AirPort On button.

✦ **Use the AirPort icon.** If the AirPort status icon is present in the menu bar, click the icon to display its menu. Then choose Turn AirPort Off or Turn AirPort On from this menu.

You may be unable to use either of these methods because the necessary menu items are missing. These conditions occur only if the AirPort port is not active, in which case the AirPort card is automatically turned off. We cover activating and deactivating network ports in "Configuring Network Ports" later in this chapter.

Configuring Network Settings

After making a connection to one of your computer's network ports — Ethernet, AirPort, or modem — you may need to change some settings in the Network pane of System Preferences (Network Preferences for short). The Network Preferences settings affect how a network connection provides access to the Internet, network printers, shared files, and other services mentioned at the beginning of this chapter.

Mac OS X maintains independent settings for each network port. Network Preferences shows the settings for one network port at a time, and you use a pop-up menu to choose the network port whose settings you want to see. Each network port has several groups of related settings. For example, each network port has a group of TCP/IP settings and a group of proxy settings. You see only one group of settings at a time, and you switch between groups by clicking tabs in Network Preferences. Figure 18-3 shows an example of the TCP/IP settings for a network connected to the built-in Ethernet port.

Figure 18-3: Configure network settings in Network Preferences (the Network pane of System Preferences).

This section describes how to configure the Network Preferences settings for Ethernet, AirPort, and modem network ports. Table 18-3 itemizes the tabs that are present in Network Preferences for each of these types of network port.

Note

After changing network settings, click the Apply Now button at the bottom of Network Preferences to retain them. If you forget to click Apply Now, Mac OS X asks you whether you want to save your changes as needed.

Table 18-3
Tabs of Network Preferences

Tab	Purpose	Type of Network Port		
		Ethernet	AirPort	Modem
AirPort	Specifying your preferred AirPort network		✓	
AppleTalk	Many Mac network printers, some file sharing, and some multiuser software	✓	✓	
Modem	Specifying the type of modem you have and some modem options			✓
PPP	Information required for an Internet connection via modem			✓
PPPoE	Information required for some Internet connections via DSL or cable modem		✓	
Proxies	Accessing some Internet sites through a firewall	✓	✓	✓
TCP/IP	Internet access, file sharing, and most other network services	✓	✓	✓

Displaying Network Preferences settings

 You can display the settings for a particular network port by doing these steps:

1. **Display Network Preferences, as previously shown in Figure 18-3.** Do one of the following:

   • Choose Apple➪Location➪Network Preferences.

   • If you can see the Network button in the System Preferences toolbar, click this button.

   • If the active application is System Preferences, choose View➪Network.

2. **Verify the network location.** Look at the Location pop-up menu near the top of Network Preferences. If this pop-up menu lists more than one network location, choose the network location whose network port configurations you want to see. You can find information on working with network locations later in this chapter.

3. **Choose the network port configuration whose settings you want to see.** Choose the port configuration from the Configure pop-up menu in Network Preferences.

Unlocking Network Preferences settings

 If Network Preferences settings are locked — the lock button at the bottom of the window looks locked and the settings are dim — you can review the settings, but you must unlock them to make changes. The settings are normally locked when you are logged in as a user who can't administer Mac OS X.

To unlock the Network Preferences settings, follow these steps:

1. **Obtain the name and password of an administrator user account.** (The first user account created for your computer is an administrator account.)

2. **In Network Preferences, click the lock button.**

3. **In the dialog that appears, enter an administrator's name and password.**

4. **Click OK.** If you entered a valid name and the correct password, you return to Network Preferences with all settings unlocked.

Configuring AirPort settings

Clicking the AirPort tab in Network Preferences reveals settings for your preferred AirPort network and a setting for showing the AirPort status icon in the menu bar. Specifying a preferred AirPort network is most convenient if you create multiple network locations, because you can set a different preferred AirPort network for each location. When you switch network locations, Mac OS X automatically joins the preferred AirPort network for the newly selected location. (We explain how to use network locations later in this chapter.) Figure 18-4 shows the AirPort settings in Network Preferences.

Setting a preferred AirPort network

To set a preferred AirPort network for the current location, simply enter the name of the AirPort network and its password in the text boxes provided. You can also click the triangle next to the Network text box to see a list of known AirPort networks; click a listed network to enter its name. Click the Apply Now button to save your changes. Mac OS X attempts to join the preferred AirPort network. If the network is not available or you make a typographical error, Mac OS X displays an error message and may turn off the AirPort card.

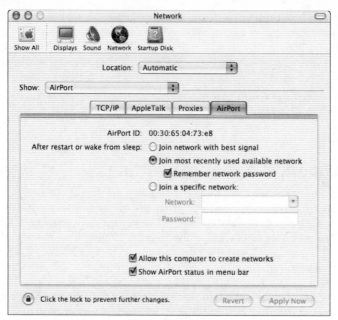

Figure 18-4: AirPort settings determine which network
Mac OS X joins automatically and whether the AirPort
status icon appears in the menu bar.

Showing the AirPort status icon

To show the AirPort status icon or hide it if it is already showing, select the aptly
named checkbox below the preferred network settings. You see the effect of selecting this checkbox immediately. If the AirPort status icon is hidden and you select
this checkbox, the AirPort status icon appears to the left of other icons on the right
side of the menu bar.

Tip   You can move the AirPort status icon by pressing the ⌘ key and dragging the icon.
Drag the icon left or right to change its position relative to other icons on the right
side of the menu bar. Drag the icon off the menu bar to make it vanish in a puff of
smoke.

Configuring TCP/IP settings

The settings in the TCP/IP tab of Network Preferences affect access to e-mail, the
Web, file sharing, and many other Internet and network services. Each network port
has its own TCP/IP settings. Figure 18-5 shows an example of an Ethernet port's
TCP/IP settings.

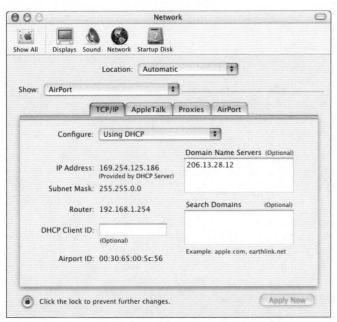

Figure 18-5: TCP/IP settings affect Internet access, file sharing, and many other network services that a network connection provides.

Note The most important TCP/IP settings for the network connection you use to access the Internet are normally configured when you first set up Mac OS X after installing it (or after first using a computer with Mac OS X already installed). You need to reconfigure these settings in the TCP/IP tab of Network Preferences if you change your Internet provider, want to access the Internet through a different network connection, or can't access the Internet.

TCP/IP settings are rather arcane, but you don't need to figure out what to enter on your own. You can ask an expert, such as your Internet provider or your local network administrator, for the following information and then enter it in the TCP/IP tab of Network Preferences:

✦ **Configure.** The method for obtaining some of the other TCP/IP settings for the network connection, such as Manually, Using PPP, Using DHCP, Using DHCP with a fixed IP address, or Using BOOTP.

✦ **DHCP client ID.** May be required by your Internet provider to authorize access to your account, especially if you have a cable modem. This setting is present only when the Configure method includes DHCP.

✦ **IP Address.** The numerical address for the network connection. This address is a set of four numbers separated by periods, such as 17.254.0.91. This setting is provided automatically by some Configure methods.

✦ **Subnet Mask.** Works in tandem with the IP address.

✦ **Router.** The IP address of a machine that connects your local network to other networks or the Internet. This setting can be changed only when the Configure method is Manually. Leave this setting blank if your network has no router or gateway.

✦ **Domain Name Servers.** One or more IP addresses of computers that translate alphabetic addresses, such as www.apple.com to IP addresses. Put each address on a separate line. This setting is provided automatically by some Configure methods. Domain Name Servers is usually abbreviated DNS.

✦ **Search Domains.** One or more domain names, such as nps.gov or berkeley.edu that Mac OS X uses to resolve a partial Internet or network address. For example, if Search Domains contains apple.com, then Mac OS X resolves the partial Internet address www as www.apple.com, livepage becomes livepage.apple.com, store becomes store.apple.com, developer becomes developer.apple.com, and so forth.

Configuring AppleTalk settings

If you're going to use a network printer, you may need to set up the AppleTalk networking protocol, because most printers use AppleTalk to communicate with Macs over a network. Some file servers and file sharing computers also use AppleTalk. In addition, AppleTalk may be required by some multiuser applications, such as a database application, but most applications now use TCP/IP instead of AppleTalk. You set up AppleTalk separately for Mac OS X applications and Classic applications.

Configuring AppleTalk for Mac OS X applications

You set up AppleTalk for Mac OS X applications by making it active in the AppleTalk tab of Network Preferences. The AppleTalk tab is present for both Ethernet and AirPort networks. Therefore you can make AppleTalk active independently for these two types of networks. You should make AppleTalk active for each network port that provides access to network services that require AppleTalk. For example, if an AppleTalk network printer is connected to your Ethernet network, make AppleTalk active for the Ethernet port. Figure 18-6 shows an example of the AppleTalk settings in Network Preferences.

Note   AppleTalk can only be active for one network port at a time—you can't enable AppleTalk for both the Built-In Ethernet and Airport network port configurations at the same time.

Assigning IP Addresses

Your computer may have a public IP address or a private IP address. If it is a *public IP address*, computers on the Internet can contact your computer. With a *private IP address*, computers on the Internet cannot contact your computer. Computers on a local network contact each other with private IP addresses or public IP addresses, whichever they have.

You can tell by looking at an IP address whether it is public or private. The following ranges of IP addresses are set aside for private networks:

✦ 192.168.0.0 through 192.168.255.255

✦ 172.16.0.0 through 172.31.255.255

✦ 10.0.0.0 through 10.255.255.255

✦ 169.254.0.0 through 169.254.254.255 (these are not officially private but are private in effect)

IP addresses outside these ranges are public IP addresses.

Your computer's IP address is private or public, and it may also be dynamic or static. A *dynamic IP address* may change each time you begin an Internet session or each time your computer starts up. A *static IP address* doesn't change. Your computer probably has a dynamic IP address if it connects to the Internet via modem or DSL with PPPoE. Some cable modem connections also provide a dynamic IP address.

A computer on a local network, Ethernet or AirPort, may get an IP address from a DHCP server on the local network each time the computer starts up. The IP address could be different each time, so it is a dynamic IP address. (The *D* in DHCP stands for Dynamic.) The AirPort base station includes a DHCP server, as do many Internet gateway and router products.

Having a dynamic IP address makes your computer hard for other computers to find, which means that your network services are hard to find. It's like a business whose phone number changes every day.

If you're setting up a small network and want to assign all your computers private static IP addresses, give each computer a different address in the 192.168.x.y series. Make *x* the same number for every computer, and make *y* different for each computer. For example, give your computers the addresses 192.168.7.1, 192.168.7.2, 192.168.7.3, and so on. When you manually enter the IP address for each computer, also enter a subnet mask of 255.255.255.0.

If you want a public IP address for each computer on your network, contact your Internet provider. You can't pick public IP addresses yourself because they may already be in use. In addition, your ISP must set up its Internet routing equipment to handle your IP address.

If your computer is connected to a network that's divided into multiple AppleTalk zones, the AppleTalk tab of Network Preferences also specifies the zone in which your computer resides. If your computer is connected to a network with only one zone, you won't have any zones from which to choose.

You should leave the Configure setting at Automatically unless you are an AppleTalk expert. If you are an expert, you know how to set the AppleTalk Node ID and Network ID, which are the settings that appear when you change the Configure setting to Manually.

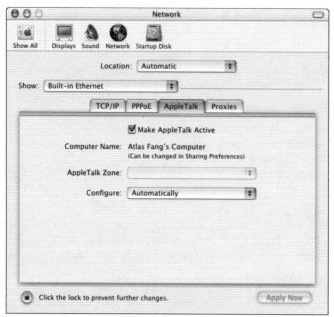

Figure 18-6: Set up AppleTalk for Mac OS X applications in the AppleTalk tab of Network Preferences.

Configuring AppleTalk for Classic applications

The AppleTalk settings in Network Preferences don't apply to Classic applications. In the Classic environment, AppleTalk can't be active on more than one network port concurrently. You choose a port for Classic AppleTalk by using the Connect Via pop-up menu in the AppleTalk control panel. All Classic applications use the chosen port to access every network service that requires AppleTalk, such as printing to an AppleTalk network printer. If the Connect Via setting in your AppleTalk control panel is static text instead of a pop-up menu, someone has locked this setting in the control panel's Administration mode (as described shortly). Figure 18-7 shows an example of the AppleTalk control panel.

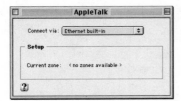

Figure 18-7: Set up AppleTalk for Classic applications in the AppleTalk control panel.

Note The Connect Via pop-up menu in the AppleTalk control panel may identify AirPort as Ethernet Slot 1. In this case, you set Classic AppleTalk to AirPort by choosing Ethernet Slot 1 from the Connect Via pop-up menu. (AirPort is actually a wireless form of Ethernet.)

If you change the connection port in the AppleTalk control panel, the AppleTalk services you were using may become unavailable. For example, an AppleTalk printer that is available via Ethernet may be unavailable via AirPort. When you close the AppleTalk control panel after changing the connection port, an alert asks if you want to save the change even though doing so may interrupt AppleTalk services. (Changing the connection port in the AppleTalk control panel does not affect AppleTalk services for Mac OS X applications or TCP/IP services for any applications.)

If your network has multiple AppleTalk zones, the AppleTalk control panel specifies which zone your computer is in. If your network is not divided into zones, the AppleTalk control panel specifies "no zones available."

You can see more settings or fewer settings in the AppleTalk control panel by changing the user mode. You have a choice of three modes: Basic, Advanced, and Administration. The Advanced and Administration modes show more settings than the Basic mode. In Administration mode, each setting can be locked so that it can't be changed in the Basic or Advanced mode. To change the user mode, choose Edit⇨User Mode and select the mode in the dialog that appears. If you select Administration mode, you can set a password that restricts future access to Administration mode.

Configuring PPPoE settings

If your computer connects to the Internet via DSL or cable modem, your Internet provider may require that you use PPPoE to start each Internet session. You can enter your account name, password, and other information by clicking the PPPoE tab in Network Preferences. If the Connect Using PPPoE option is selected, Network Preferences displays a PPPoE Options button, and clicking this button displays a dialog in which you can set options that affect the PPPoE session. Figure 18-8 shows the PPPoE settings in Network Preferences, and Figure 18-9 shows the additional settings in the PPPoE Options dialog.

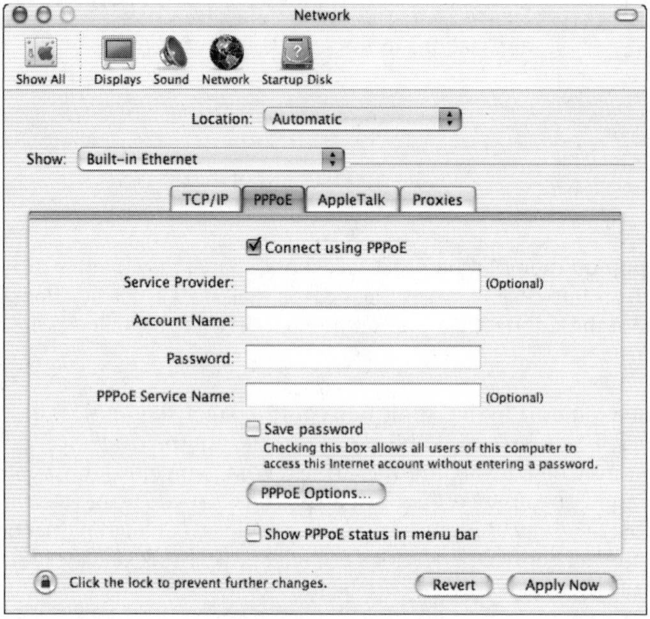

Figure 18-8: PPPoE settings are required by some DSL and cable modem Internet providers.

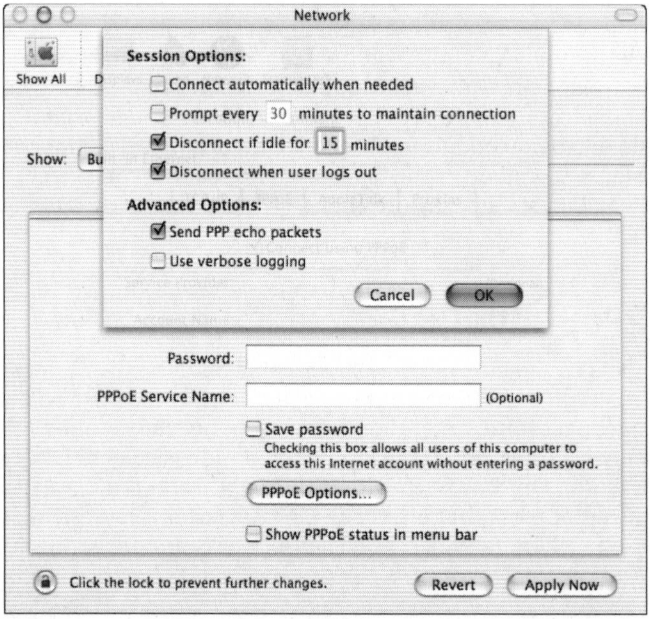

Figure 18-9: PPPoE options determine how a session gets connected, disconnected, and logged.

Configuring the PPPoE Options dialog

The settings in the PPPoE Options dialog have the following effects:

✦ **Connect automatically when needed.** Starts a PPPoE session when an application attempts to access the Internet. This attempt may actually occur some time after the application starts.

✦ **Prompt every *x* minutes to maintain connection.** A dialog appears periodically asking if you want to stay connected, and ends the PPPoE session if no one responds to the dialog.

✦ **Disconnect if idle for *x* minutes.** Automatically stops the PPPoE session if no Internet activity occurs on the PPPoE connection during the specified time interval.

✦ **Disconnect when user logs out.** Automatically stops the PPPoE session when you log out of Mac OS X, so the next person to log in can't inherit your PPPoE session.

✦ **Send PPP echo packets.** This option makes Mac OS X periodically ask your Internet provider's computer to respond and ends the PPPoE session if your Internet provider's computer stops responding. If your Internet provider doesn't support PPP echoing, then turning on this option may cause your PPPoE sessions to end prematurely.

✦ **Use verbose logging.** Creates a detailed log for troubleshooting. A detailed log uses more disk space.

Showing the PPPoE status icon

You can show or hide the PPPoE status icon in the menu bar by selecting or deselecting the option labeled "Show PPPoE status in menu bar." You see the effect of changing this setting immediately. If the PPPoE status icon is hidden and you click this checkbox, the PPPoE status icon appears to the left of other icons on the right side of the menu bar. You can use the PPPoE icon to connect to the Internet, disconnect from the Internet, and monitor the connection status, as described in Chapter 6.

Tip

You can move the PPPoE status icon by pressing the ⌘ key and dragging the icon. Drag the icon left or right to change its position relative to other icons on the right side of the menu bar. Drag the icon off the menu bar to make it vanish in a puff of smoke.

Configuring Proxies settings

If your computer connects to a local network that is protected from the Internet by a firewall, you may need to configure the Proxies settings in Network Preferences. Click the Proxies tab to specify *proxy servers,* which some firewalls use as buffers between a local network and the Internet for privacy, security, and speed. If you do enter proxy server information, you can bypass the proxy servers for specific host computers and network domains that you list. For example, may want to bypass proxy servers to access Web sites on your local network. You can also turn on Passive FTP mode, which may be necessary to access some FTP sites through your firewall. A network with proxy servers almost certainly has a network administrator who can tell you how to configure the Proxies settings. You probably can ignore these settings if you can access Web pages, FTP sites, QuickTime streaming video, and other Internet services. Figure 18-10 shows the Proxies settings in Network Preferences.

Figure 18-10: Click the Proxies tab in Network Preferences to set up Internet access through a firewall that has proxy servers.

Configuring PPP settings

Click the PPP tab in Network Preferences to configure a modem or ISDN connection to the Internet or a remote network. You can enter the name and password required for connecting to your Internet account, the telephone number that your computer must call to get connected, an alternate telephone number to call if the main number is busy, and the name of the service provider. To display a dialog of additional options that affect a PPP session, click the PPP Options button. Figure 18-11 shows the PPP settings in Network Preferences, and Figure 18-12 shows the additional settings in the PPP Options dialog.

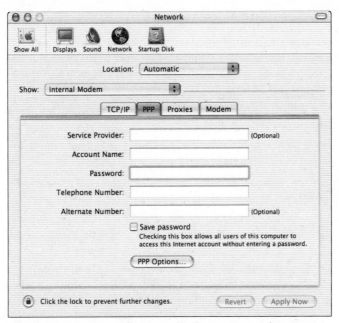

Figure 18-11: PPP settings specify the contact and account information for a modem or ISDN connection to the Internet or a remote network.

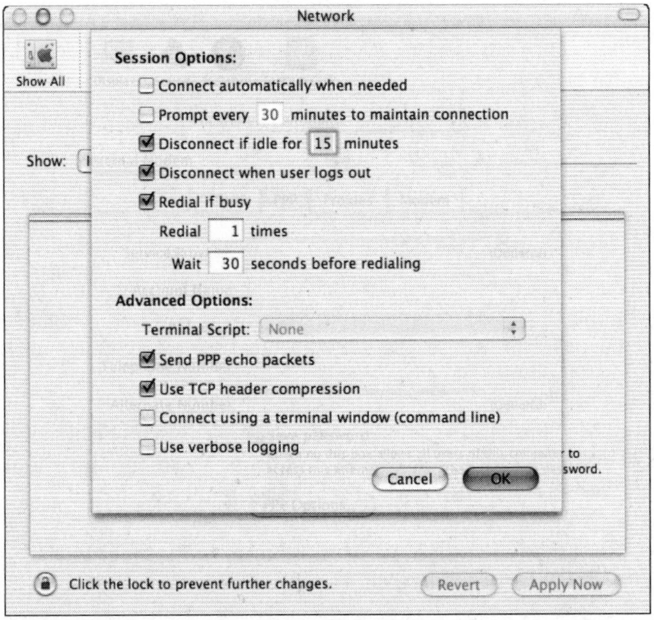

Figure 18-12: PPP options determine how a session gets connected, disconnected, verified, and logged.

The PPP options have the following effects:

✦ **Connect automatically when needed.** Starts a PPP session when an application attempts to access the Internet. This attempt may actually occur some time after the application starts.

✦ **Prompt every *x* minutes to maintain connection.** Causes a dialog to appear periodically, asking if you want to stay connected, and ends the PPP session if no one responds to the dialog.

✦ **Disconnect if idle for *x* minutes.** Automatically stops the PPP session if no Internet activity occurs on the PPP connection during the specified time interval.

✦ **Disconnect when user logs out.** Automatically stops the PPP session when you log out of Mac OS X, so the next person to log in can't inherit your PPP session.

✦ **Redial if busy.** Specifies how to redial the service provider's telephone number if it is busy.

✦ **Send PPP echo packets.** Makes Mac OS X periodically ask your Internet provider's computer to respond and ends the PPP session if your Internet provider's computer stops responding. If your Internet provider doesn't support PPP echoing, then turning on this option may cause your PPP sessions to end prematurely.

✦ **Use TCP header compression.** Makes Mac OS X try to compress TCP header information for efficiency. Leave this option turned on because the service provider can refuse header compression without causing a problem.

✦ **Connect using a terminal window (command line).** Causes a terminal window to appear while you're connecting so that you can type commands and enter requested information for your service provider.

✦ **Use verbose logging.** Creates a detailed connection log for troubleshooting purposes. A detailed log uses more disk space.

Configuring Modem settings

Click the Modem tab of Network Preferences to identify the type of modem you have and to set some dialing options. These settings are used when making a PPP connection to the Internet or a remote network. Figure 18-13 is an example of the Modem settings in Network Preferences.

You can show or hide the Modem status icon in the menu bar by selecting or deselecting the option labeled "Show Modem status in menu bar." You see the effect of changing this setting immediately. If the Modem status icon is hidden and you select this checkbox, the Modem status icon appears to the left of other icons on the right side of the menu bar. You can use the Modem icon to connect to the Internet, disconnect from the Internet, and monitor the connection status, as described in Chapter 6.

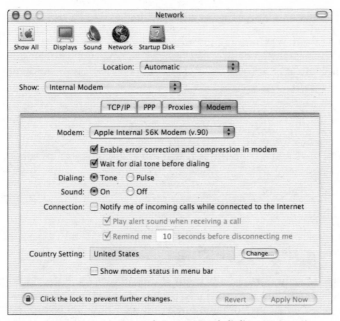

Figure 18-13: Set your modem type and dialing options in the Modem tab of Network Preferences.

Tip

You can move the Modem status icon by pressing the ⌘ key and dragging the icon. Drag the icon left or right to change its position relative to other icons on the right side of the menu bar. Drag the icon off the menu bar to make it vanish in a puff of smoke.

Configuring Network Ports

Mac OS X lets your computer have more than one network port active at the same time. Therefore, your computer can have concurrently active configurations of AirPort, Ethernet, and modem connections. You can even have multiple configurations of the same port, all of them operating in conjunction.

Multiple port configurations can provide overlapping services. On a PowerBook that you use in different locations, Ethernet can provide fast Internet access from the local network at your desk. AirPort can provide wireless Internet access when you're in meetings. A modem can provide Internet access when you're at home. On this PowerBook, the Ethernet, AirPort, and modem configurations are active all the time, and Mac OS X knows which configuration to use for Internet access.

Somehow, Mac OS X has to determine which of the available port configurations to use when you start to check your e-mail, browse the Web, print, or use some other network service. Mac OS X has a simple method of prioritizing port configurations.

It goes down a list of available port configurations, trying each in turn, and uses the first one that works. By default, Mac OS X tries port configurations in the following order: internal modem, built-in Ethernet, and AirPort.

You can change settings in Network Preferences that affect which port configuration Mac OS X uses. You can

✦ Change the priority of port configurations

✦ Turn each port configuration on or off

✦ Create additional port configurations that use the same ports as existing configurations

✦ Rename port configurations

✦ Delete port configurations

Displaying network port settings

To display the settings that affect which port configuration Mac OS X uses, choose Network Port Configurations from the Show pop-up menu in Network Preferences. If the Location pop-up menu lists more than one network location, make sure that it is set to the one whose port configurations you want to see. Figure 18-14 shows an example of Network Port Configurations settings.

Figure 18-14: Change the Network Port Configurations settings in Network Preferences to affect which port configuration Mac OS X uses.

Changing the priority of port configurations

The Network Port Configurations settings of Network Preferences include a list of all port configurations. This list shows the order in which Mac OS X tries the port configurations. You can give a port configuration a higher priority by dragging it higher on the list. You can give a port configuration a lower priority by dragging it lower on the list.

Tip   Drag the port configuration you use most often to the top of the Port Configurations list. Now Mac OS X won't waste time checking less-used port configurations.

Turning port configurations on and off

You can turn a port configuration on or off by selecting or clearing the checkbox next to its name in the Port Configurations list. When a port configuration is turned off, Mac OS X doesn't try to use it.

Tip   Turn off port configurations that you never use so that Mac OS X won't waste time checking them.

Creating port configurations

You can create additional port configurations by making new ones or duplicating existing ones.

✦ **To make a new port configuration:** Click the New button in the Network Port Configurations settings of Network Preferences. In the dialog that appears, enter a name for the new configuration and choose the new configuration's port from the pop-up menu.

✦ **To duplicate a port configuration:** Select a port configuration in the Network Port Configurations settings of Network Preferences and then click the Duplicate button. A dialog appears in which you can edit the name that Mac OS X proposes for the duplicate port configuration.

When you create a new or duplicate port configuration, Mac OS X puts it at the bottom of the list. You can drag it higher to raise its priority.

Renaming port configurations

You can rename any port configuration listed in the Network Port Configurations settings of Network Preferences by following these steps:

1. **Double-click the port configuration to select its name for editing.** You know that the name is selected when you see a heavy border around it.

2. **Edit the name as you like**.

3. **While a name is selected for editing, press Return to select the next name on the list.**

4. **Click anywhere outside the selected name to end editing.**

Deleting port configurations

You can delete a port configuration by selecting it in the Network Port Configurations settings of Network Preferences and then clicking the Delete button. An alert appears asking you to confirm that you really want to delete the port configuration.

Working with Network Locations

You may find that you need to make regular changes to settings in Network Preferences. For example, you may use your computer in locations that need to have different network settings. Every time you change locations, you have to remember what changes to make and then click and type repetitiously to make the changes. You can simplify the process of changing locations by letting Mac OS X do the repetitive part.

You can create *network locations* in Network Preferences to facilitate making regular changes to network settings. Each network location is simply one specific arrangement of all the various Network Preferences settings. When you create a network location, you give it a name. The names of network locations appear in the Apple menu and in the Location pop-up menu at the top of Network Preferences. In fact, the network locations appear in these places for all users of your computer. (User accounts don't have private network locations.)

After you create a network location for a particular arrangement of network settings, you can quickly change to that arrangement by choosing the network location by name from the Apple menu. This method of reconfiguring the Network Preferences settings is much quicker and simpler than changing all the individual settings involved in the reconfiguration.

Here are some situations in which you may want to create network locations:

✦ You use the computer in more than one place, such as at home and at work or school, with different port configurations at each place.

✦ You connect to different networks from the same port, such as a modem connection to your Internet provider and a modem connection to your network at work or school.

✦ You set different port priorities to determine which port configuration your computer will use for network services that are available on more than one network port, such as file sharing on Ethernet or AirPort.

You use the Location pop-up menu near the top of Network Preferences to create, rename, and delete network locations. You use this same pop-up menu to select a network location that you need to reconfigure. You can also use this pop-up menu to switch network locations, but the Apple menu is usually more convenient. (Earlier in this chapter, we explain several ways to display Network Preferences.)

Creating network locations

You can create additional network locations by making new ones or duplicating existing ones.

Making a new network location

To make a new network location, follow these steps:

1. **Choose New Location from the Location pop-up menu in Network Preferences.**

2. **In the dialog that appears, enter a name for the new location and then click OK.**

3. **Click the Apply Now button at the bottom of Network Preferences to retain the new location.** All port configurations for the new location have default settings.

Duplicating a network location

To duplicate a network location, do the following:

1. **Choose Edit Location from the Location pop-up menu.** A dialog appears with some buttons and a list of all existing network locations. Figure 18-15 shows this dialog.

2. **Select the network location that you want to duplicate and then click the Duplicate button.** The new network location appears in the list with the same name as the original plus the suffix Copy, and the entire name is selected so that you can change it.

3. **Change the name as you like and then click the Done button.**

4. **Click the Apply Now button at the bottom of Network Preferences to retain the duplicate location.** All port configurations for the duplicate location have the same settings as the original location.

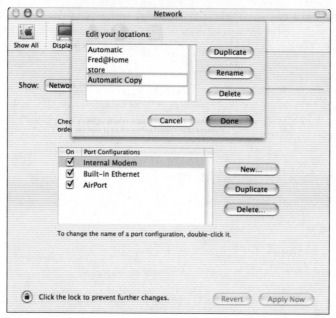

Figure 18-15: The dialog for duplicating, renaming, and deleting network locations appears when you choose Edit Location from the Location pop-up menu in Network Preferences.

Switching network locations

We already revealed the easiest way to switch to another network location, which is to use the Apple menu. Specifically, you choose the network location by name from the Location submenu in the Apple menu.

You can also switch the network location by choosing the one you want from the Location pop-up menu in Network Preferences, but you must click the Apply Now button at the bottom of Network Preferences to make the switch take effect.

Reconfiguring network locations

You can change any of the settings for a network location. To change the settings, use these steps:

1. **Choose the network location from the Location pop-up menu in Network Preferences.**

2. **Change settings as needed for each network port configuration.** Choose each port configuration in turn from the Show pop-up menu in Network Preferences. For each port configuration, click each available tab and change

settings as needed. (If you need guidance on how to configure the various network settings, refer to the information earlier in this chapter.)

3. **After you finish making changes, click Apply Now at the bottom of Network Preferences to save the changes.**

Renaming network locations

To rename a network location, do the following:

1. **Choose Edit Location from the Location pop-up menu in Network Preferences.** A dialog appears with some buttons and a list of all existing network locations. This dialog was previously shown in Figure 18-15.

2. **Select the location whose name you want to change and then click the Rename button.** Alternatively, simply double-click the location name.

3. **Change the name as you like and then click the Done button.**

4. **Click the Apply Now button at the bottom of Network Preferences to make the new name permanent.**

Deleting network locations

You can delete a network location by following these steps:

1. **Choose Edit Location from the Location pop-up menu in Network Preferences.** A dialog appears with some buttons and a list of all existing network locations. This dialog was previously shown in Figure 18-15.

2. **Select the location you want to delete and then click the Delete button.**

3. **In the alert that appears, click Delete to confirm that you really want to delete the network location.** If you change your mind about deleting, you can click Cancel instead. Whether you click Delete or Cancel, you return to the dialog for editing locations.

4. **Click Done to dismiss the dialog.**

5. **Click the Apply Now button at the bottom of Network Preferences to make the currently selected network location take effect.**

Setting up an AirPort Base Station

The computer-to-computer AirPort network we described earlier has some limitations. For one, it doesn't inherently let you share an Internet connection. What's more, a computer-to-computer network is transitory. It ceases to exist after all computers have left it.

An AirPort base station has neither of these limitations. It lets all AirPort-equipped computers share an Internet connection, share files, participate in multiplayer games, and use other multiuser software. Additionally, it can bridge a wireless network and an Ethernet network, which adds many potential benefits. Wireless computers gain access to network services on the Ethernet network, such as network printers. Computers on the Ethernet network gain access to services on the wireless network, such as the shared Internet connection. Computers on either network can share files, participate in multiplayer games, and use other multiuser software with computers on the other network. An AirPort base station has all the benefits of a computer-to-computer wireless network and more.

There are two types of AirPort base station. One is a freestanding device made by Apple (part number M7601LL/B). The other AirPort base station is a Mac, either desktop or laptop, connected to the Internet by Ethernet or modem and sharing its Internet connection to other AirPort-equipped computers.

Setting up an AirPort base station device

An AirPort base station device can connect to the Internet via its built-in 56K modem or its Ethernet port. The Ethernet port enables the AirPort base station to connect via a cable modem, DSL modem, or a local network that has an Internet gateway or router. The AirPort base station shares its one Internet connection with up to ten wireless computers concurrently. The computers must have AirPort cards or other wireless equipment that is compatible with the 802.11b standard. For example, an iBook or PowerBook G4 with an AirPort card can access the Internet completely untethered. Adding an AirPort base station to your wireless network is the easiest and most efficient way to provide wireless Internet access, but it is not the cheapest way.

Preparing for base station setup

When you set up an AirPort base station, you need to know all the details about how your base station will connect to the Internet. The details you need to know depend on how the base station connects to the Internet, as follows:

✦ **Base station internal modem.** You must know the name and password for your ISP account, ISP phone number, country, and dialing method (tone or pulse). You also specify whether to dial automatically as needed and how long to wait idle before disconnecting automatically. Additionally, you can enter one or more IP addresses of name servers (also known as DNS addresses) and default domain names.

✦ **Local network (Ethernet).** For a manual configuration, you need to know the base station's IP address and subnet mask on the local network. You also need to know the IP address of your network's Internet router or gateway. For a DHCP configuration, you need to know the DHCP client ID, if the DHCP server requires one. For either type of configuration, you can also enter one or more IP addresses of name servers (also known as DNS addresses) and default domain names.

✦ **Cable modem or DSL using DHCP or a static IP address.** For a manual configuration, you need to know the static IP address, subnet mask, and router IP address assigned by your ISP. For a DHCP configuration, you need to know the DHCP client ID, if your ISP requires one. For either type of configuration, you can also enter one or more IP addresses of name servers (also known as DNS addresses) and default domain names.

✦ **Cable modem or DSL using PPPoE.** You must know the name and password for your ISP account. You also specify whether to connect automatically as needed and how long to wait idle before disconnecting automatically. In addition, you can specify your ISP name and PPPoE service name, and you can enter one or more IP addresses of name servers (also known as DNS addresses) and default domain names.

You can learn the details of a modem, DSL, or cable modem connection from your ISP. You should know the details of a local network connection if you set up your local network. If you didn't set up your own local network, consult the person who set up or administers the network.

Using the AirPort Setup Assistant

With the details about your base station's Internet connection in hand, you are ready to configure the base station settings. You can configure an AirPort base station device by using the AirPort Setup Assistant program that's included with Mac OS X. The Airport Setup Assistant can be found in the Applications/Utilities folder. Proceed as follows:

1. **Plug in the base station's power adapter**. The base station flashes its lights as it starts up, which takes about 30 seconds. The middle light glows white when it is ready. (It's okay if you plugged in the base station ahead of time.)

2. **Make sure that the base station's middle light is glowing white. Then start the AirPort Setup Assistant program and follow the instructions on-screen.** The AirPort Setup Assistant asks you to enter the following information:

   • **Network password.** The Setup Assistant asks for this password only if the base station has been set up previously with a network password.

   • **Base station password.** The Setup Assistant does not ask for this password if the base station has the default password, which is *public*.

   • **Type of network connection.** The base station can connect to the Internet via its built-in modem, DSL, cable modem, or local Ethernet network as described previously. Figure 18-16 illustrates this stage of the AirPort Setup Assistant.

- **Internet connection details.** The details you enter depend on the type of Internet connection, as described previously.

- **Network name and password.** You give the base station network a name and password. The password is optional but strongly recommended.

- **Base station password.** The base station can use the same password as its network or you can give it a different password. A person must know this password to change base station settings.

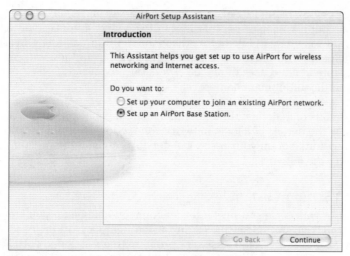

Figure 18-16: The AirPort Setup Assistant leads you through setting up a base station device.

Note   Apple has released two versions of the Airport Base Stations: the first version was graphite (gray) with three multicolored status lights, and the second version is snow (white) with three white status lights. Accordingly, the status is displayed in different ways on the two versions of the base stations. Apple has an article in the Knowledge Base defining the differences in Airport base station light status. A simple way to search the AppleCare Knowledge Base is the Apple channel in Sherlock, which is covered in Chapter 7.

Setting up AirPort base station software

As an inexpensive alternative to the freestanding Airport base station, you can set up a software base station on one Mac that has an AirPort card. The base station software can function in the background while someone uses the computer for other tasks at the same time. After you have installed and configured the AirPort base station software, the computer provides much the same capabilities as the freestanding base station. For example, a Power Mac G4 running the base station software can provide wireless Internet connection and can interconnect wireless Macs and computers on a wired network.

A software base station is attractive because you don't have to buy a separate piece of equipment, but it has several downsides. For one, a software base station is more complicated to set up. In addition, the Mac on which the software base station is running must be left on so that other wireless Macs can connect to the Internet and to computers on the interconnected wired network (if any). The software base station also uses some of the memory and processing power of the Mac on which it's running, reducing this Mac's performance on other tasks. Lastly, you probably won't be able to reposition the software base station's host Mac to optimize the wireless network signal as easily as you can move the small AirPort base station device.

To set up AirPort base station software, follow these steps:

1. **Open System Preferences and then open the Sharing pane.**

2. **Click on the Internet tab.** The Internet tab will display as shown in Figure 18-17.

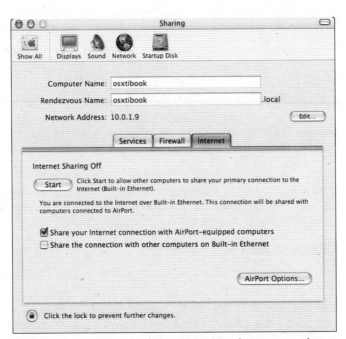

Figure 18-17: Set up your Airport-equipped Mac as a software AirPort base station in the Internet tab of the Sharing pane of System Preferences.

3. **Choose to share your Internet connection either with other AirPort-equipped computers or with other Ethernet-connected computers.**

4. **Click the Start button.** Your Mac is now acting as an Airport base station.

Administering an AirPort base station

Both the AirPort base station device and the Airport base station software have advanced features that the AirPort Setup Assistant application doesn't set up. These features include the ability to do the following:

✦ Provide Internet access to computers on an Ethernet network in addition to wireless computers.

✦ Turn on a DHCP server to automatically assign private IP addresses to computers on your AirPort network and optionally on an Ethernet network.

✦ Change individual Internet connection settings, such as the phone number for a modem connection.

✦ Allow computers on the Internet to penetrate your local network to access Web sites, FTP sites, and other services hosted by computers on your network.

✦ Limit base station access to computers with specific AirPort cards so that unauthorized computers can't join the base station's wireless network.

✦ Change individual base station settings such as the network password, channel number, and encryption.

Administering an AirPort base station device

To configure the advanced features of a base station device, you use the AirPort Admin Utility program. A Mac OS X version of this program is included with Mac OS X 10.2. Figure 18-18 shows some of the settings you can change with the AirPort Utility program.

You can find instructions for setting up the advanced features of a base station device by looking in the AirPort Help that's available in the Help Viewer application. To see these instructions, do the following:

1. **Open the AirPort Admin Utility application.**

2. **Choose Help⇨AirPort Help.** The Help Viewer opens and displays links to several categories of AirPort Help.

3. **In the text box at the top of the Help Viewer window, type** AirPort Admin Utility, **and then click Ask.** AirPort Help displays a list of articles that describe how to use the AirPort Admin Utility.

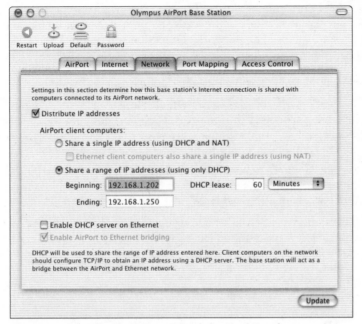

Figure 18-18: Change many settings on an AirPort base station device by using the AirPort Admin Utility application.

Summary

Here's what you know about setting up networks after reading this chapter:

✦ Setting up a network makes it possible for your computers to share an Internet connection, share printers, share files, participate in multiplayer games, and use other multiuser software.

✦ Setting up a network connection via modem is a matter of connecting the modem to a telephone jack.

✦ Wiring an Ethernet network involves running a twisted-pair cable from each computer and other network device to a hub or switch.

✦ Establishing an AirPort wireless network involves installing an AirPort card in each computer. Then you can create a computer-to-computer wireless network. An AirPort base station is optional, but allows AirPort-equipped computers to share an Internet connection and to communicate with computers on a wired Ethernet network, if you also have one of these.

✦ After making a network connection — Ethernet, AirPort, or modem — you may need to configure some settings in the Network pane of System Preferences. You configure settings for each network connection separately. Each network connection has several groups of related settings, and you switch between groups by clicking tabs in Network Preferences. The tabs include AirPort, TCP/IP, AppleTalk, PPPoE, Proxies, PPP, and Modem.

✦ The Active Network Ports settings of Network Preferences let you change the priority of network port configurations, turn each port configuration on or off, create additional configurations that use the same ports as existing configurations, rename port configurations, and delete port configurations.

✦ Network locations facilitate making regular changes to network settings. Each network location is one specific arrangement of all network settings. You can switch to any network location by choosing it from the Apple menu.

✦ An AirPort base station can be a freestanding device or software running on an AirPort-equipped Mac. A base station lets all AirPort-equipped computers share an Internet connection, and it can bridge a wireless network and an Ethernet network. You set up either kind of base station with a setup assistant application.

✦   ✦   ✦

Sharing Your Files

Just as you can share books with people who live and work near you, Mac OS X enables you to share files with people whose computers are on the same network as your computer or who can access your IP address across the Internet. You control who can connect to your computer for file sharing, and you determine what other people can do with your shared files.

This chapter explains how to share some of your files with other people on your network or even on the Internet. First, you plan for file sharing and identify your computer on the network. Next, you start the file-sharing feature in Mac OS X. Then you can make files available for sharing and create user accounts for people you want to have greater access to your files. For folders that contain shared files, you can restrict the type of access some people have.

Other people connect to and work with your shared folders and disks by using the same procedures that you use with theirs. Chapter 10 describes how to gain access to shared files on your local network, a remote computer, a remote network connect, or the Internet. If your computer is not already on a network, Chapter 18 explains how to hook your computer up to one.

Using file sharing in a small network allows all or some of the computers on that network to function as both personal computer and file server, saving the cost and space of a dedicated machine functioning as a server.

Planning for File Sharing

The personal file-sharing capabilities of Mac OS X make sharing items across a network surprisingly easy, but not without some cost. This section discusses the capabilities and limitations of Mac OS X file sharing to help you decide in advance whether it meets your needs. The alternative to file sharing is a dedicated, centralized file server.

Distributed or centralized file sharing

Your network can implement file sharing in a distributed or centralized fashion. With distributed file sharing, also known as *peer-to-peer file sharing*, each computer makes files, folders, and disks available to other computers on the network. While your computer shares your files with other computers, you are free to use your computer for other tasks. The price you pay for making files from your computer available does lead to a reduced performance of your computer while other computers are accessing it. In addition, Mac OS X file sharing limits the number of people that can share the same folder or disk at the same time, making file sharing unsuitable for serving files to large numbers of computers.

By contrast, a network with centralized file sharing dedicates one computer (or more) to providing file-sharing services. The file sharing occurs between the centralized computer and the individual computers, not between the individual computers themselves. The dedicated computer runs file server software, such as Apple's Mac OS X Server, enabling the computer to serve files to a large number of other computers. A dedicated file server needs to be fast and needs to have one or more large hard disks. Mac OS X does not include file server software; you must purchase it separately. For example, Mac OS X Server costs $499 for up to 10 simultaneous users.

Although Mac OS X file sharing capabilities are designed for distributed file sharing, you can use file sharing on a dedicated computer to create a file server for a small network. Folders or entire hard disks on that file-server computer can be made available to other computers on the network as described in the remainder of this chapter.

The problem with such a file server is its performance. Mac OS X assumes someone is using the dedicated computer for more than sharing files. As a result, Mac OS reserves more than 50 percent of the dedicated computer's processing power for nonfile sharing tasks and runs the file-sharing activities at a lower priority than non-file sharing tasks.

Mac OS X Server

The newest solution from Apple for centralized serving is Mac OS X Server. This server package, built on the Unix underpinnings of Mac OS X, offers Apple File Services support as well as sharing of many Ethernet-capable PostScript printers. Designed as a full-service Web and Internet server as well as an Apple File Services server, Mac OS X Server offers impressive performance and capabilities. One of those capabilities — NetBoot — actually allows most late-model Macs to start up from the Mac OS X server machine, making it possible for a room full of such Macs to receive their system software and applications from a centralized server. You can choose to boot from a Network Startup volume in the Startup Disk pane of System Preferences.

Centralized disk storage reduces the amount of local disk storage required by each networked computer while providing a way for people who work together to share information. People can store files on the server's disks where other people can open or copy them. Many people can access the server's disks and folders simultaneously, and new files become available to everyone instantly. Unlike the file sharing provided by Mac OS X, no one uses the server's computer to do personal work because it is dedicated to providing network services. Conversely, your computer is not burdened when someone else on the network accesses one of your shared items on the AppleShare server's disks.

A centralized file server is set up and maintained by a trained person called a *network administrator*. Mac OS X Server includes organizational, administrative, and security features to manage file access on the network. The network administrator does not control access to folders and files on the server's disks; that is the responsibility of each person who puts items on the disks.

Mac OS X Server's file server is compatible with Mac OS X file sharing. Use the methods described in this chapter to make your files available for sharing, whether those files are on your computer's hard disk or the file server's hard disks. You access the files on the file server's hard disks by using the methods described in Chapter 4.

The Mac OS X Server software runs on a Macintosh Xserve, Server G4, Power Mac G4, Power Mac G4 Cube, iMac, Macintosh Server G3, or Power Macintosh G3. Mac OS X Server requires 128MB of RAM (256MB recommended).

Guidelines for file sharing

These guidelines and tips for sharing folders and disks help optimize file sharing and help prevent problems:

✦ To share a Write-only folder (a drop box), it must be inside another shared folder that has read permission.

✦ The greater the number of accessed shared folders, the greater the memory and processing demands on your computer. Too many sharing connections slow your system to a crawl.

✦ Check or review any applicable licensing agreements before sharing programs, artwork, or sounds. Often, licensing agreements or copyright laws restrict use of such items to a single computer.

✦ Select a single computer and dedicate it to acting as a file server for the shared information. Create an ordinary user account (not an administrator account) on this computer for everyone to use when connecting for file sharing. Everyone who connects for file sharing with this account's name and password has access to the contents of the account's home folder. This method is often the most efficient way to share numerous files or to share folders with several users simultaneously.

✦ Use a router rather than a hub if your network has a DSL or cable modem connection to the Internet and each network computer has a public IP addressed assigned by your ISP. If you use a hub, network traffic from one machine travels to another machine on your network via your ISP. In addition to upsetting most ISPs, this can result in significant performance degradation. This situation does not occur if the computers on your network have private IP addresses and your network has an Internet gateway that shares a public IP address among the network computers.

Identifying Your Computer

Before your Mac can share files, it requires a network identity. There are two components to a network identity:

✦ **Computer name.** You establish the computer name in the Services tab of the Sharing pane of System Preferences, as shown in Figure 19-1.

✦ **Computer IP address.** The current IP address is also displayed in Sharing Preferences but is established or changed in the Network pane of System Preferences — an Edit button next to the IP address takes you there. When Mac OS X Setup runs the first time you start Mac OS X, you have the opportunity to establish these identity components.

Figure 19-1: Specify your Mac's network identity in Sharing Preferences.

Tip   After you have your settings the way you want them in Sharing Preferences and Network Preferences, you may want to click the lock button to prevent accidental changes. You are asked for your password to unlock the settings if you want to make changes at a later time.

Turning File Sharing On and Off

After you establish your computer's network identity in Sharing Preferences, and Network Preferences if necessary, you are ready to turn on file sharing in the same Sharing Preferences window. You don't need to turn on file sharing to access files from other computers, for example by using the Finder's Go➪Connect to Server command. However, you do need to turn on file sharing to allow users of other network computers to access the shared files on your computer. If some other computer users need to access your shared files via the AppleTalk protocol, you also need to turn on this protocol in Network Preferences.

Sharing with Microsoft Windows

For whatever reasons, far more people use Windows PCs than all other personal computers combined. Because the Windows PC is the lowest common denominator, other operating systems need to be able to coexist — something the Mac operating system has done well for quite some time. Not only can Mac OS X read and write PC-formatted disks, use Windows-format fonts, and share many hardware peripherals with Windows PCs, but it can also share files with Windows PCs. You can also enable SMB/CIFS file sharing by choosing to turn on Windows File Sharing in the Services tab of the Sharing pane of System Preferences.

In Chapter 10 you read that Mac OS X can access shared files on Windows PCs. That's fine, but what if a Windows PC user needs to access shared files on your Mac OS X computer? One solution is to install the PC MACLAN software on the Windows PC. PC MACLAN enables a Windows PC to access any AppleShare file server, and this includes Mac OS X file sharing. The PC MACLAN software is from Miramar Systems (www.miramarsys.com).

Unlike previous versions of Mac OS, simply turning on file sharing does not significantly slow down your Mac OS X computer. You may notice your computer performing more slowly while other computers are opening or copying your shared files. During this activity, your attempts to open, save, or copy files as well as network activities of your own take a bit longer.

Starting file sharing

To turn on file sharing, do the following:

1. **Open the Sharing pane of System Preferences and click the Services tab.** The Sharing pane of System Preferences is shown in Figure 19-1.

2. **Click on Personal File Sharing in the services list.** The item is highlighted in the list box.

3. **Click the Start button that's below the words File Sharing Off in the Sharing Preferences window.** (Refer back to Figure 19-1.) For a few moments, the words above this Start button change to File Sharing Starting Up and then they change to File Sharing On. At that point (File Sharing On), the Start button becomes a Stop button.

Stopping file sharing

If you want to terminate file sharing, do the following:

1. **Open the Sharing pane of System Preferences and click the Services tab.** The Sharing pane of System Preferences is shown in Figure 19-1.

2. **Click the Stop button that's below the words File Sharing On in Sharing Preferences.**

Sharing with Mac OS 9

As a Mac OS X user, you can access shared files on a Mac that's running Mac OS 9 or earlier. (Chapter 10 explains how.) The reverse is also true. Users of Mac OS 9 computers can access the shared files on your Mac OS X computer. To a Mac OS 9 user, a Mac OS X that's set up for file sharing looks like any other file server on the network. A Mac OS 9 user connects to your Mac OS X computer for file sharing by using the Network Browser, the Chooser, an alias, or any other method that connects Mac OS 9 to a file server.

In the Mac OS 9 Network Browser, your Mac OS X computer appears under the Local Network heading. This is the heading for file servers that use the TCP/IP network protocol. Mac OS X normally uses TCP/IP. If your Mac OS X computer is set up to use the AppleTalk protocol as well, the computer also appears under the AppleTalk heading in the Network Browser.

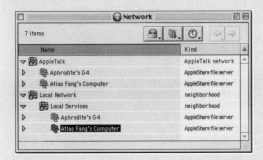

Using the Chooser, a Mac OS 9 user connects to your Mac OS X computer for file sharing by clicking the AppleShare icon on the left. If your Mac OS X computer has AppleTalk turned on in Network Preferences, then your computer's name appears in a list of file servers on the right side of the Chooser. The Mac OS 9 user can connect to your computer by clicking its name in the list. The Mac OS 9 user can connect to your computer via TCP/IP by clicking the Server IP Address button on the right side of the Chooser and entering your computer's IP address or DNS address (such as mycomputer.mydomain.com) in the dialog that appears.

Enabling file sharing via AppleTalk

Mac OS X normally uses the TCP/IP protocol for file-sharing services, but it can also use the AppleTalk protocol simultaneously. If some other computer users need or prefer to use the AppleTalk protocol for file sharing, you can configure Mac OS X to use it. You turn on AppleTalk in the Network pane of System Preferences, as described in Chapter 18.

Identifying Who Can Connect for File Sharing

In Mac OS X, unlike Mac OS 9 and earlier, you do not create users, groups, and passwords for file sharing. Generally, other computer users connect to your Mac OS X computer for file sharing as guests, without supplying a name and password. Guests have limited access to files on your computer. Users who have login accounts on your Mac can access more files if they connect to your Mac OS X computer from another computer, as described in the next section. When these users connect for file sharing, they enter their account names and passwords. In Mac OS X, names and passwords for file sharing are the same as names and passwords for login. A user gets a name and password for file sharing when you create a user account for the person in the Users pane of System Preferences.

Mac OS X automatically puts all administrator users in groups named wheel and admin. All users who have login accounts, including administrators, are automatically members of a group named staff.

Designating Your Shared Items

Inside every user account's home folder is a Public folder, and the Public folder is accessible to any individual who connects to your Mac for file sharing. Within the Public folder, by default, is a Drop Box folder. Any user who can connect to your Mac can place items in the Drop Box but cannot open it. Except for the Drop Box folder, other users can't put items in your Public folder or remove items from it. Your Public folder is normally read-only to other users. They can only open items in your Public folder and copy items from it. If you want items to be shared, place them in your Public folder.

If your computer has multiple user accounts, the Public folders from all their home folders are accessible to anyone who connects to your Mac for file sharing. This includes guests as well as registered users, who connect with a name and password.

Registered users get access to more than Public folders. A registered user connects for file sharing with the name and password of a user account on your Mac, and the registered user gets access to the account's entire home folder.

Caution

A user gains access to your entire hard drive and other volumes by connecting for file sharing as an administrator of your computer. For obvious security reasons, be very careful who you allow to connect to your computer for file sharing as an administrator. Ensure that user accounts created on your computer solely for file sharing purposes are not administrator accounts. For each of these accounts, the option in Users pane of your System Preferences that allows the account to administer Mac OS X on your computer should be turned off.

If you want to share more folders on your computer, you can create login accounts on your computer specifically for file-sharing users. When people connect to your computer for file sharing with one of these accounts, they can access everything in the account's home folder. If you want to put items in this home folder, you must log in using the account name and password. Then you can copy items into the account's home folder. Thereafter, other users can access the items in this home folder by connecting for file sharing with the account's name and password.

If you're familiar with file sharing in Mac OS 9 and earlier, the Mac OS X model seems much more constrained. For example, when using Mac OS 9 you specify which folders you want to share and you specify owners and groups for them. In Mac OS 9, you can also create users and groups who get special file sharing privileges. The Mac OS X sharing model is built atop Unix identities and groups. Changing owners and groups requires advanced system administration knowledge and use of complicated tools, such as the NetInfo Manager application (briefly discussed in Chapter 22) and the Terminal application (covered in Chapter 25). Similarly, you can't specify that specific folders are sharable in Mac OS X.

Setting Specific Access Privileges

This section explains how to use the Finder's Info window to set separate access privileges for the owner, owner's group, and everyone else.

You set access privileges for a folder or volume in its Info window. Choose File⇨Show Info (⌘-I) to display the Info window. If the window does not display the information for the folder or file in which you're interested, select that folder or file icon in the Finder and the Info window switches to the desired item. Now, select Privileges from the pop-up menu in the Info window. You set access privileges by choosing from pop-up menus for the Owner, a Group, and Everyone, as shown in Figure 19-2.

As discussed in Chapter 4, each file and folder in Mac OS X can have different access privileges for three user categories: Owner, Group, and Others. Anyone connecting to your Mac without a name and password falls into the Others category. Even if a person connects with the name and password of a login account on your computer, this person falls in the Others category for every file and folder unless they are either the owner of the file or part of the owner's group.

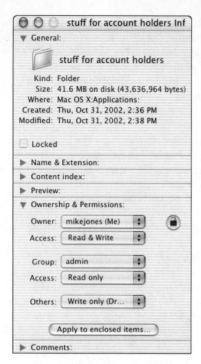

Figure 19-2: Each of your files and folders can have different privilege levels in three user categories.

You can set one of four privilege levels for each user category in the access privileges pop-up menus:

✦ **Read & Write.** Permits users to open and copy the file or folder. In the case of a folder, users can also see enclosed files and folders and can put items into the folder. In the case of a file, users can also make changes to the file.

✦ **Read only.** Permits users to open and copy the file or folder. In the case of a folder, users can see also enclosed files and folders.

✦ **Write only (Drop box).** Permits users to put files and folders into the folder, but does not allow users to open the folder. (Files can't have Write-only permission.)

✦ **None.** This level denies access to the file or folder. Users can see the item but can't open it or change it.

Note

To establish Write-only access to a folder, you must give the person or group Read privileges or Read & Write privileges to the folder containing the folder. For example, your Public folder has Read-only privileges for Others. Inside the read-only Public folder is a folder named Drop Box, which has Write-only privileges for Others. Other users couldn't access the Drop Box folder if you put it inside another folder with Write-only privileges. That would defeat the purpose.

The Owner privileges must be at least as broad as the Group privileges, and the group privileges must be at least as broad as the Others privileges. In other words, if you give Others Read & Write privileges, then both the Group and the Owner are automatically set to Read & Write.

If you wish to set the same privileges for all folders enclosed within the current folder, click the Apply to enclosed items... button. Remember that this is an all-or-nothing operation.

Dealing with Security Risks

File sharing poses security risks. Allowing other users to connect as guests is a fairly low risk if you are careful. If your computer has multiple administrator login accounts, the risk is much greater. The risks are magnified if your computer connects directly to the Internet (not to an Internet gateway that shares an connection). You can take some steps to improve file-sharing security.

Assessing the risks of guest access

Mac OS X normally allows everyone on your network to access your Public folder as a guest — without supplying a name and password. Therefore you should be careful what you put in your Public folder. The Public folder itself is normally Read only, and you can set restricted access privileges for items that you put into your Public folder. However, if everyone has write access to a folder inside your Public folder, such as to the Drop Box folder, a guest can still cause mischief by filling your disk with file after file.

Assessing the risks of administrator access

An administrator's special ability to connect to all disks and work virtually without restrictions threatens the computer's security much more than guest access. In Mac OS X 10.1, someone who connects to your computer for file sharing with an administrator's name and password can actually access the contents of all home folders and the main Library folder on your computer. This is more freedom than Mac OS X allows when you log in as an administrator. (A future update of Mac OS X may restrict an administrator's access via file sharing.) Anyone who can learn or guess an administrator's name and password can crack your computer from another computer on your network.

If your computer has multiple administrator accounts and you turn on file sharing, you either have to trust everyone with an administrator account or you have to go to a lot of trouble. You have to set specific access privileges for files and folders that you want to keep administrators from changing or deleting. There is always the risk of forgetting to deny access to an item that you don't want administrators to be able to change.

Assessing the risk of your Internet connection

The security risks of file sharing are amplified by the fact that file sharing is normally available via the Internet's TCP/IP protocol. A potential hacker does not have to be physically near your Macs — the hacker could enter by modem or Internet connection. If your computer is connected directly to the Internet, anyone in the world who learns your computer's IP address can access your Public folder anonymously via the Internet. Someone who also knows the name and password of an administrator account on your computer has very broad access via the Internet. The Internet exposure is relatively high if your computer has a static IP address from your ISP. The Internet exposure is relatively low if your ISP assigns your computer a different IP address every time you connect, as is usually the case with a modem connection or a PPPoE connection. If you share a connection via an Internet gateway, your computer probably has a private IP address that can't be accessed from the Internet unless the gateway is explicitly configured to allow such access.

Improving file-sharing security

Here are some techniques you can employ to improve file-sharing security:

✦ Be very sure to turn off the administrator option on any account that does not absolutely require it.

✦ Don't allow Write permission for guests, even to Drop Box folders. Set the Others category of every shared folder to read only.

✦ Do not overvalue the security of passwords. Someone may connect to your computer with a password and then leave his or her computer without disconnecting. A passerby can then use this computer to access all of your shared files (subject to the access privileges you set). Remind people who connect to your computer for file sharing that they must put away all your shared folders (by ejecting them) when they are finished. Also, remind users to lock their keychains or log out of the Mac when they leave it unattended. If they do not, unauthorized users may be able to access shared folders using their account, even if they do not know the password.

✦ Particularly if you have high-speed Internet access, such as cable-modem, DSL, or ISDN, you should set up a *firewall* to protect your local network. Firewalls provide a barrier to unauthorized access from outside your local network. The Internet gateways covered in Chapter 18, including the Apple AirPort Base Station, generally can be configured to provide firewall protection.

Using a personal firewall to improve security

A firewall is an application that runs on a computer to improve its security by blocking access to the computer. Mac OS X includes a firewall application that is integrated in Sharing. To see the firewall configuration, open System preferences, open the Sharing pane, and then click the Firewall tab, as shown in Figure 19-3.

Figure 19-3: Use the Firewall tab of the Sharing pane to turn the built-in firewall on and off and to change its settings.

To turn on the firewall, click the Start button. The firewall automatically stops all incoming network traffic for all services, such as Personal File Sharing, that are not turned on in the Services tab. Turning on a service in the Services tab opens the port in the firewall to allow incoming connections for that service. If you want to allow access through the firewall for a given port, either select the checkbox in the Firewall list to open that port or (if what you are looking for isn't there) click the New... button. A dialog sheet appears, as shown in figure 19-4, in which you can add less-common access or custom access.

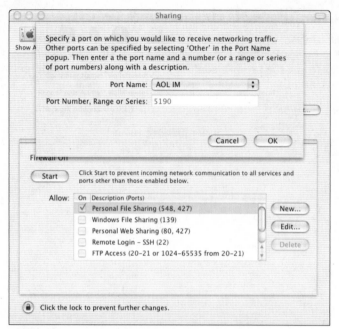

Figure 19-4: The New button on the Firewall tab of the Sharing pane enables you to add specific ports to be opened through your system's firewall.

Summary

This chapter discussed the peer-to-peer (distributed) file sharing provided by Mac OS X. Peer-to-peer file sharing in Mac OS X is great for small groups, but a dedicated file server (such as AppleShare IP or Mac OS X Server) is generally better in a large environment.

You learned how to activate and deactivate file sharing, specify privileges for folders, and take basic security precautions.

✦   ✦   ✦

Deploying More Network Services

You know from previous chapters that with Mac OS X you can share files and some USB printers with other computers on your local network. In this chapter, we take a look at the following additional services that Mac OS X can provide on your network or the Internet:

✦ Web Sharing for hosting a Web site from your computer

✦ FTP access for unprotected file copying between your computer and others

✦ Remote login for protected file copying between your computer and others and for control of your computer from others using encrypted Unix commands

In addition to all these network services, your computer can respond to messages sent from other computers on your network. These messages, called remote Apple events, are sent by AppleScript programs that are running on other computers. We cover this capability along with AppleScript in Chapter 21.

Making Network Services Available

All network services described in this chapter require a local network, an Internet connection, or both. The local network can be an Ethernet network or an AirPort wireless network. If you're not sure how to set up a local network or an Internet connection, take a look back at Chapter 18.

Each network service becomes available when you (or someone else using your computer) turns it on. While a service is available, other computers on the Internet or your local network can access it. The service remains available until someone deliberately turns off the service or shuts down your computer. If you log in, turn on a network service, and then log out, the service remains available. Network services are even available while no one is logged in — that is, while the login window is displayed. Logging in as another user does not affect availability, because users don't have private settings for the network service settings.

Shutting down your computer ends its network services, but only temporarily. The next time the computer is started up, Mac OS X automatically turns on network services that were turned on prior to shutdown.

Other computers cannot access your computer's network services if it goes into sleep mode. If another computer is connected to your computer for Web Sharing, FTP access, or remote login and your computer goes to sleep, the other computer is unable to access that service until someone wakes your computer. When your computer wakes up, computers with existing connections to your computer's network services are able to resume access. You can keep your computer from going to sleep with the Energy Saver pane of System Preferences as described in Chapter 15.

Finding your computer's IP address

Other computers need to know your computer's network identity to access the network services that it provides. For Web Sharing, FTP access, and remote login, your computer can always be identified by a numeric IP address. You can think of your computer's IP address as its telephone number.

Actually, your computer can have more than one IP address. It has different IP addresses for each network port that it's connected to. Your computer could be connected to an Internet provider via modem, an Ethernet network via its built-in Ethernet port, and an AirPort network. Each connection has its own IP address.

Displaying your computer's IP address

To see the IP address of the port currently used to provide Web Sharing, FTP access, and remote login, open System Preferences and then choose View⇨Sharing (or click the Sharing button). Click the Services tab in Sharing Preferences and look for your computer's IP address near the middle of the window, as shown in Figure 20-1.

If Sharing Preferences doesn't display an IP address, then you can look for an IP address in Network Preferences (click the Network button in System Preferences or choose Apple⇨Location⇨Network Preferences). Click the Show pop-up menu near the top of Network Preferences and choose the network port whose IP address you want to see. Then click the TCP/IP tab. The IP address is displayed below the Configure pop-up menu, as shown in Figure 20-2.

Figure 20-1: If one of your computer's network ports has an IP address, the IP address usually appears near the middle of the Sharing pane of System Preferences.

Punching holes in your firewall

If your computer has a private IP address, your local network may have an Internet gateway or router that shares a public IP address among the computers on the network. Computers on the Internet see only the shared public IP address. They can't see the private IP addresses of computers on the local network. Therefore, they have no way of contacting computers on the local network for Web, FTP, or remote login services. Because the gateway keeps Internet computers out, it provides a kind of firewall for your local network. If you want to let Internet computers through your firewall, you need to punch holes in the firewall. Each type of service — Web Sharing, FTP access, and remote login — needs a separate hole in the firewall.

You may be able to configure your Internet gateway so that it directs all incoming requests for a particular service, such as FTP access, from the shared public IP address to one computer's private IP address. This scheme is usually called *inbound port mapping*. This scheme is like an office with a main phone number and a receptionist who routes incoming calls to a different private extension for each department. Within the company, departments call each other by using the private extension numbers. With inbound port mapping, your local network has one public IP address and a gateway that routes incoming service requests to private IP addresses according to the type of service request. Computers on your local network use your private IP address to access your computer's network services.

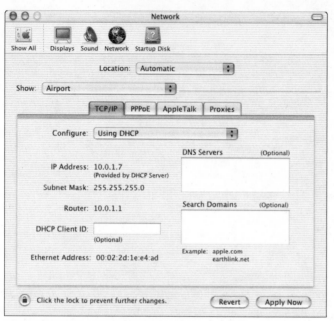

Figure 20-2: See the IP address of any network port in the Network pane of System Preferences.

The details of configuring inbound port mapping are different for each gateway product. Consult your Internet gateway's manual for specific instructions.

Dynamic and static IP address

Your computer's IP address may be dynamic or static. A *dynamic IP address* may change each time you begin an Internet session or each time your computer starts up. A *static IP address* doesn't change. Your computer probably has a dynamic IP address if it connects to the Internet via modem or DSL with PPPoE. Some cable modem connections also provide a dynamic IP address.

A computer on a local network, Ethernet or AirPort, may get an IP address from a DHCP server on the local network each time the computer starts up. The IP address could be different each time, so it is a dynamic IP address. (The *D* in DHCP stands for Dynamic.) The AirPort base station includes a DHCP server, as do many Internet gateway and router products.

Having a dynamic IP address makes your computer hard for other computers to find, which means that your network services are hard to find. It's like a business whose phone number changes every day.

Getting your computer a name

Although your Mac has an IP address for the Web Sharing, FTP access, and remote login services that it provides, an IP address is not as convenient as the names that people normally use to access Web sites and FTP servers on the Internet. In addition to its IP address, your computer can have a name for the services that it provides on the Internet and on your local network. The name is actually just another way of referring to your computer's IP address. When another computer tries to contact your computer by name, a name server on your local network or on the Internet looks up the name in a directory and finds your IP address. These name servers are known as *DNS servers* (Dynamic Name Server).

Mac OS X does not include a DNS server, nor can Mac OS X help get a name assigned to your computer and listed with DNS servers on the Internet or your local network. How you get your computer a name address for its Web Sharing, FTP access, and remote login services depends on how it connects to the Internet and whether it is on a local network. The details are beyond the scope of this book, but here are some general guidelines:

✦ Most Internet service providers provide a name, such as `www.mydomain.com` for a fee.

✦ If you have a static IP address and want to have your own domain name, you can get free DNS service from Granite Canyon Group, LLC (`www.granite canyon.com`).

✦ If you don't need your own domain name, you can get a free name like `myname.dnsalias.com` from an organization that provides dynamic DNS service, such as Dynamic DNS Network Services (`www.dyndns.org`). If you have a dynamic IP address, you also need to install software on your computer that notices each time you get a different IP address and automatically sends your new IP address to your dynamic DNS service provider. An example of this software is the free Dynamic DNS Client by James Sentman (`www.sentman.com/dyndns/`).

✦ If you want to use names instead of private IP addresses on your local network, set up a DNS server on the network. Some Internet gateway products include DNS, and DNS software is available for Mac OS 9.

Note   A computer name is displayed above the IP address in Sharing Preferences. This name is used for file sharing and other AppleTalk services, not for such TCP/IP services as Web Sharing, FTP access, and remote login.

Hosting Your Own Web Site

Ever wanted to host your own Web site? All you need, other than a network or Internet connection, is Web server software and some Web pages. Mac OS X includes the Apache Web server, which is so reliable that many commercial sites use it to host their large, active sites. This industrial strength Web server is easy to set up thanks to Mac OS X's Web Sharing feature. It gets your Web site on the Internet or your local network in about a minute. (No, this does not include the time it takes to actually create your Web pages!)

You may be able to use Web Sharing to host a large Web site, but you probably won't want to. Web Sharing is best suited to hosting a personal Web site. Your Web site is as sturdy as large Web sites, thanks to the Apache server software and Mac OS X's Unix core. System resources, not reliability, are the limiting factor. Unlike administrators of large Web sites, you probably don't want to dedicate your computer to hosting a Web site. Most likely, you want to host a Web site and use other applications at the same time. If you ask Web Sharing to host a large, busy Web site, you'll probably find that your computer is not responsive enough when you use another application at the same time. Web Sharing is perfect for distributing information to coworkers on a local network or to family and friends on the Internet.

If you want to host a Web site on the Internet, your computer needs a continuous, high-capacity Internet connection. A DSL or cable modem connection should be adequate for a personal Web site. However, many DSL and cable modem connections *upload* files (send to the Internet) much more slowly than they *download* files (receive from the Internet). For example, your computer may download files at over 140KB per second but be permitted to upload at less than 14KB per second. If this is the case with your connection, then visitors to your Web site receive Web pages from your computer at the slower upload rate. Nevertheless, DSL and cable modem connections are much faster than a modem connection. You don't want to frustrate your Web site visitors with spotty, slow service via a modem connection.

Starting Web Sharing

You really can get a Web site set up on your local network or your Internet connection in a minute. Simply open System Preferences and choose View⇨Sharing (or click the Sharing button). Click the Services tab, and then click the Start button that is below the words Web Sharing Off. Web Sharing takes a few seconds to start up. Then the Start button becomes a Stop button and the text above it reads Web Sharing On. As you probably expect, clicking the Stop button turns off Web Sharing. Figure 20-3 shows Sharing Preferences with Web Sharing ready to be turned on.

Figure 20-3: Start Web Sharing in the Sharing pane of System Preferences.

If Sharing Preferences settings are locked, you must unlock them before you can start Web Sharing. When the settings are locked, they are dim and the lock button at the bottom of the window looks locked. To unlock the settings, click the lock button and enter an administrator's user account name and password in the dialog that appears.

Loading Web site files

Turning on Web Sharing in Sharing Preferences gets a Web site on the air, but it's not your Web site until you put your Web site's files into the right folder. In the meantime, you have a provisional Web site supplied with Mac OS X, as shown in Figure 20-4.

Loading a personal Web site

You can put files for a Web site in two places. Files for a personal Web site should go in the Sites folder in your home folder, where other users of your computer can't change them. Naturally, other users of your computer can create their own personal Web sites, and you can't change them. Each user's personal Web site has a unique URL.

Figure 20-4: Visitors to your personal Web site see a provisional home page until you place your Web site's files in your home folder's Sites folder.

Loading the common Web site

Files for a joint Web site that all users of your computer can change go in the Documents folder in the WebServer folder in the main Library folder; the path is `/Library/WebServer/Documents/`. This folder initially contains a provisional home page in several languages. Each language has a separate HTML file. These files all have names beginning with `index.html` and ending with a suffix that indicates the language. For example, `index.html.en` is the English version and `index.html.es` is the Spanish (Español) version. You can make any of these HTML files the provisional home page for your Web site by removing the language-designation suffix so that the file name is just `index.html`. (You do not need to rename the `index.html.en` file because the Mac OS X Apache Web server automatically uses it if no files are named index.html.) Figure 20-5 shows the joint Web site's provisional home page in English.

Tip   If you have no other use for your computer's common Web site, make it an index to your computer's personal Web sites. This index can be a simple Web page containing a list of links to the personal Web sites. For example, if users Atlas and Medusa both have personal Web sites, the index page would have a link to `/~atlas/` and another link to `/~medusa/`.

Designing and Creating a Web Site

Designing a Web site and creating all the files that go into it can be a lot of work. If your needs are simple, you may be able to produce a satisfactory Web site with a word processing application. For example, recent versions of Microsoft Word and AppleWorks can convert a word processing document to an HTML file. Word or AppleWorks word processing documents can include formatted text, tables, graphics, and links to places in the same document or to other documents. If the original word processing document includes graphics, the graphics are converted to separate image files. You must put the image files together with the HTML file in your Sites folder or the `/Library/WebServer/Documents/` folder.

Both Microsoft Word and AppleWorks convert simple documents more accurately than complex documents. You can experiment to see whether your word processing application can generate Web site files that meet your needs.

Figure 20-5: Visitors to your computer's common Web site see another provisional Web page until someone using your computer puts Web site files in the `/Library/WebServer/Documents/` folder.

Setting up a file listing

Instead of displaying a home page, your Web site can display a list of the files in your Sites folder or in the Documents folder of the WebServer folder (path `Library/WebServer/Documents/`). To make this happen, simply remove the file named `index.html` or `index.html.en` from the folder. If the folder doesn't contain a file by either of these names, the Mac OS X Web server creates a Web page that is a list of the folder's contents, as shown in Figure 20-6.

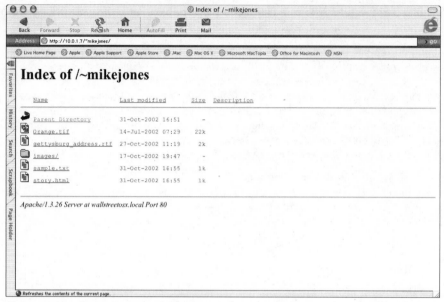

Figure 20-6: If your Web site folder has no home page, visitors see a listing of the folder's contents.

Visiting your Web site

People visit your personal Web site (the one in your Sites folder) at an Internet address (URL) like one of these:

> ✦ http://192.168.0.1/~user/

> ✦ http://mycomputer.mydomain.com/~user/

Substitute your computer's IP address or name, and substitute the short name of your user account at the end of the Internet address. Be sure to include the ending slash (/) or the Internet address won't work. Notice that neither of these Internet addresses has a www prefix. Your Web site's Internet address doesn't include the www prefix unless it is part of the name you have obtained for your computer as described at the beginning of this chapter.

The joint Web site (the one with files in Library/WebServer/Documents/) has an Internet address like one of these:

> ✦ http://192.168.0.1

> ✦ http://mycomputer.mydomain.com

Substitute your computer's IP address or name. Here again, your Web site's Internet address doesn't include the www prefix unless it is part of the name you have obtained for your computer.

Tip   If your computer has only an IP address, put a note on your home page advising people who connect to add a bookmark for your page so that they don't have to remember and retype the IP address to visit again.

Allowing FTP Access

The Mac OS X Web Sharing feature is no help when what you want to share are files. Another feature that Mac OS X inherits from Unix, known as *FTP* (file transfer protocol), enables other computers on your local network or the Internet to copy files to and from your computer.

Turning FTP access on or off

The software that provides FTP service is built into Mac OS X, and you can turn it on or off quite easily. First, open System Preferences and choose View⇨Sharing (or click the Sharing button). When Sharing Preferences appears, click the Services tab, click on FTP Access in the list box, and then click the Start button to turn it on or off. Figure 20-7 shows FTP ready to be turned on in Sharing Preferences.

Figure 20-7: Turn the built-in FTP server on or off in the Sharing pane of System Preferences.

If Sharing Preferences settings are locked, you must unlock them before you can turn FTP access on or off. The settings are dim when they are locked, and the lock button looks locked. To unlock the settings, click the security button and enter an administrator's user account name and password in the dialog that appears.

Avoiding file damage

FTP was designed to transfer plain text files. Other kinds of files such as pictures, software, and formatted text files lose vital information unless first encoded as plain text files before being transferred. Files that must be encoded before being sent over the Internet are known as *binary* files. Encoding Mac files also preserves information used by the Finder, such as the type of file and which application created it. Encoded files must be decoded after being received before they can be used.

Unlike other FTP software for Macs, the FTP server in Mac OS X is not able to automatically encode Mac files before sending them to another computer. Nor does the Mac OS X FTP server recognize encoded Mac files and automatically decode them when it receives them from another computer.

Because the Mac OS X FTP server doesn't handle any encoding or decoding automatically, you should encode files that you want other users to download from your computer by using FTP. Conversely, if other users upload encoded files to your computer by using FTP, you must decode the files before you can use them. You can use the StuffIt Expander utility application included with Mac OS X to decode files. You can encode files by using the StuffIt Deluxe application or the DropStuff application, both from Aladdin Systems (www.aladdinsys.com).

A future version of Mac OS X may include an FTP server that automatically encodes and decodes transferred files.

Considering security

Although convenient, allowing FTP access to your computer poses a serious security risk. Anyone who knows the name and password of a user account on your computer can connect to your computer from anywhere on your local network, and if your computer has an active Internet connection, from anywhere on the Internet.

Unprotected passwords

FTP's authentication method — user account name and password — protects your computer against casual snooping, but it is no defense at all against a skilled attacker. FTP does not encrypt the name and password before sending them across the network or the Internet. An attacker can use well-known tools and methods to capture names and passwords of everyone who connects to your computer for FTP access. Your name and password are just as vulnerable as those of other users of your computer. If you use FTP to get files from your computer while you're away from it, then your name and password can be captured.

Comparing FTP and File Sharing

If you've never used FTP before, you may think that it sounds like Mac OS X's file-sharing feature, which is described in the previous chapter. Actually, FTP differs from file sharing in a couple of significant ways. For one, file sharing is mainly for Macs, but FTP works across platforms. Computers running Windows and Unix operating systems can copy files to and from your computer.

Another key difference concerns how people use your files on other computers. With file sharing, other computer users see your shared files in Finder windows and Open dialogs. These computer users can open and save files directly on your computer. With FTP, other computer users see your files in FTP client applications, and these other users must copy files between your computer and theirs. They work with copies of your files on their computers.

Tip   If you allow FTP access to your computer, change your password frequently and have all other users of your computer do likewise. Never use the same password for FTP that you use for anything else, such as online banking!

Unprotected file transfers

Similarly, FTP does nothing to protect files transferred to and from your computer. Sure, you can encrypt files on your computer, and they are secure if they are transferred. In practice, keeping files encrypted on your computer is a burden. It is like keeping all your valuable possessions in locked closets so that you can leave your front door unlocked.

Protecting with privilege settings

You don't have to encrypt files inside several of the folders in your home folder to keep other users from seeing them. Other users can see and change folders and files on your computer according to the privileges set for each folder and file. In this regard, FTP access is the same as being logged in locally. For example, the preset privileges of your home folder's Desktop, Documents, Library, Movies, Music, and Pictures folders allow only you to see their contents. Anything you put in these six places, and in other folders you create with the same privilege settings, are safe from FTP access unless someone gets your user account name and password.

The preset privileges of your Public and Sites folders allow other users to see and copy their contents. Other users can't put files in these folders, although they can put files in the Drop Box folder that's inside your Public folder.

Outside your home folder and other users' home folders, the privileges of most other folders and files allow everyone with FTP access to see and copy them. In fact, many folders and files that are hidden in Finder windows can be seen by everyone with FTP access to your computer.

Everyone with FTP access to your computer can see and make changes in several of your top-level folders. Anyone with an administrator account can make changes in additional folders. People who log in to your FTP server don't see your top-level folders at first — they see their own home folder on your computer initially — but they can easily go to your top-level folders. Thus an attacker who captures a user account name and password for your computer could upload files to a folder where you may not notice them, such as the Volumes folder.

Back door to network volumes

The Volumes folder is actually an insidious security problem on a network where people use file sharing or file servers. The Volumes folder gives everyone who logs in to a computer's FTP server a back door entrance to all network volumes mounted on the computer. For example, suppose your computer has FTP access turned off but file sharing is turned on. Someone named Arachne connects to your computer as a file-sharing guest, and your Public folder is mounted on Arachne's computer. Arachne has FTP access turned on. Using a third computer, Zeus logs in to the FTP server on Arachne's computer, goes to Arachne's Volumes folder, and through it can access your Public folder. If Arachne connects to your computer as a file-sharing administrator and mounts your hard drive as a network volume, then Zeus would have access to your entire hard drive through Arachne's Volumes folder.

Allowing anonymous guest access

Considering the security problems that FTP access has, you may understandably balk at allowing guests to connect without user account names and passwords. Yet ironically, anonymous FTP access is arguably more secure than FTP access with a name and password. One reason is that anyone who connects anonymously is restricted to the contents of one folder. They can't ransack your other folders as users with passwords can. Furthermore, if everyone connects anonymously, their names and passwords aren't being sent over the network or Internet; what isn't there can't be captured.

Creating the anonymous FTP user

If you want to allow anonymous FTP access to your computer, simply create a user account with the short name ftp and a blank password. This is the anonymous FTP user's account. When anyone connects to your computer for FTP access without a name and password, this user's home folder (at /Users/ftp/) is the only folder they get to see. Initially, this home folder contains the usual assortment of folders, such as Documents, Movies, Music, Public, and Sites.

Modifying the anonymous FTP user's home folder

If you want to add files or make other changes in the anonymous user's home folder, you encounter a bit of a paradox. Although anyone can add files via FTP from another computer, you can't add files from your computer — at least not while logged in with your own user account. As usual, the privileges assigned to the

Prevent FTP Access Outside Home Folders

The FTP server normally allows remote users to go outside their home folders, but it can be configured to restrict users individually to their own home folders. This configuration requires the use of the Terminal application and the System Administrator (root user) account.

First, you create a text file containing a list of user accounts that you want to restrict. You put the short name of each user account on a separate line, making sure to press return after the last name. For example, the following list restricts users atlas and medusa to their home folders when they log in for FTP access:

```
atlas
medusa
```

In addition to restricting FTP access for individual users, you can restrict access for groups of users. For each group that you want to restrict, you simply add a line to the text file consisting of an at-sign (@) symbol followed by the group name. Because all Mac OS X user accounts belong to the staff group, a file containing the following lines (the last line being blank) restricts all users to their home directories when they log in for FTP access to your computer:

```
@staff
```

When you save the text file, name it `ftpchroot` and put it in your home folder. This file must be plain text. If you want to use the TextEdit application to create this file, you must choose Format⇨Make Plain Text before saving the file. After saving the file, change the file name so that it does not end with `.txt`.

After saving the file `ftpchroot` in your home folder, use the NetInfo Manager application to enable the root user. Make sure you know the root user's password. (If you need specific instructions, see Chapter 16.)

Next, open the Terminal application and type the following command:

```
sudo mv ~/ftpchroot /etc
```

If you are prompted in the Terminal window to enter the root password, do so. By default, sudo will require your password, although it can be configured to require the root password. (We take a closer look at the Terminal program and Unix commands in Chapter 26.) Finally, use the NetInfo Manager to disable the root user.

anonymous user's home folder and the folders inside it allow only the owner, whose name is ftp, to make changes. Therefore, you can add files and make other changes if you log out and then log in with the ftp name.

Tip You can simplify adding files, removing files, and making changes in the anonymous FTP user's home folder. First log out and then log in with user account name ftp. Next change the group privileges for the home folder (path `/Users/ftp/`) to Read & Write. Do the same for folders inside the home folder. Finally, log out and log in with your own user account.

Connecting to your FTP server

If your computer has FTP access turned on, people can use any FTP client application to connect to your computer's FTP server. They can also use a Web browser, although Web browsers have limited abilities with FTP.

Connecting with an FTP client

The FTP client needs to know the identity of the server or host, and this is just your computer's IP address or name. The client also needs to know the user's account name and password on your computer. If you have set up anonymous FTP access on your computer, the user can specify anonymous as the name (also called username or user ID) or leave the name blank. Figure 20-8 shows examples of connection dialogs in two venerable FTP clients for Mac OS 9 and Mac OS X, Fetch 4.0 from Fetch Softworks (www.fetchsoftworks.com) and Interarchy 4.0 from Stairways Software Pty Ltd (www.interarchy.com).

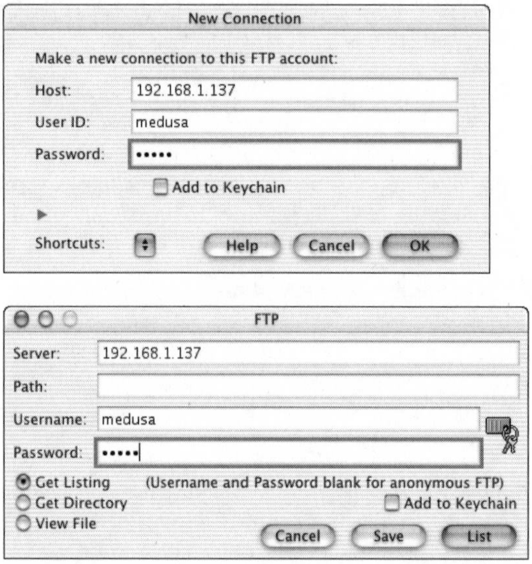

Figure 20-8: For FTP access to your computer from an FTP client, specify your computer's IP address or name as the host or server, the user account name (leave blank for anonymous FTP if you allow it), and password.

Connecting with a Web browser

Instead of connecting to your FTP server with an FTP client, people can use a Web browser, such as Internet Explorer or Netscape Communicator. A Web browser can download files from your computer but can't upload files to it. With a Web browser, people connect to your FTP server with an Internet address (URL) like one of these:

✦ `ftp://192.168.0.1`

✦ `ftp://mycomputer.mydomain.com`

Substitute your computer's IP address or name. As the Web browser is connecting to your computer, it displays a dialog asking for a user account name (also called the username or user ID) and password. Figure 20-9 shows Internet Explorer with the Internet address for an FTP server and the dialog for entering name and password.

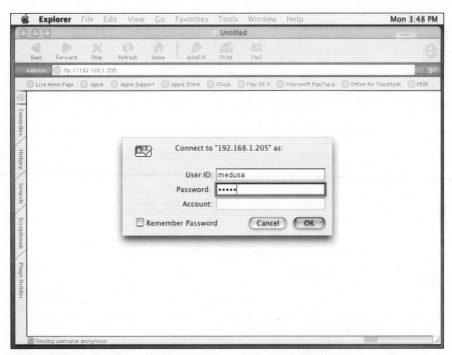

Figure 20-9: For FTP access to your computer from a Web browser, specify `ftp://` and your computer's IP address or name as the Internet address; then enter a user account name and password in a dialog.

Allowing Remote Login

Although FTP isn't secure, Mac OS X includes a different service that is. This service provides encrypted communications between your computer and others on the Internet or any network that is not secure. Other computer users can log in to your computer and copy files back and forth. These remote users of your computer can also control it with Unix commands that they type on their computers.

Mac OS X provides remote login through included OpenSSH server software. OpenSSH is a public version of SSH (secure shell), which provides secure, encrypted communications between two computers over the Internet or any network that is not secure. OpenSSH encrypts all communications and data transfer, preventing eavesdropping, hijacking of connections, and other network attacks.

OpenSSH is actually several software tools that replace several insecure Unix tools. The ssh tool provides remote login and command-line sessions, replacing login and telnet. The scp tool provides file copying, replacing rcp and some FTP functions. The sftp tool provides easier file transfer, replacing FTP.

Because OpenSSH is better for file transfer than FTP, you may wonder why more and better FTP client applications are available. The reason is simple: FTP has been around for decades, and OpenSSH has been around only a few years.

Note   Unlike Mac OS X 10.0.1 and later, Mac OS X 10.0.0 does not provide remote login through OpenSSH. Instead, Mac OS X 10.0.0 (released on 3/24/2001) provides remote login through three different Unix services: telnet, rlogin (remote login), and rsh (remote shell). If "Allow remote login" is turned on in Mac OS X 10.0.0, people using other computers can log in remotely by using a client application for telnet, rlogin, or rsh. None of these services is encrypted.

Turning remote login on or off

 You can turn remote login on or off easily. First, open System Preferences and then choose View⇨Sharing (or click the Sharing button). In Sharing Preferences, click the Services tab and then select Remote Login in the Service list. Then click the Start button to turn it on or off. Figure 20-10 shows remote login ready to be turned on in Sharing Preferences.

Caution   If Mac OS X is configured to allow System Administrator (root) access, do not turn on the Remote Login option in Sharing Preferences. The root account name is well known, and if someone guesses the root account password on your computer, they can use another computer on your local network or the Internet to damage your files or add files that covertly take over your computer. Normally, Mac OS X does not allow root access, but it can be reconfigured by using the NetInfo Manager application (see Chapter 16).

Figure 20-10: Turn Mac OS X's remote login services on or off in the Sharing pane of System Preferences.

If Sharing Preferences settings are locked, you must unlock them before you can turn remote login on or off. The settings are dim when locked, and the lock button looks locked. To unlock the settings, click the lock button and enter an administrator's user account name and password in the dialog that appears.

Note   The first time you turn on the Remote Login option, you may have to wait a minute or so before a check mark appears in the checkbox. While you're waiting for the OpenSSH service to start up, don't become impatient and click in the checkbox repeatedly, or you may induce the condition where remote login appears to be turned on but the OpenSSH service is not actually started. If this happens, remote login may appear to be turned on yet no one is able to connect to your computer by using an SSH client application on another computer. In this case, you can fix the problem by restarting your computer.

Connecting for remote login

When your computer has remote login turned on, other computer users can connect to your computer using SSH client software.

Connecting with the Terminal application

Mac OS X includes an SSH client that can be used from the Terminal window. This means another Mac OS X user can log in to your computer by opening the Terminal application and typing a Unix command similar to the following:

```
ssh username@@192.168.0.1
```

In this command, username must be replaced with the remote user's short name on your computer. The IP address must be your computer's IP address or your computer's name, if you have obtained one for it as described at the beginning of this chapter. (The username@@ part of the ssh command can be omitted if the remote user has the same short name on your computer and on the remote computer he or she is using.)

Note   You may need to wait a minute or so after entering an ssh command for the remote computer to respond.

After logging in to your computer, the remote user can type additional Unix commands in the Terminal application to control your computer. Figure 20-11 shows a Terminal session in which Medusa connects remotely to the computer whose IP address is 192.168.1.137 and then uses the finger command to see who is using the remote computer.

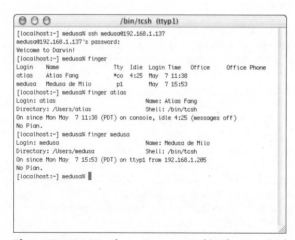

Figure 20-11: Use the ssh command in the Terminal window to log in remotely and control the remote computer with Unix commands.

Connecting with the RBrowser application

Another SSH application, RBrowser, enables copying files between computers by using Finder-like windows. RBrowser is shareware from Object Warehouse Inc. (www.rbrowser.com). Figure 20-12 shows an example of RBrowser logged in and displaying a folder from a remote computer.

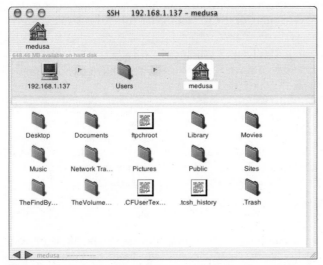

Figure 20-12: RBrowser, a shareware application, can log in remotely to another computer and securely copy files by using Finder-like windows.

Summary

Here's what you know about Web Sharing, FTP access, and remote login after reading this chapter:

✦ Every computer on a network or the Internet has an IP address. With Mac OS X, a computer can have a different IP address for Ethernet, modem, AirPort, and other network ports.

✦ If you have a public IP address, then computers on the Internet can use your computer's network services. If you have a private IP address, then Internet computers must go through a gateway on your network to use your computer's network services.

✦ A dynamic IP address may change each time you begin an Internet session or each time your computer starts up. A static IP address doesn't change.

✦ You can get your computer a name, which a name server on your network or the Internet looks up to get your IP address.

✦ You can host a Web site by turning on Web Sharing in Sharing Preferences. Your Web site files go in the Sites folder inside your home folder. Files for a joint Web site shared by all users of your computer go in the Documents folder of the WebServer folder in the main Library folder (path /Library/ WebServer/Documents/).

✦ The URL for your personal Web site has the form http://192.168.0.1/~user/ or http://mycomputer.mydomain.com/~user/. The URL for your computer's joint Web site has the form http://192.168.0.1 or http://mycomputer. mydomain.com. (Substitute your computer's address or name and the short name of your user account.)

✦ If you turn on the FTP access option in Sharing Preferences, other computer users can transfer files to and from your computer. Binary files must be encoded before FTP transfers them. FTP does not protect user account names, passwords, or file transfers from network attackers.

✦ Mac OS X does not normally allow anonymous FTP access, but you can enable it.

✦ For FTP access to your computer, other computer users specify your computer's IP address or name and their user account name and password.

✦ Turning on the Remote Login option in Sharing Preferences enables other computer users to securely log in to your computer, copy files, and send Unix commands.

✦ For remote login, other computer users specify your computer's IP address or name and their user account name and password.

✦   ✦   ✦

Automating with AppleScript

Although computers have been touted for years as the ultimate tool for "automating" our lives, too often nothing is particularly automatic about using computers at all. So far you've seen technologies in Mac OS X that help you launch documents, edit text, create multimedia, print, and perform hundreds of other tasks. And while you may be impressed by components in all of those technologies, no component does much alone—they tend to require user input.

However, *AppleScript* lessens the need for user input by providing users with the freedom to create automated tasks. The AppleScript scripting language is a simplified programming language, which enables you to tell your applications to perform certain tasks automatically. AppleScript scripts can be simple or highly complex, depending on your skill at scripting and your knowledge of AppleScript's nuances. In this chapter, you learn enough about AppleScript that even scripting novices can get scripts up and running thanks to tools, such as the Script Editor application, included with Mac OS X.

A discussion of AppleScript needs to begin with the underlying technologies that make AppleScript possible. First is a discussion of messages and events, which are the means by which applications can communicate with one another. After you understand messages and events, it's on to an introduction of AppleScript and a look at the tools that enable you to run, modify, and create scripts of your own.

Understanding Messages and Events

Mac applications perform tasks in response to events. Users originate events with the keyboard and mouse, and applications respond to the events by performing tasks. Similarly, an application can make other applications perform tasks by sending messages about events.

The events that applications send to each other in messages are called *Apple events*. AppleScript makes applications perform tasks by sending them messages about Apple events.

When an application receives a message about an Apple event, the application takes a particular action based on the specific event. This action can be anything from performing a menu command to taking some data, manipulating it, and returning the result to the source of the Apple event message.

For example, when you choose Shut Down or Restart from the Apple menu, Mac OS X sends an Apple event message to every open application saying a Quit event occurred. For this reason, applications seem to quit automatically when you choose Shut Down or Restart.

When you drop document icons on an application icon, the Finder sends a message to Mac OS X saying this event happened, and the system sends the application an Apple event message that says an Open Documents event occurred. The Open Document message includes a list of all the documents whose icons you dragged and dropped. When you double-click an application icon, the Finder sends the system a message that says this event happened, and the system sends the application an Open Application message. When you double-click a document, the application that created the document gets an Open Documents message with the name of the document you double-clicked.

Virtually all Mac applications respond to four Apple events: Open Application, Open Documents, and Quit Application. Applications that print also respond to the Apple event Print Documents. Only very old, very specialized, or poorly engineered Mac applications don't respond to these basic Apple events.

Applications that go beyond the four basic Apple events understand another two dozen core Apple events. These Apple events encompass actions and objects that almost all applications have in common, such as the Close, Save, Undo, Redo, Cut, Copy, and Paste commands. Applications with related capabilities recognize still more sets of Apple events. For example, word processing applications understand Apple events about text manipulation, and drawing applications understand Apple events about graphics manipulation. Application developers can even define private Apple events that only their applications know.

Some Classic Programs Cannot Receive Apple Event Messages

In the Classic compatibility environment, only application programs can send and receive Apple event messages; true control panels and desk accessories cannot, although these items are now uncommon. Control panels that are actually applications (listed in the Classic environment's Applications menu when open) are not subject to this limitation. And a desk accessory can work around this limitation by sending and receiving through a small surrogate application that is always open in the background. This background application does not have to appear in the Classic environment's Application menu, and the computer user does not have to know that the application is open.

Mac OS X provides the means of communicating Apple event messages between applications. The applications can be on the same computer or on different computers connected to the same network. To understand how Apple event messages work, think of them as a telephone system. Mac OS X furnishes a telephone for each application as well as the wires that connect them. Applications call each other with messages about Apple events.

Apple events offer many intriguing possibilities for the world of personal computing. No longer does one application need to handle every possible function; instead, it can send Apple event messages to helper applications. For example, iTunes handles some commands in its File menu, such as Export Song List, by sending Apple event messages to the Finder, which actually carries out the commands.

Introducing AppleScript

Apple event messages aren't just for professional software engineers. Mac enthusiasts who have little technical training can use Apple event messages to control applications by writing statements in the AppleScript language. For example, suppose that you want to quit all open applications. Mac OS X doesn't have a Quit All command, but you can create one with AppleScript. You can use AppleScript commands to automate simple tasks as well as to automate a more complicated series of tasks, as the rest of this chapter explains.

AppleScript language

AppleScript is a language that you can use to tell applications what to do. AppleScript is a programming language that is designed especially for computer users, not computer engineers. (Actually, engineers use it, too.)

You tell applications what to do by writing statements in the AppleScript language. Although AppleScript is an artificial language, its statements look like sentences in a natural language, such as English. You can look at many AppleScript statements and know right away what they're supposed to do.

The words and phrases in AppleScript statements resemble English, but they are terms that have special meanings in the context of AppleScript. Some terms are commands, and some terms are objects that the commands act on. Other terms control how AppleScript performs the statements.

A single AppleScript statement can perform a simple task, but most tasks require a series of statements that are performed one after the other. A set of AppleScript statements that accomplishes a task (or several tasks) is called a *script*. A script can rename a batch of files, change an application's preference settings, copy data from a database to another application, or automate a sequence of tasks that you previously performed one at a time by hand. You can develop your own script tools to accomplish exactly what you need.

As an added boon, AppleScript can actually watch you as you work with an application and write a script for you behind the scenes. This process is called *script recording*.

Although AppleScript is designed for end users, it offers all the capabilities of a traditional programming language and won't frustrate programmers and more-advanced users. You can store information in variables for later use; write if...then statements to perform commands selectively according to a condition that you specify; or repeat a set of commands as many times as you want. AppleScript also offers error checking and object-oriented programming.

Scripting additions

AppleScript has an expandable lexicon of terms. It knows meanings of basic terms, and it augments this knowledge with terms from other sources. Many additional AppleScript terms come from the very applications that AppleScript controls. We explore this source of AppleScript terms in greater detail later.

 Additional AppleScript terms also come from special files called *scripting additions*. AppleScript looks for scripting addition files in the following folders:

✦ **ScriptingAdditions.** In the Library folder of the System folder (path /System/Library/ScriptingAdditions/)—contains standard scripting additions from Apple that are available to all users of your computer. (This folder may also contain other files that are not scripting additions.)

✦ **Scripts.** In the main Library folder (path /Library/Scripts/)—contains more scripting additions that are available to all users of your computer.

✦ **Scripting Additions.** In the folder named System Folder (path `/System Folder/Scripting Additions/` unless you have moved or renamed System Folder) — contains more scripting additions that are available in the Classic environment to all users of your computer.

✦ **Scripting Additions and Scripts.** In the Extensions folder of the folder named System Folder (path `/System Folder/Extensions/Scripting Additions/` and path `/System Folder/Extensions/Scripts/` unless you have moved or renamed System Folder) — contains more scripting additions that are available in the Classic environment to all users of your computer. (This Scripting Additions folder usually exists only on computers that previously used Mac OS 8.)

You need separate scripting additions for Mac OS X and the Classic environment. Scripting additions made for Mac OS X do not work in the Classic environment. Conversely, scripting additions made for Mac OS 9 and earlier work only in the Classic environment. If you get more scripting additions made for Mac OS X, put them in one of the ScriptingAdditions folders that is inside a Library folder. If you get more scripting additions made for Mac OS 9, put them in one of the Scripting Additions folders that is inside the System Folder used for the Classic environment.

Tip If the ScriptingAdditions folder doesn't exist in a Library folder where you want to put a scripting addition file, create a new folder and name it ScriptingAdditions (put no spaces in the name). Put your scripting addition file in this new folder.

Introducing Script Editor

For creating and editing AppleScript scripts, you can use the Script Editor application included with Mac OS X. Script Editor can also run scripts, and it can make scripts into self-contained applications that run when you double-click them in the Finder. Script Editor is normally located in the AppleScript folder, which is in the Applications folder.

Tip If you end up doing a lot of scripting, you may want to replace Script Editor with a more capable script development application, such as or Script Debugger from Late Night Software (`www.latenightsw.com`). Make sure you get a version made for Mac OS X.

Scriptable applications and environments

The scripts you create with Script Editor can control any *scriptable application*. A prime example of a scriptable application is the Finder. Other scriptable applications included with Mac OS X are Apple System Profiler, ColorSync Scripting, Internet Connect, Internet Explorer, Mail, Print Center, QuickTime Player, Sherlock, StuffIt Expander, Terminal, TextEdit, and URL Access Scripting. In addition, many Mac OS X applications not made by Apple are scriptable.

Plenty of Classic applications are also scriptable. Although a Classic version of Script Editor is included with Mac OS 9, you can use the Mac OS X version of Script Editor to make scripts for the Classic environment as well as for Mac OS X.

Looking at a script window

When you open Script Editor, an empty script window appears. Each script window can contain one script. The bottom part of the script window is the script editing area, where you type and edit the text of the script just as you type and edit in any text editing application. The top part of the window is the script description area. You use this area to type a description of what the script does. Figure 21-1 shows an empty script window.

Figure 21-1: A new script window appears when Script Editor opens.

Tip   You can change the default size of a new script window. First, make the script window the size you want and then choose Set Default Window Size from the File menu in Script Editor.

The middle area of a script window has four buttons. You find out more about each of them in later sections, but the following list summarizes their functions:

✦ **Record.** AppleScript goes into recording mode and creates script statements corresponding to your actions in applications that support script recording. You can also press ⌘-D to start recording. You cannot record scripts for every scriptable application because software developers must do more work to make an application recordable than to make it scriptable. You can find out whether an application is recordable by trying to record some actions in it.

✦ **Stop.** Takes AppleScript out of recording mode or stops a script that is running, depending on which action is relevant at the time. Pressing ⌘-period (.) on the keyboard is the same as clicking Stop.

✦ **Run.** Starts running the script that is displayed in the script editing area. You also can press ⌘-R to run the script.

Before running the script, Script Editor scans the script to see if you changed any part of it since you last ran it or checked its syntax (as described next). If the script has changed, Script Editor checks the script's syntax.

✦ **Check Syntax.** Checks for errors in the script, such as incorrect punctuation or missing parts of commands. If any errors turn up, Script Editor highlights the error and displays a dialog explaining the problem. Script Editor also formats the text to make keywords stand out and the structure of the script more apparent. Script Editor may even change the text, but the changes do not affect the meaning of the script.

If the script's syntax is correct, Script Editor tells AppleScript to *compile* the script, which means it converts the text of the script into codes. These codes are what Apple event messages actually contain and what applications understand. You don't usually see these codes in Script Editor, because AppleScript translates them into words for the enlightenment of human beings.

 Note   If you use the Classic version of Script Editor to run or check the syntax of a script that controls an application that isn't open, the script may fail while waiting for the application to open. Wait until the needed application opens and then try the script again.

Creating a Simple Script

An easy way to see how a script looks and works is to type a simple script into a new script window. If Script Editor is not already the active application, open it or switch to it. If you need to create a new script window, choose File⇨New Script. In the script editing area at the bottom of the new script window, type the following statements:

```
tell application "Finder"
activate
set the bounds of the first Finder window to {128, 74, 671,
479}
set the current view of the first Finder window to icon view
set the icon size of the icon view options of the first Finder
window to 32
select the first item of the first Finder window
end tell
```

Check your script for typographical errors by clicking the Check Syntax button in the script window. If Script Editor reports an error, carefully compare the statement you typed in the script window to the same statement in the book. Pay particular attention to spelling, punctuation, omitted words, and omitted spaces.

When you click Check Syntax, Script Editor formats your script, changing the text formatting as it compiles the script using different type styles to show different kinds of terms. The statements that you typed probably changed from Courier font to Geneva font after you clicked Check Syntax. Script Editor normally formats text that hasn't been compiled as 10-point Courier. Most other words, including commands from scripting additions and application dictionaries, are normally formatted in plain 10-point Geneva. Geneva 10-point Bold normally indicates native words in the AppleScript language. Figure 21-2 shows how Script Editor formats the script that you typed.

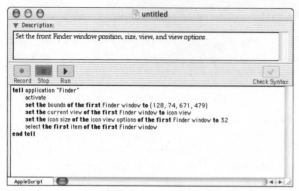

Figure 21-2: Check your script for errors and format it for readability by clicking the Check Syntax button.

Before running this script, return to the Finder and make sure a Finder window is displayed. If you really want to see the script in action, set the front Finder window to list view and resize the window so that it is very small.

After setting the stage for the script, switch back to Script Editor and click Run in your script's window. AppleScript executes each script statement in turn. When the script finishes running, the Finder window should be a standard size and set to icon view. The item that comes first alphabetically in the window should be selected.

Switch to Script Editor again and examine the script. You find that the script is fairly understandable. It may not be fluent English, but many of the commands should make sense as you read them.

Analyzing a Script

Having looked through the script that you wrote in the previous example, you may be surprised to learn that AppleScript doesn't know anything about the Finder's operations. Although your recorded script contains commands that set the position, size, and view of a Finder window and selects an item in it, AppleScript doesn't know anything about these or other Finder operations. In fact, AppleScript knows how to perform only the six following commands:

    ✦ Copy

    ✦ Count

    ✦ Error

    ✦ Get

    ✦ Run

    ✦ Set

AppleScript learns about moving and resizing Finder windows from the Finder. More generally, AppleScript learns about commands in a script from the application that the script controls. The application has a dictionary of AppleScript commands that work with the application. The dictionary defines the syntax of each command. AppleScript learns about more commands from scripting addition files on your computer. Each scripting addition file contains a dictionary of supplemental AppleScript commands.

Learning application commands and objects

Look at the sample script you created. The first statement says,

```
tell application "Finder"
```

To AppleScript, this statement means "start working with the application named Finder." When AppleScript sees a `tell application` statement, it looks at the dictionary for the specified application and figures out what commands the application understands. For example, by looking at the Finder's dictionary, AppleScript learns that the Finder understands the `select` command. The dictionary also tells AppleScript what objects the application knows how to work with, such as files and windows. In addition, an application's dictionary tells AppleScript how to compile the words and phrases that you write in scripts into Apple event codes that the application understands.

After learning from the `tell application` statement which application it will send event messages to, AppleScript compiles the remaining statements to determine what Apple event messages to send. One by one, AppleScript translates every statement it encounters in your script into an Apple event message based on the application's dictionary. When the script runs, the Apple event messages will be sent to the application named in the `tell` statement. The application will receive the messages and take the appropriate action in response to the Apple events.

AppleScript stops using the application dictionary when it encounters the `end tell` statement at the end of your script.

A complex script may have several `tell application` statements that name different scriptable applications. In each case, AppleScript starts using the dictionary of the application named by the `tell application` statement, compiles subsequent statements using this dictionary, and stops using this dictionary when it encounters the next `end tell` statement. Because AppleScript gets all the information about an application's commands and objects from the application itself, you never have to worry about controlling a new application. As long as the application has a dictionary, AppleScript can work with it.

Inspecting a dictionary

Just as AppleScript can get information about an application's commands and objects from its dictionary, so can you. Using Script Editor, you can display the AppleScript dictionary of an application to see what commands the application understands and what objects the commands work with. You can also look at the dictionaries of scripting addition files.

Displaying a dictionary window

In Script Editor, choose Open Dictionary from the File menu. A dialog appears, listing scriptable applications and scripting additions. Select an application or scripting addition file in the list and click Open. Script Editor displays a dictionary window for the application or scripting addition you selected, as shown in Figure 21-3.

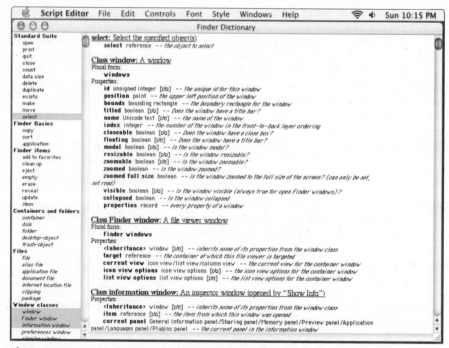

Figure 21-3: An AppleScript dictionary defines suites of commands and objects for a scriptable application or a scripting addition file.

Tip　In the Open Dictionary dialog, you can select several applications and scripting additions whose dictionaries you want to display (each in a separate window). To select adjacent items in the list, drag across or Shift-click the items. To select non-adjacent items, ⌘-click each item that you want to select.

Looking at a dictionary window

The left side of a dictionary window displays a list of commands and objects. The commands are displayed in plain text, and objects are displayed in italics. Script Editor groups related commands and objects into suites and displays the names of suites in bold. You don't have to worry about suites when you're scripting.

The right side of a dictionary window displays detailed information about the term or terms selected on the left. To see a detailed description of one term, click it on the left side of the window. To see detailed descriptions of all terms in a suite, click the suite name.

Tip   You can also see descriptions of several adjacent terms by dragging across them on the left. You can see descriptions of nonadjacent terms by Shift-clicking or ⌘-clicking each term on the left. Note that Shift-clicking works differently in Script Editor dictionary windows than in most other contexts. (Usually, Shift-clicking selects a range of items.)

The description of a command briefly explains what the command does and defines its syntax. In the syntax definition, bold words are command words that you must type exactly as written. Words in plain text represent information that you provide, such as a value or an object for the command to work on. Any parts of a syntax definition that are enclosed in brackets are optional.

The description of an object very briefly describes the object and may list the following:

✦ **Plural Form.** States how to refer to refer to multiple objects collectively. For example, you can refer to a specific window or to all windows.

✦ **Elements.** Enumerates items that can belong to the object. In a script, you would refer to *item* of *object*. For example, you could refer to a file named index.html in the folder named Sites as `file "index.html" of folder "Sites"`.

✦ **Properties.** Lists attributes of an object. Each property has a name, which is displayed in bold, and a value, which is described in plain text. Scripts can get and set property values, except that properties designated [r/o] (means read only) can't be changed.

Saving a Script

In Script Editor, you save a script by choosing Save, Save As, or Save As Run-Only from the File menu. When you choose one of these three commands, Script Editor displays a Save dialog. (The dialog does not appear when you choose Save for a script that has been saved.) In the dialog, you can choose any of several different file formats for the saved script. Figure 21-4 shows the Save dialog.

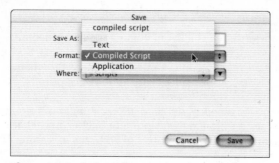

Figure 21-4: Script Editor can save a script in several formats.

Choosing Save or Save As Run-Only

Choosing Save or Save As from the File menu has almost the same effect as choosing Save As Run-Only. All three menu commands produce similar script files. The difference lies in whether the script file can be opened later. Choosing Save or Save As produces a file that can be opened, viewed, and changed. Choosing Save As Run-Only produces a file that can't be opened or changed. Run-only script files are perfect for distributing to people who you don't want to be able to modify your scripts, potentially causing the scripts to malfunction.

Caution   Be sure to save every script as a file that you can open so that you can revise the script in the future. If you need to revise a script that exists only as a run-only file, you have to recreate the script.

Looking at script file formats

Script Editor can save a script in three file formats. (Only two of the formats are available when you choose Save As Run-Only from the File menu.) When you save a new script or a copy of a script, you specify a file format by choosing the format from the Format pop-up menu in the Save dialog. Script Editor can save in the following file formats:

  ✦ **Text.** Saves the script as a plain text document. You can open it in Script Editor, in a word processing application, and in many other applications. Although adaptable, this format is not as efficient as the others, because the script must be compiled before it can be run. The Text format is not an option when you choose File➪Save As Run-Only.

  ✦ **Compiled Script.** Saves the script as Apple event codes rather than plain text. You can open it with Script Editor and then run or change it. You can also run compiled scripts by using the Script Runner application and applications that have a script menu, such as AppleWorks.

✦ **Application.** Saves the script as an application, complete with an icon. Opening the icon (by double-clicking it, for example) runs the script. When you choose the application format, the following two options appear at the bottom of the Save dialog:

- **Stay Open.** Causes the application to stay open after its script finishes running. If this option is turned off, the application quits automatically after running its script.

- **Never Show Startup Screen.** Suppresses the display of an identifying window that otherwise appears when the application is opened.

Creating a More Complex Script

You now know how to use Script Editor to create a simple AppleScript script. This type of script, however, has limited value. A simple script that doesn't take advantage of the full AppleScript language is not very intelligent.

More frequently, you'll use AppleScript to create more complex scripts. This section explains how to create a full-blown script quickly and use the resulting custom utility to augment an application's capabilities.

Making a Finder utility

Your Mac OS X disk is full of special folders, but when someone sends you a file, it's up to you to figure out where the file belongs. For example, you have to sort TIFF and JPEG files into your Pictures folder, QuickTime files into your Movies folder, and MP3 files into your Music folder. You also have to classify and put away fonts, sounds, and so on. The Finder doesn't help you sort out any of this.

You can, however, write a simple script that recognizes certain types of files and uses the Finder to move files to the folders where you want the files to go. The destination folders can be any folders that you have permission to change. These include all the folders in your home folder. If you log in as a user with administrator privileges, the destination folders can also include folders in the main Library folder.

Beginning the script

To begin writing a new script in Script Editor, choose File⇨New Script. Then type the following statement in the script editing area of the new script window:

```
choose file
```

This command gives the script user a way to specify the file to be moved. The `choose file` command displays a dialog for choosing a file. This command is part of a scripting addition that is preinstalled in Mac OS X. The name of this scripting addition is Standard Additions.

Changing AppleScript Formatting

You can change the way Script Editor formats text by choosing Edit⇨AppleScript Formatting. A dialog appears listing various components of AppleScript commands and the text format of each component. You can change the format of any component by selecting it in the dialog and then choosing different formatting from the Font and Style menus.

Seeing the script's results

The script isn't finished, but you can run it now to see the results of the one statement you have entered thus far. Click Run to run the script in its current condition. When AppleScript performs the `choose file` statement, it displays a dialog for choosing a file. Go ahead and select any file and click Choose. Because there aren't any more script statements, AppleScript stops the script.

AppleScript shows you the result of the last script action in the result window. If this window isn't open, choose Show Result from the Script Editor Controls menu. The result window contains the word alias and the path through your folders to the file you selected. This wording does not mean that the file is an alias file. In the context of a script, *alias* means the same thing as *file path*. Figure 21-5 is an example of the result window.

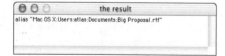

Figure 21-5: Script Editor's result window shows the result of running a script.

Using variables

The result of the `choose file` statement is called a file specification, or *file spec*. A file spec tells Mac OS X exactly where to find a file or folder. You need the file spec later in the script, so you must put it in a *variable,* which is a container for information. You can place data in a variable and then retrieve it whenever you want to before the script finishes running. The data in a variable is called the variable's *value.* You can change a variable's value by placing new data in it during the course of the script.

On the next line of the script, type the following statement:

```
copy the result to thisFile
```

This statement places the result of the `choose file` statement in a variable named `thisFile`. You can include the `thisFile` variable in any subsequent script statements that need to know the file spec of the chosen file. When AppleScript sees a variable name, it uses the current value of the variable. In this case, the value of variable `thisFile` is the file spec you got from the first statement.

When you run the script, you see that the `copy` command doesn't change the result of the script (as displayed in the result window). Because the result is just being copied to a variable, the result doesn't change.

Capitalizing script statements

You may notice the capital F in the `thisFile` variable and wonder whether capitalization is important when entering AppleScript statements. In general, you can capitalize any way that makes statements easier to read. Many AppleScript authors adopt the convention of capitalizing each word in a variable name except the first word, hence `thisFile`. This practice helps you distinguish variables from other terms in statements, which are generally all lowercase.

Getting file information

Ultimately, the script you are creating decides where to move a selected file based on the type of file it is. In Mac OS X, a file's type may be indicated by an extension (suffix) at the end of the file's name or by a hidden four-letter code known as the *file type*. Therefore, the script needs to determine the name and the file type of the selected file. You can use another command from the Standard Additions scripting addition to get this information. (Standard Additions is preinstalled in Mac OS X.) Enter the following statements beginning on the third line of the script:

```
copy the info for thisFile to fileInfo
copy the name extension of the fileInfo to nameExtension
copy the file type of the fileInfo to fileType
```

The first of these statements uses the `info for` command to get an information record about the selected file that is now identified by the variable `thisFile`. The first statement also copies the entire information record into a variable named `fileInfo`.

A record in AppleScript is a structured collection of data. Each data item in a record has a name and a value. AppleScript statements can refer to a particular item of a record by name, using a phrase similar to item of record. This is the phrasing used in the second two statements above.

Each of the second two statements gets an item of a record and copies it into a variable. The item names in these statements, name extension and file type, are taken from the AppleScript dictionary definition of the record. In this script, the record was obtained by the info for command in a previous statement. Figure 21-6 shows the AppleScript dictionary entries for the info for command and the record it provides.

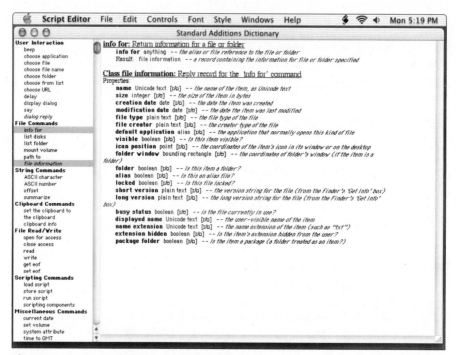

Figure 21-6: An AppleScript dictionary defines the structure of a record provided by an AppleScript command.

To test the script so far, run it, choose a file, and look at the result. The result window contains the four-letter file type of the file you chose, displayed as a piece of text. Figure 21-7 shows the whole example script so far.

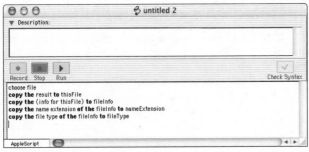

Figure 21-7: This script uses the `info for` command to get file name and file type information.

Using parentheses

You may notice that when AppleScript compiles the example script, which happens when you run the script or check its syntax, AppleScript adds parentheses around `info for thisFile` but does not add parentheses in other statements. AppleScript adds parentheses around a command that returns a value, which any `info for` command does. However, AppleScript does not add parentheses around a command at the end of a statement, such as the `choose file` command in the first statement of the example script. Nor does AppleScript add parentheses around elements that refer to a property, such as `the name extension of the fileInfo` in the example script.

Parentheses group elements of a command together. You can type your own parentheses around elements that you want to group in a statement. Parentheses make a complex AppleScript statement easier to read. Parentheses may also affect the result of a statement, because AppleScript evaluates elements within parentheses before evaluating other elements of a statement.

Working with an application

For the next part of the script, you need to add statements that move the chosen file to the folder where it belongs. The script can use an application—the Finder—to move the file. Add the following statement to have AppleScript start using the Finder:

```
tell application "Finder"
```

After AppleScript encounters this statement, it knows all the commands and objects from the Finder's AppleScript dictionary. This means that subsequent statements use commands and objects that the Finder understands. AppleScript sends these commands and objects to the Finder in Apple event messages. The script doesn't yet include any statements for the Finder, but we add some next. Later we add an `end tell` statement to have AppleScript stop using the Finder.

Performing script statements conditionally

For a situation like this, you include a series of conditional statements, or *conditionals* for short. Each conditional begins with an `if` statement, which defines the condition to be evaluated. The `if` statement is followed by one or more other statements to be performed only if the condition is true. The conditional ends with an `end if` statement. In AppleScript, a simple conditional looks like this:

```
if the fileType is "MooV" or the nameExtension is "mov" then
move thisFile to folder "Movies" of home
end if
```

In this example, the `if` statement contains a two-part condition. The first part of the condition determines whether the current value of the `fileType` variable is `MooV`, which is the four-letter file type of QuickTime movie files. The second part of the condition determines whether the file name ends with `mov`, which is the file name extension of a QuickTime movie file. If either part of the condition is true, AppleScript performs the included `move` statement. If both parts are false, AppleScript skips the included `move` statement and goes on to the statement that follows the `end if` statement. Remember that AppleScript sends the `move` command to the Finder because of the `tell application` statement earlier in the script.

Note   AppleScript considers the dot, or period, between the file name and the extension to be a separator. The dot is not part of the extension or the file name as far as AppleScript is concerned.

Include as many conditionals in the example script as you want. In each conditional, use the four-character file type and corresponding file name extension for a different type of file, and specify the path of the folder to which you want AppleScript to move files of that type. A quick way to enter several conditionals is to select one conditional (from the `if` statement through the `end if` statement), copy it, paste it at the end of the script, and change the relevant pieces of information. You can repeat this for each conditional you want to include.

Finding a Folder Path

If you don't know the full path of a folder, you can use a script to get this information. Open a new window in Script Editor and type the following script in the script editing area:

```
choose folder
```

Run the script and select a folder. The result is a file spec for the folder you selected. You can copy the text from the result window and paste it in any script.

You may notice that the file spec has a colon after each folder name. AppleScript uses colons in file specs to maintain compatibility with Mac OS 9 and earlier. Outside of AppleScript, Mac OS X generally follows the UNIX and Internet convention of putting a slash after each folder name.

Finding a File's Type

You may not know the file type of the files that you want to move. For example, you may know that you want to put font files in your Fonts folder, but you may not know that the four-letter file type of a font file is FFIL. To make a script that reports the file type, copy the following three-line script to a new Script Editor window:

```
choose file
copy the result to thisFile
copy the file type of the info for thisFile to fileType
```

Run this three-line script and select a file whose four-character file type you need to learn. If the result window is not visible, choose Show Result from the Controls menu. The result of the script is the file type of the selected file. You can copy and paste the result from the result window into a conditional statement in any script window.

If you choose a file that has no file type, one of two things happens. The result window displays an empty value (indicated by quotation marks with nothing between them) or AppleScript reports an error, saying that it can't get the file type.

Breaking long statements

When you type a long statement, Script Editor never breaks it automatically (as a word processor does). You can break a long statement manually by pressing Option-Return. (Do not break a statement in the middle of a quoted text string, however.) AppleScript displays a special symbol (¬) to indicate a manual break. Here's an example:

```
if the fileType is "JPEG" or ¬
the nameExtension is "jpg" or ¬
the nameExtension is "jpeg" then
move thisFile to folder "Pictures" of home
end if
```

In this example, the first statement, which goes from `if` through `then`, takes three lines because it has two manual line breaks.

Ending the use of an application

After the last statement that is directed at the Finder, the script needs a statement that makes AppleScript stop using the application. Type the following statement at the end of the script:

```
end tell
```

This statement doesn't include the name of the application to stop using because AppleScript automatically pairs an `end tell` statement with the most recent `tell` statement. Subsequent statements in the script can't use the commands and objects of that application.

Now is a good time to recheck the script's syntax. If you tried to check syntax recently, you got an error message about a missing end tell statement. Click Check Syntax now, and after AppleScript compiles the script you see Script Editor neatly indent statements to make the structure of the script more apparent. If AppleScript encounters any errors while compiling your script, Script Editor advises you of them one by one.

Trying out your script

After creating a new script, you must run it and test it thoroughly. To test the script that moves files according to their type, follow these steps:

1. **Run your script.**

2. **When the dialog appears, select a file that is of a type your script should recognize but that is not in the destination folder; then click Choose.**

3. **Switch to the Finder, and make sure that the file you selected actually moved from the source folder to the destination folder.**

4. **Repeat the test, selecting a different file type that your script should recognize.**

Figure 21-8 shows an example of a script with four conditional statements that move a selected file depending on its file type or file name extension.

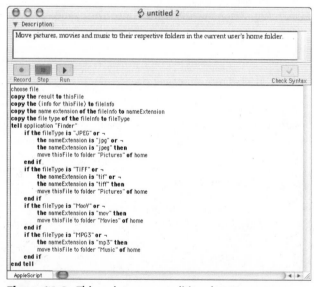

Figure 21-8: This script uses conditional statements to determine where to put a file.

Creating a drag-and-drop script application

Although the sample script you created is useful, it would be more useful as an application with an icon on your Desktop. Then you could drag files that you wanted to sort into folders and drop them on the application's icon. This would cause the application to run and move the files to their appropriate folders. You wouldn't have to open Script Editor every time you wanted to sort files into folders, and you could sort more than one file at a time. AppleScript gives you this capability.

You already know that AppleScript can save a script as an application. With a little extra work, you can make an application with drag-and-drop capability so that you can simply drag files to it.

Retrieving dropped files

Remember that when you drop a set of icons on an application in a Finder window, the Finder sends that application an Open Documents message that includes a list of the files you dropped on the icon. This message is sent to all applications, even to applications that you create yourself with AppleScript.

You need to tell your script to intercept that event message and retrieve the list of items that were dropped on to the application icon. Place the following statement at the beginning of your script:

```
on open itemList
```

Now enter the following statement at the end of your script:

```
end open
```

This on open statement enables the script to intercept an Open Documents event message and puts the message's list of files in a variable named itemList. The end open statement helps AppleScript know which statements to perform when the open message is received. Any statements between the on open and end open statements are performed when the script receives an Open Documents event message.

Save this script by choosing the Save As command from the File menu. From the Format pop-up menu in the Save As dialog, choose the Application option. (You may want to save the script on the Desktop, at least for experimental purposes.) If you switch to the Finder and look at the icon of the application you just created, you can see that the icon includes an arrow, which indicates that the icon represents a drag-and-drop application. The application has this kind of icon because its script includes an on open statement.

Processing dropped files

The script won't be fully operational until you make a few more changes. As the script stands, it places the list of files in a variable, but it doesn't do anything with that information. If you dropped several files on the application now, the script would still display a dialog asking you to pick a file and then quit, having accomplished nothing.

First, you need to eliminate the script statements that obtain the file to be processed from a dialog. Delete what now are the second and third lines of the script (the ones beginning with the words choose and copy) and replace them with the following:

```
repeat with x from 1 to the number of items in the itemList
copy item x of the itemList to thisFile
```

Between the end tell and end open statements, which are the last two lines of the script, enter the following statement:

```
end repeat
```

Figure 21-9 shows the complete sample script modified for drag-and-drop operation.

Save the script so that your changes take effect and then switch back to the Finder. You now have a drag-and-drop application that you can use to move certain types of files to specific folders.

Figure 21-9: This script application processes items dropped on its icon.

Using a repeat loop

In the modified script, AppleScript repeatedly performs the statements between the repeat and end repeat statements for the number of times specified in the repeat statement. This arrangement is called a *repeat loop*. The first time AppleScript performs the repeat statement, it sets variable x to 1, as specified by from 1. Then AppleScript performs statements sequentially until it encounters the end repeat statement.

In the first statement of the repeat loop, variable x determines which file spec to copy from variable itemList to variable thisFile. The rest of the statements in the repeat loop are carried over from the previous version of the script.

When AppleScript encounters the end repeat statement, it loops back to the repeat statement, adds 1 to variable x, and compares the new value of x with the number of items that were dragged to the icon (as specified by the phrase the number of items in the itemList). If the two values are not equal, AppleScript performs the statements in the repeat loop again. If the two values are equal, these statements are performed one last time, and AppleScript goes to the statement immediately following end repeat. This is the end open statement, which ends the script.

Extending the script

Anytime you want the application to handle another type of file, open the script application in Script Editor, add a conditional that covers that type of file, and save the script.

Tip You can't open a script application by double-clicking it because doing so causes the application to run. To open a script application in Script Editor, choose File ➪ Open command in Script Editor or drop the script application on the Script Editor icon in the Finder.

Borrowing Scripts

An easy way to make a script is to modify an existing script that does something close to what you want. You simply duplicate the script file in the Finder, open the duplicate copy, and make changes. You can do this with scripts that have been saved as applications, compiled scripts, or text files. (You can't open a script that has been saved as a run-only script.)

Apple has developed a number of scripts that you can use as starting points or models for your own scripts. You can find some scripts in the Example Scripts folder, which is in the AppleScript folder in the Applications folder. Another place to look is the Scripts folder, which is in the ColorSync folder of main Library folder (the path is /Library/ColorSync/Scripts/). For some complex scripts that really give the Finder a workout, look in the Scripts folder of the Image Capture folder in the main Library folder (path /Library/Image Capture/Scripts/). More scripts are available on the Web. The official AppleScript site has some (www.apple.com/applescript/). Check out the Learn AppleScript, Help & Examples, and Download Scripts areas of this site. Part of the AppleScript site has scripting examples specifically for Mac OS X (www.apple.com/applescript/macosx/).

If you have upgraded to Mac OS X from a previous version of the Mac OS, look for Mac OS 9 scripts in the Automated Tasks folder of the Apple Menu Items folder, which is located in the System Folder. You may find more Mac OS 9 scripts in the AppleScript folder of the Apple Extras folder, which is normally in the folder named Applications (Mac OS 9). Additional Mac OS 9 scripts are located in the AppleScript Extras folder of the CD Extras folder on the Mac OS 9 CD-ROM.

Note   Some Mac OS 9 scripts work as-is with Mac OS X, but many require some tweaking. In particular, scripts made to control the Mac OS 9 Finder are likely to require modification, and some parts may not work at all.

Running Scripts

After you've built up a collection of scripts that you run frequently, you're not going to want to switch to Script Editor every time you want to run one. This reason is precisely why Mac OS X includes the Script Menu in 10.2, which replaces the Script Runner application in 10.1 and earlier. The Script Menu sits in the OS toolbar at the top of the screen as shown in Figure 21-10. You can run any of the listed scripts by choosing it from the pop-up menu.

Figure 21-10: Scripts listed in Script Menu's pop-up menu are always available no matter which application is currently active.

Running Scripts from the Menu Bar in OS 9

For a script menu in the Classic environment, you need the OSA Menu software. OSA Menu allows you to quickly run Mac OS 9 scripts while any Classic application is the active application. The scripts are listed in a permanent menu near the right end of the Classic menu bar. You can also use the script menu to start recording a script or open the Classic version of Script Editor. OSA Menu is a system extension for Mac OS 9. It's on the Mac OS 9 CD in the AppleScript Extras folder, which is in the CD Extras folder.

Tip   The Script Menu is not limited to just AppleScript, it can be used to launch Perl and shell scripts as well. Perl and shell scripts are discussed in Chapter 26.

Linking Programs

You have seen how AppleScript can automate tasks on your own computer. Beginning with Mac OS X 10.1, AppleScript can also send Apple events messages to open applications on other Macs in a network. As a result, you can use AppleScript to control applications on other people's computers. Of course, the reverse is also true; other people can use AppleScript to control applications on your computer. To send and receive Apple events over a network your Mac must be running with Mac OS X 10.1, 10.2, or Mac OS 9.

Sharing programs by sending and receiving Apple events messages across a network is called *program linking*. For security reasons, program linking is normally disabled. Computers that you want to control with AppleScript must be set to allow remote Apple events. Likewise you must set your computer to allow remote Apple events.

Mac OS X 10.1 and up use the TCP/IP protocol to send and receive Apple events messages over a network. Therefore, Mac OS X 10.1 and 10.2 can send and receive Apple events messages over the Internet as well as a local network. Mac OS X 10.1 or 10.2 can't use the AppleTalk protocol to send or receive Apple events over a remote network as can Mac OS 9 and earlier. Mac OS X 10.0–10.0.4 can't send or receive remote Apple events.

Allowing remote Apple events

If you want a Mac OS X computer to receive Apple events from remote computers, you must set it to allow remote Apple events. First, open System Preferences and then choose View⇨Sharing (or click the Sharing button). In Sharing Preferences, click the Application tab and then turn on the option labeled Allow remote Apple events. If you want the computer to receive Apple events from remote Mac OS 9 computers, turn on the option labeled Allow Mac OS 9 computer to use remote

Apple events. If you turn on this option, a dialog appears in which you must enter a password that Mac OS 9 users will have to use when sending Apple events messages to the computer. You can change this password later by clicking Set Password in Sharing Preferences. Figure 21-11 shows remote Apple events turned on in Sharing Preferences.

Figure 21-11: Set Mac OS X to receive remote Apple events by using the Sharing pane of System Preferences.

Scripting across a network

Using AppleScript to run a program across the network doesn't take much more work than writing a script to use a program on the same computer. For example, the following script sends commands to the Finder on the computer at IP address 192.168.1.203:

```
set remoteMachine to machine "eppc://192.168.203"
tell application "Finder" of remoteMachine
   using terms from application "Finder"
        activate
        open the trash
   end using terms from
end tell
```

Turning On Program Linking in Mac OS 9

If you want a computer that's using Mac OS 9 to receive remote Apple events messages from your computer, the Mac OS 9 computer must have program linking turned on. To do this, open the Mac OS 9 computer's File Sharing control panel and click the Start button in the control panel's Program Linking section. In addition, turn on the option labeled Enable Program Linking clients to connect over TCP/IP. The Mac OS 9 computer is ready for program linking when the button's label changes to Stop and the File Sharing control panel reports "Program Linking on," as shown in the following figure.

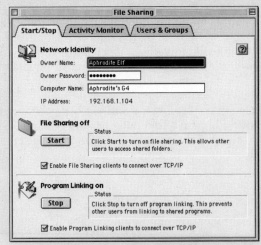

A Mac OS 9 computer can receive remote Apple events when program linking is turned on and set to use TCP/IP.

Mac OS 9 can be configured to receive remote Apple events only from specific users. These access restrictions are set up with the Users & Groups tab in the File Sharing control panel. In addition, each application on a Mac OS 9 computer can be set to not receive any remote Apple events. This restriction is set in each application's Info window in the Finder.

The example script begins by setting the value of variable `remoteMachine` to the URL of a remote computer. A URL for remote Apple events begins with `eppc://` and is followed by the remote computer's IP address or DNS name. (The prefix `eppc` stands for event program-to-program communication.)

The second statement of the example script names the application, in this case Finder, and uses the variable `remoteMachine` to identify the remote computer.

Inside the `tell application...end tell` block is another block that is bracketed by the statements `using terms from` and `end using terms from`. When AppleScript encounters the statement `using terms from`, it compiles subsequent statements using the named application's scripting dictionary but does not send the resulting Apple events to this application. The Apple events from a `using terms from` block are sent to the application named in the enclosing `tell application` block. In the example script, AppleScript compiles the `activate` and `open the trash` statements using terms from the Finder's scripting dictionary on the local computer (your computer) but sends the resulting Apple events to the Finder on the remote computer.

When you run a script that sends remote Apple events, AppleScript has to connect to the remote application. Before doing this, AppleScript displays a dialog in which you must enter a name and password of a user account on the remote computer. If you connect successfully, the script continues. At this point the example script should cause the remote computer's Finder to become the active application and open the Trash in a Finder window.

If you run the script again, you don't have to go through the authentication process. After AppleScript is connected to an application on a particular remote computer, you don't have to go through the authentication dialog each time you want to send an Apple event.

Summary

Here's what you learned in this chapter:

✦ AppleScript makes applications perform tasks by sending them Apple event messages.

✦ AppleScript is a programming language designed with everyday users in mind, but with enough power for advanced users and programmers.

✦ Many AppleScript terms come from the applications it controls. AppleScript terms also come from files called scripting additions.

✦ Use the Script Editor application to create, edit, and run AppleScript scripts. Script Editor can also make scripts into applications.

✦ Script Editor can display the AppleScript dictionary of an application to see what commands an application or scripting addition understands and what objects the commands work with.

✦ You can save a script in any of three formats: text, compiled script, or Application.

✦ You type AppleScript statements into a new Script Editor window, check the syntax for errors, and run the script to test it. Your script can use a copy statement to set the value of a variable. To start controlling an application, you use a tell application statement. A matching end tell statement stops controlling the application. With if statements, you can have AppleScript perform some operations only when specified conditions are met. Repeat loops execute a group of statements over and over. To make a drag-and-drop script application, you include an on open statement and a matching end open statement.

✦ Apple has developed a number of scripts that you can use as starting points or models for your own scripts.

✦ You can use Script Runner or Script Menu to run compiled scripts no matter what application is currently active.

✦ AppleScript can control applications over a network or the Internet on computers that are set to allow remote Apple events.

✦   ✦   ✦

Making the Most of Mac OS X

Working with Included Programs

Mac OS X provides a collection of useful and necessary programs as well as some diversions (games). A CD only has so much space available, so not all applications are initially installed on your disk. Apple makes a growing and changing collection of Mac OS X programs available through your iDisk. In this chapter, we briefly describe each of the programs that Apple provides in your Applications folder. Apple may change the mix or produce new versions of some programs as Mac OS X becomes more commonly used. We also give you an introduction to some of the Apple-provided programs available via your iDisk and attempt to explain, for the longtime Mac users in our readership, what happened to some of the programs to which you've become accustomed.

Changing with the Times

As you've probably gathered by now, Mac OS X is more a revolution than an evolution in the way that you use your Mac. With the Classic environment available, you have the temptation to continue doing things in a familiar way by using familiar tools. Because much of the software that you find in stores and on the Internet is still for Classic or is carbonized for use under both Mac OS 9 and Mac OS X, there is a tendency for documents to launch a Classic version or application.

The first bit of advice we're going to give you is to remove all copies of SimpleText from your system. Many applications, even in the days of Mac OS X, save text files with a default creator of SimpleText — particularly files downloaded from the Internet. Further, if you have a Classic application that's equivalent to a Mac OS X application, remove the Classic application unless you know that you're going to be using it in the Classic environment. Two Classic applications that have Mac OS X equivalents — Internet Explorer and Picture Viewer — come immediately to mind.

Unless you know that you're going to be starting in Mac OS 9 and that you need the Classic versions of these applications, the applications in the left column can go. The right column shows the new Mac OS X equivalent.

Table 22-1	
Archaic Applications and Their Replacements	
Classic Application to Remove	*Mac OS X Replacement*
Apple Applet Runner	Applet Launcher
AppleCD Audio Player	iTunes
Disk First Aid	Disk Utility
iMovie 2	iMovie 2 for Mac OS X
SimpleText	TextEdit

Using Mac OS X Applications

As we remarked earlier in this chapter, Mac OS X comes with a number of applications and utilities in the Applications folder and its subdirectories. This section lists the applications in this hierarchy and briefly describes them and their use or points you to another chapter where we cover the applications in detail.

Acrobat Reader

With Acrobat Reader, you can read and print documents in the common PDF (Portable Document Format). You can do the same with the Preview application (described later), but with Acrobat Reader you can do more. You can search for text in a PDF document, and you can copy text or graphics for pasting in another application. If you're viewing a PDF document with bookmarks or thumbnails, Acrobat Reader can display them and you can use them to navigate the document. In addition, Acrobat Reader can display facing pages side by side. Not only is PDF the native format for Mac OS X graphics, it is also the most common format used for distributing fully formatted documents on CD and the Internet. Adobe makes the free Acrobat Reader application, and Apple includes it as part of Mac OS X 10.1. Figure 22-1 shows an example of Acrobat Reader. (Compare to the Preview application's display of the PDF file, shown later in Figure 22-7.)

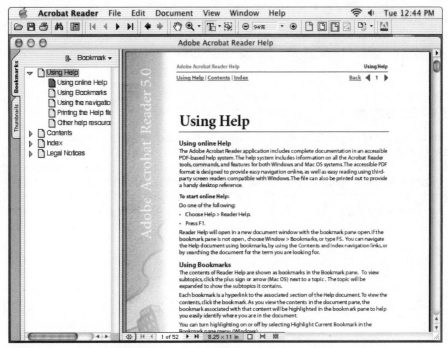

Figure 22-1: Flip through a PDF document in Acrobat Reader by clicking bookmarks on the left side of the document window.

Address Book

The Mac OS X Address Book not only functions as a personal card file, but is integrated with the Mail application (covered in Chapter 6) and allows access to Web-based directory services, such as BigFoot, Four11, and WhoWhere. Figure 22-2 shows an example of the Address Book main window.

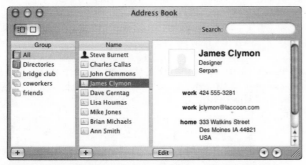

Figure 22-2: A big step forward from the traditional little black book.

AppleScript (folder)

The AppleScript folder contains two applications, Script Editor and Script Runner as well as a folder of example AppleScripts. Refer to Chapter 21 for complete coverage of these items.

Calculator

For those of you familiar with the venerable Calculator desk accessory, which has been included with every Mac OS release since the dawn of time (1984), this Calculator looks very familiar. However, the two buttons just below the numerical display add functionality. The Advanced button adds a wide range of advanced math functions, and the Paper Tape button adds a pane on the right emulating a scrolling paper tape. Figure 22-3 shows the expanded version of the Calculator.

Figure 22-3: Much more than the service station giveaway calculator in a pretty Aqua case it used to be.

Chess

Chess is one of the most engrossing games of strategy in human history. People have played it for many centuries, and it is considered by many to be a very good test of machine intelligence. This piece of software gives you the choice of two boards, a beautiful wooden set with a 3-D perspective or a more traditional 2-dimensional representation. Both are shown in Figure 22-4.

Not only can you play chess against the computer, but you can also set the level of how well the computer can play by limiting the time available for it to calculate its moves. The chess program behind the beautiful interface is the GNU (Gnu's Not Unix) offering of the Free Software Foundation with its famous *copyleft* notice saying that any software based on the code must be made available in source form, if you want it.

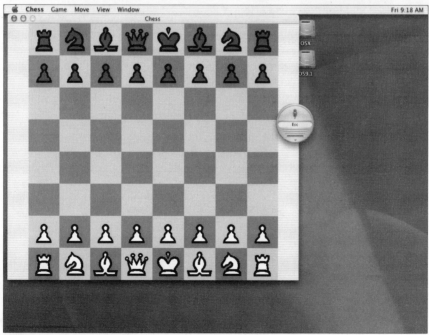

Figure 22-4: You can play chess on either 3-D or 2-D boards.

If you want a list of the moves in a game, choose Game⇨List to save the game record. The Move menu gives you the following choices:

✦ **Hint (⌘-Shift-H):** Tells Chess to give you a hint as to your best move in the current position.

✦ **Show Last Move (⌘-Shift-M):** Tells Chess to remind you of the last move you (or it) made. This command can be handy when you are playing at intermittent intervals.

✦ **Take Back Move (⌘-Z):** Tells Chess to let you undo your last move.

Choose Game⇨Controls to set piece colors or have the computer play against itself.

Clock

The clock is one of the less useful accessories in our opinion, considering that you have a clock in the menu bar; however, it does give you an analog clock that can float around as a window or sit in your Dock.

iChat

iChat is an AOL-compatible Instant Messaging (IM) client included with 10.2. You can connect to AOL's AIM service, and have a separate window for a list of IM "buddies" on the local Rendezvous network. Figure 22-5 shows the Rendezvous and AOL IM Buddy windows, and preferences for a given account.

Figure 22-5: iChat is an AOL IM–compatible instant messaging client.

Image Capture

Apple CEO Steve Jobs calls your Mac the hub of your multimedia experience. Well, if digital cameras are any indication, Image Capture starts putting action to those words. Although not all USB camera models are recognized (according to reports on the Internet and Apple's Web-based user forums), the mainstream ones, which store their images in an accepted format, such as JPEG, are. Plug your USB camera into the Mac, turn it on if necessary, and its icon appears in the Finder like the icon of a removable disk.

By using Image Capture, you can download the pictures from your camera to disk, scaling to particular sizes if desired. You can even tell Image Capture to create a Web page of your photos for you, such as the one shown in Figure 22-6.

Figure 22-6: Image Capture even runs an automatic AppleScript to create a Web page of your photos.

iMovie

Use iMovie to turn raw video footage from a digital camcorder into a movie by removing unwanted footage, rearranging scenes, and adding titles, transitions, visual effects, sound effects, and other audio. We describe iMovie in more detail in Chapter 13. Figure 22-7 shows what movie making is like in iMovie.

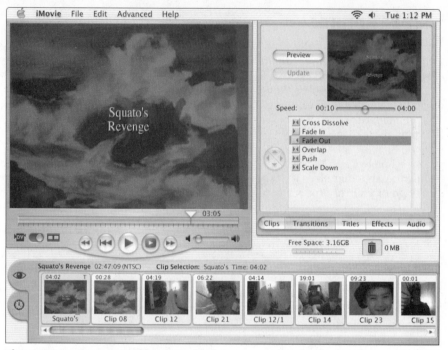

Figure 22-7: Amaze your friends and influence people with the movies you create using iMovie and a digital camcorder.

Internet Connect

If you have a dial-up connection to the Internet, or even if you use PPPoE (Point-to-Point Protocol over Ethernet) on a DSL connection, Internet Connect is the tool to use to initiate your connection. You can also use it to connect to an Airport network or to have your AirPort base station connect to the Internet. Refer to Chapter 6 for detailed coverage of Internet Connect.

Internet Explorer

Internet Explorer, Microsoft's Web browser, is included with your Mac OS X software. Version 5.2 was shipped with Mac OS X for 10.2; however, a later version may be included with your Mac OS X release. Internet Explorer is also covered in Chapter 6.

iPhoto

iPhoto is a new application in OS X that works with digital photographs. Using iPhoto, you transfer pictures from a digital camera into your Mac and then view, sort, label, and categorize photos. Albums and webpage slide galleries can be created easily. Figure 22-8 shows the starting window of iPhoto and the preferences window.

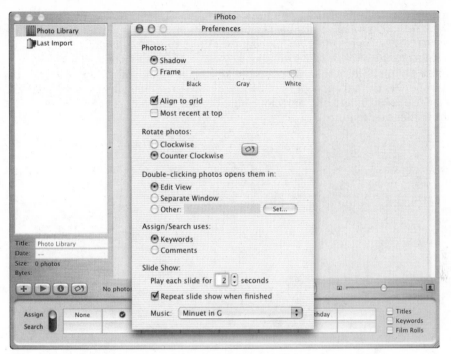

Figure 22-8: iPhoto is used to import and manage digital photographs.

iTunes

With iTunes, you can have music coming in your ears from a mixture of sources including audio CDs, MP3 files from the Internet, an MP3 player, and an Internet radio station. You can create your own playlists of songs from CD and MP3, and if your Mac has a CD recorder, you can use iTunes to burn audio CDs. If you have an Apple iPod, you can copy songs to it and organize songs on it by using iTunes 3. Chapter 14 covers iTunes in detail.

Mail

Mail is another application that we cover in Chapter 6. Apple's Mail application is a very capable and flexible e-mail program. It offers excellent integration with the Address Book application (covered earlier in this section), handles multiple mail-boxes including your iTools e-mail account, and lets you define rules for the automatic processing of incoming mail.

Preview

Preview is a small application that does a lot. As described in Chapter 9, Preview is integrated into the printing process, enabling you to preview any Mac OS X print job. Additionally, it enables you to view any QuickTime-readable graphics file and PDF (Adobe Acrobat's Portable Document Format) files. Any print job can be saved as PDF (File⇨Save As PDF). Choosing the File⇨Export command enables you to save a graphics file in TIFF format or any other graphics format QuickTime recognizes. Figure 22-9 shows a graphics file and a PDF displayed in Preview. (Compare to Acrobat Reader's display of the PDF file, shown previously in Figure 22-1.) Preview can also zoom in and out, and can rotate the image to left and right, as well as several other new features.

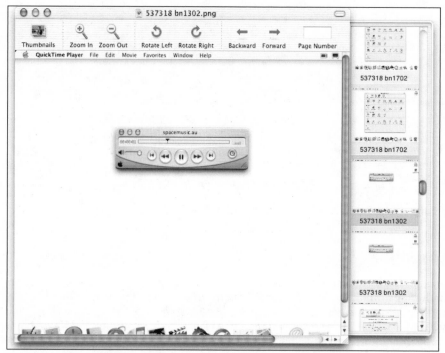

Figure 22-9: The Preview application opens PDF files and a variety of graphics files; it can also convert graphics files to other formats.

QuickTime Player

QuickTime is Apple's award-winning cross-platform multimedia technology. The QuickTime Player application plays digital movie files, QuickTime TV and other streaming QuickTime media from the Internet, QuickTime VR (virtual reality) panoramas and objects, and MP3 and other audio files. Apple provides QuickTime Player and the technology behind it with Mac OS X and as a free download for any interested Mac or Windows user. You can read all about QuickTime and QuickTime Player in Chapter 13. Figure 22-10 shows a QuickTime Player movie window (together with some Stickies notes).

Sherlock

First introduced with Mac OS 8.5, Sherlock helps you find things, whether they're on your disk or on the Internet. Chapter 7 details what Sherlock can do—check it out.

Stickies

Is anything so ubiquitous in today's offices and homes as the Post-it note? Stickies is the electronic equivalent—just create a Stickies note and leave it on your screen for notes or reminders. Stickies has been part of the Mac OS since System 7.5, but the Mac OS X version takes these handy little gadgets to new heights. They now support multiple fonts and styles and can even contain embedded graphics. Best of all, they lend themselves as a Service. Refer to Chapter 11 for a discussion of the Make Sticky service. Figure 22-10 shows several Stickies notes (together with a QuickTime Player window).

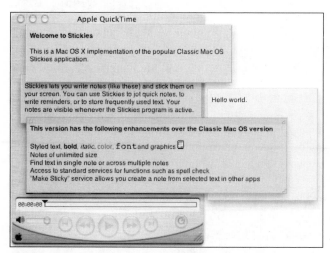

Figure 22-10: Stickies posts notes on your screen; QuickTime Player displays movies.

System Preferences

Chapter 15 is devoted to covering this essential collection of panels—the nerve center of your Mac OS where you establish how Mac OS X works for you.

TextEdit

This little gem begins life bearing the burden of (at least) two serious misconceptions: The first is that TextEdit is the Mac OS X version of the venerable SimpleText application, which is the successor to the even more venerable TeachText. The second misconception is due to its name—the belief that it is just a simple text editor. Both of these ideas are without foundation, although you can use TextEdit as a simple text editor if you wish, as described later in this section.

TextEdit is a word-processor. No, it's not competitive with Microsoft Word or with AppleWorks, but it is all the word-processor many people ever need. When you first launch TextEdit, you may think that it really is SimpleText in new clothes, as shown in Figure 22-11.

Figure 22-11: TextEdit looks pretty barren at first glance . . .

If, however, you explore the menus just a bit, then great power is revealed, as shown in Figure 22-12, where you have a ruler with various tab stops and different paragraphs formatted in different manners with differing margins.

As you insert tabs or adjust the margins or the first line indent, TextEdit provides feedback as to just where the margins are, as seen in Figure 22-12. TextEdit's Preferences, shown in Figure 22-13 and outlined in the following list, hint at the flexibility of this little word processor.

✦ **New Document Attributes:** Where you specify whether the default document format is in plain text or rich text. There is also a check box, Wrap to Page, where you can specify that the window's contents rewrap when the length matches that of a printed page. The default setting (off) has TextEdit wrapping at the window's width, somewhat like a Web page. All of these settings are adjustable on a document-by-document basis.

✦ **Default Fonts:** Where you establish the default font to use for both rich text and plain text documents. Initially, TextEdit defaults to 12 point Helvetica for rich text and 10 point Monaco for plain text documents.

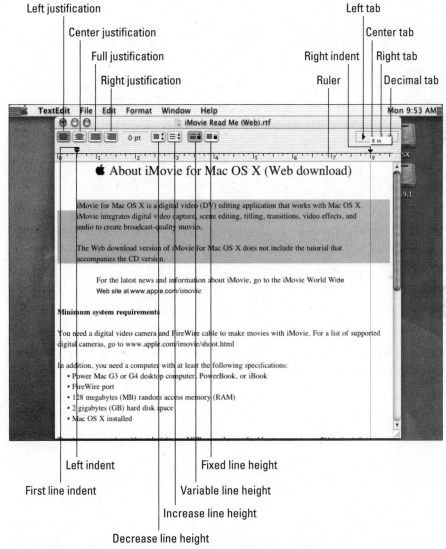

Figure 22-12: But TextEdit has great power under the hood.

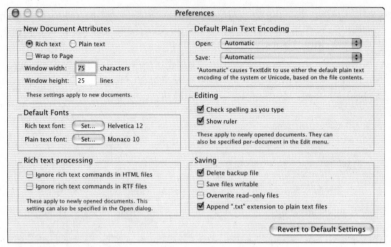

Figure 22-13: TextEdit has plenty of Preferences at hand.

✦ **Rich text processing:** Where you can tell TextEdit to ignore embedded Rich Text commands in HTML or RTF files. Ignoring these commands results in plain text being read and figures ignored.

✦ **Default Plain Text Encoding:** Allows you to specify the text encoding (character set mapping) for files you open or save. Automatic is the default choice for both, but can be changed. When Automatic is chosen, TextEdit uses either Unicode or the default encoding for your System, depending upon the document's contents.

✦ **Editing:** Lets you turn on spell-checking-as-you-type. When you type a word that the spell-checker doesn't recognize, the word is underlined with small red dots. Control-click on the word, and the contextual menu gives you a choice of possible corrections as well as the opportunity to have the word added to your dictionary or for the spelling to be ignored for this instance only, as shown in Figure 22-14.

✦ **Saving:** Lets you set preferences for actions to be taken when you save a document. *Delete backup file* tells TextEdit not to save the previous version as a backup file. *Save files writable* sets write privileges on for everyone, not just the owner or group. *Overwrite read-only files* reverses the standard behavior of not letting you edit and save changes to read-only files. *Append ".txt" extension to plain text files* tells TextEdit to put the extension on the filename for plain text files. Although not necessary for Mac OS X users, this option comes in handy for cross-platform users and is a good visual clue as to the file's character.

✦ **Revert to Default Settings:** The button at the bottom of the dialog that sets all preferences back to their factory defaults.

Figure 22-14: Use the contextual menu to correct spelling errors in TextEdit.

Utilizing Mac OS X Utilities

The Utilities folder within the Applications folder is the repository of another large collection of applications, although used less frequently. Exceptions to that, for example, are Print Center and Disk Copy, both of which may be used quite frequently.

AirPort Admin Utility

If you have an AirPort base station device, you can use the AirPort Admin Utility to change settings that the AirPort Setup Assistant (described next) doesn't handle. For example, by changing settings with AirPort Admin Utility you can do the following:

✦ Change the AirPort network name, wireless channel number, and so on.

✦ Change individual Internet connection settings, such as the phone number for a modem connection.

✦ Share a single public IP address on your AirPort network and optionally on an Ethernet network, as shown in Figure 22-15.

✦ Turn on a DHCP server to automatically assign private IP addresses to computers on your AirPort network. and optionally on an Ethernet network.

✦ Restrict use of the wireless network to computers that you identify.

✦ Designate computers on your network to provide particular Internet services such as Web server (Web sharing) and FTP server.

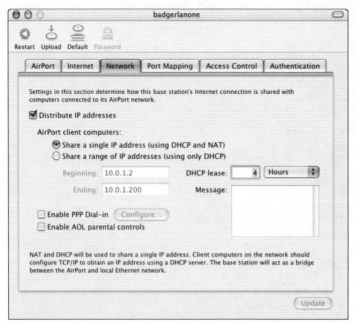

Figure 22-15: Change many settings on an AirPort base station device by using the AirPort Admin Utility application.

AirPort Setup Assistant

The AirPort Setup Assistant leads you through the process of setting up or reconfiguring an Apple AirPort Base Station, which is a piece of equipment that establishes a wireless network. Macs equipped with AirPort cards can join the wireless network, as can other computers that have cards or circuitry that is compatible with the 802.11b standard for wireless networking. The AirPort Setup Assistant can also help you set your computer to join an AirPort wireless network. Chapter 18 covers the AirPort Setup Assistant in more detail.

You can't use the AirPort Setup Assistant included with Mac OS X 10.2 to set up or reconfigure a software base station. In this case, the wireless network is established by turning on Sharing in the Internet tab of the Sharing pane of System Preferences.

Apple System Profiler

The Apple System Profiler tells you what you may need to know if you ever need to call Apple Computer (or some other hardware or software vendor) for technical assistance. You can find out what your processor type is, exactly which version of Mac OS you're running (including any updates), which bus your startup drive is on, how much RAM is present and where it is located, and what frameworks, extensions, and applications are installed. Figure 22-16 shows an example of the details that Apple System Profiler reports.

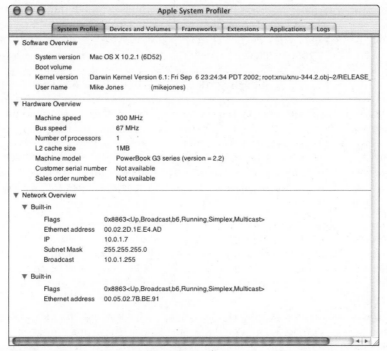

Figure 22-16: Apple System Profiler tells you more than you may want to know about your hardware and software.

You can choose from among these categories of information:

✦ **System Profile category:** Provides details about your system's software, memory, hardware, network, and production information. This category has six subcategories that you can show or hide by clicking the disclosure triangle next to the subcategory name in the application window. The six subcategories are:

- **Software overview:** Provides information about the version of the Mac OS running on your computer. The software overview also identifies your startup device.

- **Memory overview:** Provides details about built-in memory and external caches.

- **Hardware overview:** Identifies the machine ID, model name, keyboard type, processor type, and machine speed, if applicable.

- **Network overview:** Displays details about networking options that are installed and active. For TCP/IP, you can get the broadcast address, netmask, IP address, and hardware address.

- **Production information:** Tells you which ROM revision the computer is using, the hardware serial number, and the Apple part number (sales order number).

✦ **Devices and Volumes category:** Provides a hierarchical chart of information about all the devices connected to your computer. The highest level of the hierarchy is the type of device: SCSI bus, PCI slot, network, USB, Firewire, ATA bus, and so on. As you read across the pane you see more-detailed information about each type of device. For example, for SCSI devices, a list of all devices attached to the SCSI bus in order by SCSI ID number displays. For each device, you can see what type of device it is, what driver it's using, and the vendor, revision number, product ID, and serial number. For a removable-media drive, you can see whether a disk is currently inserted. For a storage device, you can see information about all the volumes on it; for each volume, you can check the format, size, space available, percent full, and whether the volume is write protected or file sharing is on. You determine the level of detail displayed by clicking disclosure triangles that hide or reveal more details about each device.

✦ **Frameworks category:** Lists all of the *frameworks* (support libraries) currently available, displaying the name, version, and whether the framework is from Apple. Clicking a framework's disclosure triangle reveals more information, such as what the framework is called, how it is recognized by the defaults system, copyright information, source version, build version, and release status.

✦ **Extensions category:** Lists all of the extensions currently available, including the name and version of each extension. This feature also tells you whether an extension is from Apple. Clicking an extension's disclosure triangle reveals more information, similar to that of a framework.

✦ **Applications category:** Lists all of the application programs on your startup volume. This feature displays the name, version number, and whether it's an Apple application. Clicking an application's disclosure triangle reveals information about the application. Some applications also display a brief description of their functions in the Get Info string field when selected.

Each time you open System Profiler, it gathers information for the System Profile category. You can also set up System Profiler to gather other categories of information at launch.

You can also create reports of System Profiler information by choosing New Report from the File menu. A dialog in which you select the categories of information you want in the report appears. Reports can be in Apple System Profiler format or in text format. You select the report format at the top of the report window. In addition, you can set a standard report format with the Preferences command.

The Commands menu enables you to update a system profile at any time. For the Frameworks, Extensions, and Applications sections of the Apple System Profiler, you determine which volumes the Apple System Profiler searches by choosing Commands⇨Search Options (⌘-F) and then selecting the volumes you want in the dialog that appears.

In a nice touch, Apple added a shortcut in 10.2. Select the Apple menu, then the About This Mac... command from the Apple menu. The More Info... button shown in Figure 22-17 opens the Apple System Profiler.

Figure 22-17: The Apple System Profiler can be opened by clicking the More Info... button in the About This Mac window.

Applet Launcher

The Java programming language has received a lot of press. By using Java, you can easily create small, platform-independent applications, called *applets*, that can be automatically retrieved from a Web page by your browser, extending the functionality of that Web page. The divergence from original platform-independent intent (particularly by Microsoft) has made this vision less than fully realized, resulting in Java applets being one of the principal causes of browser instability and crashes.

Other than being able to run applets in Web pages, how important is Java? So far, not very important; however, Mac OS X goes to great lengths to make Java a full partner in developing full-featured applications.

If you want to run some Java applets without a Web browser's interaction, you can do it with Applet Launcher. After you launch Applet Launcher, you can open an applet's HTML file and launch the applet. The Applet Launcher is found in the Java folder in the Utilities folder.

AudioMIDI Setup

The AudioMIDI Setup utility provides control of the audio and MIDI inputs ond outputs on the various ports of your computer. Audio can be routed between the CD/DVD drive, the headphone port, the built-in speakers (if present), attached USB devices, and so on. Figure 22-18 shows the AudioMIDI setup utility.

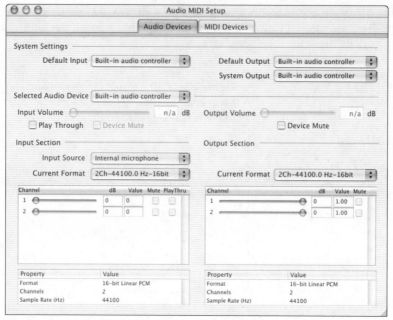

Figure 22-18: The AudioMIDI Setup utility provides control of the audio and MIDI inputs ond outputs on the computer.

Bluetooth File Exchange

Bluetooth is a wireless network protocol that is essentially wireless capability for USB. Bluetooth File Exchange can be used to update a Bluetooth-compliant cellphone with information from your computer's Address Book, can transfer graphics, can synchronize appointment and calendar information from iCal on your computer to a Bluetooth-compliant cellular phone or personal digital assistant (PDA) such as a Palm Pilot.

ColorSync Utility

Use the ColorSync Utility to verify and repair the ICC (International Color Consortium) profiles installed on your computer. You would use the ColorSync utility to coordinate the color spaces employed by different devices, such as a printer and your screen, so that the colors you see are rendered consistently and correctly.

Console

The Console is a monitoring tool that displays all the messages being sent by applications and system processes to the Unix console hidden behind the Mac OS X interface. Unless you are experienced with Unix system administration, these messages are unlikely to be of any interest or help to you; however, they can be utilized to discern where problems are arising, or if you're a programmer they can be helpful in debugging your software. Figure 22-19 shows an example of a Console window full of messages.

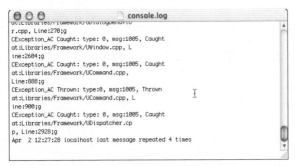

Figure 22-19: The Console displays all the error and informational messages sent by applications and processes.

CPU Monitor

The CPU Monitor displays a variety of windows depicting the level of processor activity on your Mac. It can display a small bar that floats above just about everything, including the menu bar. This floating window can be oriented horizontally or vertically, and you can move it by dragging any part of it. CPU Monitor can also display a standard window and an expanded window. The floating window and standard window show the overall processor activity at the moment. The expanded window shows processor activity over time, and it shows system software activity in one color and user software activity in another color. The wider you make the expanded window, the more historical information it shows. Be sure to investigate the preferences settings, where you can change colors, transparency, window orientation, and whether the CPU Monitor icon in the Dock also displays processor activity. Figure 22-20 shows the three CPU Monitor windows.

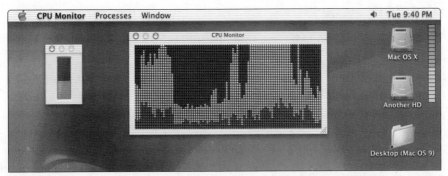

Figure 22-20: CPU Monitor can display the processor activity in a standard window (left), an expanded window (middle), and a floating bar window (right).

DigitalColor Meter

This little gadget is similar to a Photoshop function in that it tells you what color is beneath the pointer, as shown in Figure 22-21. The frame on the left of the window shows a zoomed-in view of the area around your pointer. You can view the color information as RGB in percentage, decimal (Actual Value), or hexadecimal format; CIE 1931, CIE 1976, or CIE L*a*b (CIE is short for Commission Internationale de l'Eclairage, which is the French title of the international commission on light), or *tristimulus* (a three-dimensional color space in X, Y, and Z coordinates). Not all devices provide color translation tables for CIE or tristimulus — for example, the Color LCD in the figure does not.

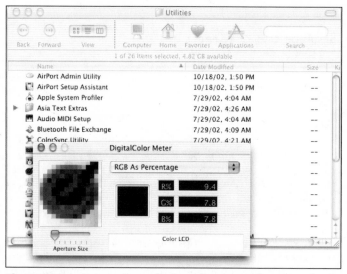

Figure 22-21: Know what color is under your pointer anywhere on the screen.

Directory Access

Mac OS X and some applications obtain information about users, servers, and other entities that may be located on a network from directories that are listed in the Directory Access utility. You can use Directory Access to change the directory that Mac OS X uses to authenticate users during login, define LDAP data and attribute mapping, configure search policies, select NetInfo domains, and so on.

If you think the settings in Directory Access are rather esoteric, you're right. Directory Access is primarily for the use of a network administrator. If your computer is not connected to a local network or is connected to a home network or a small office network, you don't need to touch the settings in Directory Access. If your computer is connected to a corporate or school network, ask the network administrator whether you need to make changes in Directory Access.

Disk Copy

The Disk Copy utility provided with Mac OS X 10.1 enables you to create disk image files. *Disk image files* are files that, when opened, are mounted as removable volumes. Apple and many software vendors distribute software and updaters as disk image files.

You can create your own image files with Disk Copy by choosing Image⇨New Blank Image and setting the options in the dialog that appears. Figure 22-22 shows the New Blank Image dialog.

Figure 22-22: Create your own disk image files with Disk Copy.

After creating a disk image file, you can convert it to several different formats:

✦ **Read only.** Mounts as a volume that can't be changed, like a CD-ROM.

✦ **Read/write.** Mounts as a volume whose contents you can change, like a hard drive.

✦ **Compressed.** Makes the image file smaller. Mounts as a volume that can't be changed.

✦ **CD/DVD master.** Mounts as a volume that's optimized for burning on a recordable CD or DVD.

Disk Utility

The Disk Utility program combines the functionality of the Mac OS 9 programs Drive Setup and Disk First Aid for repairing, erasing (formatting), and partitioning hard drives, CDs, and other storage devices. Beginning with Mac OS X 10.1, Disk Utility can also set up multiple hard drives as a RAID set. You select the type of operation that you want to perform by clicking a tab at the top of the Disk Utility window. From a list on the left side of the window, you select the storage device or volume that you want to work on. Figures 22-23 and 22-24 show two views of the Disk Utility window.

Information tab

Click Disk Utility's Information tab and select a device or a volume to see the following details:

✦ **Hard drive, CD, DVD, or other device.** You see the manufacturer's product identification, total capacity in MB or GB and in bytes, connection bus, connection type, and connection ID.

✦ **Volume.** You see its mount point in the file system, format, capacity, available space, used space, number of files, and number of folders.

First Aid tab

Click the First Aid tab to check the condition of a volume directory. (Mac OS X uses a volume directory to keep track of which files are on the volume and where they're stored.) If you have any problems with a volume directory, Disk Copy's First Aid can often fix them.

To have First Aid check a volume, select the volume on the left side of the window and click the Verify button. If First Aid discovers problems, it informs you of them, and you can click the Repair button to try to remedy matters. Figure 22-23 shows the results of using First Aid to check a volume that has no problems.

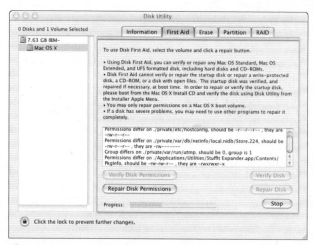

Figure 22-23: Verify or repair a volume directory by clicking Disk Utility's First Aid tab.

Erase tab

Click the Erase tab in Disk Utility to erase the contents of a volume or an entire disk. If you're sure you want to erase a volume or disk, select it on the left side of the Disk Copy window, choose a volume format, type a name, and click the Erase button.

Caution You can't recover the contents of a volume or disk after erasing it unless you have the resources of the FBI. Make sure you have an up-to-date backup copy of all important files on a volume before you erase it.

Partition tab

Click the Partition tab in the Disk Utility window to change the number of volumes or the sizes of volumes on the currently selected disk. (You can't change the partitioning of the startup disk or a read-only disk.) You can choose the number of volumes you desire from the Volume Scheme pop-up menu. You can adjust volume sizes either by dragging the divider handles in the figure on the left or by typing numbers into the Size text box. When you select a volume on the left, you can use the Split and Delete buttons to, respectively, split that volume in two or delete it from the scheme. The Revert button returns you to the settings you had before you made any changes — Revert is disabled until you've made a change. The OK button tells Drive Setup to proceed with the settings you've made. Figure 22-24 shows the settings for partitioning a disk into multiple volumes.

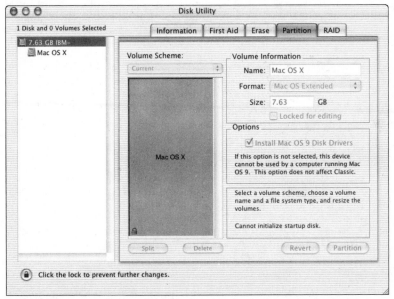

Figure 22-24: Partition a disk into multiple volumes by clicking Disk Utility's Partition tab.

RAID tab

If your computer has multiple hard drives, the version of Disk Utility included with Mac OS X 10.1 can create a RAID (redundant array of independent disks) set. A RAID set coordinates two or more hard drives to optimize storage capacity, improve performance, or increase reliability. When you click the RAID tab in the Disk Utility window, you can designate which disks you want to be part of the RAID set, choose a RAID scheme, name the RAID set, and choose a volume format. You can find more information about using the RAID feature of Disk Utility in article 106594 of the AppleCare KnowledgeBase Web site (`http://docs.info.apple.com/ article.html?artnum=106594`).

Display Calibrator

Display Calibrator is actually an Assistant (those coming from the Windows world call it a Wizard) that walks you through the process of creating a custom ColorSync profile for your display. If your ColorSync profile accurately reflects the behavior of your display, applications that take advantage of ColorSync can better display images in their intended colors. Similarly, if you have a proper profile for your printer, the colors match when printed — that's the *sync* in ColorSync.

You can use Display Calibrator to create a custom profile for your display and your viewing preferences. A custom profile accounts for your display's age and individual manufacturing variations. What's more, you can configure custom profiles for different resolutions, white points, and gamma corrections (more on all these terms shortly). Display Calibrator walks you through the process that calibrates your display and creates a new ColorSync profile. Figure 22-25 shows the Calibrator's introduction.

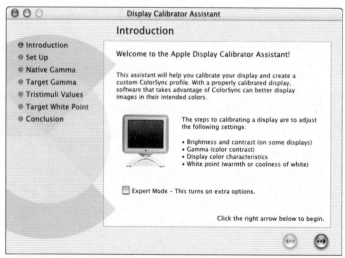

Figure 22-25: Display Calibrator walks you through calibrating a display and creating a custom profile.

The Display Calibrator Assistant takes you through the following steps:

1. **Introduction.** Decide whether to use expert calibration settings instead of basic settings. There isn't much difference to the casual user, but professionals who use ColorSync for important projects may find it useful to place a

check next to Expert Mode before moving on to the next step. (Expert mode gives you a little more control over the settings in Display Calibrator, although it doesn't change Display Calibrator dramatically.)

2. **Set Up.** Set your display to its highest contrast setting and then adjust the brightness. A test image helps you find the proper setting. This step is omitted on some displays.

3. **Native Gamma.** Provide information about the display's current gamma correction. *Gamma* refers to the relationship between the intensity of color and its luminance. Gamma correction compensates for the loss of detail that the human eye perceives in dark areas. In regular mode, you make adjustments to a gray image; in Expert mode, you determine the current gamma by adjusting sliders until red, green, and blue test images look right.

4. **Target Gamma.** Specify the gamma correction that you want the display to use:

   • 1.0 is the gamma of most scanners

   • 1.8 is the standard gamma for Mac displays

   • 2.2 is the standard gamma for television displays, video editing equipment, and Windows computers

   A low gamma setting makes colors appear more washed out. A high gamma setting makes colors appear more brilliant and with higher contrast. In this step, the Expert mode allows you to use a slider to choose a very specific gamma setting.

5. **Tristimuli Values.** Select your display type from a scrolling list. If your display's specific make and model is not listed, choose a generic description that fits your display, such as Generic LCD Color, Generic sRGB Display, or Generic Trinitron Display. This step is omitted for some displays.

6. **Target White Point.** Select your preferred *white point,* which determines whether colors look warm (reddish) or cool (bluish). You can also choose to make no white-point correction. In Expert mode, you can use a slider to choose a specific white point measured in degrees Kelvin, which is a temperature scale commonly used in science.

7. **Conclusion.** Name and save the custom profile for future use.

You can repeat the calibration process to create a number of profiles if you use your display at different resolutions or for different purposes.

Grab

The Grab utility lets you save pictures of your screen or rectangular selections on your screen. If you have upgraded to Mac OS X from Mac OS 9 or earlier, you can probably find some advantages and disadvantages of Grab when compared to Mac OS 9's screen capture keystrokes, ⌘-Shift-3 and ⌘-Shift-4 (or ⌘-Shift-4 with Caps Lock).

Grab has the following advantages:

✦ You can set a ten-second timer in Grab so that you can set up your screen, such as opening a menu.

✦ You can use Preferences to specify the pointer to display or no pointer.

✦ Capturing a selection displays the size of the selection while you're dragging the selection rectangle.

✦ You get to see the image immediately and name it as you want, not saving it if you don't like the results.

Grab has the following disadvantages:

✦ You can't click in and specify just a single window.

✦ If the pointer isn't one of those offered by Preferences, it may not show up in the image.

Grab offers itself as a service to other Mac OS X applications. Refer to Chapter 11 for more information on Grab as a service.

Beginning with Mac OS X version 10.1, you can use keystrokes instead of Grab to save screen pictures, as follows:

✦ ⌘-Shift-3 saves a picture of the entire screen as a TIFF file on the Desktop.

✦ ⌘-Shift-4 lets you select a rectangular area of the screen, and saves the selected area as a TIFF file on the Desktop.

✦ ⌘-Control-Shift-3 copies a picture of the entire screen to the Clipboard, ready for pasting.

✦ ⌘-Control-Shift-4 copies a picture of the rectangular area that you select to the Clipboard.

Installer

The Installer is a utility that installs software packages, such as System Updates, which are assembled in a specific format. Software vendors will usually use disk images when all you need to do is place the proffered application in your Applications folder; however, if support files (such as frameworks) also need to be installed, the software company may choose to provide an installer package.

Java Web Start

The Java Web Start utility facilitates opening applications that use the Java Web Start technology, which is built into Mac OS X 10.2. This technology lets you launch applications by clicking links on Web pages. These applications do not have to be installed on your computer. When you click a link to launch an application that uses the Java Web Start technology, the application is downloaded to your computer, the application opens, and an icon for the application is added to the Java Web Start utility. You can launch the downloaded application again later by double-clicking its icon in the Java Web Start utility. (Choose View⇨Downloaded Applications to see the Java Web Start applications that are on your computer.) An icon for the down-loaded application also appears in the Finder, and you can also launch the applica-tion by double-clicking the icon in the Finder. Figure 22-26 shows the Java Web Start utility with a couple of downloaded application icons in it and on the Desktop, and one of the downloaded applications is open in the background.

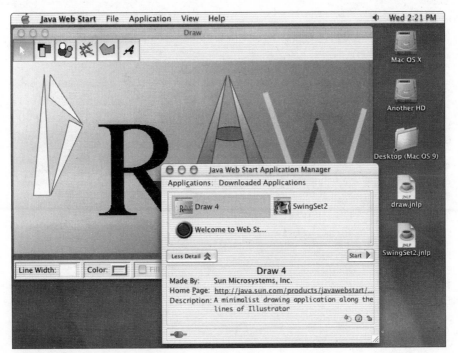

Figure 22-26: The Java Web Start utility (foreground window) lets you launch Web-based applications (background window).

The Java Web Start technology provides automatic installation of applications and automatic updating as well. You pay a price for this convenience. Applications that use the Java Web Start technology take longer to open than conventional applica-tions. In addition, Java Web Start applications have somewhat nonstandard inter-faces, and these applications take longer to launch than regular applications. Applications must be specifically designed to use the Java Web Start technology, and must be written in the Java programming language.

Key Caps

Key Caps lets you see all the characters that are available in any installed font, and Key Caps shows you how to enter any character. You choose the font from the Key Caps Font menu. Key Caps changes the display to show the effect of pressing any key or key combination. Figure 22-27 shows Key Caps with the Font menu open.

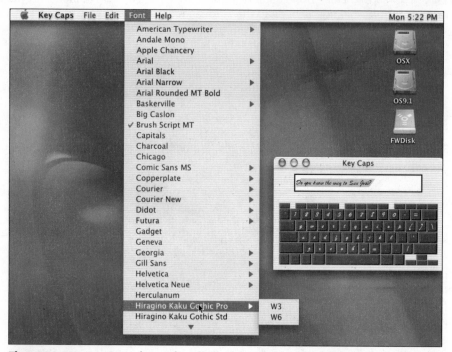

Figure 22-27: Key Caps shows the effect of pressing any combination of keys in any installed font.

Pressing the Option key outlines each of the Option-key combinations. Called *dead keys*, you can use them to add an accent or other diacritic to certain subsequently typed keys. Pressing a dead key—for example, Option-U for an umlaut—outlines the keys that can have that diacritic added. Figure 22-28 shows some accented characters and how dead keys appear in Key Caps.

Keychain Access

Keychain Access is where you manage your collections of user ids and passwords that you don't want to have to remember individually and type in repeatedly. By using the Keychain, you need only remember the passphrase that opens the Keychain and it feeds the information required to any Keychain-aware application, as described in detail in Chapter 10.

Figure 22-28: Seeing the dead keys and some of their effects.

NetInfo Manager

This utility is one of great power and complexity. In this utility, you can enable the System Administrator account and wreak havoc on your System. This account is also known by its short name, root, and in Unix circles is also called the *superuser* account. To enable this account, you need the name and password of an administrator account. Apple advises that if you don't already know how to use this account, and you don't know how to administer a Unix system, then you should just leave this account alone.

Aside from the dubious ability to enable the System Administrator account, NetInfo Manager presumably can be used to manage a NetInfo database. We say presumably, because Apple supplies no manuals or help files of any value for NetInfo Manager, and they have no useful documentation in the Apple Knowledge Base on the Web. Apple expects NetInfo to be set up by a system or network administrator using special applications that are included with the Mac OS X Server software. A 62-page document that describes NetInfo in more detail is available on the Mac OS X Server Web site at www.apple.com/macosx/server/pdf/UnderstandingUsingNetInfo.pdf.

We can tell you that NetInfo is database of information about network users and network devices such as printers and servers. For example, NetInfo can contain user account information including name, password, and the location of the account's home folder on a network file server. Mac OS X is designed to hook into NetInfo automatically. If you have a user account in NetInfo, you can log in from different Mac OS X computers on a network. No matter which computer you use to log in, Mac OS X always gives you the same home folder from the network file server where it is stored. (You can still log in without NetInfo by using the name and password of an account that's set up in Users Preferences of the computer where you're logging in.)

When you first launch NetInfo Manager, you are presented with the window shown in Figure 22-29. Most of NetInfo Manager is initially locked, as you can see by the lock icon in the lower-left corner of the window and the disabled (dim) items in the window. Even many menu items are disabled.

Whole books, large ones, are written covering Unix system administration, and we aren't even going to touch on that subject here. We just tell you that if you have a need to administer your Mac's Unix innards, you do so here. The traditional modification of files, such as /etc/group are only valid if you start up in single-user mode by holding down the S key while starting up.

Figure 22-29: If you unlock this window, you've released the safety and cocked the gun — made it easy to shoot yourself.

Network Utility

This handy little utility is your interface to the arcane mysteries of networking. By using its various tabs (shown in Figure 22-30), you can perform such tasks as:

✦ **Netstat:** Provides a statistical summary of the network activity on your Mac.

✦ **Ping:** Lets you send answer-back messages to another IP address to discern how long it takes to communicate with that location.

✦ **Lookup:** Enables you to ascertain various details about an Internet address, for example, what server hosts it and its IP address after resolution by a *DNS* (Domain Name Server).

✦ **Traceroute:** Reports back to you the route taken to get a message between your Mac and the address entered.

✦ **Whois:** Communicates with the servers where Internet domains are registered and returns to you the information as to who has registered a given domain name, when they registered it, and what its name servers are.

✦ **Finger:** Feed this Internet lookup tool a username and domain name, such as `steve@mac.com`, and it queries the host for that domain to retrieve any published information about that account. Not all domains provide finger information on their users.

✦ **Port Scan:** Scans a domain for open ports. You can limit the scan to only ports within a given range.

✦ **Info:** Tells you about your particular network connection.

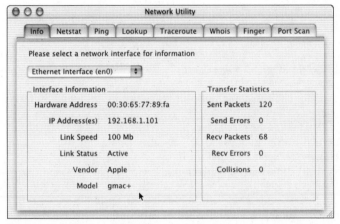

Figure 22-30: Network Utility comprises a graphic interface to a collection of Unix-based network search commands.

ODBC Administrator

The ODBC (Open DataBase Connectivity) Administrator, shown in Figure 22-31, is included in OS X as of 10.2 to aid users in ODBC data sources. If you're familiar with ODBC, this utility should be of use to you. Most OS X users are unlikely to need it.

The Print Center is the clearinghouse for adding, deleting, and managing the printers to which your Mac communicates and is covered in Chapter 9.

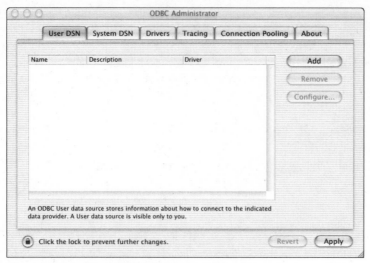

Figure 22-31: The ODBC Administrator Print Center

Process Viewer

As we mention frequently, underneath Mac OS X beats a heart of Unix, and Unix is a multi-user, multitasking system. At any given time, a wide variety of *processes* (programs) are running behind the scenes. You can use Process Viewer, as shown in Figure 22-32, to see what all those processes are, which user is running them (yes, invisible users run the background tasks that enable your applications and hardware peripherals to work), and detailed information about each process.

You can filter the process listing to include only processes whose names contain the text you enter in the Find box. For example, if you type init in the Find box, only the processes whose names contain init are shown.

Choose from the Show pop-up menu to show all processes, only user processes (those run by a logged-in account), administrator processes (those run by *root*), or NetBoot processes (those that are running to enable starting up across the network).

Click the disclosure triangle that's labeled either More Info or Less Info to show or hide detailed information about a process selected in the process listing.

Choose Processes⇨Export to create a text file, actually a plist (property list) file, containing the information in the table. Plist files are written in XML (eXtended Markup Language) and may be displayed by most modern Web browsers.

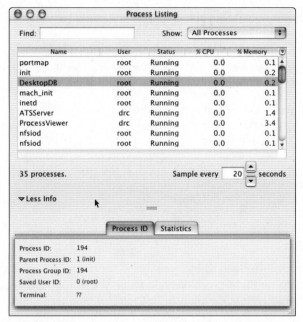

Figure 22-32: Did you ever wonder what programs were running in the background? Now you can find out.

StuffIt Expander

StuffIt Expander is an excellent little tool provided to Apple for free redistribution by Aladdin Systems (www.aladdinsys.com). StuffIt Expander decodes and decompresses a wide variety of formats used on Mac, Windows, and Unix computers. Many of the files you download from the Internet are automatically decoded and decompressed by StuffIt Expander; it opens, does its work, and quits. You can also use StuffIt Expander with files that aren't processed automatically. Just drag the files over the StuffIt Expander icon and let go. Expander decodes and decompresses them for you. If you receive many encoded or compressed files, we recommend keeping StuffIt Expander in your Dock for quick and easy use.

Terminal

Terminal is the window into the world of the Unix command line. When you're running Terminal, you can enter such cryptic commands as mv *.pdf ~/Documents to copy all the PDF files in your current directory to the Documents folder in your home directory. *Directory* is the Unix term for folder.

We cover Terminal in Chapter 26, where we give an introduction to the Unix command-line interface available to you.

Adding Goodies from Your iDisk

Not just a repository for 20 MB of your Web pages, pictures, movies, and other files, your iDisk is also a portal to a treasure trove of software from Apple and other vendors. See Chapter 10 for more information on iDisk.

When you open your iDisk, you see a folder named Software, and inside it are additional folders. Browse through these inner folders to find such enhancements to your Mac as additional effects for iMovie (Chapter 13).

Other software companies provide free or trial versions of their software via this mechanism as well. In addition, you often find updated drivers for your printer or other peripheral devices available in the Software folder.

Summary

In this chapter, you learned about the programs available to you in the Applications folder and its subfolders, or you received a pointer to the chapter where we cover that application in detail.

You also saw that Apple makes more applications available through your iDisk. You can check your iDisk regularly to see what goodies Apple wants to offer you.

✦   ✦   ✦

Enhancing Your System with Utility Software

Every system software upgrade, including Mac OS X, offers significant enhancements in performance and ease of use over older Mac system software. Nevertheless, even Mac OS X can benefit from utility software created by individuals and companies other than Apple Computer. Software that enhances Mac OS X and the Classic environment to increase your productivity and enjoyment is the subject of this chapter.

Finding Utility Software

Nowadays, most utility software is distributed via the Internet. Software developers have their own Web sites where you can find more information about their products and download the latest versions. New versions typically come out much more often for noncommercial utility software than for products from major commercial developers.

The software mentioned in this chapter is a small fraction of what's available. You may discover additional interesting products while you're visiting a developer's Web site to obtain one of the utilities listed in this chapter. You can also go looking for software that you don't see listed here.

You can look for additional noncommercial software and trial copies of commercial software to use with Mac OS X or the Classic environment in several places. Start with these sources:

✦ **Software folder of your iDisk.** This folder has Mac OS X software and Mac OS 9 software (which you can use in the Classic environment) from Apple and many other developers. To check your iDisk, switch to the Finder and choose Go⇨iDisk. (Your .Mac account information must be entered in the Internet pane of System Preferences.)

✦ **Mac OS X Downloads pages** (`www.apple.com/downloads/macosx/`). Apple provides an extensive collection of current software that you can download for Mac OS X. This site has shareware, software updates, demo software, and free software in every category. You can search the entire collection.

✦ **OSX Page** (`http://osx.hyperjeff.net/Apps/`). Maintains a categorized, searchable list of Mac OS X applications.

✦ **Apple's Mac OS X Applications page** (`http://guide.apple.com/macosx/`). Has a database that you can search for Mac OS X applications. You can also search separately for Classic applications.

✦ **VersionTracker Online** (`www.versiontracker.com`). This is a great Web site that keeps up with the latest new Macintosh shareware, free software, demos, and free updates to commercial software. You can search it for a particular software title or for keywords that describe a type of software you're trying to find.

✦ **Info-Mac.Archive.** This archive is a major storehouse of shareware, freeware, and demo versions of retail software. All software is submitted to a central location and redistributed to mirror sites throughout the world, such as Apple's FTP mirror site (`ftp://mirror.apple.com/mirrors/Info-Mac.Archive/`). At most mirror sites, you browse for files by category. MIT's HyperArchive mirror has an Info-Mac search facility (`http://hyperarchive.lcs.mit.edu/HyperArchive.html`).

✦ **CNET's software library** (`www.download.com`). This library offers extensive shareware, demo software, and freeware. And if you can't find what you're looking for at this site, you may find a shareware or freeware title you're seeking at its sister site, `shareware.cnet.com`.

✦ **Applelinks.com** (`http://search.applelinks.com`). Here's another major storehouse of shareware, freeware, and demo versions of retail software.

Trying Out Shareware and Freeware

Much of the software you download from the Internet is not available from any retail store or mail-order company. Some of this software, called *shareware,* is distributed on a trial basis. You pay nothing to obtain and try out shareware aside from the cost of your Internet connection. Authors of shareware encourage you to try their software and to share copies with your friends and coworkers.

Each person who decides to keep a shareware product is expected to pay for it. Some shareware authors accept payment directly. Many authors accept payment on the Internet through a clearinghouse, such as Kagi (`www.kagi.com`). Look for payment instructions in the Read Me file or other documentation files that come with the software.

Support Shareware Authors

Shareware depends on the honor and honesty of the people who use it. If you decide to keep shareware installed on your disk, the Honorable Society of Civilized People politely insists that you immediately send payment to the author. The fees that you pay for the shareware you use today (generally $5 to $50) help fund development of even greater shareware. For detailed information about the amount of payment requested for a particular shareware product and where to send payment, check the product's Read Me file, About menu command, or on-screen help.

In some cases, the shareware has a couple of key features removed, or it expires after a period of time. When you pay for this software, you get a registration code that you enter to remove the restrictions. Crippled trial versions of shareware are becoming more commonplace as authors try to come up with ways to get people to pay for what they keep.

You may find that some utility software that's distributed via the Internet is actually free or nearly free. This type of utility software is sometimes called *freeware*. The software developer may ask that you send a postcard or some other token of appreciation.

Understanding that free software and shareware do not become your property is important. Most freeware authors (and all shareware authors) retain the copyrights to their work. Their products are not in the public domain. You have a license to use the shareware and freeware, and you can generally pass it around, but you can't sell it. For specific rules about distributing a particular product, read the license agreement that comes with the product.

Using shareware and freeware

This chapter describes shareware and free software (freeware) but does not include detailed operating instructions. Because such software is usually distributed on the Internet, it doesn't come with printed manuals. Instead, this software usually comes with a documentation file, frequently named Read Me. You should also check for on-screen help in the Help menu while the software is running.

Shareware and freeware programs aren't always as stable as commercial software. Be sure to follow the instructions and discussions provided by the authors in their Read Me or Help files before using any of these programs.

Caution You use shareware and freeware at your own risk.

Getting support for shareware and freeware

Shareware and free software are typically developed by enthusiasts who can't afford to provide technical support by telephone. Some developers provide support by e-mail.

Although the developers of shareware and free software may not be able to hold your hand, they tend to release new versions of their products frequently. Each new version may introduce minor improvements and fix a few bugs that users reported via e-mail.

If you're having trouble with shareware or free software, check the developer's Web site for a new version. Look for a description of what has changed since your version of the software was released. You may find that the problem you're experiencing has been fixed in a newer version of the software. You may also find a list of frequently asked questions (FAQs) and other information that was not included with the software. You'll probably find an e-mail address where you can submit a bug report describing a problem you've discovered that doesn't appear to have been fixed in the latest version.

Utilities List

Apple, commercial developers, and shareware and freeware authors offer thousands of utility programs to the Macintosh community. Many new programs become available each day. The software listed in this chapter is not meant to be all-inclusive, but rather to be an example of the types of software that are available to enhance the performance of your computer with Mac OS X, including the Classic environment.

The great variation in computer models and configurations makes predicting accurately whether a particular shareware or free software product works on your system impossible. Authors of shareware and free software don't typically have the facilities to test their products with a variety of software combinations and computer models. Instead, they fix problems reported by people who try out the software.

Note   Some Read Me files and documentation mention the systems and configurations required and known conflicts, but others do not. If you decide to try some software, check the Read Me file or other included documentation for compatibility information of the version you get. If the compatibility information doesn't assure you that the software you want to try is compatible with your computer model and Mac OS version, you should take the precaution of making a backup of your hard drive before trying the software. (Chapter 25 discusses backups.)

The software items described in this chapter are listed alphabetically, with a short description of each of their features, the names of their authors, and their prices. Software (especially noncommercial software) is updated often, and you may find that newer versions of programs have features not described here.

Note

The prices and Web addresses listed in this chapter were correct at the time this book was written, but (of course) the individual software authors and developers who provide such prices and addresses may change them without notice. If you have trouble with a Web address listed here, try using Sherlock to search the Internet for the product name.

AMICO (Classic)

AMICO (Apple Menu Items Custom Order) lets you change the order of items in the Classic environment's Apple menu without renaming them. You can also add gray divider lines and divider titles between groups of items. AMICO is $10 shareware by Dennis Chronopoulos and is available at www.versiontracker.com/moreinfo .fcgi?id=253.

ASCII Table

True to its name, ASCII Table displays a table of Mac characters (in your choice of fonts) and their ASCII codes. You type a character or click it in the table and see its ASCII code displayed at the bottom of the table as decimal, hexadecimal, and octal numbers. This code can then be copied and pasted into other applications. ASCII Table, shown in Figure 23-1, is free software from ælius Productions and is available at www.aelius.com/products/asciitable.phtml.

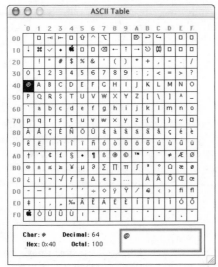

Figure 23-1: ASCII Table displays a table of Mac characters and their ASCII codes.

CDFinder

Looking for a file on a stack of CD-ROMs, Zip disks, or other removable disks? The Finder can't help you, and Sherlock can't help you, but CDFinder can. Feed CDFinder your CDs and disks and let it create a catalog. Then use CDFinder to search the catalog and tell you which CD or disk has the file you want. It even finds compressed files inside StuffIt, Compact Pro, Zip, and Apple Installer (Tome) archive files. Pick up this $25 shareware by Norbert M. Doerner at www.cdfinder.de/.

ChangeFileFolderProps

With ChangeFileFolderProps, you can change privileges and other settings that aren't available in the Finder's Info window. For instance, you can change the identity of the owner and the group for a file or folder. The ChangeFileFolderProps application lets you make these changes with pop-up menus rather than by typing the Unix commands chflags, chmod, and chown in the Terminal application. Obtain this free software from Bryan L. Blackburn at www.withay.com/macosx/sw.html.

Clean Text

For those times when you want to paste text without the formatting it had when you copied it, you can run it through the Clean Text laundry. Clean Text removes the font, size, style, color, and other formatting that is present in text copied to the Clipboard when you choose Edit⇨Copy in many word processors and some other applications. Clean Text can also rid copied text of empty lines, multiple spaces, e-mail reply characters, tab characters, and other blemishes. Find this $15 shareware from Applimac at www.apimac.com.

CopyPaste (Classic)

CopyPaste enhances the Clipboard functionality by remembering the last 100 items copied in Classic applications and keeping them accessible via menu or key commands; and it also includes hot keys for switching between applications you're copying and pasting between. CopyPaste can also save all 100 Clipboards on shutdown or restart. Get this $20 shareware from Script Software at www.scriptsoftware.com.

DAVE X

With the DAVE software installed on your Mac, you can share files and Postscript printers with Windows PCs. The Windows PCs don't have to install any software or hardware to make this work, although they do have to set up Windows file sharing. Therefore, DAVE is a good choice for cross-platform file sharing on networks that have more PCs than Macs.

On a network that has more Macs than PCs, you may prefer to install PC MACLAN from Miramar Systems (www.miramarsystems.com) on the Windows computers.

You can find out more about DAVE X from Thursby Software Systems at www.thursby.com.

Default Folder (Classic)

Default Folder enhances Open and Save dialogs in Classic applications, making file management easier by letting you specify where files should always be saved by certain applications, providing a pop-up menu of recently used folders, moving items to the Trash from within dialogs, and adjusting multiple Save options. Obtain this $34.95 shareware from St. Clair Software at www.stclairsoft.com/DefaultFolder/.

Delocalizer

A default install of OS X 10.2 includes language support for a vast array of languages other than the one you chose as native at the beginning of the Installer. If you have no need for the foreign language files and also need more disk space, Delocalizer allows you to remove the unwanted language support files for any or all of the languages support is installed for. This can regain almost half a gigabyte of disk space. Delocalizer can be found at www.versiontracker.com/moreinfo.fcgi?id=13503 on the Web.

Dialog Director (Classic)

Dialog Director is a scripting addition file that adds the ability to display almost any kind of dialog with AppleScript in the Classic environment. You can use it to create simple or complex dialogs and floating windows to enhance a Classic AppleScript applet's user interface. The dialogs can include push buttons, checkboxes, radio buttons, pop-up menus, scrolling text list boxes, static and editable text, QuickTime movie controllers, and much more. Check out this free software from Christopher Hyde at www.hylight.demon.co.uk/DialogDirector/.

Dialog Studio Lite (Classic)

Dialog Studio simplifies the process of including dialogs based on Dialog Director (described previously) in your AppleScript scripts. Dialog Studio Lite provides a convenient drag-and-drop interface and a variety of tools to help in creating dialogs. This product relieves you of writing the numerous, intricate AppleScript statements necessary to create a dialog with Dialog Director. You can create dialogs containing push buttons, text fields, checkboxes, radio buttons, gauges, and more, all without typing a single line of AppleScript. Obtain this free software from David Kanzu at www.macscripter.net/dialog_studio.html.

Docking Maneuvers

You need all the vertical space you can get for Web pages and document windows, but the Dock restricts the vertical space available (unless you make the Dock less convenient by hiding it). You probably have more room for the Dock on the side edge of your screen than at the bottom because your screen is wider than it is tall. The Docking Maneuvers software lets you change Mac OS X settings to move the Dock to either side of the screen and to pin one end of the Dock so that it grows only from the opposite end. Download this free software by Austin Shoemaker at http://www.versiontracker.com/moreinfo.fcgi?id=10291.

DragThing

DragThing has been tidying up Mac Desktops since 1995 and knows how to do it right. Use DragThing to create as many docks as you like, and populate each dock with your choice of applications, files, folders, disks, file servers, and Internet addresses. Click a docked application to open it or bring it to the front. You can customize the look of your docks with icons, folder tabs, or just text. DragThing provides some of the same features as Drop Drawers X and PocketDock. Be sure to look at all of them and see which works better for you. DragThing, shown in Figure 23-2, is $25 shareware from TLA Systems at www.dragthing.com.

Figure 23-2: DragThing provides multiple docks, whose appearance and location you can customize.

Drop Drawers X

Drop Drawers provides handy places to keep snippets of text, Web addresses and other URLs, pictures, sounds, movies, and more. The drawers can hold aliases of applications, documents, and so forth. You can also have a drawer that lists applications and processes that are currently running on your computer. The drawers pull out conveniently from the sides of your screen, so their contents are always at hand. You can configure each drawer to your liking, and you can even protect drawers with passwords. The Dock is nowhere near as versatile as Drop Drawers X. Drop Drawers X provides some of the same features as DragThing and PocketDock. Be sure to look at all of them and see which works better for you. Drop Drawers X, shown in Figure 23-3, is $20 shareware from Sig Software at www.sigsoftware.com.

Figure 23-3: Drop Drawers provides handy places to keep a wide variety of objects.

DropStuff

DropStuff creates compressed StuffIt archives when you drag your files and folders onto the DropStuff icon. The compressed files can be decompressed with StuffIt Expander, included with Mac OS X (in the Utilities folder). A version of Expander is also available for Microsoft Windows computers. DropStuff is available for $30 from Aladdin Systems at www.aladdinsys.com.

epicware screen savers

Would you like more choices of screen saver modules in the Screen Saver pane of System Preferences? This collection of 22 screen saver modules includes whales, gears, a rotating galaxy, paper airplanes, psychedelic, basic black, and more. Pick up the free software by epicware at www.epicware.com/macosxsavers.html.

Felt Tip Sound Studio

Record and edit audio on your Mac with Felt Tip Sound Studio. This application features one- or two-channel sound editing, several effects filters, and pitch shifting. It can convert the sampling rate. Use it with many file formats, including AIFF, Sound Designer II, System 7 sound, WAVE, CD track, as well as any formats that QuickTime supports, such as MP3 importing. Check out this $50 shareware from Lucius Kwok of Felt Tip Software at www.felttip.com/products/soundstudio/.

FileTyper (Classic)

Drop files on the FileTyper icon to change types, creators, attribute flags, and date stamps on files quickly. It also supports processing batches of files, filtering, and directory searches. Get this $10 shareware by Daniel Azuma at `www.ugcs.caltech.edu/~dazuma/filetyper/`.

FinderNote

FinderNote is a simple text editor whose documents are saved as clippings and can be read in the Finder (on the Desktop) without needing to run any application. When this free software by Jae Ho Chang is ready for Mac OS X, it will be available at `www.macupdate.com/info.php/id/2249`.

Fink

Fink is an open-source project intended to port much of the free Unix software to OS X and manage its installation in a coherent manner. For more information, see Chapter 26 and `http://fink.sourceforge.net/`.

FontManager

FontManager displays the Mac OS X standard Font Panel, so you can edit your font sets and favorites. FontManager saves you the trouble of opening an application that lets you change font settings, such as TextEdit. Obtain this free software by Amar Sagoo at `http://homepage.mac.com/asagoo/fontmanager/`.

GetInfo for App

If you ever want to know whether a Mac OS X application is built on the Cocoa framework or the Carbon framework, GetInfo for App can tell you. It also reveals whether the application is a single file or a package, what kind of binary library the application uses, and the application's path. Travel to `www.saryo.org/basuke/osx/getinfo4app/` to obtain the free software from SiestaWare.

GraphicConverter

GraphicConverter converts an amazing number of graphics file formats found on Mac, Windows, Unix, Amiga, and Atari computers. GraphicConverter imports 100 different file formats and exports more than 40 different file formats. In addition, the program has tools and filters for editing pictures. Get this $35 shareware by Thorsten Lemke at `www.lemkesoft.com`.

Helium (Classic)

Helium enhances the Classic environment's Balloon Help feature by enabling you to use key commands to make help balloons appear and disappear automatically or to toggle balloon help on and off, as well as set a more legible font size for the help text. Obtain this $12 shareware from Tiger Technologies at www.tigertech.com/helium.html.

HourWorld (Classic)

HourWorld displays a map of the world that indicates where the sun is currently shining and where it has set. HourWorld can display up to nine clocks set to the local time of cities around the world. In addition, it provides times of sunrise, sunset, moonrise, moonset, lunar phase, location on horizon of sun and moon, solar radiation, and more. Depending on the amount of features you want, you can shell out from $15 to $35 for this shareware from Paul Software Engineering at www.hourworld.com/prod01.htm.

IconFactory

At the IconFactory Web site, you find elegant alternative icons optimized for Mac OS X. The free icons from The IconFactory are available at www.iconfactory.com.

Interarchy

With Interarchy, you can copy files to and from another Mac OS X computer that is configured to allow FTP access (as described in Chapter 20). You can also use Interarchy to copy files to and from an FTP server on the Internet or on your local network. In addition, Interarchy can search the Internet, provide information about your network connection, and let you remotely control your Mac. Purchase this handy $45 shareware from Stairways Software Pty Ltd at www.interarchy.com.

iView MediaPro

Organize, catalog, archive, view, print, and convert your image, audio, and video files with iView MediaPro. View each catalog as a list, as thumbnails, or as full-size images. Create slide shows and Web site galleries. iView MediaPro reads 128 file formats for graphics, audio, and video. You can review this software and purchase it for $80 from iView Multimedia Ltd. at www.iview-multimedia.com.

L2CacheConfig

If you've managed to install Mac OS X on an old Power Mac that has been upgraded from a PowerPC 604 processor to a G3 or G4 processor, you may be able to get better performance with Mac OS X by enabling and configuring the processor's L2 backside cache. This is advanced work, but you're probably up to the task if you successfully installed Mac OS X on a Power Mac 7300, 7500, 7600, 8500, 8600, 9500, or 9600; a UMAX S900 or J700; or a Power Computing Power Wave or Power Tower Pro. Obtain this free software (and information about using Mac OS X on an upgraded old computer) from Ryan Rempel at `http://build.versiontracker.com/moreinfo.fcgi?id=9077`.

Note   You don't need this software if your Mac was originally equipped with a G3 or G4 processor. In this case, your computer enables and configures the L2 backside cache automatically.

LoadInDock

This convenient program keeps an eye on how hard your Mac's processor is working. LoadInDock displays a graph of this information in the Dock. Pick up this free software by Takashi T. Hamada at `http://build.versiontracker.com/moreinfo.fcgi?id=9849`.

MacJanitor

MacJanitor provides a way to perform important maintenance tasks on demand or according to a set schedule. These tasks, which include backing up and resetting system log files so they don't grow too large, are performed by a number of standard Unix utilities that are included with Mac OS X. Historically, these tasks are scheduled to take place between 3 a.m. and 5 a.m. on Unix machines, which typically operate 24 hours a day. Some tasks are supposed to happen every night, some once a week, and others once a month. (MacJanitor includes a complete list.)

If you're like most Mac Users, you probably shut down your computer or have it go into sleep mode overnight. While your Mac is shut down or sleeping, the housekeeping utilities can't do their work. With MacJanitor, you can start the maintenance tasks with the click of a button. Obtain this useful and free software from Brian Hill at `http://personalpages.tds.net/~brian_hill/macjanitor.html`.

ManOpen

Buried on your hard disk are documentation files for some of the Unix commands (which are actually Unix programs) and other Unix components included with Mac OS X. Why should you read these documentation files, which are known as *man pages,* by typing Unix commands in the Terminal application when you can display the man pages in the Aqua windows of ManOpen? You can specify the man page you want to read by typing its title in a ManOpen window or by selecting it from a list of man page titles. ManOpen, shown in Figure 23-4, is free software and can be downloaded from Carl Lindberg at `www.clindberg.org/projects/ManOpen.html`.

Note The ManOpen list of available man pages is taken from a database that's supposed to be generated automatically very early every Saturday morning. If you have never left your computer running overnight on a Friday night, this database of titles does not exist. The ManOpen documentation explains how to update the database, or you can use MacJanitor (described previously) to take care of the update.

Figure 23-4: ManOpen provides a graphical interface for viewing the Unix manual pages that are included with Mac OS X.

MenuStrip

The MenuStrip software places several handy controls in the Mac OS X menu bar or in a floating window. The most useful controls are buttons that hide all applications or show all applications. Other controls let you set the sound volume and the display resolution and number of colors. A menu bar clock with chime and alarm functions is also part of MenuStrip. You determine which controls appear in the menu bar, and you can adjust the position of the controls in the menu bar. Pick up this $12 shareware from MacPowerUser.com at www.macpoweruser.com/.

MyEyes (Classic)

MyEyes draws a pair of eyes on the Classic menu bar that constantly follow the pointer's movement. MyEyes helps PowerBook users who have trouble seeing the pointer find it more quickly. Download the $10 shareware from Federico Filipponi and Factor Software at `www.factor-software.com/myeyes.php`.

NameCleaner X

This utility makes files with file name extensions (suffixes) have the correct internal Macintosh file type and file creator codes. Also does the reverse, adding the correct file name extension based on a Macintosh file's internal type and creator codes. Use NameCleaner X to prepare files created on a Mac for use in Windows or Unix, or vice versa. Check out this $20 shareware from Sig Software at `www.sigsoftware.com`.

OroboroSX

OroboroSX is a X11 windowing environment that runs of OS X. For users with a long history with Unix, this gives a familiar working environment. OrobroroSX can be found on the web at `http://oroborosx.sourceforge.net/`.

OSA Menu (Classic)

OSA Menu adds a menu to the Classic menu bar that lists AppleScript scripts you can run while using a Classic application. This menu also lists scripts written with UserLand Frontier, QuicKeys, tclScript, or MacPerl. Besides running scripts, you can start and stop recording a script directly from OSA Menu. You can also use the menu to open a script for editing or to open the folders that contain scripts listed in the menu. (To run AppleScript scripts while using Mac OS X applications, use the Script Runner application in your Utilities folder.) OSA Menu is free software by Leonard Rosenthol, and can be found at `www.lazerware.com/software.html`.

PocketDock

If your Dock has become overcrowded or you get frustrated trying to keep it organized, PocketDock gives you an alternative. You can create one or more PocketDock windows. Each PocketDock window has multiple drawers that slide out to reveal collections of links to applications, documents, Web addresses, and e-mail addresses. You can customize the appearance of each PocketDock window for esthetic or space-saving reasons. PocketDock provides some of the same features as DragThing and Drop Drawers X. Be sure to look at all of them and see which works better for you. Figure 23-5 shows an example of PocketDock. Pocket Software offers this $20 shareware at `www.pocketsw.com/PocketDock.html`.

Figure 23-5: Organize your applications, documents, Web addresses, and e-mail addresses with PocketDock windows.

PopChar Pro (Classic)

PopChar Pro simplifies "typing" of unusual characters in Classic applications. Pull down the PopChar menu and select the character you want; PopChar Pro automatically inserts it in the current document as if you had typed the proper key combination on the keyboard. This $29 shareware is available from Uni Software Plus at www.macility.com/products/popcharpro/index.html.

PTHClock

An alternate clock for your menu bar is available from PTH as freeware, donations accepted, at www.pth.com/PTHClock/.

RBrowser

RBrowser is both an OpenSSH client and an FTP client application. Therefore you can use it to copy files to and from another Mac OS X computer that has remote login turned on. (This "other computer" could be your computer, and you could log in to it from another computer.) You can also use RBrowser to copy files to and from an FTP server. You can find information on allowing remote login (via OpenSSH) or FTP access to a Mac OS X computer in Chapter 20. Preliminary versions of RBrowser are free, but finished versions may not be. Pick up this software by Robert Vasvari of Object Warehouse Inc. at www.rbrowser.com.

Sharity

Sharity enables you to access shared files on Windows computers. It also enables you to access Microsoft Windows, IBM OS/2, Samba, and other file servers that use the CIFS (Common Internet File System) protocol on your network. Sharity mounts shared volumes and lets you open shared files directly from servers. You don't have to copy files to and from servers, as you must do with Samba's client software.

Free software for limited noncommercial home users, students, and noncommercial, nonmilitary educational institutions; $59 and up for less limited noncommercial use and commercial use; from Objective Development at www.obdev.at/products/sharity/.

Snard

Snard reduces clutter in the Dock by replacing numerous application and document icons in the Dock with a single icon. Clicking the Snard icon in the Dock pops up a menu of the applications and documents that you've set up. You can organize items by group, and each group has a submenu in the Snard menu. You can also set up worksets to open a whole slew of documents in different applications all at once. In addition, Snard features a submenu that lists every pane of System Preferences. Figure 23-6 shows an example of Snard. This $10 shareware from GideonSoftworks downloads from www.gideonsoftworks.com/snard.html.

Figure 23-6: Snard reduces clutter in the Dock by replacing numerous application and document icons with a pop-up menu.

Son of Weather Grok

Son of Weather Grok displays the current weather conditions from reporting stations in cities and airports around the world. For each reporting station that you want to monitor, Son of Weather Grok displays temperature, sky conditions, humidity, wind speed, barometric pressure, cloud ceiling, visibility, and more. These statistics are usually updated hourly from NOAA (National Oceanic and Atmospheric Administration). Figure 23-7 shows Son of Weather Grok. Pick up the free software from StimpSoft, Inc., at www.stimpsoft.com/products/sonofgrok.html.

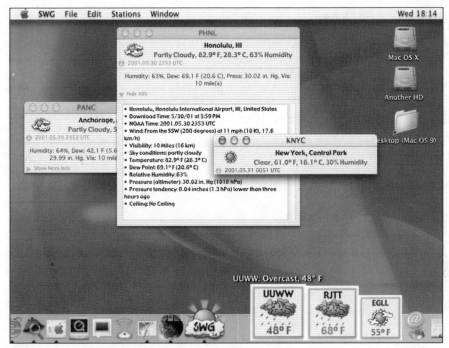

Figure 23-7: Son of Weather Grok displays the current weather conditions from reporting stations in cities and airports around the world.

Super Comments (Classic)

Super Comments enables you to see comments for the selected item in an Open dialog of a Classic application. You can also enter comments in a Save dialog. These are the same comments that you see and edit in the Info window of the Mac OS 9 Finder after starting up the computer with Mac OS 9. You do not see these comments in the Info window of the Mac OS X Finder. Download this $10 shareware from Maurice Volaski and Flux Software at www.fluxsoft.com.

Super GetInfo

BareBones (www.barebones.com/) provides SuperGetInfo as a feature-enhanced version of the Get Info window, with integration into BBEdit. The shareware cost is $20.

Tex-Edit Plus

Tex-Edit Plus is a small, fast text editor that offers more word-processing features than the TextEdit application included with Mac OS X. For example, Tex-Edit Plus has a more elaborate find and replace feature. You can configure Tex-Edit Plus to clean up strange characters, extra spaces, line breaks, and other detritus in text that you get from e-mail, the Internet, Windows computers, and so on. Tex-Edit Plus can read text aloud and it can record sound from your computer's microphone. Pick up this useful $15 shareware from Tom Bender, Trans-Tex Software at `www.versiontracker.com/moreinfo.fcgi?id=9013`.

The Moose's Apprentice

The Moose's Apprentice provides a graphical interface that allows you to inspect, edit, change, and create important Unix configuration files, such as `hosts.allow`, `hosts.deny`, `ftpwelcome`, and many others. You can find this $15 shareware from Wundermoosen at `www.wundermoosen.com/wmTMA.htm`.

Thoth

Thoth is a full-featured Usenet newsreader. It includes automatic viewing of download images, binary posting, flexible article filtering and sorting, and reference-based article threading. It also has multiple character set support for reading and posting in non-English-language and non-Latin-alphabet newsgroups. For more information on using newsreaders to participate in Usenet newsgroups, see Chapter 6. Pick up a shareware copy of Thoth for $25 from Thoth Software at `www.thothsw.com/thoth/`.

TinkerTool

With TinkerTool, you can activate hidden options of Mac OS X. You can control font smoothing, select default fonts used in Cocoa applications, activate transparent Terminal windows, display the Trash on the Desktop, and more. None of these options requires typing Unix commands. Instead you use familiar Aqua controls such as checkboxes and pop-up menus, as you can see in Figure 23-8. TinkerTool is free software from Marcel Bresink Software-Systeme and can be downloaded from `www.bresink.com/osx/TinkerTool.html`.

TitlePop (Classic)

TitlePop turns the title of a Classic window into a pop-up menu that enables you to quickly bring another Classic window to the front. The pop-up menu lists other windows that belong to the same Classic application as the front window. The pop-up menu also lists all Classic and Mac OS X applications that are open, and a submenu for each of the open Classic applications lists the application's windows. TitlePop is $15 shareware by Jouko Pakkanen and is available at `www.datavasara.fi/titlepop/`.

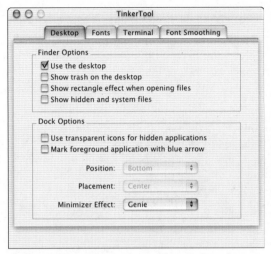

Figure 23-8: TinkerTool provides settings for a host of hidden Mac OS X options.

TypeIt4Me (Classic)

TypeIt4Me works inside any Classic application that allows text-entry, letting you type small abbreviations for predefined strings like names, addresses, and difficult-to-type phrases. It's similar to the auto-correct feature in Microsoft Word, but TypeIt4Me works in all Classic applications. Pick up the $27 shareware ($14 for students) by Riccardo Ettore at www.r-ettore.dircon.co.uk/.

Unix Date

The Unix Date scripting addition file lets you use AppleScript to convert a date and time format from the standard U.S. format used by Mac OS X to a format commonly used by Unix computers. It converts from the format "Day, Month Date, Year HH:MM:SS" to either "Day, Month Date, HH:MM:SS, Year" or to this same format with a time zone abbreviation included before the year. The converted time uses 24-hour notation, and all numbers less than 10 in the converted date and time have leading zeroes. This scripting addition does not change the date and time format used by Mac OS X; to change that, use the Date & Time pane of System Preferences. Pick up this free software from Public Access Software at http://www.versiontracker. com/moreinfo.fcgi?id=8045.

VisualRoute

VisualRoute is a visually oriented version of the Unix traceroute tool, and also includes the Unix commands ping and whois. VisualRoute can be found on the Web at www.visualware.com/visualroute/index.html.

wClock

Besides displaying the time and date in the menu bar, wClock provides one-click access to a slide-out monthly calendar. You can modify the time and date formats and position. Figure 23-9 shows wClock. wClock is free and available from Christopher Wolf at www.wolfware.com/wclock/.

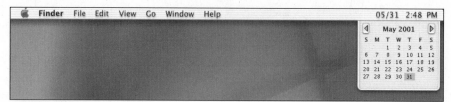

Figure 23-9: wClock displays the time and date in the menu bar and provides one-click access to a slide-out monthly calendar.

X-Assist

X-Assist provides Mac OS X with a menu that's much like a combination of the Apple and Application menus in Mac OS 9. This new menu appears at the right end of the Mac OS X menu bar. It provides the following:

- ✦ Provides commands for hiding and showing applications
- ✦ Lists currently open applications so you can switch to them
- ✦ Lists more than five recent applications
- ✦ Lists every pane of System Preferences

You can add your own applications, documents, and folders to the new menu by putting aliases into a special X-Assist Items folder. Figure 23-10 shows an example of the X-Assist menu. X-Assist is free and available from Peter Li at http://members.ozemail.com.au/~pli/x-assist/.

Xicons

At the Xicons Web site, you can find countless icons expressly made for Mac OS X. That site has all kinds of icons for applications, folders, disks, games, hardware, and more. The free icons are located at http://xicons.com/.

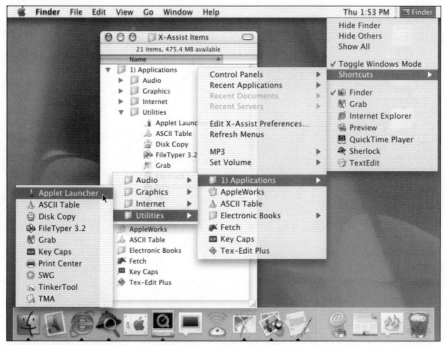

Figure 23-10: X-Assist provides Mac OS X with a combination of the Apple and Application menus from Mac OS 9.

Summary

In this chapter, you saw that many shareware and freeware programs are available from Internet sites, user groups, and Apple Computer. You can distribute copies of most shareware and freeware, but authors generally retain copyrights to their software. Shareware authors ask that you send payment for products that you decide to keep, but freeware authors don't ask for payment. The utilities listed in this chapter are a sample of the utility shareware and freeware that's available to enhance the Mac OS.

✦ ✦ ✦

Uncovering Tips and Secrets

S cattered throughout the previous chapters of this book are scores of tips and secrets for getting more out of Mac OS X and the Classic environment. For your convenience, this chapter contains a digest of the most useful tips and secrets, plus some tips that don't appear elsewhere in this book.

Using Menus

Keep the tips in this section in mind when you use the menu bar, pop-up menus, and contextual menus.

Conventional menu operations

When you click a Mac OS X menu, it stays open until you click elsewhere. If you're used to the way Macintosh menus work in Mac OS 9, you can still use them that way. If you click a menu title and keep holding down the mouse button while moving the pointer, the menu goes away as soon as you release the mouse button. To choose a menu item, just click and hold, move to the menu item, and release. With this method, you click only once, but you have to keep pressing the mouse button.

Kinesthetic confusion

Don't count on your kinesthetic memory to help you move efficiently to a particular standard menu. Menu positions are less predictable in Mac OS X than in previous Mac OS versions. All menus to the right of the Application menu may appear in slightly different positions on the menu bar, depending on the application that you are currently using, because the width of the Application menu's title varies according to the length of the application's name.

Right-click for contextual menu

If your Mac has a two-button mouse or trackball, you may be able to display contextual menus by pressing the right button without simultaneously pressing Control. If your multibutton mouse or trackball doesn't already work this way, you may be able to program it to simulate simultaneously pressing the left mouse button and the Control key whenever you press the right button. For instructions on programming a multibutton mouse or trackball, see the documentation that came with it. These alternative pointing devices are made by a number of companies, including Logitech (www.logitech.com) and Kensington Technology (www.kensington.com), but not by Apple; check with the vendor to see whether the device supports multiple buttons in Mac OS X.

Rearranging and removing icon menus

You can rearrange the icon menus on the right side of the menu bar — including sound, AirPort, modem, PPPoE, displays, script, and even the clock — by pressing the ⌘ key and dragging the icons left or right. As you ⌘-drag one of the menu icons, the other menu icons move aside to make space for the icon you're dragging.

You can remove a menu icon from the menu bar by pressing ⌘ while dragging the icon off the menu bar. When you have dragged an icon off the menu bar, release the mouse button; the icon disappears in a puff of smoke.

Replacing icon menus

If you removed an icon from the right side of the menu bar and want to get the icon back, here's what to do:

- ✦ **AirPort status.** Do either of the following:
    - • In the Network pane of System Preferences, choose AirPort from the Show pop-up menu, click the AirPort tab, and select "Show AirPort status in menu bar."
    - • In Internet Connect, choose AirPort from the Configuration pop-up menu and select "Show AirPort status in menu bar."
- ✦ **Clock.** In the Date & Time pane of System Preferences, click the Menu Bar Clock tab and select "Show the clock in the menu bar."
- ✦ **Displays.** In the Displays pane of System Preferences, click the Display tab and select "Show displays in menu bar."
- ✦ **Modem status.** Do either of the following:
    - • In the Network pane of System Preferences, choose a modem port from the Show pop-up menu, click the Modem tab, and select "Show modem status in menu bar."
    - • In Internet Connect, choose a modem port from the Configuration pop-up menu and select "Show modem status in menu bar."

✦ **PPPoE status menu.** Do either of the following:

- In the Network pane of System Preferences, choose an Ethernet port from the Show pop-up menu, click the PPPoE tab, and select "Show PPPoE status in menu bar."

- In Internet Connect, choose an Ethernet port from the Configuration pop-up menu and select "Show PPPoE status in menu bar."

✦ **Script menu.** Download the Script Menu software from the AppleScript Web site (`www.apple.com/applescript/macosx/script_menu/`). Then drag the ScriptMenu.menu file to the right side of the menu bar.

✦ **Sound menu.** In the Sound pane of System Preferences, select "Show volume in the menu bar."

Getting Organized with the Dock

Use the tips in this section to get more organized with the Dock. In addition, see Chapter 23 for utility software that customizes the Dock.

Hiding Dock icons

The Dock can become clogged with icons, especially if you minimize many windows. You can hide all the window icons that are in the Dock from one application by clicking the application's icon in the Dock to make the application active, and then Option-clicking the Desktop or any icon in the Dock.

Bring all windows forward

Normally, clicking a Mac OS X window brings only that window to the front. If you want to bring all windows belonging to the same application forward together, simply click the application's icon in the Dock. Alternatively, if the application has a Window menu and is the active application, you can choose Bring All To Front from the Window menu.

Dragging to a frozen Dock

When you drag an icon from a Finder window to a folder in the Dock, the folder icon may move aside to make space in the Dock for the icon you're dragging. To make the Dock icons hold still when you drag an icon to the Dock, press ⌘ while dragging.

Identifying folders in the dock

Prime candidates for custom icons are folders that you keep in the Dock. Ordinary folders all look the same in the Dock unless you scrub them with the mouse to see their names. By giving each folder icon a distinctive custom icon, you can identify it in the Dock much more easily, as shown in Figure 24-1.

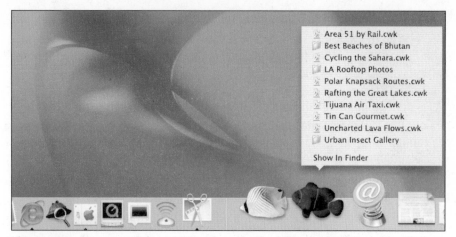

Figure 24-1: You can see how custom icons make folder icons easy to identify in the Dock.

(Fish icons courtesy of John Schilling, Stimpsoft, www.stimpsoft.com*.)*

Showing a Dock item in the Finder

The quickest way to show where a Dock item is located in the Finder is to ⌘-click the item in the Dock. You can also Control-click the Dock item and choose Show in Finder from the item's Dock menu.

Resizing the Dock

To make the Dock and its icons larger or smaller, place the pointer over the vertical line that separates application icons from other icons in the Dock. When the icon changes to look like a two-headed arrow, drag up or down to change the size of the Dock and the icons in it.

You can scale the Dock up or down incrementally, so that the icon size is always a multiple of 16 pixels, by pressing Option while you drag the separator line.

Working in Windows and Dialogs

This section presents some tricks for working in the windows and dialogs of most Mac OS X applications and Classic applications.

Minimizing all windows

While working in a Mac OS X application with several windows open, you can minimize all of them to the Dock by Option-clicking the minimize button of any of them.

To minimize all windows of an application that's in the background, ⌘-Option-click the minimize button of any of these windows.

For Classic windows, Option-click the collapse box of any window that belongs to the same application as the active window.

Background window tricks

You can move and minimize most inactive windows without bringing them to the front. The following window tricks work even on windows that don't have visible controls, as is the case with all inactive Classic windows:

✦ To move an inactive window, press ⌘ while dragging the window's title bar. Alternatively, you can ⌘-drag the frame of an inactive Classic window to move the window.

✦ To minimize a Mac OS X window that's in the background, click its minimize button. Minimize all background windows belonging to the same application by ⌘-Option-clicking one of their minimize buttons.

✦ To collapse or expand an inactive Classic window, press ⌘ while double-clicking its title bar.

✦ To scroll or resize a background window of some applications, press ⌘ while operating the background window's scroll bar or dragging the background window's resize control. (These tricks work with Mac OS X applications built on the Cocoa framework but not with Mac OS X applications built on the Carbon framework or with Classic applications.)

Note that with inactive Classic windows, these tricks work only if the active window belongs to the same application as the inactive window that you want to affect. If the active window is a Mac OS X window, then applying these tricks to any inactive Classic window brings the Classic window to the front.

First or last in a hurry

In most Finder windows, you can highlight the item that comes first alphabetically by pressing the space bar. In most cases, you can highlight the item that comes last alphabetically by pressing Option-P. These tricks stem from the capability to select an item by typing the first part of its name. If the item you select by typing isn't visible in the Finder window before you select it, the window may not automatically scroll to show the item you selected. An update to Mac OS X may make the automatic scrolling more reliable.

If nothing is selected in the active Finder window and it is set to icon view, you can highlight the first or last icon by pressing Tab or Shift-Tab. With an icon highlighted, pressing Tab or Shift-Tab highlights the icon that follows or precedes it alphabetically, and pressing an arrow key highlights the closest icon in the window in the direction of the arrow. In a Finder window set to list view or column view, pressing Tab or Shift-Tab has a different effect.

Hide windows while switching

To hide the active application's windows as you switch to another application, Option-click the other application's icon in the Dock or any of its windows. You can hide windows and switch to the Finder by Option-clicking the Desktop (or a Finder window or the Finder's icon in the Dock).

Hiding all other applications

To hide the windows of all applications except the windows of the application you want to use, ⌘-Option-click the Dock icon of the application you want to use. The application that you ⌘-Option-click can be the one you're currently using or another application that you want to switch to. After doing this, you see all the windows of the application that you ⌘-Option-clicked, but no windows of other applications.

Advancing to the next text box

In a dialog that has more than one box for entering text, you can move from one text box to the next by pressing Tab. You can move to the previous text box by pressing Shift-Tab.

Reversing the scroll bar setting

In Mac OS X 10.1 and above, you can specify what normally happens when you click a scroll track above or below the scroller. You can have this action scroll one page or scroll to where you clicked the scroll track. To temporarily reverse the normal behavior, press Option while clicking the scroll track. (You specify the behavior that you want to be normal by using the General pane of System Preferences.)

Hidden options of Classic scroll bars

Classic scroll bars are actually more configurable than it may appear from the Smart Scrolling option in the Options pane of the Appearance control panel. With a utility application like Smart Scroll by Marc Moini (www.marcmoini.com), you can have one scroll arrow at each end of the scroll bar, both arrows at one end, or both at both ends. You can also turn proportional scroll boxes on or off, independent of the scroll arrow setting.

Switch view format for Finder windows

In a Finder window, the View as Icons, View as List, and View in Column formats have the keyboard shortcuts option-1, option-2, and option-3, respectively.

Modifying Toolbars

Windows in the Finder, Mail, Address Book, and many other applications have standard Mac OS X toolbars. You can hide a standard Mac OS X toolbar or modify it in other ways by using the toolbar's contextual menu, a toolbar item's contextual menu, or the lozenge-shaped toolbar button in the upper-right corner of the window. (You can display the toolbar's contextual menu by Control-clicking the toolbar, and you can display a toolbar item's contextual menu by Control-clicking the item.)

 The methods described in this section don't work in all toolbars, because some applications have their own unique toolbars instead of standard Mac OS X toolbars like the ones in Finder window.

Hide or show toolbar

Hide the toolbar, or show it if it is hidden, by clicking the lozenge-shaped toolbar button in the upper-right corner of the window. Alternatively, choose Hide Toolbar or Show Toolbar from the toolbar's contextual menu.

Change toolbar mode

Show items as icons with names, icons only, or names only by choosing the mode you want from the toolbar's contextual menu.

Add toolbar items

Add items by choosing Customize Toolbar from the toolbar's contextual menu or by Shift-clicking the lozenge-shaped toolbar button. Either action displays a dialog that contains items you can drag into the toolbar.

Remove toolbar items

You can remove items from a toolbar by choosing Remove Item from the button's contextual menu. Alternatively, ⌘-drag an item away from the toolbar to see it vanish in a puff of smoke. If the Customize Toolbar dialog is displayed (as described above for adding buttons), you don't have to press ⌘ to drag an item away from the toolbar.

Rearranging toolbar items

Move an item to a different place on a toolbar by ⌘-dragging the item right or left. If the Customize Toolbar dialog is displayed (as described above for adding buttons), you don't have to press ⌘ to drag an item to another place on the toolbar.

Saving Time in the Finder

This section contains tips for saving time and effort with Finder windows and icons.

Shortcuts in Go To Folder

When you choose Go To Folder from the Finder's Go menu, a dialog appears in the frontmost Finder window. You're supposed to type the path to the folder that you want to go to. You can use Unix pathname shortcuts. For example, a tilde character (~) is a shortcut for your home folder, so ~/Sites is the path to the Sites folder in your home folder. Similarly, to get to the Public folder of the user named spenser, you can type ~spenser/Public. See Chapter 26 for more on Unix.

Folder icon makes new window

Normally, a new window doesn't open when you double-click a folder icon in a Finder window. Press the ⌘ key while double-clicking a folder icon to make a new window showing the folder's contents.

Toolbar button makes new window

Clicking a toolbar button at the top of a Finder window doesn't normally open a new window. But if you ⌘-click a toolbar button, a new Finder window opens to show the contents of the folder corresponding to the button that you clicked.

Moving disk to disk

When you drag an item from a folder on one disk to a folder on another disk, the Finder normally copies the item on the destination disk. The original item that you dragged remains on the source disk. If you want to move an item from one disk to another, press ⌘ while dragging. This method copies the dragged item to the destination and deletes it from the source.

Move items to main level

If you're working in a list view of a Finder window and want to move an item from an enclosed folder to the main level of the window, just drag the item to the column header.

Cancel a drag

If you realize while dragging an item in the Finder that you want to leave the item where it was, just drag it up to the menu bar, the title bar, or the status bar (if showing) and release the mouse button. The Finder returns the item to its original location.

Undo in the Finder

If you realize too late that you have moved an item to the wrong place, choose Edit⇨Undo (or press ⌘-Z). The Undo command actually works under these circumstances in Mac OS X's Finder.

In fact, Mac OS X's Finder lets you undo far more operations than any previous Finder. Not only can you undo moving a file (including moving it to the Trash), you can also undo renaming an icon, copying an icon, or duplicating an icon. You still can't undo emptying the Trash, creating a new folder, or changing which window or view is being displayed.

Organizing your favorites

After you add more than a few items to your list of favorites, the Finder's Favorites submenu becomes a mess. You can group different types of items by prefixing different numbers of blank spaces to their names — the more blank spaces, the higher on the list of favorites.

Prefixing a name with a hyphen, exclamation point, or other punctuation mark makes the name appear below names that are prefixed with spaces, and makes the name appear above names that have no prefixes. To make items appear at the bottom of the Favorites menu, prefix them with the character that you get by typing Option-0 (zero), Option-S, Option-2, Option-Z, Option-M, or Option-P. Figure 24-2 shows how these prefixes affect the order of items.

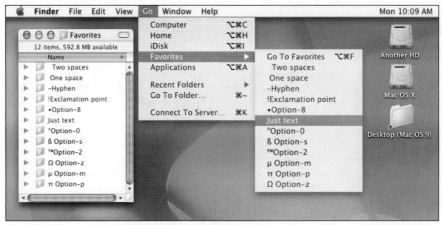

Figure 24-2: Prefix names of favorites with blank spaces or special characters to arrange the order of the favorites.

Drag to scroll

You can scroll a list view or an icon view of a Finder window without using the scroll bars. Hold down ⌘-Option and start dragging inside a folder or disk window. The pointer changes to look like a gloved hand and the window contents scroll as you ⌘-Option-drag. It's like you're pulling the contents of the window into view.

Expanding multiple folders

You can use keyboard commands to see the contents of multiple folders in a Finder window that's set to list view. Select the folders (press ⌘-A to select all) and press ⌘-→ (Right Arrow) to expand the selected folders and see their contents. To also expand all folders contained in the selected folders, press ⌘-Option-→ (Right Arrow). Pressing ⌘-← (Left Arrow) collapses all selected folders, and pressing ⌘-Option-← (Left Arrow) collapses all selected folders and all folders in them.

Spotting empty folders

You can force empty folders to the bottom of a Finder window that is set to list view. Just select the Calculate Folder Sizes option with the Show View Options command in the View menu, and then click the Size column heading to sort the list by size.

Selecting item names for editing in the Finder

If you have trouble editing icon names, it may be because methods that work in list view don't work in icon and column views. In list view, you can click the item name (not the icon!), wait briefly, and the name is highlighted and ready for editing. The wait time between your click and the name being highlighted depends on the double-click speed set in Mouse Preferences: A slower double-click speed means a longer wait for the name to highlight.

These methods of clicking the item name have worked for at least 10 years in list and icon views of Mac OS 9 and earlier, but they don't work in icon and column views of Mac OS X. In Mac OS X's icon and column views, you must click the name (or the icon), wait briefly, and then click again to have the name highlighted and ready for editing.

The most reliable, consistent method works in all views (and all versions of the Mac OS): Select the item and press Return. You're immediately in editing mode. (You can select the item by clicking its icon, clicking its name, typing the first part of its name, or pressing Tab, Shift-Tab, or arrow keys until the item is selected.)

Copy/paste icon names

While you are editing an item name in a Finder window, you can use the Undo, Cut, Copy, Paste, and Select All commands in the Edit menu. You can also copy the entire name of any item by selecting its icon (or its whole name) and then choosing Edit⇨Copy.

You can copy the name of a locked item—simply select the item and use the Copy command—but you can't change the name of a locked item. (Unlock an item by choosing File⇨Show Info.)

The Mac OS doesn't limit you to copying one icon name at a time. If you select several items and then use the Copy command, the names of all the items are put on the Clipboard, with one name per line.

Reverting to standard icons

You can revert to an item's standard icon after giving it a custom icon. Just select the item and use the Finder's Show Info command (⌘-I) to display the item's Info window. Select the icon in the Info window and a box appears around the icon to indicate that you have selected the icon, and then choose Cut from the Edit menu.

Making Aliases

Try the tips in this section for making aliases and using them. (An alias is a file that acts as a stand-in or agent for an actual program, document, folder, or disk. The alias does not duplicate the item it represents; instead, the alias points to the item it represents.)

Removing the alias from alias names

When you use the Finder's Make Alias command, the resulting alias has the word *alias* at the end of its name. To remove the word *alias* from the end of an icon name, select the name for editing, press the Right Arrow (→) or Down Arrow (↓) key to move the insertion point to the end of the name, and press Delete five or six times. Pressing Delete five times leaves a blank space at the end of the alias name to distinguish it from the original name; pressing Delete six times removes this space.

Aliases where you want them

Making an alias of an item that's not on the same disk as the alias is a three-step process if you use Finder's Make Alias command. First, make the alias on the same disk as its original item; second, copy the alias to the destination disk; and third, delete the first alias. A better way is to make an alias exactly where you want it in the first place. Simply hold down ⌘-Option while dragging the original item to the disk where you want an alias.

Making many aliases

You can make aliases for several items in the same window at the same time. First, select all the items. Then ⌘-Option-drag the selected items to a different window or to the Desktop. Alternatively, you can use the Make Alias command (⌘-L). An alias appears for each item that you selected.

Proxy icon becomes alias

You can make an alias of an open document in a Mac OS X application without going to the Finder and displaying the document's icon in a Finder window. Simply drag the proxy icon from the title bar of a document window to the Desktop, the Dock, a Finder window, or any folder icon that you can see in the Finder.

Zooming through Open and Save Dialogs

The tips in this section help you zoom through the dialogs that appear when you choose Open, Save, Save As, and other disk-related commands.

Open more than one

In some Mac OS X applications, you can select several items in the Open dialog, and each item opens in a separate window. To select adjacent items in the Open dialog's list, either drag across the items or Shift-click. To select nonadjacent items, ⌘-click each one in the list. You can't tell in advance whether these tricks work in a particular application. You have to experiment.

Dealing with duplicate names in Favorites

You can't add the currently selected folder in an Open dialog to your favorites list if you already have a favorite with the same name. If you try — by clicking the Add to Favorites button in the Open dialog — an alert asks if you want to replace the existing favorite with the same name.

If you want to add this new favorite and keep the existing favorite, switch to the Finder, click Favorites in any Finder window's toolbar (or choose Go⇨Favorites⇨Go To Favorites), and rename the existing favorite. The favorite is just an alias, which you can rename without affecting the item it refers to.

Copy, cut, and paste while saving

While you are entering a name for the document to save in a Save dialog, the Cut, Copy, and Paste commands are available from the Edit menu. This means that you can copy a name for a document from within the document before choosing the Save command, and then paste the copied name into the dialog. You can also use the keyboard equivalents: ⌘-X for Cut, ⌘-C for Copy, and ⌘-V for Paste.

Unsaved changes telltale

If you see a small dot at the center of a document window's Close button, it means that the document has unsaved changes. This telltale dot appears in Mac OS X applications that are built on the Cocoa framework. The telltale dot doesn't appear in Mac OS X applications that are built on the Carbon framework or in any Classic applications.

Navigating Save dialogs by keyboard

Do you know the trick to navigating with the keyboard in a Save dialog? You must select the scrolling list in the dialog so that your keystrokes don't end up as part of the document name. You can alternate between the scrolling list and the name entry area by pressing Tab. Clicking in either area also makes it the keyboard target. Mac OS X indicates that your typing affects the scrolling list by outlining it with a gray border. If instead you see a flashing insertion point or highlighted text in the document name, you know that your typing affects the name.

When the scrolling list is receiving keystrokes in a Save dialog, you can navigate the list by pressing the arrow keys. You can also select a listed item by typing the first part of the item's name. For example, type the letter M to select the first listed item whose name begins with an M.

Folder switching

If you find that you frequently go back and forth between two folders, put an alias of each folder in the other. Whichever folder you are in, you can go to the other in one step by opening its alias. Also, you can bookmark your frequently visited folders by clicking the Add to Favorites button in an Open dialog of any Mac OS X application. (In a Classic application that uses Navigation Services dialogs, choose Add to Favorites from the Favorites pop-up menu in the dialog.)

Find an alias's original item

In the Open, Save, or Navigation Services dialog of a Classic application, you can go quickly to an alias's original item by Option-double-clicking the alias. Alternatively, select the alias in the dialog and then Option-click the Open button. Alias names appear in italics in these dialogs. (If you don't press the Option key, the alias's original item opens.)

Sidestepping a Classic double-click

If in the midst of double-clicking an item in the Open dialog of a Classic application you realize that you double-clicked the wrong item, continue holding down the mouse button and drag the pointer to the item that you want to open. When you release the mouse button, the currently selected item opens. This trick also works when you are opening a folder in a Save dialog.

This trick doesn't work in Mac OS X applications or in Classic applications that use Navigation Services dialogs (see the next tip, however).

Canceling a Classic double-click

To cancel a double-click in an Open, Save, or Navigation Services dialog of a Classic application, keep holding down the mouse button on the second click and drag the pointer outside the dialog before releasing the mouse button. This trick doesn't work in Mac OS X applications.

Working with Applications and Documents

This section has some tips that apply to most applications, followed by tips for these specific applications: Internet Explorer, Help Browser, QuickTime Player, iMovie, iTunes, Script Editor, and Script Runner.

Switching applications

You can switch to another open application by pressing ⌘-Tab or ⌘-Shift-Tab until the application you want to use is highlighted in the Dock. Release the keys to switch to the highlighted application.

Forcing open

If you want to force an application to try to open a document that it doesn't think it can open, press ⌘ and Option while dragging the document icon to the application's icon in the Dock. This trick doesn't work when you drag to an application icon in a Finder window or on the Desktop.

Applications in the Shared folder

For convenient access to applications installed in the Shared folder, put them in a folder that you create inside the Shared folder. For example, create a folder named Shared Applications inside the Shared folder. Then put an alias of the Shared Applications folder in the Applications folder. You need to log in as an administrator to put the alias in the Applications folder, but thereafter anyone can easily use this alias to access applications that are in the Shared Applications folder.

Take a clipping

When you want to save a text excerpt or a picture from a Web page or a document in another application, you can make a clipping file. Select the text or picture that you want to save and try to drag it to the Desktop or to a Finder window. If the application that you're dragging from supports drag-and-drop editing between applications, Mac OS X creates a clipping file containing what you dragged. If nothing happens, or if the selection changes when you try to drag to the Desktop, the application that you're dragging from doesn't work with drag-and-drop editing.

After you've created your clipping file, rename it so that you can tell at a glance what's in it. If you forget what it contains, just double-click the clipping file; the clipping appears in its own window in the Finder.

You may be able to insert the contents of a clipping file into an open document by dragging the clipping file to the document window. The document window that you drag to must belong to an application that supports drag-and-drop editing between applications.

Stop Internet Explorer's autocompletion

When you type a URL in the address bar of Internet Explorer, it normally tries to complete the URL for you as you type. You can turn off the automatic completion of URLs by choosing Explorer⇨Preferences, clicking Browser Display on the left side of the Preferences dialog, and then turning off the Use Address AutoComplete option.

Resize the Explorer Bar

While the Explorer bar is expanded on the left side of an Internet Explorer window, you can resize it. Start by placing the pointer over the gray border that's immediately to the left of the Explorer bar's five tabs. When the pointer shape changes to two small arrows pointing left and right, you can drag right or left to make the Explorer bar wider or narrower.

Autocompletion in Mail

Mail remembers the addresses of people to whom you have recently sent e-mail. When you start to type an address on the To line, Mail autocompletes the address for you, or provides a drop-down list if more than one address matches what you're typing. If you don't want to use Mail's suggested address, just continue typing the address that you do want to use.

Getting general help

You can always get general help by going to the Finder and using the Help menu from there.

Help you've already seen

While using the Help Viewer, you can tell which articles you have already seen. Links to articles that you previously visited are green instead of blue. When you quit the Help Viewer, it forgets which links you have visited. The next time you open the Help Viewer, all links are blue until you visit them again.

Search in Help Viewer

If the words that you search for in the Help Viewer don't turn up the help articles that you want, try different search words. The Help Viewer looks up your search words in an index of help articles. The index is prepared using Sherlock technology.

QuickTime fast-forward and rewind

While you view a QuickTime movie, you can fast forward it or rewind it by holding down the appropriate step button. If you hold down the forward-step (or backward-step) button while a movie is playing, you speed up the audio (or play it backward) as well.

QuickTime Player audio controls

In addition to the clearly visible volume control, QuickTime Player has several hidden audio controls. To reveal the hidden controls — Balance, Bass, and Treble — simply click the audio equalizer at the right end of the play bar. If you prefer to use menus, choose Movie⇨Show Sound Controls.

Quickly setting QuickTime Player audio controls

In a QuickTime Player window, you can change the volume quickly by clicking in the slider track instead of dragging the slider. For example, to set full volume, click at the right end of the slider track. When the Balance, Bass, and Treble controls are showing, you can drag the mouse over the settings instead of clicking the plus and minus buttons. To raise the sound level beyond its normal maximum, press Shift-Up Arrow (↑).

Rearranging QuickTime Player favorites

In QuickTime Player, you can rearrange the favorites window by dragging icons to different positions in the window. You can remove a favorite by Control-clicking its icon in the favorites window and choosing Delete Favorite from the contextual menu that appears.

Optimum streaming video

For optimum streaming video, QuickTime Player consults the settings in the Connection panel of your QuickTime System Preferences. You get better playback from streaming video if you make sure that these settings are accurate. You won't get better video by setting a faster connection speed than you actually have.

Adding text to your QuickTime movie

If you're creating a QuickTime movie or slide show, here's a quick way to add a title or silent-movie style text block. Type your text in TextEdit or any application that handles text, set the format that you want it to have (font, size, style), and copy the text to the Clipboard. Now go to the spot in your movie where you want this text and then paste it. QuickTime Player Pro inserts the text as a two-second block of white text against a black background — formatting and all. You can even drag a text file directly to the QuickTime Player screen to make it a two-second insert at the current frame.

Adding still pictures to your QuickTime movie

While creating a QuickTime movie or slide show, you can easily add an image as a still picture. In an image-viewing or editing application, copy the image to the Clipboard. Then in QuickTime Player Pro, go to the frame in your movie where you want to insert the image. Choose Edit⇨Paste and the image is inserted as a two-second still. You can even drag an image file directly to the QuickTime Player window to insert it at the current frame.

iMovie likes big screens

The higher the screen resolution, the easier it is to work with iMovie. Although you can make do at an 800 x 600 resolution by scrolling the iMovie shelf, we recommend that you operate at 1024 x 768 or greater resolution. (Of course, we recommend that for Mac OS X in general.)

Extracting audio in iMovie

In iMovie, you can extract the audio portion of your video clip onto one of the Timeline's audio tracks by choosing Advanced⇨Extract Audio (⌘-J). Then, if you turn the volume for the video track off or down low, you can move the audio tracks around in the Timeline to give effects similar to those of a television news broadcast where you continue to hear the newscaster speak while you're being shown footage taken in the field.

Clearing iMovie crop markers

If you want to remove iMovie crop markers, just click the clip's icon on the Shelf. This immediately clears all crop markers.

Retrieving trashed material in iMovie

Until you empty iMovie's Trash, you can recover material that you put there. Just repeatedly choose Edit⇨Undo until you get back to where you want to be.

QuickTime controller shortcuts

The QuickTime movie controller responds to all kinds of keyboard shortcuts. The most popular shortcuts are the following:

- ✦ Press Return or Spacebar to alternately start and pause play forward.
- ✦ Press ⌘-.(period) to pause playing.
- ✦ Press ⌘-→ (Right Arrow) to play forward.
- ✦ Press ⌘-← (Left Arrow) to play backward.
- ✦ Press → (Right Arrow) to step forward.
- ✦ Press ← (Left Arrow) to step backward.
- ✦ Press ↑ (Up Arrow) or ↓ (Down Arrow) to raise or lower the sound level.
- ✦ Press Shift-↑ (Up Arrow) to raise the sound level beyond its normal maximum.

Internet radio performance in iTunes

When picking an Internet radio station in iTunes, select a radio station that transmits less data per second, as indicated in the Bit Rate column of the iTunes window, than your actual Internet connection speed. If, for example, your modem can't connect at a full 56K, then you should avoid 56kbps streams.

iTunes window sizes

Clicking the iTunes window zoom button (+) reduces the window to just the controls at the top-left plus the progress area. Further, the buttons are now positioned vertically at the left edge of the window with close (X) on top, minimize to Dock (–) in the middle, and zoom (+) on the bottom. Clicking zoom again pops you back to the original size. The small size is a handy way to keep the window around in an unobtrusive manner.

You can also quickly resize the iTunes window to the full height of the screen by Option-clicking the zoom button. Click the zoom button again to reduce the window to its small size.

Get bigger scripting windows

Script Editor makes new windows kind of small, but you don't have to resize every new script's window by hand. Just leave the script windows small and scroll, scroll, scroll instead—just kidding! Actually, you can change the standard size of a new script window. First, make the script window the size that you want—be sure to make it wide enough to show a healthy line of AppleScript—and then choose

File⇨Set Default Window Size. Yes, this menu command is right there in plain sight, but lots of scripters overlook it.

Descriptions of several AppleScript terms

When you're looking at an AppleScript dictionary in Script Editor, you can see descriptions of several terms at once. To see descriptions of adjacent terms, drag across the terms on the left side of the dictionary window. To see descriptions of nonadjacent terms, Shift-click or ⌘-click each term on the left side of the window.

How to edit an AppleScript application

You can't open an AppleScript application for editing by double-clicking it. Doing this causes the application's script to run! To edit an application's script, either use the File⇨Open command in Script Editor or drag the application to the Script Editor icon in the Finder.

Opening scripts with Script Runner

Normally a script runs when you choose it from the Script Runner pop-up menu. You can use Script Runner to open scripts in Script Editor instead of running them. To do this, press the ⌘ key while choosing the script from the Script Runner pop-up menu.

Finding a folder path

If you need the full path of a folder for a script you're working on, you can use a small script to get this information. Open a new window in Script Editor and type the following script in the script editing area:

```
choose folder
```

Run the script and select a folder. The result is a file spec for the folder you selected. You can copy the text from the result window and paste it in any script.

Execute a command as root

In the Terminal application, you can execute a single command as root, even if you haven't enabled root login. Use the `sudo` command followed by the desired command as an argument to `sudo`. For example, the following command typed in the Terminal executes the `chown` (change owner) command, causing the file, `myfile`, to belong to root:

```
sudo chown root myfile
```

Screen capture without Grab

Beginning with Mac OS X 10.1, you can capture the full screen or a selected area without using the Grab utility. The following keystrokes do the trick:

✦ ⌘-Shift-3 captures the full screen.

✦ ⌘-Shift-4 provides a cross-hairs pointer to select the area you want captured.

With either keystroke, the screen shot is saved as a PDF picture file on the Desktop.

Login, Logout, and Security

In this section, you find a couple of tricks for logging in and logging out plus several tips for making your computer more secure.

Typing to select a listed account

If your login window is set to show a list of your computer's user accounts, you can select an account by typing instead of clicking its name. As soon as you begin typing, the first name that matches your typing is selected. For example, type the letter A and the first account whose name begins with A is selected. If more than one account begins with the same letter, type additional letters to select the account you want. When the account you want to use is selected, press Return to go on to the second login window where you enter the account password.

Logout and shutdown items

Mac OS X has no formal mechanism for designating items that you want to have open just before logging out. However, if the Classic environment is running when you log out, you can piggyback on its shutdown items mechanism. Simply place aliases of the Mac OS X applications, AppleScript applets, sound files, or what have you into the Shut Down Items folder of the System Folder that the Classic environment uses. When the Classic environment shuts down during the logout process, the Mac OS X items open. Of course, these items also open if you manually shut down the Classic environment with the Stop button in the Classic pane of System Preferences.

Login messages

Do you like to have reminders pop up when you log in? Put your reminders in Stickies notes (text, graphics, movies, you name it) and add Stickies to the list of login items in the Login pane of System Preferences.

Don't want to use Stickies? Create a clipping file of your notes and add it to the list of login items in the Login pane of System Preferences. Drag the clipping file to the bottom of the list of login items so that it opens last. At login, the Finder does not have to open an application to display the note, which you can easily dismiss with ⌘-W.

The Keychain unlocked during login

If you have more than one Keychain, you can designate the one that you want automatically unlocked when you log in to Mac OS X. Open Keychain Access. Bring up the desired Keychain by choosing it from the Keychains menu and then choose Keychains⇨Make "Keychain name" Default.

Picking a secure password

Pick a password that you can remember easily but one that is difficult for other people to guess. For better security, mix letters with numbers; try replacing the letters I and O with the numbers 1 and 0. Another trick is to use the initial letters of an easy-to-remember phrase. For example, "The White House is at 1600 Pennsylvania Avenue" becomes TWHia1600PA. Don't use birthdays, anniversaries, or the names of family members or pets. Don't use your social security number, phone number, or driver's license number. Don't use any one word that appears in a dictionary of any language; hackers have programs that try every word in a dictionary.

No restarts or shut downs

You can configure your computer so that the Restart and Shut Down buttons don't work in the login window. This configuration makes it more difficult, although not impossible, for someone to restart the computer with Mac OS 9 or a CD and access your Mac OS X files. You disable the Restart and Shut Down buttons in the login window by changing clearly labeled settings in the Login pane of System Preferences.

Locking with the screen saver

To make the computer more secure against tampering by a passerby, set the Screen Saver pane of System Preferences to require the user account password to wake the screen saver. In addition, make the top-right corner of the screen a hot corner for activating the screen saver. Then you can activate your locked screen saver by slinging the pointer into this corner.

Locking with the keychain

Open System Preferences and then click on the Keychain Access icon to show the Keychain Access pane. Select "Show status in menu bar" on the pane and close System preferences. In addition to the ability to lock and unlock keychains from the Keychain menu, you can lock the screen as well with the Lock Screen command. FTP password

If you allow FTP access to your computer, change your password frequently and have all other users of your computer do likewise. Never use the same password for FTP that you use for anything else, such as online banking! The password you use for FTP is not encrypted when it is sent over your network or the Internet. A hacker can easily capture this password.

Prevent FTP access outside home folders

The FTP server normally allows remote users to go outside their home folders, but it can be configured to restrict users individually to their own home folders. This configuration requires the use of the Terminal application and the root user (System Administrator) account.

First, you create a text file containing a list of user accounts that you want to restrict. You put the short name of each user account on a separate line, making sure to press return after the last name. For example, the following list restricts users atlas and medusa to their home folders when they log in for FTP access:

```
atlas
medusa
```

In addition to restricting FTP access for individual users, you can restrict access for groups of users. For each group that you want to restrict, you simply add a line to the text file consisting of an @ symbol followed by the group name. Because all Mac OS X user accounts belong to the staff group, a file containing the following lines (the last line being blank) restricts all users to their home directories when they log in for FTP access to your computer:

```
@staff
```

When you save the text file, name it `ftpchroot` and put it in your home folder. This file must be plain text. If you want to use the TextEdit application to create this file, you must choose Format⇨Make Plain Text before saving the file. After saving the file, change the file name so that it does not end with `.txt`. After saving the file `ftpchroot` in your home folder, use the NetInfo Manager application to enable the root user. Make sure that you know the root user's password. (If you need specific instructions, see Chapter 16.) Next, open the Terminal application and type the following command:

```
sudo ~/ftpchroot /etc
```

If you are prompted in the Terminal window to enter a password, do so. By default, sudo will require your password, although it can be configured to require the root password. We take a closer look at the Terminal program and Unix commands in Chapter 26. Finally, use the NetInfo Manager to disable the root user.

Dealing with a Network

The first couple of tips in this section apply to all kinds of networks. Then come several tips specifically for AirPort networks. These are followed by a tip for personal Web sharing and a tip for FTP access to your computer.

Optimize your network connection

Drag the network connection you use most often to the top of the list in Network Preferences' advanced settings. While you're there, turn off network connections that you never use. Now Mac OS X won't waste time checking the less used or unused network connections.

Lock network settings

After you have your network settings the way you want them, it is a good idea to click the lock button to prevent accidental changes. Anyone who wants to make changes at a later time has to unlock the settings by entering the name and password of an administrator account. (The first account created is an administrator account.)

Creating an ad hoc AirPort network

You can create a computer-to-computer network by using the AirPort status icon in the menu bar. Click this icon to display its menu and choose Create Network... from this menu. In the dialog that appears, enter a name, password, and channel number. Don't leave the password blank unless you want to permit any nearby computer with an AirPort card (or other IEEE 802.11 card) to join the network. If you have more than one wireless network in the same vicinity, leave two unused channel numbers between each used channel, because adjacent channels overlap.

Joining an AirPort network

You can join an AirPort network (or other IBSS wireless network) by using the AirPort status icon in the menu bar. Just click the icon to display its menu and choose a network from this menu. Choose Other from this menu to join a closed network. To join a closed network, you have to type the name of the network; you don't get to choose it from a list.

Leaving an AirPort network

If you want to leave an AirPort network without joining another and without turning off AirPort, have Mac OS X try to join a nonexistent AirPort network. You can do this by choosing Other from the Network pop-up menu in the Internet Connect application. Alternatively, you can choose Other from the menu of the AirPort status icon in the menu bar. In the dialog that appears, enter a phony AirPort network name and click OK. An alert appears telling you that an error occurred. This is not a serious problem. The computer is now not connected to any AirPort network.

How they find your personal Web site

If you have turned on Web Sharing in the Sharing pane of System Preferences and your computer has only an IP address, put a note on your home page advising viewers to add a bookmark for your page. By adding a bookmark, they don't have to remember your IP address and retype it to visit again. However, your Internet connection may change its IP address for your computer, depending on the type of connection you have.

The anonymous FTP user's home folder

If you create a user account named ftp to provide anonymous FTP access to your computer, you can simplify adding files, removing files, and making changes in the anonymous FTP user's home folder. First log out and then log in with user name ftp. Next change the group privileges for the ftp home folder (path `/Users/ftp/`) to Read & Write. Do the same for folders inside the ftp home folder. Finally, log out and log in with your own user name.

Getting More out of Sound and Speech

Try the tricks in this section to get more out of the Mac OS X text-to-speech and speech recognition capabilities.

Adding and removing Classic sounds

You can add and remove sounds from the System file used by the Classic environment without restarting your computer with Mac OS 9 if you can use another computer with Mac OS 9 on your network. First you stop the Classic environment and start file sharing on your computer. Then go to the other computer and connect to your computer. From the other computer, open your computer's System file and move sound files in or out as you like. Close the System file and disconnect from your computer. When you return to your computer, you can start the Classic environment, and the Classic environment uses the modified System file.

Speech loudness

To set the speaking volume for both the Mac OS X voice and the Classic environment's voice, use the Sound icon in the menu bar to change the system volume level. If the Sound icon isn't present, use the Sound pane of System Preferences. (The Classic Sound control panel's settings do not affect the speaking volume in the Classic environment.)

Making speech sound more natural

The Mac does a pretty good job of speaking text, but you can adjust the cadence and pronunciation of the speech to make it sound more natural. You make these adjustments by adding punctuation and emphasis codes.

When the Mac reads text, it tends to pause less often than a person would. You can make the Mac pause more often by inserting extra commas where you want pauses. For example:

```
You have a lunch date at 12:30, on Tuesday, at the Sam & Ella
Cafe.
```

To insert a brief pause, put single quotation marks around a phrase. For example:

```
Exclusive to the 'Coast Starlight' is the 'Pacific Parlor Car.'
```

Also, the Mac tends to emphasize too many words, making it hard to tell which words are important. You can insert the [[emph -]] code before a word you want to have less emphasis. This code must have one space before the hyphen, and none anywhere else. Here is an example:

```
The shuttle bus runs every half [[emph -]] hour, on the half
[[emph -]] hour.
```

As this example illustrates, sentences with repeated words are likely to have unwanted emphasis. You may also want to remove emphasis from words that are easily inferred. In addition, the Mac may overemphasize the last noun in a phrase that modifies the noun, such as Apple [[emph -]] menu, home [[emph -]] folder, and Big [[emph -]] Ben.

If you need to add emphasis, insert the [[emph +]] code. This code also has one space in it. Here is an example:

```
Are you [[emph +]] sure you want to delete the selected items?
```

Naming speakable items

Apple offers a little help when it comes to naming items that you add to the Speakable Items folder. Here are some of Apple's suggestions:

✦ Try to name items so that they don't sound too much alike (Navigator and Communicator are probably better than Netscape Navigator and Netscape Communicator, at least in our experience).

✦ Long command names are more easily recognized.

✦ If you need acronyms or a series of letters in a name, put spaces in between. Connect using P P P is better than Connect using PPP.

✦ Avoid using numerals in your file names. For example, speech recognition doesn't recognize the difference between AppleWorks 5 and AppleWorks 6.

✦ Make the names of speakable items sound different from each other. If speakable items have names that sound similar, the computer may have trouble distinguishing them. If the computer frequently mistakes one speakable item for another, try changing the name of one or both so that they don't sound alike.

Sing it to me

Four of the Mac's text-to-speech voices sing rather than speak text.

✦ The Bad News voice sings to the tune of a Chopin prelude.

✦ The Good News voice sings to the tune of "Pomp and Circumstance."

✦ The Pipe Organ voice sings to the tune of "Funeral March of a Marionette" by Gounod (also known as the theme music for the *Alfred Hitchcock Presents* television show).

✦ The Cellos voice sings to the tune of Edvard Grieg's "In the Hall of the Mountain King" from *Peer Gynt*.

To hear the tunes clearly, you need to have these voices sing (speak) a selection of text without punctuation marks. When these voices encounter punctuation, they start their tunes over.

Try this:

1. **Open an application that uses Mac text-to-speech voices to speak text, such as AppleWorks or the Classic SimpleText application.**

2. **Create a new document and type** la la la **several times in succession.**

3. **Select what you have typed, copy it, click at the end of the document, and keep pasting it until you have a dozen lines of "la la la" in the document.**

4. **Set the speaking voice to one of the singing voices named in the foregoing list and start text-to-speech.** You do this in SimpleText by choosing one of the singing voices from the Voices submenu of the Sound menu and then by choosing Speak All from the Sound menu to hear the voice sing.

Bonus: Some of the novelty voices, such as Boing, Bubbles, and Hysterical, also sound pretty weird when you have them speak this text.

Tell me a joke

If you have Speakable Items turned on in the Speech Recognition panel of Speech Preferences, you can get your computer to tell you knock-knock jokes. You say, "Tell me a joke." The computer responds, "Knock, knock." You reply, "Who is there?" The computer answers with a name or some word, such as "Wayne." You repeat the word and then say "who?" Figure 24-3 shows a transcript of one of these jokes in the Speech Commands window.

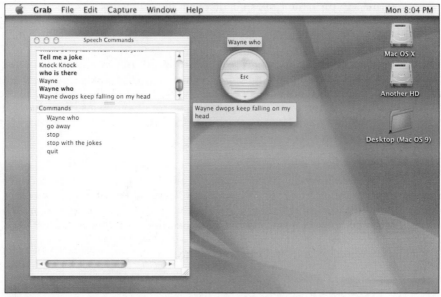

Figure 24-3: Get Speakable Items to tell you a joke.

Maintenance, Easter Egg, and Troubleshooting

In this section, you find a tip about software updates, a hidden Easter egg, and two tips for dealing with common problems.

Getting all software updates

Sometimes one software update must be installed before your computer is eligible for other updates that are available. This situation is especially likely if you haven't checked for updates in quite a while. To make sure that you're not missing any updates, install all listed updates and then click Update Now in Software Update Preferences. If the list is empty, you know you're completely up-to-date.

Ill will for Bill

Although Apple's software engineers reportedly have been under strict orders not to include any *Easter eggs,* which are cute or funny animations or other surprising actions, in Mac OS X. Nevertheless, at least one inadvertent Easter egg does exist. To see it, open the Terminal application and type the following command:

```
bill gates
```

When you press Return, the Unix shell displays the following:

```
OK? kill gates?
```

Despite appearances, this response probably does not reflect any ill will on the part of the Unix shell, the Terminal application, Mac OS X, or engineers involved with any of these programs. This response is a wry side effect of the Unix shell's attempt to correct what it perceives as a typographical error. It supposes that you meant to type `kill`, which is a valid Unix command. In fact, you get similar results by typing `bill clinton` or `ill will`.

Another Easter egg that exists in 10.2.1 is the "Cupertino File Sharing" Easter egg. Under normal circumstances, if you open System Preferences, then click on the Sharing icon, then the Services tab, and select Personal File Sharing, the text in the right side of the pane will read "Personal File Sharing On – Click Stop to prevent users of other computers from accessing Public folders on this computer." However, under other circumstances the text will read "Cupertino Sharing On – Lots of information for you. and you. and timmy."

About This Mac

When you choose Apple⇨About This Mac in Mac OS X 10.1, you normally see the Mac OS X version number displayed in the middle of the window. Click the version number line several times to cycle from version number to build number.

Totally Unix

Want to see what computer life was like before the Mac popularized the graphical interface. You can easily take your high-powered computer 20 years back in time, when the command-line interface ruled the computer world. We're not talking about using a command line in a terminal window that's surrounded by the comfort of the menu bar, Dock, and so on. We're talking about white text on a black screen and that's all.

Here's how you can expose the Unix beast beneath the Mac OS X's Aqua façade and then return to Aqua:

1. **Log out.**

2. **Log in with the name** >console **and a blank password.** After a few seconds, the screen goes black and you see a Darwin login prompt in white text, which should look like this:

```
Darwin/BSD (localhost) (console)

login:
```

If your login window displays a list of user accounts, you must click Other in the list to get a login window in which you can type the login name. If your login window's account list doesn't include Other, you must log in using one of the listed accounts and select the option to include Other in the list. This option is set in the Login pane of System Preferences.

3. **When you see the prompt** Login: **displayed, type the short name of your user account and press Return.** If you don't see this prompt, try pressing Return and waiting for a few seconds to see if the prompt appears.

4. **When you see the prompt** Password:, **type your password and press Return.** You should see the message Welcome to Darwin! followed on the next line by a Unix prompt, which includes your name, like this:

```
Darwin/BSD (localhost) (console)

login: atlas
Password:
Welcome to Darwin!
[localhost:~] atlas%
```

5. **If you know any Unix commands, you can enter them now.** For example, try typing ls and pressing Return. In response to the ls command, Unix lists the names of the items in the current directory, which is your home directory. (Directory is the Unix term for folder.) Therefore entering the ls command should result in a list of names including Desktop, Documents, Library, Movies, Music, Pictures, Public, and Sites. These are all standard folders in your home folder.

6. **When you've had enough of the command line, type the command** exit **and press Return.** Wait a minute or so and the login window appears.

Thawing a frozen program

Applications sometimes freeze and don't respond to ordinary controls, such as clicking Cancel buttons, pressing ⌘-period (.) to stop the current operation, or pressing ⌘-Q to quit the active application. If an application stops responding, choose Apple➪Force Quit or press ⌘-Option-Escape to display the Force Quit window. In this window, select the application that's misbehaving and then click Force Quit. Mac OS X forces the selected application to quit. You can also force an application to quit from the Dock in Mac OS X 10.1 and above. Control-click the application's icon in the Dock and then press Option to change the Quit choice to Force Quit in the application's Dock menu.

 Caution

When you force an application to quit, you don't get an opportunity to save changes in the application. Make sure that the application is not responding before you resort to forcing it to quit.

If you force a Mac OS X application to quit, none of the other applications is affected. If you force a Classic application to quit, other Classic applications that are open may be affected. You should quit all other Classic applications in the conventional manner, saving changes as necessary. Then restart the Classic environment by using the Restart button in the Classic pane of System Preferences.

Stuck in the past

If your computer's clock insists that it's really 1956 or some other date in the past, you aren't stuck in a time warp — you probably need to have the computer's internal battery replaced. When the computer is off, the battery keeps the clock ticking. You can find Apple part numbers for batteries for all but the latest Macs, which shouldn't need batteries yet, in Apple's Technical Information Library article 11751, which is available on the Web (`http://docs.info.apple.com/article.html?artnum=11751`) Apple recommends having a qualified service technician replace the internal battery.

Summary

In this chapter, you read about the following kinds of tips, tricks, and shortcuts:

✦ Using menus, getting more organized with the Dock, and working in windows and dialogs

✦ Saving time and effort with Finder windows and icons

✦ Making aliases

✦ Tweaking searches in Sherlock

✦ Zooming through the dialogs that appear when you choose Open, Save, Save As, and other disk-related commands

✦ Working with applications and documents, especially the following: Internet Explorer, Help Browser, QuickTime Player, iMovie, iTunes, Script Editor, and Script Runner

✦ Logging in, logging out, and making your computer more secure

✦ Dealing with network connections, personal Web Sharing, and FTP access to your computer

✦ Getting more out of text-to-speech and speech recognition

✦ Getting all software updates, finding an Easter egg, and solving a couple of common problems

✦   ✦   ✦

Maintaining Mac OS X

As a multiuser operating system with built-in file system security, Mac OS X compartmentalizes files in various folders. You'll be better able to maintain your Mac OS X computer if you understand where Mac OS X keeps system-related files. From your perspective as a user, there are three layers of what are traditionally thought of as "System stuff." There are the files that the operating system has to have to function, the files that can be organized for all users to access, and the files that belong to you. For example, you may have font files in three Fonts folders. One Fonts folder is in the Library folder of your home folder (path ~/Library/Fonts), another is in the main Library folder (path /Library/Fonts), and the third is in the Library folder of the folder named System (path /System/Library/Fonts).

Exploring the Mac OS X Library Folders

The files that comprise the Mac OS X core and that aren't accessible to user modification or management are kept in the /System folder hierarchy. You can look in the /System folder hierarchy, but don't touch. This structure belongs to the system. About the only thing you see here is a Library subfolder, and it contains a large number of subfolders holding the code and resources required for core Mac OS X functionality.

The main Library folder, at the top level of your system disk, is where someone who logs in with an administrator account can place things that are available to all users. It holds the fonts, sounds, screen savers, and so forth available to everyone who has an account on your Mac, as well as the resources required by installed applications and drivers for peripheral devices, such as printers.

In your home folder, another Library folder appears. This one stores all your personal settings, fonts, sounds, and other configuration objects.

Managing the main Library folder

The main Library folder (path `/Library`) is the repository of all the files required to make your Mac OS X user experience work. This folder is the closest thing you'll find to the System Folder of Mac OS 9 or the Windows directory on a PC. It contains all the files that support the applications installed in the Applications folder (path `/Applications`) as well as any preference settings that apply to the Mac as a whole. The following list enumerates the folders present in the main Library folder after a standard installation of Mac OS X and tells you what sorts of files can be found within them.

✦ **Application Support.** Contains shared libraries used by installed applications, such as the StuffIt Engine used by StuffIt Expander, other Aladdin Systems products, or third-party applications that make use of Aladdin's compression libraries.

✦ **Audio.** A repository for sounds used systemwide and sound-related plug-ins. If you wish to make an alert sound available, save it as an AIFF sound and put it in the Alerts folder of the Sounds folder in this Audio folder (path `/Library/Audio/Sounds/Alerts`).

✦ **Caches.** Holds temporary and permanent cache files used by applications.

✦ **ColorSync.** Holds the ColorSync profiles for a wide variety of devices and monitors in the Profiles subfolder and support AppleScripts in the Scripts subfolder. You can save some space by removing profiles for devices you don't have.

✦ **Desktop Pictures.** A collection of the TIFF and JPEG files available for use as a background picture for the Desktop. Each user can set a Desktop picture by using the Desktop pane of System Preferences.

✦ **Documentation.** Holds user manuals, help files, and copyright information for installed applications and services.

✦ **Fonts.** Contains the various font files that are not required by the System but are available to all users of your Mac. As discussed in Chapter 12, Mac OS X supports a wide range of font formats. This Fonts folder (path `/Library/Fonts`) is where you install fonts you want all users to be able to access, and if there are fonts in here that you do not wish to use, you can remove them. Having said that, certain fonts (such as Arial, Helvetica, Times New Roman, and Courier New) are default fonts for a number of applications, and you should probably leave those in place.

✦ **Frameworks.** Frameworks are another kind of shared library that is dynamic: only loaded into memory when being used. Frameworks can be compared to System Extensions in OS 9.

✦ **Image Capture.** Contains a Scripts folder in which the AppleScripts that perform the Image Capture application's hot-plug actions (see Chapter 22) reside.

✦ **Internet Plug-Ins.** Holds the plug-ins that add functionality to Web browsers and other Internet applications. Examples include the QuickTime Plug-in, which allows you to watch QuickTime movies in your Web browser.

✦ **Java.** Contains, by default, an alias to the Java support files and libraries in the Library folder hierarchy of the System folder (path `/System/Library`). It also contains Java libraries installed for use by various Java applications.

✦ **Keyboard Layouts.** Where keyboard layouts (analogous to keyboard scripts under OS 9) can be stored. Detailed information can be found in Apple Technical Note TN2056, `http://developer.apple.com/technotes/tn2002/tn2056.html`.

✦ **Logs.** Holds the log histories (viewable with the Console utility — see Chapter 22) for applications that send debug and status information to the system console.

✦ **Modem Scripts.** A collection of files describing the characteristics and capabilities of a wide variety of modems. You can feel free to remove the files for modems you don't have. If you acquire a new modem, you might have to reinstall its modem script into this folder.

✦ **Perl.** Where the scripting language Perl is installed by default on OS X.

✦ **Preferences.** Holds the `.plist` (property list) files describing preference and state settings for systemwide services. For example, `com.apple.loginwindow.plist` contains the user number (as maintained in NetInfo) for the last user to log into Mac OS X, whether that user is currently logged in; and `com.apple.PowerManagement.plist` contains the settings made for Energy Saver in System Preferences.

✦ **Printers.** Contains the printer drivers and PPD files used by Print Center in recognizing, configuring, and enabling your printers. More on printers in Chapter 9.

✦ **QuickTime.** Where additional codecs and other QuickTime support files should be installed. For example, Roxio Toast includes a QuickTime codec to convert to VCD MPEG (VideoCD-ready MPEG-1) format, and that file is installed here.

✦ **Receipts.** Contains files required by the Installer relating to your Mac OS X installation.

✦ **Screen Savers.** A folder you can fill with screen saver modules to be available to all users of your Mac via the Screen Saver pane of Systems Preferences.

✦ **Scripts.** Contains folders of AppleScript scripts that are available to all users of your computer. The scripts in this folder appear in Script Runner's pop-up menu and in the menu of the Script Menu icon, as described in Chapter 21.

✦ **User Pictures.** Contains folders of small pictures suitable for assigning to user accounts. Each user account can have a picture that appears in the login window's list of user accounts. Pictures are assigned to user accounts in the Users pane of System Preferences.

✦ **WebServer.** Holds the *CGI* (Common Gateway Interface) scripts that enable add-on Web server functions, such as forms submittal, for Mac OS X Web Sharing. (Turn on Web Sharing in the Sharing pane of Systems Preferences.) This folder also contains the documentation for Apache, the software that turns your Mac into a Web server.

Exploring your personal Library folder

Located in your home folder, you also see a folder named Library. Many of the folders in this folder have the same names as those discussed earlier in this chapter ("Managing the main Library folder"). When you encounter a folder with the same name, it has the same functionality, except that it contains items specific to *your* use of the Mac rather than items for all users. As an example, you install fonts for your personal use in the Fonts folder of the Library folder in your home folder (path ~/Library/Fonts) if you aren't making them available to other users of the Mac. Similarly, alert sounds or screen savers that aren't shared would go in a folder of your personal Library folder.

Some of the other folders you're likely to see in your personal Library folder include:

✦ **Addresses.** The folder containing information from your Address Book and possibly other address book and contact-management applications.

✦ **Application Support.** Contains shared libraries used by applications installed by you when not acting as an administrator. For example, the folder for information from your Address Book was located in Library as Addresses, but in 10.2 the Addresses folder has moved to inside the Application Support folder.

✦ **Assistants.** Contains files used by various Assistants. For example, if you were unable to connect during your initial setup to register Mac OS X, a file named SendRegistration.setup (a .plist file) is saved here with your registration information and preferences.

✦ **Audio.** Sounds and plug-ins installed by you when not acting as an administrator.

✦ **ColorPickers.** Where you find additional ColorPickers to augment the collection Apple provides.

✦ **Documentation.** Holds user manuals, help files, and copyright information for installed applications and services installed by you. Like the other files associated with applications installed by you when not acting as an administrator, these are not accessible to other users on the system.

✦ **Favorites.** Where your Favorites are stored.

✦ **FontCollections.** Where your choices for font collections (see Chapter 12) are cached.

✦ **Frameworks.** Where the support frameworks (shared program libraries) for personal applications are stored.

✦ **Internet Search Sites.** Contains folders for each of your Sherlock channels, each containing the search-site plug-in files for that channel. See Chapter 7 for more about Sherlock and its channels. You might not see this folder until you've performed at least one Internet search in Sherlock.

✦ **Keyboards.** Contains any custom keyboard layouts you've installed.

✦ **Keychains.** Holds your Keychain files (see Chapter 10 for more information about the Keychain).

✦ **Mail.** Your personal mail folder. The Mail application (see Chapter 6) keeps its databases and other files here.

✦ **Recent Servers.** Contains the URL files to the servers that you've recently used. These are the servers that show up under Recent Servers in the Connect to Server dialog's pop-up menu.

✦ **Scripts.** The repository for your personal AppleScripts, if you have any. This is one of the locations Script Runner and Script Menu check by default when you use them.

Depending upon what other applications you have installed or run, there can be other folders in your personal Library folder, such as OmniWeb, if you've installed that Web browser. Apple's iTunes and iMovie also create folders in the user's Library folder when they first run.

Exploring the Classic (Mac OS 9) System Folder

In addition to the three levels of Library folders described previously in this chapter, there is yet another folder full of configuration and system files to know about — the Mac OS 9 System Folder used by the Classic environment.

Note   As discussed in numerous other chapters, Classic is a Mac OS X application that runs your Mac OS 9 system and its applications. It is sometimes referred to as the *blue box*, because in the early days of planning for the new operating system, the classic Mac OS was called "Blue," and the Mac OS of the future was called "Pink." Now, what we have as Mac OS X bears almost no relationship to the object-oriented environment originally envisioned. (That became part of Taligent, the joint development of Apple and IBM, which never quite shipped.) But Classic is, to all intents and purposes, the compatibility environment that started life as Blue.

Probing the System Folder

The heart of the Classic environment is the System file in your Mac OS 9 System Folder. This file contains the code that makes Mac OS 9 possible — it provides the basic system services and protocols through which everything else communicates.

In the early days of Mac OS, the System file contained almost everything — fonts, sounds, desk accessories (the original Apple menu items), keyboards, you name it. Due to architectural and space limitations, many of these resources were moved out of the System file to stand alone as files in your System Folder. From this reorganization arose a new problem — System Folder clutter. All of a sudden, there were so many files and folders inside System Folders that most users couldn't find what they were looking for.

Apple addressed this by introducing specialized folders for classes of System support files — Extensions, Control Panels, Fonts, Preferences, and so forth. Of course, even this organizational setup grew unwieldy as more and more capabilities became available, each capability requiring its own collection of support files in the System Folder. Then, there was the problem of users putting the right files in the right folders when installing new software or accidentally dragging a file to a folder where it didn't belong.

Tip   Before you read the next two sections, let us just give you the following advice. If you have sufficient disk space to partition your disk or you have a second hard disk, we strongly recommend that you keep *two* Mac OS 9 Systems, one on the partition or disk with Mac OS X to act as your Classic environment and one on another disk or partition into which you restart when you want to run old applications not compatible with the Classic environment under Mac OS X. The Mac OS 9 used for Classic should have a minimum of extensions and control panels, and the one used for serious Classic work should be the customized environment. This results in faster startup time for Classic under Mac OS X and more stability in the Classic environment.

Adding items to the System Folder

In response to the location difficulties, Apple provided *autorouting* intelligence to the Finder — certain file types could be dropped on the System Folder, and the Finder would place them in the correct subfolder for you. Control panels and even applications that were typed to work like control panels were placed in the Control Panels folder; extensions, printer drivers, shared libraries, and the like were routed to the Extensions folder; Sherlock plug-in files were placed in Internet Search Sites; fonts were placed in the Fonts folder; and so forth.

In general, if you have a file that needs to be in the System Folder, just drag it onto the System Folder's icon (not into a window that is displaying the System Folder), and it is usually placed where it is supposed to be. As shown in Figure 25-1, the Mac OS X Finder has the smarts to tell you about the autorouting of items into the Classic environment's System Folder and then putting them where they need to be. On a rare occasion, you might have a need to place a file in a specific location within the System Folder — such as when you want to add something to your Classic Apple menu. When that is the case, open the System Folder in a Finder window and drag the file to the folder where it needs to be.

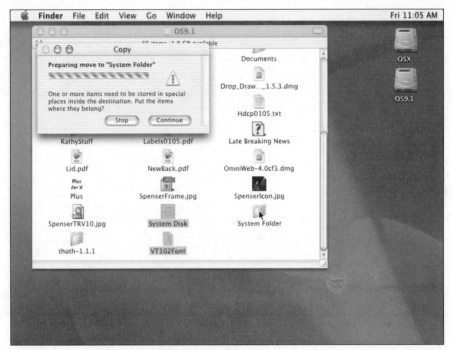

Figure 25-1: Mac OS X autoroutes files in the Classic environment's System Folder.

Removing items from the System Folder

Unfortunately, Apple has never developed an automated process for removing items from the System Folder or its subfolders, nor does there exist a really intelligent uninstaller that can determine which items can safely be removed without compromising the usability of existing applications. Some third-party solutions come close, for example Aladdin Systems' Spring Cleaning, but they do not cover all contingencies.

To manage extensions and control panels, you should employ the Extensions Manager that comes with Mac OS 9 or an alternative extensions manager, such as Conflict Catcher 8 from Casady & Greene (www.casadyg.com). Deactivate the items you wish to remove and restart Classic. The deactivated items are now in folders named Extensions (Disabled) and Control Panels (Disabled), and you can safely remove them if you want to free up some disk space. Of course, you can remove items from the Classic environment's System Folder when Classic isn't running without going through these steps. Removing fonts requires that no Classic applications be running.

Invisible Folders

Apple and the graphical user interface try very hard to conceal the sometimes cryptic Unix underpinnings of Mac OS X from you. One thing they do is to hide the standard command-line directories (folders) from you when you're in the Finder or using an Open or Save dialog. These directories have such revealing names as .bin (binary executables), .dev (devices), .etc (et cetera, miscellaneous items), .sbin (more binary executables, mostly run at startup time), and .usr (user directory hierarchy).

Now, you may ask, if the Finder hides these from us, how do we ever find out where they are? There are two easy ways to find out: use Unix commands in a Terminal window as described in Chapter 26 or use OS X's Find command to search for items whose visibility is off.

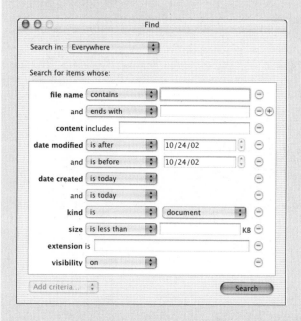

Because these folders are invisible, Sherlock won't let you double-click them to open them in the Finder. To see what they contain, you're pretty much constrained to use Terminal and enter Unix commands — ls -F /bin, for example, gives you a listing of all the files in the /bin directory and indicates whether they are directories (appending a slash), executables (appending an asterisk), or a link (appending an at-sign).

Opening Classic applications automatically

Just as you can add items to a list in the Login pane of System Preferences (see Chapter 15) that you want opened automatically when you log in, you can specify applications and documents you want to open automatically when Classic starts up or shuts down.

You place the items (in general, it's better to place aliases to the items) into the System Folder's Startup Items and Shutdown Items folders. By placing aliases into the folders, you gain the advantage of not having to navigate into or out of your System Folder hierarchy for changed documents, nor do you have to place support files that need to be co-located with their applications in the folder with the application items.

Now, each time you start Classic, the applications and documents in your Startup Items folder opens. Similarly, each time you quit Classic, the items in your Shutdown Items folder open.

Investigating preferences

Well-behaved Classic applications store their preferences in the Preferences folder of the System Folder. This is one place where the compartmentalization of ownership and individualized preferences breaks down in Mac OS X. For Mac OS X applications, your preferences are kept in your home folder's Library folder structure, and the preferences of other users are kept in the Library folders of their home folders. Everyone shares Classic applications, though, and whoever sets preferences in a Classic application last leaves those behind to benefit or bedevil the next user of the application.

Practicing Good Housekeeping

As with any disk-based operating system, debris accumulates, and storage space becomes fragmented over time. A few basic maintenance operations, performed on a regular basis, provide improved performance and stability. The most critical of these is to *back up your data*. We cannot stress enough how important a regular backup routine can be — the first time you accidentally delete or overwrite some file(s) you need, you'll be very glad to have a backup from which to restore them.

Backups

A computer user who doesn't make backups is like a parachutist who doesn't check his or her equipment before jumping — they may be lucky for a while, but their luck runs out eventually, usually at a really inopportune time. It's not a matter of *if* you encounter a problem with one of your files, it's merely a matter of *when* that the problem occurs.

Software and media

At one time, personal computer users could back up all their files on diskettes — in fact, the first IBM PCs and the first Macs didn't even have hard disks, and everything was on diskettes. Now that multigigabyte sizes are required for Mac OS X, it is no longer practical. Even Zip disks in 100MB to 250MB sizes are starting to look impractical as a general backup medium. Tape drives, CD-RW, and DVD-RAM drives are becoming the media of preference. Long the leading purveyor of backup software, Dantz Development (www.dantz.com) produces Mac OS X versions of their Retrospect backup software.

In this constantly changing arena, there is no way we could make any up-to-date recommendations — reviews appear regularly in publications like *Macworld* magazine and on Web sites.

Regardless of the hardware and software you choose, you should perform backups regularly. A month-old copy of your magnum opus won't be of much use if you've been updating it steadily over the past few weeks — all those changes and additions are lost.

Backup rotation

A useful backup strategy includes regular rotation of your media and periodic archiving of your backups. Writing repeatedly to the same media can frequently be problematic — not only does media degrade under frequent use, but you could easily be overwriting a good copy of a file with a corrupted copy.

If you're backing up data that is really important to you or your employer, you'll want to make your plan as fail-safe as possible. This plan requires quite a few sets of backup media. One such plan follows:

1. Every other day, back up to a new disk or tape. A good rule, for instance, would be to back up on Monday, Wednesday, and Friday. For the first week, each backup requires a full backup, because you'll be using a new disk or tape. Subsequently, you can use your backup software's incremental backup feature to back up *some* of the disks more quickly.

2. After the first week, drop the Friday disk or tape out of the rotation and save it in a secure location (off-site, in a safety deposit box, in secure storage). This is your archive disk or tape for the week.

3. On the following Monday and Wednesday, you can perform an incremental update to the backups. On the following Friday, create a new, full backup that is again archived.

In this scheme, you're able to keep your backup data relatively fresh while guarding against catastrophe and data corruption. At the most, you've lost two days (often one business day) of data in the event of hard disk failure. (If your disk fails on Thursday, you have Wednesday's backup. If it fails on Sunday, you have Friday's backup.)

If you receive a virus or notice disk corruption at some point, you have a number of backups to choose from, including backups that are one day old, three days old, a week old, two weeks old, and so on. (If you find corruption on Thursday, you have Wednesday's backup, Monday's backup, and the previous Friday's archive. Then you have previous week's archives as well.) Hopefully, there is a recent version that lacks the corruption. If your data is even more mission-critical, you should back up every day, and possibly begin each backup on a fresh tape or disk.

For personal backup, the scheme can be a little less arduous. We recommend backing up once or twice a week, rotating between at least two different disks or tapes, and then archiving your data every two weeks or once a month, depending on the sensitivity of the data. It can be a pain to enter two weeks worth of Quicken checkbook data or lose changes in files over the past few weeks, but at least you'll probably have a good backup to work with. Although you probably don't need to back up applications and system software, because you can reinstall them if necessary, you should back up your documents regularly. (You can also back up the Preferences folder of the Library folder in your home folder and the Preferences folder the Classic environment's System Folder often so you can restore changes to application preferences in the case of a hard disk crash.) You may also want an archive of application updates and software downloaded from the Internet, just so you can get to those patches and updates quickly if you need to reinstall. It's best to archive data periodically and keep at least two different backup tapes or disks active at once for some measure of redundancy.

Maintaining the file system

Although Mac OS X can read and write a wide variety of disk formats, it (at least currently) can only start up from two different formats, Mac OS Extended (also known as HFS Plus or HFS+ for *hierarchical file system plus*) and UFS (Unix File System, sometimes called ffs for *fast file system*). Apple recommends the use of the Mac OS Extended format and so do we — if you run any Classic applications, you definitely want the Mac OS Extended format, and most Carbon applications perform better in the Mac OS Extended format because they do not require the file system to do translation to emulate to multiform files to which Mac applications are accustomed.

Mac OS X comes with a pretty good disk diagnostic and disk-directory repair tool — Disk Utility, covered in Chapter 22. Other vendors of well-regarded disk utilities include Micromat with TechTool Pro (www.micromat.com), Alsoft with DiskWarrior (www.alsoft.com), and Symantec with Norton Utilities (www.symantec.com). At the time we're writing this, only Alsoft has released a Mac OS X version of their product. Alsoft claims that DiskWarrior fixes problems that are peculiar to Mac OS Extended format and Mac OS X. None recognize UFS disks at this time.

Note
    If you restart in single-user mode (hold down ⌘-S during startup), you can run the Unix command-line tool fsck (File System CHeck), with the -y option, to repair many problems with the directory structures. If you choose this route, you should rerun it repeatedly until it comes back with no errors found.

Protecting against viruses

Although computer viruses are not nearly as prevalent on Macs as on Microsoft Windows PCs, Mac viruses do exist, and many of the so-called "macro viruses" developed on PCs (generally infecting Microsoft Office documents) can infect Macs.

Viruses invade your computer through documents or applications that you have downloaded from the Internet, through electronic mail attachments, or through any type of removable disk (including floppy disks) you may use with your computer. Although some viruses may be relatively innocuous, doing little more than taking up space on disk and slowing down your computer a bit, others can be highly destructive, causing crashes and erasing files. The Unix system of file permissions underlying Mac OS X make infection from viruses even less likely to cause extensive damage — at least so long as you don't log in with the System Administrator (root) account.

The only way to protect your Mac from computer viruses is to install an antivirus utility on your computer. Antivirus software warns you if a virus attempts to infect your system, scans your disks for viruses that may be lurking (or may already have caused some damage), and eradicates almost any virus that it finds. Symantec's Norton Antivirus, Virex X, and Sophos Anti-Virus, among others, are available for Mac OS X.

Whichever antivirus software package you choose, you need to keep it up-to-date; each time a new virus appears, the antivirus packages must generally be updated to recognize it. Most of the time, you receive updates by downloading them from the software publisher's Web site or accessing them in public download Web sites or FTP sites. In some cases, you may have a limited "subscription" to updates to the virus software itself. With Virex, you can pay an additional fee to have updates e-mailed directly to you. Norton AntiVirus includes a LiveUpdate feature that can automatically download the latest virus definitions for you. Norton AntiVirus also offers a free trial version that you can download directly from the company's Web site. Both Network Associates and Symantec post new virus definitions to their Web sites monthly (on the first of the month), possibly more frequently if a particularly destructive virus is discovered. If you are either a Virex or Norton AntiVirus customer, you should consider marking your calendar to check on the first of the month and to bookmark the company's virus definitions page for easy access.

Keeping software up-to-date

It is an unfortunate fact of life in the computer age that no software of any consequential size and complexity is completely bug-free (bugs being improperly programmed instructions). Some bugs may be features that do not function as planned to more serious errors, causing crashes or data corruption. Many bugs are so obscure, requiring an unusual confluence of events, that you are likely never to encounter them, but a few bugs appear to take a nip at you. As one of the largest bodies of code on your Mac, Mac OS X also is not completely bug-free.

Customarily, after software publishers become aware of a problem with their product, they take action to correct the anomaly by either one of the following:

✦ Documents a work-around while they work on a new version that fixes the problem

✦ Provide an *updater* that runs and updates the application to a new version with the problem fixed

Computer Viruses, Worms, and Trojan Horses

A *computer virus* is a piece of software designed to spread itself by illicitly attaching copies of itself to legitimate software. Although not all viruses perform malicious actions (such as erasing your hard disk), any virus can interfere with the normal functioning of your computer.

A *macro virus* is a virus written in the *macro language* of an application (a programming language that enables you to automate multiple-step operations in an application). By far, most macro viruses infect Microsoft Word (Version 6.0 and later) and Excel (Version 5.0 and later) documents. Like other viruses, macro viruses can be very destructive.

Viruses, alas, are not the only potentially destructive software that you may encounter. *Worms* are similar to viruses in that they replicate, but they do not attach themselves to files. A worm replaces a legitimate program or file on your system and performs its mischief whenever that legitimate program is run. A *Trojan horse* is an intentionally destructive program masquerading as something useful, such as a utility, software updater, or game. Although worms and Trojan horses are not viruses, most commercial antivirus programs can detect and remove them.

Registering your software (either by sending in the postcard that came with it or via the Internet, as you did when you performed your Mac OS X Setup) and checking the publisher's Web site regularly are two good ways to keep informed of workarounds and updaters.

Mac OS X, like Mac OS 9 before it, provides a live Software Update capability. The Software Update pane of System Preferences is discussed in more depth in Chapter 15. Keeping your operating system software up-to-date with the latest enhancements and bug fixes from Apple should be part of your maintenance regimen. Many software publishers, such as Aladdin Systems, include in their applications the ability to automatically check the publisher for updates just as Apple does with Mac OS X and QuickTime.

You should also check your iDisk for new and updated applications and utilities from Apple, as discussed in Chapter 10. There, you find such goodies as iTunes, iMovie, and the AppleWorks updaters in addition to new and updated printer drivers for Mac OS X. Here are some excellent sources to check:

- ◆ Apple's Mac OS X Web site (www.apple.com/macosx/)
- ◆ Apple's Software Updates library (www.apple.com/swupdates)
- ◆ VersionTracker (www.versiontracker.com/macosx)

Despite testing by Apple and various software publishers, some older software products are incompatible with the Classic environment. Assuming that you have already verified that they work with Mac OS 9, you should keep them separate and run them only when you start up with Mac OS 9 until a Mac OS X-compatible version becomes available.

Scheduling maintenance

Taken together, all of the maintenance tasks discussed in the preceding sections —
backing up, virus checking, securing your system, and periodic cleaning up — can
help ensure that your Mac experience is relatively error and hassle free. Here, then,
is a quick summary of the steps to take to maintain your Mac and the recommended frequency:

✦ **Daily.** For the most part, you should turn on and shut down your Mac only
once per day (at the beginning and end of your work day or Mac session), if
you elect to do so at all. You can put your Mac to sleep, spin down the hard
disk, and make other energy-saving settings in the Energy Saver pane of
System Preferences (see Chapter 15). Otherwise, more harm than good comes
from powering down and up more than once per day. You may find it useful to
restart the Mac (using the Restart command in the Apple menu) more than
once per day if, for instance, you find that some application is not recognizing
newly installed hardware.

You should also check your disk space levels — open the Macintosh HD icon
and look at the status section of the window at the top (you may have to
choose View⇨Show Status Bar to make it visible) to make sure that you have
disk space available. Having less than 20 percent free disk space could begin
to create problems, so you should back up and archive unnecessary documents or applications. In a business setting, you may also want to back up on
a daily basis or every other day, according to a well-planned rotation schedule. If you share your Mac, you should also coordinate with the other users so
that they can also clean out unnecessary files from their home folders.

✦ **Weekly.** On a weekly basis, you should run your virus-checking software if it's
not already designed to run in the background. If your machine is for personal
use, you may want to back up on a weekly basis, again according to a media
rotation schedule. You may also want to run Disk Utility's Disk First Aid on a
weekly basis.

✦ **Monthly.** On a monthly basis, you should update your virus definitions if your
virus software doesn't do this for you automatically. Check for updates to Mac
OS X at least once a month. You can do this by going to the Apple software
page of the Mac OS X Downloads site on the Web (http://www.apple.com/
downloads/macosx/apple/) or by configuring the Software Updates pane
of System Preferences to check for updates automatically on a weekly or
monthly basis. Even if you configure the Software Updates pane of System
Preferences to update automatically, go to this pane at least once a month and
click the Update Now button to initiate an update manually. In addition, every
one to three months you should consider defragmenting your hard disk.

✦ **Every three to six months.** Every three to six months, perform a more-serious
tune-up session. Start up from a Mac OS X CD or utility CD and run a session

from Alsoft's Disk Express or Micromat's TechTool Pro. You should also perform a disk housecleaning session, removing applications, preference files, and other software that your Mac no longer needs. A tool such as Aladdin's Spring Cleaning can help with this. If you haven't defragmented your hard disk in the last three months, do it now.

Monitoring system performance

Some Mac problems manifest themselves in slow performance rather than in crashes or system errors. The causes of performance problems are often the same as the causes of other problems, and the general troubleshooting techniques presented in this chapter can often solve performance problems as well.

If your Mac has been performing more slowly than usual, here are a few possible causes and solutions.

Memory problems

If you open memory-consumptive applications or documents, Mac OS X employs *virtual memory* (treating part of your hard disk as memory, also called the *swap space*) to continue to work. If your software has to continually access the disk to retrieve data because of this, you experience a significant performance degradation. Other than dealing with smaller documents or using applications with lesser appetites, the solution here is to purchase and install more RAM. Although Mac OS X recommends at least 128MB of RAM, more is better.

Disk fragmentation

When the files on a disk become fragmented, disk performance suffers considerably. In addition, files themselves (including applications) can become fragmented on a disk. A single file may be split into several pieces spread around in different locations physically on a disk. Fragmentation degrades disk performance because the disk drive must take extra time to move from one piece of a file to the next.

A fragmented file is analogous to a single track on an audio CD being split into multiple segments, so that the beginning of the track may be at the beginning of the CD, the middle at the end, and the end of the track some place in the middle. If audio CDs were mastered in that fashion (which, fortunately, they are not), you would likely notice a delay as the CD player's laser moves to play the next segment.

In a disk with no fragmentation, each file physically resides in a single contiguous block. As a disk begins to fill up and new files are created and deleted with increasing frequency, files and the free space start to become fragmented. A heavily fragmented disk is more likely to experience a variety of problems, including corrupted directory structures and damaged files.

Without any special software, you can eliminate fragmentation by copying the entire contents of a disk to another disk, erasing the disk, and copying everything back. An easier solution is to use a commercial disk defragmentation utility, such as the SpeedDisk component of the Norton Utilities from Symantec (www.symantec.com), or DiskWarrior from Alsoft (www.alsoft.com). Note, however, that older disk optimization utilities are not compatible with the Unix File System (UFS); you should check for compatibility before attempting to run a disk optimizer on a UFS volume.

Before optimizing any disk, it is especially important to make a full backup, because virtually every byte on the disk may be erased and moved to a different location.

Summary

In this chapter, you learned where different system, application, and personal support and preferences files are stored in Mac OS X. You also learned how to manage a Classic environment's System Folder and the files within it as well as how to perform preventive and basic remedial maintenance on your hard disk(s). You also been shown the outlines of a backup strategy to maintain your data and recover in the event of a disk or system problem.

✦   ✦   ✦

Commanding Unix

By now, you are aware that Mac OS X is built upon a foundation known as Unix. Apple has named this foundation *Darwin* and has made the source to Darwin downloadable on the Internet. Much has been said and written about how this foundation provides Mac OS with modern Mac OS capabilities, and that is all true. The humorous aspect of these assertions is that Unix, having been developed at Bell Laboratories in the early 1970s and based on Ken Thompson's experiments with file systems in 1969 at Bell Labs, is far older than Mac OS, or even the DOS that preceded and lay the foundation for Windows.

In this chapter, we present a brief history of Unix and show you how to use some of the power Unix provides. Unix is a large, complex system with literally hundreds of commands, each of which may have multiple options. Much (most) of this, you never really need to see; however, if your curiosity gets the better of you, there are some excellent Unix references available, such as *Unix For Dummies,* 4th Edition, by John R. Levine and Margaret Levine Young (Wiley, Inc.).

Introduction to Unix

The flexibility and raw power available through Unix can easily overwhelm those who are not familiar with it. You might say that Unix gives you the power and freedom to shoot yourself in the foot if you aren't careful.

As mentioned earlier, Unix was developed at Bell Laboratories. Unix was designed to be *machine-independent* — in other words, an operating system that was not wedded to the underlying processor in the way that the traditional Mac OS is coupled to the PowerPC chips and Windows is tied to the

Intel chip family. Apple first produced a Unix-based system for its Macintosh line, A/UX (Apple Unix), in the late 1980s and early 1990s. Additionally, the NeXT operating system, acquired by Apple with the purchase of NeXT, is a Unix-based operating system — the same Unix-based system underlying Mac OS X.

Unix supports multiple users while they are performing multiple tasks simultaneously. This support includes managing memory and the file system and other resources without user supervision or involvement.

A standard Unix implementation includes a large variety of built-in and standard commands that enables the user to perform a variety of standard functions, from editing text to managing individual files and folders. In the beginning, Unix ran on computers with limited memory. The most powerful computers of the late 1960s and early 1970s were large, slow, cumbersome, and limited tools as compared with today's iMac. One effect of the limited memory and disk storage of these early computers was that Unix implementers traded clarity for space, particularly in naming the tools and commands available. Thus, commands such as "Change Directory to" became `cd` and Archive to/from Tape became `tar`.

Command-Line versus Graphical Interface

History, or at least folklore, tells us that Apple's *GUI* (graphical user interface) development arose from a visit to Xerox PARC (Palo Alto Research Center). Apple executives, including Steve Jobs, were impressed with the fledgling foray into a new user experience — the graphical user interface that was implemented on Xerox's Star and Alto workstations. Until that time, the developing personal computer industry was dominated by operating systems and applications directed solely from the keyboard. Pointing devices, such as mice, were virtually unheard of, although some games supported joysticks as optional control devices.

Apple's Lisa was the first consumer line to be introduced with a GUI, but at $10,000 each, a small software base, and limited (and proprietary) development tools, this machine was soon eclipsed by another Apple product, introduced a year later — the Macintosh. From the beginning, traditionalists decried the Mac and its GUI as a toy and opined that "real computer users use the command line." Thus began a religious argument that still flares up today, albeit with slightly less heat and frequency, concerning the relative advantages and disadvantages of the two approaches. The evolution, by Microsoft, from DOS to Windows dragged all but the most vocal opponents of GUIs into the current era, and the advent of windowing systems for Unix has quieted most of the rest.

As is true with most religious arguments, both sides have credible arguments and both draw overly broad conclusions from those arguments. Although GUIs currently hold sway in the vast majority of user environments, the inclusion of a *CLI* (command-line interface) or its equivalent can significantly augment user productivity in some situations.

Whether it is easier to select a desired folder from a Window menu, navigate a file browser to locate it, or type cd directoryname depends greatly upon the context, the user's typing ability, and the user's memory.

> **Note** What we visualize as folders in our graphical interface are generally referred to as directories in a Unix (or almost any other command-line) operating system. Throughout this chapter, we use *folder* when talking about the GUI view and *directory* when dealing with the CLI.

The traditional Unix interface is a CLI, although various GUIs exist to shield the user from that experience if they so desire. These GUIs include an assortment of window managers running under X (not "ten"), also known as X Windows, and such vendor-specific GUIs as BeOS, OpenStep (or NextStep), and Solaris.

> **Note** A version of the X Windows interface is available for OS X under the name OroboroSX, and is described in Chapter 23.

Almost without exception, anything that can be accomplished by using one interface is also possible with the other. A common example of a CLI's power is to delete all files with a particular extension. Using Mac OS X or Mac OS 9, you usually launch Sherlock to find all names with the same extension and drag the found set to the Trash. Same result, different methodology.

You can access the Unix command line in Mac OS X by using the Terminal application (found in the Utility folder of the Applications folder). The initial, and not very enlightening, Terminal window is shown in Figure 26-1. The Terminal window presents a few clues, if you know how to read them. Those clues are:

✦ The path to your current directory (the Unix term for folder) is shown in square brackets to the left of the prompt. In Figure 26-1, the localhost followed by the tilde (~) indicates that you are in your home directory on the machine, localhost.

✦ The user ID (short name) of the current user follows — that's you, almost always.

✦ The % indicates that you are not logged in as the System Administrator (the root user) and serves as your command prompt.

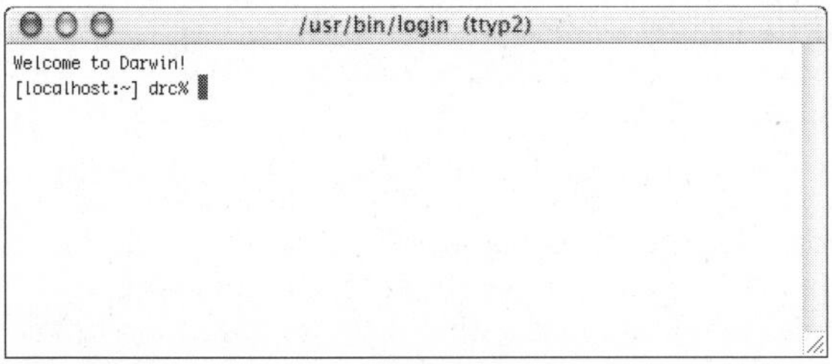

Figure 26-1: The Terminal window doesn't give you many hints on how to proceed.

The command-line interpreter in Unix is called a *shell*. In the next section, we delve a little deeper into the default shell and the other shell choices available to you. Apple has actually had a shell available as part of a package for Macintosh programmers (and other users) since 1986 (and as a free download for almost a decade) called *MPW*. The MPW shell differs from the shells available in the Terminal mostly in the following ways:

✦ The command names are different.

✦ The wildcards used are different.

✦ MPW Shell is also a full-featured text-editing environment.

✦ A Unix shell can spawn processes and has more control due to Unix's multi-tasking model.

Tip   Sometimes applications have options available from the command line that aren't necessarily available through the GUI. For an example, open a Terminal window, type the word screencapture and press the Return key. Read the options for use of the screencapture command carefully, as they are much more extensive than the ⌘-Shift-3 and ⌘-Shift-4 keyboard shortcuts allow you to use.

Shells

The shell is just an application, and various shells exist, such as sh (standard Unix Bourne shell), csh (Berkeley Unix c-shell), and ksh (Korn shell). The default shell included with Mac OS X is called tcsh and is a significantly enhanced version of csh. Another of the shells provided is zsh, which is to ksh what tcsh is to csh. A Mac OS X installation provides four shells in the standard distribution: sh, csh, tcsh, and zsh. You can find other shells (such as ksh and bash) by checking the Darwin distribution on Apple's Web site. Shells fall into two general camps: sh derivatives and csh derivatives. These camps don't differ by much superficially, but they do some things differently. For example, csh derivatives use setenv to set environment variables while sh derivatives use a combination of set and export to set these variables.

In many respects, you can think of the different shells as different dialects of the same language. After you learned one shell, you can pretty much communicate in any of them; however, you occasionally find differences in syntax, and you may not command the full power of the new shell's enhancements. For example, if you are fully proficient in every aspect of csh, all of that knowledge is usable in tcsh. But to get the full power of tcsh, you can take advantage of its history mechanism and spelling correction. Moving to zsh, you would learn different techniques for some of these enhancements.

Some common special characters

Unix, as noted earlier in this chapter, originated in an era of extremely limited memory and disk space. One of your authors, for example, programmed the real-time tracking system used by the Deep Space Network at the Jet Propulsion Laboratory on a minicomputer with 64K words (128K bytes) of memory and two 5MB disk packs, each of which was approximately 15 inches in diameter and two inches thick. Conservation of resources was critical; therefore, command names were abbreviated. Commands and file names were case-sensitive, because that provided for more diversity in short names and eliminated the need to provide code-parsing commands into a consistent case for comparisons.

Additionally, a number of special and punctuation characters were employed as shortcuts or abbreviations. Some are shown in the following list:

~	home directory
.	current directory
..	parent directory to the current directory
/	topmost or root directory

Scripting the shell

These shells all support *shell scripting*, or programmatic control. Although these scripting languages are not as Englishlike as AppleScript, they are incredibly powerful and flexible. In addition to supporting variables and such programming constructs as conditionals and loops, shell scripting supports a number of *control* and *redirection* operators.

Control operators enable you to set precedence, group, and have commands proceed *asynchronously* (start it running and continue without waiting for the background process to complete). You use redirection to specify from where input to a command should come or where a command's output or error messages should go.

When you log in to Mac OS X, `tcsh` executes two scripts behind the scenes, one called `login` and one called `rc`, that initialize a wide variety of Unix variables. Similarly, when you choose Logout, Shut Down, or Restart from the Apple menu, `tcsh` runs a logout script to clean up after you. When you make any changes in the System Preferences application, shell settings and variables are changed. In fact, the shell command *defaults* lets you access and change the settings in the Mac OS X user defaults system from the command line. You can find entire books devoted to Unix shell scripting. All we can give you here are the basics to get you started and pointers to where you can find more information. (The `man pages` for `sh`, `csh`, and `tcsh` are a good place to begin.)

Note   The AppleScript Script Menu shown in Chapter 21 will run shell and perl scripts as well as AppleScripts. In addition to shell scripting and AppleScript language interpreters, Mac OS X 10.2 ships with Perl, PHP, Python, Ruby, and Tcl.

Basic Unix Commands

Unix has literally hundreds of standard commands, many of which you may never need to use; however, these commands are present just in case you find a need, or so Apple can say that they provide a complete Unix installation.

Unix command syntax

The basic form of a Unix command is

```
command-name switches arguments
```

The *command-name* is the Unix name of the command, such as `ls` or `mv`. *Switches* are the options you can specify to modify the default behavior of the command and are usually preceded by a minus sign (`-`). *Arguments* are strings (frequently, but not always, file names) that provide the command's input and may also specify the output destination.

Unix commands are the CLI equivalent of Mac OS X applications and menu selections. Although Unix commands can be placed anywhere you have permission to access and execute them, traditional organization has them in one of the directories specified by the PATH environment variable (type `echo $PATH` in the Terminal to see what directories, separated by colons, are automatically searched for commands). If the command is not located in one of these directories, its location must be fully specified for the shell to execute the command.

A traditional Unix file system is case-sensitive in the naming of files and directories — that is, the file `INSTALL` is different from the file `Install`, which is also different from the file `install`. Mac OS X modifies this behavior so that file names are not case-sensitive in the GUI, but case-sensitivity is still the rule when you are working in the shell.

Note   Although Mac OS X eliminates case-sensitivity from file names, it does not eliminate case-sensitivity from switches or built-in commands. You must still enter them in the proper case.

Log in and log out

As we belabor endlessly throughout this book, Unix is a multiuser system. Even if you are the only person who uses the computer, it's still multiuser. As the Process Viewer application shows you (see Chapter 22), a user named *root* executes all sorts of system-level processes, even when you're the actual person using the computer.

Specifying File Names

The Macintosh file system is a hierarchy in that you use folders to contain files and other folders, and this process can be carried to an arbitrary depth. You can consider each volume to be a separate hierarchy, or you can consider the Desktop as being the top of the hierarchy, containing the various volumes.

With one significant alteration, Unix takes the Desktop View of your file hierarchy. Viewed as an upside-down tree, the top of the Unix hierarchy is called by a single-character name, /, called the *root* of the tree. The one difference from the Desktop analogy is that in a Unix file system, the mount points are not necessarily mounted directly below the root level — they can reside within folders.

The slash character is also used to separate levels in the *path* from root (or any other reference point) to a given file. For example, the full path to a file named `Diary.rtf` in the Documents folder of a user named Spenser would be:

```
/Users/Spenser/Documents/Diary.rtf
```

If you omit the leading slash, you are assumed to be specifying a path *relative* to your current directory rather than an *absolute* path specification.

When you first installed Mac OS X and the Setup program ran, you created an administrator account and gave it a password. To make things easier for you, this account logs in automatically when you start your computer; but you can turn that off in the Login pane of System Preferences (see Chapter 16) if your computer is going to have multiple users because you might not want your business partner to be logged in as you when he or she restarts the computer.

Just as you are always logged in as a specific user when using the Mac OS X GUI, you are also logged in as a specific user when you use the Terminal application — the CLI. One difference is that you can use Unix commands to change which user identity is in effect for part of your Terminal session. The command used to change users is called `su` (for switch user). Until you create other accounts or enable root login in NetInfo Manager, no other identities are available to you.

 Tip You can execute a single command as root, even if you haven't enabled the root login by using the `sudo` command followed by the desired command as an argument to `sudo`. For example, `sudo chown root myfile` executes the `chown` (change owner) command, causing the file, `myfile`, to belong to `root`. As a caution, you will be prompted for an administrator password when using a command through sudo. A freeware utility named Pseudo is available via `www.version-tracker.com`, which enables you to execute root level commands without going into the Terminal application.

The most visible effect of each user having a distinct identity is that, when each user creates files, the files are marked as belonging to that user. You can see this in the Finder by choosing File⇨Show Info and then choosing Privileges in the Info window's pop-up menu. In Terminal, type `ls -l thefile` (assuming `thefile` is the file's name).

As shown in Figure 26-1, the command line prompt (unless you change it) reminds you who you are. If that isn't enough, you can type the `whoami` command, and the shell tells you.

One big advantage in using Terminal to execute a few commands as another user is that you don't have to log out (losing your context — running applications, open documents, and so on), log in as the other user, log out as that user, log in as yourself again, and then reestablish your context. You can just `su` as that user, as shown in Figure 26-2, execute the commands, and terminate their shell session with `exit` or Control-D.

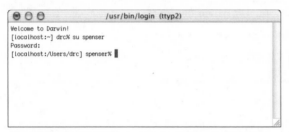

Figure 26-2: Use the `su` command to temporarily change your identity.

Managing files and directories

Just as you always have an active window in the Finder or a current folder in which an application opens or saves files, you have a *current directory* (also known as *working directory*) when using the Terminal application. As you can see in Figures 26-1 and 26-2, the default shell prompt provides your current directory and user account name. However, you can customize the shell prompt, possibly to make it shorter and still find out your working directory by entering the `pwd` (print working directory) command.

As we noted earlier in this chapter, some shortcut symbols are used with the shell. In particular, shortcut symbols for directories are ~ (user's home directory), . (current directory), and .. (parent directory to the current directory).

To change your current directory, you use the `cd` (change directory) command. For example, `cd ~` takes you back to your home directory, and `cd /` takes you to the root of the file system.

Obtaining a list of the files in a directory is as simple as entering the `ls` command. This command has a number of switches available that you can use to modify its behavior; the more useful and common ones are described in the following list:

`-a`	Show all files, even invisible (those whose names start with a `.`) ones
`-F`	Append a character to the names of executables (*), directories (/), and links or aliases (@). Characters for sockets are (=), whiteouts (%), and queues (|), which we aren't going to get into here.
`-f`	Don't sort the output (default is to sort alphabetically)
`-L`	If the file is a link, resolve the link and list that file
`-l`	Long listing, including owner, group, size, permissions
`-n`	Use the user and group ID numbers rather than names in a long listing
`-R`	Recursively list all subdirectories as well
`-r`	Reverse the sorting order
`-S`	Sort by size, largest first
`-s`	List the number of 512-byte blocks actually used by each file
`-t`	Sort by time modified, most recent first
`-x`	Sort multicolumn output across page rather than in columns
`-1`	Force output to one item per line (screen output defaults to multicolumn)

Another useful command when dealing with files and directories is the `file` command. If you type `file /Users`, the `file` command attempts to tell you what kind of file `/Users` is — in this case, a directory. `file` also recognizes other file types, such as `TIFF`, `rtf`, `text`, and so forth.

Autocompletion of file names

One of the really nice features of `tcsh` is that you don't have to type quite so much. Just as Internet Explorer attempts to complete URLs as you type, `tcsh` attempts to complete the name for you if you press the Tab key while typing a file name. Assuming that you have only one choice that completes what you have typed thus far, `tcsh` completes the name; however, if multiple possibilities exist, `tcsh` prints a list (as shown in Figure 26-3) and beeps at you, waiting for you to type more characters and press Tab again. This process continues until such time as your typing prior to you pressing the Tab uniquely identifies a file or, using wildcards as described shortly, a group of files.

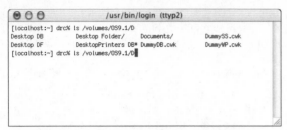

Figure 26-3: The shell provides choices if it is unable to fully resolve your partial file name.

Unix wildcards and regular expressions

You're probably getting the idea by now that one of Unix's tenets is to express the most information in a terse manner. Through the use of *regular expressions*, a shorthand notation for arbitrary strings of characters, the shell buttresses this impression. If you've used BBEdit (BareBones Software, www.barebones.com) or any of a number of other applications, you've encountered *grep* (global regular expression parser) and the power that this shorthand provides in matching patterns and strings.

Regular expressions can be used on the command line in arguments to a command or within applications (particularly editors) to perform searches or find and replace operations.

In its simplest form, an *expression* is a string of characters, such as document name. Two special wildcards are used in regular expressions:

✦ Asterisk (*), which stands for any sequence of characters.

✦ Question mark (?), which stands for any individual character.

You can also tell the shell to match any character from a list by enclosing the list in square brackets; for example, [aeiou] would indicate that any lowercase vowel would be a matching character. You can even tell the shell to match any character that is not in the list by preceding the list with a caret (^). Additionally, special characters are available if you want it to match at the beginning of a line (^) or end of a line ($).

Note   Yes, the caret is used for both negation and to denote beginning-of-line. Here, you need to be aware of the context. If the caret is the first character within square brackets (a set of characters), it means "anything except the characters enumerated." But, if the caret is outside the brackets and is the first character of the expression, it means "beginning of line."

Giving you even more to remember (but less to type), you can specify ranges of characters, for example [a-z] to specify any lowercase alphabetic character. Now, the obvious question arises, "But what if I want to match a hyphen?" The so-called *escape character* (\) comes into play here—any character following the escape character is to be taken literally, and to specify a backslash, escape it as well.

Tip

Certain escaped characters have special meaning in regular expressions. To denote a line break, you use \n. To specify a tab character, use \t; and to match a page break, type \f.

You can use metacharacters to specify how many times a pattern may repeat. The pattern may be a literal character, a wildcard character, a character class, or a special character. The asterisk (*) denotes zero or more occurrences of the pattern — therefore, the pattern is always true. Similarly, the question mark (?) signifies zero or one occurrence of the pattern and also indicates a match for every character scanned. Finally, the plus sign (+) tells the shell to find one or more occurrences of the pattern.

Note

There is actually another repetition indicator. You can enter a {n}, where n is a digit, to indicate matching exactly n occurrences of the pattern. Entering {n,} specifies matching n or more occurrences of the pattern, and entering {n,m} indicates matching at least n but no more than m occurrences of the pattern.

Just as you can combine patterns to form more-complex patterns, you are provided with an *alternate* character (an or operator), enabling you to match any of a collection of patterns. This character is the vertical bar (|).

Table 26-1 illustrates some of the ways that you can use wildcards and regular expressions to find matches.

Table 26-1
Use of Wildcards and Regular Expressions to Find Matches

Pattern	Meaning
[Ff]ile[0-9]	Match anything spelled file, whether or not the f is capitalized and followed by a single digit
*.rtf	Match any string ending in .rtf
^From*Spenser$	Any line starting with From and ending with Spenser
^[^a-z]	The first character of any line that does not start with a lowercase letter
1[01]:##[\t][Pp]\.[Mm]\.	Any time entry starting at 10:00pm, but before midnight
tom|dick|harry	Find any tom, dick, or harry (not on the command line; only in grep, Unix's "global regular expression parser" command)

You can even create remembered patterns by enclosing the pattern within parentheses. These remembered patterns are often referred to as *tagged regular expressions*. Within the same command, you can specify the remembered patterns by specifying \1 for the first, \2 for the second, and so forth in a subsequent argument. Such references are referred to as *back references*. Back references can take considerable time to evaluate; however, they are of particular advantage when doing search-and-replace operations in an editor.

Note   Operators function in precedence (order) in regular expressions. Repetition operators are evaluated before concatenation operators, and concatenation takes precedence over alternation.

Creating and deleting directories and files

Analogous to the Finder's New Folder command, the shell offers you the mkdir command to create a new directory. You can even create a new (empty) file by using the touch command and specifying a file that does not already exist. The touch command on an existing file changes the file's modification date and time to the current date and time.

Unix doesn't really need a rename command, because it has something just as good — the mv (move) command. If you move a file with a new name rather than copy it into the directory in which it already resides, you have renamed it. Moving a file deletes the original. Of course, you use a cp (copy) command when you don't want to delete the original. Both commands can take one of two forms. They have two arguments (source and destination file names), or they have multiple arguments, the last of which is the directory into which all the other arguments are moved or copied.

Both cp and mv have a number of switches available, and you can read about them by typing man cp or man mv in a Terminal window. The type that we're going to tell you about here is the one that you're probably going to use the most — the -R switch tells the shell to recursively copy or move the contents when a source argument is a directory.

You delete files with the rm (remove) command. Here is where Unix shows a different mindset from that typical of the Mac OS or even Windows — the effects of rm are immediate and irrevocable. If you want to provide a little bit of safety while possibly increasing the annoyance factor, you can use the -i option, which interrogates you on every file that the command is going to delete, as shown in Figure 26-4. A y is an affirmative response; anything else is taken as a negative response.

```
000                  /usr/bin/login  (ttyp2)
[localhost:~] drc% cd Public
[localhost:~/Public] drc% ls
Drop Box   a2.txt    a4.txt    a6.txt    a8.txt
a1.txt     a3.txt    a5.txt    a7.txt    a9.txt
[localhost:~/Public] drc% rm -i a*
remove a1.txt? y
remove a2.txt? y
remove a3.txt? ▮
```

Figure 26-4: Using the -i switch with rm.

To remove an empty directory, you use the `rmdir` command. If the directory isn't empty, you receive an error message to that effect, and the directory is not deleted. You can, however, use the `rm` command with either the `-R` or `-r` switch to recursively delete a directory and its contents. Again, adding the `-i` switch causes the shell to interrogate you for each file and directory before deleting it.

Another useful tool is the `diff` command. The `diff` command takes two arguments, a source and destination file to compare. If one argument is a directory and the other a file, `diff` compares a file within the directory that has the same name as the other argument. If both arguments are directories, all files with matching names in the two directories are compared. Again, you can discover a plethora of seldom-used options by reading the `man` page; however, a couple of options are used frequently. Some commonly used options include the `-B` and `-b` options which, respectively, tell `diff` to ignore changes that just add or delete blank lines (B) or treat runs of white space (spaces and tabs) as the same (b). Another is the `-i` option to ignore case changes. Figure 26-5 shows the results of a `diff` comparison of two files.

```
[localhost:~/Public] drc% cd ~/Documents
[localhost:~/Documents] drc% cat file1.txt
Now is
the time
for all
good men
to come
to the aid
of their country.
[localhost:~/Documents] drc% cat file2.txt
Now is
the time
for all
good women
to come
to the aid
of their
country.
[localhost:~/Documents] drc% diff file1.txt file2.txt
4c4
< good men
---
> good women
7c7,8
< of their country.
---
> of their
> country.
[localhost:~/Documents] drc% █
```

Figure 26-5: `diff` compares files.

As you can see in Figure 26-5, the output is a bit cryptic until you become accustomed to it. Source file lines are preceded by a less than (<) sign, and destination file lines are preceded by a greater than (>) sign. The line number(s) from the source file precede the kind-of-change indicator (changed, added, or deleted lines).

Disk and file system statistics

Two commands, du (disk utilization) and df (display free-space), let you find out how much space you are using for your files and directories and how much space is available for use.

Displaying free space

By default, the df command gives you a report such as the one shown in Figure 26-6. It gives you a list of all the file systems you have mounted, where they are mounted, how many 512-byte blocks are on the file system, how many are used, how many are still available, and the percentage of capacity utilized. Divide the number of blocks by 2 to get the number of kilobytes or use the -k option to specify that you want the results in kilobytes.

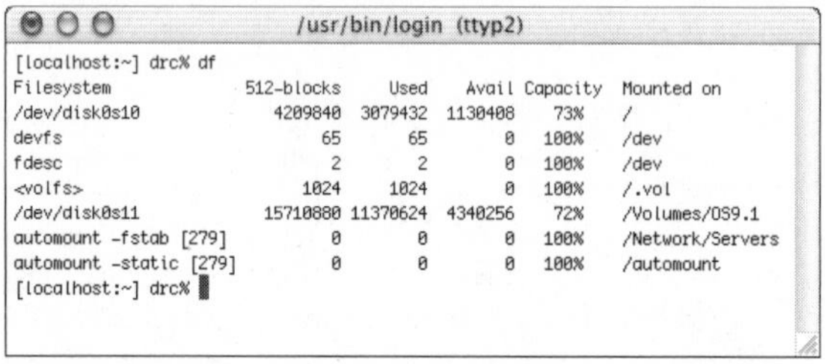

```
● ● ●                   /usr/bin/login  (ttyp2)
[localhost:~] drc% df
Filesystem            512-blocks      Used     Avail Capacity  Mounted on
/dev/disk0s10           4209840   3079432   1130408     73%   /
devfs                        65        65         0    100%   /dev
fdesc                         2         2         0    100%   /dev
<volfs>                    1024      1024         0    100%   /.vol
/dev/disk0s11          15710880  11370624   4340256     72%   /Volumes/OS9.1
automount -fstab [279]        0         0         0    100%   /Network/Servers
automount -static [279]       0         0         0    100%   /automount
[localhost:~] drc%
```

Figure 26-6: df tells you how much space each file system has and how much is being used.

You can give a single file as an argument to df to get statistics for just the file system on which the specified file resides. Notice that the file system names are not normally the names of the volume (such as Macintosh HD) but rather the cryptic device names.

Disk utilization

The du command breaks the information down into finer increments, giving you statistics for files and directories, as shown in Figure 26-7. With no argument(s), du reports on utilization by all files and directories, recursively, from the current directory. With a file for an argument, you get the number of 512-byte blocks used by that file. With a directory as an argument, du gives you the information for that directory and recurses through any directories contained within the directory (see Figure 26-7). Employing the -s option tells du to summarize (not enumerate), also shown in Figure 26-6.

```
000                    /usr/bin/login  (ttyp2)
[localhost:~] drc% du Documents
8        Documents/.FBCLockFolder
0        Documents/AppleWorks User Data/AutoSave
32       Documents/AppleWorks User Data/Dictionaries
0        Documents/AppleWorks User Data/Starting Points/Disabled Items
8        Documents/AppleWorks User Data/Starting Points/Recent Items
8        Documents/AppleWorks User Data/Starting Points
40       Documents/AppleWorks User Data
15200    Documents/iTunes/iTunes Music/Louis Armstrong/Ken Burns Jazz
15200    Documents/iTunes/iTunes Music/Louis Armstrong
15200    Documents/iTunes/iTunes Music
15208    Documents/iTunes
15400    Documents
[localhost:~] drc% du -s Documents
15400    Documents
[localhost:~] drc% █
```

Figure 26-7: To get an itemized breakdown of disk space used, use d f without options — the -s option gives a summary.

Viewing and Editing Files

Unix's origin as a command-line environment brings with it a number of erstwhile tools for dealing with files. You have tools to display file contents and many kinds of editors, from ones that execute commands a line at a time, through screen editors, and on to stream editors that process commands against entire files. To use these editors, you type (or store) your commands rather than use a mouse and menus; all editors are keyboard driven.

Standard input, standard output, and pipes

To the shell, any place it obtains or places data is a file. The keyboard data stream is a file, the window in which output is displayed is a file, and files on your disk are files. The input stream from your keyboard is the default for a special file called standard input (stdin). The default file for output, your Terminal window, is called standard output. You can redirect standard input to come from some other file by preceding the file name with a less than sign (<). Similarly, you can redirect standard output by using a greater than sign (>). If, for example, you wanted to create a file containing a directory listing of your Documents folder, you could type ls Documents >docdir.txt, as shown in Figure 26-8. A number of commands display the contents of files. Among these commands are cat, more, pr, head, and tail. The meaning for each command is provided in Table 26-2.

Tip

You can append output to an existing file by using two successive greater than signs. For example, ls Movies >>docdir.txt would append the directory listing for your Movies folder to the file docdir.txt created above.

Paths and Variables

With few exceptions, such as cd, almost every command you enter at the Unix prompt is a program stored on your disk. The shell is a programming environment, complete with loops, conditionals, and variables. Shell programs are usually called *scripts*. Shell programs are *interpreted* rather than *compiled*. This means that when a shell script or command executes, the shell parses the command, evaluates the variables, and then executes rather than having the instructions reduced to binary machine instructions.

You create shell variables by using the set command. For example, set myPath = "~/MyApps" would create a variable named myPath which had the value /Users/drc/ MyApps (assuming that your username is drc). You can determine the current value of any shell variable by issuing the echo command, with the variable name, preceded by a dollar sign ($), as an argument. One very important shell variable is PATH. PATH is the variable the shell evaluates to determine where it should look for commands you issue. The figure below shows the initial value of PATH for the user drc.

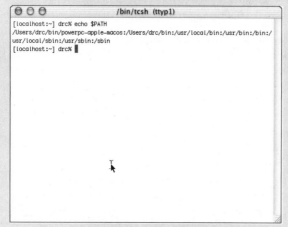

```
[localhost:~] drc% echo $PATH
/Users/drc/bin/powerpc-apple-macos:/Users/drc/bin:/usr/local/bin:/usr/bin:/bin:/
usr/local/sbin:/usr/sbin:/sbin
[localhost:~] drc%
```

The PATH variable tells you the directories the shell searches for commands.

As you can determine, PATH is a series of directory specifications that is separated by colons. Every time you issue a command, such as ls or cp, the shell starts checking each directory in PATH until it finds the command and executes it. If the command cannot be found in any directory in PATH, you receive an error message to that effect. If the program is not in one of the PATH directories, you need to specify a directory path to it. To execute a command in your current directory, you precede it with ./. If you are curious as to which directory holds the command you want to execute, you can use the which command (a built-in shell command). This which can come in handy if, for example, you are attempting to execute a newly installed command, and the wrong command executes—because a command with the same name was located in an earlier PATH directory.

Table 26-2
Commands that Display Contents of Files

Command	Meaning
cat	Concatenate the files given as arguments and display on standard output.
more	Display the arguments on standard output a page (windowfull) at a time. You type a space to get to the next screen; type a b to go back a screen. Typing a return advances one line, and typing a q terminates the command.
pr	Similar to more, but it includes page headers and footers at would-be page breaks if the output were directed to a printer.
head	Display the first *n* (default is 10) lines of a file on standard output.
tail	Display the last *n* (default is 10) lines of a file on standard output.

```
⊖ ⊖ ⊖              /usr/bin/login (ttyp2)
[localhost:~] drc% ls Documents > docdir.txt
[localhost:~] drc% cat docdir.txt
AppleWorks User Data
BerkeleyUSD.pdf
CD.pdf
Cosby2000.cwk
Elvis4-5.cwk
ElvisSheet.cwk
Fax Cover Page.cwk
Jan&Dean.cwk
LittleLabels.cwk
file1.txt
file2.txt
iTunes
president@whitehouse.gov
spensericon.tiff
[localhost:~] drc% ▊
```

Figure 26-8: You can create and display files from the command line.

You can even chain commands together with the pipe symbol — a vertical bar (|) — so that the output from the first command is the input to the next. For example, ls -R|more would display a recursive directory listing one screen at a time.

Most commands default to taking their input from standard input. For example, if you omit the file argument from the cat command, cat patiently waits for you to enter it from the keyboard. When you enter data from the keyboard, you need to indicate that you're finished by entering the Unix end-of-input character (Control-d[CS2]).

About permissions

In addition to the read and write permissions (refer to Chapter 16), you find an execute permission at the file level. Because Unix commands aren't applications with an APPL file type (or a bundle with an .app extension), the shell needs some way to indicate that a particular file is executable, and Unix has used this method for over three decades now.

Permissions on directories have a slightly different but analogous meaning compared to files as shown in Table 26-3.

Table 26-3
Unix Permissions and Meanings

Permission	Meaning for a File	Meaning for a Directory
r read	read a file	list files in …
w write	write a file	create file in … rename file in … delete file …
x execute	execute a shell script, command, or program	read a file in … write to a file in … execute a file in … execute a shell script in …

Commands, programs, and shell scripts are examples of files for which execute permission should be enabled. As with any other file, this file has three levels of permission: owner, group, and everybody.

Note

In typical geekspeak, Unix users typically refer to permissions as three (octal) digit numbers. In this jargon, read permission is worth four points, write permission is worth two, and execute permission is worth one. Therefore, when you hear that a file has 740 permission, the first digit being 7 means that the owner can read, write, and execute the file (4+2+1=7); the second digit being 4 means members of the group can read the file (4+0+0=4); and the third digit being 0 means everyone else has no permissions with respect to the file (0-0+0=0).

Changing permissions

The chmod command enables the owner or root to change the permissions on a file. The simplest form of this command is to follow chmod with the new permissions and then the file or list of files to receive those permissions. For example, chmod 777 myscript.sh would give read, write, and execute permission to everyone for the file myscript.sh.

If you don't want to do the math, you only need to remember six letters — *u* for user, *g* for group, *a* for all, *r* for read, *w* for write, and *x* for execute. You also need to remember three symbols as well — + to add a permission, - to subtract a permission, and = to set permissions. For example, chmod g+w dirdoc.txt would add write permission for members of the group to the file dirdoc.txt without affecting any other permissions.

Changing owner and groups

Only the root user (System Administrator) has the authority to change a file's owner. Assuming that you have logged in as root or are running from an administrator account and using the sudo command, the syntax to change a file's owner is chown *newownerid filelist*. The newownerid is either the new owner's login name or her numeric ID, as displayed in NetInfo Manager, and filelist is the file or files whose ownership is to be changed.

If you are a member of the group to which you want to change group ownership and you have write and execute permissions to the files and directories in question, you can change the group ownership of a file with the chgrp command, whose form is the same as chown command except that you use a group name or number rather than a user name or number.

Tip To determine to which groups you belong, you can enter the groups command. You can also determine to which groups another user belongs by typing groups with their username as an argument.

These commands should be avoided, and their NetInfo Manager equivalents used, according to Apple.

Advanced Unix Topics

Unix is a highly configurable environment with a wealth of tools, and a jargon all its own. In this section, we give you a very brief introduction to some tools and commands available to you when running a Terminal shell.

Environment and shell variables

Every time you log in, open a new Terminal window, or switch shells, the shell checks its initialization files to establish your environment and your shell variables. Each shell handles its initialization files and environment settings somewhat differently. We cover the default shell (tcsh) in this section.

First, tcsh reads the hidden file .tcshrc and then the .login file. Both of these files contain a number of environment variables as well as some local shell variables that are not *exported* to the shell; they are local to this shell and not available to you when the shell has finished executing. When you start a new shell process, it just checks the .tcshrc file.

Note By convention, environment variables are all uppercase, and shell variables are all lowercase. Thus, the environment variable PATH and the shell variable path can (and usually do) have different values. Further convention holds that you should set your shell variables in the .tcshrc file and environment variables in the .login file. You can, however, make sure that all settings are as you want them by setting all of them in the .tcshrc file.

Enter the env command to see a list of your current environment variables and the set command to see a list of your current shell variables. Examples of both are shown in Figure 26-9.

Changing environment variables

You can change environment variable settings or declare new environment variables for the current session by entering a command of the form: setenv *VARIABLENAME* new_value where *VARIABLENAME* is the environment variable you want to change or declare and new_value is the value you want to give it. This value persists until you log out or exit the shell in which you're working.

If you want to make the change apply to future sessions as well, you need to edit the .tcshrc file. You can do this with a shell editor, such as vi or emacs. You can also do so with Mac OS X or Classic text editor, such as TextEdit, BBEdit, or SimpleText. But you first have to make a non-hidden copy in the shell (the Open dialogs won't display hidden files), edit that copy, and make sure to save the result as plain text, and then replace the hidden file with the edited copy. Proceed as follows:

1. **If it is a new variable, add the above** setenv **command to the** .tcshrc **file. If it is a change to an existing variable, find the line where that variable is declared and change the line.**

2. **Save the file and exit the editor.**

3. **If you want the change to take effect, enter the command** source .tcshrc.

Note The default location of .tcshrc is your HOME directory.

The source command feeds the contents of the file arguments to the shell as input.

Changing shell variables

To define a temporary value to a shell variable, use the following command:

```
set variable_name=value
```

The value of this variable remains set until you exit from this shell. The value of this variable is not exported to other TC shells when they are invoked.

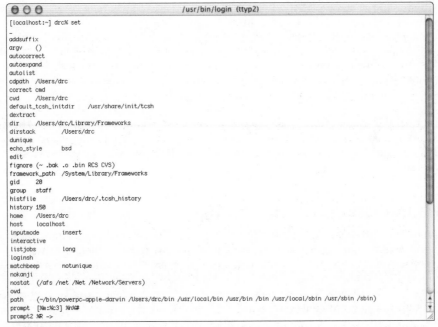

Figure 26-9: The env and set commands display environment and shell variables, respectively.

To give a lasting value to a shell variable, follow these steps:

1. **Use an editor to open your** .tcshrc **file and add the line:** set variable_name=value.

2. **Save the file and leave the editor.**

3. **Enter the command** source .tcshrc.

Doing so adds the value of the shell variable to your shell's present environment. When subsequent TC shells are invoked, they will also have this variable set.

Creating aliases

No, these aren't the same aliases available under Mac OS. Unix aliases are pseudonyms for other Unix commands. To create an alias for use with the TC shell, add the command alias aliasname what-it-stands-for to the .tcshrc file and enter the source .tcshrc command, making the obvious substitutions.

One example of an alias is the following:

```
alias what 'ps -aux | grep $USER | more'
```

This command sequence pipes (sends) the output of the process status command as input to grep, which searches that input for the processes you're running and then displays the results a screen at a time.

You can even chain multiple commands together in an alias by separating them with semicolons. For example, alias tree 'cd; ls -R' would display a complete directory hierarchy of a user's home directory when the command tree was entered.

Manipulating text file contents

Just as Unix provides you the cat, pr, head, tail, more, and less commands (mentioned earlier in this chapter) to display files or parts of files, it provides you a variety of editors and other tools with which to create, edit, and summarize text file contents. In addition to the ancient command-line editor, ed, you also have vi, pico, and emacs, all of which are screen editors. Screen editors were the segue between line editors where you entered commands describing the editing action you wanted to take and the current direct manipulation windowing editors, such as TextEdit. In a screen editor, file contents were displayed on a terminal screen, and you moved the cursor around via the keyboard and shifted modes between overstrike and insert, with the option of still using the commands of the old-line editors. Although multiple editors are available in the Unix of Mac OS X, among the screen editors, only vi is guaranteed to be included with every Unix distribution, so a knowledge of vi, whether or not it is your editor of choice, is recommended.

Each editor is well documented in its man pages, and full books are written about their use. Which is the best for you is going to be a decision only you can make after trying them out. Each has a devoted, almost religious, following.

Some other tools you can use to work with file contents are listed in Table 26-4.

	Table 26-4 Text File Tools	
Command	**Description**	
compress	Reduce the size of files by encoding, similar to StuffIt or Zip, but only compresses individual files. Use uncompress to restore the file to its original state. Convention has it that the .z extension indicates a compressed file. To create compressed archives, use tar to create the archive and then compress to reduce its size.	
cut	Selects portions of each line of a file.	
diff	Compares two files (described earlier).	
fmt	Reformats the files given to have consistent line lengths — default is 65, maximum is 75 characters. This tool originated primarily for the manipulation of line breaks in e-mail messages.	
grep	The (in)famous regular expression parser is used to find all instances of patterns within a file or list of files.	
sed	A stream editor, it reads the file(s) specified, modifying the input based upon the command(s) listed and passing the result to standard output. The editing commands may be stored in a file, one per line.	
sort	Reorders the lines of a file into lexicographic order.	
split	Divides a file into multiple parts, each (except possibly the last part) of the same size. Use cat to recombine the files at a later time.	
tar	Creates (uncompressed) archives of the files given as arguments. Short for tape archiver, it is used to package files together.	
uniq	Removes duplicate adjacent lines. Pipe the output of sort to uniq if you want to remove all duplicates.	
wc	Reports the number of characters, words, and lines in a file.	

Additionally, whole languages, such as perl, awk, and tcl, can scan and process the contents of text files.

Writing shell scripts

You can do more with the shell than just execute commands. The shell has a built-in programming language so that you can write your own text programs or commands. These programs are called *shell scripts*. The main strength of shell scripts is that you can use them to invoke a possibly long and complex sequence of instructions, with logical branches, as though the sequence were a simple command.

Writing a shell script is similar to entering the commands manually in a Terminal window, with a few significant differences:

✦ You may want your command to accept arguments. The shell automatically assigns any strings following your script's name on the command line to a set of parameters: shell variables named $1 through $9. You don't have to do anything special to obtain arguments from the command line — they're already available in the parameter variables when your script begins its execution. If you need more than nine arguments, you can use the shift operator in your script to access later variables.

✦ You may want your new command to support options. The shell passes options to your script the same as any other arguments: each command-line string is set into the $n variables (also accessible in the special shell array variable argv[n]).

✦ Usually you enter keyboard commands with all information explicitly stated; however, commands inside shell scripts are often parameterized and can be executed conditionally. You parameterize a command by providing variable references and file name substitutions as the command's arguments instead of literal text. You need to use the shell's if, switch, while, and foreach commands to handle alternative paths of executions. You rarely use these commands at the keyboard, but they occur often in shell scripts.

Regardless of the use to which you're going to put a shell script, almost all shell scripts are developed using the following general plan:

1. Develop a text file containing the required commands.

2. Mark the text file executable, using the chmod command chmod +x *filename* to make it executable for all users.

3. Test the shell script.

4. Install the script in its permanent location.

5. Use it.

If the script is for your personal use, create a ~/bin directory and add it to your search path, as described earlier in this chapter ("Changing shell variables"). After you create a new script, you can just mark the script executable and drop it in your personal `bin` directory, and it will be available for use.

When testing a script, you may want to see which commands are being executed so that you can track an unexpected behavior. To do so, invoke your script with the command `tcsh -x scriptname` or embed a `set echo` command in your script.

> **Tip**
>
> If you are only interested in a specific range of included commands, you can `set echo` just before the commands and `unset echo` immediately after the commands. Remember to remove these `set` and `unset` commands after testing.

As with most any other programming language, internal documentation in the form of *comments* — lines which are not executed, but are meant to explain what is going on — is considered very good form. Lines beginning with a *splat* (Unix jargon for the sharp or number sign character, #) are taken as comments by the shell. In fact, the shell ignores anything starting with a splat to the end of that line as a comment unless the splat is escaped with the backslash character.

Using conditionals

Using alternative courses of action based upon a test of some sort is a standard part of any programming language, and shell scripts are no exception. The TC shell includes both `if` and `switch` statements to provide for conditional execution.

An `if` statement takes one of two forms, single-line and multiline. The single-line command is of the form `if (`*expression*`)` *command*, where *expression* evaluates false if equal to zero and true otherwise. Use this form only in the situation in which you have exactly one command to execute if the test is true.

The multiline form of the if statement looks like the following:

```
if (expression) then
    commands
else if (expression2) then
    commands
else
    commands
endif
```

Here *commands* can be one or more shell commands. The `else if` section can occur zero or more times, and the `else` section is optional. The main point to remember is that an `endif` statement terminates the structure.

The `switch` statement is really nothing but an `if` statement on steroids. Rather than testing for whether an expression is true or false, the `switch` statement chooses from a series of alternative actions, depending upon the value to which an expression evaluates. The general form for a `switch` statement follows

```
switch (expression)
case value1:
commands
case value2:
commands
default:
commands
endsw
```

where *expression* is evaluated and lines skipped until a `case` statement is encountered where the value being tested matches — *expression* and value are strings and may be expressed as patterns. Then the commands up to the next case or default statement are executed, followed by executing subsequent lines (ignoring case and default statements) through the `endsw` statement. The default statement occurs last and is optional, giving a sequence of commands to be executed if none of the alternative values match the current value of expression. If you don't want the execution to continue through the latter case statements, use a `breaksw` statement as the final command in a case group.

The following is an example of a switch statement:

```
echo -n "Do you really want to move this file? "
set reply=$<
switch $reply
case y*:
case Y*:
mv $1 ~/bin
breaksw
default:
echo $1 not moved
endsw
```

In this example script, the command receives as an argument a file to be moved to the `bin` subdirectory of your `HOME` directory. You are asked whether you really want to move it; the shell variable reply is set to the answer you give. The `-n` option to `echo` tells `echo` not to advance to the next line. If that answer starts with a lowercase or uppercase `y`, the file is moved, otherwise you see a message that the file was not moved.

Looping constructs

You use looping or iterative constructs to repetitively execute a sequence of commands. The two looping constructs in the TC shell are `while` and `foreach`.

The `while` statement takes the following general form:

```
while (expression)
  commands
end
```

The while loop executes the commands so long as expression evaluates to something other than zero. The shell evaluates *expression* before each (including the first) iteration of the loop. Therefore, if *expression* initially evaluates to zero, the loop never executes.

The following is a fairly typical example of a while loop in a shell script. It tests each file name given as an argument to see whether it exists and gives you a message for any missing files.

```
while ($#argv > 0)
  if (! -f $1) echo $1: missing
  shift
end
```

The primary use of the foreach loop is to process lists. The general form of a foreach loop is as follows:

```
foreach variablename (wordlist)
commands
end
```

variablename is the name you're giving your variable, and *wordlist* is a list of strings, such as those returned by an ls command. Each string in *wordlist* is assigned to *variablename* in turn as the loop iterates. When the loop is done executing, the variable holds the last value derived.

An example of a foreach loop would be:

```
foreach namen (`ls ~/bin`)
mv $namen $namen.sh
end
```

This loop would rename each file in your personal bin directory to have a .sh suffix (a conventional indication that it is a shell script).

 Note Two additional commands can be used within the body of a loop structure. continue tells the shell to skip any remaining commands and proceed to the next iteration of the loop. break tells the shell to terminate the loop process and execute the next command after the loop.

More Information

Unix is, as we stated earlier, a large and complex environment, and we can only touch on the surface of it in this book. Fortunately, Unix comes with a lot of information and internal documentation in the form of man pages. Enter man followed by the name of the command, and you receive chapter and verse about that command. If you aren't quite sure about the name of the command but you know roughly what it does, you may be able to find it by using the apropos command followed by a keyword, assuming that `apropos`'s database has been created — it wasn't supplied with early releases of Mac OS X. First, you should investigate the `man` command — type `man man`.

Tip   Instead of displaying man pages in the Terminal window, you can display them in a Mac OS X application such as ManOpen by Carl Lindberg (`www.clindberg.org/projects/ManOpen.html`). This application has a Find command to help you find the man page that you want to read. You can also select a man page from a list of available pages in another window.

There are huge numbers of applications already written for UNIX. Fink is an open-source project intended to port much of the free UNIX software to OS X and manage its installation in a coherent manner. You can think of fink as analogous to Apple's Software Update in System Preferences, except fink manages installations and upgrades of UNIX applications. For an experienced UNIX user, fink is invaluable by providing many UNIX applications they're already familiar with for OS X, in addition to the extensive amount of UNIX software ported by Apple and installed with OS X. See `http://fink.sourceforge.net/` for a more thorough explanation of what fink is and how to install and use it.

You can find a number of excellent books on UNIX. If you want a gentle introduction, we would recommend *Unix For Dummies[CS3],* 4th Edition, by John R. Levine and Margaret Levine Young.

As always, the Internet provides a wealth of references. Some Web sites for Unix issues we particularly recommend include:

✦ A Unix Guide at `www.ed.com/unixguide`

✦ Unix is a four-letter word at `www.msoe.edu/~taylor/4ltrwrd/`

✦ An introduction to Terminal at `homepage.mac.com/x_freedom/tips/terminal.html`

✦ Unix concepts at `www.bpsi.net/~kingery/unix/unix-concepts.html`

You can find literally hundreds of others. Use Sherlock to Do an Internet search for Unix and you will be amazed at the number of sites that have Unix as a keyword.

Summary

In this chapter, you discovered a little bit about how to use the Mac OS X Unix underpinnings, known as Darwin, as well as a little history about Unix in general. You saw how to use the Terminal application, modify your Unix shell environment, enter commands in the shell, switch from one shell to another, and write shell scripts. You also saw that we barely touch the surface of this complex subject, and we've given you some pointers to learn more if you're interested.

✦   ✦   ✦

Appendixes

◆ ◆ ◆ ◆

In This Part

Appendix A
Installing Mac OS X

Appendix B
Installing
Applications

Appendix C
Exploiting Keyboard
Shortcuts

◆ ◆ ◆ ◆

Installing Mac OS X

Installing a newer Mac OS version on your computer is not something you do casually. This chapter describes what you need to do to prepare for installation. First, you need to assess the equipment requirements and consider upgrading your applications and other software for Mac OS X. Next, you need to prepare for installation by gathering setup information that you will use after installing Mac OS X. You also need to make a backup copy of your disk and possibly partition your hard drive.

With the preliminaries finished, you are ready to install and set up Mac OS X. You may also need to install Mac OS 9.1 or later for the Classic environment.

Preinstallation Considerations

Before installing Mac OS X, you need to answer several questions. Is your Mac model qualified to use Mac OS X? Does your computer have enough memory and disk space available? If you have a PCI video card, will it work? How compatible are your printer, other hardware, applications, and other software that you need to use? Do you need to upgrade or install Mac OS 9 for the Classic environment? This section helps you answer these questions.

Qualified Mac models

Mac OS X can be installed on the following models if they have enough RAM and disk space:

✦ Power Mac G4 (all)

✦ Power Mac G4 cube

✦ Power Mac G3 (all)

✦ PowerBook G4

✦ PowerBook G3 (except original PowerBook G3 without large white Apple logo on case)

✦ iMac (all)

✦ iBook (all)

People will manage to successfully install Mac OS X on older Macs that have been upgraded with G3 and G4 processors. In fact, the makers of some upgrades have developed software expressly enabling the installation of Mac OS X on upgraded old Macs. For example, Sonnet Technology (www.sonnettech.com) has a $30 installer for using Mac OS X on the following models when they are equipped with a Sonnet Crescendo/PCI G3 or G4 upgrade card or a Newer Technology MAXpowr PCI processor upgrade card:

✦ Apple Power Mac 7300, 7500, 7600, 8500, 8600, 9500, and 9600

✦ Power Computing PowerTower Pro and Power Wave

✦ UMAX J700 and S900

✦ DayStar Genesis and Millennium

Caution

If you decide to install Mac OS X on any of these older models, take into consideration that there is no support from Apple for any problems that may arise. If Apple updates Mac OS X to fix problems and add features, the updated versions may not work on your older Mac. Proceed with caution.

Memory requirements

If you're upgrading from Mac OS 9, chances are you need to install more memory. Mac OS X requires a minimum of 128MB, and it performs much better with more memory. We recommend at least 192MB, especially if you expect to use Mac OS 9 applications a lot. The more memory you install, the better Mac OS X performs. If you're not sure how much memory is installed in your computer, choose About This Computer from the Apple menu while using the Finder in Mac OS 9. The amount of built-in memory reported in the About This Computer window must be 128MB or more, as shown in Figure A-1.

Tip

For an up-to-date comparison of memory prices, check out the Ramseeker Web site (www.ramseeker.com) and the Mac Resource Page RAMWatch site (http://macresource.pair.com/mrp/ramwatch.shtml).

Figure A-1: The About This Computer window reports the amount of memory installed in your computer as Built-in Memory.

Disk space requirements

Your computer needs about 1GB of disk space available to install Mac OS X. While Mac OS X is in use, it performs best with significant amounts of additional disk space for virtual memory. The amount of space you should plan on for virtual memory depends on which applications you use and which applications are open at the same time. Certainly it would not be out of line to allow several hundred MBof disk space free. Altogether, plan on devoting 1.5GB to 2GB of disk space to Mac OS X and its working files. If you're not sure how much disk space you have available, look at the top of any folder or disk window in Mac OS 9, as shown in Figure A-2.

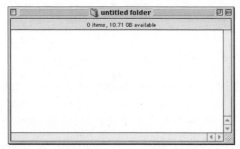

Figure A-2: Just below the title of every disk and folder window in Mac OS 9 is the amount of available disk space.

Note   Mac OS X can't be installed on a FireWire disk or USB disk. A future update to Mac OS X may remove this restriction.

You need additional disk space for Mac OS 9 if you expect to use Mac OS 9 applications in the Classic compatibility environment of Mac OS X. You can have Mac OS 9 installed on the same volume as Mac OS X or on a different volume. Plan on Mac OS 9 occupying 200MB to 300MB of disk space. In addition to the disk space occupied by Mac OS X and Mac OS 9, you need more space available for applications and document files.

You have several options for arranging the operating systems, applications, and documents. Your options include the following:

✦ Use one disk for everything—Mac OS X, Mac OS 9, applications, and documents

✦ Have more than one disk, with Mac OS X on one disk, Mac OS 9 on another, and applications and documents on any or all disks

✦ Partition a disk into two or more volumes, with Mac OS X on one volume, Mac OS 9 on another, and applications and documents on any or all volumes

If you need to start up your computer with Mac OS 9 to use software that doesn't work in Mac OS X's Classic environment, we recommend you have a separate disk or a separate volume expressly for this purpose. On this volume, install Mac OS 9 (or even Mac OS 8) and never use it to start the Classic environment. This copy of Mac OS 9 can include system extensions and control panels that don't work or aren't needed in the Classic environment.

Display requirements

Mac OS X has more stringent display and video card requirements than Mac OS 9. Apple certifies that the following display and video connections work with Mac OS X:

✦ **iMac.** Built-in display and external video port (on iMacs that have one)

✦ **PowerBook.** Built-in display and external video ports (on PowerBooks that have them)

✦ **iBook.** Built-in display and external video port (on iBooks that have one)

✦ **Power Mac G3 All-in-one.** Built-in display

✦ **Power Mac G3.** Built-in video port (not counting the video port of a PCI video card)

✦ **Power Mac G3 or G4.** Video card either factory installed or custom made for Apple by IXMicro, ATI, or Nvidia

Other video cards made for Power Mac G3 and Power Mac G4 expansion slots, including video cards from ATI, may also work. In general, the more recently a card was made, the more likely it is to work with Mac OS X. If you depend on a video card not supplied by Apple, ask its manufacturer if the card works with Mac OS X.

Hardware compatibility

Before installing Mac OS X, you should find out whether your printer, digital camera, or other hardware device is compatible with Mac OS X. Mac OS X works with PostScript printers that connect to the computer via network. Mac OS X also includes printer driver software that provides basic printing support for many inkjet printers made by Canon, Epson, and Hewlett-Packard. Table A-1 lists the inkjet models that Mac OS X initially supports.

The initial printer driver software may not support all features of a particular printer model. Support for features such as custom paper sizes, banner printing, booklet printing, watermarks, and network printer adapters as well as additional printer models should become available in later versions.

Driver software may be available for other printers directly from their manufacturers. Check with your printer's manufacturer for the latest information.

Table A-1
Some Mac OS X Compatible Inkjet Printers

Printer Brand	Initially Supported Printer Models

Canon
`http://consumer.usa.canon.com/`
`techsupport/downloads/index.html`
	BJC85, BJC2100, BJC8200, BFJ210, BJF360, BJF660, BFJ850, BJF870, BJM70, BJS600, BJS630, BJS6300,S400, S450, S600, S630, S800, S6300

Epson `http://support.epson.com`	Stylus Color 680, 740, 760, 777, 860, 880 PM-720C, PM-780C, PM-780CS, PM-880C, PM-900C, PM-3500C

Hewlett-Packard
`www.hewlettpackard.com/`
`cposupport/software.html`
	Deskjet 810, 812 , 816, 830, 832, 840, 842, 880, 882, 895, 930, 932, 935, 950, 952, 955, 957, 960, 970, 990

Mac OS X also works with many USB cameras from Fuji, Hewlett-Packard, Kodak, Panasonic, Pentax, and Sony.

Software upgrades

Eventually, you will need to replace your applications and other software made for Mac OS 9 with software made for Mac OS X. The new and revised software will be built on the Carbon or Cocoa frameworks and will take advantage of such major Mac OS X features as the Aqua interface. The following sources may help you determine whether a Mac OS X version of each application is available:

✦ VersionTracker Mac OS X Web site at www.versiontracker.com/vt_mac_osx.shtml

✦ MacUpdate Web site at www.macupdate.com

✦ Version Master Web site (Sherlock 2 for Classic plug-in available) at www.versionmaster.com

✦ Publisher or distributor of each application

Mac OS 9.1 or later for Classic

Until you can replace all your Mac OS 9 software with Mac OS X software, you'll use the Mac OS 9 software in the Mac OS X Classic environment. The Classic environment requires Mac OS 9.1 or later. If your computer has Mac OS 9.0.4 or earlier installed and you want to use it for the Classic environment, you must upgrade it to Mac OS 9.1 or later. An installation CD for Mac OS 9.1 or later was included with Mac OS X 10.1, but no version of OS 9 is included with the 10.2 OS boxed set. (Although the Classic environment may be installed on Macs purchased from Apple with OS X 10.2.)

Mac OS 9.1 is not the final version of Mac OS 9. As of this writing, the most current version of OS 9 is 9.2.2. You can upgrade to the latest version by obtaining upgrade software from Apple's software updates site on the Web (http://asu.info.apple.com).

Preparing for Installation

After you have decided to install Mac OS X, prepare for installation by performing the following tasks:

✦ Gather the information you need to set up Mac OS X after installing it.

✦ Make a backup of your hard drive and of any RAM disk you have.

✦ Update disk driver software.

✦ Optionally, partition your hard drive into two or more volumes.

✦ If you are installing on a PowerBook, make sure that it's plugged in.

✦ Read the PDF files on the installation disk, Read Before You Install.pdf, and Welcome to Mac OS X.pdf.

The remainder of this section discusses the first four of these tasks in more detail. The last two tasks are self-explanatory.

Gather setup information

If you want your computer to use the same Internet and network settings after you install Mac OS X on it, you need to make a note of the current settings. In Mac OS 9, the settings are located in the TCP/IP control panel, Remote Access control panel, and Modem control panel. In addition, you need to get the settings for your e-mail account from your e-mail reader application.

TCP/IP settings

In the TCP/IP control panel note the following basic settings: Connect via, Configure, DHCP Client ID, IP Address, Subnet mask, Router address, Name server addr., and Search domains. If any of these settings are blank or "will be supplied by server," then you do not need to note it. Figure A-3 shows examples of the TCP/IP control panel settings for an Ethernet connection.

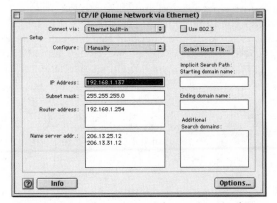

Figure A-3: Make a note of the settings in the TCP/IP control panel.

Your TCP/IP control panel may be set to Advanced mode or Administrator mode, in which case it has the following additional settings: Use 802.3, Starting Domain Name, Ending Domain Name, Additional Search domains. If any of these settings is absent or blank, then you do not need to note it.

Remote Access settings

If you connect to the Internet or a remote network via modem, open the Remote Access control panel and note the Name and Number settings. If you don't see these settings, click the disclosure triangle near the top of the Remote Access window to expand the window so that it shows the settings. Figure A-4 shows examples of the Remote Access settings.

You can't make a note of the password in this control panel because it is displayed as a series of dots for security purposes. You do need to know the password, so track it down.

Figure A-4: Make a note of the settings in the Remote Access control panel.

Next, click the Options button in the Remote Access control panel. In the Options dialog, click the Redialing tab and note whether Redialing is set to Off or something else (doesn't matter what else). Click the Connection tab and note the following settings: Use verbose logging, Prompt every x minutes. . ., and Disconnect if idle for x minutes. In addition, click the Protocol tab and note the settings of Connect automatically. . . and Use TCP header compression. Figure A-5 shows examples of all these settings except redialing.

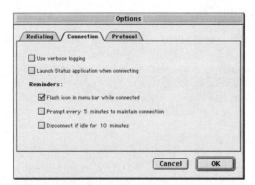

Figure A-5: Make a note of the settings in the Options dialog of the Remote Access control panel.

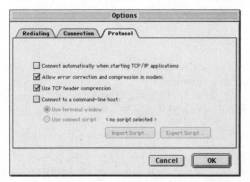

Modem settings

If you connect to the Internet or a remote network via modem, you also need to open the Modem control panel and note all the settings in it, as shown in Figure A-6.

Figure A-6: Make a note of the settings in the Modem control panel.

E-mail settings

If you have an e-mail account, you need to get the following settings from your e-mail application: e-mail address, incoming mail server, account type (POP or IMAP), user account ID, password, and outgoing mail server. If you have more than one account, get these settings for each account. You do not need to get the settings for an account provided by a Web site, such as Yahoo!

Backing up disks

The next step in getting ready to install Mac OS X is to make backup copies of your computer's hard drive. If you use more than one hard drive or if your hard drive is partitioned into multiple volumes, make backups of all of them. Making backups is like buying insurance — it's a terrific imposition, and you hope it's a total waste of effort. Do it anyway.

RAM disk backup

If you have a RAM disk, copy its contents to another disk before upgrading or installing any Mac OS version. Alternatively, you can save the RAM disk as a disk image file by using Apple's free Disk Copy program or Aladdin Systems' ShrinkWrap shareware. If you don't back up your RAM disk, its contents are lost during the installation process.

Hard drive backup

To back up today's large hard drives, you need some type of high-capacity backup storage device, either another hard drive of equal or greater capacity, a tape drive, or a recordable CD drive. In a pinch use a removable-media disk with 100MB or 250MB cartridges, but you'll probably need a lot of them to make a complete backup. Moreover, these removable cartridges are not as reliable as another hard drive, tape, or recordable CDs. What good is a backup if you can't restore from it?

If you have a second hard drive, you can back up your main hard drive by simply dragging its icon to the backup disk's icon. That method isn't very efficient if you want to keep your backup up-to-date on a regular basis, but it's adequate for preinstallation purposes.

Note   At a typical capacity of 100 to 250MB, it can take a lot of removable disks to completely back up your hard drive. (Some removable drives can store gigabytes of data on one disk, which is ideal for this sort of backup.) Even just backing up your System Folder can easily take more than one typical removable disk. It may be cheaper to simply buy a second hard drive than to buy enough backup disks to mirror your entire hard drive. An external hard drive — whether SCSI, USB, or FireWire-based — can be handy for other troubleshooting tasks, too.

You could back up to removable disks by dragging folder icons, but it's simpler to use a special backup utility, such as Retrospect Express from Dantz Development (www.dantz.com). This utility automates the process of backing up a large hard drive to several smaller removable disks. Retrospect Express also makes it easy to keep your backup files current. Each time you back up, Retrospect Express copies only the files and folders that have changed since the last backup. That minimizes the amount of time and number of removable disks needed for backup.

If you're up to the investment, a CD-R (CD-Recordable), CD-RW (CD-Rewriteable), DVD-RAM (DVD-Random Access Memory) drive), DVD-R (DVD-Recordable), or DVD-RW (DVD-Record/Write) is another option for backup. Many Macintoshes ship with one of these drives now. With these drives, you can generally write about 700MB to a CD or up to 4.7GB to each side of a DVD. This gives you an easy-to-store archive of your files that can often be read in any CD-ROM drive (or DVD-ROM drive, if you're creating a DVD-RAM disc). The downside is that creating a CD or DVD tends to be slow.

If you have a tape drive, you must use backup software, such as Dantz's Retrospect. You can't back up folders to a tape by dragging icons in the Finder.

Tip   If backing up your entire hard drive isn't feasible, you can back up only your document files and System Folder. This backup method is easier if you have all of your document files in one place. If you use this method, remember that you don't have a backup of your applications. To restore your entire hard drive, you have to reinstall the applications from scratch.

Updating disk driver software

The driver software that resides on every hard drive and removable disk cartridge must be compatible with the Mac OS version in use or problems may result. Updating driver software takes just a minute and generally doesn't affect drive contents in any way.

If you're installing Mac OS X on an Apple hard drive, the installer program updates the driver for you—there's no need to run a separate program. If you're not installing on an Apple hard drive, you need to use the most recent version of the formatting utility program last used on the drive.

Partitioning a hard drive (optional)

If you want to keep Mac OS X separate from Mac OS 9, you can partition your hard drive into two or more volumes. You must back up a disk before partitioning it, because partitioning a disk erases its contents. After partitioning, you can restore from the backup.

Partitioning your hard drive — a restriction

As you plan the number of volumes and their sizes, consider the following restriction. Some Mac models have a limitation on installing Mac OS X on a hard drive that is larger than 8GB and has been partitioned into more than one volume. The limitation requires that Mac OS X be installed on a volume that is completely within the first 8GB of the hard drive. The following models are affected:

- ✦ Any PowerBook G3 Series without USB ports
- ✦ Any beige Power Mac G3
- ✦ An iMac Rev. A, B, C, or D; that is, the original Bondi Blue iMacs with 233MHz processors and the Five Flavors iMacs with 266MHz and 333MHz processors

Using the Disk Utility application

You partition an Apple hard drive with the Drive Setup application. This utility also works with some hard drives sold by other companies. If you try Drive Setup and it says it can't deal with your hard drive, you need to use the disk utility application that came with the hard drive.

To partition the startup disk and prepare your Mac for Mac OS X, follow these steps:

1. **Restart from the Mac OS X installation CD.** Put the CD into the computer and restart while holding down the C key.

2. **When the Installer window appears, choose Installer⇨Open Disk Utility.** This action opens the Disk Utility application.

3. **In the Disk Utility window, click the Partition tab and select the disk you want to partition from the list of your disks.** Disk Utility displays the settings that you use to specify how many volumes you want and the size of each, as shown in Figure A-7.

4. **Choose the number of volumes you want from the Volume Scheme pop-up menu.**

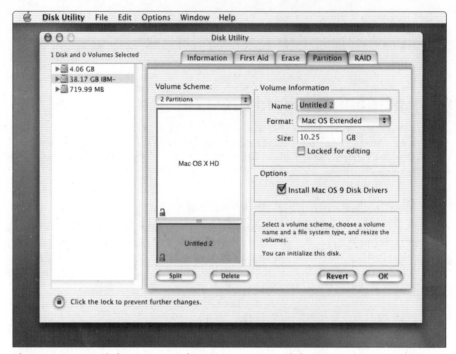

Figure A-7: Specify how many volumes you want and the name, format, and size of each.

5. **Set the size, name, and format of each volume.** The Name, Format, and Size settings apply to the currently selected volume, which is represented by a dark box below the Volume Scheme pop-up menu. You can select a different volume by clicking its box. You can adjust the size of the selected volume by typing a new size in the Size box or by dragging the bar below the dark box that represents the volume. When setting the volume format, choose Mac OS Extended unless you have a particular reason for picking a different format.

Note   OS X 10.2 requires the volume it is installed on be HFS+ (Mac OS Extended) if you wish to run the Classic environment within OS X. If you have an older Mac with OS 9 on a nonextended HFS volume, you will not be able to install 10.2 onto that volume without reformatting the partition.

6. **When you have finished setting up volumes, click OK.** A dialog appears, warning you that partitioning the drive erases its entire contents. This reason is why you have a reliable backup of the drive already. Think for a minute about your backup, because you're about to pass the point of no return. Are you sure that you know how to restore from your backup and that you won't need any files, such as a catalog file from the disk you're about to initialize?

7. **If you're sure you want to proceed, click Partition.**

Restore

After Disk Setup partitions your disk and initializes all the volumes, restore from your backup.

Installing Mac OS X

You install Mac OS X by using an installation program on the Mac OS X CD. This program leads you through the installation process. You need to select a language, read installation information, agree to a software license, select a destination volume, and then start installation.

Starting up from the installation CD

Immediately before installing Mac OS X, the computer must start up from the Mac OS X Install CD. You can accomplish this in two ways. One is to insert the CD into your computer, restart your Mac, and hold down the C key as soon as you hear the startup chime.

You can also start up the computer from the Mac OS X CD by inserting the CD and then double-clicking the Install Mac OS X icon in the CD's window, which is titled Welcome to Mac OS X. A window appears with a Restart button. Click this button to restart the computer with the Mac OS X Install CD and begin installation. If your computer is already using Mac OS X when you carry out this procedure, a dialog appears asking you to enter the name and password of an administrator account. You must provide this information to continue the installation process. No such dialog appears if your computer is using Mac OS 9 when you double-click the Install Mac OS X icon in the CD's window. Figure A-8 shows the Restart button in the Install Mac OS X window.

Figure A-8: The Restart button in the Install Mac OS X program restarts the computer with the Mac OS X Install CD to begin installation.

Selecting a language

When the computer starts from the Mac OS X Install CD, the Installer program starts automatically. In the Installer window, you select the language you want to use and click the Continue button.

Reading installation information

After you select a language, the Installer displays a welcome message, which explains that the Installer will guide you through the installation process. You click Continue and the Installer displays last-minute installation information for Mac OS X. It's tempting to skip this document, but the information provided is important, so you should at least skim it for the mention of your computer model, printers you use, and software you use. After reading the information, click Continue to go to the next step.

Agreeing to the software license

In the next installation step, the Installer window displays a license agreement. The license agreement is filled with lawyerspeak, but you should look through it so you know what you're agreeing to. For example, one provision states that you may only install the software on one computer at a time.

Tip   The Software License Agreement screen offers a small pop-up menu where you can choose a different language if you'd prefer to read the agreement in something other than English.

Click Continue when you're ready to go to the last step. A dialog appears, asking if you agree or disagree with the terms of the license. You cannot continue with the installation unless you click Agree.

Selecting a destination

Before beginning the next installation step, the Installer checks the version of Mac OS 9 that's installed on your computer to see if you will be able to use Classic applications after installing Mac OS X. If the Installer cannot find Mac OS 9.1 or later on one of your disk volumes, the Installer displays a message explaining that you must upgrade to Mac OS 9.1 or later to use your Classic applications. If the Installer finds Mac OS 9.1, it displays a message explaining that you can update it to Mac OS 9.2.1. You can perform these upgrades at any time after installing Mac OS X. After reading this message, click OK to continue installing Mac OS X. (If you prefer, after clicking OK you can stop installing Mac OS X, upgrade to Mac OS 9.1 or later, and then begin installing Mac OS X again. We discuss how to stop installing Mac OS X later under "Stopping installation.")

In the next installation step, you select the volume where you want Mac OS X installed. An icon appears for each volume, and you click the one you want to use.

At the bottom of the window is an option to erase the selected volume and format it. Do not turn on this option if the destination contains software that you want to continue using.

Note   If you are installing Mac OS X on a disk that has been partitioned into two or more volumes and one of the other volumes already has the Public Beta version of Mac OS X installed, you may need to install Mac OS X on a lower-numbered volume. This special requirement applies to the following Mac models: any beige Power Mac G3, a PowerBook G3 Series, and an original Bondi Blue iMac Rev. A or B.

Customizing the installation

In the last step before installation begins, you can customize the installation.

To customize your installation, click the Customize button to reveal a checklist of available Mac OS X modules. You can exclude a couple of the modules by clicking their checkboxes, but you probably won't want to. One of the excludable modules, BSD Subsystem, contains software needed for connecting to the Internet or a local network. The Additional Print Drivers module contains printer driver software for some Canon, Epson, and Hewlett-Packard printers.

Starting installation

When you're ready to get the installation process under way, click the Install button. The Installer checks the destination disk to make sure that it doesn't have any problems that would interfere with installation and prepares the software modules you selected. Then each module is installed. Figure A-9 shows the Install button for a standard (not customized) installation of Mac OS X.

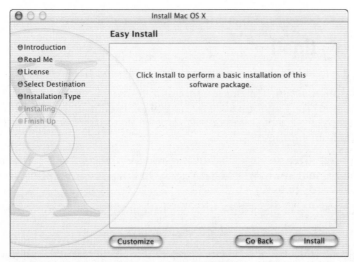

Figure A-9: Click Install to begin installation.

If you install Mac OS X on a disk or disk partition that already contains Mac OS 9, the existing contents of the disk or disk partition are placed in a folder named Mac OS 9. The disk or disk partition that contains Mac OS 9 must be formatted with the Mac OS Extended format.

Stopping installation

Until you click the Install button to get the installation process under way, you can stop installation by choosing Installer⇨Quit Installer. If you do this, the Installer displays a dialog that asks to confirm that you really want to stop installation. Click the Restart button in this dialog to have installation stop and your computer restart. When you hear your computer's startup chime, hold down the Option key to start up using your current version of the Mac OS. To start up using the Mac OS X CD, hold down the C key as the computer starts up.

Caution

After the installation process has begun, quitting the Installer may leave your computer in an unstable state. The Installer displays an alert informing you of this danger and giving you a chance to resume installation.

Using the Mac OS X Setup Assistant

When the Installer finishes installing the Mac OS X software, the computer restarts, and the Mac OS X Setup Assistant starts automatically. The Assistant asks for some basic information about the computer and you. The Assistant requests this information in several panes, which it displays one at a time. You go from one pane to the next by clicking the Continue button.

The Assistant asks for the following information:

- ✦ **Country.** Hard to believe, but the answer to this part affects some of the registration information asked for later.

- ✦ **Keyboard layout.** This information sets the formats for time, date, text, and numbers.

- ✦ **Registration information.** This information is automatically sent to Apple in an upcoming step. You cannot leave anything blank except the e-mail address and the company or school. If you do not want Apple to have a dossier on you, enter fictitious information here.

- ✦ **Marketing survey.** The survey asks whether you use the computer at home, school, business, and so on; what you do; and whether you want Apple and other companies to contact you.

- ✦ **User account.** Enter a name, a short name, a password, and an optional password hint for the first Mac OS X user account. This account has administrator privileges, which means anyone logging in with this account can create additional user accounts, change all system preference settings, and install other

Choose Your Password with Care

An easy-to-guess password is as good as no password at all. Even if you are the only user of your Mac and you have enabled Automatic Login, choosing a good password is still important if you connect to the Internet.

Here are a few suggestions on how to pick a secure password:

✦ Do not use any word that can be found in *any* dictionary, including foreign language dictionaries. Hackers use programs that attempt to log into machines by automatically trying words from dictionaries.

✦ Choose a password that is at least eight characters long.

✦ Include in the password at least one character from each of these groups: uppercase letters, lowercase letters, numbers, and special symbols, such as punctuation marks.

✦ Do not choose any obvious passwords, such as your birthday or variants of your name or the names of family members or pets.

Following these guidelines helps ensure that your password is difficult to guess. Be sure to safeguard your password. Do not write your password down in an obvious place and do not share it with anyone whom you would not trust with all your data.

Not forgetting your password is also important, especially the Administrator password; if you do, you may need to reinstall the Mac OS. Also, remember to log out whenever you end a session of using your Mac.

software. Therefore be sure you remember the name and password for this user account. Your account is created as soon as you click Continue. You cannot go back and change any of the information you have entered so far. For more information on user accounts, see Chapter 16.

At this point, the Assistant gives you the choice of setting up trial Internet service with EarthLink, setting up Mac OS X to use your existing Internet service, or not setting up for the Internet at this time. If you choose to set up for your existing Internet service, the Assistant asks for the following information:

✦ **How you connect.** Connect by telephone modem, local network, cable modem, DSL, or AirPort wireless.

✦ **Connection details.** These details vary depending on your connection method. Use the information gathered earlier from Mac OS 9 control panels (TCP/IP, Remote Access, and Modem) to help you here.

Next, the Assistant offers to set up an .Mac account for you. A .Mac account provides an e-mail address @mac.com, a personal Web site, and storage space on the Internet. You can create an .Mac account on the spot or enter the member name and password for an existing .Mac account.

After dealing with .Mac, the Assistant advises that it's ready to send your registration and configure your computer. Click Continue. The Assistant connects with Apple to send your registration information. You can cancel the connection and stop sending the registration information by quickly clicking the Cancel button.

Next the Assistant asks for information to set up your e-mail account. If you've already set up a .Mac account, the Assistant uses the e-mail account included with the .Mac account. If you want to use another account, you can select an option to add your existing e-mail account. Then you enter your e-mail address, incoming mail server, account type (POP or IMAP), user account ID, password, and outgoing mail server.

The Assistant wants more information from you. It asks for the time zone, which you specify by clicking your region of the world on a map and choosing a time zone from a pop-up menu. The Assistant may also ask for the date and time, which set your computer's clock and calendar. They establish the creation date and modification date for each of your files, set the date on e-mail you send, and so forth. The Assistant asks you for the date and time only if it can't get the information on its own via the Internet. Finally, click the Done button to start using Mac OS X.

Installing Mac OS 9.x for Classic

As mentioned earlier, Mac OS 9.1 or later must be installed on your computer if you want to use the Classic environment of Mac OS X. The Classic environment cannot use Mac OS 9.0.4 or earlier. This section describes how to install Mac OS 9.1 or later. For simplicity, we refer to Mac OS 9.1, Mac OS 9.2, and any later versions of Mac OS 9 as Mac OS 9.x. If Mac OS 9.x is already installed on your computer or you don't want to use the Classic environment, you can skip this section.

Note   OS 9 installation CDs were included with OS X for 10.0 and 10.1, but are not included in the 10.2 Jaguar boxed set as of this writing.

You install Mac OS 9.1 or later using the Mac OS Install program on the Mac OS 9.x CD. The Mac OS Install program leads you through the steps necessary to install Mac OS 9.x. In these steps, you select a destination disk, read a document about installing Mac OS 9.x, and agree to a software license. Then you may select the modules to be installed and start the installation.

Start up from the installation CD

Begin by starting up the computer with the Mac OS 9.x CD. To do this, you insert the CD and restart the computer while holding down the C key. Continue holding it down until see the Mac OS 9.x welcome screen.

Hiding the Mac OS X Applications folder

If you're going to install Mac OS 9.1 or later on the disk on which Mac OS X is already installed, you must hide Mac OS X's Applications folder. If you fail to take this precaution, you may have to reinstall Mac OS X. To hide the Mac OS X Application folder, do the following:

1. **After the computer has started up from the Mac OS 9.x CD, create a new folder.** (Choose File➪New Folder.)

2. **Open the icon of the disk where Mac OS X is installed and locate the Applications folder there.**

3. **Drag this Applications folder to the new folder you created.**

You have now hidden Mac OS X's Application's folder and can proceed with installing Mac OS 9.1 or later. When the installation has finished, you must move the Applications folder back to its original location. We discuss this move later.

Starting the Mac OS Install program

Having started up from the Mac OS 9.x CD and, if necessary, hidden the Applications folder, you're ready to start the Mac OS X Install program. Double-click its icon, and in a few seconds, the Install Mac OS 9.x window appears, displaying some introductory information. Click Continue to begin installation. Figure A-10 shows the introductory information in the Install Mac OS 9.x window.

Figure A-10: Read the introductory information in the Install Mac OS 9.x window.

Selecting a destination

The first step to installing the Mac OS is to choose a disk for it. A pop-up menu lists the available disks. When you choose a disk from the pop-up menu, the Mac OS Install program reports the disk's system software version and the amount of free space available. This step also gives you the option of selecting a clean installation. Figure A-11 shows this first step in the Install Mac OS 9 window.

Figure A-11: Choose a hard drive and optionally select a clean installation.

If Mac OS 9.*x* is already installed on the disk you chose as the destination, you may want to perform a clean installation. A clean installation provides a completely new System Folder that does not include any third-party system extensions, control panels, or fonts. In addition, all preferences for Mac OS 9.*x* and for Classic applications are reset to their default settings. If you want to do a clean installation, click Options at the bottom of the Install Mac OS 9.*x* window. In the dialog that appears, turn on the option Perform Clean Installation and click OK.

Click Select at the bottom of the Install Mac OS 9.*x* window to go to the second step. If you chose a destination disk that already has Mac OS 9.*x* installed, the Mac OS Install program displays an alert explaining the situation and giving you three choices: Cancel, Reinstall, or Add/Remove. If you want to choose a different destination disk, click Cancel. If you want to replace the system software with a clean copy, click Reinstall. If you want to add or remove portions of the system software, click Add/Remove. If you click Add/Remove, the Mac OS Install program skips the second and third installation steps and switches from a standard installation to a custom installation. In this case, you should continue reading at "Setting options and customizing installation."

Reading installation information

In the second installation step, the Install Mac OS 9.x window displays a document containing last-minute installation information for Mac OS 9.x. Read the information and then click Continue at the bottom of the window to go to the third step.

Agreeing to the software license

In the third installation step, the Install Mac OS 9.x window displays a license agreement. Make sure you understand the terms of the license and then click Continue. A small dialog appears, asking if you agree or disagree with the terms of the license. You must click Agree to continue with the installation.

Setting options and customizing installation

In the last installation step, you can set some options and set up a custom installation before beginning installation. Figure A-12 shows the last step of the Mac OS Install program for Mac OS 9.x.

Figure A-12: Set options, customize installation, and start installing Mac OS 9.x.

Clicking the Options button displays a dialog in which you can set two options. One option determines whether the Installer creates a report of its actions. The other option controls whether the Installer updates the driver software on Apple hard drives. Both options are normally turned on.

Clicking the Customize button in the Install Mac OS 9.x window reveals a checklist of available system software modules. Each module can be included or excluded individually. You can also include or exclude portions of some modules. Some customizations you can do include the following:

✦ You can exclude a number of modules that Mac OS X makes obsolete. This customization saves some disk space and reduces the time it takes to start the Classic environment in Mac OS X. You can exclude any or all the following modules from an installation of Mac OS 9.x for the Classic environment: AirPort, Apple DVD Software, Internet Access, Apple Remote Access, Personal Web Sharing, Mac OS Runtime for Java, ColorSync, English Speech Recognition, and Network Assistant Client. None of these modules is needed for the Classic environment.

✦ You must include the Mac OS 9.x module.

✦ You may want to include the Text-to-Speech module, which lets your computer speak text aloud in Classic applications.

✦ You may also want to include the Language Kits module, which enables you to display and edit in languages other than English in your Classic applications.

Note　If you expect to start up your computer with the Mac OS 9.x that you are about to install, then be sure to include the following modules even though they are obsolete in the Classic environment: AirPort, Apple DVD Software, Internet Access, Apple Remote Access, and ColorSync. Depending on how you use the computer with Mac OS 9.x, you may also want to include some other modules that are obsolete in the Classic environment.

Starting installation

To begin the installation, click Start in the Install Mac OS window. The Mac OS Install program checks the destination disk's directory to ensure that files can be written to the disk properly. Next, the Mac OS Install program may update the drivers of Apple hard drives. These procedures in no way affect the contents of your disk.

After checking the disk directory and updating Apple drivers, the Mac OS Install program begins installing system software modules. Installation proceeds automatically unless a problem occurs.

You can always cancel an installation that is under way by clicking Cancel. If you cancel an installation in progress, the Mac OS Install program displays an alert asking how you want to proceed. You can stop installation, skip installation of the module currently being installed, or try installing again.

Finishing installation

When the installation of Mac OS 9.*x* is finished, quit the Installer but do not restart the computer yet. If you hid the Mac OS X Applications folder before starting installation of Mac OS 9.*x*, you must now move it from the folder in which you hid it back to its former location. Simply drag the Applications folder from its hiding place to the icon of the disk where you just installed Mac OS 9.*x*.

After installing Mac OS 9.*x*, the computer is set to start up with Mac OS 9.*x*. To change this setting so the computer starts up with Mac OS X, open the Startup Disk control panel and select the Mac OS X disk. You can open the Startup Disk control panel by choosing Apple⇨Control Panels and then double-clicking the Startup Disk icon. Figure A-13 shows this control panel in Mac OS 9.1.

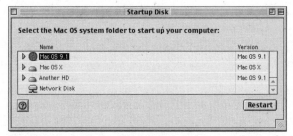

Figure A-13: After installing Mac OS 9.*x*, use the Startup Disk control panel to set the computer to start up with Mac OS X.

✦   ✦   ✦

Installing Applications

With Mac OS X, Apple includes a new Installer program and some applications take advantage of it by distributing packages that Installer opens and distributes to the appropriate folders. Early releases of this Installer had some problems, the most serious of which was deleting folders when it removed old versions of a file before installing the new one. These issues have since been resolved in subsequent updates — another reason to use the Software Update pane of System Preferences periodically to make sure that your system software is up-to-date. Meanwhile, MindVision and Aladdin have carbonized their installers so that they run natively under Mac OS X.

First, one of things you need to know about installing an application is that, if you want to install it in the Applications folder so that all users of your Mac can access it, you need to be logged in with an administrator account.

Using the Installer Utility

Unless Mac OS X was preinstalled on your Mac or somebody else installed Mac OS X for you, you have seen the Mac OS X Installer in action. Apple uses the Installer for installing Mac OS X, updating Mac OS X via the Software Update pane of System Preferences, and using applications.

The Installer utility is located in, ta-da, the Utilities folder of the Applications folder. The Installer's documents are installer *packages* and generally have a .PKG extension on their file name and an icon similar to the one shown in Figure B-1. The Installer application's icon is also seen in Figure B-1.

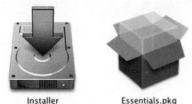

Figure B-1: The Installer (left) and a typical Installer package (right).

Installer   Essentials.pkg

A typical installation follows these steps:

1. **Double-click the Installer icon and initiate the installation process.**

2. **Verify your administrator status by clicking the padlock icon (see Figure B-2) and entering your administrator password confirming that you are authorized to install software on this Mac.**

   After you are authorized to install software, you see an Introduction screen, as shown in Figure B-3.

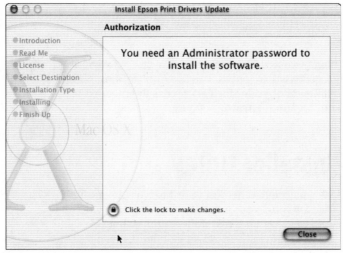

Figure B-2: The Installer requires proper authorization before allowing you to install software.

3. **Click the Continue button to proceed to the next step.** The screen reveals important information (the Read Me document) about the software product and adds four buttons along the bottom of the window, as seen in Figure B-4.

   The Read Me document often includes directions on things you need to do or know before you install. You can print the Read Me file (click the Print button at the bottom) or save it to your disk (click the Save button), if you want to refer to it at a later time. The Go Back button allows you to retrace your steps, in case you want to change an earlier selection (although there isn't much point in that, yet).

Note

On the left of the Installer window is a task bar listing the steps taken during the installation process. Although you cannot use it to navigate the installation process, it is a handy reference for where you are and which steps remain.

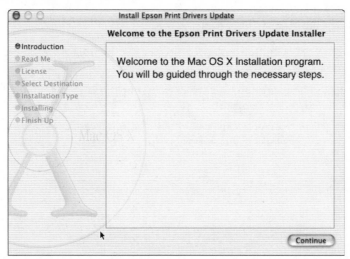

Figure B-3: Greetings from the Installer. Click Continue to proceed.

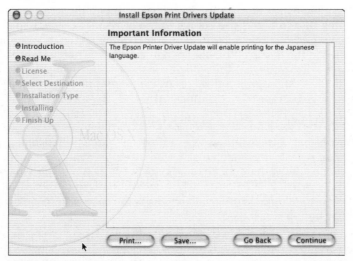

Figure B-4: Release notes provided by the software provider in the Read Me file.

4. **Click Continue.** The software license agreement appears. In most cases (at least for software from Apple), you need to agree to the license before the installation takes place.

5. **After reading the license agreement (and you'll read every word, won't you?), click Continue.** The Install screen appears, asking you to agree or disagree to the terms of the license agreement, as shown in Figure B-5.

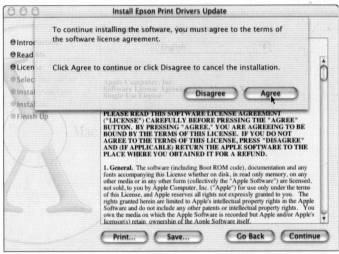

Figure B-5: Agree to the license and proceed with the installation or disagree and exit the Installer after it takes you back a step.

6. **Click Agree to continue with the installation. If you disagree with the agreement, click Disagree and you return to the previous screen.** Usually, if you disagree with the agreement, you cannot install the software. Assuming that you agreed to the terms of the license agreement, you are asked to choose the volume on which you want the software installed. The available volumes appear in the destination window. (Because there is no documentation, the Print and Save buttons have disappeared.)

7. **Select the volume you want and click Continue.**

   Near the bottom of the window, where the Print and Save buttons used to be, the Installer reveals how much disk space is required to do the installation after selecting the volume's icon, as shown in Figure B-6. A fairly bare screen (Figure B-7) appears. The Continue button has changed to the Install button. If no customization options are available (as is the case with this example), the Customize button is disabled.

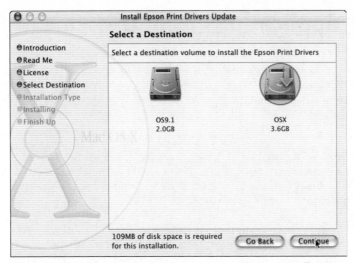

Figure B-6: Select the destination of your software installation.

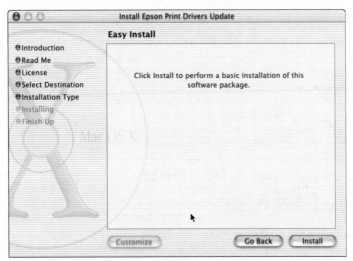

Figure B-7: The point of no return—time to install.

8. **Click Install.** A progress bar appears in the right pane of the window. When the installation is complete, you are notified and you can quit from the Installer. Some installations, particularly many involving updates to the System, require you to restart. When that is the case, the Installer tells you that you need to restart (via a dialog) and restarts the Mac when you dismiss the dialog.

Installing Applications from Disk Images

With the advent of packages (see Chapter 5), applications rarely continue to require installation of additional components in scattered locations. In fact, it is now normal for an application to be just one file, a package (a special folder type that the Mac OS X presents to you like a single file), or a small group of files maintained in the same folder as the application. Thus, the ease of the drag install is currently the norm for Mac OS X applications.

Because of the ease of drag installations, shipping applications as disk image files (see Chapter 11 and Chapter 22) is one of the most common distribution methods for applications. In fact, Apple uses it for distribution of Mac OS X applications, such as iTunes, iMovie, and AppleWorks.

Disk image files are usually obtained via download from the Internet, which includes the software folder of your iDisk where Apple provides a veritable cornucopia of software for Mac OS X—both from Apple and from third-party developers.

Copy the disk image file to your hard disk and double-click it. The disk image usually has a .IMG, .DMG, or .SMI file name extension (suffix). If the image has a .SMI extension, you may want to just drag it to the Disk Copy window (after launching Disk Copy, of course). Why? Because double-clicking a .SMI file may launch the Classic version of Disk Copy if it is present.

Figure B-8 illustrates an example of a mounted disk image file, ready for you to install your software. Remember, to install the file in the Applications folder, you need to be logged in with an administrator account. Just drag the file to the folder where you want it to reside—in Figure B-8, we're dragging TinkerTool to the Utilities folder.

Installing Applications from Compressed Archives

Just as you use Disk Copy to mount disk images, you use a decompression utility to make the contents of compressed archives installable. Until quite recently, a Mac user would rarely encounter a compressed archive in any format other than that of Aladdin Systems' StuffIt Deluxe. In the rare situation where a user encountered a WinZip file, the free StuffIt Expander would also decompress WinZip as well. While there were other compressors and archivers (Disk Doubler and Compact Pro, to name two), anything other than .SIT (StuffIt) or .ZIP (WinZip) was extremely uncommon.

Figure B-8: Drag from the mounted disk image to install new software.

Thanks to the Unix underpinnings of Mac OS X, a couple of other formats are becoming semistandard. As noted in Chapter 26, `tar` files are the Unix standard for archiving, and compression is achieved with compress or gzip. gzip files typically have a `.gz` file name extension and compressed files have a `.z` extension. The multitalented StuffIt Expander also recognizes these formats and decompresses and expands tar archives, although some other utilities, such as OpenUp — a freeware offering by Scott Anguish, obtained from `www.stepwise.com/Software/OpenUp/` — also decompresses these formats. If you have both StuffIt Expander and OpenUp, you should be ready for just about any compressed archive that can come your way.

To install from a compressed archive, decompress the archive and then extract the archive's contents. If there are installation instructions (such as a Unix script to run in a Terminal shell), follow them. If there are no installation instructions, just drag the application where you want it, remembering that you need administrator permissions to install it in the Applications folder.

Installing Applications with Custom Installers

Some application providers feel the need to "roll their own" installation utility or script. When you encounter one of these situations, just follow the instructions, which accompany the custom installer — every one will be different. Other than telling you to follow the accompanying instructions, no general rule applies.

✦   ✦   ✦

Exploiting Keyboard Shortcuts

Using the keyboard is sometimes faster or more convenient than moving your hand to the mouse, trackball, or trackpad. Setting bold or italic for the next text you type while you're in the process of typing is such an example — it is easier to keep typing and press ⌘-B (bold) or ⌘-I (italic), assuming that you know and remember these keyboard shortcuts.

Most keyboard shortcuts are visible to you in the active application's menus, and not too many of those are covered in this appendix. However, a number of keyboard shortcuts aren't easily visible.

Finder Shortcuts

The Mac OS X Finder has more keyboard shortcuts available in its menus than any preceding Mac OS or System release. Most of these are brand new and representative of changes to a Unix-based folder structure. Others are changes to keyboard shortcuts present in Mac OS 9, such as the shortcut for New Folder.

When it comes to the shortcuts not in menus, the Mac OS X Finder has a few that may facilitate your Finder experiences, as shown in Table C-1. You can also go to a specific item in the front window by typing the first characters of its name.

Table C-1
Finder Keyboard Shortcuts

Shortcut	Meaning
Tab	Takes you to the next item alphabetically in an icon or list view, inactive in a column view
Shift-Tab	Takes you to the next item alphabetically in an icon or list view, inactive in a column view
↑	Takes you to the item above the current item (to the bottom item if none are selected)
↓	Takes you to the item below the current item (to the topmost item if none are selected)
→	Expands a folder in a list or column view, takes you to the next item to the right in an icon view
←	Collapses a folder in a list view, moves back (left) one column in column view, takes you to the icon to the left in an icon view
⌘-↑	Displays the folder containing the currently displayed folder in a new Finder window if the toolbar is hidden or in the same Finder window if the toolbar is showing
⌘-↓	Opens the selected item(s) in new windows if the toolbar is hidden or in the same window if the toolbar is showing — launches applications to open document icons, launches selected applications
⌘-Option-W	Closes all Finder windows
Shift-⌘-delete	Empties the Trash
⌘-H	Hide the Finder application
⌘-Option-H	Hides non-Finder application windows
⌘-Shift-Y	Makes a new Sticky Note (see Chapter 11, "Harnessing Standard Services")
⌘-N	New Finder window
⌘-Shift-N	New folder
⌘-W	Close active window
⌘-I	Get Info on a selected item or group of items
⌘-D	Duplicate selected item
⌘-L	Make Alias to selected item
⌘-R	Show Original item of selected alias
⌘-T	Add item to Favorites
⌘-delete	Move selected item to Trash folder

Shortcut	Meaning
⌘-E	Eject removable disk or other mounted volume
⌘-F	Find (opens the Find window)
⌘-Z	Undo move of item and return item to previous location
@-A	Select All items in current folder or window
⌘-1	View window items as icons
⌘-2	View window items as list
⌘-3	View window items in column view
⌘-B	Hide Toolbar of active window
⌘-J	Show View Options for Desktop or window
Shift-⌘-C	Go (change active window to show) Computer
Shift-⌘-H	Go (change active window to show) Home
Shift-⌘-I	Go (change active window to show) iDisk
Shift-⌘-A	Go (change active window to show) Applications
Shift-⌘-F	Go (change active window to show) Favorites
Shift-⌘-G	Go (change active window to show) to Folder.... A dialog window will appear asking for the name of the folder to go to.
⌘-K	Connect to Server
⌘-M	Minimize active window to Dock
⌘-Option-M	Minimizes all Finder windows to the Dock
⌘-?	Mac Help

Note One shortcut that will probably cause experienced Mac users a bit of a problem until they become accustomed is that ⌘-N now opens a new Finder window rather than creating a new folder. (New folder is now ⌘-Shift-N.) While the new meaning for this keystroke is probably more logical and consistent with the use of ⌘-N in other applications, over 15 years of ingrained experience with one of the most commonly used Finder shortcuts is not going to be without cost.

Common Application Shortcuts

Certain keyboard shortcuts are considered to be standard by Apple's Human Interface Guidelines. Historically, applications that diverge from these recommended uses receive a markedly negative reception from Mac users. In this respect, Mac OS X is no different with one caveat: If the command doesn't make sense in an application, its keyboard shortcut is considered "fair game" to be employed in another way. Under Mac OS 9 and earlier, the keyboard shortcuts were semi-sacred.

How Key Shortcuts Work

If you've ever wondered why ⌘-N with the Caps Lock key down isn't equivalent to pressing ⌘-Shift-N or similar things, the reason is fairly straightforward, if a bit geeky.

Mac applications (including Mac OS X applications) respond to *events*, such as a window activating or pressing a key. One such event is the *keydown event*. Keys such as Shift, Option, Control, and Caps Lock do not generate an event—their state (up or down) is recorded in what is called the *modifier field* of the event record. Thus, when you press the *n* key, the programmer writing the code needs to check the state of the various modifier keys to determine whether it is just text being typed or whether it is some sort of a command. Every key on the keyboard has a separate state entry in the modifier field.

Just so you know, this method is not peculiar to Macs. The same techniques are used in Windows programming.

One example is the Hide Toolbar command in the Finder — ⌘-B. Previously, this shortcut was pretty much reserved for setting a bold font, even when there was no such capability in the application (like the Finder). Another example is the universal Undo shortcut — ⌘-Z. In Apple's Grab utility, Undo doesn't make sense (how do you undo taking a screenshot?), so Undo doesn't appear in the Edit menu. The ⌘-Z keystroke is reassigned to take a full-screen picture.

Note   Quite frankly, we think that this decision is a poor one. There is no strong reason to not continue with the keyboard shortcut ⌘-Shift-3 to which veteran Mac users are accustomed. Further, Grab often has no windows open and a user can easily believe that they are in another application and get frustrated when ⌘-Z doesn't Undo the last action.

In Mac OS 9 and earlier, ⌘-H was a semistandard shortcut for Find Selection. All applications using that keystroke have to change because ⌘-H is now the shortcut for Hide application.

To switch from one application to the next (in the stacking order), press ⌘-Tab. ⌘-Shift-Tab switches to the previous application. Note that when you press these shortcuts, the new item's name flashes in the Dock, even if the Dock is hidden. If you continue holding down the ⌘ key, the name displays until you release the key.

For any application that sports a Window menu (and pretty much all Mac OS X applications do), you're accustomed to seeing ⌘-M as the keystroke to minimize the frontmost (active) window to the Dock. Using ⌘-Option-M minimizes all that application's open windows to the Dock. Similarly, ⌘-Option-W modifies the standard close window behavior to close all of an application's open windows.

One particularly nice feature of Mac OS X-native applications is that the Page Down and Page Up keys work to scroll the front-most window. Similarly, the Home key takes you to the top of the document, and the End key takes you to the bottom.

Standard Dialog Shortcuts

Regardless whether an application implements Save and Print as an independent dialog or as a sheet attached to a document window, the dialog's manipulation remains the same, whether you're using the mouse or the keyboard. Tab moves you from one text box or list to the next, previewing any effects from the typing you do. For example, if a text box is selected, typing enters characters in that text box; however, if a list is selected, typing functions as it does in a Finder column view. (See "Finder Shortcuts" earlier in this chapter.)

Note
> The keyboard shortcut ⌘-N (or even ⌘-Shift-N, if Apple wants to be consistent with the Mac OS X Finder) is particularly annoying to experienced Mac users because the shortcut does not equate to clicking the New Folder button in a Save dialog — something to which they have long been accustomed and something which is logical to expect.

If there is a Cancel button, either ⌘-. (period) or the Esc key function is an equivalent. Likewise, either Enter or Return functions as an equivalent to the default (pulsating) button.

✦　　✦　　✦

Glossary

Absolute path A path that specifies the location of a file or folder starting at the root of the file system, which is designated by a single slash character (/).

Active application The application displaying menus in the menu bar.

Administrator account A user account that can be used for changing system preference settings and installing software in the Applications and Library folders.

Adorn The process of changing the formatting of a *subscriber* in a Classic application.

AirPort Apple's name for its implementation of the IEEE 802.11 standard for wireless networking.

AirPort Base Station A device sold by Apple that wirelessly connects Airport-equipped computers to connect to an Ethernet network, a modem connection to the Internet, or both.

Alert A window in which Mac OS X or an application program notifies you of a hazardous situation, a limitation in your proposed course of action, or an error condition.

Alias A stand-in or agent for an actual program, document, folder, or disk. The alias does not duplicate the item it represents; instead, the alias points to the item it represents.

Anti-alias The process of smoothing text or graphics by blending jagged edges with the color of the background. In the Classic environment, text smoothing is an option of the Appearance control panel.

Apple events Apple's name for *event messages*.

Apple Guide A type of on-screen help that is available in some Classic applications. It provides step-by-step interactive instructions for completing a task in a Classic application.

AppleScript An English-like language that you can use to write your own programs, called *scripts*, to automate tasks involving one or more applications. For example, you can use an AppleScript script to move data between applications. AppleScript sends *event messages* to programs.

AppleTalk The networking protocol used to communicate with all Apple network printers, many other network printers, and some multiuser software. The content that is passed back and forth could be *event messages*, page images to be printed, e-mail, file contents, or any other kind of information. The content and the protocol can be transmitted through *Ethernet* cabling, a wireless *Airport* connection, or other means.

Applets A small application program. Often refers to small Java-language programs that are commonly embedded in Web pages to make them more interesting or useful. Also refers to AppleScript scripts that have been saved as small applications.

Application Software that enables a computer to perform a set of related tasks for a specific purpose, such as word processing, working with spreadsheets or graphics, or Web browsing. See *program* and *software*.

Application Programming Interfaces (API) The means by which application programs take advantage of operating system features.

Application Switcher The floating Classic window that facilitates switching Classic applications. It appears when you "tear-off" the Classic Application menu (select the menu and drag straight down with the mouse).

Argument The part of a Unix command that specifies its input source and may specify its output destination.

ASCII A standard for using the numbers 0 through 255 to represent the letters of the Roman alphabet, digits, punctuation marks, and other symbols. Text characters are encoded as numbers so that computers can work with them.

Asynchronously Able to proceed independently.

Authentication The process of validating a username and password to allow logging in to a computer or making a network connection.

Autorouting The Finder's ability to place files dropped on the System Folder into the correct folders inside the System Folder.

Autoscrolling The process of scrolling through a window or a list without using the scroll bars by placing the mouse pointer in the window or the list, pressing the mouse button, and dragging toward the area you want to view.

Background program A program that runs without input from the keyboard or mouse and generally without displaying anything on the screen with the possible exception of discreet status information.

Balloon Help A type of help that makes a cartoon-like balloon appear when you place the mouse pointer over an object in a Classic application. The balloon may tell you what the object is, what it does, or what happens when you click it. Not all objects have help balloons. The equivalent in a Mac OS X application are *Help tags*.

Bevel button A displayed control with a beveled edge that gives it a three-dimensional look. It bears a label that indicates its function. Bevel buttons mimic the function and behavior of other items: *push buttons, radio buttons, checkboxes,* or *pop-up menus*.

Binary file A file of formatted text, pictures, sound, movies, other data, or program code.

BinHex A method of encoding a *binary file* into a plain text file so that it can be sent over a network. A BinHexed file must be decoded back into a binary file before it can be used on the receiving computer.

Bit A single binary digit.

Bit depth See *color depth* and *pixel depth*.

Bitmap font Same as *fixed-size font*.

Blessed A term used to denote the System Folder currently being used by the Classic environment. (Also denotes the active System Folder on a computer that is using Mac OS 9 or earlier.)

Bookmark A way to store *Web page* locations (*URLs*) that you want to remember and go to frequently.

Bridge Software or hardware used to connect two different types of networking hardware. For example, a bridge is used to connect *Ethernet* and *AirPort* wireless networks so that they can exchange data.

Bundle See *package*.

Bug A programming error or other flaw in software. A minor bug may affect what you see or how a program works in a noncritical way. A serious bug may cause a program to quit unexpectedly or a loss of data.

Built-in memory Apple's term for physical *RAM*, that is, the memory chips that are actually installed in the Mac.

Burn To burn means to record a CD.

Burn-in A condition affecting display screens in which a vestige of an unchanging screen image remains visible when the screen image finally changes.

Button See *push button*.

Case-sensitive Describes a password in which capitalization matters; a capital *A* is not the same as lowercase *a*.

Character A written representation of a letter, digit, or symbol — a basic element of a written language.

Checkbox A displayed control that lets you turn a setting on or off. When a setting is on, a check mark appears in the checkbox. When a setting is off, the checkbox is empty. When a setting is partly on and partly off because it indicates the state of more than one item, such as the format of a range of text, a dash appears in the checkbox.

Clarus See *DogCow*.

Clean installation This type of installation installs a new System Folder with unused copies of Mac OS 9 files for the Classic environment. The existing System Folder is deactivated and renamed Previous System Folder.

CLI See *command-line interface*.

Click-and-a-half A gesture used to make a disk or folder spring open. To perform the gesture, begin to double-click the disk or folder, but do not release the mouse button after the second click.

Click-through The ability to interact directly with an item in an inactive window. For example, you can operate the Close, Minimize, and Zoom buttons in most inactive Aqua windows.

Client A program (or a computer running a program) that requests and receives information or services from a *server*.

Clipping file A file created by the Finder to hold material that has been dragged from a document to the Desktop or a Finder window.

Closed network An AirPort network that requires you to type its name (not simply pick the name from a list) to connect to it.

Codec Compressor-decompressor software or hardware. See *compressor*.

Collated Multiple printed copies of a document with each copy having all its pages in the correct order.

Color depth The number of bits of information that are required to represent the number of colors available on the screen. For example, a screen that can display thousands of colors is set at a color depth of 16 bits. Compare to *pixel depth*.

Color picker The dialog in which you specify a custom color either by clicking a color wheel, clicking a color sample, or entering color values.

Command Line Interface A means of interacting with and controlling a computer by typing commands one line at a time.

Comment An AppleScript line that begins with a hyphen, or a Unix command line that begins with a number sign character (#), which in either case means that the line is descriptive and not a command to be performed.

Compile To convert the human-readable text of an AppleScript *script* into command codes that a Mac can execute. As part of this process, AppleScript checks the script for nonconformance with AppleScript grammar, such as a missing parenthesis.

Compression algorithm A method for compressing data so that it fits in less space and can be transferred more quickly. Each compression algorithm generally works best with one type of data, such as sound, photographs, video or motion pictures, and computer-generated animation. Three characteristics of a compression algorithm determine how effectively it compresses — *compression ratio*, fidelity to the original data, and speed.

Compression ratio Indicates the amount of compression and is calculated by dividing the size of the original source data by the size of the compressed data. Larger compression ratios mean greater compression and generally (although not always) a loss of quality in the compressed data.

Compressor-decompressor Something that compresses data so that it takes less space to store and decompresses compressed data back to its original form for playing or other use. A compressor may consist of software, hardware, or both. Sometimes called by the shortened form *codec*.

Conditional A programming command that evaluates a condition (stated as part of the conditional) to determine whether another command or set of commands should be performed. (Also referred to as a *conditional statement*.)

Contextual menu A contextual menu lists commands, relevant to an item that you Control-click.

Control Panel A small Classic application that you use to set the way some part of the Classic environment looks and behaves.

Cooperative multitasking A scheme of *multitasking* used by Classic applications whereby multiple applications are open in the Classic environment and voluntarily taking turns using the Classic environment's processing time. While each Classic application is idle, it allows other Classic applications to use the processor. Compare *preemptive multitasking*.

Cracker A person who overcomes a computer's security and gains unauthorized access. Compare to *hacker*.

Crop markers Small triangles that indicate the beginning and end of a selected part of a movie in iMovie.

Crossover cable A cable whose wires are reversed inside the plug at one end of the cable.

Custom installation You can selectively install Mac OS X packages. You can also selectively install Mac OS 9 modules for the Classic environment.

Daisy chaining The process of connecting one peripheral or network device to another device, linking them so that they can share data. This is often done with Ethernet networking hubs to extend the size of an Ethernet network. It's also how multiple FireWire and SCSI devices are connected to a single Macintosh computer so that they can all be accessed by that computer.

Dead keys The keys that generate accented characters when typed in combination with the Option key and in proper sequence. For example, typing Option-E followed by O generates ó on a U.S. keyboard. The Key Caps program highlights the dead keys when you press Option.

Default button The one button that pulsates in an Aqua dialog or alert box; in a Classic dialog or alert box, the default button has a heavy border. In either case it represents the action you'll most often want to take. If the most common action is dangerous, a button representing a safer action may be the default button. Usually, pressing Return or Enter has the same effect as click the default button.

Default browser The Web browser application that opens when you click a link to a Web page in Sherlock's list of search results; open an Internet *location file;* otherwise don't specify a particular browser application.

Desktop database Invisible files used by the Finder to associate Classic applications and their documents. Mac OS X keeps the Desktop database hidden because you don't use it directly. You can use the Classic pane of System Preferences to rebuild the Desktop database.

Device driver Software that controls a device, such as a printer, and transfers data to and from it.

Dialog A window that displays options you can set or select. A dialog has a button for accepting the changes and another button for canceling the changes. Both buttons close the dialog.

Digital signature Functions as a handwritten signature, identifying the person who vouches for the accuracy and authenticity of the signed document.

DIMM A dual in-line memory module is a small circuit board containing memory chips.

Directory A folder or the *root level* of a disk. Also refers to a list of the items contained in a folder or the root level of a disk.

Disclosure triangle A displayed control that regulates how much detail you see in a window. When the window is displaying minimal detail, clicking a disclosure triangle reveals additional detail and may automatically enlarge the window to accommodate it. Clicking the same triangle again hides detail and may automatically shrink the window to fit.

Disk cache Improves system performance by storing recently used information from disk in a dedicated part of memory. Accessing information in memory is much faster than accessing information on disk.

Disk image A file that, when mounted using Disk Copy or a similar utility, appears on the Desktop as if it were a removable disk.

Display mirroring See *video mirroring.*

DNS server Software that looks up a computer's name on the Internet (or a local network) and determines the computer's *IP address.* DNS stands for Dynamic Name Server.

DogCow Also known as Clarus, it is the official mascot of Mac hackers and is pictured in the Page Setup Options dialog of Classic applications.

Domain name The part of a *URL* that identifies the owner of an Internet location. A domain name has the form `companyname.com`, `organizationname.net`, `schoolname.edu`, `militaryunitname.mil`, `governmentagencyname.gov`, and so forth.

Double-click speed The rate at which you have to click so that Mac OS X perceives two clicks in a row as a single event.

Download The process of receiving software or other computer files from another computer, over the Internet or a local network.

dpi (dots-per-inch) A measure of how fine or coarse the dots are that make up a printed image. More dots-per-inch means smaller dots, and smaller dots mean finer (less coarse) printing.

Drag To move the mouse while holding down the mouse button.

Drag-and-drop editing To copy or move selected text, graphics, and other material by dragging it to another place in the same window, a different window, or the Desktop. Some applications do not support drag-and-drop editing.

Drag-and-drop open To drag a document to a compatible application in the Finder, thereby highlighting the application, and then releasing the mouse button, causing the application to open the document.

Drop box A shared folder in which network users may place items, but only the folder's owner can see them.

DSL (Digital Subscriber Line) An add-on for standard telephone service that enables you to maintain a constant, high-speed Internet connection over a standard telephone line.

Duplex A method of printing on both sides of the page that does not need a person there to flip the pages.

Dynamic IP address An *IP address* that may change each time you begin an Internet session or start up your computer.

Dynamic RAM allocation An operating system technology that allows the operating system to respond to an application's request for more or less memory, as needed.

Easter eggs Cute or funny animations or other surprising actions hidden in a program. You reveal them by performing secret combinations of keystrokes and mouse clicks.

Edition A file that contains a live copy of the material in the *publisher* portion of a document belonging to a Classic application. When the publisher changes, the edition is updated. *Subscribers* contain copies of editions.

Enclosing folder The enclosing folder contains another folder.

Encryption The process of making messages or files unrecognizable, for example to keep someone from reading a sensitive document.

Escape character A backslash (\) in a Unix command. Used to indicate that the next character is to be used literally, not interpreted as a *wildcard* or other special character.

Ethernet A high-speed standard for connecting computers and other devices in a network. Ethernet ports are built into all Macs that can use Mac OS X and in many network printers. Ethernet networks can be wireless, as exemplified by AirPort wireless networks.

Event message A means of *interprocess communication*. Applications can send event messages to one another. When an application receives an event message, it takes an action according to the content of the message. This action can be anything from executing a particular command to taking some data, working with it, and then returning a result to the program that sent the message.

Extension The last part of a file name that follows a period and indicates the kind of file on the Internet and a DOS or Windows computer (along with some other computer systems). Also referred to as a file name suffix. See also *system extension*.

Fair use Defines the criteria that must be considered before using another person's copyrighted work (printed or recorded materials).

Favorites Often-accessed items. Aliases can be added to the Favorites folder, which then appear on the Favorites menu in the Finder's Go menu and in Open and Save dialogs of Mac OS X applications.

File ID number The number that Mac OS X uses internally to identify the original item to which an alias is attached even if you have renamed or moved that original item.

File mapping The technique used by Mac OS X of treating a program file as part of *virtual memory* so that fragments of a program are only loaded into memory as needed.

File name extension See *extension*.

File server A computer running a program that makes files centrally available for other computers on a network.

File sharing Enables you to share files in your Public folder with people whose computers are connected to yours in a network.

File spec (specification) Tells Mac OS X exactly where to find a file or folder.

Filter A technology that applies special effects to an image, such as a visual effect to a QuickTime movie.

File type A four-letter code that identifies the general characteristics of a file's contents, such as plain text, formatted text, picture, or sound.

Firewall A device or software that prevents Internet users from getting access to computers on a local network. A firewall may also stop local network users from sending sensitive information out.

Fixed-size font Contains exact pictures of every letter, digit, and symbol for one size of a font. Fixed-size fonts are called *bitmap fonts* because each picture precisely maps the dots, or *bits*, to be displayed or printed for one character.

Folder-action script An AppleScript script that is attached to a folder so that it can watch and respond to user interaction with that folder in the Finder.

Font A set of *characters* that have a common and consistent design.

Font family A collection of differently styled variations (such as bold, italic, and plain) of a single *font*. Many *fixed-size*, *TrueType*, and *PostScript* fonts come in the four basic styles: plain, bold, italic, and bold italic. Some PostScript font families include 20 or more styled versions.

Fonts folder Located in the System Folder used for the Classic environment, this folder includes all *fixed-size*, *PostScript*, and *TrueType* fonts available in the Classic environment.

Font suitcase A folder-like container specifically for *fixed-size* and *TrueType* fonts in the Classic environment.

Fork Part of a Mac OS file. Many Mac OS files include a data fork and a resource fork where different types of information are stored.

fps (frames-per-second) Measures how smoothly a motion picture plays. More frames-per-second means smoother playback. This measurement is used when discussing the *frame rate* of time-based media.

Frame One still image that is part of a series of still images, which, when shown in sequence, produce the illusion of movement.

Frame rate The number of frames displayed in one second. The TV frame rate is 30 fps in the United States and other countries that use the NTSC broadcasting standard; 25 fps in countries that use the PAL or SEACAM standard. The standard movie frame rate is 24 fps. See also *fps*.

Freeware Free software primarily distributed over the Internet and from person to person. Most freeware is still copyrighted by the person who created it. You can use it and give it to other people, but you can't sell it. See also *shareware*.

FTP A data communications *protocol* used by the Internet and other TCP/IP networks to transfer files between computers. FTP stands for File Transfer Protocol.

FTP site A collection of files on an FTP server available for downloading.

Full motion Video displayed at frame rates of 24 to 30 fps. The human eye perceives fairly smooth motion at frame rates of 12 to 18 fps. See also *fps* and *frame rate*.

Gamma The relationship between the intensity of color and its luminance.

Gamma correction A method of compensating for the loss of detail that the human eye perceives in dark areas.

Glyph A distinct visual representation of one character (such as a lowercase *z*), multiple characters treated as one (such as the ligature æ), or a nonprinting character (such as a space).

Grid fitting The process of modifying characters at small point sizes so that they fit the grid of dots on the relatively coarse display screen. The font designer provides a set of instructions (also known as *hints*) for a *TrueType* or *PostScript* font that tells Mac OS X how to modify character outlines to fit the grid.

Group A collection of users who can log in to a Mac OS X system. You can grant a group specific access privileges for your folders and files.

Guest A network user who is not identified by a name and password.

GUI (Graphical User Interface) A means of interacting with and controlling a computer by manipulating graphical objects shown on the display, such as windows, menus, and icons. GUI stands for graphical user interface.

Hack A programming effort that accomplishes something ingenious or unconventional.

Hacker A person who likes to tinker with computers and especially with computer software code. Some hackers create new software, but many hackers use programs such as ResEdit to make unauthorized changes to existing software. Compare to *cracker*.

Handler A named set of *AppleScript* commands that you can execute by naming the handler elsewhere in the same script. Instead of repeating a set of commands several times in different parts of a script, you can make the set of commands a handler and invoke the handler each place you would have repeated the set of commands. This is also sometimes called a subroutine.

Help tag A short description of the object under the mouse pointer in a Mac OS X application. The description appears in a small yellow box near the object. Many objects do not have help tags. The equivalent in Classic applications is *Balloon Help*.

Helper application A program that handles a particular kind of media or other data encountered on the Internet.

Home page This term refers to the main page of a Web site, and it is also the page that a Web browser displays when you first open it.

Hot spots Places in a QuickTime VR panorama that you can click to go to another scene in the panorama or to a QuickTime VR object.

Hub A device on an Ethernet network that passes signals from any device connected to one of the hub's RJ-45 ports to all other devices connected to the hub.

Hyperlink Underlined text or an image on a *Web page* that takes you to another page on the same or a different Web site when clicked.

Icon A small picture that represents an entity such as a program, document, folder, or disk.

Inbound port mapping A scheme for directing all requests coming into a local network from the Internet for a particular service, such as a Web server, to a particular computer on the local network.

Initialization A process that creates a blank disk directory. The effect is the same as erasing the disk. Initialization actually wipes out the means of accessing the existing files on the disk without actually touching the content of files.

Insertion point A blinking vertical bar that indicates where text is inserted when you start typing.

Installation The process of putting a new or updated version of software on your disk.

Internet A worldwide network that provides e-mail, Web pages, news, file storage and retrieval, and other services and information.

Internet gateway A device or software that enables all the computers on a local network to connect to the Internet, optionally sharing a single public IP address on the Internet.

Internet Service Provider (ISP) A company that gives you access to the Internet via your modem.

Interpreted The technique used by Unix shells and other scripting languages such as Perl to perform each command as it is encountered rather than converting all commands to machine instructions in advance.

Interprocess communication The technology that enables programs to send each other messages requesting action and receiving the results of requested actions. Mac OS X has several forms of interprocess communication, one of which is *Apple events,* which is the basis of *AppleScript.*

IP address A four-part number, such as 192.168.0.1, that uniquely identifies a computer or other device on a network.

ISDN (Integrated Services Digital Technology) A special telephone technology that allows for medium-speed network transmissions over long distances.

Kernel The kernel is the core of Mac OS X. It provides essential services such as *preemptive multitasking, virtual memory, memory protection, symmetric multiprocessing,* multiple user accounts, *device drivers,* file systems, and networking.

Kerning Adjusting the space between pairs of letters so that the spacing within the word looks consistent.

Keychain Technology that enables you to store password and passphrases for network connections, file servers, some types of secure Web sites, and encrypted files.

Label A means of categorizing files, folders, and disks. Each label has its own color and text. The Mac OS X Finder can show labels in list views, but doesn't let you set the label of a file, folder, or disk. To set labels, you must start up the computer with Mac OS 9.

LAN See *local network*.

Landscape A printed page that is wider than it is tall.

Language script system Software that enables the Mac OS to use an additional natural language, such as Japanese. Multiple languages can use one language script system (for example, the Roman script is used for English, French, Italian, Spanish, and German).

Launch To get an application started.

Ligature A glyph composed of two merged characters. For example, *f* and *l* can be merged to form fl.

Link See *hyperlink*.

Little arrows Displayed controls that let you raise or lower a value incrementally. Clicking an arrow changes the value one increment at a time. Pressing an arrow on the keyboard continuously changes the value until it reaches the end of its range.

Local area network (LAN) A complicated term for *local network*.

Localization The development of software whose dialogs, screens, menus, and other screen elements use the language spoken in the region in which the software is sold.

Local network A system of computers that are interconnected for sharing information and services and are located in proximity such as in an office, home, school, or campus.

LocalTalk A relatively low-speed standard for connecting computers, printers, and other devices to create an *AppleTalk* network. LocalTalk uses the built-in serial printer ports of Mac OS computers (or specialized adapters for Macs that don't include a serial port) and the LocalTalk ports of many LaserWriter printers.

Location file A file that, when opened, takes you to a location on the Internet or a local network.

Log in The process of entering a username and password to begin a session with Mac OS X or another a secured resource such as a network connection.

Loop To repeat a movie, a song, or a *playlist*.

Lossless A type of compression algorithm that regenerates exactly the same data as the uncompressed original.

MacBinary A scheme for encoding the special information in a Macintosh file's data and resource forks into a file format appropriate for transmission over the Internet.

Man pages Documentation for some of the Mac OS X Unix commands (which are actually Unix programs) and other Unix components.

Memory protection An operating system technology that makes it impossible for one active application to read and write data from another active application's space in memory. Memory protection helps applications run with fewer crashes.

MIDI The acronym for Musical Instrument Digital Interface. Developed in 1983 by several of the music industry's electronics manufacturers, MIDI is a data transmission protocol that permits devices to work together in a performance context. MIDI doesn't transfer music, it transfers information about the notes and their characteristics in a format another MIDI device can reconstruct the music from.

Modem A device that connects a computer to telephone lines. It converts digital information from the computer into sounds for transmission over phone lines and converts sounds from phone lines to digital information for the computer. (The term *modem* is a shortened form of *modulator-demodulator*.) This term is also used informally for devices that connect computers by using digital technologies — for example, TV cable, DSL, and ISDN connections.

Modem script Software consisting of the modem commands necessary to start and stop a remote access connection for a particular type of modem.

Mount To mount means to make the contents of a disk or other volume available to the computer. In the case of hard drives, this occurs every time you start up the computer.

Movie Any time-related data, such as video, sound, animation, and graphs, that change over time; Apple's format for organizing, storing, and exchanging time-related data.

Multimedia A presentation combining text or graphics with video, animation, or sound, and presented on a computer.

Multitasking The capability to have multiple programs open and executing concurrently.

Multithreading An operating system technology that allows tasks in an application to share processor time.

Navigate To open disks and folders until you have opened the one that contains the item you need; to go from one *Web page* to another.

Network A collection of interconnected, individually controlled computers, printers, and other devices together with the hardware, software, and protocols used to connect them. A network lets connected devices exchange messages and information.

Network administrator Someone who sets up and/or maintains a centralized file server and other network services.

Network Interface Card (NIC) An internal adapter card that provides a network port.

Network location A specific arrangement of all the various Network Preferences settings that can be put into effect all at once (for example, by choosing from the Location submenu of the Apple menu).

Network time servers Computers on a network or the Internet that provide the current time of day.

Networking protocol A set of rules for exchanging data over a *network*.

Newsgroup A subject on the Internet's *Usenet*. It is a collection of people and messages pertaining to that particular subject.

Nonblocking alert An alert from a background Classic application that appears in a floating window so that the current application's activities are not halted.

Object A kind of information, such as words, paragraphs, and characters, that an application knows how to work with. An application's *AppleScript* dictionary lists the kinds of objects it can work with under script control.

Operating system Software that controls the basic activities of a computer system. Also known as *system software*.

Original item A file, folder, or disk to which an *alias* points, and which opens when you open its alias.

Orphaned alias An *alias* that has lost its link with its original item (and, therefore, Mac OS X cannot find it).

Outline font A font whose *glyphs* are outlined by curves and straight lines that can be smoothly enlarged or reduced to any size and then filled with dots.

Owner The user who can assign access privileges to a file or folder.

Package A folder that the Finder displays as if it were a single application file. The Finder normally hides the files inside a package so users can't change them. A package is also a logical grouping of files that are related, such as all of the items that make up fax software or all of the parts of QuickTime.

Palette An auxiliary window that contains controls or tools or displays information for an application. A palette usually floats above regular windows of the same application.

Pane A tabbed page or section of a window.

Partition To divide a hard drive into several smaller volumes, each of which the computer treats as a separate disk. Also, another name for any of the volumes created by dividing a hard drive.

Passphrase Like a password, but generally consisting of more than one word. (The larger a password or passphrase, the more difficult it is to guess or otherwise discover.)

Password A combination of letters, digits, and symbols that must be typed accurately to gain access to information or services on the Internet or a *local network*.

Path A way of writing the location of a file or folder by specifying each folder that must be opened to get at the file. The outermost folder name is written first, and each folder name is followed by a slash (/). See also *absolute path* and *relative path*.

Peer-to-peer file sharing A technology for allowing other computers to access folders located on your computer—not a central file server—and reciprocally allowing your computer to access folders on other people's computers. The computers access each other's folders and files over a *network*.

Pipe A means of directing the output of one Unix command to the input of the next Unix command. Expressed in a Unix command line with a vertical bar symbol (|).

Pixel Short for picture element, a pixel is the smallest dot that the computer and a display can show.

Pixel depth The number of memory bits used to store each pixel of an image. The number of bits determines the number of different colors that could be in the image. For example, thousands of colors require 16 bits per pixel. Compare to *color depth*.

Playhead A marker that tracks movie frames as they are shown, always indicating the location of the current frame in relationship to the beginning and end of the movie.

Playlist A collection of songs arranged for playing in a particular sequence.

Plug-ins Software that works with an application to extend its capabilities. For example, plug-ins for the Sherlock application enable it to search additional Internet sites.

Point Of Presence (POP) An entry point to the Internet. Also, a telephone number that gains access to the Internet through an Internet service provider.

Pop-up menu A menu that is not in the menu bar, but that is marked with an arrowhead and pops open when you click it.

Portrait A printed page that is taller than it is wide.

PostScript font An outline font that conforms to the specifications of the PostScript page description language. PostScript fonts can be smoothly scaled to any size, rotated, and laid out along a curved path. (Compare *TrueType*.)

PostScript printers Printers that interpret PostScript commands to create printable images.

PPD (PostScript Printer Description) A file that contains the optional features of a PostScript printer, such as its resolution and paper tray configuration.

PRAM (parameter RAM) A small amount of battery-powered memory that stores system settings, such as time and date.

Preemptive multitasking A scheme for *multitasking* used in Mac OS X whereby multiple applications are open, and the operating system controls how much processor time each application can use. Compare *cooperative multitasking*.

Preferences folder Holds files that contain the settings you make in System Preferences and with the Preferences commands of application programs.

Primary script The *language script system* used by system dialogs and menus. If you are working on a computer that is set up for English, Roman is your primary script; your secondary script can be any other installed language script, such as Japanese.

Printer driver Software that prepares pages for and communicates with a particular type of printer.

Print job A file of page descriptions that is sent to a particular type of printer. Also called a *print request* or *spool file*.

Print request See *print job*.

Print server A device or a software that manages one or more shared printers on a network.

Private IP address An *IP address* for use on a local network. Compare *public IP address*.

Process A program that is currently running on the computer.

Program A set of coded instructions that direct a computer in performing a specific task.

Program linking The process of sharing programs by sending and receiving *event messages* across a network.

Protocol See *networking protocol*.

Proxy icon A little icon next to the title of a Finder window. It represents the folder whose contents are currently displayed in the window. You can drag the proxy icon to any folder, volume, or the Trash.

Proxy server A device or software that serves as a buffer between a local network and the Internet for purposes of privacy, security, and speed.

Public IP address An *IP address* for use on the Internet. Compare *private IP address.*

Publisher A section of a document that is saved as an *edition,* which can appear as *subscribers* in other documents. The documents all belong to Classic applications.

Push button A displayed control that when clicked causes an action to take place. A label on the button indicates the action that the button performs. The label may be text or graphic. Push buttons with text labels are generally rectangular with rounded ends. Buttons with graphic labels may be any shape.

Radio buttons A group of displayed controls that let you select one setting from a group. They work like the station presets on a car radio. Just as you can select only one radio station at a time, you can select only one radio button from a group.

RAM Random-access memory, which is physical memory built into the computer in the form of electronic chips or small circuit boards called *DIMMs.*

RAM disk Memory that is set aside to be used as if it were a very fast hard drive.

Raster image An image made of lines of discrete dots for the display screen or the printer.

Record A structured collection of data in AppleScript (and in other programming languages), in which each data item has a name and a value.

Regular expression A shorthand method of expressing a string of characters or various permutations of a string of characters. Used in Unix command lines.

Relative path A *path* that does not begin with a slash character (/) and is therefore assumed to start in the current folder.

Repeat loop An arrangement of *AppleScript* commands that begins with a Repeat command and ends with an End Repeat command. AppleScript executes the commands between the Repeat and End Repeat commands for the number of times specified in the Repeat command.

Resolution The horizontal and vertical dimensions of a display, measured in pixels. Also refers to the perceived smoothness of a displayed or printed image. Printed resolution is measured in dots-per-inch (*dpi*). A high-resolution image has more dots-per-inch than a low-resolution image.

Resolve an alias What Mac OS X does to find the original item that is represented by an *alias.*

Resources Information such as text, menus, icons, pictures, or patterns used by Mac OS X, an application, or other software. Also refers to a computer's processing power, memory, and disk space.

Rip To convert tracks from audio CDs into MP3 format.

RIP (Raster Image Processor) Software that translates PostScript code into an image made of lines of dots.

ROM Read-only memory.

Root The name of the user account that has control over all folders and files on a computer, including the contents of the normally off-limits System folder.

Root level The main level of a disk, which is what you see when you open the disk icon.

Router See *Internet gateway.*

Screen saver Software that protects against *burn-in* by showing a constantly changing image on the display while the computer is idle.

Script A collection of *AppleScript* commands that perform a specific task. Also, short for *language script system*, which is software that defines a method of writing (vertical or horizontal, left-to-right, or right-to-left). A language script also provides rules for text sorting, word breaking, and the formatting of dates, times, and numbers.

Scriptable application An application that can be controlled by *AppleScript* commands.

Script applet *AppleScript* scripts saved as applets or small applications.

Scripting additions Files that add commands to the *AppleScript* language, such as plug-ins add features to applications.

Script recording A process in which *AppleScript* watches as you work with an application and automatically writes a corresponding *script.*

Scrolling list Displays a list of values in a box with an adjacent scroll bar. Clicking a listed item selects it. You may be able to select multiple items by pressing Shift or ⌘ while clicking.

Scrub To move quickly forward or backward through a movie by dragging the *playhead.*

Selection rectangle A dotted-line box that you drag around items to select them all.

Server Software or a device that provides information or services to *clients* on demand.

Shareware Software distributed over the Internet and from person to person on a trial basis. You pay for it if you decide to keep using it. See also *freeware*.

Sheet A *dialog* that applies to and is attached to another window, ensuring you won't lose track of which window the dialog applies to.

Shell Part of the Unix operating system that interprets command lines.

Slider A displayed control consisting of a track that displays a range of values or magnitudes and the slider itself, also known as the thumb, which indicates the current setting. You can change the setting by dragging the slider.

Smoothing See *anti-alias*.

Software One or more programs that consist of coded instructions that direct a computer in performing tasks.

Sound track The audible part of a movie.

Splat Unix jargon for the number sign symbol (#).

Spool file See *print job*.

Spooling A printer-driver operation in which the driver saves page descriptions in a file (called a *spool file*) for later printing.

Standard input The source of Unix commands, which is the keyboard by default.

Standard output The destination for the result of Unix commands, which is the Terminal window by default.

Startup disk A disk that contains the software needed for the computer to begin operation.

Static IP address An *IP address* that doesn't change when you begin an Internet session or when your computer starts up.

Stationery pad A template document that contains preset format and contents.

Status bar A strip in the top part of a Finder window that shows how much free space is available on the volume that contains the currently displayed folder.

Streaming media Movies designed to be played over the Internet as they are downloaded.

Stuffed file A file (or group of files) that has been compressed in the StuffIt file format from Aladdin Systems.

Submenu A secondary menu that pops out from the side of another menu. A submenu appears when you place the pointer on a menu item that has an arrowhead at the right side of the menu. Submenus are sometimes referred to as hierarchical menus.

Subscriber A copy of an *edition* that has been placed in a document belonging to a Classic application. A subscriber can be updated automatically when the edition is updated by its *publisher*.

Suite In *AppleScript*, a group of related commands and other items.

Superuser The user who has complete control over all folders and files on a computer, including the contents of the normally off-limits System folder.

Switch A device on an Ethernet network that passes signals from any device connected to one of the hub's RJ-45 ports to one of the other devices connected to the hub. Also refers to options you can specify as part of a Unix command.

Symmetrical multiprocessing An operating system technology that allows the operating system and applications to take advantage of two or more processors installed in the computer.

System administrator A person who has the knowledge and authority to make changes to settings that affect the fundamental operation of a computer's operating system.

System extension A software module loads when the Classic environment starts up. It adds features or capabilities to Mac OS 9 for the Classic environment.

System file Contains sounds, keyboard layouts, and language script systems, as well as the basic Mac OS 9 software for the Classic environment.

System Folder Stores the Mac OS 9 software used by the Classic environment.

System software Software that controls the basic activities of a computer system. Also known as the *operating system*.

Tabs Controls that look like the tabs on dividers used in card files. They divide the contents of a window into discrete pages called panes, with each tab connected to one pane of window content.

Text behavior The set of rules used in a particular language for alphabetizing, capitalizing, and distinguishing words.

Theme A group of all the settings in the Classic environment's Appearance control panel.

Thread A string of messages about the same subject in a newsgroup. Also refers to a single task being executed within an application that may have multiple threads.

Thumb The movable part of a *slider* control that indicates the current setting.

Track One channel of a QuickTime movie, containing video, sound, closed-captioned text, MIDI data, time codes, or other time-related data.

Tracking The overall spacing between letters in an entire document or text selection. Text with loose tracking has extra space between the characters in words. Text with tight tracking has characters squeezed close together.

Tracking speed The rate at which the pointer moves as you drag the mouse.

Translator A program that translates your documents from one file format to another file format, such as a PICT graphic to a GIF graphic.

Tristimulus A three-dimensional color space expressed in terms of X, Y, and Z coordinates.

Trojan horse Destructive software that masquerades as something useful, such as a utility program or game. Compare to *virus* and *worm*.

TrueType The outline font technology built into the Mac OS (and Microsoft Windows). TrueType fonts can be smoothly scaled to any size on-screen or to any type of printer.

Type 1 font A PostScript font that includes instructions for grid fitting so that the font can be scaled to small sizes and low printer resolutions with good results.

Unix A complex and powerful operating system whose TCP/IP networking protocol is the basis of the Internet.

Unmount To remove a disk's icon from the Desktop and make the disk's contents unavailable without deleting the items in that disk permanently.

Unshielded twisted-pair (UTP) The type of cable used in a 10Base-T, 100Base-T, or Gigabit Ethernet network.

Upload The process of sending files from your computer to another computer.

URL (Uniform Resource Locator) An *Internet* address. This can be the address of a *Web page*, a file on an *FTP* site, or anything else that you can access on the Internet.

Usenet A worldwide *Internet* bulletin board system that enables people to post messages and join discussions about subjects that interest them.

User group An organization that provides information and assistance to people who use computers. For the names and phone numbers of user groups near you, check Apple's Web page for looking up user groups (www.apple.com/usergroups/find.html).

User Someone who can log into your computer with a unique name and a password.

Username A name that can be used to log into a Mac OS X system.

Variable A container for information in a *script*. You can place data in a variable and then use it elsewhere in the script.

Video mirroring The duplication of one screen image on two displays connected to a computer.

Virtual memory Additional memory made available by Mac OS X treating part of a hard drive as if it were built-in memory.

Virus Software designed to spread itself by illicitly attaching copies of itself to legitimate software. Some viruses perform malicious actions, such as erasing your hard drive. Even seemingly innocuous viruses can interfere with the normal functioning of your computer. Compare to *Trojan horse* and *worm*.

Volume A disk or a part of a disk that the computer treats as a separate storage device. Each volume can have an icon on the Desktop.

Web browser A program that displays *Web pages* from the Internet.

Web page A basic unit that the Web uses to display information (including text, pictures, animation, audio, and video clips). A Web page can also contain *hyperlinks* to the same page or to other Web pages (on the same or a different Web server).

Web server A computer or a program running on a computer that provides information to a Web browser program.

White point A setting that determines whether colors look warm (reddish) or cool (bluish). Measured in degrees Kelvin, with warm white points having lower temperatures than cool white points.

White space A run of blank spaces, tab characters, or both.

Wildcard A character that represents a range of characters in a *regular expression*. For example, an asterisk stands for any individual character.

Worm Software that replicates like a virus but without attaching itself to other software. It may be benign or malicious. Compare to *Trojan horse* and *Virus*.

Write-protect The process of locking a disk so that it cannot be erased, have its name changed, have files copied to it or duplicated from it, or have files or folders it contains moved to the Desktop or trash.

Zipped file A file (or group of files) that has been compressed by using the PKZip or WinZip format. Also, a file compressed by using the Unix gzip standard.

Index

                                                    Continued

Continued

Continued

Continued

Continued

Continued

Continued